THE CIVILIZING PROCESS

Dedicated to the Memory of My Parents
Hermann Elias, d. Breslau 1940
Sophie Elias, d. Auschwitz 1941 (?)

Norbert Elias

THE CIVILIZING PROCESS

The History of Manners

and

State Formation and Civilization

Translated by Edmund Jephcott

BLACKWELL

Oxford UK & Cambridge USA

This edition copyright © Norbert Elias Stichting 1994;

The History of Manners: © Norbert Elias 1939, 1968. English translation
© Basil Blackwell Ltd. 1978.

State Formation and Civilization: © Norbert Elias 1939, 1969, 1976. English translation
© Basil Blackwell Ltd. 1982.
Originally published as *Über den Prozess der Zivilisation* as two separate volumes in
1939 by Haus zum Falker, Basel.

Blackwell Publishers
108 Cowley Road
Oxford OX4 1JF
UK

238 Main Street
Cambridge, Massachusetts 02142
USA

British Library Cataloguing in Publication Data

A CIP catalogue record for this book is available from the British Library.

Library of Congress Cataloging-in-Publication Data

Elias, Norbert.
[Über den Prozess der Zivilisation. English]
The civilizing process / Norbert Elias ; translated by Edmund
Jephcott.
p.   cm.
Contents: The history of manners – State formation and
civilization.
Includes bibliographical references and index.
ISBN 0–631–19221–2 (alk. paper). – ISBN 0–631–19222–0 (pbk.:
alk. paper)
1. Civilization—History.   2. Civilization—Philosophy.
I. Title.
CB83.E413   1994   93–37350
909—dc20   CIP

Typeset in 10 on 12pt Garamond by Photoprint, Torquay, S. Devon
Printed in Great Britain by Biddles Ltd, Guildford

This book is printed on acid-free paper

Contents

The History of Manners

Translated by Edmund Jephcott

Table of Contents

Preface*

Central to this study are modes of behavior considered typical of Western civilized man. The problem they pose is simple enough. Western man has not always behaved in the manner we are accustomed to regard as typical or as the hallmark of "civilized" man. If a member of present-day Western civilized society were to find himself suddenly transported into a past epoch of his own society, such as the medieval-feudal period, he would find there much that he esteems "uncivilized" in other societies today. His reaction would scarcely differ from that produced in him at present by the behavior of people in feudal societies outside the Western world. He would, depending on his situation and inclinations, be either attracted by the wilder, more unrestrained and adventurous life of the upper classes in this society, or repulsed by the "barbaric" customs, the squalor and coarseness that he encountered there. And whatever he understands by his own "civilization," he would at any rate feel quite unequivocally that society in this past period of Western history was not "civilized" in the same sense and to the same degree as Western society today.

This state of affairs may seem obvious to many people, and it might appear unnecessary to refer to it here. But it necessarily gives rise to questions which cannot with equal justice be said to be clearly present in the consciousness of living generations, although these questions are not without importance for an understanding of ourselves. How did this change, this "civilizing" of the West,

* The Introduction to the 1968 German edition can be found on p. 181

actually happen? Of what did it consist? And what were its causes or motive forces? It is to the solution of these main questions that this study attempts to contribute.

To facilitate understanding of this book, and thus as an introduction to the questions themselves, it seems necessary to examine the different meanings and evaluations assigned to the concept of "civilization" in Germany and France. This inquiry makes up the first Part. It may help the reader to see the concepts of *Kultur* and *civilisation* as somewhat less rigidly and self-evidently opposed. And it may also make a small contribution toward improving the German historical understanding of the behavior of Frenchmen and Englishmen, and the French and English understanding of the behavior of Germans. But in the end it will also serve to clarify certain typical features of the civilizing process.

To gain access to the main questions, it is necessary first to obtain a clearer picture of how the behavior and affective life of Western peoples slowly changed after the Middle Ages. To show this is the task of the second chapter. It attempts as simply and clearly as possible to open the way to an understanding of the psychical process of civilization. It may be that the idea of a psychical process extending over many generations appears hazardous and dubious to present-day historical thinking. But it is not possible to decide in a purely theoretical, speculative way whether the changes in psychical makeup observable in the course of Western history took place in a particular order and direction. Only a scrutiny of documents of historical experience can show what is correct and what is incorrect in such theories. That is why it is not possible here, when knowledge of this documentary material cannot be presupposed, to give a brief preliminary sketch of the structure and central ideas of the whole book. They themselves take on a firmer form only gradually, in a continuous observation of historical facts and a constant checking and revision of what has been seen previously through what entered later into the field of observation. And thus the individual parts of this study, its structure and method, will probably be completely intelligible only when they are perceived in their entirety. It must suffice here, to facilitate the reader's understanding, to pick out a few problems.

The second Part contains a number of series of examples. They serve to show development in an accelerated fashion. In a few pages we see how in the course of centuries the standard of human behavior on the same occasion very gradually shifts in a specific direction. We see people at table, we see them going to bed or in hostile clashes. In these and other elementary activities the manner in which the individual behaves and feels slowly changes. This change is in the direction of a gradual "civilization," but only historical experience makes clearer what this word actually means. It shows, for example, the decisive role played in this civilizing process by a very specific change in the feelings of shame and delicacy. The standard of what society demands and prohibits changes; in conjunction with this, the threshold of socially instilled displeasure and fear moves; and the question of sociogenic fears thus emerges as one of the central problems of the civilizing process.

Very closely related to this is a further range of questions. The distance in behavior and whole psychical structure between children and adults increases in the course of the civilizing process. Here, for example, lies the key to the question of why some peoples or groups of peoples appear to us as "younger" or "more childlike," others as "older" or "more grown-up." What we are trying to express in this way are differences in the kind and stage of the civilizing process that these societies have attained; but that is a separate question which cannot be included within the framework of this study. The series of examples and the interpretations of them in Part Two show one thing very clearly: the specific process of psychological "growing up" in Western societies, which frequently occupies the minds of psychologists and pedagogues today, is nothing other than the individual civilizing process to which each young person, as a result of the social civilizing process over many centuries, is automatically subjected from earliest childhood, to a greater or lesser degree and with greater or lesser success. The psychogenesis of the adult makeup in civilized society cannot, therefore, be understood if considered independently of the sociogenesis of our "civilization." By a kind of basic "sociogenetic law"** the individual, in his short history, passes once more through some of the processes that his society has traversed in its long history.

It is the purpose of Part One of *State Formation and Civilization* to make certain processes in this long history of society more accessible to understanding. It attempts, within a number of precisely defined areas, to clarify how and why in the course of its history the structure of Western society continuously changes, and points at the same time to an answer to the question of why, in the same areas, the standard of behavior and the psychical makeup of Western peoples change.

We see, for example, the social landscape of the early Middle Ages. There is a

---

** This expression should not be understood to mean that all the individual phases of a society's history are reproduced in the history of the civilized individual. Nothing would be more absurd than to look for an "agrarian feudal age" or a "Renaissance" or a "courtly-absolutist period" in the life of the individual. All concepts of this kind refer to the structure of whole social groups.

What must be pointed out here is the simple fact that even in civilized society no human being comes into the world civilized, and that the individual civilizing process that he compulsorily undergoes is a function of the social civilizing process. Therefore, the structure of the child's affects and consciousness no doubt bears a certain resemblance to that of "uncivilized" peoples, and the same applies to the psychological stratum in grown-ups which, with the advance of civilization is subjected to more or less heavy censorship and consequently finds an outlet in dreams, for example. But since in our society each human being is exposed from the first moment of life to the influence and the molding intervention of civilized grown-ups, he must indeed pass through a civilizing process in order to reach the standard attained by his society in the course of its history, but not through the individual phases of the social civilizing process.

multitude of greater and smaller castles; even the town settlements of earlier times have become feudalized. Their centers too are formed by the castles and estates of lords from the warrior class. The question is: What are the sets of social relationships that press toward the development of what we call the "feudal system"? The attempt is made to demonstrate some of these "mechanisms of feudalization." We see further how, from the castle landscape, together with a number of free, urban craft and commercial settlements, a number of larger and richer feudal estates slowly emerge. Within the warrior class itself a kind of upper stratum forms more and more distinctly; their dwelling places are the real centers of minnesong and the lyrics of the troubadours, on the one hand, and of *courtois* forms of behavior on the other. If earlier in the book the *courtois* standard of conduct is placed at the starting point of a number of sequences of examples giving a picture of the subsequent change of psychical makeup, here we gain access to the sociogenesis of these *courtois* forms of behavior themselves.

Or we see, for example, how the early form of what we call a "state" develops. In the age of absolutism, under the watchword of *civilité*, behavior moves very perceptibly toward the standard that we denote today by a derivative of the word *civilité* as "civilized" behavior. It therefore seems necessary, in elucidating this civilizing process, to obtain a clearer picture of what gave rise to the absolutist regimes and therefore to the absolutist state. It is not only the observation of the past that points in this direction; a wealth of contemporary observations suggest strongly that the structure of civilized behavior is closely interrelated with the organization of Western societies in the form of states. The question, in other words, is: How did the extremely decentralized society of the early Middle Ages, in which numerous greater and smaller warriors were the real rulers of Western territory, become one of the internally more or less pacified but outwardly embattled societies that we call states? Which dynamics of human interdependencies push toward the integration of ever larger areas under a relatively stable and centralized government apparatus?

It may perhaps seem at first sight an unnecessary complication to investigate the genesis of each historical formation. But since every historical phenomenon, human attitudes as much as social institutions, did actually once "develop," how can modes of thought prove either simple or adequate in explaining these phenomena if, by a kind of artificial abstraction, they isolate the phenomena from their natural, historical flow, deprive them of their character as movement and process, and try to understand them as static formations without regard to the way in which they have come into being and change? It is not theoretical prejudice but experience itself which urges us to seek intellectual ways and means of steering a course between the Scylla of this "statism," which tends to express all historical movement as something motionless and without evolution, the Charybdis of the "historical relativism" which sees in history only constant transformation, without penetrating to the order underlying this transformation and to the laws governing the formation of historical structures. That is what is attempted here. The sociogenetic and psychogenetic investigation sets out to reveal the *order* underlying historical *changes*, their mechanics and their concrete mechanisms; and it seems that in this way a large number of questions that appear complicated or even beyond understanding today can be given fairly simple and precise answers.

For this reason, this study also inquires into the sociogenesis of the state. There is, to take one aspect of the history of the state's formation and structure, the problem of the "monopoly of force." Max Weber pointed out, mainly for the sake of definition, that one of the constitutive institutions required by the social organization we call a state is a monopoly in the exercise of physical force. Here the attempt is made to reveal something of the concrete historical processes that, from the time when the exercise of force was the privilege of a host of rival warriors, gradually impelled society toward this centralization and monopoliz-ation of the use of physical violence and its instruments. It can be shown that the tendency to form such monopolies in this past epoch of our history is neither easier nor more difficult to understand than, for example, the strong tendency toward monopolization in our own epoch. And it is then not difficult to understand that with this monopolization of physical violence as the point of intersection of a multitude of social interconnections, the whole apparatus which shapes the individual, the mode of operation of the social demands and prohibitions which mold his social makeup, and above all the kinds of fear that play a part in his life are decisively changed.

Finally, the concluding Part of *State Formation and Civilization*, "Towards a Theory of Civilizing Processes", underlines once more the connections between changes in the structure of society and changes in the structure of behavior and psychical makeup. Much of what could only be hinted at earlier, in depicting concrete historical processes, is now stated explicitly. We find here, for example, a short sketch of the structure of the fears experienced as shame and delicacy, as a kind of theoretical summing-up of what previously emerged of itself from the study of historical documents; we find an explanation of precisely why fears of this kind play an especially important role in the advance of the civilizing process; and at the same time, some light is shed on the formation of the "super-ego" and on the relation of the conscious and unconscious impulses in the psyche of civilized man. Here an answer is given to the question of historical processes; the question of how all these processes, consisting of nothing but the actions of individual people, nevertheless give rise to institutions and formations which were neither intended nor planned by any single individual in the form they actually take. And finally, in a broad survey, these insights from the past are combined into a single picture with experiences from the present.

This study therefore poses and develops a very wide-ranging problem; it does not pretend to solve it.

It marks out a field of observation that has hitherto received relatively little attention, and undertakes the first steps toward an explanation. Others must follow.

Many questions and aspects which presented themselves in the course of this study I deliberately did not pursue. It was not so much my purpose to build a general theory of civilization in the air, and then afterward find out whether it agreed with experience; rather, it seemed the primary task to begin by regaining within a limited area the lost perception of the process in question, the peculiar transformation of human behavior, then to seek a certain understanding of its causes, and finally to gather together such theoretical insights as have been encountered on the way. If I have succeeded in providing a tolerably secure foundation for further reflection and research in this direction, this study has achieved everything it set out to achieve. It will need the thought of many people and the cooperation of different branches of scholarship, which are often divided by artificial barriers today, gradually to answer the questions that have arisen in the course of this study. They concern psychology, philology, ethnology, and anthropology no less than sociology or the different special branches of historical research.

However, the issues raised by the book have their origin less in scholarly tradition, in the narrower sense of the word, than in the experiences in whose shadow we all live, experiences of the crisis and transformation of Western civilization as it had existed hitherto, and the simple need to understand what this "civilization" really amounts to. But I have not been guided in this study by the idea that our civilized mode of behavior is the most advanced of all humanly possible modes of behavior, nor by the opinion that "civilization" is the worst form of life and one that is doomed. All that can be seen today is that with gradual civilization a number of specific civilizational difficulties arise. But it cannot be said that we already understand why we actually torment ourselves in this way. We feel that we have got ourselves, through civilization, into certain entanglements unknown to less civilized peoples; but we also know that these less civilized peoples are for their part often plagued by difficulties and fears from which we no longer suffer, or at least not to the same degree. Perhaps all this can be seen somewhat more clearly if it is understood how such civilizing processes actually take place. At any rate, that was one of the wishes with which I set to work on this book. It may be that, through clearer understanding, we shall one day succeed in making accessible to more conscious control these processes which today take place in and around us not very differently from natural events, and which we confront as medieval man confronted the forces of nature.

I myself was obliged in the course of this study to revise my thinking on a large number of points, and I cannot spare the reader from becoming acquainted with a number of unfamiliar aspects and expressions. Above all, the nature of historical processes, of what might be called the "developmental mechanics of history," has become clearer to me, as has their relation to psychical processes. Terms such as socio- and psychogenesis, affective life and instinct-molding, external and internal compulsions, embarrassment threshold, social power, monopoly mechanism, and a number of others give expression to this. But the least possible concession has been made of the necessity to express new things that have become visible by new words.

So much for the subject of this book.

For the present study and for a number of necessary preliminary investigations, I have received advice and support from many sides. It is my wish here to thank expressly all the people and institutions that have helped me.

The enlargement of my *Habilitationschrift* and an extended study of nobility, royalty, and courtly society in France which is the basis of *The History of Manners*, was made possible by the support of the Steun-Fond of Amsterdam. My thanks are due to this foundation, and to Professor Frijda of Amsterdam and Professor Bouglé of Paris for the great kindness and interest they showed me during my work in Paris.

For the period of my work in London I received the generous support of Woburn House, London. To it and above all to Professor Ginsberg of London, Professor H. Loewe of Cambridge, and A. Makower, M.A., of London I owe very great thanks. Without their help my work would not have come to fruition. Professor K. Mannheim of London I thank for the help and advice he gave me. And I am not least indebted to my friends Giséle Freund, D.Phil., Paris; M. Braun, D.Phil., Ph.D., Cambridge; A. Glücksmann, D.Med., Cambridge; H. Rosenhaupt, D.Phil., Chicago; and R. Bonwit, London, for their help and for the discussions in which many things were made clear to me, and I thank them.

September, 1936   Norbert Elias

PART ONE

On the Sociogenesis of the Concepts "Civilization" and "Culture"

Chapter One

Sociogenesis of the Difference Between Kultur and Zivilisation in German Usage

I

Introduction

1. The concept of "civilization" refers to a wide variety of facts: to the level of technology, to the type of manners, to the development of scientific knowledge, to religious ideas and customs. It can refer to the type of dwelling or the manner in which men and women live together, to the form of judicial punishment, or to the way in which food is prepared. Strictly speaking, there is almost nothing which cannot be done in a "civilized" or an "uncivilized" way; hence, it always seems somewhat difficult to summarize in a few words everything that can he described as civilization.

But when one examines what the general function of the concept of civilization really is, and what common quality causes all these various human attitudes and activities to be described as civilized, one starts with a very simple discovery: this concept expresses the self-consciousness of the West. One could even say: the national consciousness. It sums up everything in which Western society of the last two or three centuries believes itself superior to earlier societies or "more primitive" contemporary ones. By this term Western society seeks to describe what constitutes its special character and what it is proud of: the level of *its* technology, the nature of *its* manners, the development of *its* scientific knowledge or view of the world, and much more.

2. But "civilization" does not mean the same thing to different Western nations. Above all, there is a great difference between the English and French use of the word, on the one hand, and the German use of it, on the other. For the former, the concept sums up in a single term their pride in the significance of their own nations for the progress of the West and of mankind. But in German usage, *Zivilisation* means something which is indeed useful, but nevertheless only a value of the second rank, comprising only the outer appearance of human beings, the surface of human existence. The word through which Germans interpret themselves, which more than any other expresses their pride in their own achievement and their own being, is *Kultur*.

3. A peculiar phenomenon: Words like the English and French "civilization" or the German *Kultur* appear completely clear in the internal usage of the society to which they belong. But the way in which a piece of the world is bound up in them, the manner in which they include certain areas and exclude others as a matter of course, the hidden evaluations which they implicitly bring with them, all this makes them difficult to define for any outsider.

The French and English concept of civilization can refer to political or economic, religious or technical, moral or social facts. The German concept of *Kultur* refers essentially to intellectual, artistic, and religious facts, and has a tendency to draw a sharp dividing line between facts of this sort, on the one side, and political, economic, and social facts, on the other. The French and English concept of civilization can refer to accomplishments, but it refers equally to the attitudes or "behavior" of people, irrespective of whether or nor they have accomplished anything. In the German concept of *Kultur*, by contrast, the reference to "behavior," to the value which a person has by virtue of his mere existence and conduct, without any accomplishment at all, is very minor. The specifically German sense of the concept of *Kultur* finds its clearest expression in its derivative, the adjective *kulturell*, which describes the value and character of particular human products rather than the intrinsic value of a person. But this word, the concept embodied in *kulturell*, cannot be exactly translated into French and English.

The word *kultiviert* (cultivated) is very close to the Western concept of civilization. To some extent, it represents the highest form of being civilized. Even people and families who have accomplished nothing *kulturell* can be *kultiviert*. Like the term "civilized," *kultiviert* refers primarily to the form of people's conduct or behavior. It describes a social quality of people, their housing, their manners, their speech, their clothing, unlike *kulturell*, which does not refer directly to people themselves, but exclusively to particular human accomplishments.

4. Another difference between the two concepts is very closely bound up with this. "Civilization" describes a process or at least the result of a process. It refers to something which is constantly in motion, constantly moving "forward." The

German concept of *Kultur*, in current usage, has a different relation to motion. It refers to human products which are there like "flowers of the field,"[1] to works of art, books, religious or philosophical systems, in which the individuality of a people expresses itself. The concept of *Kultur* delimits.

To a certain extent, the concept of civilization plays down the national differences between peoples; it emphasizes what is common to all human beings or—in the view of its bearers—should be. It expresses the self-assurance of peoples whose national boundaries and national identity have for centuries been so fully established that they have ceased to be the subject of any particular discussion, peoples which have long expanded outside their borders and colonized beyond them.

In contrast, the German concept of *Kultur* places special stress on national differences and the particular identity of groups; primarily by virtue of this, it has acquired in such fields as ethnological and anthropological research a significance far beyond the German linguistic area and the situation in which the concept originated. But that situation is the situation of a people which, by Western standards, arrived at political unification and consolidation only very late, and from whose boundaries, for centuries and even down to the present, territories have again and again crumbled away or threatened to crumble away. Whereas the concept of civilization has the function of giving expression to the continuously expansionist tendency of colonizing groups, the concept of *Kultur* mirrors the self-consciousness of a nation which had constantly to seek out and constitute its boundaries anew, in a political as well as a spiritual sense, and again and again had to ask itself: "What is really our identity?" The orientation of the German concept of culture, with its tendency toward demarcation and the emphasis on and detailing of differences between groups, corresponds to this historical process. The questions "What is really French? What is really English?" have long since ceased to be a matter of much discussion for the French and English. But for centuries the question "What is really German?" has not been laid to rest. One answer to this question—one among others—lies in a particular aspect of the concept of *Kultur*.

5. Thus the national self-images represented by concepts such as *Kultur* and "civilization" take very different forms. But however different the self-image of the Germans, who speak with pride of their *Kultur*, and that of the French and English, who think with pride of their "civilization," they all regard it as completely self-evident that theirs is the way in which the world of men as a whole wants to be viewed and judged. The German can perhaps try to explain to the French and English what he means by the concept of *Kultur*. But he can communicate hardly anything of the specific national background and the self-evident emotional values which envelop the word for him.

The Frenchman or Englishman can perhaps tell the German what elements make the concept of civilization the sum of the national self-image. But however reasonable and rational this concept may appear to them, it too grows out of a specific set of historical situations, it too is surrounded by an emotional and traditional atmosphere which is hard to define but which nevertheless represents an integral part of its meaning. And the discussion really becomes futile when the German tries to show the Frenchman and Englishman why the concept of *Zivilisation* does indeed represent a value for him, but only one of the second rank.

6. Concepts like these two have something of the character of those words which from time to time make their appearance in some narrower group, such as a family or a sect, a school class or an association, and which say much to the initiate and little to the outsider. They take form on the basis of common experiences. They grow and change with the group whose expression they are. The situation and history of the group are mirrored in them. And they remain colorless, they never become fully alive for those who do not share these experiences, who do not speak from the same tradition and the same situation.

The concepts of *Kultur* and "civilization," to be sure, bear the stamp not of sects or families but of whole peoples, or perhaps only of certain classes of these peoples. But in many respects what is true of the specific words of smaller groups is also true of them: they are primarily used by and for people who share a particular tradition and a particular situation.

Mathematical concepts can be separated from the group which uses them. Triangles may be explicable without reference to historical situations. Concepts such as "civilization" and *Kultur* are not. It may be that particular individuals formed them from the existing linguistic material of their group, or at least gave them new meaning. But they took root. They established themselves. Others picked them up in their new meaning and form, developing and polishing them in speech or writing. They were tossed back and forth until they became efficient instruments for expressing what people had jointly experienced and wanted to communicate about. They became fashionable words, concepts current in the everyday speech of a particular society. This shows that they met not merely individual but collective needs for expression. The collective history has crystallized in them and resonates in them. The individual finds this crystallization already in their possibilities of use. He does not know very precisely why this meaning and this delimitation are bound up with the words, why exactly this nuance and that new possibility can be drawn from them. He makes use of them because it seems to him a matter of course, because from childhood he learns to see the world through the lens of these concepts. The social process of their genesis may be long forgotten. One generation hands them on to another without being aware of the process as a whole, and the concepts live as long as this crystallization of past experiences and situations retains an existential value, a function in the actual being of society—that is, as long as succeeding generations can hear their own experiences in the meaning of the words. The terms gradually die when the functions and experiences in the actual life of society cease to be bound up with them. At times, too, they only sleep, or sleep in certain respects, and acquire a new existential value from a new social situation. They are recalled then because something in the present state of society finds expression in the crystallization of the past embodied in the words.

II

The Development of the Antithesis of *Kultur* and *Zivilisation*[2]

7. It is clear that the function of the German concept of *Kultur* took on new life in the year 1919, and in the preceding years, partly because a war was waged against Germany in the name of "civilization" and because the self-image of the Germans had to define itself anew in the situation created by the peace treaty.

But it is just as clear, and can be proved, that to a certain extent the historical situation of Germany after the war only gave a new impulse to an antithesis which had long found expression through these two concepts, even as far back as the eighteenth century.

It seems to have been Kant who first expressed a specific experience and antithesis of his society in related concepts. In 1784 he wrote in his *Ideas on a Universal History from the Point of View of a Citizen of the World*: "Cultivated to a high degree by art and science, we are civilized to the point where we are overburdened with all sorts of social propriety and decency . . ."

"The idea of morality," he added, "is a part of culture. But the application of this idea, which results only in the similitude of morality in the love of honor and in outward decency, amounts only to civilizing."

Related as this formulation of the antithesis already seems, in the moment of its genesis, to our formulation, its concrete point of departure in the experiences and situation in the late eighteenth century, though not without a historical connection to the experiences on which its present-day use rests, is nevertheless significantly different. The contraposition here, where the spokesmen of the developing German bourgeoisie, the middle-class German intelligentsia,[3] still speak in large part "from the point of view of a citizen of the world," relates only vaguely and at best secondarily to a national contrast. Its primary aspect is an internal contrast within the society, a social contrast which nevertheless bears within itself in a significant way the germ of the national contraposition: the contrast between the courtly nobility, predominantly French-speaking and "civilized" on the French model, and a German-speaking, middle-class stratum of intelligentsia recruited chiefly from the bourgeois "servers of princes" or officials in the broadest sense, and occasionally also from the landed nobility.

This latter is a stratum far removed from political activity, scarcely thinking in political terms and only tentatively in national ones, whose legitimation consists primarily in its intellectual, scientific, or artistic *accomplishments*. Counterposed to it is an upper class which "accomplishes" nothing in the sense in which the others do, but for which the shaping of its distinguished and distinctive *behavior* is central to its self-image and self-justification. And this is the class which Kant has in mind when he speaks of being "civilized to the point where we are overburdened," of mere "social propriety and decency," of "the similitude of morality in the love of honor." It is in the polemic of the stratum of German middle-class intelligentsia against the etiquette of the ruling courtly upper class that the conceptual contraposition of *Kultur* and *Zivilisation* originates in Germany. But this polemic is older and broader than its crystallization in these two concepts.

8. It can be traced long before the middle of the eighteenth century, even if only as an undertone in thought much more muted than after the middle of the century. A good idea of this can be obtained from the articles on *Hof*, *Höflichkeit*, and *Hofmann* (Court, Courtesy, Courtier), too long to be reproduced here in full, in the *Zedler Universal Lexicon* of 1736.[4]

> Courtesy undoubtedly gets its name from the court and court life. The courts of great lords are a theater where everyone wants to make his fortune. This can only be done by winning the favor of the prince and the most important people of his court. One therefore takes all conceivable pains to make oneself agreeable to them. Nothing does this better than making the other believe that we are ready to serve him to the utmost of our capacity under all conditions. Nevertheless, we are not always in a position to do this, and may not want to, often for good reasons. Courtesy serves as a substitute for all this. By it we give the other so much reassurance, through our outward show, that he has a favorable anticipation of our readiness to serve him. This wins us the other's trust, from which an affection for us develops imperceptibly, as a result of which he becomes eager to do good to us. This is so common with courtesy that it gives a special advantage to him who possesses it. To be sure, it should really be ability and virtue which earn us people's esteem. But how few are the correct judges of these two! And how many fewer hold them worthy of honor! People, all too concerned with externals, are far more moved by what reaches their senses externally, especially when the accompanying circumstances are such as particularly affect their will. This works out exactly in the case of a courtier.

Simply, without philosophical interpretation and in clear relation to specific social configurations, the same antithesis is here expressed which eventuates in Kant, refined and deepened, in the contraposition of culture and civilization: deceptive external "courtesy" and true "virtue." But the author only speaks of this in passing, with a sigh of resignation. After the middle of the century the tone gradually changes. The self-legitimation of the middle classes by virtue and accomplishment becomes more precise and emphatic, and the polemic against the external and superficial manners to be found in the courts becomes more explicit.

III
Examples of Courtly Attitudes in Germany

9. It is not easy to speak of Germany in general, since at this time there are special characteristics in each of the many states. But only a few are eventually decisive for the development of the whole; the rest follow. And certain general phenomena present themselves more or less clearly everywhere.

To begin with, there is the depopulation and the dreadful economic devastation of the country after the Thirty Years War. In the seventeenth century, and even still in the eighteenth, Germany and in particular the German bourgeoisie are poor by French and English standards. Trade, and especially the foreign trade which was highly developed in parts of Germany in the sixteenth century, is in ruins. The huge wealth of the great mercantile houses is destroyed, partly by the shift in trade routes due to the overseas discoveries, and partly as a direct consequence of the long chaos of the war. What is left is a small-town bourgeoisie with narrow horizons, living essentially by supplying local needs.

There is not much money available for luxuries such as literature and art. In the courts, wherever there is enough money to do so, people inadequately imitate the conduct of the court of Louis XIV and speak French. German, the language of the lower and middle classes, is unwieldy and awkward. Leibniz, Germany's only courtly philosopher, the only great German of this time whose name wins acclaim in wider courtly circles, writes and speaks French or Latin, seldom German. And the language problem, the problem of what could be done with this awkward German language, occupies him as it has occupied many others.

French spreads from the courts to the upper layer of the bourgeoisie. All *honnêtes gens* (decent people), all people of "consequence" speak it. To speak French is the status symbol of all the upper classes.

In 1730, Gottsched's bride writes her betrothed: "Nothing is more plebeian than to write letters in German."[5]

If one speaks German, it is considered good form to introduce as many French words as possible. In 1740, E. de Mauvillon writes in his *Lettres Françoises et Germaniques*: "It is only a few years since one did not say four words of German without two of French." That was *le bel usage* (good usage).[6] And he has more to say about the barbaric quality of the German language. Its nature, he says, is "d'être rude et barbare" (to be rude and barbarous).[7] There are the Saxons, who assert "qu'on parle mieux l'Allemand en Saxe, qu'en aucun autre endroit de l'Empire" (German is spoken better in Saxony than in any other part of the

Empire). The Austrians make the same assertion in regard to themselves, as do the Bavarians, the Brandenburgers, and the Swiss. A few scholars, Mauvillon continues, want to establish rules of grammar, but "il est difficile, qu'une Nation, qui contient dans son sein tant de Peuples indépendans les uns des autres, se soumette aux décisions d'un petit nombre des Savans" (it is difficult for a nation that embraces so many peoples independent of one another to submit to the decisions of a small number of savants).

Here as in many other fields, a small, powerless, middle-class intelligentsia falls heir to tasks which in France and England were undertaken largely by the court and the aristocratic upper class. It is learned middle-class "servers of princes" who first attempt to create, in a particular intellectual class, models of what German is, and thus to establish at least in this intellectual sphere a German unity which does not yet seem realizable in the political sphere. The concept of *Kultur* has the same function.

But at first most of what he sees in Germany appears crude and backward to Mauvillon, an observer grounded in French civilization. He speaks of the literature as well as the language in these terms: "Milton, Boileau, Pope, Racine, Tasso, Molière, and practically all poets of consequence have been translated into most European languages; your poets, for the most part, are themselves only translators."

He goes on: "Name me a creative spirit on your Parnassus, name me a German poet who has drawn from his own resources a work of some reputation; I defy you to."[8]

10. One might say that this was the unauthoritative opinion of a badly oriented Frenchman. But in 1780, forty years after Mauvillon and nine years before the French Revolution, when France and England have already passed through decisive phases of their cultural and national development, when the languages of the two Western countries have long since found their classic and permanent form, Frederick the Great publishes a work called *De la littérature allemande*,[9] in which he laments the meager and inadequate development of German writing, makes approximately the same assertions about the German language as Mauvillon, and explains how in his opinion this lamentable situation may be remedied.

Of the German language he says: "I find a half-barbarous language, which breaks down into as many different dialects as Germany has provinces. Each local group is convinced that its patois is the best." He describes the low estate of German literature and laments the pedantry of German scholars and the meager development of German science. But he also sees the reasons for it: he speaks of Germany's impoverishment as a result of continuous wars, and of the inadequate development of trade and bourgeoisie.

"It is," he says, "not to the spirit or the genius of the nation that one must attribute the slight progress we have made, but we should lay the blame only on a succession of sad events, a string of wars which have ruined us and left us poor in men as well as money."

He speaks of the slowly beginning recovery of prosperity: "The Third Estate no longer languishes in shameful degradation. Fathers educate their children without going into debt. Behold, a beginning has been made in the happy revolution which we await." And he prophesies that with growing prosperity there will also come a blossoming of German art and science, a civilizing of the Germans which will give them an equal place among the other nations: this is the happy revolution of which he speaks. And he compares himself to Moses, who saw the new blossoming of his people approaching without experiencing it.

11. Was Frederick right? A year after the appearance of his work, in 1781, Schiller's *Die Räuber* and Kant's *Critique of Pure Reason* appeared, to be followed in 1787 by Schiller's *Don Carlos* and Goethe's *Iphigenie*. There followed the whole blossoming of German literature and philosophy which we know. All of this seems to confirm his prediction.

But this new blooming had been long in preparation. The German language did not achieve its new expressive power in two or three years. In 1780, when *De la littérature allemande* appeared, this language had long ceased to be the half-barbaric "patois" of which Frederick speaks. A whole collection of works to which today, in retrospect, we assign considerable importance had already appeared. Goethe's *Götz von Berlichingen* had been produced seven years earlier, *Werther* was in circulation, Lessing had already published the major part of his dramatic and theoretical works, including *Laokoon* in 1766 and *Die Hamburgische Dramaturgie* in 1767. Frederick died in 1781, a year after the appearance of his work. Klopstock's writings had been published much earlier; his *Messias* appeared in 1748. This is without counting Herder, the *Sturm und Drang* plays, and a whole collection of widely read novels such as Sophie de la Roche's *Das Fräulein von Sternheim*. There had long since developed in Germany a class of buyers, a bourgeois public—even if still a relatively small one—which was interested in such works. Waves of great intellectual excitement had flowed over Germany and found expression in articles, books, plays, and other works. The German language had become rich and flexible.

Of all this Frederick gives no hint in his work. He either does not see it or assigns it no significance. He mentions a single work of the young generation, the greatest work of the period of *Sturm und Drang* and enthusiasm for Shakespeare, *Götz von Berlichingen*. He mentions it, characteristically, in connection with the education and forms of entertainment of the *basses classes*, the lower strata of the population:

> To convince yourself of the lack of taste which has reigned in Germany until our day, you only need go to the public spectacles. There you will see presented the abominable works of Shakespeare, translated into our language; the whole audience goes into

raptures when it listens to these ridiculous farces worthy of the savages of Canada. I describe them in these terms because they sin against all the rules of the theater, rules which are not at all arbitrary.

Look at the porters and gravediggers who come on stage and make speeches worthy of them; after them come the kings and queens. How can such a jumble of lowliness and grandeur, of buffoonery and tragedy, be touching and pleasing?

One can pardon Shakespeare for these bizarre errors; the beginning of the arts is never their point of maturity.

But then look at *Götz von Berlichingen* making its appearance on stage, a detestable imitation of these bad English pieces, while the public applauds and enthusiastically demands the repetition of these disgusting stupidities.

And he continues: "After having spoken of the lower classes, it is necessary for me to go on with the same frankness in regard to the universities."

12. The man who speaks thus is the man who did more than any of his contemporaries for the political and economic development of Prussia and perhaps indirectly for the political development of Germany. But the intellectual tradition in which he grew up and which finds expression through him is the common tradition of Europe's "good society," the aristocratic tradition of prenational court society. He speaks its language, French. By the standard of its taste he measures the intellectual life of Germany. Its prescribed models determine his judgment. Others of this society have long spoken of Shakespeare in a way altogether similar to his. Thus, in 1730, Voltaire gave expression to very similar thoughts in the *Discours sur la tragédie*, which introduces the tragedy *Brutus*: "I certainly do not pretend to approve the barbarous irregularities with which it [Shakespeare's tragedy *Julius Caesar*] is filled. It is only surprising that there are not more in a work composed in an age of ignorance by a man who did not even know Latin and had no teacher except his own genius."

What Frederick the Great says about Shakespeare is, in fact, the standard opinion of the French-speaking upper class of Europe. He does not "copy" or "plagiarize" Voltaire; what he writes is his sincere personal opinion. He takes no pleasure in the rude and uncivilized jests of gravediggers and similar folks, the more so if they are mixed in with the great tragic sentiments of princes and kings. He feels that all of this has no clear and concise form; these are the "pleasures of the lower classes." This is the way in which his comments are to be understood; they are no more and no less individual than the French language he uses. Like it, they bear witness to his membership in a particular society. And the paradox that while his politics were Prussian his aesthetic tradition was French (or, more precisely, absolutist-courtly) is less great than present-day concepts of national uniformity may suggest. It is bound up with the special structure of this court society, whose political institutions and interests were multifariously fissured, but whose social stratification was into estates whose taste, style, and language were by and large the same throughout Europe.

The peculiarities of this situation occasionally produced inner conflicts in the young Frederick, as he slowly became aware that the interests of the ruler of Prussia could not always be brought into accord with reverence for France and adherence to courtly customs.[10] Throughout his life they produced a certain disharmony between what he did as a ruler and what he wrote and published as a human being and philosopher.

The feelings of the German bourgeois intelligentsia toward him were also sometimes correspondingly paradoxical. His military and political successes gave their German self-awareness a tonic it had long lacked, and for many he became a national hero. But his attitude in matters of language and taste, which found expression in his work on German literature though by no means there alone, was exactly what the German intelligentsia, precisely as a *German* intelligentsia, had to fight against.

Their situation had its analogue in almost all the greater German states and in many of the smaller ones. At the top almost everywhere in Germany were individuals or groups of men who spoke French and decided policy. On the other side, there was a German-speaking intelligentsia, who by and large had no influence on political developments. From their ranks, essentially, came the men on whose account Germany has been called the land of poets and thinkers. And from them concepts such as *Bildung* and *Kultur* received their specifically German imprint and tenor.

IV

The Middle Class and the Court Nobility in Germany

13. It would be a special project (and a very fascinating one) to show how much the specific spiritual condition and ideals of a courtly-absolutist society found expression in classical French tragedy, which Frederick the Great counterposes to the Shakespearean tragedies and *Götz*. The importance of good form, the specific mark of every genuine "society"; the control of individual feelings by reason, a vital necessity for every courtier; the reserved behavior and elimination of every plebeian expression, the specific mark of a particular stage on the road to "civilization"—all this finds its purest expression in classical tragedy. What must be hidden in court life, all vulgar feelings and attitudes, everything of which "one" does not speak, does not appear in tragedy either. People of low rank, which for this class also means of base character, have no place in it. Its form is clear, transparent, precisely regulated, like etiquette and court life in general.[11] It shows the courtly people as they would like to be and, at the same time, as the absolute prince wants to see them. And all who lived under the impress of this

social situation, be they English or Prussian or French, had their taste forced into the same pattern. Even Dryden, next to Pope the best-known courtly poet of England, wrote about earlier English drama very much in the vein of Frederick the Great and Voltaire in the epilogue to the *Conquest of Granada*:

> Wit's now arrived to a more high degree;
> Our native language more refined and free,
> Our ladies and our men now speak more wit
> In conversation, than those poets writ.

The connection with social stratification is particularly clear in this aesthetic judgment. Frederick, too, defends himself against the tastelessness of juxtaposing on the stage the "tragic grandeur" of princes and queens and the "baseness" of porters and gravediggers. How could he have understood and approved a dramatic and literary work which had central to it precisely the struggle against class differences, a work which was intended to show that not merely the sorrows of princes and kings and the courtly aristocracy but those of people lower on the social scale have their greatness and their tragedy.

In Germany, too, the bourgeoisie slowly becomes more prosperous. The King of Prussia sees this and promises himself that it will lead to an awakening of art and science, a "happy revolution." But this bourgeoisie speaks a different language from the king. The ideals and taste of the bourgeois youth, the models for its behavior, are almost the opposite of his.

In *Dichtung und Wahrheit* (*Poetry and Truth*), Book 9, Goethe writes: "In Strasbourg, on the French border, we were at once freed from the spirit of the French. We found their way of life much too ordered and too aristocratic, their poetry cold, their criticism destructive, their philosophy abstruse and unsatisfying."

He writes *Götz* from this mood. How could Frederick the Great, the man of enlightened, rational absolutism and aristocratic-courtly taste, have understood it? How could the King have approved the dramas and theories of Lessing, who praises in Shakespeare precisely what Frederick condemns: that his works fit the taste of the people far more than do the French classics?

"If someone had translated the masterpieces of Shakespeare . . . for our Germans, I know well that it would have a better result than thus making them acquainted with Corneille or Racine. In the first place, the people would take far more delight in him than in them."

Lessing writes this in his *Letters Concerning the Most Recent Literature* (part I, letter 17), and he demands and writes bourgeois dramas, appropriate to the newly awakening self-consciousness of the bourgeois classes, because courtly people do not have the exclusive privilege to be great. "This hateful distinction which men have made between themselves," he says, "is not known to nature. She parcels out the qualities of the heart without any preference for the nobles and the rich."[12]

The whole literary movement of the second half of the eighteenth century is the product of a social class—and, accordingly, of aesthetic ideals—in opposition to Frederick's social and aesthetic inclinations. Thus, they have nothing to say to him, and he therefore overlooks the vital forces already active around him and condemns what he cannot overlook, like *Götz*. This German literary movement, whose exponents include Klopstock, Herder, Lessing, the poets of *Sturm und Drang* (Storm and Stress), the poets of "sensibility," and the circle known as the *Göttinger Hain*, the young Goethe, the young Schiller, and many others, is certainly no political movement. With isolated exceptions, one finds in Germany before 1789 no idea of concrete political action, nothing reminiscent of the formation of a political party or a political party program. One does find, particularly in Prussian officialdom, proposals and also the practical beginning of reforms in terms of enlightened absolutism. In philosophers such as Kant one finds the development of general basic principles which are, in part, in direct opposition to the prevailing conditions. In the writings of the young generation of the *Göttinger Hain* one finds expressions of wild hatred of princes, courts, aristocrats. Frenchifiers, courtly immorality, and intellectual frigidity. And everywhere among middle-class youth one finds vague dreams of a new united Germany, of a "natural" life—"natural" as opposed to the "unnatural" life of court society—and again and again an overwhelming delight in their own exuberance of feeling.

Thoughts, feelings—nothing which was able in any sense to lead to concrete political action. The structure of this absolutist society of petty states offered no opening for it. Bourgeois elements gained self-assurance, but the framework of the absolute states was completely unshaken. The bourgeois elements were excluded from any political activity. At most, they could "think and write" independently; they could not act independently.

In this situation, writing becomes the most important outlet. Here the new self-confidence and the vague discontent with what exists find a more or less covert expression. Here, in a sphere which the apparatus of the absolute states had surrendered to a certain extent, the young middle-class generation counterposed its new dreams and oppositional ideas, and with them the German language, to the courtly ideals.

As has been said, the literary movement of the second half of the eighteenth century is not a political one, but in the fullest sense of the word it is the expression of a social movement, a transformation of society. To be sure, the bourgeoisie as a whole did not yet find expression in it. It was at first the expression of a sort of bourgeois vanguard, what is here described as the middle-class intelligentsia: many individuals in the same position and of similar social origin scattered throughout the country, individuals who understood one another because they were in the same position. Only occasionally do individuals of this vanguard find themselves together in some place as a group, for a shorter or longer time; often they live in isolation or solitude, an elite in relation to the people, persons of the second rank in the eyes of the courtly aristocracy.

Again and again one can see in these works the connection between this social situation and the ideals of which they speak: the love of nature and freedom, the solitary exaltation, the surrender to the excitement of one's own heart, unhindered by "cold reason." In *Werther,* whose success shows how typical these sentiments were of a particular generation, it is occasionally said quite unequivocally.

In the letter of December 24, 1771, one reads: "The resplendent misery, the boredom among the detestable people gathered together here, the competition for rank among them, the way they are constantly looking for a chance to get a step ahead of one another. . . ."

And under January 8, 1772: "What sort of people are these whose whole soul is rooted in ceremonial, and whose thoughts and desires the year round are centered on how they can move up a chair at table."

Under March 15, 1772: "I gnash my teeth . . . I eat at the Count's house and after dinner we walk back and forth in the great park. The social hour approaches. I think, God knows, about nothing." He remains, the nobles arrive. The women whisper, something circulates among the men. Finally the Count, somewhat embarrassed, asks him to leave. The nobility feel insulted at seeing a bourgeois among them.

" 'You know,' " says the Count, " 'I notice that the company is displeased at seeing you here.' . . . . I stole away from the distinguished company, and drove to M., to watch the sunset from the hill there while reading in my Homer the noble song of how Ulysses was hospitably received by the excellent swineherds."

On the one hand, superficiality, ceremony, formal conversation; on the other, inwardness, depth of feeling, immersion in books, development of the individual personality. It is the same contrast which is expressed by Kant in the antithesis between *Kultur* and civilization, relating to a very specific social situation.

In *Werther,* Goethe also shows particularly clearly the two fronts between which the bourgeoisie lives. "What irritates me most of all," we read in the entry of December 24, 1771, "is our odious bourgeois situation. To be sure, I know as well as any other how necessary class differences are, how many advantages I owe to them myself, only they should not stand directly in my way." Nothing better characterizes middle-class consciousness than this statement. The doors below must remain shut. Those above must open. And like any other middle class, this one was imprisoned in a peculiarly middle-class way: it could not think of breaking down the walls that blocked the way up, for fear that those separating it from the lower strata might also give way in the assault.

The whole movement was one of upward mobility: Goethe's great-grandfather was a blacksmith,[13] his grandfather a tailor, then an innkeeper with a courtly clientele and courtly-bourgeois manners. Already well-to-do, his father becomes an imperial councellor, a rich bourgeois of independent means, with a title. His mother is the daughter of a Frankfurt patrician family.

Schiller's father was a surgeon, later a badly paid major; his grandfather, great-grandfather, and great-great-grandfather were bakers. From similar social origins, now closer, now farther off, from the crafts and the middle administration, come Schubart, Bürger, Winkelmann, Herder, Friedrich August Wolff, Fichte, and many other members of this movement.

14. There was an analogous movement in France. There, too, in conjunction with a similar social change, a profusion of outstanding people emerged from middle-class circles. They include Voltaire and Diderot. But in France these talents were received and assimilated without great difficulty by the large court society of Paris. In Germany, on the other hand, sons of the rising middle class who were distinguished by talent and intelligence were debarred, in their great majority, from courtly-aristocratic life. A few, like Goethe, achieved a kind of elevation to these circles. But aside from the fact that the court at Weimar was small and relatively poor, Goethe was an exception. By and large, the walls between the middle-class intelligentsia and the aristocratic upper class in Germany remained, by Western standards, very high. In 1740 the Frenchman Mauvillon notes that "one observes in the German gentleman an air that is haughty to the point of arrogance. Swollen with a lineage the length of which they are always ready to prove, they despise anyone not similarly endowed. Seldom," he continues, "do they contract *mésalliances*. But no less seldom are they seen behaving simply and amiably toward middle-class people. And if they spurn connubiality with them, how much less do they seek out their company, whatever their merit may be."[14]

In this particularly sharp social division between nobility and middle class, to which countless documents bear witness, a decisive factor was no doubt the relative indigence of both. This impelled the nobles to cut themselves off, using proof of ancestry as the most important instrument for preserving their privileged social existence. On the other hand, it blocked to the German middle class the main route by which in the Western countries bourgeois elements rose, intermarried with, and were received by the aristocracy: through money.

But whatever the causes—doubtless highly complex—of this very pronounced separation, the resulting low degree of fusion between the courtly-aristocratic models and values based on intrinsic worth, on the one hand, and the bourgeois models and values based on achievement, on the other, protractedly influenced the German national character as it emerged from now on. This division explains why a main linguistic stream, the language of educated Germans, and almost the entire recent intellectual tradition deposited in literature received their decisive impulses and their stamp from a middle-class intellectual stratum which was far more purely and specifically middle-class than the corresponding French intelligentsia and even than the English, the latter seeming to occupy an intermediate position between those of France and Germany.

The gesture of self-isolation, the accentuation of the specific and distinctive, which was seen earlier in the comparison of the German concept of *Kultur* with Western "civilization," reappears here as a characteristic of German historical development.

It was not only externally that France expanded and colonized early in comparison with Germany. Internally, too, similar movements are frequently seen throughout her more recent history. Particularly important in this connection is the diffusion of courtly-aristocratic manners, the tendency of the courtly aristocracy to assimilate and, so to speak, colonize elements from other classes. The social pride of the French aristocracy is always considerable, and the stress on class differences never loses its importance for them. But the walls surrounding them have more openings; access to the aristocracy (and thus the assimilation of other groups) plays a far greater role here than in Germany.

The most vigorous expansion of the German empire occurs, by contrast, in the Middle Ages. From this time on, the German Reich diminishes slowly but steadily. Even before the Thirty Years War and more so after it, German territories are hemmed in on all sides, and strong pressure is exerted on almost all the external frontiers. Correspondingly, the struggles within Germany between the various social groups competing for the limited opportunities and for survival, and therefore the tendencies toward distinctions and mutual exclusiveness, were generally more intense than in the expanding Western countries. As much as the fragmentation of the German territory into a multiplicity of sovereign states, it was this extreme isolation of large parts of the nobility from the German middle class that stood in the way of the formation of a unified, model-setting, central society, which in other countries attained decisive importance at least as a stage on the way to nationhood, setting its stamp in certain phases on language, on the arts, on the manners, and on the structure of emotions.

V

Literary Examples of the Relationship of the German Middle-Class Intelligentsia to the Court

15. The books of the middle classes which had great public success after the mid-eighteenth century—that is, in the period when these classes were gaining in prosperity and self-assurance—show very clearly how strongly this dissimilarity was felt. They also demonstrate that the differences between the

structure and life of the middle class, on the one hand, and the courtly upper class, on the other, were matched by differences in the structure of behavior, emotional life, aspirations, and morality; they show—necessarily one-sidedly—how these differences were perceived in the middle-class camp.

An example of this is the well-known novel by Sophie de la Roche, *Das Fräulein von Sternheim*,[15] which made the authoress one of the most celebrated women of her time. "My whole ideal of a young woman," wrote Caroline Flachsland to Herder after reading *Sternheim*, "gentle, delicate, charitable, proud, virtuous, and deceived. I have spent precious, wonderful hours reading the book. Alas, how far I still am from my ideal, from myself."[16]

The curious paradox residing in the fact that Caroline Flachsland, like many others of similar makeup, loves her own suffering—that she includes being deceived, along with charity, pride, and virtue, among the features of the ideal heroine whom she wishes to resemble—is highly characteristic of the emotional condition of the middle-class intelligentsia, and particularly of the women among them, in the age of sensibility. The middle-class heroine is deceived by the aristocratic courtier. The warning, the fear of the socially superior "seducer" who cannot marry the girl because of the social discrepancy, and the secret wish for his approach, the fascination that lies in the idea of penetrating the closed and dangerous circle, finally the identifying empathy with the deceived girl: all this is an example of the specific ambivalence besetting the emotional life of middle-class people—and not only women—with regard to the aristocracy. *Das Fräulein von Sternheim* is, in this respect, a feminine counterpart of *Werther*. Both works point to specific entanglements of their class, which find expression in sentimentality, sensibility, and related shades of emotion.

The problem presented in the novel: A high-minded country girl, from a family of landed gentry with bourgeois origins, arrives at court. The Prince, related to her on her mother's side, desires her as his mistress. Having no other escape, she seeks refuge with the "scoundrel" of the novel, an English lord living at the court, who speaks just as many middle-class circles would have imagined an "aristocratic seducer" to speak, and who produces a comic effect because he utters middle-class reproaches to his type as his own thoughts. But from him, too, the heroine preserves her virtue, her moral superiority, the compensation for her class inferiority, and dies.

This is how the heroine, Fräulein von Sternheim, the daughter of an ennobled colonel, speaks:[17]

> To see how the tone, the modish spirit of the court suppresses the noblest movements of a heart admirably nature, to see how avoiding the sneers of the ladies and gentlemen of fashion means laughing and agreeing with them, fills me with contempt and pity. The thirst for amusement, for new finery, for admiration of a dress, a piece of furniture, a new noxious dish—oh, my Emilie, how anxious and sick my soul grows. . . . I will not speak of the false ambition that hatches so many base intrigues, grovels before vice

ensconced in prosperity, regards virtue and merit with contempt, and unfeelingly makes others wretched.

"I am convinced, Aunt," she says after a few days of court life, "that life at court does not suit my character. My taste, my inclinations, diverge from it in every way. And I confess to my gracious aunt that I would leave more happily than I came."

"Dearest Sophie," her aunt tells her, "you are really a most charming girl, but the old vicar has filled your head with pedantic ideas. Let go of them a little."[18]

In another place Sophie writes: "My love of Germany has just involved me in a conversation in which I sought to defend the merits of my Fatherland. I talked so zealously that my aunt told me afterward that I had given a pretty demonstration of being the granddaughter of a professor. . . . This reproach vexed me. The ashes of my father and grandfather had been offended."

The clergyman and the professor—these are indeed two of the most important representatives of the middle-class administrative intelligentsia, two social figures who played a decisive part in the formation and diffusion of the new German educated language. This example shows quite clearly how the vague national feeling of these circles, with its spiritual, nonpolitical leanings, appears as bourgeois to the aristocracy at the petty courts. At the same time, both the clergyman and the professor point to the social center most important in fashioning and disseminating the German middle-class culture: the university. From it generation after generation of students carried into the country, as teachers, clergymen, and middle-rank administrators, a complex of ideas and ideals stamped in a particular way. The German university was, in a sense, the middle-class counterweight to the court.

Thus it is in words with which the pastor might thunder against him from the pulpit that the court scoundrel expressed himself in the middle-class imagination:[19]

> You know that I have never granted love any other power than over my senses, whose most delicate and lively pleasures it affords. . . . All classes of beauty have pandered to me. . . . I grew sated with them. . . . The moralists . . . may have their say on the fine nets and snares in which I have captured the virtue and pride, the wisdom and the frigidity, the coquetry and even the piety of the whole feminine world. . . . Amour indulged my vanity. He brought forth from the most wretched corner of the countryside a colonel's daughter whose form, mind, and character are so charming that . . .

Twenty-five years later, similar antitheses and related ideals and problems can still earn a book success. In 1796, *Agnes von Lilien*,[20] by Caroline von Wolzogen, appeared in Schiller's *Horen*. In this novel the mother, of the high aristocracy, who must for mysterious reasons have her daughter educated outside the court circle, says:

I am almost thankful for the prudence that compels me to keep you far from the circle in which I became unhappy. A serious, sound formation of the mind is rare in high society. You might have become a little doll that danced to and fro at the side of opinion.

And the heroine says of herself:[21]

I knew but little of conventional life and the language of worldly people. My simple principles found many things paradoxical to which a mind made pliable by habit is reconciled without effort. To me it was as natural as that night follows day to lament the deceived girl and hate the deceiver, to prefer virtue to honor and honor to one's own advantage. In the judgment of this society I saw all these notions overturned.

She then sketches the prince, a product of French civilization:[22]

The prince was been sixty and seventy, and oppressive to himself and others with the stiff, old French etiquette which the sons of German princes had learned at the court of the French king and transplanted to their own soil, admittedly in somewhat reduced dimensions. The prince had learned through age and habit to move almost naturally under this heavy armor of ceremony. Toward women he observed the elegant, exaggerated courtesy of the bygone age of chivalry, so that his person was not unpleasing to them, but he could not leave the sphere of fine manners for an instant without becoming insufferable. His children . . . saw in their father only the despot.

The caricatures among the courtly people seemed to me now ridiculous, now pitiable. The reverence that they were able, on the appearance of their lord, to summon instantly from their hearts to their hands and feet, the gracious or angry glance that passed through their bodies like an electric shock . . . the immediate compliance of their opinions to the most recent utterance from the princely lips, all this I found incomprehensible. I seemed to be watching a puppet theater.

Courtesy, compliance, fine manners, on the one hand, sound education and preference of virtue to honor, on the other: German literature in the second half of the eighteenth century is full of such antitheses. As late as October 23, 1828, Eckermann says to Goethe: "An education as thorough as the Grand-Duke appears to have had is doubtless rare among princely personages." "Very rare," Goethe replies. "There are many, to be sure, who are able to converse cleverly on any subject, but they do not possess their learning inwardly, and merely tickle the surface. And it is no wonder, if one thinks of the appalling diversions and truncations that court life brings with it."

On occasion he uses the concept of *Kultur* quite expressly in this context. "The people around me," he says, "had no idea of scholarship. They were German courtiers, and this class had not the slightest *Kultur*."[23] And Knigge once observes explicitly: "Where more than here [in Germany] did the courtiers form a separate species."

16. In all these statements a quite definite social situation is reflected. It is the

same situation that is discernible behind Kant's opposition of *Kultur* to civilization. But even independently of these concepts, this phase and the experiences deriving from it imprinted themselves deeply in the German tradition. What is expressed in this concept of *Kultur*, in the antithesis between depth and superficiality and in many related concepts, is primarily the self-image of a middle-class intellectual stratum. This is a relatively thin layer scattered over the whole area, and therefore individualized to a high degree and in a particular form. It does not constitute, as does the court, a closed circle, a "society." It is composed predominantly of administrators, of civil servants in the broadest sense of the word—that is, of people who directly or indirectly derive their income from the court, but who, with few exceptions, do not themselves belong to courtly "good society," to the aristocratic upper class. It is a class of intellectuals without a broad middle-class background. The commercial professional bourgeoisie, who might have served as a public for the writers, is relatively undeveloped in most German states in the eighteenth century. The rise to prosperity is only beginning in this period. The German writers and intellectuals are therefore floating in the air to some extent. Mind and books are their refuge and their domain, achievements in scholarship and art their pride. Scope for political activity, political goals, scarcely exists for this class. Commerce and the economic order are for them, in keeping with the structure of their life and society, marginal concerns. Trade, communications, and industry are comparatively undeveloped and still need, for the most part, protection and promotion by mercantilist policy rather than liberation from its constraints. What legitimizes this eighteenth-century middle-class intelligentsia to itself, what supplies the foundation of its self-image and pride, is situated beyond economics and politics. It exists in what is called for precisely this reason *das rein Geistige* (the purely spiritual), in books, scholarship, religion, art, philosophy, in the inner enrichment, the intellectual formation (*Bildung*) of the individual, primarily through the medium of books, in the personality. Accordingly, the watchwords expressing this self-image of the German intellectual class, terms such as *Bildung* and *Kultur*, tend to draw a sharp distinction between accomplishments in the areas just mentioned, between this purely spiritual sphere as the only one of genuine value, and the political, economic, and social sphere, in complete contrast to the watchwords of the rising bourgeoisie in France and England. The peculiar fate of the German bourgeoisie, its long political impotence, and the late unification of the nation acted continuously in one direction, reinforcing concepts and ideals of this kind. Thus the development of the concept *Kultur* and the ideals it embodied reflected the position of the German intelligentsia without a significant social hinterland, which, being the first bourgeois formation in Germany, develop an expressly bourgeois self-image, specifically middle-class ideas, and an arsenal of trenchant concepts directed against the courtly upper class.

Also in keeping with their situation was what this intelligentsia saw as most to be opposed in the upper class, as the antithesis of *Bildung* and *Kultur*. The attack is directed only infrequently, hesitantly, and usually resignedly against the political or social privileges of the courtly aristocracy. Instead, it is directed predominantly against their human behavior.

A very illuminating description of the difference between this German intellectual class and its French counterpart is likewise to be found in Goethe's conversations with Eckermann: Ampère has come to Weimar. (Goethe did not know him personally but had often praised him to Eckermann.) To everyone's astonishment the celebrated Monsieur Ampère turns out to be a "cheerful youth of some twenty years." Eckermann expresses surprise, and Goethe replies (Thursday, May 3, 1827):

> It has not been easy for you on your heath, and we in middle Germany have had to buy dearly enough such little wisdom as we possess. For at bottom we lead an isolated, miserable life! Very little culture comes to us from the people itself, and all our men of talent are scattered across the country. One is in Vienna, another in Berlin, another in Königsberg, another in Bonn or Düsseldorf, all separated from each other by fifty or a hundred miles, so that personal contact or a personal exchange of ideas is a rarity. I feel what this means when men like Alexander von Humboldt pass through, and advance my studies further in a single day than I would otherwise have traveled in a year on my solitary path.
>
> But now imagine a city like Paris, where the outstanding minds of the whole realm are gathered in a single place, and in their daily intercourse, competition, and rivalry teach and spur each other on, where the best from every sphere of nature and art, from the whole surface of the earth, can be viewed at all times. Imagine this metropolis where every walk over a bridge or across a square summons up a great past. And in all this do not think of the Paris of a dull, mindless epoch, but the Paris of the nineteenth century, where for three generations, through men like Molière, Voltaire, and Diderot, such a wealth of ideas has been put into circulation as is not found anywhere else on the entire globe, and you will understand that a good mind like Ampère, having grown up in such plenitude, can very well amount to something in his twenty-fourth year.

Further on, Goethe says with reference to Mérimée: "In Germany we cannot hope to produce such mature work when still so young. This is not the fault of the individual, but of the cultural state of the nation, and the great difficulty that we all experience in making our way in isolation."

From such statements, which in this introductory context must suffice as documentation, it is very clear how the political fragmentation of Germany is connected to a quite specific structure, both of the German intellectual class and of its social behavior and way of thinking. In France the members of the intelligentsia are collected in one place, held together within a more or less unified and central "good society"; in Germany, with its numerous, relatively small capitals, there is no central and unified "good society." Here the intelligentsia is dispersed over the entire country. In France conversation is one of the most important means of communication and, in addition, has been for centuries an art; in Germany the most important means of communication is the book, and it is a unified written language, rather than a unified spoken one, that this German intellectual class develops. In France even young people live in a milieu of rich and stimulating intellectuality; the young member of the German middle class must work his way up in relative solitude and isolation. The mechanisms of social advancement are different in both countries. And finally, this statement of Goethe's also shows very clearly what a middle-class intelligentsia without social hinterland really means. Earlier a passage was quoted in which he attributed little culture to the courtiers. Here he says the same of the common people. *Kultur* and *Bildung* are the watchwords and characteristics of a thin intermediate stratum that has risen out of the people. Not only the small courtly class above it, but even the broader strata below still show relatively little understanding for the endeavors of their own elite.

However, precisely this underdevelopment of the broader, professional bourgeois classes is one of the reasons why the struggle of the middle-class vanguard, the bourgeois intelligentsia, against the courtly upper class is waged almost entirely outside the political sphere, and why the attack is directed predominantly against the conduct of the upper class, against general human characteristics like "superficiality," "outward politeness," "insincerity," and so on. Even the few quotations that were used here show these connections extremely clearly. Admittedly, it is only rarely and without great emphasis that the attack focuses on specific concepts antithetical to those which served as self-legitimization for the German intellectual class, concepts such as *Bildung* and *Kultur*. One of the few specific counter-concepts is "civilization" in the Kantian sense.

VI

The Recession of the Social and the Advance of the National Element in the Antithesis of *Kultur* and *Zivilisation*

17. Whether the antithesis is expressed by these or other concepts, one thing is always clear: the contraposition of particular human characteristics which later serve primarily to express a national antithesis here appears primarily as the expression of a social antithesis. As the experience underlying the formulation of pairs of opposites such as "depth" and "superficiality," "honesty" and "falsity," "outward politeness" and "true virtue," and from which, among other things,

the antithesis between *Zivilisation* and *Kultur* grows up, we find at a particular phase of German development the tension between the middle-class intelligentsia and the courtly aristocracy. Certainly, there is never a complete lack of awareness that courtliness and French are related entities. G. C. H. Lichtenberg expresses this very clearly in one of his aphorisms, in which he speaks of the difference between the French *promesse* and the German *Versprechung* (Part 3, 1775–1779[24]). "The latter is kept," he says, "and not the former. The usefulness of French words in German. I am surprised that it has not been noticed. The French word gives the German idea with an admixture of humbug, or in its court meaning. . . . An invention (*Erfindung*) is something new and a *découverte* something old with a new name. Columbus discovered (*entdeckte*) America and it was Americus Vesputius's *découverte*. Indeed, *goût* and taste (*Geschmack*) are almost antithetical, and people of *goût* seldom have much taste."

But it is only after the French Revolution that the idea of the German courtly aristocracy unmistakably recedes, and the idea of France and the Western powers in general moves toward the foreground in the concept of "civilization" and related ideas.

One typical example: in 1797 there appeared a small book by the French émigré Menuret, *Essay sur la ville d'Hambourg*. A citizen of Hamburg, Canon Meyer, writes the following commentary on it:

> Hamburg is still backward. After a famous epoch (famous enough, when swarms of emigrants are settling here), it has made progress (really?); but to increase, to complete I do not say its happiness (that would be addressing his God) but its civilization, its advance in the career of science and art (in which, as you know, we are still in the North), in that of luxury, comfort, frivolity (his special field!) it still needs a number of years, or events which draw to it new throngs of foreigners (provided they are not more swarms of his civilized compatriots) and an increase of opulence.

Here, therefore, the concepts "civilized" and "civilization" are already quite unequivocally linked with the image of the Frenchman.

With the slow rise of the German bourgeoisie from a second-rank class to the bearer of German national consciousness, and finally—very late and conditionally— to the ruling class, from a class which was first obliged to perceive or legitimize itself primarily by contrasting itself to the courtly-aristocratic upper class, and then by defining itself against competing nations, the antithesis between *Kultur* and Zivilisation, with all its accompanying meanings, changes in significance and function: *from a primarily social it becomes a primarily national antithesis.*

And a parallel development is undergone by what is thought specifically German: here, likewise, many originally middle-class social characteristics, imprinted in people by their social situation, become national characteristics. Honesty and sincerity, for example, are now opposed as German characteristics to dissimulating courtesy. But sincerity, as it is used here, originally emerged as a specific trait of the middle-class person, in contrast to the worldling or courtier. This, too, is seen clearly in a conversation between Eckermann and Goethe.

"I usually carry into society," says Eckermann on May 2, 1824, "my personal likes and dislikes and a certain need to love and be loved. I seek a personality conforming to my nature; to that person I should like to give myself entirely and have nothing to do with the others."

"This natural tendency of yours," Goethe answers, "is indeed not of a sociable kind; yet what would all our education be if we were not willing to overcome our natural tendencies. It is a great folly to demand that people should harmonize with us, I have never done so. I have thereby attained the ability to converse with all people, and only thus is knowledge of human character gained, as well as the necessary adroitness in life. For with opposed natures one must take a grip on oneself if one is to get on with them. You ought to do likewise. There's no help for it, you must go into society. No matter what you say."

The sociogenesis and psychogenesis of human behavior are still largely unknown. Even to raise the questions may seem odd. It is nevertheless observable that people from different social units behave differently in quite specific ways. We are accustomed to take this for granted. We speak of the peasant or the courtier, of the Englishman or the German, of the medieval man or the man of the twentieth century, and we mean that the people of the social units indicated by such concepts behave uniformly in a specific manner which transcends all individual differences when measured against the individuals of a contrasting group: for example, the peasant behaves in many respects differently from the courtier, the Englishman or Frenchman from the German, and the medieval man from the man of the twentieth century, no matter how much else they may have in common as human beings.

Modes of behavior differing in this way are apparent in the conversation just quoted between Eckermann and Goethe. Goethe is certainly a man individualized to a particularly high degree. As a result of his social destiny, modes of behavior with different social origins merge in him into a specific unity. He, his opinions, and his behavior are certainly never entirely typical of any of the social groups and situations through which he has passed. But in this quotation he speaks quite expertly as a man of the world, as a courtier, from experiences which are necessarily foreign to Eckermann. He perceives the compulsion to hold back one's own feelings, to suppress antipathies and sympathies, which is inherent in court life, and which is often interpreted by people of a different social situation, and therefore with a different affect structure, as dishonesty or insincerity. And with a degree of consciousness that distinguishes as a relative outsider from all social groups, he emphasizes the beneficial, human aspect of his moderation of individual affects. His comment is one of the few German utterances of this time to acknowledge something of the social value of "courtesy" and to say something positive about social adroitness. In France and England, where "society" played a far greater role in the overall development of the nation, the behavioral tendencies he speaks of also play—though less consciously than in his case—a far more important part. And ideas of a similar kind, including the notion that people should seek to harmonize with and show consideration for each other, that the individual may not always give way to his emotions, recur quite frequently, with the same specifically social meaning as in Goethe, in the court literature of France, for example. As a reflection, these thoughts were the individual property of Goethe. But related social situations, life in the *monde*, led everywhere in Europe to related precepts and modes of behavior.

Similarly, the behavior which Eckermann describes as his own is—as compared to the outward serenity and amiability concealing opposed feelings that is first developed in this phase in the courtly-aristocratic world—clearly recognizable as originating from the small-town, middle-class sphere of the time. And it is certainly found not only in Germany in this sphere. But in Germany, owing to the particularly pure representation of the middle-class outlook by the intelligentsia, these and related attitudes become visible to an exceptional degree in literature. And they recur in this relatively pure form produced by the sharper, more rigorous division between courtly and middle-class circles, above all in the national behavior of the Germans.

The social units that we call nations differ widely in the personality structure of their members, in the schemata by which the emotional life of the individual is molded under the pressure of institutionalized tradition and of the present situation. What is typical in the behavior described by Eckermann is a specific form of "economy of affects," the open admission of individual inclination that Goethe considers unsociable and contrary to the affect formation necessary for "society."

For Nietzsche, many decades later, this attitude had long been the typical national attitude of Germans. Certainly, it has undergone modifications in the course of history, and no longer has the same social purpose as at Eckermann's time. Nietzsche ridicules it: "The German," he says in *Beyond Good and Evil* (Aphorism 244), "loves 'sincerity' and 'uprightness.' How comforting it is to be sincere and upright. It is today perhaps the most dangerous and deceptive of all the disguises in which the German is expert, this confidential, obliging, German honesty that always shows its cards. The German lets himself go, looking the while with trustful blue empty German eyes—and foreigners immediately mistake him for his nightshirt." This—leaving aside the one-sided value judgment—is one of the many illustrations of how, with the slow rise of the middle classes, their specific social characteristics gradually become national characteristics.

And the same is clear from the following judgment of Fontane on England, to be found in *Ein Sommer in London* (Dessau, 1852):

England and Germany are related in the same way as form and content, appearance and reality. Unlike things, which in no other country in the world exhibit the same solidity as in England, people are distinguished by form, their most outward packing. You need not be a gentleman, you must only have the means to appear one, and you are one. You need not be right, you must only find yourself within the forms of rightness, and you are right. . . . Everywhere appearance. Nowhere is one more inclined to abandon oneself blindly to the mere luster of a name. The German lives in order to live, the Englishman to represent. The German lives for his own sake, the Englishman for the sake of others.

It is perhaps necessary to point out how exactly this last idea coincides with the antithesis between Eckermann and Goethe: "I give open expression to my personal likes and dislikes," says Eckermann. "One must seek, even if unwillingly, to harmonize with others," argues Goethe.

"The Englishman," Fontane observes, "has a thousand comforts, but no comfort. The place of comfort is taken by ambition. He is always ready to receive, to give audiences. . . . He changes his suit three times a day; he observes at table—in the sitting room and drawing room—certain prescribed laws of propriety. He is a distinguished man, a phenomenon that impresses us, a teacher from whom we take lessons. But in the midst of our wonderment is mixed an infinite nostalgia for our petty-bourgeois Germany, where people have not the faintest idea how to represent, but are able so splendidly, so comfortably and cozily, to live."

The concept of "civilization" is not mentioned here. And the idea of German *Kultur* appears in this account only from afar. But we see from it, as from all these reflections, that the German antithesis between *Zivilisation* and *Kultur* does not stand alone; it is part of a larger context. It is an expression of the German self-image. And it points back to differences of self-legitimization, of character and total behavior, that first existed preponderantly, even if not exclusively, between particular German classes, and then between the German nation and other nations.

Chapter Two

Sociogenesis of the Concept of Civilisation *in France*

I

Introduction

1. It would be incomprehensible that, in the German antithesis of genuine *Bildung* and *Kultur* on the one hand and mere outward *Zivilisation* on the other, the internal social antithesis should recede and the national become dominant, had not the development of the French bourgeoisie followed, in certain respects, exactly the opposite course from the German.

In France the bourgeois intelligentsia and the leading groups of the middle class were drawn relatively early into court society. The German nobility's old means of distinction, the proof of ancestry—which later, in a bourgeois transformation, took on new life in German racial legislation—was certainly not entirely absent in the French tradition, but particularly after the establishment and consolidation of the "absolute monarchy," it no longer played a very decisive role as a barrier between the classes. The permeation of bourgeois circles by specifically aristocratic traditions (which in Germany, with the more rigorous separation of the classes, had a deep effect only in certain spheres such as the military, being elsewhere very limited) had quite different proportions in France. Here, as early as the eighteenth century, there was no longer any considerable difference of manners between the leading bourgeois groups and the courtly aristocracy. And even if, with the stronger upsurge of the middle class from the mid-eighteenth century onward—or, stated differently, with the enlargement of aristocratic society through the increased assimilation of leading middle-class groups—behavior and manners slowly changed, this happened without rupture as a direct continuation of the courtly-aristocratic tradition of the seventeenth century. Both the courtly bourgeoisie and the courtly aristocracy spoke the same language, read the same books, and had, with particular gradations, the same manners. And when the social and economic disproportionalities burst the institutional framework of the *ancien régime*, when the bourgeoisie became a nation, much of what had originally been the specific and distinctive social character of the courtly aristocracy and then also of the courtly-bourgeois groups, became, in an ever-widening movement and doubtless with some modification, the national character. Stylistic conventions, the forms of social intercourse, affect-molding, esteem for courtesy, the importance of good speech and conversation, articulateness of language and much else—all this is first formed in France within courtly society, then slowly changes, in a continuous diffusion, from a social into a national character.

Here, too, Nietzsche saw the difference very clearly. "Wherever there was a court," he says in *Beyond Good and Evil* (Aphorism 101), "there was a law of right speaking, and therefore also a law of style for all who wrote. Courtly language, however, is the language of the courtier who has no special subject, and who even in conversation on scholarly matters prohibits all technical expressions because they smack of specialization; this is why, in countries with a courtly culture, the technical term and everything that betrays the specialist is a stylistic blemish. Now that all courts have become caricatures . . . one is surprised to find even Voltaire very particular on this point. The fact is that we are all emancipated from court taste, while Voltaire was its consummation!"

In Germany the aspiring middle-class intelligentsia of the eighteenth century, trained at universities specializing in particular subjects, developed its self-expression, its own specific culture, in the arts and sciences. In France the bourgeoisie was already developed and prosperous to an entirely different degree. The rising intelligentsia had, besides the aristocracy, a broad bourgeois public, too. The intelligentsia itself, like certain other middle-class formations, was assimilated by the courtly circle. And so it came about that the German middle classes, with their very gradual rise to nationhood, increasingly perceived as the national character of their neighbor those modes of behavior which they had first observed predominantly at their own courts. And, having either judged this behavior second-rate or rejected it as incompatible with their own affect structure, so they also disapproved it to a greater or lesser degree in their neighbors.

2. It may seem paradoxical that in Germany, where the social walls between the middle class and the aristocracy were higher, social contacts fewer, and differences in manners more considerable, for a long time the discrepancies and

tensions between the classes found no political expression; whereas in France, where the class barriers were lower and social contact between the classes incomparably more intimate, the political activity of the bourgeoisie developed earlier and the tension between the classes reached an early political resolution.

But the paradox is only apparent. The long denial of political functions to the French nobility by royal policy, the early involvement of bourgeois elements in government and administration, their access to even the highest governmental functions, their influence and advancement at the court—all this had two consequences: on the one hand, continuous close social contact between elements of differing social origin; on the other, the opportunity for bourgeois elements to engage in political activity when the social situation was ripe and, prior to this, a strongly political training, a tendency to think in political categories. In the German states, by and large, almost exactly the reverse was the case. The highest government posts were generally reserved for the nobility. At the least, unlike their French counterparts, the German nobility played a decisive role in higher state administration. Its strength as an autonomous class had never been so radically broken as in France. In contrast, the class strength of the bourgeoisie, in keeping with its economic power, was relatively low in Germany until well into the nineteenth century. The sharper social severance of German middle-class elements from the courtly aristocracy reflected their relative economic weakness and their exclusion from most key positions in the state.

3. The social structure of France made it possible for the moderate opposition, which had been slowly growing from about the mid-eighteenth century, to be represented with a certain success in the innermost court circles. Its representatives did not yet form a party. Other forms of political struggle fitted the institutional structure of the *ancien régime*. They formed a clique at the court without a definite organization, but were supported by people and groups within the broader court society and in the country itself. The variety of social interests found expression at court in the conflicts between such cliques, admittedly in a somewhat vague form and with a strong admixture of the most diverse personal interests; nevertheless, these conflicts were expressed and resolved.

The French concept of *civilisation*, exactly like the corresponding German concept of *Kultur*, was formed within this opposition movement in the second half of the eighteenth century. Its process of formation, its function, and its meaning are as different from those of the German concept as are the circumstances and manners of the middle classes in the two countries.

It is not uninteresting to observe how similar is the French concept of *civilisation*, as first encountered in literature, to the concept to which many years later Kant opposed his concept of *Kultur*. The first literary evidence of the evolution of the verb *civiliser* into the concept *civilisation* is to be found, according to present-day findings,[25] in the work of the elder Mirabeau in the 1760s.

"I marvel to see," he says, "how our learned views, false on all points, are wrong on what we take to be civilization. If they were asked what civilization is, most people would answer: softening of manners, urbanity, politeness, and a dissemination of knowledge such that propriety is established in place of laws of detail: all that only presents me with the mask of virtue and not its face, and civilization does nothing for society if it does not give it both the form and the substance of virtue."[26] This sounds very similar to what was also being said in Germany against courtly manners. Mirabeau, too, contrasts what most people, according to him, consider to be civilization (i.e., politeness and good manners) against the ideal in whose name everywhere in Europe the middle classes were aligning themselves against the courtly-aristocratic upper class, and through which they legitimized themselves—the ideal of virtue. He, too, exactly like Kant, links the concept of civilization to the specific characteristics of the courtly aristocracy, with reason: for the *homme civilisé* was nothing other than a somewhat extended version of that human type which represented the true ideal of court society, the *honnête homme*.

Civilisé was, like *cultivé*, *poli*, or *policé*, one of the many terms, often used almost as synonyms, by which the courtly people wished to designate, in a broad or narrow sense, the specific quality of their own behavior, and by which they contrasted the refinement of their own social manners, their "standard," to the manners of simpler and socially inferior people.

Concepts such as *politesse* or *civilité* had, before the concept *civilisation* was formed and established, practically the same function as the new concept: to express the self-image of the European upper class in relation to others whom its members considered simpler or more primitive, and at the same time to characterize the specific kind of behavior through which this upper class felt itself different to all simpler and more primitive people. Mirabeau's statement makes it quite clear to what extent the concept of civilization was at first a direct continuation of other incarnations of courtly self-consciousness: "If they were asked what 'civilization' is, people would answer: softening of manners, politeness, and suchlike." And Mirabeau, like Rousseau, if more moderately, inverts the existing valuations. You and your civilization, he says, all that you are so proud of, believing that it raises you above the simple people, is of very little value: "In all the languages . . . of all ages, the depiction of the love of shepherds for their flocks and their dogs finds its way into our soul, deadened as it is by the pursuit of luxury and a false civilization."[27]

A person's attitude toward the "simple man"—above all, toward the "simple man" in his most extreme form, the "savage"—is everywhere in the second half of the eighteenth century a symbol of his position in the internal, social debate. Rousseau launched the most radical attack on the dominant order of values of his time, and for this very reason his direct importance for the courtly/middle-class reform movement of the French intelligentsia was less than might be suggested by his resonance among the unpolitical yet intellectually more radical middle-class intelligentsia of Germany. But Rousseau, for all the radicalism of his social criticism, had not yet fashioned an inclusive, unified counterconcept against which to hurl the accumulated reproaches. Mirabeau creates it, or is at least the first to use it in his writings; perhaps it had previously existed in conversation. From the *homme civilisé* he derives a general characteristic of society: *civilisation*. But his social criticism, like that of the other Physiocrats, is moderate. It remains entirely within the framework of the existing social system. It is, indeed, the criticism of reformers. While members of the German middle-class intelligentsia, at least in the mind, in the daydreams of their books, forge concepts diverging absolutely from the models of the upper class, and thus fight on politically neutral ground all the battles which they are unable to fight on the political and social plane because the existing institutions and power relationships deny them instruments and even targets; while they, in their books, oppose to the human characteristics of the upper class their own new ideals and behavioral models; the courtly-reformist intelligentsia in France remains for a long time within the framework of courtly tradition. These Frenchmen desire to improve, modify, adapt. Apart from a few outsiders like Rousseau, they do not oppose radically different ideals and models to the dominant order, but reformed ideals and models of that order. In the words "false civilization" the whole difference from the German movement is contained. The French writers imply that the false civilization ought to be replaced by a genuine one. They do not oppose to the *homme civilisé* a radically different human model, as did the German bourgeois intelligentsia with the term *gebildeter Mensch* (educated man) and with the idea of the "personality"; instead, they pick up courtly models in order to develop and transform them. They address themselves to a critical intelligentsia which, directly or indirectly, is itself writing and struggling within the extensive network of court society.

II

Sociogenesis of Physiocratism and the French Reform Movement

4. Let us recall the situation of France after the middle of the eighteenth century.

The principles by which France was governed and on which, in particular, taxation and customs legislation was based were broadly the same as at Colbert's time. But the internal relationships of power and interest, the social structure of France itself, had shifted in crucial ways. Strict protectionism, the shielding of national manufacturing and commercial activity against foreign competition, had actually contributed decisively to the development of French economic life, and so to furthering what mattered more than anything else to the king and his representatives—the taxable capacity of the country. The barriers in the grain trade, monopolies, the granary system, and the customs walls between provinces had partly protected local interests but, above all, had from time to time preserved the district most important to the king's peace and perhaps to that of all France, Paris, from the extreme consequences of bad harvests and rising prices—starvation and revolt.

But in the meantime, the capital and the population of the country had increased. Compared to Colbert's time, the trade network had become denser and more extensive, industrial activity more vigorous, communications better, and the economic integration and interdependence of French territory closer. Sections of the bourgeoisie began to find the traditional taxation and customs systems, under whose protection they had grown up, irksome and absurd. Progressive country gentry and landowners like Mirabeau saw in the mercantilist restraints on the grain economy an impediment rather than an inducement to agricultural production; in this they profited not a little from the lessons of the freer English trading system. And most important of all, a section of the higher administrators themselves recognized the ill effects of the existing system; at their head was their most progressive type, the provincial intendants, the representatives of the single modern form of bureaucracy which the *ancien régime* had produced, the only administrative function which was not, like the others, purchasable and therefore hereditary. These progressive elements in the administration formed one of the most important bridges between the demand for reform making itself felt in the country, and the court. Directly or indirectly they played, in the struggle of court cliques for key political positions (primarily the ministries), a not inconsiderable part.

That these struggles were not yet the more impersonal, political conflicts they later became, when the various interests would be represented by parties within a parliamentary framework, has already been pointed out. But the courtly groups which, for the most diverse reasons, competed for influence and posts at the court were, at the same time, social nuclei through which the interests of broader groups and classes could find expression at the controlling center of the country. In this way reformist tendencies, too, were represented at court.

By the second half of the eighteenth century, the kings had long ceased to rule arbitrarily. Far more perceptibly than Louis XIV, for example, they were the prisoners of social processes and dependent on court cliques and factions, some of which extended far into the country and deep into middle-class circles.

Physiocratism is one of the theoretical expressions of these interfactional struggles. It is by no means confined to economics, being a large-scale system of political and social reform. It contains, in a pointed, abstract, and dogmatically hardened form, ideas which—expressed less theoretically, dogmatically, and rigorously, i.e., as practical demands for reform—characterize the whole movement of which Turgot, who was for a time in charge of finance, was an exponent. If this tendency (which had neither a name nor a unified organization) is to be given a name, it might be called the reformist bureaucracy. But these reformist administrators doubtless also had sections of the intelligentsia and of the commercial bourgeoisie behind them.

Among those desiring and demanding reform, moreover, there were considerable differences of opinion concerning the kind of reform that was needed. Some were wholly in favor of a reform of the taxation system and the state machinery, yet were far more protectionist than the Physiocrats, for example. Forbonnais is one of the leading representatives of this tendency, and it is to misunderstand him and like-minded people to include them, on account of their more strongly protectionist attitude, indiscriminately among the "mercantilists." The debate between Forbonnais and the Physiocrats was an early expression of a divergence within modern industrial society which was to lead to ever-recurring conflicts between the exponents of free trade and protectionism. Both sides are part of the middle-class reform movement.

On the other hand, it was by no means the case that the *whole* bourgeoisie desired reform while the aristocracy exclusively opposed it. There were a number of clearly definable middle-class groups which resisted to the utmost any serious attempt at reform, and whose existence was indeed bound up with the conservation of the *ancien régime* in its unreformed state. These groups included the majority of the higher administrators, the *noblesse de robe*, whose offices were family possessions in the same sense that a factory or business today is hereditary property. They also included the craft guilds and a good proportion of the financiers. And if reform failed in France, if the disproportions of society finally burst the institutional structure of the *ancien régime* violently asunder, the opposition of these middle-class groups to reform bears a large measure of responsibility.

This whole survey shows very clearly one thing which is important in this context: whereas the middle classes already played a political role in France at this time, in Germany they did not. In Germany the intellectual stratum is confined to the sphere of mind and ideas; in France, along with all the other human questions, social, economic, administrative, and political issues come within the range of interests of the courtly/middle-class intelligentsia. The German systems of thought, by contrast, are purely academic. Their social base is the university. The social base from which Physiocratism emerged is the court and court society, where intellectual effort has specific concrete aims, such as influencing the king or his mistress.

5. The basic ideas of Quesnay and the Physiocrats are well known. In his *Tableau économique* (1758), Quesnay depicts the economic life of society as a more or less autonomous process, a closed cycle of the production, circulation, and reproduction of commodities. He speaks of the natural laws of a social life in harmony with reason. Basing his argument on this idea, Quesnay opposes

arbitrary intervention by rulers into the economic cycle. He wishes them to be aware of its laws in order to guide its processes, instead of issuing uninformed decrees at whim. He demands freedom of trade, particularly the grain trade, because self-regulation, the free play of forces, creates in his view a more beneficial order for consumers and producers than the traditional regulations from above and the countless trade barriers between province and province, country and country.

But he fully concedes that the self-regulating processes ought to be understood, and guided, by a wise and enlightened bureaucracy. Here, above all, lies the difference between the way in which the French reformers and the English reformers react to the discovery of self-regulation in economic life. Quesnay and his fellows remain wholly within the framework of the existing monarchic system. He leaves the basic elements of the *ancien régime* and its institutional structure untouched. And this applies all the more to the sections of the administration and intelligentsia whose position was close to his, and who, in a less abstract, less extreme, and more practically minded form, arrive at results similar to those of the central group of the Physiocrats. Fundamentally, the position common to all of them is extremely simple: roughly, it is not true that rulers are almighty and can regulate all human affairs as they think fit. Society and the economy have their own laws, which resist the irrational interference of rulers and force. Therefore an enlightened, rational administration must be created which governs in accordance with the "natural laws" of social processes, and thus in accordance with reason.

6. The term *civilisation* was, at the moment of its formation, a clear reflection of these reformist ideas. If in this term the idea of the *homme civilisé* leads to a concept designating the manners and conditions of existing society as a whole, it is first and foremost an expression of insights derived from opposition, from social criticism. To this is added the realization that government cannot issue decrees at will, but is automatically resisted by anonymous social forces if its ordinances are not guided by an exact knowledge of these forces and laws; the realization that even the most absolute government is helpless in the face of the dynamisms of social development, and that disaster and chaos, misery and distress, are unleashed by arbitrary, "unnatural," "irrational" government. As already stated, this realization finds expression in the Physiocratic idea that social events, like natural phenomena, form part of an ordered process. This same realization manifests itself in the evolution of the earlier *civilisé* into the noun *civilisation*, helping to give it a meaning that transcends the individual.

The birth pangs of the industrial revolution, which could no longer be understood as the result of government, taught men, briefly and for the first time, to think of themselves and their social existence as a process. If we first pursue the use of the term *civilisation* in the work of Mirabeau, we see clearly how this discovery causes him to view the entire morality of his time in a new light.

He comes to regard this morality, this "civilization" too as a cyclical manifestation, and wishes rulers to perceive its laws in order to use them. That is the meaning of the term *civilisation* at this early stage of its use.

In his *Ami des hommes*, Mirabeau argues in one place that a superfluity of money reduces population, so that consumption by each individual is increased. He considers that this excess of money, should it grow too large, "banishes industry and the arts, so casting states into poverty and depopulation." And he continues: "From this we perceive how the cycle from barbarism to decadence through civilization and wealth might be reversed by an alert and skillful minister, and the machine wound up again before it has run down."[28] This sentence really sums up all that was to become characteristic, in very general terms, of the fundamental standpoint of the Physiocrats: the conception of economy, population, and finally manners as an interrelated whole, developing cyclically; and the reformist political tendency which intends this knowledge finally for the rulers, to enable them, from an understanding of these laws, to guide social processes in a more enlightened and rational way than hitherto.

In Mirabeau's dedication of his *Théorie de l'impôt* to the king in 1760, in which he recommends to the monarch the Physiocratic plan for tax reform, exactly the same idea is still present: "The example of all the empires that have preceded yours, and which have run the circle of civilization, would be detailed evidence of what I have just advanced."

The critical attitude of Mirabeau, the landed nobleman, toward wealth, luxury, and the whole of prevailing manners gives his ideas a special tinge. Genuine civilization, he thinks, stands in a cycle between barbarism and a false, "decadent" civilization engendered by a superabundance of money. The task of enlightened government is to steer this automatism so that society can flourish on a middle course between barbarism and decadence. Here, the whole range of problems latent in "civilization" is already discernible at the moment of the concept's formation. Even at this stage it is connected to the idea of decadence or "decline," which has reemerged again and again, in an open or veiled form, to the rhythm of cyclical crises. But we can also see quite clearly that this desire for reform remains wholly within the framework of the existing social system manipulated from above, and that it does not oppose to what it criticizes in present manners an absolutely new image or concept, but instead takes its departure from the existing order, desiring to improve it: through skillful and enlightened measures by the government, "false civilization" shall again become a good and true civilization.

7. In this conception of civilization there may at first be many individual shades of meaning. But it contains elements corresponding to the general needs and experience of the reformist and progressive circles of Parisian society. And the concept becomes all the more widely used in these circles the more the reform movement is accelerated by growing commercialization and industrialization.

The last period of Louis XV's reign is a time of visible debility and disorder in the old system. The internal and external tensions grow. The signals for social transformation multiply.

In 1773 tea chests are thrown into Boston harbor. In 1776 comes the Declaration of Independence by England's American colony: the government, it proclaims, is appointed to ensure the happiness of the people. Should it not succeed in this purpose, a majority of the people has the right to dismiss it.

The French middle-class circles sympathetic to reform observe what is happening across the sea with the utmost attention, and a sympathy in which their reformist social tendencies mingle with growing national hostility toward England, even though their leading minds are thinking of anything but an overthrow of the monarchy.

At the same time, from 1774 onward, there is a growing feeling that a confrontation with England is inevitable and that preparations must be made for war. In the same year, 1774, Louis XV dies. Under the new king the struggle for the reform of the administrative and taxation systems is immediately renewed with intensified force in both the narrower and the wider court circles. As a result of these conflicts, Turgot is welcomed in the same year as *contrôleur général des finances* by all the reformist and progressive elements in the country.

"At last the belated hour of justice has come," writes the Physiocrat Baudeau on Turgot's appointment. D'Alembert writes on the same occasion: "If good does not prevail now, it is because good is impossible." And Voltaire regrets being at the gates of death at the moment when he can observe "virtue and reason in their place."[29]

In the same years, *civilisation* appears for the first time as a widely used and more or less fixed concept. In the first edition of Raynal's *Histoire philosophique et politique des établissements et du commerce des Européens dans les deux Indes* (1770) the word does not occur once; in the second (1774) it is "used frequently and without any variation of meaning as an indispensable term that is obviously generally understood."[30]

Holbach's *Système de la nature* of 1770 does not yet contain the word *civilisation*. In his *Système sociale* of 1774, *civilisation* is used frequently. He says, for example, "There is nothing that places more obstacles in the way of public happiness, of the progress of human reason, of the entire civilization of men than the continual wars into which thoughtless princes are drawn at every moment."[31] Or, in another place: "Human reason is not yet sufficiently exercised; *the civilization of peoples is not yet complete*; obstacles without number have hitherto opposed the progress of useful knowledge, the advance of which can alone contribute to perfecting our government, our laws, our education, our institutions, and our morals."[32]

The concept underlying this enlightened, socially critical reform movement is always the same: that the improvement of institutions, education, and law will be brought about by the advance of knowledge. This does not mean "scholarship" in the eighteenth-century German sense, for the speakers are not university people but independent writers, officials, intellectuals, courtly citizens of the most diverse kind united through the medium of "good society," the *salons*. Progress will be achieved, therefore, first by the enlightenment of kings and rulers in conformity with "reason" or "nature," which come to the same thing, and then by placing in leading positions enlightened (i e., reformist) men. A certain aspect of this whole progressive process of reform, came to be designated by a fixed concept: *civilisation*. What was visible in Mirabeau's individual version of the concept, which had not yet been polished by society, and what is characteristic of any reform movement is to be found here also: a half-affirmation and half-negation of the existing order. Society, from this point of view, has reached a particular stage on the road to civilization. But it is insufficient. Society cannot stand still there. The process continues and ought to be pushed further: "the civilization of peoples is not yet complete."

Two ideas are fused in the concept of civilization. On the one hand, it constitutes a general counterconcept to another stage of society, barbarism. This feeling had long pervaded courtly society. It had found its courtly-aristocratic expression in terms such as *politesse* or *civilité*.

But peoples are not yet civilized enough, say the men of the courtly/middle-class reform movement. Civilization is not only a state, it is a process which must be taken further. That is the new element expressed in the term *civilisation*. It absorbs much of what has always made court society believe itself, as compared to those living in a simpler, more uncivilized or more barbaric way, a higher kind of society: the idea of a standard of morals and manners, i.e., social tact, consideration for others, and many related complexes. But in the hands of the rising middle class, in the mouth of the reform movement, the idea of what is needed to make a society civilized is extended. The civilizing of the state, the constitution, education, and therefore of broader sections of the population, the liberation from all that was still barbaric or irrational in existing conditions, whether it be the legal penalties or the class restrictions on the bourgeoisie or the barriers impeding a freer development of trade—this civilizing must follow the refinement of manners and the internal pacification of the country by the kings.

"The king succeeded," Voltaire once said of the age of Louis XIV, "in making of a hitherto turbulent nation a peaceful people dangerous only to its enemies. . . . Manners were softened. . . ."[33] It will be seen in more detail later how important this internal pacification was for the civilizing process. Condorcet, however, who was by comparison to Voltaire a reformist of the younger generation and already far more inclined to opposition, comments as follows on this reflection of Voltaire's: "Despite the barbarity of some of the laws, despite the faults of the administrative principles, the increase in duties, their burdensome form, the harshness of fiscal laws, despite the pernicious maxims which direct the government's legislation on commerce and manufacture, and finally despite the persecution of the Protestants, one may observe that the peoples within the realm lived in peace under the protection of law."

This enumeration, itself not entirely without affirmation of the existing order, gives a picture of the many things thought in need of reform. Whether or not the term *civilisation* is here used explicitly, it relates to all this, everything which is still "barbaric."

This discussion makes very clear the divergence from developments in Germany and German concepts: it shows how members of the rising middle-class intelligentsia in France stand partly within the court circle, and so within the courtly-aristocratic tradition. They speak the language of this circle and develop it further. Their behavior and affects are, with certain modifications, modeled on the pattern of this tradition. Their concepts and ideas are by no means mere antitheses of those of the courtly aristocracy. Around courtly-aristocratic concepts such as the idea of "being civilized," they crystallize, in conformity with their social position within the court circle, further ideas from the area of their political and economic demands, ideas which, owing to the different social situation and range of experience of the German intelligentsia, were largely alien to it and at any rate far less relevant.

The French bourgeoisie—politically active, at least partly eager for reform, and even, for a short period, revolutionary—remained strongly bound to the courtly tradition in its behavior and its affect-molding even after the edifice of the old regime had been demolished. For through the close contact between aristocratic and middle-class circles, a great part of courtly manners had long before the revolution become middle-class manners. So it can be understood that the bourgeois revolution in France, though it destroyed the old political structure, did not disrupt the unity of traditional manners.

The German middle-class intelligentsia, politically entirely impotent but intellectually radical, forged a purely bourgeois tradition of its own, diverging widely from the courtly-aristocratic tradition and its models. The German national character which slowly emerged in the nineteenth century was not, to be sure, entirely lacking in aristocratic elements assimilated by the bourgeoisie. Nevertheless, for large areas of the German cultural tradition and German behavior, the specifically middle-class characteristics were predominant, particularly as the sharper social division between bourgeois and aristocratic circles, and with it a relative heterogeneity of German manners, survived long after the eighteenth century.

The French concept of *civilisation* reflects the specific social fortunes of the French bourgeoisie to exactly the same degree that the concept of *Kultur* reflects the German. The concept of *civilisation* is first, like *Kultur*, an instrument of middle-class circles—above all, the middle-class intelligentsia—in the internal social conflict. With the rise of the bourgeoisie, it too comes to epitomize the nation, to express the national self-image. In the revolution itself *civilisation* (which, of course, refers essentially to a gradual process, an evolution, and has not yet discarded its original meaning as a watchword of reform) does not play any considerable part among the revolutionary slogans. As the revolution grows more moderate, shortly before the turn of the century, it starts on its journey as a rallying cry throughout the world. Even as early as this, it has a level of meaning justifying French aspirations to national expansion and colonization. In 1798, as Napoleon sets off for Egypt, he shouts to his troops: "Soldiers, you are undertaking a conquest with incalculable consequences for civilization." Unlike the situation when the concept was formed, from now on nations consider the *process* of civilization as completed within their own societies; they see themselves as bearers of an existing or finished civilization to others, as standard-bearers of expanding civilization. Of the whole preceding process of civilization nothing remains in their consciousness except a vague residue. Its outcome is taken simply as an expression of their own higher gifts; the fact that, and the question of how, in the course of many centuries, civilized behavior has been attained is of no interest. And the consciousness of their own superiority, the consciousness of this "civilization," from now on serves at least those nations which have become colonial conquerors, and therefore a kind of upper class to large sections of the non-European world, as a justification of their rule, to the same degree that earlier the ancestors of the concept of civilization, *politesse* and *civilité*, had served the courtly-aristocratic upper class as a justification of theirs.

Indeed, an essential phase of the civilizing process was concluded at exactly the time when the *consciousness* of civilization, the consciousness of the superiority of their own behavior and its embodiments in science, technology, or art began to spread over whole nations of the West.

This earlier phase of the civilizing process, the phase in which the consciousness of the process scarcely existed and the concept of civilization did not exist at all, will be discussed in Part Two.

PART TWO

Civilization as a Specific Transformation of Human Behavior

I

The Development of the Concept of *Civilité*

1. The decisive antithesis expressing the self-image of the West during the Middle Ages is that between Christianity and paganism or, more exactly, between correct, Roman-Latin Christianity, on the one hand, and paganism and heresy, including Greek and Eastern Christianity, on the other.[1]

In the name of the Cross, and later in that of civilization, Western society wages, during the Middle Ages, its wars of colonization and expansion. And for all its secularization, the watchword "civilization" always retains an echo of Latin Christendom and the knightly-feudal crusade. The memory that chivalry and the Roman-Latin faith bear witness to a particular stage of Western society, a stage which all the major Western peoples have passed through, has certainly not disappeared.

The concept of *civilité* acquired its meaning for Western society at a time when chivalrous society and the unity of the Catholic church were disintegrating. It is the incarnation of a society which, as a specific stage in the formation of Western manners or "civilization," was no less important than the feudal society before it. The concept of *civilité*, too, is an expression and symbol of a social formation embracing the most diverse nationalities, in which, as in the Church, a common language is spoken, first Italian and then increasingly French. These languages take over the function earlier performed by Latin. They manifest the unity of Europe, and at the same time the new social formation which forms its backbone, court society. The situation, the self-image, and the characteristics of this society find expression in the concept of *civilité*.

2. The concept of *civilité* received the specific stamp and function under discussion here in the second quarter of the sixteenth century. Its individual starting point can be exactly determined. It owes the specific meaning adopted by society to a short treatise by Erasmus of Rotterdam, *De civilitate morum puerilium* (On civility in children), which appeared in 1530. This work clearly treated a theme that was ripe for discussion. It immediately achieved an enormous circulation, going through edition after edition. Even within Erasmus's lifetime—that is, in the first six years after its publication—it was reprinted more than thirty times.[2] In all, more than 130 editions may be counted, 13 of them as late as the eighteenth century. The multitude of translations, imitations, and sequels is almost without limit. Two years after the publication of the treatise the first English translation appeared. In 1534 it was published in catechism form, and at this time it was already being introduced as a schoolbook for the education of boys. German and Czech translations followed. In 1537, 1559, 1569, and 1613 it appeared in French, newly translated each time.

As early as the sixteenth century a particular French type face was given the name *civilité*, after a French work by Mathurin Cordier which combined doctrines from Erasmus's treatise with those of another humanist, Johannes Sulpicius. And a whole genre of books, directly or indirectly influenced by Erasmus's treatise, appeared under the title *Civilité* or *Civilité puérile*; these were printed up to the end of the eighteenth century in this *civilité* type.[3]

3. Here, as so often in the history of words, and as was to happen later in the evolution of the concept *civilité* into *civilisation*, an individual was the instigator. By his treatise, Erasmus gave new sharpness and impetus to the long-established and commonplace word *civilitas*. Wittingly or not, he obviously expressed in it something that met a social need of the time. The concept *civilitas* was henceforth fixed in the consciousness of people with the special sense it received from his treatise. And corresponding words were developed in the various popular languages: the French *civilité*, the English "civility," the Italian *civiltà*, and the German *Zivilität*, which, admittedly, was never so widely adopted as the corresponding words in the other great cultures.

The more or less sudden emergence of words within languages nearly always points to changes in the lives of people themselves, particularly when the new concepts are destined to become as central and long-lived as these.

Erasmus himself may not have attributed any particular importance to his short treatise *De civilitate morum puerilium* within his total *oeuvre*. He says in the introduction that the art of forming young people involves various disciplines, but that the *civilitas morum* is only one of them, and he does not deny that it is *crassissima philosophiae pars* (the grossest part of philosophy). This treatise has its special importance less as an individual phenomenon or work than as a symptom of change, an embodiment of social processes. Above all, it is the resonance, the elevation of the title word to a central expression of the self-interpretation of European society, which draws our attention to this treatise.

4. What is the treatise about? Its theme must explain to us for what purpose and in what sense the new concept was needed. It must contain indications of the social changes and processes which made the word fashionable.

Erasmus's book is about something very simple: the behavior of people in society—above all, but not solely, "outward bodily propriety." It is dedicated to a noble boy, a prince's son, and written for the instruction of boys. It contains simple thoughts delivered with great seriousness, yet at the same time with much mockery and irony, in clear, polished language and with enviable precision. It can be said that none of its successors ever equaled this treatise in force, clarity, and personal character. Looking more closely, one perceives beyond it a world and a pattern of life which in many respects, to be sure, are close to our own, yet in others still quite remote; the treatise points to attitudes that we have lost, that some among us would perhaps call "barbaric" or "uncivilized." It speaks of many things that have in the meantime become unspeakable, and of many others that are now taken for granted.[4]

Erasmus speaks, for example, of the way people look. Though his comments are meant as instruction, they also bear witness to the direct and lively observation of people of which he was capable. "Sint oculi placidi, verecundi, compositi," he says, "non torvi, quod est truculentiae . . . non vagi ac volubiles, quod est insaniae, non limi quod est suspiciosorum et insidias molentium. . . ." This can only with difficulty be translated without an appreciable alteration of tone: a wide-eyed look is a sign of stupidity, staring a sign of inertia; the looks of those prone to anger are too sharp; too lively and eloquent those of the immodest; if your look shows a calm mind and a respectful amiability, that is best. Not by chance do the ancients say: the seat of the soul is in the eyes. "Animi sedem esse in oculis."

Bodily carriage, gestures, dress, facial expressions—this "outward" behavior with which the treatise concerns itself is the expression of the inner, the whole man. Erasmus knows this and on occasion states it explicitly: "Although this outward bodily propriety proceeds from a well-composed mind, nevertheless we sometimes find that, for want of instruction, such grace is lacking in excellent and learned men."

There should be no snot on the nostrils, he says somewhat later. A peasant wipes his nose on his cap and coat, a sausage maker on his arm and elbow. It does not show much more propriety to use one's hand and then wipe it on one's clothing. It is more decent to take up the snot in a cloth, preferably while turning away. If when blowing the nose with two fingers somethings falls to the ground, it must be immediately trodden away with the foot. The same applies to spittle.

With the same infinite care and matter-of-factness with which these things are said—the mere mention of which shocks the "civilized" man of a later stage with a different affective molding—we are told how one ought to sit or greet. Gestures are described that have become strange to us, e.g., standing on one leg. And we might reflect that many of the bizarre movements of walkers and dancers that we see in medieval paintings or statues not only represent the "manner" of the painter or sculptor but also preserve actual gestures and movements that have grown strange to us, embodiments of a different mental and emotional structure.

The more one immerses oneself in the little treatise, the clearer becomes this picture of a society with modes of behavior in some respects related to ours, and in many ways remote. We see people seated at table: "A dextris sit poculum, et cultellus escarius rite purgatus, ad laevam panis," says Erasmus. The goblet and the well-cleaned knife on the right, on the left the bread. That is how the table is laid. Most people carry a knife, hence the precept to keep it clean. Forks scarcely exist, or at most for taking meat from the dish. Knives and spoons are very often used communally. There is not always a special implement for everyone: if you are offered something liquid, says Erasmus, taste it and return the spoon after you have wiped it.

When dishes of meat are brought in, usually everyone cuts himself a piece, takes it in his hand, and puts it on his plate if there are plates, otherwise on a thick slice of bread. The expression *quadra* used by Erasmus can clearly mean either a metal plate or a slice of bread.

"Quidam ubi vix bene considerint mox manus in epulas conjiciunt." Some put their hands into the dishes when they are scarcely seated, says Erasmus. Wolves or gluttons do that. Do not be the first to take from a dish that is brought in. Leave dipping your fingers into the broth to the peasants. Do not poke around in the dish but take the first piece that presents itself. And just as it shows a want of forbearance to search the whole dish with one's hand—"in omnes patinae plagas manum mittere"—neither is it very polite to turn the dish round so that a better piece comes to you. What you cannot take with your hands, take on your *quadra*. If someone passes you a piece of cake or pastry with a spoon, either take it with your *quadra* or take the spoon offered to you, put the food on the *quadra*, and return the spoon.

As has been mentioned, plates too are uncommon. Paintings of table scenes from this or earlier times always offer the same spectacle, unfamiliar to us, that is indicated by Erasmus's treatise. The table is sometimes covered with rich cloths, sometimes not, but always there is little on it: drinking vessels, saltcellar, knives, spoons, that is all. Sometimes we see the slices of bread, the *quadrae*, that in French are called *tranchoir* or *tailloir*. Everyone, from the king and queen to the peasant and his wife, eats with the hands. In the upper class there are more refined forms of this. One ought to wash one's hands before a meal, says Erasmus. But there is as yet no soap for this purpose. Usually the guest holds out his hands, and a page pours water over them. The water is sometimes slightly scented with chamomile or rosemary.[5] In good society one does not put both hands into the dish. It is most refined to use only three fingers of the hand. This is one of the marks of distinction between the upper and lower classes.

The fingers become greasy. "Digitos unctos vel ore praelingere vel ad tunicam extergere . . . incivile est," says Erasmus. It is not polite to lick them or wipe them on one's coat. Often you offer others your glass, or all drink from a communal tankard. Erasmus admonishes: "Wipe your mouth beforehand." You may want to offer someone you like some of the meat you are eating. "Refrain from that," says Erasmus, "it is not very decorous to offer something half-eaten to another." And he says further: "To dip bread you have bitten into the sauce is to behave like a peasant, and it shows little elegance to remove chewed food from the mouth and put it back on the *quadra*. If you cannot swallow a piece of food, turn round discreetly and throw it somewhere."

Then he says again: "It is good if conversation interrupts the meal from time to time. Some people eat and drink without stopping, not because they are hungry or thirsty, but because they can control their movements in no other way. They have to scratch their heads, poke their teeth, gesticulate with their hands, or play with a knife, or they can't help coughing, snorting, and spitting. All this really comes from a rustic embarrassment and looks like a form of madness."

But it is also necessary, and possible, for Erasmus to say: Do not expose without necessity "the parts to which Nature has attached modesty." Some prescribe, he says, that boys should "retain the wind by compressing the belly." But you can contract an illness that way. And in another place: "Reprimere sonitum, quem natura fert, ineptorum est, qui plus tribuunt civilitati, quam saluti" (Fools who value civility more than health repress natural sounds.) Do not be afraid of vomiting if you must; "for it is not vomiting but holding the vomit in your throat that is foul."

5. With great care Erasmus marks out in his treatise the whole range of human conduct, the chief situations of social and convivial life. He speaks with the same matter-of-factness of the most elementary as of the subtlest questions of human intercourse. In the first chapter he treats "the seemly and unseemly condition of the whole body," in the second "bodily culture," in the third "manners at holy places," in the fourth banquets, in the fifth meetings, in the sixth amusement, and in the seventh the bedchamber. This is the range of questions in the discussion of which Erasmus gave new impetus to the concept of *civilitas*.

Not always is our consciousness able to recall this other stage of our own history without hesitation. The unconcerned frankness with which Erasmus and his time could discuss all areas of human conduct is lost to us. Much of what he says oversteps our threshold of delicacy.

But precisely this is one of the problems to be considered here. In tracing the transformation of the concepts by which different societies have tried to express themselves, in following back the concept of civilization to its ancestor *civilité*, one finds oneself suddenly on the track of the civilizing process itself, of the actual change in behavior that took place in the West. That it is embarrassing for us to speak or even hear of much that Erasmus discusses is one of the symptoms of this civilizing process. The greater or lesser discomfort we feel toward people who discuss or mention their bodily functions more openly, who conceal and restrain these functions less than we do, is one of the dominant feelings expressed in the judgment "barbaric" or "uncivilized." Such, then, is the nature of "barbarism and its discontents" or, in more precise and less evaluative terms, the discontent with the different structure of affects, the different standard of repugnance which is still to be found today in many societies which we term "uncivilized," the standard of repugnance which preceded our own and is its precondition. The question arises as to how and why Western society actually moved from one standard to the other, how it was "civilized." In considering this process of civilization, we cannot avoid arousing feelings of discomfort and embarrassment. It is valuable to be aware of them. It is necessary, at least while considering this process, to attempt to suspend all the feelings of embarrassment and superiority, all the value judgments and criticism associated with the concepts "civilization" or "uncivilized." Our kind of behavior has grown out of that which we call uncivilized. But these concepts grasp the actual change too statically and coarsely. In reality, our terms "civilized" and "uncivilized" do not constitute an antithesis of the kind that exists between "good" and "bad," but represent stages in a development which, moreover, is still continuing. It might well happen that our stage of civilization, our behavior, will arouse in our descendants feelings of embarrassment similar to those we sometimes feel concerning the behavior of our ancestors. Social behavior and the expression of emotions passed from a form and a standard which was not a beginning, which could not in any absolute and undifferentiated sense be designated "uncivilized," to our own, which we denote by the word "civilized." And to understand the latter we must go back in time to that from which it emerged. The "civilization" which we are accustomed to regard as a possession that comes to us apparently ready-made, without our asking how we actually came to possess it, is a process or part of a process in which we are ourselves involved. Every particular characteristic that we attribute to it—machinery, scientific discovery, forms of state, or whatever else—bears witness to a particular structure of human relations, to a particular social structure, and to the corresponding forms of behavior. The question remains whether the change in behavior, in the social process of the "civilization" of man, can be understood, at least in isolated phases and in its elementary features, with any degree of precision.

II

On Medieval Manners

1. In Erasmus of Rotterdam's *De civilitate morum puerilium* a particular kind of social behavior is discernible. Even here, the simple antithesis of "civilized" and "uncivilized" hardly applies.

What came before Erasmus? Was he the first to concern himself with such matters?

By no means. Similar questions occupied the men of the Middle Ages, of Greco-Roman antiquity, and doubtless also of the related, preceding "civilizations."

This process that has no beginning cannot here be traced back indefinitely. Wherever we start, there is movement, something that went before. Limits must necessarily be set to a retrospective inquiry, preferably corresponding to the phases of the process itself. Here the medieval standard must suffice as a starting point, without itself being closely examined, so that the movement, the developmental curve joining it to the modern age may be pursued.

The Middle Ages have left us an abundance of information on what was considered socially acceptable behavior. Here, too, precepts on conduct while eating had a special importance. Eating and drinking then occupied a far more central position in social life than today, when they provide—frequently, not always—rather the framework and introduction for conversation and conviviality.

Learned ecclesiastics sometimes set down, in Latin, precepts for behavior that testify to the standard of their society. Hugh of St. Victor (d. 1141), in his *De institutione novitiarum*, is concerned with these questions among others. The baptized Spanish Jew Petrus Alphonsi deals with them in his *Disciplina clericalis* of the early twelfth century; Johannes von Garland devotes to manners, and particularly to table manners, a number of the 662 Latin verses bearing the title *Morale scolarium* of 1241.

Besides these precepts on behavior from the Latin-speaking clerical society, there are, from about the thirteenth century on, corresponding documents in the various lay languages—above all, at first, from the courts of the warrior nobility.

The earliest records of the manners prevalent in the secular upper class are doubtless those from Provence and neighboring, culturally related Italy. The earliest German work on *courtoisie* is also by an Italian, Thomasin von Zirklaria, and is called *The Italian Guest* (*Der wälsche Gast*, put into modern German by Rückert). Another such writing by Thomasin, in Italian, transmits to us in its German title an early form of the concept of "courtesy" (*Höflichkeit*). He refers to this book, which has been lost, as a "buoch von der hüfscheit."

Originating from the same knightly-courtly circles are the fifty *Courtesies* by

Bonvicino da Riva and the *Hofzucht* (Courtly manners) attributed to Tannhäuser. Such precepts are also occasionally found in the great epic poems of chivalrous society, e.g., the *Roman de la rose*[6] of the fourteenth century. John Russell's *Book of Nurture*, written in English verse probably in the fifteenth century, already gives a complete compendium of behavior for the young nobleman in the service of a great lord, as does more briefly *The Babees Book*.[7]

In addition there is, primarily in fourteenth- or fifteenth-century versions but probably, in part, older in substance, a whole series of poems designed as mnemonics to inculcate table manners, *Tischzuchten* of varying length and in the most diverse languages. Learning by heart as a means of educating or conditioning played a far greater part in medieval society, where books were comparatively rare and expensive, than it does today, and these rhymed precepts were one of the means used to try to impress on people's memories what they should and should not do in society, above all at table.

2. These *Tischzuchten*, or table disciplines, like medieval writings on manners of known authorship, are not individual products in the modern sense, records of the personal ideas of particular people within an extensively individualized society. What has come down to us in writing are fragments of a great oral tradition, reflections of what actually was customary in that society; these fragments are significant precisely because they transmit not the great or the extraordinary but the typical aspects of society. Even poems handed down under a specific name, like Tannhäuser's *Hofzucht* or John Russell's *Book of Nurture*, are nothing other than individual versions of one of the many strands of tradition corresponding to the structure of this society. Those who wrote them down were not the legislators or creators of these precepts but collectors, arrangers of the commands and taboos customary society; for this reason, whether or not there is a literary connection, similar precepts recur in almost all these writings. They are reflections of the same customs, testimonies to a particular handbook of behavior and emotions in the life of society itself.

It is perhaps possible on closer examination to discover certain differences of customs between individual national traditions, and variations in the social standards. Perhaps the material may also reveal certain changes within the same tradition. It appears, for example, that the tenor and perhaps also the customs of society underwent certain changes in the fourteenth or fifteenth century with the rise of guild and burgher elements, much as in modern times behavior-models originating in the court aristocracy here adopted in bourgeois circles.

A closer study of these modifications within medieval behavior remains to be carried out. It must suffice here to note them, bearing in mind that this medieval standard is not without inner movement and certainly is not a beginning or "bottom rung" of the process of civilization, nor does it represent, as has sometimes been asserted, the stage of "barbarism" or "primitiveness."

It was a different standard from our own—whether better or worse is not here at issue. And if, in our *recherche du temps perdu*, we have been led back step by step from the eighteenth to the sixteenth and from the sixteenth to the thirteenth and twelfth centuries, this does not imply that we are, as already stated, in anticipation of finding the "beginning" of the process of civilization. It is a sufficient task to present purposes, to take the short journey from the medieval to the early modern stage in an attempt to understand what actually happened to human beings in this transition.

3. The standard of "good behavior" in the Middle Ages is, like all later standards, represented by a quite definite concept. Through it the secular upper class of the Middle Ages, or at least some of its leading groups, gave expression to their self-image, to what, in their own estimation, made them exceptional. The concept epitomizing aristocratic self-consciousness and socially acceptable behavior appeared in French as *courtoisie*, in English "courtesy," in Italian *cortezia*, along with other related terms, often in divergent forms. In German it was, likewise in different versions, *hövescheit* or *hübescheit* and also *zuht*. All these concepts refer quite directly (and far more overtly than later ones with the same function) to a particular place in society. They say: That is how people behave at court. By these terms certain leading groups in the secular upper stratum, which does not mean the knightly class as a whole, but primarily the courtly circles around the great feudal lords, designated what distinguished them in their own eyes, namely the specific code of behavior that has first formed at the great feudal courts, then spread to rather broader strata; this process of differentiation may, however, be disregarded here. Measured against later periods, the great uniformity in the good and bad manners referred to—what is called here a particular "standard"—is especially impressive.

What is this standard like? What emerges as typical behavior, as the pervasive character of its precepts?

Something, in the first place, that in comparison to later times might be called its simplicity, its naïveté. There are, as in all societies where the emotions are expressed more violently and directly, fewer psychological nuances and complexities in the general stock of ideas. There are friend and foe, desire and aversion, good and bad people.

> You should follow honorable men and vent your wrath on the wicked.

We read this in a German translation of the *Disticha Catonis*,[8] the code of behavior encountered throughout the Middle Ages under the name of Cato. Or in another place:

> When your companions anger you, my son, see that you are not so hot-tempered that you regret it afterward.[9]

In eating, too, everything is simpler, impulses and inclinations are less restrained:

A man of refinement should not slurp with his spoon when in company; this is the way people at court behave who often indulge in unrefined conduct.

This is from Tannhäuser's *Hofzucht*.[10] *Hübsche Leute* (fine people) are the nobles, the courtly people. The precepts of the *Hofzucht* are meant expressly for the upper class, the knights who lived at court. Noble, courteous behavior is constantly contrasted to "coarse manners," the conduct of peasants.

Some people bite a slice and then dunk it in the dish in a coarse way; refined people reject such bad manners.[11]

If you have taken a bite from the bread, do not dip it in the common dish again. Peasants may do that, not "fine people."

A number of people gnaw a bone and then put it back in the dish—this is a serious offense.[12]

Do not throw gnawed bones back into the communal dish. From other accounts we know that it was customary to drop them on the floor. Another precept reads:

A man who clears his throat when he eats and one who blows his nose in the tablecloth are both ill-bred, I assure you.[13]

Here is another:

If a man wipes his nose on his hand at table because he knows no better, then he is a fool, believe me.[14]

To use the hand to wipe one's nose was a matter of course. Handkerchiefs did not yet exist. But at table a certain care should be exercised; and one should on no account blow one's nose into the tablecloth. Avoid lip-smacking and snorting, eaters are further instructed:

If a man snorts like a seal when he eats, as some people do, and smacks his chops like a Bavarian yokel, he has given up all good breeding.[15]

If you have to scratch yourself, do not do so with your bare hand but use your coat:

Do not scrape your throat with your bare hand while eating; but if you have to, do it politely with your coat.[16]

Everyone used his hands to take food from the common dish. For this reason one was not to touch one's ears, nose, or eyes:

> It is not decent to poke your fingers into your ears or eyes, as some people do, or to pick
> your nose while eating. These three habits are bad.[17]

Hands must be washed before meals:

> I hear that some eat unwashed (if it is true, it is a bad sign). May their fingers be
> palsied![18]

And in *Ein spruch der ze tische kêrt* (A word to those at table)[19] another *Tischzucht* of
which Tannhäuser's *Hofzucht* has many echoes, it is demanded that one eat with
only one hand, and if one is eating from the same plate or slice of bread as
another, as often happened, with the outside hand:

> You should always eat with the outside hand; if your companion sits on your right, eat
> with your left hand. Refrain from eating with both hands.[20]

If you have no towel, we read in the same work, do not wipe your hands on your
coat but let the air dry them.[21] Or:

> Take care that, whatever your need, you do not flush with embarrassment.[22]

Nor is it good manners to loosen one's belt at table.[23]

All this is said to adults, not only to children. To our minds these are very
elementary precepts to be given to upper-class people, more elementary in many
respects than what, at the present stage of behavior, is generally accepted as the
norm in rural-peasant strata. And the same standard emerges with certain
variations from the *courtois* writings of other linguistic areas.

4. In the case of one of these different strands of tradition, which leads from
certain Latin forms primarily to French, but perhaps also to Italian and to a
Provençal code of table manners, a compilation has been made of the rules
recurring in most or all of the variants.[24] They are by and large the same as in the
German *Tischzuchten*. First there is the instruction to say grace, which is also
found in Tannhäuser. Again and again we find the injunctions to take one's
allotted place and not to touch nose and ears at table. Do not put your elbow on
the table, they often say. Show a cheerful countenance. Do not talk too much.
There are very frequent reminders not to scratch oneself or fall greedily on the
food. Nor should one put a piece that one has had in one's mouth back into the
communal dish; this, too, is often repeated. Not less frequent is the instruction
to wash one's hands before eating, or not to dip food into the saltcellar. Then it is
repeated over and over again: do not clean your teeth with your knife. Do not spit
on or over the table. Do not ask for more from a dish that has already been taken
away. Do not let yourself go at table is a frequent command. Wipe your lips
before you drink. Say nothing disparaging about the meal nor anything that

might irritate others. If you have dipped bread into the wine, drink it up or pour the rest away. Do not clean your teeth with the tablecloth. Do not offer others the remainder of your soup or the bread you have already bitten into. Do not blow your nose too noisily. Do not fall asleep at table. And so on.

Indications of the same code of good and bad manners are also found in other collections of related mnemonic verses on etiquette, in traditions not directly related to the French one just mentioned. All bear witness to a certain standard of relationships between people, to the structure of medieval society and of the medieval psyche. The similarities between these collections are sociogenetic and psychogenetic; there may but need not be a literary relationship between all these French, English, Italian, German, and Latin precepts. The differences between them are less significant than the common features, which correspond to the unity of actual behavior in the medieval upper class, measured against the modern period.

For example, the *Courtesies* of Bonvicino da Riva, one of the most personal and—in keeping with Italian development—most "advanced" of table guides, contains, apart from the precepts mentioned from the French collection, the instructions to turn round when coughing and sneezing, and not to lick one's fingers. One should, he says, refrain from searching out the best pieces in the dish, and cut the bread decently. One should not touch the rim of the communal glass with one's fingers, and one should hold the glass with both hands. But here, too, the tenor of *courtoisie*, the standard, the customs are by and large the same. And it is not uninteresting that when Bonvicino da Riva's *Courtesies* were revised three centuries after him, of all the rules given by Da Riva only two not very important ones were altered: the editor advises not to touch the edge of the communal glass and to hold it with both hands, and if several are drinking from the same glass, one should refrain altogether from dipping bread into it (Da Riva only required that the wine thus used should be tipped away or drunk).[25]

A similar picture could be drawn from the German tradition. German *Tischzuchten*, of which we have copies from the fifteenth century, are perhaps somewhat coarser in tone than the *Italian Guest* of Thomasin von Zirklaria or Tannhäuser's *Hofzucht* from the thirteenth century. But the standard of good and bad manners seems scarcely to have altered to any considerable extent. It has been pointed out that in one of the later codes which has much in common with the earlier ones already mentioned, the new injunction appears that one should spit not on the table but only under it or against the wall. And this has been interpreted as a symptom of a coarsening of manners. But it is more than questionable whether things were done very differently in the preceding centuries, particularly as similar precepts from earlier periods are transmitted by the French tradition, for example. And what is to be derived from literature in the broadest sense is confirmed by paintings. Here, too, more detailed studies are needed; but compared to the later age, pictures of people at table show, until well into the fifteenth century, very sparse table utensils, even if, in some details, certain changes are undoubtedly present. In the houses of the more wealthy, the platters are usually taken from the sideboard, frequently in no particular order. Everyone takes—or sends for—what he fancies at the moment. People help themselves from communal dishes. Solids (above all, meat) are taken by hand, liquids with ladles or spoons. But soups and sauces are still very frequently drunk. Plates and dishes are lifted to the mouth. For a long period, too, there are no special implements for different foods. The same knife or spoon is used. The same glasses are drunk from. Frequently two diners eat from the same board.

This is, if it may so be called, the standard eating technique during the Middle Ages, which corresponds to a very particular standard of human relationships and structure of feeling. Within this standard there is, as has been said, an abundance of modifications and nuances. If people of different rank are eating at the same time, the person of higher rank is given precedence when washing hands, for example, or when taking from the dish. The forms of utensils vary considerably in the course of centuries. There are fashions, but also a very definite trend that persists through the fluctuations of fashion. The secular upper class, for example, indulges in extraordinary luxury at table. It is not a poverty of utensils that maintains the standard, it is quite simply that nothing else is needed. To eat in this fashion is taken for granted. It suits these people. But it also suits them to make visible their wealth and rank by the opulence of their utensils and table decoration. At the rich tables of the thirteenth century the spoons are of gold, crystal, coral, ophite. It is occasionally mentioned that during Lent knives with ebony handles are used, at Easter knives with ivory handles, and inlaid knives at Whitsun. The soupspoons are round and rather flat to begin with, so that one is forced when using them to open one's mouth wide. From the fourteenth century onward, soupspoons take on an oval form.

At the end of the Middle Ages the fork appears as an instrument for taking food from the common dish. A whole dozen forks are to be found among the valuables of Charles V. The inventory of Charles of Savoyen, which is very rich in opulent table utensils, counts only a single fork.[26]

5. It is sometimes said, "How far we have progressed beyond this standard," although it is not usually quite clear who is the "we" with whom the speaker identifies himself on such occasions, as if he deserved part of the credIt.

The opposite judgment is also possible: "What has really changed? A few customs, no more." And some observers seem inclined to judge these customs in much the same way as one would today judge children: "If a man of sense had come and told these people that their practices were unappetizing and unhygienic, if they had been taught to eat with knives and forks, these bad manners would rapidly have disappeared."

But conduct while eating cannot be isolated. It is a segment—a very characteristic one—of the totality of socially instilled forms of conduct. Its standard corresponds to a quite definite social structure. It remains to be ascertained what this structure is. The behavior of medieval people was no less tightly bound to their total way of life, to the whole structure of their existence, than our own behavior and social code are bound to ours.

At times, some minor statement shows how firmly rooted these customs were, and makes it apparent that they must be understood not merely as something "negative," as a "lack of civilization" or of "knowledge" (as it is easy to suppose from our standpoint), but as something that fitted the needs of these people and that seemed meaningful and necessary to them in exactly this form.

In the eleventh century a Venetian doge married a Greek princess. In her Byzantine circle the fork was clearly in use. At any rate, we hear that she lifted food to her mouth "by means of little golden forks with two prongs."[27]

This gave rise in Venice to a dreadful scandal: "This novelty was regarded as so excessive a sign of refinement that the dogaressa was severely rebuked by the ecclesiastics who called down divine wrath upon her. Shortly afterward she was afflicted by a repulsive illness and St. Bonaventure did not hesitate to declare that this was a punishment of God."

Five more centuries were to pass before the structure of human relations had so changed that the use of this instrument met a more general need. From the sixteenth century on, at least among the upper classes, the fork comes into use as an eating instrument, arriving by way of Italy first in France and then in England and Germany, after having served for a time only for taking solid foods from the dish. Henri III brought it to France, probably from Venice. His courtiers were not a little derided for this "affected" manner of eating, and at first they were not very adept in the use of the instrument: at least it was said that half the food fell off the fork as it traveled from plate to mouth. As late as the seventeenth century the fork was still essentially a luxury article of the upper class, usually made of gold or silver. What we take entirely for granted, because we have been adapted and conditioned to this social standard from earliest childhood, had first to be slowly and laboriously acquired and developed by society as a whole. This applies to such a small and seemingly insignificant thing as a fork no less than to forms of behavior that appear to us larger and more important.[28]

However, the attitude that has just been described toward the "innovation" of the fork shows one thing with special clarity. People who ate together in the way customary in the Middle Ages, taking meat with their fingers from the same dish, wine from the same goblet, soup from the same pot or the same plate, with all the other peculiarities of which examples have been and will further be given—such people stood in a different relationship to one another than we do. And this involves not only the level of clear, rational consciousness; their emotional life also had a different structure and character. Their affects were conditioned to forms of relationship and conduct which, by today's standard of conditioning, are embarrassing or at least unattractive. What was lacking in this *courtois* world, or at least had not been developed to the same degree, was the invisible wall of affects which seems now to rise between one human body and another, repelling and separating, the hall which is often perceptible today at the mere approach of something that has been in contact with the mouth or hands of someone else, and which manifests itself as embarrassment at the mere sight of many bodily functions of others, and often at their mere mention, or as a feeling of shame when one's own functions are exposed to the gaze of others, and by no means only then.

III

The Problem of the Change in Behavior during the Renaissance

1. Were the thresholds of embarrassment and shame raised at the time of Erasmus? Does his treatise contain indications that the frontiers of sensibility and the reserve which they expected of each other were increasing? There are good reasons for supposing so. The humanists' works on manners form a kind of bridge between those of the Middle Ages and modern times. Erasmus's treatise, the high point in the succession of humanist writings on manners, also has this double face. In many respects it stands entirely within medieval tradition. A good part of the rules and precepts from the *courtois* writings recur in his treatise. But at the same time, it clearly contains the beginnings of something new. In it a concept is gradually developing which was to force the knightly-feudal concept of courtesy into the background. In the course of the sixteenth century the use of the concept of *courtoisie* slowly recedes in the upper class, while *civilité* grows more common and finally gains the upper hand, at least in France, in the seventeenth century.

This is a sign of a behavioral change of considerable proportions. It did not take place, of course, in such a way that one ideal of good behavior was suddenly opposed by another radically different to it. The *De civilitate morum puerilium* of Erasmus—to confine the discussion to this work for the time being—stands in many respects, as we have said, entirely within medieval tradition. Almost all the rules of *courtois* society reappear in it. Meat is still eaten with the hand, even if Erasmus stresses that it should be picked up with three fingers, not the whole hand. The precept not to fall upon the meal like a glutton is also repeated, as are the direction to wash one's hands before dining and the strictures on spitting, blowing the nose, the use of the knife, and many others. It may be that Erasmus knew one or another of the rhymed *Tischzuchten* or the clerical writings in which such questions were treated. Many of these writings were no doubt in wide circulation; it is unlikely that they escaped Erasmus. More precisely demonstrable is his relation to the heritage of antiquity. In the case of this treatise, it was partly shown by the commentaries of his contemporaries. Its place in the rich humanist discussion of these problems of education and propriety remains to be examined in more detail.[29] But whatever the literary interconnections may be, of primary interest in this context are the sociogenetic ones. Erasmus certainly did not merely compile this treatise from other books; like anyone who reflects on such questions, he had a particular social code, a particular standard of manners directly before his eyes. This treatise on manners is a collection of observations from the life of his society. It is, as someone said later, "a little the work of everyone." And if nothing else, its success, its rapid dissemination, and its use as an educational manual for boys show how much it met a social need, and how it recorded the models of behavior for which the time was ripe, which society—or, more exactly, the upper class first of all—demanded.

2. Society was "in transition." So, too, were works on manners. Even in the tone, the manner of seeing, we feel that despite all their attachment to the Middle Ages something new is on the way. "Simplicity" as we experience it, the simple opposition of "good" and "bad," "pious" and "wicked," has been lost. People see things with more differentiation, i.e., with a stronger restraint of their emotions.

It is not so much, or at least not exclusively, the rules themselves or the manners to which they refer that distinguish a part of the humanistic writings—above all, the treatise of Erasmus—from the *courtois* codes. It is first of all their tone, their way of seeing. The same social rules which in the Middle Ages were passed impersonally from mouth to mouth are now spoken in the manner and with the emphasis of someone who is not merely passing on tradition, no matter how many medieval and, above all, ancient writings he may have absorbed, but who has observed all this personally, who is recording experience.

Even if this were not seen in *De civilitate morum puerilium* itself, we should know it from Erasmus's earlier writings, in which the permeation of medieval and ancient tradition with his own experience is expressed perhaps more clearly and directly. In his *Colloquies*, which in part certainly draw on ancient models (above all, Lucian), and particularly in the dialogue *Diversoria* (Basel, 1523), Erasmus describes directly experiences elaborated in the later treatise.

The *Diversoria* is concerned with the difference between manners at German and French inns. He describes, for example, the interior of a German inn: some eighty or ninety people are sitting together, and it is stressed that they are not only common people but also rich men and nobles, men, women, and children, all mixed together. And each is doing what he considers necessary. One washes his clothes and hangs the soaking articles on the stove. Another washes his hands. But the bowl is so clean, says the speaker, that one needs a second one to cleanse oneself of the water. Garlic smells and other bad odors rise. People spit everywhere. Someone is cleaning his boots on the table. Then the meal is brought in. Everyone dips his bread into the general dish, bites the bread, and dips it in again. The place is dirty, the wine bad. And if one asks for a better wine the innkeeper replies: I have put up enough nobles and counts. If it does not suit you, look for other quarters.

The stranger to the country has a particularly difficult time. The others stare at him fixedly as if he were a fabulous animal from Africa. Moreover, these people acknowledge as human beings only the nobles of their own country.

The room is overheated; everyone is sweating and steaming and wiping himself. There are doubtless many among them who have some hidden disease: "Probably," says the speaker, "most of them have the Spanish disease, and are thus no less to be feared than lepers."

"Brave people," says the other, "they jest and care nothing for it."

"But this bravery has already cost many lives."

"What are they to do? They are used to it, and a stouthearted man does not break with his habits."

3. It can be seen that Erasmus, like others who wrote before or after him about conduct, is in the first place a collector of good and bad manners that he finds present in social life itself. It is primarily this that explains both the agreement and the differences between such writers. That their writings do not contain as much as others to which we habitually give more attention, the extraordinary ideas of an outstanding individual, that they are forced by their subject itself to adhere closely to social reality, gives them their special significance as a source of information on social processes.

But the observations of Erasmus on this subject are nevertheless to be numbered, along with a few by other authors from the same phase, among the exceptions in the tradition of writing on manners. For in them the presentation of partly very ancient precepts and commands is permeated by a very individual temperament. And precisely that is, in its turn, a "sign of the times," an expression of a transformation of society, a symptom of what is somewhat misleadingly called "individualization." It also points to something else: the problem of behavior in society had obviously taken on such importance in this period that even people of extraordinary talent and renown did not disdain to concern themselves with it. Later this task falls back in general to minds of the second and third rank, who imitate, continue, extend, thus giving rise once more, even if not so strongly as in the Middle Ages, to a more impersonal tradition of books on manners.

The social transitions connected with the changes in conduct, manners, and feelings of embarrassment will be studied separately later. However, an indication of them is needed here for an understanding of Erasmus's own position, and therefore of his way of speaking about manners.

Erasmus's treatise comes at a time of social regrouping. It is the expression of the fruitful transitional period after the loosening of the medieval social hierarchy and before the stabilizing of the modern one. It belongs to the phase in which the old, feudal knights nobility was still in decline, while the new aristocracy of the absolutist courts was still in the process of formation. This situation gave, among others, the representatives of a small, secular-bourgeois intellectual class, the humanists, and thus Erasmus, not only an opportunity to rise in social station, to gain renown and authority, but also a possibility of candor and detachment that was not present to the same degree either before or afterward. This chance of distancing themselves, which permitted individual representatives of the intellectual class to identify totally and unconditionally with none of the social groups of their world—though, of course, they always stood closer to one of them, that of the princes and of the courts, than to the others—also finds expression in *De civilitate morum puerilium*. Erasmus in no way overlooks or conceals social differences. He sees very exactly that the real nurseries of what is regarded as good manners in his time are the princely courts. He says, for example, to the young prince to whom he dedicates his treatise: "I shall address your youth on the manners fitting to a boy not because you are so greatly in need of these precepts; from childhood you have been educated among courtly people and you early had an excellent instructor . . . or because all that is said in this treatise applies to you; for you are of princely blood and are born to rule."

But Erasmus also manifests, in a particularly pronounced form, the characteristic self-confidence of the intellectual who has ascended through knowledge and writing, who is legitimized by books, the self-assurance of a member of the humanistic intellectual class who is able to keep his distance even from ruling strata and their opinions, however bound to them he may be. "Modesty, above all, befits a boy," he says at the close of the dedication to the young prince, "and particularly a noble boy." And he also says: "Let others paint lions, eagles, and other creatures on their coats of arms. More true nobility is possessed by those who can inscribe on their shields all that they have achieved through the cultivation of the arts and sciences."

This is the language, the typical self-image of the intellectual in this phase of social development. The sociogenetic and psychogenetic kinship of such ideas with those of the German intellectual class of the eighteenth century, who were epitomized to themselves by concepts such as *Kultur* and *Bildung*, is immediately visible. But in the period immediately after Erasmus's time, few people would have had the assurance or even the social opportunity to express such thoughts openly in a dedication to a noble. With the increasing stabilization of the social hierarchy, such an utterance would have been increasingly seen as an error of tact, perhaps even as an attack. The most exact observance of differences of rank in behavior becomes from now on the essence of courtesy, the basic requirement of *civilité*, at least in France. The aristocracy and the bourgeois intelligentsia mix socially, but it is an imperative of tact to observe social differences and to give them unambiguous expression in social conduct. In Germany, by contrast, there is always, from the time of the humanists onward, a bourgeois intelligentsia whose members, with few exceptions, live more or less in isolation from aristocratic court society, an intellectual class of specifically middle-class character.

4. The development of German writings on manners and the way these writings differ from the French give numerous clear illustrations of this. It would lead too far to pursue this in detail, but one need only think of a work like Dedekind's *Grobianus*[30] and its widely disseminated and influential German translation by Kaspar Scheidt to be aware of the difference. The whole German *grobianisch* (boorish) literature in which, spiced with mockery and scorn, a very serious need for a "softening of manners" finds expression, shows unambiguously and more purely than any of the corresponding traditions of other nationalities the specifically middle-class character of its writers, who include Protestant clergymen and teachers. And the case is similar with most of what was written in the ensuing period about manners and etiquette in Germany. Certainly, manners here too are stamped primarily at the courts; but since the social walls between the bourgeoisie and court nobility are relatively high, the later bourgeois authors of books on manners usually speak of them as something alien that has to be learned because that is the way things are done at court. However familiar with the subject these authors may be, they speak of it as outsiders, very often with noticeable clumsiness. It is a relatively constricted, regional, and penurious intellectual stratum which writes in Germany in the following period, and particularly after the Thirty Years War. And only in the second half of the eighteenth century, when the German bourgeois intelligentsia, as a kind of vanguard of the commercial bourgeoisie, attains new opportunities for social advance and rather more freedom of movement, do we again hear the language and expression of a self-image related to that of the humanists, especially Erasmus. Even now, however, the nobles are hardly ever told so openly that all their coats of arms are worth less than the cultivation of the *artes liberales*, even if this is often enough what is really meant.

What has been shown in the introductory chapter on the movement of the late eighteenth century goes back to a far older tradition, to a pervasive structural characteristic of German society following the particularly vigorous development of the German cities and burgher class toward the end of the Middle Ages. In France, and periodically in England and Italy also, a proportion of the bourgeois writers feel themselves to belong to the circles of the court aristocracies; in Germany this is far less the case. In the other countries, bourgeois writers not only write largely for circles of the court aristocracies but also identify extensively with their manners, customs, and views. In Germany this identification of members of the intelligentsia with the courtly upper class is much weaker, less taken for granted and far more rare. Their dubious position (along with a certain mistrust of those who legitimize themselves primarily by their manners, courtesy, and ease of behavior) is part of a long tradition, particularly as the values of the German court aristocracy—which is split up into numerous greater or lesser circles, not unified in a large, central "society," and moreover is bureaucratized at an early stage—cannot be developed as fully as in the Western countries. Instead, there emerges here more sharply than in the Western countries a split between the university-based cultural-bureaucratic tradition of "Kultur" of the middle-class, on the one hand, and the no less bureaucratic-military tradition of the nobility, on the other.

5. Erasmus's treatise on manners has an influence both on Germany and on England, France, and Italy. What links his attitude with that of the later German intelligentsia is the lack of identification with the courtly upper class; and his observation that the treatment of "civility" is without doubt *crassissima philosophiae pars* points to a scale of values which was not without a certain kinship to the later evaluation of *Zivilisation* and *Kultur* in the German tradition.

Accordingly, Erasmus does not see his precepts as intended for a particular class. He places no particular emphasis on social distinctions, if we disregard occasional criticism of peasants and small tradesmen. It is precisely this lack of a specific social orientation in the precepts, their presentation as general human rules, that distinguishes his treatise from its successors in the Italian and especially the French traditions.

Erasmus simply says, for example, "Incessus nec fractus sit, nec praeceps" (The step should be neither too slow nor too quick). Shortly afterward, in his *Galateo*, the Italian Giovanni della Casa says the same thing (ch. VI, 5, pt. III). But for him the same precept has a direct and obvious function as a means of social distinction: "Non dee l'huomo nobile correre per via, ne troppo affrettarsi, che cio conviene a palafreniere e non a gentilhuomo. Ne percio si dee andare sì lento, ne sì conregnoso come femmina o come sposa." (The noblemen ought not to run like a lackey, or walk as slowly as women or brides.) It is characteristic, and in agreement with all our other observations, that a German translation of *Galateo*—in a five-language edition of 1609 (Geneva)—regularly seeks, like the Latin translation and unlike all the others, to efface the social differentiations in the original. The passage quoted, for example, is translated as follows: "Therefore a noble, or any other *honorable man*, should not run in the street or hurry too much, since this befits a lackey and not a gentleman. . . . Nor should one walk unduly slowly like a stately matron or a young bride" (p. 562).

The words "honorable man" are inserted here, possibly referring to burgher councillors, and similar changes are found in many other places; when the Italian says simply *gentilhuomo* and the French *gentilhomme*, the German speaks of the "virtuous, honorable man" and the Latin of "homo honestus et bene moratus." These examples could be multiplied.

Erasmus proceeds similarly. As a result, the precepts that he gives without any social characteristics appear again and again in the Italian and French traditions with a sharper limitation to the upper class, while in Germany the tendency to obliterate the social characteristics remains, even if for a long period hardly a single writer achieves the degree of social detachment possessed by Erasmus. In this respect he occupies a unique position among all those who write on the subject. It stems from his personal character. But at the same time, it points beyond his personal character to this relatively brief phase of relaxation between two great epochs characterized by more inflexible social hierarchies.

The fertility of this loosening transitional situation is perceptible again and again in Erasmus's way of observing people. It enables him to criticize "rustic," "vulgar," or "coarse" qualities without accepting unconditionally (as did most who came later) the behavior of the great courtly lords, whose circle was finally, as he himself puts it, the nursery of refined conduct. He sees very exactly the exaggerated, forced nature of many courtly practices, and is not afraid to say so. Speaking of how to hold the lips, for example, he says: "It is still less becoming to purse the lips from time to time as if whistling to oneself. This can be left to the great lords when they stroll among the crowd." Or he says: "You should leave to a few courtiers the pleasure of squeezing bread in the hand and then breaking it off with the fingertips. You should cut it decently with a knife."

6. But here again we see very clearly the difference between this and the medieval manner of giving directions on behavior. Earlier, people were simply told, to give one example, "The bread cut fayre and do not breake."[31] Such rules are embedded by Erasmus directly in his experience and observation of people. The traditional precepts, mirrors of ever-recurring customs, awaken in his observation from a kind of petrifaction. An old rule ran: "Do not fall greedily upon the food."

Do not eat bread before the meat is served, for this would appear greedy.

Remember to empty and wipe your mouth before drinking.[32]

Erasmus gives the same advice, but in so doing he sees people directly before him: some, he says, devour rather than eat, as if they were about to be carried off to prison, or were thieves wolfing down their booty. Others push so much into their mouths that their cheeks bulge like bellows. Others pull their lips apart while eating, so that they make a noise like pigs. And then follows the general rule that was, and obviously had to be, repeated over and again: "Ore pleno vel bibere vel loqui, nec honestum, nec tutum." (To eat or drink with a full mouth is neither becoming nor safe.)

In all this, besides the medieval tradition, there is certainly much from antiquity. But reading has sharpened seeing, and seeing has enriched reading and writing.

Clothing, he says in one place, is in a sense the body of the body. From it we can deduce the attitude of the soul. And then Erasmus gives examples of what manner of dress corresponds to this or that spiritual condition. This is the beginning of the mode of observation that will at a later stage be termed "psychological." The new stage of courtesy and its representation, summed up in the concept of *civilité*, is very closely bound up with this manner of seeing, and gradually becomes more so. In order to be really "courteous" by the standards of *civilité*, one is to some extent obliged to observe, to look about oneself and pay attention to people and their motives. In this, too, a new relationship of man to man, a new form of integration is announced.

Not quite 150 years later, when *civilité* has become a firm and stable form of behavior in the courtly upper class of France, in the *monde*, one of its members begins his exposition of the *science du monde* with these words: "It seems to me that to acquire what is called the science of the world one must first apply oneself to knowing men as they are in general, and then gain particular knowledge of those with whom we have to live, that is to say, knowledge of their inclinations and their good and bad opinions, of their virtues and their faults."[33]

What is here said with great precision and lucidity was anticipated by Erasmus. But this increased tendency of society and therefore of writers to observe, to connect the particular with the general, seeing with reading, is found not only in Erasmus but also in the other Renaissance books on manners, and certainly not only in these.

7. If one is asked, therefore, about the new tendencies[34] that make their appearance in Erasmus's way of observing the behavior of people—this is one of them. In the process of transformation and innovation that we designate by the term "Renaissance," what was regarded as "fitting" and "unfitting" in human intercourse no doubt changed to a certain degree. But the rupture is not marked by a sudden demand for new modes of behavior opposed to the old. The tradition of courtoisie is continued in many respects by the society which adopts the concept of *civilitas*, as in *Civilitas morum puerilium*, to designate social "good behavior."

The increased tendency of people to observe themselves and others is one sign of how the whole question of behavior is now taking on a different character: people mold themselves and others more deliberately than in the Middle Ages.

Then they were told, do this and not that; but by and large a great deal was let pass. For centuries roughly the same rules, elementary by our standards, were repeated, obviously without producing firmly established habits. This now changes. The coercion exerted by people on one another increases, the demand for "good behavior" is raised more emphatically. All problems concerned with behavior take on new importance. The fact that Erasmus brought together in a prose work rules of conduct that had previously been uttered chiefly in mnemonic verses or scattered in treatises on other subjects, and for the first time devoted a separate book to the whole question of behavior in society, not only at table, is a clear sign of the growing importance of the question, as is the book's success.[35]

And the emergence of related writings, like the *Courtier* of Castiglione or the *Galateo* of Della Casa, to name only the most well-known, points in the same direction. The underlying social processes have already been indicated and will be discussed in more detail later: the old social ties are, if not broken, extensively loosened and are in a process of transformation. Individuals of different social origins are thrown together. The social circulation of ascending and descending groups and individuals speeds up.

Then, slowly, in the course of the sixteenth century, earlier here and later there and almost everywhere with numerous reverses until well into the seventeenth century, a more rigid social hierarchy begins to establish itself once more, and from elements of diverse social origins a new upper class, a new aristocracy forms. For this very reason the question of uniform good behavior becomes increasingly acute, particularly as the changed structure of the new upper class exposes each individual member to an unprecedented extent to the pressure of others and of social control. It is in this context that the writings on manners of Erasmus, Castiglione, Della Casa, and others are produced. People, forced to live with one another in a new way, become more sensitive to the impulses of others. Not abruptly but very gradually the code of behavior becomes stricter and the degree of consideration expected of others becomes greater. The sense of what to do and what not to do in order not to offend or shock others becomes subtler, and in conjunction with the new power relationships the social imperative not to offend others becomes more binding, as compared to the preceding phase.

The rules of *courtoisie* also prescribed, "Say nothing that can arouse conflict, or anger others":

> Non dicas verbum
> cuiquam quod ei sit acerbum.[36]

"Be a good table companion":

> Awayte my chylde, ye be have you manerly,
> When at you mete ye sitte at the table
> In every prees and in every company
> Dispose you to be so compenable
> That men may of you reporte for commendable
> For thrusteth wel upon your berynge
> Men wil you blame or gyue preysynge. . . .

So we read in an English *Book of Curtesye*.[37] In purely factual terms, much of what Erasmus says has a similar tendency. But the change of tone, the increased sensitivity, the heightened human observation, and the sharper understanding of what is going on in others are unmistakable. They are particularly clear in a remark at the end of his treatise. There he breaks through the fixed pattern of "good behavior," together with the arrogance that usually accompanies it, and relates conduct back to a more comprehensive humanity: "Be lenient toward the offenses of others. This is the chief virtue of *civilitas*, of courtesy. A companion ought not to be less dear to you because he has worse manners. There are people who make up for the awkwardness of their behavior by other gifts." And further on he says: "If one of your comrades unknowingly gives offense . . . tell him so alone and say it kindly. That is civility."

But this attitude only expresses again how little Erasmus, for all his closeness to the courtly upper class of his time, identifies with it, keeping his distance from its code, too.

Galateo takes its name from an account in which Erasmus's precept "Tell him alone and say it kindly" applies in reality; an offense is corrected in that very way. But here the courtly character of such customs is emphasized as far more self-evident than in Erasmus.

The Bishop of Verona, the Italian work relates,[38] one day receives a visit from a Duke Richard. He appears to the Bishop and his court as "gentilissime cavaliere e di bellissime maniere." The host notes in his guest a single fault. But he says nothing. On the Duke's departure the Bishop sends a man of his court, Galateo, to accompany him. Galateo has particularly good manners, acquired at the courts of the great: "molto havea de' suoi dì usato alle corti de' gran Signori." This is explicitly emphasized.

This Galateo therefore accompanies Duke Richard part of the way, and says the following to him before taking his leave: His master, the Bishop, would like to make the Duke a parting gift. The Bishop has never in his life seen a nobleman with better manners than the Duke. He has discovered in him only a single fault—he smacks his lips too loudly while eating, so making a noise that is unpleasant for others to hear. To inform him of this is the Bishop's parting gift, which he begs will not be ill-received.

The precept not to smack the lips while eating is also found frequently in medieval instructions. But its occurrence at the beginning of *Galateo* shows clearly what has changed. It not only demonstrates how much importance is now attached to "good behavior." It shows, above all, how the pressure people now exert on one another in this direction has increased. It is immediately apparent that this polite, extremely gentle, and comparatively considerate way of correcting is, particularly when exercised by a social superior, much more compelling as a means of social control, much more effective in inculcating lasting habits, than insults, mockery, or any threat of outward physical violence.

Within countries, pacified societies are formed. The old code of behavior is transformed only step by step. But social control becomes more binding. And above all, the nature and mechanism of affect-molding by society are slowly changed. In the course of the Middle Ages the standard of good and bad manners, for all the regional and social differences, clearly did not undergo any decisive change. Over and again, down the centuries, the same good and bad manners are mentioned. The social code hardened into lasting habits only to a limited extent in people themselves. Now, with the structural transformation of society, with the new pattern of human relationships, a change slowly comes about: the compulsion to check one's own behavior increases. In conjunction with this the standard of behavior is set in motion.

Caxton's *Book of Curtesye*, probably of the late fifteenth century, already gives unambiguous expression to this feeling that habits, customs, and rules of conduct are in flux:[39]

> Thingis whilom used ben now leyd a syde
> And newe feetis, dayly ben contreuide
> Mennys actes can in no plyte abyde
> They be changeable ande ofte meuide
> Thingis somtyme alowed is now repreuid
> And after this shal thines up aryse
> That men set now but at lytyl pryse.

This sounds, indeed, like a motto for the whole movement that is now coming: "Thingis somtyme alowed is now repreuid." The sixteenth century is still wholly within the transition. Erasmus and his contemporaries are still permitted to speak about things, functions, and ways of behaving that one or two centuries later are overlaid with feelings of shame and embarrassment, and whose public exposure or mention are proscribed in society. With the same simplicity and clarity with which he and Della Casa discuss questions of the greatest tact and propriety, Erasmus also says: Do not move back and forth on your chair. Whoever does that "speciem habet subinde ventris flatum emittentis ant emittere conantis" (gives the impression of constantly breaking or trying to break wind). This still shows the old unconcern in referring to bodily functions that was characteristic of medieval people, but enriched by observation, by consideration of "what others *might* think." Comments of this kind occur frequently.

Consideration of the behavior of people in the sixteenth century, and of their code of behavior, casts the observer back and forth between the impressions "That's still utterly medieval" and "That's exactly the way we feel today." And precisely this apparent contradiction clearly corresponds to reality. The people of this time have a double face. They stand on a bridge. Behavior and the code of behavior are in motion, but the movement is quite slow. And above all, in observing a single stage, we lack a sure measure. What is accidental fluctuation? When and where is something advancing? When is something falling behind? Are we really concerned with a change in a definite direction? Is European society really, under the watchword *civilité*, slowly moving toward that kind of refined behavior, that standard of conduct, habits, and affect formation, which is characteristic in our minds of "civilized" society, of Western "civilization"?

8. It is not very easy to make this movement clearly visible precisely because it takes place so slowly—in very small steps, as it were—and because it also shows manifold fluctuations, following smaller and larger curves. It clearly does not suffice to consider in isolation each single stage to which this or that statement on customs and manners bears witness. We must attempt to see the movement itself, or at least a large segment of it, as a whole, as if speeded up. Images must be placed together in a series to give an overall view, from one particular aspect, of the process: the gradual transformation of behavior and the emotions, the expanding threshold of aversion.

The books on manners offer an opportunity for this. On individual aspects of human behavior, particularly eating habits, they give us detailed information— always on the same feature of social life—which extends relatively unbroken, even if at rather fortuitous intervals, from at least the thirteenth to the nineteenth and twentieth centuries. Here images can be seen in a series, and segments of the total process can be made visible. And it is perhaps an advantage, rather than a disadvantage, that modes of behavior of a relatively simple and elementary kind are observed, in which scope for individual variation within the social standard is relatively small.

These *Tischzuchten* and books on manners are a literary genre in their own right. If the written heritage of the past is examined primarily from the point of view of what we are accustomed to call "literary significance," then most of them have no great value. But if we examine the modes of behavior which in every age a particular society has expected of its members, attempting to condition individuals to them; if we wish to observe changes in habits, social rules and taboos; then these instructions on correct behavior, though perhaps worthless as literature, take on a special significance. They throw some light on elements in the social process on which we possess, at least from the past, very little direct information. They show precisely what we are seeking—namely, the standard of habits and behavior to which society at a given time sought to accustom the individual. These poems and treatises are themselves direct instruments of "conditioning" or "fashioning,"[40] of the adaptation of the individual to those modes of behavior which the structure and situation of his society make necessary. And they show at the same time, through what they censure and what they praise, the divergence between what was regarded at different times as good and bad manners.

IV

On Behavior at Table

Part One

Examples

(a) Examples representing upper-class behavior in a fairly pure form:

A

Thirteenth century

This is Tannhäuser's poem of courtly good manners:[41]

1 I consider a well-bred man to be one who always recognizes good manners and is never ill-mannered.

2 There are many forms of good manners, and they serve many good purposes. The man who adopts them will never err.

25 When you eat do not forget the poor. God will reward you if you treat them kindly.

33 A man of refinement should not slurp with his spoon when in company; that is the way people at court behave who often indulge in unrefined conduct.

37 It is not polite to drink from the dish, although some who approve of this rude habit insolently pick up the dish and pour it down as if they were mad.

41 Those who fall upon the dishes like swine while eating, snorting disgustingly and smacking their lips . . .

45 Some people bite a slice and then dunk it in the dish in a coarse way; refined people reject such bad manners.

49 A number of people gnaw a bone and then put it back in the dish—this is a serious offense.

On v. 25, cf. the first rule of Bonvicino da Riva:

The first is this: when at table, think first of the poor and needy.

From *Ein spruch der ze tische kêrt* (A word to those at table):[42]

313 You should not drink from the dish, but with a spoon as is proper.

315 Those who stand up and snort disgustingly over the dishes like swine belong with other farmyard beasts.

319 To snort like a salmon, gobble like a badger, and complain while eating—these three things are quite improper.

or

In the *Courtesies* of Bonvicino da Riva:

Do not slurp with your mouth when eating from a spoon. This is a bestial habit.

or

In *The Book of Nurture and School of Good Manners*:[43]

201 And suppe not lowde of thy Pottage
no tyme in all thy lyfe.

53 Those who like mustard and salt should take care to avoid the filthy habit of putting their fingers into them.

57 A man who clears his throat when he eats and one who blows his nose in the tablecloth are both ill-bred, I assure you.

65 A man who wants to talk and eat at the same time, and talks in his sleep, will never rest peacefully.

69 Do not be noisy at table, as some people are. Remember, my friends, that nothing is so ill-mannered.

81 I find it very bad manners whenever I see someone with food in his mouth and drinking at the same time, like an animal.

On v. 45, cf. *Ein spruch der ze tische kêrt*:

346 May refined people be preserved from those who gnaw their bones and put them back in the dish.

or

From *Quisquis es in mensa* (For those at table):[44]

A morsel that has been tasted should not be returned to the dish.

On v. 65, cf. from *Stans puer in mensam* (The boy at table):[45]

22 Numquam ridebis nec faberis
ore repleto.
   Never laugh or talk with a full
mouth.

On v. 81, cf. from *Quisquis es in mensa*:

15 Qui vult potare debet prius
os vacuare.
   If you wish to drink, first empty
your mouth.

or

From *The Babees Book*:

149 And withe fulle mouthe drinke in no wyse.

85 You should not blow into your drink, as some are fond of doing; this is an ill-mannered habit that should be avoided.

94 Before drinking, wipe your mouth so that you do not dirty the drink; this act of courtesy should be observed at all times.

105 It is bad manners to lean against the table while eating, as it is to keep your helmet on when serving the ladies.

109 Do not scrape your throat with your bare hand while eating; but if you have to, do it politely with your coat.

113 And it is more fitting to scratch with that than to soil your hand; onlookers notice people who behave like this.

117 You should not poke your teeth with your knife, as some do; it is a bad habit.

On v. 85, cf. *The Book of Curtesye*:[46]

111 Ne blow not on thy drinke ne mete,
   Nether for colde, nether for hete.

On 94, cf. *The Babees Book*:

155 Whanne ye shalle drynke,
your mouthe clence withe a clothe.

or

From a *Contenance de table* (Guide to behavior at table):[47]

Do not slobber while you drink, for this is a shameful habit.

On v. 105, cf. *The Babees Book*:

Nor on the borde lenynge be yee nat sene.

On v. 117, cf. *Stans puer in mensam*:[48]

30 Mensa cultello, dentes mundare
caveto.
    Avoid cleaning your teeth with a
knife at table.

125 If anyone is accustomed to loosening his belt at table, take it from me that he is
not a true courtier.

129 If a man wipes his nose on his hand at table because he knows no better, then he
is a fool, believe me.

141 I hear that some eat unwashed (if it is true, it is a bad sign). May their fingers be
palsied!

157 It is not decent to poke your fingers into your ears or eyes, as some people do, or
to pick your nose while eating. These three habits are bad.

B

Fifteenth century?

From *S'ensuivent les contenances de la table* (These are good table manners):[49]

I

Learn these rules.

II

Take care to cut and clean your nails; dirt under the nails is dangerous when
scratching.

III

Wash your hands when you get up and before every meal.

On v. 141, cf. *Stans puer in mensam*:

11 Illotis manibus escas ne sumpseris
unquam.
    Never pick up food with unwashed
hands.

On v. 157, cf. *Quisquis es in mensa*:

9 Non tangas aures nudis digitis
neque nares.
      Touch neither your ears nor your nostrils
with your bare fingers.

> This small selection of passages was compiled from a brief perusal of various guides to behavior at table and court. It is very far from exhaustive. It is intended only to give an impression of how similar in tone and content were the rules in different traditions and in different centuries of the Middle Ages. Originals may be found in Appendix II.

XII
Do not be the first to take from the dish.

XIII
Do not put back on your plate what has been in your mouth.

XIV
Do not offer anyone a piece of food you have bitten into.

XV
Do not chew anything you have to spit out again.

XVII
It is bad manners to dip food into the saltcellar.

XXIV
Be peaceable, quiet, and courteous at table.

XXVI
If you have crumbled bread into your wineglass, drink up the wine or throw it away.

XXXI
Do not stuff too much into yourself, or you will be obliged to commit a breach of good manners.

XXXIV
Do not scratch at table, with your hands or with the tablecloth.

C

1530

From De civilitate morum puerilium (On civility in boys), by Erasmus of Rotterdam, ch. 4:

If a serviette is given, lay it on your left shoulder or arm.

If you are seated with people of rank, take off your hat and see that your hair is well combed.

Your goblet and knife, duly cleansed, should be on the right, your bread on the left.

Some people put their hands in the dishes the moment they have sat down. Wolves do that.

Do not be the first to touch the dish that has been brought in, not only because this shows you greedy, but also because it is dangerous. For someone who puts something hot into his mouth unawares must either spit it out or, if he swallows it, burn his throat. In either case he is as ridiculous as he is pitiable.

It is a good thing to wait a short while before eating, so that the boy grows accustomed to tempering his affects.

To dip the fingers in the sauce is rustic. You should take what you want with your knife and fork; you should not search through the whole dish as epicures are wont to do, but take what happens to be in front of you.

What you cannot take with your fingers should be taken with the *quadra*.

If you are offered a piece of cake or pie on a spoon, hold out your plate or take the spoon that is held out to you, put the food on your plate, and return the spoon.

If you are offered something liquid, taste it and return the spoon, but first wipe it on your serviette.

To lick greasy fingers or to wipe them on your coat is impolite. It is better to use the tablecloth or the serviette.

D

1558

From *Galateo*, by Giovanni della Casa, Archbishop of Benevento, quoted from the five-language edition (Geneva, 1609), p. 68:

> What do you think this Bishop and his noble company (*il Vescove e la sua nobile brigata*) would have said to those whom we sometimes see lying like swine with their snouts in the soup, not once lifting their heads and turning their eyes, still less their hands, from the food, puffing out both cheeks as if they were blowing a trumpet or trying to fan a fire, not eating but gorging themselves, dirtying their arms almost to the elbows and then reducing their serviettes to a state that would make a kitchen rag look clean.
>
> Nonetheless, these hogs are not ashamed to use the serviettes thus sullied to wipe away their sweat (which, owing to their hasty and excessive feeding, often runs down their foreheads and faces to their necks), and even to blow their noses into them as often as they please.

E

1560

From a *Civilité* by C. Calviac[50] (based heavily on Erasmus, but with some independent comments):

When the child is seated, if there is a serviette on the plate in front of him, he shall take it and place it on his left arm or shoulder; then he shall place his bread on the left and the knife on the right, like the glass, if he wishes to leave it on the table, and if it can be conveniently left there without annoying anyone. For it might happen that the glass could not be left on the table or on his right without being in someone's way.

The child must have the discretion to understand the needs of the situation he is in.

When eating . . . he should take the first piece that comes to his hand on his cutting board.

If there are sauces, the child may dip into them decently, without turning his food over after having dipped one side. . . .

It is very necessary for a child to learn at an early age how to carve a leg of mutton, a partridge, a rabbit, and such things.

It is a far too dirty thing for a child to offer others something he has gnawed, or something he disdains to eat himself, *unless it be to his servant.* [Author's emphasis]

Nor is it decent to take from the mouth something he has already chewed, and put it on the cutting board, unless it be a small bone from which he has sucked the marrow to pass time while awaiting the dessert; for after sucking it he should put it on his plate, where he should also place the stones of cherries, plums, and suchlike, as it is not good either to swallow them or to drop them on the floor.

The child should not gnaw bones indecently, as dogs do.

When the child would like salt, he shall take it with the point of his knife and not with three fingers.

The child must cut his meat into very small pieces on his cutting board . . . and he must not lift the meat to his mouth now with one hand and now with the other, like little children who are learning to eat; he should always do so with his right hand, taking the bread or meat decently with three fingers only.

As for the manner of chewing, it varies according to the country. The Germans chew with the mouth closed, and find it ugly to do otherwise. The French, on the other hand, half open the mouth, and find the procedure of the Germans rather dirty. The Italians proceed in a very slack manner and the French more roundly, finding the Italian way too delicate and precious.

And so each nation has something of its own, different to the others. So that the child will proceed in accordance with the customs of the place where he is.

Further, the Germans use sans when eating soup and everything liquid, and the Italians forks. The French use either, as they think fit and as is most convenient. The Italians generally prefer to have a knife for each person. But the Germans place special importance on this, to the extent that they are greatly displeased if one asks for or takes the knife in front of them. The French way is quite different: a whole table full of people will use two or three knives, without making difficulties in asking for or taking a knife, or passing it if they have it. So that if someone asks the child for his knife, he should pass it after wiping it with his serviette, holding it by the point and offering the handle to the person requesting it: for it would not be polite to do otherwise.

F

Between 1640 and 1680
From a song by the Marquis de Coulanges:[51]

In times past, people ate from the common dish and dipped their bread and fingers in the sauce.

Today everyone eats with spoon and fork from his own plate, and a valet washes the cutlery from time to time at the buffet.

G

1672
From Antoine de Courtin, *Nouveau traité de civilité*, pp. 127, 273:

If everyone is eating from the same dish, you should take care not to put your hand into it *before those of higher rank have done so*, and to take food only from the part of the dish opposite you. Still less should you take the best pieces, even though you might be the last to help yourself.

It must also be pointed out that you should always wipe your spoon when, after using it, you want to take something from another dish, *there being people so delicate that they would not wish to eat soup into which you had dipped it after putting it into your mouth.* [Author's emphasis]

And even, if you are at the table of very refined people, it is not enough to wipe your spoon; you should not use it but ask for another. Also, in many places, spoons are brought in with the dishes, *and these serve only for taking soup and sauce.* [Author's emphasis]

You should not eat soup from the dish, but put it neatly on your plate; 'if it is too hot, it is impolite to blow on each spoonful; you should wait until it has cooled.

If you have the misfortune to burn your mouth, you should endure it patiently if you can, without showing it; but if the burn is unbearable, as sometimes happens, you should, before the others have noticed, take your plate promptly in one hand and lift it to your mouth and, while covering your mouth with the other hand, return to the plate what you have in your mouth, and quickly pass it to a footman behind you. Civility requires you to be polite, but it does not expect you to be homicidal toward yourself. It is very impolite to touch anything greasy, a sauce or syrup, etc., with your fingers, apart from the fact that it obliges you to commit two or three more improper acts. One is to wipe your hand frequently on your serviette and to soil it like a kitchen cloth, so that those who see you wipe your mouth with it feel nauseated. Another is to wipe your fingers on your bread, which again is very improper. The third is to lick them, which is the height of impropriety.

. . . As there are many [customs] which have already changed, I do not doubt that several of these will likewise change in the future.

Formerly one was permitted . . . to dip one's bread into the sauce, provided only that one had not already bitten it. Nowadays that would be a kind of rusticity.

Formerly one was allowed to take from one's mouth what one could not eat and drop it on the floor, provided it was done skillfully. Now that would be very disgusting. . . .

H

1717

From François de Callières, *De la science du monde et des connoissances utiles à la conduite de la vie*, pp. 97, 101:

In Germany and the Northern Kingdoms it is civil and decent for a prince to drink first to the health of those he is entertaining, and then to offer them the same glass or goblet usually filled with the same wine; nor is it a lack of politeness in them to drink from the same glass, but a mark of candor and friendship. The women also drink first and then give their glass, or have it taken, to the person they are addressing, with the same wine from which they have drunk his health, *without this being taken as a special favor, as it is among us*. . . . [Author's emphasis]

"I cannot approve," a lady answers "—without offense to the gentlemen from the north—this manner of drinking from the same glass, and still less of drinking what the ladies have left; it has an air of impropriety that makes me wish they might show other marks of their candor."

(b) Examples from books which either, like La Salle's *Les Règles de la bienséance et de la civilité chrétienne*, represent the spreading of courtly manners and models to broader bourgeois strata, or, like Example I, reflect fairly purely the bourgeois and probably the provincial standard of their time.

In Example I, from about 1714, people still eat from a communal dish. Nothing is said against touching the meat on one's own plate with the hands. And the "bad manners" that are mentioned have largely disappeared from the upper class.

The *Civilité* of 1780 (Example L) is a little book of forty-eight pages in bad *civilité* type, printed in Caen but undated. The British Museum catalogue has a question mark after the date. In any case, this book is an example of the multitude of cheap books or pamphlets on *civilité* that were disseminated throughout France in the eighteenth century. This one, to judge from its general attitude, was clearly intended for provincial town-dwellers. In no other eighteenth-century work on *civilité* quoted here are bodily functions discussed so openly. The standard the book points to recalls in many respects the one that Erasmus's *De civilitate* had marked for the upper class. It is still a matter of course to take food in the hands. This example seemed useful here to complement the other quotations, and particularly to remind the reader that the movement ought to be seen in its full multilayered polyphony, not as a line but as a kind of fugue with a succession of related movement-motifs on different levels.

Example M from 1786 shows the dissemination from above to below very directly. It is particularly characteristic because it contains a large number of customs that have subsequently been adopted by "civilized society" as a whole, but are here clearly visible as specific customs of the courtly upper class which still seem relatively alien to the bourgeoisie. Many customs have been arrested, as "civilized customs," in exactly the form they have here as courtly manners.

The quotation from 1859 (Example N) is meant to remind the reader that in the nineteenth century, as today, the whole movement had already been entirely forgotten, that the standard of "civilization" which in reality had been attained only quite recently was taken for granted, what preceded it being seen as "barbaric."

I

1714

From an anonymous *Civilité française* (Liège, 1714?), p. 48:

> It is not . . . polite to drink your soup from the bowl unless you are in your own family, and only then if you have drunk the most part with your spoon.
>
> If the soup is in a communal dish, take some with your spoon in your turn, without precipitation.
>
> Do not keep your knife always in your hand, as village people do, but take it only when you need it.
>
> When you are being served meat, it is not seemly to take it in your hand. You should hold out your plate in your left hand while holding your fork or knife in your right.
>
> It is against propriety to give people meat to smell, and you should under no circumstances put meat back into the common dish if you have smelled it yourself. If you take meat from a common dish, do not choose the best pieces. Cut with the knife, holding still the piece of meat in the dish with the fork, which you will use to put on your plate the piece you have cut off; do not, therefore, take the meat with your hand [nothing is said here against touching the meat on one's own plate with the hand].
>
> You should not throw bones or eggshells or the skin of any fruit onto the floor.
>
> The same is true of fruit stones. It is more polite to remove them from the mouth with two fingers than to spit them into one's hand.

J

1729

From La Salle, *Les Régles de la bienséance et de la civilité chrétienne* (Rouen, 1729), p. 87:

On Things to Be Used at Table

At table you should use a serviette, a plate, a knife, a spoon, and a fork. It would be entirely contrary to propriety to be without any of these things while eating.

It is for the person of highest rank in the company to unfold his serviette first, and the others should wait until he has done so before unfolding theirs. When the people are approximately equal, all should unfold it together without ceremony. [N.B. With the "democratization" of society and the family, this becomes the rule. The social structure, here still of the hierarchical-aristocratic type, is mirrored in the most elementary human relationships.]

It is improper to use the serviette to wipe your face; it is far more so to rub your teeth with it, and it would be one of the grossest offenses against civility to use it to blow your nose. . . . The use you may and must make of the serviette when at table is for wiping your mouth, lips, and fingers when they are greasy, wiping the knife before cutting bread, and cleaning the spoon and fork after using them. [N.B. This is one of many examples of the extraordinary control of behavior embedded in our eating habits. The use of each utensil is limited and defined by a multiplicity of very precise rules. None of them is simply self-evident, as they appear to later generations. Their use is formed very gradually in conjunction with the structure and changes of human relationships.]

When the fingers are very greasy, wipe them first on a piece of bread, which should then be left on the plate, before cleaning them on the serviette, in order not to soil it too much.

When the spoon, fork, and knife are dirty or greasy, it is very improper to lick them, and it is not at all decent to wipe them, or anything else, on the tablecloth. On these and similar occasions you should use the serviette, and regarding the tablecloth you should take care to keep it always very clean, and not to drop on it water, wine, or anything that might soil it.

When the plate is dirty, you should be sure not to scrape it with the spoon or fork to clean it, or to clean your plate or the bottom of any dish with your fingers: that is very impolite. Either they should not be touched or, if you have the opportunity of exchanging them, you should ask for another.

When at table you should not keep the knife always in your hand; it is sufficient to pick it up when you wish to use it.

It is also very impolite to put a piece of bread into your mouth while holding the knife in your hand; it is even more so to do this with the point of the knife. The same thing must be observed in eating apples, pears, or some other fruits. [N.B. Examples of taboos relating to knives.]

It is against propriety to hold the fork or spoon with the whole hand, like a stick; you should always hold them between your fingers.

You should not use your fork to lift liquids to the mouth . . . it is the spoon that is intended for such uses.

It is polite always to use the fork to put meat into your mouth, for *propriety does not permit the touching of anything greasy with the fingers* [Author's emphasis], neither sauces nor syrups; and if anyone did so, he could not escape subsequently commiting several further incivilities, such as frequently wiping his fingers on his serviette, which would make it very dirty, or on his bread, which would be very impolite, or licking his fingers, which is not permitted to well-born, refined people.

This whole passage, like several others, is taken from A. de Courtin's *Nouveau traité* of 1672; cf. Example G, p. 75. It also reappears in other eighteenth-century works on *civilité*. The reason given for the prohibition on eating with the fingers is particularly instructive. In Courtin, too, it applies in the first place only to greasy foods, especially those in sauces, since this gives rise to actions that are "distasteful" to behold. In La Salle this is not entirely consistent with what he says in another place: "If your fingers are greasy . . ." etc. The prohibition is not remotely so self-evident as today. We see how gradually it becomes an internalized habit, a piece of "self-control."

In the critical period at the end of the reign of Louis XV—in which, as shown earlier, the urge for reform is intensified as an outward sign of social changes, and in which the concept of "civilization" comes to the fore—La Salle's *Civilité*, which had previously passed through several editions largely unchanged, was revised. The changes in the standard are very instructive (Example K, below). They are in some respects very considerable. The difference is partly discernible in what no longer needs to be said. Many chapters are shorter. Many "bad manners" earlier discussed in detail are mentioned only briefly in passing. The same applies to many bodily functions originally dealt with at length and in great detail. The tone is generally less mild, and often incomparably harsher than in the first version.

K

1774

From La Salle, *Les Règles de la bienséance et de la civilité chrétienne* (1774 ed.), pp. 45ff.:

The serviette which is placed on the plate, being intended to preserve clothing from spots and other soiling inseparable from meals, should be spread over you so far that it covers the front of your body to the knees, going under the collar and not being passed inside it. The spoon, fork, and knife should always be placed on the right.

The spoon is intended for liquids, and the fork for solid meats.

When one or the other is dirty, they can be cleaned with the serviette, if another service cannot be procured. You should avoid wiping them with the tablecloth, which is an unpardonable impropriety.

When the plate is dirty you should ask for another; it would be revoltingly gross to clean spoon, fork, or knife with the fingers.

At good tables, attentive servants change plates without being called upon.

Nothing is more improper than to lick your fingers, to touch the meats and put them into your mouth with your hand, to stir sauce with your fingers, or to dip bread into it with your fork and then suck it.

You should never take salt with your fingers. It is very common for children to pile pieces one on top of the other, and even to take out of their mouths something they have chewed, and flick pieces with their fingers. [All these were mentioned earlier as general misdemeanors, but are here mentioned only as the "bad" manners of children. Grown-ups no longer do such things.] Nothing is more impolite [than] to lift meat to your nose to smell it; to let others smell it is a further impoliteness toward the master of the table; if you should happen to find dirt in the food, you should get rid of the food without showing it.

L

1780?

From an anonymous work, *La Civilité honete pour les enfants* (Caen, n.d.), p. 35:

Afterward, he shall place his serviette on him, his bread on the left and his knife on the right, to cut the meat without breaking it. [The sequence described here is found in many other documents. The most elementary procedure, earlier usual among the upper class as well, is to break up the meat with the hands. Here the next stage is described, when the meat is cut with the knife. The use of the fork is not mentioned. To break off pieces of meat is regarded here as a mark of the peasant, cutting it as clearly the manners of the town.] He will also take care not to put his knife into his mouth. He should not leave his hands on his plate . . . nor rest his elbow on it, for this is done only by the aged and infirm.

The well-behaved child will be the last to help himself if he is with his superiors. . . . next, if it is meat, he will cut it politely with his knife and eat it with his bread.

It is a rustic, dirty habit to take chewed meat from your mouth and put it on your plate. Nor should you ever put back into the dish something you have taken from it.

M

1786

From a conversation between the poet Delille and Abbé Cosson:[52]

A short while ago Abbé Cosson, Professor of Belles Lettres at the Collège Mazarin, told me about a dinner he had attended a few days previously with some *court people* . . . at Versailles.

"I'll wager," I told him, "that you perpetrated a hundred incongruities."

"What do you mean?" Abbé Cosson asked quickly, greatly perturbed. "I believe I did everything in the same way as everyone else."

"What presumption! I'll bet you did nothing in the same way as anyone else. But I'll limit myself to the dinner. First, what did you do with your serviette when you sat down?"

"With my serviette? I did the same as everyone else. I unfolded it, spread it out, and fixed it by a corner to my buttonhole."

"Well, my dear fellow, you are the only one who did that. One does not spread out one's serviette, one keeps it on one's knees. And how did you eat your soup?"

"Like everyone else, I think. I took my spoon in one hand and my fork in the other. . . ."

"Your fork? Good heavens! No one uses his fork to eat soup. . . . But tell me how you ate your bread."

"Certainly, like everyone else: I cut it neatly with my knife."

"Oh dear, you break bread, you do not cut it. . . . Let's go on. The coffee—how did you drink it?"

"Like everyone, to be sure. It was boiling hot, so I poured it little by little from my cup into my saucer."

"Well, you certainly did not drink it like anyone else. Everyone drinks coffee from the cup, never from the saucer. . . ."

N

1859

From *The Habits of Good Society* (London, 1859; 2d ed., verbatim, 1889), p. 257:

Forks were undoubtedly a later invention than fingers, but as we are not *cannibals* I am inclined to think they were a good one.

Part Two

Comments on the Quotations on Table Manners

Group 1:

A Brief Survey of the Societies to which the Texts were Addressed

1. The quotations have been assembled to illustrate a real process, a change in the behavior of people. In general, the examples have been so selected that they may stand as typical of at least certain social groups or strata. No single person, not even so pronounced an individual as Erasmus, invented the *savoir-vivre* of his time.

We hear people of different ages speaking on roughly the same subject. In this way, the changes become more distinct than if we had described them in our own words. From at least the sixteenth century onward, the commands and prohibitions by which the individual is shaped (in conformity with the standard of society) are in continuous movement. This movement, certainly, is not perfectly rectilinear, but through all its fluctuations and individual curves a definite overall trend is nevertheless perceptible if these voices from past centuries are heard together in context.

Sixteenth-century writings on manners are embodiments of the new court aristocracy that is slowly coalescing from elements of diverse social origin. With it grows a different code of behavior.

De Courtin, in the second half of the seventeenth century, speaks from a court society which is consolidated to the highest degree—the court society of Louis XIV. And he speaks primarily to people of rank, people who do not live directly at court but who wish to familiarize themselves with the manners and customs of the court.

He says in his foreword: "This treatise is not intended for printing but only to satisfy a provincial gentleman who had requested the author, as a particular friend, to give some precepts on civility to his son, whom he intended to send to the court on completing his studies. . . . He [the author] undertook this work only for well-bred people; *it is only to them that it is addressed*; and particularly to youth, which might derive some utility from these small pieces of advice, as not everyone has the opportunity nor the means of coming to the court at Paris to learn the fine points of politeness."

People living in the example-setting circle do not need books in order to know how "one" behaves. This is obvious; it is therefore important to ascertain with what intentions and for which public these precepts are written and printed-precepts which are originally the distinguishing secret of the narrow circles of the court aristocracy.

The intended public is quite clear. It is stressed that the advice is only for *honnêtes gens*, i.e., by and large for upper-class people. Primarily the book meets the need of the provincial nobility to know about behavior at court, and in addition that of distinguished foreigners. But it may be assumed that the not inconsiderable success of this book resulted, among other things, from the interest of leading bourgeois strata. There is ample evidence to show that at this period customs, behavior, and fashions from the court are continuously penetrating the upper middle classes, where they are imitated and more or less altered in accordance with the different social situation. They thereby lose, to some extent, their character as means of distinguishing the upper class. They are somewhat devalued. This compels those above to further refinement and development of behavior. And from this mechanism—the development of courtly customs, their dissemination downward, their slight social deformation, their devaluation as marks of distinction—the constant movement in behavior patterns through the upper class receives part of its motivation. What is important is that in this change, in the inventions and fashions of courtly behavior, which are at first sight perhaps chaotic and accidental, over extended time spans certain directions or lines of development emerge. These include, for example, what may be described as an advance of the threshold of embarrassment and shame, as "refinement," or as "civilization." A particular social dynamism triggers a particular psychological one, which has its own regularities.

2. In the eighteenth century wealth increases, and with it the advance of the bourgeois classes. The court circle now includes, directly alongside aristocratic elements, a larger number of bourgeois elements than in the preceding century, without the differences in social rank ever being lost. Shortly before the French Revolution the tendency toward self-encapsulation of the socially weakening aristocracy is intensified once more.

Nevertheless, this extended court society, in which aristocratic and bourgeois elements intermingle, and which has no distinct boundaries barring entry from below must be envisaged as a whole. It comprises the hierarchically structured elite of the country. The compulsion to penetrate or at least imitate it constantly increases with the growing interdependence and prosperity of broad strata. Clerical circles, above all, become popularizers of the courtly customs. The moderated restraint of the emotions and the disciplined shaping of behavior as a whole, which under the name of *civilité* have been developed in the upper class as a purely secular and social phenomenon, a consequence of certain forms of social life, have affinities to particular tendencies in traditional ecclesiastical behavior. *Civilité* is given a new Christian religious foundation. The Church proves, as so often, one of the most important organs of the downward diffusion of behavioral models.

"It is a surprising thing," says the venerable Father La Salle at the beginning of the preface to his rules of Christian *civilité*, "that the majority of Christians regard decency and civility only as a *purely human and worldly quality* and, not thinking to elevate their minds more highly, do not consider it a virtue related to God, our neighbor, and ourselves. This well shows how little Christianity there is in the world." And as a good deal of the education in France lay in the hands of ecclesiastical bodies, it was above all, if not exclusively, through their mediation that a growing flood of *civilité* tracts now inundated the country. They were used as manuals in the elementary education of children, and were often printed and distributed together with the first instructions on reading and writing.

Precisely thereby the concept of *civilité* is increasingly devalued for the social elite. It begins to undergo a process similar to that which earlier overtook the concept of *courtoisie*.

Excursus on the Rise and Decline of the Concepts of *Courtoisie* and *Civilité*

3. *Courtoisie* originally referred to the forms of behavior that developed at the courts of the great feudal lords. Even during the Middle Ages the meaning of the word clearly lost much of its original social restriction to the "court," coming into use in bourgeois circles as well. With the slow extinction of the knightly-feudal warrior nobility and the formation of a new absolute court aristocracy in the course of the sixteenth and seventeenth centuries, the concept of *civilité* is slowly elevated as the expression of socially acceptable behavior. *Courtoisie* and *civilité* exist side by side during the French transitional society of the sixteenth century, with its half knightly-feudal, half absolute court character. In the course of the seventeenth century, however, the concept *courtoisie* gradually goes out of fashion in France.

"The words *courtois* and *courtoisie*," says a French writer in 1675,[53] "are beginning to age and are no longer good usage. We say *civil, honneste; civilité, honnesteté.*"

Indeed, the word *courtoisie* now actually appears as a bourgeois concept. "My neighbor, the bourgeois, . . . says in accordance with the language of the bourgeoisie of Paris 'affable' and 'courteous' (*courtois*) . . . he does not express himself politely because the words 'courteous' and 'affable' are scarcely in use among people of the world, and the words 'civil' and 'decent' (*honnête*) have taken their place, just as 'civility' and 'decency' have taken the place of 'courtesy' and 'affability.' " So we read in a conversation with the title *On Good and Bad Usage in Expressing Oneself: On Bourgeois Manners of Speaking*, by F. de Callières (1694, pp. 110ff.).

In a very similar way, in the course of the eighteenth century, the concept of *civilité* slowly loses its hold among the upper class of court society. This class is now in its turn undergoing a very slow process of transformation, of bourgeoisification, which, at least up to 1750, is always combined with an inverse process assimilating bourgeois elements to the court. Something of the resultant problem is perceptible, for example, when in 1745 Abbé Gedoyn, in an essay "De l'urbanité romaine" (*Oeuvres diverses*, p. 173), discusses the question of why, in his own society, the expression *urbanité*, though it refers to something very fine, has never come into use as much as *civilité*, *humanité*, *politesse*, or *galanterie*, and he replies: "*Urbanitas* signified that *politesse* of language, mind, and manners attached singularly to the city of Rome, which was called par excellence *Urbs*, the city, whereas among us, where this politeness is not the privilege of any city in particular, not even of the capital, but solely of the court, the term urbanity becomes a term . . . with which we may dispense."

If one realizes that "city" at this time refers more or less to "bourgeois good society" as against the narrower court society, one readily perceives the topical importance of the question raised here.

In most of the statements from this period, the use of *civilité* has receded, as here, in the face of *politesse*, and the identification of this whole complex of ideas with *humanité* emerges more sharply.

As early as 1733, Voltaire, in the dedication of his *Zaïre* to a bourgeois, A. M. Faulkner, an English merchant, expressed these tendencies very clearly: "Since the regency of Anne of Austria the French have been the most sociable and the most polite people in the world . . . and *this politeness is not in the least an arbitrary matter, like that which is called* civilité, *but is a law of nature* which they have happily cultivated more than other peoples."

Like the concept of *courtoisie* earlier, *civilité* now is slowly beginning to sink. Shortly afterward, the content of this and related terms is taken up and extended in a new concept, the expression of a new form of self-consciousness, the concept of *civilisation*. *Courtoisie*, *civilité*, and *civilisation* mark three stages of a social development. They indicate which society is speaking and being addressed at a given time. However, the actual change in the behavior of the upper classes, the development of the models of behavior which will henceforth be called "civilized," takes place—at least so far as it is visible in the areas discussed here—in the middle phase. The concept of *civilisation* indicates quite clearly in its nineteenth-century usage that the *process* of civilization—or, more strictly speaking, a phase of this *process*—has been completed and forgotten. People only want to accomplish this process for other nations, and also, for a period, for the lower classes of their own society. To the upper and middle classes of their own society, civilization appears as a firm possession. They wish above all to disseminate it, and at most to develop it within the framework of the standard already reached.

The examples quoted clearly express the movement toward this standard in the preceding stage of the absolute courts.

A Review of the Curve Marking the "Civilization" of Eating Habits

4. At the end of the eighteenth century, shortly before the revolution, the French upper class attained approximately the standard of eating manners, and certainly not only of eating manners, that was gradually to be taken for granted in the whole of civilized society. Example M from the year 1786 is instructive enough: it shows as still a decidedly courtly custom exactly the same use of the serviette which in the meantime has become customary in the whole of civilized bourgeois society. It shows the exclusion of the fork from the eating of soup, the necessity of which, to be sure, is only understood if we recall that soup often used to contain, and still contains in France, more solid content than it does now. It further shows the requirement not to cut but to break one's bread at table, a requirement that has in the meantime been democratized, as a courtly demand. And the same applies to the way in which one drinks coffee.

These are a few examples of how our everyday ritual was formed. If this series were continued up to the present day, further changes of detail would be seen: new imperatives are added, old ones are relaxed; a wealth of national and social variations on table manners emerges; the penetration of the middle classes, the working class, the peasantry by the uniform ritual of civilization, and by the regulation of drives that its acquisition requires, is of varying strength. But the essential basis of what is required and what is forbidden in civilized society—the standard eating technique, the manner of using knife, fork, spoon, plate, serviette, and other eating utensils—these remain in their essential features unchanged. Even the development of technology in all areas—even that of cooking—by the introduction of new sources of energy has left the techniques of eating and other forms of behavior essentially unchanged. Only on very close inspection does one observe traces of a trend that is continuing to develop.

What is still changing now is, above all, the technology of production. The technology of consumption was developed and kept in motion by social formations which were, to a degree never since equaled, consumption classes.

With their social decline, the rapid and intensive elaboration of consumption techniques ceases and is delegated into what now becomes the private (in contrast to the occupational) sphere of life. Correspondingly, the tempo of movement and change in these spheres which during the stage of the absolute courts was relatively fast, slows down once again.

Even the shapes of eating utensils—plates, dishes, knives, forks, and spoons—are from now on no more than variations on themes of the *dix-huitième* and preceding centuries. Certainly there are still very many changes of detail. One example is the differentiation of utensils. On many occasions, not only the plates are changed after each course but the eating utensils, too. It does not suffice to eat simply with knife, fork, and spoon instead of with one's hands. More and more in the upper class a special implement is used for each kind of food. Soupspoons, fish knives, and meat knives are on one side of the plate. Forks for the hors d'oeuvre, fish, and meat on the other. Above the plate are fork, spoon, or knife—according to the custom of the country—for sweet foods. And for the dessert and fruit yet another implement is brought in. All these utensils are differently shaped and equipped. They are now larger, now smaller, now more round, now more pointed. But on closer consideration they do not represent anything actually new. They, too, are variations on the same theme, differentiations within the same standard. And only on a few points—above all, in the use of the knife—do slow movements begin to show themselves that lead beyond the standard already attained. Later there will be more to say on this.

5. In a sense, something similar is true of the period up to the fifteenth century. Up to then—for very different reasons—the standard eating technique, the basic stock of what is socially prohibited and permitted, like the behavior of people toward one another and toward themselves (of which these prohibitions and commands are expressions), remains fairly constant in its essential features, even if here too fashions, fluctuations, regional and social variations, and a slow movement in a particular direction are by no means entirely absent.

Nor are the transitions from one phase to another to be ascertained with complete exactness. The more rapid movement begins later here, earlier there, and everywhere one finds slight preparatory shifts. Nevertheless, the overall shape of the curve is everywhere broadly the same: first the medieval phase, with a certain climax in the flowering of knightly-courtly society, marked by eating with the hands. Then a phase of relatively rapid movement and change, embracing roughly the sixteenth, seventeenth, and eighteenth centuries, in which the compulsions to elaborate eating behavior press constantly in one direction, toward a new standard of table manners.

From then on, one again observes a phase which remains within the framework of the standard already reached, though with a very slow movement in a certain direction. The elaboration of everyday conduct never entirely loses, in this period either, its importance as an instrument of social distinction. But from now on, it no longer plays the same role as in the preceding phase. More exclusively than before, money becomes the basis of social differences. And what people actually achieve and produce becomes more important than their manners.

6. Taken together, the examples show very clearly how this movement progresses. The prohibitions of medieval society, even at the feudal courts do not yet impose any very great restraint on the play of emotions. Compared to later eras, social control is mild. Manners, measured against later ones, are relaxed in all senses of the word. One ought not to snort or smack one's lips while eating. One ought not to spit across the table or blow one's nose on the tablecloth (for this is used for wiping greasy fingers) or into the fingers (with which one holds the common dish). Eating from the same dish or plate as others is taken for granted. One must only refrain from falling on the dish like a pig, and from dipping bitten food into the communal sauce.

Many of these customs are still mentioned in Erasmus's treatise and in its adaptation by Calviac. More clearly than by inspecting particular accounts of contemporary manners, by surveying the whole movement one sees how it progresses. Table utensils are still limited; on the left the bread, on the right the glass and knife. That is all. The fork is already mentioned, although with a limited function as an instrument for lifting food from the common dish. And, like the handkerchief, the napkin also appears already, both still—a symbol of transition—as optional rather than necessary implements: if you have a handkerchief, the precepts say, use it rather than your fingers. If a napkin is provided, lay it over your left shoulder. One hundred and fifty years later both napkin and handkerchief are, like the fork, more or less indispensable utensils in the courtly class.

The curve followed by other habits and customs is similar. First the soup is often drunk, whether from the common dish or from ladles used by several people. In the *courtois* writings the use of the spoon is prescribed. It, too, will first of all serve several together. A further step is shown by the quotation from Calviac of 1560. He mentions that it was customary among Germans to allow each guest his own spoon. The next step is shown by Courtin's text from the year 1672. Now one no longer eats the soup directly from the common dish, but pours some into one's own plate, first of all using one's own spoon; but there are even people, we read here, who are so *delicate* that they do not wish to eat from a dish into which others have dipped a spoon already used. It is therefore necessary to wipe one's spoon with the serviette before dipping it into the dish. And some people are not satisfied even with this. For them, one is not allowed to dip a used spoon back into the common dish at all; instead, one must ask for a clean one for this purpose.

Statements like these show not only how the whole ritual of living together is in flux, but also how people themselves are aware of this change.

Here, step by step, the now accepted way of taking soup is being established:

everyone has his own plate and his own spoon, and the soup is distributed with a specialized implement. Eating has acquired a new style corresponding to the new necessities of social life.

Nothing in table manners is self-evident or the product, as it were, of a "natural" feeling of delicacy. The spoon, fork, and napkin are not invented by individuals as technical implements with obvious purposes and clear directions for use. Over centuries, in direct social intercourse and use, their functions are gradually defined, their forms sought and consolidated. Each custom in the changing ritual, however minute, establishes itself infinitely slowly, even forms of behavior that to us seem quite elementary or simply "reasonable," such as the custom of taking liquid only with the spoon. Every movement of the hand—for example, the way in which one holds and moves knife, spoon, or fork—is standardized only step by step. And the social mechanism of standardization is itself seen in outline if the series of images is surveyed as a whole. There is a more or less limited courtly circle which first stamps the models only for the needs of its own social situation and in conformity with the psychological condition corresponding to it. But clearly the structure and development of French society as a whole gradually makes ever broader strata willing and anxious to adopt the models developed above them: they spread, also very gradually, throughout the whole of society, certainly not without undergoing some modification in the process.

The passage of models from one social unit to another, now from the centers of a society to its outposts (e.g., from the Parisian court to other courts), now within the same political-social unit (e.g., within France or Saxony, from above to below or from below to above), is to be counted, in the whole civilizing process, among the most important individual movements. What the examples show is only a limited segment of these. Not only the eating manners but also forms of thinking or speaking, in short, of behavior in general, are molded in a similar way throughout France, even if there are significant differences in the timing and structure of their patterns of development. The elaboration of a particular ritual of human relations in the course of social and psychological development cannot be isolated, even if here, as a first attempt, it has only been possible to follow a single strand. A short example from the process of the "civilization" of speech may serve as a reminder that the observation of manners and their transformation exposes to view only a very simple and easily accessible segment of a much more far-reaching process of social change.

Excursus on the Modeling of Speech at Court

7. For speech, too, a limited circle first develops certain standards.

As in Germany, though to a far lesser extent, the language spoken in court society was different from the language spoken by the bourgeoisie.

"You know," we read in a little work which in its time was much read, *Mots à la mode* by Callières, in the edition of 1693 (p. 46), "that the bourgeois speak very differently from us."

If we examine more closely what is termed "bourgeois" speech, and what is referred to as the expression of the courtly upper class, we encounter the same phenomenon that can be observed in eating-customs and manners in general: much of what in the seventeenth and to some extent the eighteenth century was the distinguishing form of expression and language of court society gradually becomes the French national language.

The young son of bourgeois parents, M. Thibault, is presented to us visiting a small aristocratic society. The lady of the house asks after his father. "He is your very humble servant, Madame," Thibault answers, "and he is still poorly, as you well know, since you have graciously sent oftentimes to inquire about the state of his health."

The situation is clear. A certain social contact exists between the aristocratic circle and the bourgeois family. The lady of the house has mentioned it previously. She also says that the elder Thibault is a very nice man, not without adding that such acquaintances are sometimes quite useful to the aristocracy because these people, after all, have money.[54] And at this point one recalls the very different structure of German society.

But social contacts at this time are clearly not close enough, leaving aside the bourgeois intelligentsia, to have effaced the linguistic differences between the classes. Every other word the young Thibault says is, by the standards of court society, awkward and gross, smelling bourgeois—as the courtiers put it, "from the mouth." In court society one does not say "as you well know" or "oftentimes" or "poorly" (*comme bien sçavez, souventes fois, maladif*).

One does not say, like M. Thibault in the ensuing conversation, "Je vous demande excuse" (I beg to be excused). In courtly society one says, as today in bourgeois society, "Je vous demande pardon" (I beg your pardon).

M. Thibault says: "Un mien ami, un mien parent, un mien cousin" (A friend of mine, etc.), instead of the courtly "un de mes amis, un de mes parents" (p. 20). He says "deffunct mon père, le pauvre deffunct" (deceased). And he is instructed that that too is not one of the expressions "which civility has introduced among well-spoken people. People of the world do not say that a man is deceased when they mean that he is dead" (p. 22). The word can be used at most when saying "we must pray to God for the soul of the deceased . . . but those who speak well say rather: my late father, the late Duke, etc." (feu mon père, etc.). And it is pointed out that "for the poor deceased" is "a very bourgeois Nm of phrase."

8. Here, too, as with manners, there is a kind of double movement: the bourgeois are, as it were, "courtified," and the aristocracy, "bourgeoisified." Or, more precisely: bourgeois people are influenced by the behavior of courtly people,

and vice versa. The influence from below to above is certainly very much weaker in the seventeenth century in France than in the eighteenth. But it is not entirely absent: the château Vaux-le Vicomte of the bourgeois intendant of finances, Nicolas Fouquet, antedates the royal Versailles, and is in many ways its model. That is a clear example. The wealth of leading bourgeois strata compels those above to compete. And the incessant influx of bourgeois people to the circle of the court also produces a specific movement in speech: with the new human substance it brings new linguistic substance, the slang of the bourgeoisie, into the circle of the court. Elements of it are constantly being assimilated into courtly language, polished, refined, transformed; they are made, in a word, "courtly," i.e., adapted to the standard of sensibility of the court circles. They are thereby turned into means of distinguishing the *gens de la cour* from the bourgeoisie, and then perhaps, after some time, penetrate the bourgeoisie once more, thus refined and modified, to become "specifically bourgeois."

There is, says the Duke in one of the conversations quoted from Callières (*Du bon et do mauvais usage*, p. 98), a manner of speaking "most common among the bourgeois of Paris and even among some courtiers raised among the bourgeoisie. It is to say 'Let us go and see' (*voyons voir*), instead of saying 'Let us see' (*voyons*), and avoiding the word 'go,' which is perfectly useless and disagreeable in this place."

But there has recently come into use, the Duke continues, "another bad turn of phrase, which began among the lowest people and made its fortune at the court, like those favorites without merit who got themselves elevated there in the old days. It is 'il en sçait bien long,' meaning that someone is subtle and clever. The ladies of the court are beginning to use it, too."

So it goes on. The bourgeois and even some court people say "il faut que nous faisions cela" instead of "il faut que nous fassions cela." Some say "l'on za" and "l'on zest" instead of the courtly "l'on a" and "l'on est." They say "Je le l'ai" instead of "Je l'ai."

In almost all these cases the linguistic form which here appears as courtly has indeed become the national usage. But there are also examples of courtly linguistic formations being gradually discarded as "too refined," "too affected."

9. All this elucidates at the same time what was said earlier about the sociogenetic differences between the German and French national characters. Language is one of the most accessible manifestations of what we perceive as national character. Here it can be seen from a single concrete example how this peculiar and typical character is elaborated in conjunction with certain social formations. The French language was decisively stamped by the court and court society. For the German language the Imperial Chamber and Chancellery for a time played a similar role, even if they did not have remotely the same influence as the French court. As late as 1643, someone claims his language to be exemplary "because it is modeled on writings from the Chamber at Speyer."[55]

Then it was the universities that attained almost the same importance for German culture and language as the court in France. But these two socially closely related entities, Chancellery and university, influenced speech less than writing; they formed the German written language not through conversation but through documents, letters, and books. And if Nietzsche observes that even the German drinking song is erudite, or if he contrasts the elimination of specialist terms by the courtly Voltaire to the practice of the Germans, he sees very clearly the results of these different historical developments.

10. If in France the *gens de la cour* say "This is spoken well and this badly," a large question is raised that must be at least touched on in passing: "By what standards are they actually judging what is good and bad in language? What are their criteria for selecting, polishing, and modifying expressions?"

Sometimes they reflect on this themselves. What they say on the subject is at first sight rather surprising, and at any rate significant beyond the area of language. Phrases, words, and nuances are good *because* they, the members of the social elite, use them; and they are bad *because* social inferiors speak in this way.

M. Thibault sometimes defends himself when he is told that this or that turn of phrase is bad. "I am much obliged to you, Madame," he says (*Do bon et du mauvais usage*, p. 23), "for the trouble you are taking to instruct me, yet it seems to me that the term 'deceased' is a well-established word used by a great many well-bred people (*honnêtes gens*)."

"It is very possible," the lady answers, "that there are many well-bred people who are insufficiently familiar with the delicacy of our language . . . a delicacy which is known to only a small number of well-spoken people and causes them not to say that a man is deceased in order to say that he is dead."

A small circle of people is versed in this delicacy of language; to speak as they do is to speak correctly. What the others say does not count. The judgments are apodictic. A reason other than that "We, the elite, speak thus, and only we have sensitivity to language" is neither needed nor known. "With regard to errors committed against good usage," it is expressly stated in another place, "as there are no definite rules it depends only on the consent of a certain number of elite people whose ears are accustomed to certain ways of speaking and to preferring them to others" (p. 98). And then the words are listed that should be avoided.

Antiquated words are unsuited to ordinary, serious speech. Very new words must arouse suspicion of affectation—we might perhaps say, of snobbery. Learned words that smack of Latin and Greek must be suspect to all *gens du monde*. They surround anyone using them with an atmosphere of pedantry, if other words are known that express the same thing simply.

Low words used by the common people must be carefully avoided, for those who use them show that they have had a "low education." "And it is of these words, that is, low words," says the courtly speaker, "that we speak in this connection"—he means in the contraposition of courtly and bourgeois language.

The reason given for the expurgation of "bad" words from language is the refinement of feeling that plays no small role in the whole civilizing process. But this refinement is the possession of a relatively small group. Either one has this sensitivity or one has not—that, roughly, is the speaker's attitude. The people who possess this delicacy, a small circle, determine by their consensus what is held to be good or bad.

In other words, of all the rational arguments that might be put forward for the selection of expressions, the social argument, that something is better because it is the usage of the upper class, or even of only an elite within the upper class, is by far the most prominent.

"Antiquated words," words that have gone out of fashion, are used by the older generation or by those who are not permanently involved directly in court life, the déclassé. "Too new words" are used by the clique of young people who have yet to be accepted, who speak their special "slang," a part of which will perhaps be tomorrow's fashion. "Learned words" are used, as in Germany, by those educated at the universities, especially lawyers and the higher administrators, i.e., in France, the *noblesse de robe*. "Low expressions" are all the words used by the bourgeoisie down to the populace. The linguistic polemic corresponds to a quite definite, very characteristic social stratification. It shows and delimits the group which at a given moment exerts control over language: in a broader sense the *gens de la cour*, but in a narrower sense a smaller, particularly aristo "Antiquated words," words that have gone out of fashion, are used by the older generation or by those who are not permanently involved directly in court life, the déclassé. "Too new words" are used by the clique of young people who have yet to be accepted, who speak their special "slang," a part of which will perhaps be tomorrow's fashion. "Learned words" are used, as in Germany, by those educated at the universities, especially lawyers and the higher administrators, i.e., in France, the *noblesse de robe*. "Low expressions" are all the words used by the bourgeoisie down to the populace. The linguistic polemic corresponds to a quite definite, very characteristic social stratification. It shows and delimits the group which at a given moment exerts control over language: in a broader sense the *gens de la cour*, but in a narrower sense a smaller, particularly aristocratic circle of people who temporarily have influence at court, and who carefully distinguish themselves. from the social chambers, the courtiers from bourgeois nurseries, from the "antiquated," from the "young people," the "snobbish" competitors of the rising generation, and last but not least, from the specialized officials emanating from the university. ThIs circle is the predominant influence on language formation at this time. How the members of these narrower and broader court circles speak is "how to speak," to speak *comme il faut*. Here the models of speech are formed that subsequently spread out in longer or shorter waves. The manner in which language develops and is stamped corresponds to a certain social structure. Accordingly, from the mid-eighteenth century onward, bourgeois influence on the French language slowly gains in strength. But this long passage through a stage dominated by the court aristocracy remains perceptible in the French language today, as does the passage of German through a stage of dominance by a learned middle-class intelligentsia. And wherever elites or pseudo-elites form within French bourgeois society, they attach themselves to these older, distinguishing tendencies in their language.

Reasons Given by People for Distinguishing Between "Good" and "Bad" Behavior

11. Language is one of the embodiments of social or mental life. Much that can be observed in the way language is molded is also evident in other embodiments of society. For example, the way people argue that this behavior or this custom at table is better than that, is scarcely distinguishable from the way they claim one linguistic expression to be preferable to another.

This does not entirely correspond to the expectation that a twentieth-century observer may have. For example, he expects to find the elimination of "eating with the hands," the introduction of the fork, individual cutlery and crockery, and all the other rituals of his own standard explained by "hygienic reasons." For that is the way in which he himself in general explains these customs. But as late as the second half of the eighteenth century, hardly anything of this kind is found to motivate the greater restraint that people impose upon themselves. At any rate, the so-called "rational explanations" are very far in the background compared to others.

In the earliest stages the need for restraint was usually explained by saying: Do this and not that, for it is not *courtois*, not "courtly"; a "noble" man does not do such things. At most, the reason given is consideration for the embarrassment of others, as in Tannhäuser's *Hofzucht*, where he says, in effect, "Do not scratch yourself with your hand, with which you also hold the common dish; your table companions might notice it, so use your coat to scratch yourself" (Example A, v. 109ff.). And clearly here the threshold of embarrassment differs from that of the following period.

Later on, a similar argument is used for everything: Do not do that, for it is not *civil* or *bienséant*. Or such an argument is used to explain the respect due to those of higher social rank.

As in the molding of speech, so too in the molding of other aspects of behavior in society, social motivations, adaptations of behavior to the models of influential circles, are by far the most important. Even the expressions used in motivating "good behavior" at table are very frequently exactly the same as those used in motivating "good speech."

In Callières's *Du bon et du mauvais usage dans les manières de s'exprimer*, reference is made, for example, to this or that expression "which civility has introduced among people who speak well" (p. 22).

Exactly the same concept of *civilité* is also used again and again by Courtin and La Salle to express what is good and bad in manners. And exactly as Callières here speaks simply of the people *qui parlent bien*, Courtin (at the end of Example G) says, in effect, "Formerly one was allowed to do this or that, but today one is no longer allowed to." Callières says in 1694 that there are a great many people who are not sufficiently conversant with the *délicatesse* of the language: "C'est cette délicatesse qui n'est connu que d'une petite nombre de gens." Courtin uses the same expression in 1672 when he says that it is necessary always to wipe one's spoon before dipping it into the common dish if one has already used it, "there being people so *delicate* that they would not wish to eat soup in which you had dipped it after putting it into your mouth" (Example G).

This *délicatesse*, this sensibility and a highly developed feeling for the "embarrassing," is at first all a distinguishing feature of small courtly circles, then of court society as a whole. This applies to language in exactly the same way as to eating habits. On what this delicacy is based, and why it demands that this be done and not that, is not said and not asked. What is observed is simply that "delicacy"—or, rather, the embarrassment threshold—is advancing. In conjunction with a very specific social situation, the feelings and affects are first transformed in the upper class, and the structure of society as a whole permits this changed affect standard to spread slowly throughout society. Nothing indicates that the affective condition, the degree of sensitivity, is changed for reasons that we describe as "clearly rational" from a demonstrable understanding of particular causal connections. Courtin does not say, as would be said later, that some people feel it to be "unhygienic" or "detrimental to health" to take soup from the same dish as others. Certainly, delicacy of feeling is heightened under the pressure of the courtly situation in a way which is later justified partly by scientific investigations, even though a major part of the taboos that people gradually impose on themselves in their dealings with each other, a far larger part than is usually thought, has not the slightest connection with "hygiene" but is concerned even today merely with "delicacy of feeling." At any rate, the process moves in some respects in a way that is exactly opposite to what is commonly assumed today. First, over a long period and in conjunction with a specific change in human relationships, that is in society, the embarrassment threshold is raised. The structure of emotions, the sensitivity, and the behavior of people change, despite fluctuations, in a quite definite direction. Then, at a certain point, this behavior is recognized as "hygienically correct," i.e., it is justified by clear insight into causal connections and taken further in the same direction or consolidated. The expansion of the threshold of embarrassment may be connected at some points with more or less indefinite and, at first, rationally inexplicable experiences of the way in which certain diseases are passed on or, more precisely, with indefinite and therefore rationally undefined fears and anxieties which point vaguely in the direction subsequently confirmed by clear understanding. But "rational understanding" is not the motor of the "civilizing" of eating or of other behavior.

The close parallel between the "civilizing" of eating and that of speech is highly instructive in this context. It makes clear that the change in behavior at table is part of a very extensive transformation of human feelings and attitudes. It also illustrates to what degree the motive forces of this development come from the social structure, from the way in which people are connected to each other. We see more clearly how relatively small circles first form the center of the movement and how the process then gradually passes to broader sections. But this diffusion presupposes very specific contacts, and therefore a quite definite structure of society. Moreover, it could certainly not have taken place had there not been established for larger classes, as well as for the model-forming circles, conditions of life—or, in other words, a social situation—that made both possible and necessary a gradual transformation of the emotions and behavior, an advance in the threshold of embarrassment.

The process that emerges resembles in form—though not in substance— chemical processes in which a liquid, the whole of which is subjected to conditions of chemical change (e.g., crystallization), first takes on crystalline form at a small nucleus, while the rest then gradually crystallizes around this core. Nothing would be more erroneous than to take the core of crystallization for the cause of the transformation.

The fact that a particular class in one or another phase of social development forms the center of a process and thus supplies models for other classes, and that these models are diffused to other classes and received by them, itself presupposes a social situation and a special structure of society as a whole, by virtue of which one circle is allotted the function of creating models and the other that of spreading and assimilating them. What kinds of change in the integration of society set these behavioral changes in motion will be discussed in detail later.

Group 2:

On the Eating of Meat

1. Although human phenomena—whether attitudes, wishes, or products of human action may be looked at on their own, independently of their connections with the social life of men, they are by nature nothing but substantializations of human relations and of human behavior, embodiments of social and mental life. This is true of speech, which is nothing other than human relations turned into sound; it is true of art, science, economics, and politics; it is true both of phenomena which rank high on our scale of values and of others which seem

trivial or worthless. Often it is precisely these latter, trivial phenomena that give us clear and simple insights into the structure and development of the psyche and its relations which are denied us by the former. The attitudes of men to meat-eating, for example, is highly illuminating with regard to the dynamics of human relationships and personality structures.

In the Middle Ages, people move between at least three different sets of behavior toward meat. Here, as with a hundred other phenomena, we see the extreme diversity of behavior characteristic of medieval society as compared with its modern counterpart. The medieval social structure is far less conducive to the permeation of models developed in a specific social center through the society as a whole. Certain modes of behavior often predominate in a particular social class throughout the Western world, while in a different class or estate behavior is very different. For this reason, the behavioral differences between different classes in the same region are often greater than those between regionally separate representatives of the same social class. And if modes of behavior pass from one class to another, which certainly happens, they change their face more radically in accordance with the greater isolation of the classes.

The relation to meat-eating moves in the medieval world between the following poles. On the one hand, in the secular upper class the consumption of meat is extraordinarily high, compared to the standard of our own times. A tendency prevails to devour quantities of meat that to us seem fantastic. On the other hand, in the monasteries an ascetic abstention from all meat-eating largely prevails, an absention resulting from self-denial, not from shortage, and often accompanied by a radical depreciation or restriction of eating. From these circles come expressions of strong aversion to the "gluttony" among the upper-class laymen.

The meat consumption of the lowest class, the peasants, is also frequently extremely limited—not from a spiritual need, a voluntary renunciation with regard to God and the next world, but from shortage. Cattle are expensive and therefore destined, for a long period, essentially for the rulers' tables. "If the peasant reared cattle," it has been said "it was largely for the privileged, the nobility, and the burghers," not forgetting the clerics, who ranged in varying degrees from asceticism to approximately the behavior of the secular upper class. Exact data on the meat consumption of the upper classes in the Middle Ages and at the beginning of the modem age are sparse. There were, no doubt, considerable differences between the lesser, poorer knights and the great feudal lords. The standards of the knights will frequently have been scarcely removed from those of the peasants.

A calculation of the meat consumption of a north German court from relatively recent times, the seventeenth century, indicates a consumption of two pounds per head per day, in addition to large quantities of venison, birds, and fish.[57] Spices play a major, vegetables a relatively minor role. Other information points fairly unanimously in the same direction. The subject remains to be investigated in detail.

2. Another change can be documented more exactly. The manner in which meat is served changes considerably from the Middle Ages to modern times. The curve of this change is very instructive. In the upper class of medieval society, the dead animal or large parts of it are often brought whole to the table. Not only whole fish and whole birds (sometimes with their feathers) but also whole rabbits, lambs, and quarters of veal appear on the table, not to mention the larger venison or the pigs and oxen roasted on the spit.[58]

The animal is carved on the table. This is why the books on manners repeat, up to the seventeenth and sometimes even the eighteenth century, how important it is for a well-bred man to be good at carving meat. "Discenda a primis statim annis secandi ratio . . ." (The correct way to carve should be taught from the first years) says Erasmus in 1530.

"When serving," says Courtin in 1672,

one must always give away the best portion and keep the smallest, and touch nothing except with the fork; this is why, if a person of rank asks you for something that is in front of you, it is important to know how to cut meat with propriety and method, and to know the best portions, in order to be able to serve them with civility. The way to cut them is not prescribed here, because it is a subject on which special books have been written, in which all the pieces are illustrated to show where the meat must first be held with a fork to cut it, for as we have just said, *the meat must never be touched . . . by hand, not even while eating*; then where the knife must be placed to cut it; what must be lifted first . . . what is the best piece, and the piece of honor that must be served to the person of highest rank. It is easy to learn how to carve when one has eaten three or four times at a good table, and for the same reason it is no disgrace to excuse oneself and leave to another what one cannot do oneself.

And the German parallel, the *New vermehrtes Trincier-Büchlein* (New, enlarged carving manual), printed in Rintelen in 1650, says:

Because the office of carver at princely courts is not reckoned as the lowest but among the most honorable, the same must therefore be either of the nobility or other good origin, of straight and well-proportioned body, good straight arms and nimble hands. In all public cutting he should . . . abstain from large movements and useless and foolish ceremonies . . . and make quite sure that he is not nervous, *so that he does not bring dishonor through trembling of the body and hands* and because in any case this does not befit those at princely tables.

Both carving and distributing the meat are particular honors. It usually falls to the master of the house or to distinguished guests whom he requests to perform the office. "The young and those of lower rank should not interfere in serving, but only take for themselves in their turn," says the anonymous *Civilité française* of 1714.

In the seventeenth century the carving of meat at table gradually ceases, in the French upper class, to be an indispensable accomplishment of the man of the world, like hunting, fencing, and dancing. The passage quoted from Courtin points to this.

3. That the serving of large parts of the animal to be carved at table slowly goes out of use is connected with many factors. One of the most important may be the gradual reduction in the size of the household[59] as part of the movement from larger to smaller family units; then comes the removal of production and processing activities like weaving, spinning, and slaughtering from the household, and their gradual transference to specialists, craftsmen, merchants, and manufacturers, who practice them professionally while the household becomes essentially a consumption unit.

Here, too, the psychological tendency matches the large social process: today it would arouse rather uneasy feelings in many people if they or others had to carve half a calf or pig at table or cut meat from a pheasant still adorned with its feathers.

There are even *des gens si délicats*—to repeat the phrase of Courtin, which refers to a related process—to whom the sight of butchers' shops with the bodies of dead animals is distasteful, and others who from more or less rationally disguised feelings of disgust refuse to eat meat altogether. But these are forward thrusts in the threshold of repugnance that go beyond the standard of civilized society in the twentieth century, and are therefore considered "abnormal." Nevertheless, it cannot be ignored that it was advances of this kind (if they coincided with the direction of social development in general) that led in the past to changes of standards, and that this particular advance in the threshold of repugnance is proceeding in the same direction that has been followed thus far.

This direction is quite clear. From a standard of feeling by which the sight and carving of a dead animal on the table are actually pleasurable, or at least not at all unpleasant, the development leads to another standard by which reminders that the meat dish has something to do with the killing of an animal are avoided to the utmost. In many of our meat dishes the animal form is so concealed and changed by the art of its preparation and carving that while eating one is scarcely reminded of its origin.

It will be shown how people, in the course of the civilizing process, seek to suppress in themselves every characteristic that they feel to be "animal." They likewise suppress such characteristics in their food.

In this area, too, the development is certainly not uniform everywhere. In England, for example, where in many aspects of life older forms are more prominently preserved than on the Continent, the serving of large portions of meat (and with it the task, which falls to the master of the house, of carving and distributing it) survives in the form of the "joint" to a greater extent than in the urban society of Germany and France. However, quite apart from the fact that the present-day joint is itself a very reduced form of the serving of large pieces of meat, there has been no lack of reactions to it that mark the advance in the threshold of repugnance. The adoption of the "Russian system" of table manners in society about the middle of the last century acted in this direction. "Our chief thanks to the new system," says an English book on manners, *The Habits of Good Society* (1859), "are due for its ostracising that unwieldy barbarism—the joint. Nothing can make a joint look elegant, while it hides the master of the house, and condemns him into the misery of carving. . . . The truth is, *that unless our appetites are very keen, the sight of much meat reeking in its gravy is sufficient to destroy them entirely*, and a huge joint especially is calculated to disgust the epicure. If joints are eaten at all, they should be placed on the side-table, *where they will be out of sight*" (p. 314).

The increasingly strong tendency to remove the distasteful from the sight of society clearly applies, with few exceptions, to the carving of the whole animal.

This carving, as the examples show, was formerly a direct part of social life in the upper class. Then the spectacle is felt more and more to be distasteful. Carving itself does not disappear, since the animal must, of course, be cut when being eaten. But the distasteful is *removed behind the scenes of social life*. Specialists take care of it in the shop or the kitchen. It will be seen again and again how characteristic of the whole process that we call civilization is this movement of segregation, this hiding "behind the scenes" of what has become distasteful. The curve running from the carving of a large part of the animal or even the whole animal at table, through the advance in the threshold of repugnance at the sight of dead animals, to the removal of carving to specialized enclaves behind the scenes is a typical civilization-curve.

It remains to be investigated how far similar processes underlie similar phenomena in other societies. In earlier Chinese civilisation, above all, the concealment of carving behind the scenes was effected much earlier and more radically than in the West. There the process is taken so far that the meat is carved and cut up entirely behind the scenes, and the knife is banished altogether from use at table.

Use of the Knife at Table

4. The knife, too, by the nature of its social use, reflects changes in the human personality with its changing drives and wishes. It is an embodiment of historical situations and structural regularities of society.

One thing above all is characteristic of its use as an eating implement in present-day Western society: the innumerable prohibitions and taboos surrounding it.

Certainly the knife is a dangerous instrument in what may be called a rational sense. It is a weapon of attack. It inflicts wounds and cuts up animals that have been killed.

But this obviously dangerous quality is beset with emotions. The knife becomes a symbol of the most diverse feelings, which are connected to its function and shape but are not deduced "logically" from its purpose. The fear it awakens goes beyond what is rational and is greater than the "calculable," probable danger. And the same is true of the pleasure its use and appearance arouse, even if this aspect is less evident today. In keeping with the structure of our society, the everyday ritual of its use is today determined more by the displeasure and fear than by the pleasure surrounding it. Therefore its use even while eating is restricted by a multitude of prohibitions. These, we have said, extend far beyond the "purely functional"; but for every one of them a rational explanation, usually vague and not easily proved, is in everyone's mouth. Only when these taboos are considered together does the supposition arise that the social attitude toward the knife and the rules governing its use while eating—and, above all, the taboos surrounding it—are primarily emotional in nature. Fear, distaste, guilt, associations and emotions of the most disparate kinds exaggerate the real danger. It is precisely this which anchors such prohibitions so firmly and deeply in the personality and which gives them their taboo character.

5. In the Middle Ages, with their upper class of warriors and the constant readiness of people to fight, and in keeping with the stage of affect control and the relatively lenient regulations imposed on drives, the prohibitions concerning knives are quite few. "Do not clean your teeth with your knife" is a frequent demand. This is the chief prohibition, but it does indicate the direction of future restrictions on the implement. Moreover, the knife is by far the most important eating utensil. That it is lifted to the mouth is taken for granted.

But there are indications in the late Middle Ages, even more direct ones than in any later period, that the caution required in using a knife results not only from the rational consideration that one might cut or harm oneself, but above all from the emotion aroused by the sight or the idea of a knife pointed at one's own face.

> Bere not your knyf to warde your visage
> For therein is parelle and mykyl drede

we read in Caxton's *Book of Curtesye* (v. 28). Here, as everywhere later, an element of rationally calculable danger is indeed present, and the warning refers to this. But it is the general memory of and association with death and danger, it is the *symbolic* meaning of the instrument that leads, with the advancing internal pacification of society, to the preponderance of feelings of displeasure at the sight of it, and to the limitation and final exclusion of its use in society. The mere sight of a knife pointed at the face arouses fear: "Bear not your knife toward your face, for therein lies much dread." This is the emotional basis of the powerful taboo of a later phase, which forbids the lifting of the knife to the mouth.

The case is similar with the prohibition which in our series of examples was mentioned first by Calviac in 1560 (at the end of Example E): If you pass someone a knife, take the point in your hand and offer him the handle, 'for it would not be polite to do otherwise."

Here, as so often until the later stage when the child is given a "rational" explanation for every prohibition, no reason is given for the social ritual except that "it would not be polite to do otherwise." But it is not difficult to see the emotional meaning of this command: one should not move the point of the knife toward someone as in an attack. The mere symbolic meaning of this act, the memory of the warlike threat, is unpleasant. Here, too, the knife ritual contains a rational element. Someone might use the passing of the knife in order suddenly to stab someone. But a social ritual is formed from this danger because the dangerous gesture establishes itself on an emotional level as a general source of displeasure, a symbol of death and danger. Society, which is beginning at this time more and more to limit the real dangers threatening men, and consequently to remodel the affective life of the individual, increasingly places a barrier around the symbols as well, the gestures and instruments of danger. Thus the restrictions and prohibitions on the use of the knife increase, along with the restraints imposed on the individual.

6. If we leave aside the details of this development and only consider the result, the present form of the knife ritual, we find an astonishing abundance of taboos of varying severity. The imperative never to put a knife to one's mouth is one of the gravest and best known. That it greatly exaggerates the actual, probable danger scarcely needs to be said; for social groups accustomed to using knives and eating with them hardly ever injure their mouths with them. The prohibition has become a means of social distinction. In the uneasy feeling that comes over us at the mere sight of someone putting his knife into his mouth, all this is present at once: the general fear that the dangerous symbol arouses, and the more specific fear of social degradation which parents and educators have from early on linked to this practice with their admonitions that "it is not done."

But there are other prohibitions surrounding the knife that have little or nothing to do with a direct danger to the body, and which seem to point to symbolic meanings of the knife other than the association with war. The fairly strict prohibition on eating fish with a knife-circumvented and modified today by the introduction of a special fish knife—seems at first sight rather obscure in its emotional meaning, though psychoanalytical theory points at least in the direction of an explanation. There is a well-known prohibition on holding cutlery, particularly knives, with the whole hand, "like a stick," as La Salle put it, though he was only at that time referring to fork and spoon (Example J). Then there is obviously a general tendency to eliminate or at least restrict the contact of the knife with round or egg-shaped objects. The best-known and one of the gravest of such prohibitions is on cutting potatoes with a knife. But the rather less strict prohibition on cutting dumplings with a knife or opening boiled eggs with one also point in the same direction, and occasionally, in especially sensitive circles, one finds a tendency to avoid cutting apples or even oranges with a knife. "I may hint that no epicure ever yet put knife to apple, and that an orange should be peeled with a spoon," says *The Habits of Good Society* of 1859 and 1889.

7. But these more or less strict particular prohibitions, the list of which could certainly be extended, are in a sense only examples of a general line of development in the use of the knife that is fairly distinct. There is a tendency that slowly permeates civilized society, from the top to the bottom, to restrict the use of the knife (within the framework of existing eating techniques) and wherever possible not to use the instrument at all.

This tendency makes its first appearance in a precept as apparently trivial and obvious as that quoted in Example I: "Do not keep your knife always in your hand, as village people do, but take it only when you need it." It is clearly very strong in the middle of the last century, when the English book on manners just quoted, *The Habits of Good Society*, says: "Let me give you a rule—everything that can be cut without a knife, should be cut with fork alone." And one need only observe present-day usage to find this tendency confirmed. This is one of the few distinct cases of a development which is beginning to go beyond the standard of eating technique and ritual attained by court society. But this is not, of course, to say that the "civilization" of the West will actually continue in this direction. It is a beginning, a possibility like many others that exist in any society. All the same, it is not inconceivable that the preparation of food in the kitchen will develop in a direction that restricts the use of the knife at table still further, displacing it even more than hitherto to specialized enclaves behind the scenes.

Strong retroactive movements are certainly not inconceivable. It is sufficiently known that the conditions of life in the World War I automatically enforced a breakdown of some of the taboos of peacetime civilization. In the trenches, officers and soldiers again ate when necessary with knives and hands. The threshold of delicacy shrank rather rapidly under the pressure of the inescapable situation.

Apart from such breaches, which are always possible and can also lead to new consolidations, the line of development in the use of the knife is quite clear.[60] The regulation and control of emotions intensifies. The commands and prohibitions surround the menacing instrument become ever more numerous and differentiated. Finally, the use of the threatening symbol is limited as far as possible.

One cannot avoid comparing the direction of this civilization-curve with the custom long practiced in China. There, as has been said, the knife disappeared many centuries ago from use at table. To many Chinese the manner in which Europeans eat is quite uncivilized. "The Europeans are barbarians," people say there, "they eat with swords." One may surmise that this custom is connected with the fact that for a long time in China the model-making upper class has not been a warrior class but a class pacified to a particularly high degree, a society of scholarly officials.

On the Use of the Fork at Table

8. What is the real use of the fork? It serves to lift food that has been cut up to the mouth. Why do we need a fork for this? Why do we not use our fingers? Because it is "cannibal," as the "Man in the Club-Window," the anonymous author of *The Habits of Good Society* said in 1859. Why is it "cannibal" to eat with one's fingers? That is not a question; it is self-evidently cannibal, barbaric, uncivilized, or whatever else it is called.

But that is precisely the question. Why is it more civilized to eat with a fork?

"Because it is unhygienic to eat with one's fingers." That sounds convincing. To our sensibility it is unhygienic if different people put their fingers into the same dish, because there is a danger of contracting disease through contact with others. Each of us seems to fear that the others are diseased.

But this explanation is not entirely satisfactory. Nowadays we do not eat from common dishes. Everyone puts food into his mouth from his own plate. To pick it up from one's own plate with one's fingers cannot be more "unhygienic" than to put cake, bread, chocolate, or anything else into one's mouth with one's own fingers.

So why does one really need a fork? Why is it "barbaric" and "uncivilized" to put food into one's mouth by hand from one's own plate? Because it is distasteful to dirty one's fingers, or at least to be seen in society with dirty fingers. The suppression of eating by hand from one's own plate has very little to do with the danger of illness, the so-called "rational" explanation. In observing our feelings toward the fork ritual, we can see with particular clarity that the first authority in our decision between "civilized" and "uncivilized" behavior at table is our feeling of distaste. The fork is nothing other than the embodiment of a specific standard of emotions and a specific level of revulsion. Behind the change in eating techniques between the Middle Ages and modern times appears the same process that emerged in the analysis of other incarnations of this kind: a change in the structure of drives and emotions.

Modes of behavior which in the Middle Ages were not felt to be in the least distasteful are increasingly surrounded by unpleasurable feelings. The standard of delicacy finds expression in corresponding social prohibitions. These taboos, so far as one can be ascertained, are nothing other than ritualized or institutionalized feelings of displeasure, distaste, disgust, fear, or shame, feelings which have been socially nurtured under quite specific conditions and which are constantly reproduced, not solely but mainly because they have become institutionally embedded in a particular ritual, in particular forms of conduct.

The examples show—certainly only in a narrow cross-section and in the relatively randomly selected statements of individuals—how, in a phase of development in which the use of the fork was not yet taken for granted, the feeling of distaste that first formed within a narrow circle is slowly extended. "It is very impolite," says Courtin in 1672 (Example G), "to touch anything greasy, a sauce or syrup, etc., with your fingers, apart from the fact that it obliges you to commit two or three more improper acts. One is to wipe your hand frequently on your serviette and to soil it like a kitchen cloth, so that those who see you wipe your mouth with it feel nauseated. Another is to wipe your fingers on your bread, which again is very improper. [N.B. The French terms *propre* and *malpropre* used by Courtin and explain in one of his chapters coincide less with the German terms for clean and unclean (*sauber* and *unsauber*) than with the word frequently used earlier, *proper*.] The third is to lick them, which is the height of impropriety."

The *Civilité* of 1729 by La Salle (Example J), which transmits the behavior of the upper class to broader circles, says on one page: "When the fingers are very greasy, wipe them first on a piece of bread." This shows how far from general acceptance, even at this time, was the standard of delicacy that Courtin had already represented decades earlier. On the other hand, La Salle takes over fairly literally Courtin's precept that "*Bienséance* does not permit anything greasy, a sauce or a syrup, to be touched with the fingers." And, exactly like Courtin, he mentions among the ensuing *incivilités* wiping the hands on bread and licking the fingers, as well as soiling the napkin.

It can be seen that manners are here still in the process of formation. The new standard does not appear suddenly. Certain forms of behavior are placed under prohibition, not because they are unhealthy but because they lead to an offensive sight and disagreeable associations; shame at offering such a spectacle, originally absent, and fear of arousing such associations are gradually spread from the standard setting circles to larger circles by numerous authorities and institutions. However, once such feelings are aroused and firmly established in society by means of certain rituals like that involving the fork, they are constantly reproduced so long as the structure of human relations is not fundamentally altered. The older generation, for whom such a standard of conduct is accepted as a matter of course, urges the children, who do not come into the world already equipped with these feelings and this standard, to control themselves more or less rigorously in accordance with it, and to restrain their drives and inclinations. If a child tries to touch something sticky, wet, or greasy with his fingers he is told, "You must not do that, people do not do things like that." And the displeasure toward such conduct which is thus aroused by the adult finally arises through habit, without being induced by another person.

To a large extent, however, the conduct and instinctual life of the child are forced even without words into the same mold and in the same direction by the fact that a particular use of knife and fork, for example, is completely established in the adult world—that is, by the example of the environment. Since the pressure or coercion of individual adults is allied to the pressure and example of the whole surrounding world, most children, as they grow up, forget or repress relatively early the fact that their feelings of shame and embarrassment, of pleasure and displeasure, are molded into conformity with a certain standard by external pressure and compulsion. All this appears to them as highly personal, something "inward," implanted in them by nature. While it is still directly visible in the writings of Courtin and La Salle that adults, too, were at first dissuaded from eating with their fingers by consideration for each other, by "politeness," to spare others a distasteful spectacle and themselves the shame of being seen with soiled hands, later it becomes more and more an inner automatism, the imprint of society on the inner self, the superego, that forbids the individual to eat in any other way than with a fork. The social standard to which the individual was first made to conform by external restraint is finally reproduced more or less smoothly within him, through a self-restraint which may operate even against his conscious wishes.

Thus the sociohistorical process of centuries, in the course of which the standard of what is felt to be shameful and offensive is slowly raised, is reenacted in abbreviated form in the life of the individual human being. If one wished to express recurrent processes of this kind in the form of laws, one could speak, as a parallel to the laws of biogenesis, of a fundamental law of sociogenesis and psychogenesis.

V

Changes in Attitude Toward the Natural Functions

Examples

Fifteenth century?

A

From *S'ensuivent les contenances de la table*:

VIII
Before you sit down, make sure your seat has not been fouled.

B

From *Ein spruch der ze tische kêrt*:[61]

> 329 Do not touch yourself under your clothes with your bare hands.

C

1530

From *De civilitate morum puerilium*, by Erasmus. The glosses are taken from a Cologne edition of 1530 which was probably already intended for educational purposes. Under the title is the following note: "Recognized by the author, and elucidated with new scholia by Gisbertus Longolius Ultratraiectinus, Cologne, in the year XXX." The fact that these questions were discussed in such a way in schoolbooks makes the difference from later attitudes particularly clear:

> It is impolite to greet someone who is urinating or defecating. . . .
>
> A well-bred person should always avoid exposing without necessity the parts to which nature has attached modesty. If necessity compels this, it should be done with decency and reserve, even if no witness is present. For angels are always present, and nothing is more welcome to them in a boy than modesty, the companion and guardian of decency. If it arouses shame to show them to the eyes of others, still less should they be exposed to their touch.
>
> To hold back urine is harmful to health, to pass it in secret betokens modesty. There are those who teach that the boy should retain wind by compressing the belly. Yet it is not pleasing, while striving to appear urbane, to contract an illness. If it is possible to withdraw, it should be done alone. But if not, in accordance with the ancient proverb, let a cough hide the sound. Moreover, why do not the same works teach that boys should not defecate, since it is more dangerous to hold back wind than to constrict the bowel?
>
> [This is glossed as follows in the scholia, p. 33:]
>
> To contract an illness: Listen to the old maxim about the sound of wind. If it can be purged without a noise that is best. But it is better that it be emitted with a noise than that it be held back.
>
> At this point, however, it would have been useful to suppress the feeling of embarrassment so as to either calm your body or, following the advice of all doctors, to press your buttocks together and to act according to the suggestions in Aethon's epigrams: Even though he had to be careful not to fart explosively in the holy place, he nevertheless prayed to Zeus, though with compressed buttocks. The sound of farting, especially of those who stand on elevated ground, is horrible. One should make sacrifices with the buttocks firmly pressed together.
>
> To let a cough hide the explosive sound: Those who, because they are embarrassed, want the explosive wind to be heard, simulate a cough. Follow the law of Chiliades: Replace farts with coughs.
>
> Regarding the unhealthiness of retaining the wind: There are some verses in volume two of Nicharchos' epigrams where he describes the illness-bearing power of the

retained fart, but since these lines are quoted by everybody I will not comment on them here.

The unabashed care and seriousness with which questions are publicly discussed here that have subsequently become highly private and strictly prohibited in society emphasizes the shift of the frontier of embarrassment. That feelings of shame are frequently mentioned explicitly in the discussion underlines the difference in the shame standard.

D

1558

From *Galateo*, by Della Casa, quoted from the five-language edition (Geneva, 1609), p. 32:

> Moreover, it does not befit a modest, honorable man to prepare to relieve nature in the presence of other people, nor to do up his clothes afterward in their presence. Similarly, he will not wash his hands on returning to decent society from private places, as the reason for his washing will arouse disagreeable thoughts in people. For the same reason it is not a refined habit, when coming across something disgusting in the sheet, as sometimes happens, to turn at once to one's companion and point it out to him.
>
>   It is far less proper to hold out the stinking thing for the other to smell, as some are wont, who even urge the other to do so, lifting the foul-smelling thing to his nostrils and saying, "I should like to know how much that stinks," when it would be better to say, "Because it stinks do not smell it."

E

1570

From the Wernigerode Court Regulations of 1570:[62]

> One should not, like rustics who have not been to court or lived among refined and honorable people, relieve oneself without shame or reserve in front of ladies, or before the doors or windows of court chambers or other rooms. Rather, everyone ought at all times and in all places to show himself reasonable, courteous, and respectful in word and gesture.

F

1589

From the Brunswick Court Regulations of 1589:[63]

> Let no one, whoever he may be, before, at, or after meals, early or late, foul the staircases, corridors, or closets with urine or other filth, but go to suitable, prescribed places for such relief.

G

c. 1619

Richard Weste, *The Booke of Demeanor and the Allowance and Disallowance of Certaine Misdemeanors in Companie*:[64]

143 Let not thy privy members be
    layd open to be view'd,
    it is most shameful and abhord,
    detestable and rude.
    Retaine not urine nor the winde
    which doth thy body vex
    so it be done with secresie
    let that not thee perplex.

H

1694

From the correspondence of the Duchess of Orléans (October 9, 1694; date also given as August 25, 1718):

> The smell of the mire is horrible. Paris is a dreadful place. The streets smell so badly that you cannot go out. The extreme heat is causing large quantities of meat and fish to rot in them, and this, coupled to the multitude of people who . . . in the street, produces a smell so detestable that it cannot be endured.

I

1729

From La Salle, *Les Règles de la bienséance et de la civilité chrétienne* (Rouen, 1729), pp. 45ff.:

> It is a part of decency and modesty to cover all parts of the body except the head and hands. You should care, so far as you can, not to touch with your bare hand any part of the body that is not normally uncovered. And if you are obliged to do so, it should be done with great precaution. You should get used to suffering small discomforts without twisting, rubbing, or scratching. . . .
>
> It is far more contrary to decency and propriety to touch or see in another person, particularly of the other sex, that which Heaven forbids you to look at in yourself. When you need to pass water, you should always withdraw to some unfrequented place. And it is proper (even for children) to perform other natural functions where you cannot be seen.
>
> *It is very impolite to emit wind from your body when in company, either from above or from below, even if it is done without noise*[This rule, in line with more recent custom, is the exact opposite of what is prescribed in Examples C and G]; and it is shameful and indecent to do it in a way that can be heard by others.

It is never proper to speak of the parts of the body that should be hidden, nor of certain bodily necessities to which Nature has subjected us, nor even to mention them.

German developments were somewhat slower than French. As the following selection shows, as late as the first half of the eighteenth century a precept is given which represents the same standard of manners as that found in the passage by Erasmus quoted above: "It is impolite to greet someone who is urinating or defacating."

J

1731

From Johann Christian Barth, *The Gallant Ethic, in which it is shown how a young man should commend himself to polite society through refined acts and complaisant words. Prepared for the special advantage and pleasure of all amateurs of present-day good manners*, 4th ed. (Dresden and Leipzig, 1731), p. 288:

If you pass a person who is relieving himself you should act as if you had not seen him, and so it is impolite to greet him.

K

1774

From La Salle, *Les Règles de la bienséance et de la civilité chrétienne* (1774 ed.), p. 24. The chapter "On the Parts of the Body That Should Be Hidden, and on Natural Necessities" covers a good two and one-half pages in the earlier edition and scarcely one and one-half in that of 1774. The passage "You should take care . . . not to touch, etc." is missing. Much that could be and had to be expressed earlier is no longer spoken of:

It is a part of decency and modesty to cover all parts of the body except the head and hands.

As far as natural needs are concerned, it is proper (even for children) to satisfy them only where one cannot be seen.

It is never proper to speak of the parts of the body that should always be hidden, or of certain bodily necessities to which nature has subjected us, or even to mention them.

L

1768

Letter from Madame du Deffand to Madame de Choiseul, May 9, 1768;[65] quoted as an example of the prestige value of the utensil

I should like to tell you, dear Grandmother, as I told the Grand-Abbé, how great was my surprise when a large bag from you was brought to me at my bed yesterday morning. I hasten to open it, put in my hand, and find some green peas . . . and then a vase . . . that I quickly pull out: it is a chamber pot. But of such beauty and magnificence that my people say in unison *that it ought to be used as a sauce boat. The chamber pot was on display the whole of yesterday evening and was admired by everyone.* The peas . . . were eaten till not one was left.

Some Remarks on the Examples
and on these Changes in General

1. The *courtois* verses say little on this subject. The social commands and prohibitions surrounding this area of life are relatively few. In this respect, too, at least in secular society, everything is far more lax. Neither the functions themselves, nor speaking about them or associations with them, are so intimate and private, so invested with feelings of shame and embarrassment, as they later become.

Erasmus's treatise marks, for these areas too, a point on the curve of civilization which represents, on the one hand, a notable rise of the shame threshold, compared to the preceding epoch; and on the other, compared to more recent times, a freedom in speaking of natural functions, a "lack of shame," which to most people adhering to the present-day standard may at first appear incomprehensible and often "embarrassing."

But at the same time, it is quite clear that this treatise has precisely the function of cultivating feelings of shame. Reference to the omnipresence of angels, used to justify the restraint on impulses to which the child is to be accustomed, is very characteristic. The manner in which anxiety is aroused in young people, in order to force them to repress display of pleasure in accordance with the standard of social conduct, changes in the course of centuries. Here, the anxiety aroused in connection with the renunciation of instinctual gratification is explained to oneself and others in terms of external spirits. Somewhat later, the restraint imposed on oneself, along with the fear, shame, and distaste toward any infringement, often appears, at least in the upper class, in courtly-aristocratic society, as social restraint, as shame and fear of men. In wider circles, admittedly, reference to the guardian angel clearly remains very long in use as an instrument for conditioning children. It recedes somewhat when health and "hygienic reasons" are given more emphasis in bringing about a certain degree of restraint of impulses and emotions. These hygienic reasons then play an important role in adult ideas on civilization, usually without their relation to the arsenal of childhood conditioning being realized. It is only from such a realization, however, that what is rational in them can be distinguished from what is only seemingly rational, i.e., founded primarily on the disgust and shame feelings of adults.

2. As already mentioned, Erasmus in his treatise acts as a cursor of a new

standard of shame and repugnance which first begins to form slowly in the secular upper class. Yet he also speaks as a matter of course about things which it has since become embarrassing to mention. He, whose delicacy of feeling is demonstrated again and again by this very treatise, finds nothing amiss in calling by their names bodily functions which, by our present standards, may not be even mentioned in company, and still less in books on etiquette. But between this delicacy and this unconcern there is no contradiction. He speaks from another stage of control and restraint of emotions.

The different standard of society at Erasmus's time becomes clear if one reads how commonplace it is to meet someone "qui urinam reddit aut alvum exonerat" (urinating or defecating). And the greater freedom with which people were able at this time to perform and speak about their bodily functions before others recalls the behavior that can still be encountered throughout the Orient today. But delicacy forbids that one greet anyone encountered in this position.

The different standard is also visible when Erasmus says it is not civil to require that the young man "ventris flatum retineat" (hold back his wind), for in doing so he might, under the appearance of urbanity, contract an illness; and Erasmus comments similarly on sneezing and related acts.

Medical arguments are not found very frequently in this treatise. When they occur it is almost always, as here, to oppose demands for the restraint of natural functions; whereas later, above all in the nineteenth century, they nearly always serve as instruments to compel restraint and renunciation of instinctual gratification. It is only in the twentieth century that a slight relaxation appears.

3. The examples from La Salle must suffice to indicate how the feeling of delicacy is advancing. Again the difference between the editions of 1729 and 1774 is very instructive. Certainly, even the earlier edition already embodies a quite different standard of delicacy than Erasmus's treatise. The demand that all natural functions be removed from the view of other people is raised quite unequivocally, even if the uttering of this demand indicates that the actual behavior of people—both adults and children—did not yet conform to it. Although La Salle says that it is not very polite even to speak of such functions or the parts of the body concerned, he himself still speaks of them with a minuteness of detail astonishing to us; he calls things by their names, whereas the corresponding terms are missing in Courtin's *Civilité* of 1672, which was intended for the upper classes.

In the later edition of La Salle, too, all detailed references are avoided. More and more these necessities are "passed over in silence." The mere reminder of them becomes embarrassing to people in the presence of others who are not close acquaintances, and in society everything that might even remotely or associatively recall such necessities is avoided.

At the same time, the examples make it apparent how slowly the real process of suppressing these functions from social life took place. Sufficient material[66] has been passed down to us precisely because the silence on these subjects did not exist earlier, or was less strictly observed. What is usually lacking is the idea that information of this kind has more than curiosity value, so that it is seldom synthesised into a picture of the overall line of development. However, if one takes a comprehensive view, a pattern emerges that is typical of the civilizing process.

4. At first these functions and their exhibition are invested only slightly with feelings of shame and repugnance, and are therefore subjected only mildly to isolation and restraint. They are taken as much for granted as combing one's hair or putting on one's shoes. Children are conditioned accordingly.

"Tell me in exact sequence," says the teacher to a pupil in a schoolbook of 1568, Mathurin Cordier's dialogues for schoolboys,[67] "what you did between getting up and having your breakfast. Listen carefully, boys, so that you learn to imitate your fellow pupil." "I woke up," says the pupil, "got out of bed, put on my shirt, stockings, and shoes, buckled my belt, urinated against the courtyard wall, took fresh water from the bucket, washed my hands and face and dried them on the cloth, etc."

In later times the action in the courtyard, at least in a book written like this one expressly as a manual of instruction and example, would have been simply passed over as "unimportant." Here it is neither particularly "unimportant" nor particularly "important." It is taken for granted as much as anything else.

The pupil who wished to report on this necessity today would do so either as a kind of joke, taking the invitation of the teacher "too literally," or would speak of it in circumlocutions. But most probably he would conceal his embarrassment with a smile, and an "understanding" smile of the others, the expression of minor infringement of a taboo, would be the response.

The conduct of adults corresponds to these different kinds of conditioning. For a long period the street, and almost any place one happened to be, served the same and related purposes as the courtyard wall above. It is not even unusual to turn to the staircase, the corners of rooms, or the hangings on the walls of a castle if one is overtaken by a need. Examples E and F make this clear. But they also show how, given the specific and permanent interdependence of many people living together at the courts, the pressure exerted from above toward a stricter regulation of impulses, and therefore toward greater restraint.

Stricter control of impulses and emotions is first imposed by those of high social rank on their social inferiors or, at most, their social equals. It is only comparatively late, when bourgeois classes comprising a large number of social equals have become the upper, ruling class, that the family becomes the only—or, more exactly, the primary and dominant—institution with the function of installing drive control. Only then does the social dependence of the child on its parents become particularly important as a leverage for the socially required regulation and molding of impulses and emotions.

In the stage of the feudal courts, and still more in that of the absolute courts, the courts themselves largely fulfilled this function for the upper class. In the latter stage, much of what has been made "second nature" to us has not yet been inculcated in this form, as an automatic self-restraint, a habit that, within certain limits, also functions when a person is alone. Rather, restraint on the instincts is at first imposed only in the company of others, i.e., more consciously for social reasons. And both the kind and the degree of restraint correspond to the social position of the person imposing them, relative to the position of those in whose company he is. This slowly changes as people move closer together socially and as the hierarchical character of society becomes less rigid. As the interdependence of men increases with the increasing division of labor, everyone becomes increasingly dependent on everyone else, those of high social rank on those socially inferior and weaker. The latter become so much the equals of the former that they, the socially superior, feel shame even before their inferiors. It is only now that the armor of restraints is fastened to the degree which is gradually taken for granted by people in democratic industrial societies.

To take from the wealth of examples one instance which shows the contrast particularly clearly and which, correctly understood, throws light on the whole development, Della Casa gives in his *Galateo* a list of malpractices to be avoided. One should not fall asleep in society, he says; one should not take out letters and read them; one should not pare or clean one's fingernails. "Furthermore," he continues (p. 92), "one should not sit with one's back or posterior turned toward another, nor raise a thigh so high that the members of the human body, which should properly be covered with clothing at all times, might be exposed to view. *For this and similar things are not done, except among people before whom one is not ashamed* (se non tra quelle persone, che l'huom non riverisce). *It is true that a great lord might do so before one of his servants or in the presence of a friend of lower rank; for in this he would not show him arrogance but rather a particular affection and friendship.*"

There are people before whom one is ashamed, and others before whom one is not. The feeling of shame is clearly a social function molded according to the social structure. This is perhaps not often *expressed* so clearly. But the corresponding *behavior* is amply documented. In France,[68] as late as the seventeenth century, kings and great lords receive specially favored inferiors on occasions on which, a German saying was later to run, even the emperor should be alone. To receive inferiors when getting up and being dressed, or on going to bed, was for a whole period a matter of course. And it shows exactly the same stage of the shame-feeling when Voltaire's mistress, the Marquise de Châtelet, shows herself naked to her servant while bathing in a way that casts him into confusion, and then with total unconcern scolds him because he is not pouring in the hot water properly.[69]

Behavior which in more democratized industrial societies is surrounded on all sides with taboos, with trained feelings of shame or embarrassment of varying degrees, is here only partially affected. It is omitted in the company of those of higher or equal rank. In this area, too, coercion and restraint are self-imposed on the same pattern as was visible earlier in table manners. "Nor do I believe," we read in *Galateo* (p. 580), "that it is fitting to serve from the common dish intended for all guests, unless the server is of higher rank so that the other, who is served, is thereby especially honored. For when this is done among equals, it appears as if the server is partly placing himself above the others."

In this hierarchically structured society, every act performed in the presence of many people took on prestige value. For this reason the restraint of the emotions, that we call "politeness," also had a different form than later, when outward differences of rank had been partly leveled. What is mentioned here as a special case in intercourse between equals; that one should not serve another, later becomes a general practice. In society everyone helps himself, and everyone begins eating at the same time.

The situation is similar with the exposure of the body. First it becomes a distasteful offense to show oneself exposed in any way before those of higher or equal rank; with inferiors it can even be a sign of benevolence. Then, as all become socially more equal, it slowly becomes a general offense. The social reference of shame and embarrassment recedes more and more from consciousness. Precisely because the social command not to show oneself exposed or performing natural functions now operates with regard to everyone and is imprinted in this form on the child, it seems to the adult a command of his own inner self and takes on the form of a more or less total and automatic self-restraint.

5. But this isolation of the natural functions from public life, and the corresponding regulation or molding of instinctual urges, was only possible because, together with growing sensitivity, a technical apparatus was developed which solved fairly satisfactorily the problem of eliminating these functions from social life and displacing them behind the scenes. The situation was not unlike that regarding table manners. The process of social change, the advance in the frontiers of shame and the threshold of repugnance, cannot be explained by any one thing, and certainly not by the development of technology or by scientific discoveries. On the contrary, it would not be difficult to demonstrate the sociogenetic and psychogenetic bases of these inventions and discoveries.

After a reshaping of human needs had once been set in motion with the general transformation of human relations, the development of a technical apparatus corresponding to the changed standard consolidated the changed habits to an extraordinary degree. This apparatus served both the constant reproduction of the standard and its dissemination.

It is not uninteresting to observe that today [in the 1930s, the translator], when this standard of conduct has been so heavily consolidated that it is taken for granted, a certain relaxation is setting in, particularly in comparison to the nineteenth century, at least with regard to speech about the natural functions. The freedom and unconcern with which people say what has to be said without embarrassment, without the forced smile and laughter of a taboo infringement, has clearly increased in the postwar period. But this, like modern bathing and dancing practices, is only possible because the level of habitual, technically and institutionally consolidated self-control, the individual capacity to restrain one's urges and behavior in correspondence with the more advanced feelings for what is offensive, has been on the whole secured. It is a relaxation within the framework of an already established standard.

6. The standard which is emerging in our phase of civilization is characterized by a profound discrepancy between the behavior of so-called "adults" and children. The children have in the space of a few years to attain the advanced level of shame and revulsion that has developed over many centuries. Their instinctual life must be rapidly subjected to the strict control and specific molding that gives our societies their stamp, and which developed very slowly over centuries. In this the parents are only the (often inadequate) instruments, the primary agents of conditioning; through them and thousands of other instruments it is always society as a whole, the entire figuration of human beings, that exerts its pressure on the new generation, bending them more or less perfectly to its purpose.

In the Middle Ages, too, it was society as a whole that exerted this formative pressure, even if—as will be shown in more detail—the mechanisms and organs of conditioning, particularly in the upper class, were largely different from those of today. But above all, the control and restraint to which the instinctual life of adults was subjected was considerably less than in the following phase of civilization, as consequently was the difference in behavior between adults and children.

The individual inclinations and tendencies which medieval writings on etiquette were concerned to control were often the same as can be frequently observed in children today. However, they are now dealt with so early that certain kinds of "misbehavior" which were quite commonplace in the medieval world scarcely manifest themselves in present-day social life.

Children today are admonished not to snatch whatever they want from the table, and not to scratch themselves or touch their noses, ears, eyes, or other parts of their bodies at table. The child is instructed not to speak or drink with a full mouth, or to sprawl on the table, and so on. Many of these precepts are also to be found in Tannhäuser's *Hofzucht*, for example, but there they are addressed not to children but unequivocally to adults. This becomes still more apparent if one considers the way in which adults earlier satisfied their natural needs. This very often happened—as the examples show—in a manner that would be just tolerated in children today. Often enough, needs were satisfied where and when they happened to be felt. The degree of instinctual restraint and control expected by adults of each other was not much greater than that imposed on children. The distance between adults and children, measured by that of today, was slight.

Today the circle of precepts and regulations is drawn so tightly about people, the censorship and pressure of social life forming their habits are so strong, that young people have only two alternatives: to submit to the pattern of behavior demanded by society, or to be excluded from life in "decent society." A child that does not attain the level of control of emotions demanded by society is regarded in varying gradations as "ill," "abnormal," "criminal," or just "impossible" from the point of view of a particular caste or class, and is accordingly excluded from the life of that class. Indeed, from the psychological point of view, the terms "sick," "abnormal," "criminal," and "impossible" have, within certain limits, no other meaning; how they are understood varies with the historically mutable models of affect formation.

Very instructive in this regard is the conclusion of Example D: "It is far less proper to hold out the stinking thing for the other to smell, etc." Instinctual tendencies and behavior of this kind would, by today's standard of shame and revulsion, simply exclude a person as "sick," "pathological," or "perverse" from mixing with others. If the inclination to such behavior were manifested publicly, he would, depending on his social position, be confined indoors or in an institution. At best, if this tendency were only manifested behind the scenes, a specialist in nervous disorders would be assigned the task of correcting this person's unsuccessful conditioning. In general, impulses of this kind have disappeared from the waking consciousness of adults under the pressure of conditioning. Only psychoanalysis uncovers them in the form of unsatisfied and unsatisfiable desires which can be described as the unconscious or the dream level of the mind. And these desires have indeed in our society the character of an "infantile" residue, because the social standard of adults makes a complete suppression and transformation of such tendencies necessary, so that they appear, when occurring in adults, as a "remnant" from childhood.

The standard of delicacy represented by *Galateo* also demands a detachment from these instinctual tendencies. But the pressure to transform such inclinations exerted on the individual by society is minimal compared to that of today. The feeling of revulsion, distaste, or disgust aroused by such behavior is, in keeping with the earlier standard, incomparably weaker than ours. Consequently, the social prohibition on the expression of such feelings is much less grave. This behavior is not regarded as a "pathological anomaly" or a "perversion," but rather as an offense against tact, politeness, or good form.

Della Casa speaks of this "misdemeanor" with scarcely more emphasis than we might today speak of someone biting his nails in society. The very fact that he speaks of "such things" at all shows how harmless this practice then appeared.

Nevertheless, in one way this example marks a turning point. It may be supposed that the expression of these feelings was not lacking in the preceding period. But only now does it begin to attract attention. Society is gradually beginning to suppress the positive pleasure component in certain functions more and more strongly by the arousal of anxiety; or, more exactly, it is rendering this pleasure "private" and "secret" (i.e., suppressing it within the individual), while fostering the negatively charged affects—displeasure, revulsion, distaste—as the only feelings customary in society. But precisely by this increased social proscription of many impulses, by their "repression" from the surface both of social life and of consciousness, the distance between the personality structure and behavior of adults and children is necessarily increased.

VI

On Blowing One's Nose

Examples

A

Thirteenth century

From Bonvesin de la Riva (Bonvicino da Riva), *De la zinquanta cortexie da tavola* (Fifty table courtesies):

(a) Precept for gentlemen:

> When you blow your nose or cough, turn round so that nothing falls on the table.

(b) Precept for pages or servants:

> Pox la trentena è questa:
>   zaschun cortese donzello
> Che se vore mondà lo naxo,
>   con li drapi se faza bello;
> Chi mangia, over chi menestra,
>   no de'sofià con le die;
> Con li drapi da pey se monda
>   vostra cortexia.*

---

* The meaning of passage (b) is not entirely clear. What is apparent is that it is addressed especially to people who serve at table. A commentator, Uguccione Pisano, says: "Those are called *donizelli* who are handsome, young, and the servants of great lords. . . ." These *donizelli* were not allowed to sit at the same table as the knights; or, if this was permitted, they had to sit on a lower chair. They, pages of a kind and at any rate social inferiors, are told: The thirty-first courtesy is this—every *courtois* "donzel" who wishes to blow his nose should beautify himself with a cloth. When he is eating or serving he should not blow (his nose?) through his fingers. It is *courtois* to use the foot bandage.

B

Fifteenth century

From *Ein spruch der ze tische kêrt*:

It is unseemly to blow your nose into the tablecloth.

C

From *S'ensuivent les contenances de la table*:

XXXIII

Do not blow your nose with the same hand that you use to hold the meat.**

D

From A. Cabanès, *Moeurs intimes du temps passé* (Paris, 1910), 1st series, p. 101:

In the fifteenth century people blew their noses into their fingers, and the sculptors of the age were not afraid to reproduce the gesture, in a passably realistic form, in their monuments.

Among the knights, the plourans, at the grave of Philip the Bold at Dijon, one is seen blowing his nose into his coat, another into his fingers.

E

Sixteenth century

From *De civilitate morum puerilium*, by Erasmus, ch. 1:

To blow your nose on your hat or clothing is rustic, and to do so with the arm or elbow befits a tradesman; nor is it much more polite to use the hand, if you immediately smear the snot on your garment. It is proper to wipe the nostrils with a handkerchief, and to do this while turning away, *if more honorable people are present*.

If anything falls to the ground when blowing the nose with two fingers, it should immediately be trodden away.

[From the scholia on this passage:]

Between snot and spit there is little difference, except that the former fluid is to be interpreted as coarser and the latter more unclean. The Latin writers constantly confuse a breastband, a napkin, or any piece of linen with a handkerchief.

F

1558

From *Galateo*, by Della Casa, quoted from the five-language edition (Geneva, 1609), pp. 72, 44, 618:

** According to an editor's note (*The Babees Book*, vol. 2, p. 14), courtesy consisted in blowing the nose with the fingers of the left hand if one ate and took meat from the common dish with the right.

You should not offer your handkerchief to anyone unless it has been freshly washed. . . .

Nor is it seemly, after wiping your nose, to spread out your handkerchief and peer into it as if pearls and rubies might have fallen out of your head.

. . . What, then, shall I say of those . . . who carry their handkerchiefs about in their mouths? . . .

G

From Cabanès, *Moeurs intimes*, pp. 103, 168, 102:

[From Martial d'Auvergue, "Love decrees"] . . . in order that she might remember him, he decided to have one of the most beautiful and sumptuous handkerchiefs made for her, in which his name was in letters entwined in the prettiest fashion, for it was joined to a fine golden heart bordered with tiny heart's eases.***

[From Lestoil, *Journal d'Henri IV*] In 1594, Henri IV asked his valet how many shirts he had, and the latter replied: "A dozen, sire, and some torn ones." "And how many handkerchiefs?" asked the king. "Have I not eight?" "For the moment there are only five," he said.

In 1599, after her death, the inventory of Henri IV's mistress is found to contain "five handkerchiefs worked in gold, silver and silk, worth 100 crowns."

In the sixteenth century, Monteil tells us, in France as everywhere else, the common people blow their noses without a handkerchief, but among the bourgeoisie it is accepted practice to use the sleeve. As for the rich, they carry a handkerchief in their pockets; therefore, to say that a man has wealth, one says that he does not blow his nose on his sleeve.

H

Late seventeenth century
The Peak of Refinement
First Highpoint of Modeling and Restrictions

1672

From Courtin, *Nouveau traité de civilité*:

[At table] to blow your nose openly into your handkerchief, without concealing yourself with your serviette, and to wipe away your sweat with it . . . are filthy habits fit to make everyone's gorge rise. . . .

You should avoid yawning, blowing your nose, and spitting. If you are obliged to do so in places that are kept clean, do it in your handkerchief, while turning your face away and shielding yourself with your left hand, and do not look into your handkerchief afterward.

*** This cloth was intended to be hung from the lady's girdle, with her keys. Like the fork, night-commode, etc., the handkerchief is first an expensive luxury article.

I

1694

From Ménage, *Dictionnaire étymologique de la langue française*:

Handkerchief for blowing the nose.
As this expression "blowing the nose" gives a very disagreeable impression, ladies ought to call this a pocket handkerchief, as one says neckerchief, rather than a handkerchief for blowing the nose. [N.B. *Mouchoir de poche, Taschentuch*, handkerchief as more polite expressions; the word for functions that have become distasteful is repressed.]

Eighteenth century

Note the increasing distance between adults and children. Only children are still allowed, at least in the middle classes, to behave as adults did in the Middle Ages.

J

1714

From an anonymous *Civilité française* (Liège, 1714), p. 141:

Take good care not to blow your nose with your fingers or on your sleeve *like children*; use your handkerchief and do not look into it afterward.

K

1729

From La Salle, *Les Règles de la bienséance et de la civilité chrétienne* (Rouen, 1729), in a chapter called "On the Nose, and the Manner of Blowing the Nose and Sneezing," p. 23:

It is very impolite to keep poking your finger into your nostrils, and still more insupportable to put what you have pulled from your nose into your mouth. . . .
It is vile to wipe your nose with your bare hand, or to blow it on your sleeve or your clothes. It is very contrary to decency to blow your nose with two fingers and then to throw the filth onto the ground and wipe your fingers on your clothes. It is well known how improper it is to see such uncleanliness on clothes, which should always be very clean, no matter how poor they may be.
There are some who put a finger on one nostril and by blowing through their nose cast onto the ground the filth inside; those who act thus are people who do not know what decency is.
You should always use your handkerchief to blow your nose, and never anything else, and in doing so usually hide your face with your hat. [A particularly clear example of the dissemination of courtly customs through this work.]
You should avoid making a noise when blowing your nose. . . . Before blowing it, it is impolite to spend a long time taking out your handkerchief. *It shows a lack of respect*

toward the people you are with to unfold it in different places to see where you are to use it. You should take your handkerchief from your pocket and use it quickly in such a way that you are scarcely noticed by others.

After blowing your nose you should take care not to look into your handkerchief. It is correct to fold it immediately and replace it in your pocket.

L

1774

From La Salle, *Les Règles de la bienséance et de la civilité chrétienne* (1774 ed.), pp. 14f. The chapter is now called only "On the Nose" and is shortened:

> Every voluntary movement of the nose, whether caused by the hand or otherwise, is impolite and puerile. To put your fingers into your nose is a revolting impropriety, and from touching it too often *discomforts may arise which are felt for a long time.** Children are sufficiently in the habit of committing this lapse; *parents should correct them carefully*.

> You should observe, in blowing your nose, all the rules of propriety and cleanliness.

All details are avoided. The "conspiracy of silence" is spreading. It is based on the presupposition—which evidently could not be made at the time of the earlier edition—that all the details are known to adults and can be controlled within the family.

M

1797

From La Mésangère, *Le voyageur de Paris* (1797), vol. 2, p. 95. This is probably seen, to a greater extent than the preceding eighteenth-century examples, from the point of view of the younger members of "good society":

> Some years ago people made an art of blowing the nose. One imitated the sound of the trumpet, another the screech of a cat. Perfection lay in making neither too much noise nor too little.

Comments on the Quotations on Nose-Blowing

1. In medieval society people generally blew their noses into their hands, just as they ate with their hands. That necessitated special precepts for nose-cleaning at table. Politeness, *courtoisie*, required that one blow one's nose with the left hand if one took meat with the right. But this precept was in fact restricted to the

---

* This argument, absent in the earlier edition, shows clearly how the reference to damage to health is gradually beginning to emerge as an instrument of conditioning, often in place of the remainder about the respect due to social superiors.

table. It arose solely out of consideration for others. The distasteful feeling frequently aroused today by the mere thought of soiling the fingers in this way was at first entirely absent.

Again the examples show very clearly how slowly the seemingly simplest instruments of civilization have developed. They also illustrate to a certain degree the particular social and psychological preconditions that were required to make the need for and use of so simple an instrument general. The use of the handkerchief—like that of the fork—first established itself in Italy, and was diffused on account of its prestige value. The ladies hang the precious, richly embroidered cloth from their girdles. The young "snobs" of the Renaissance offer it to others or carry it about in their mouths. And since it is precious and relatively expensive, at first there are not many of them even among the upper class. Henri IV, at the end of the sixteenth century, possessed (as we hear in Example G) five handkerchiefs. And it is generally taken as a sign of wealth not to blow one's nose into one's hand or sleeve but into a handkerchief. Louis XIV is the first to have an abundant supply of handkerchiefs, and under him the use of them becomes general, at least in courtly circles.

2. Here, as so often, the transitional situation is clearly visible in Erasmus. It is proper to use a handkerchief, he says, and if people of a higher social position are present, turn away when blowing your nose. But he also says: If you blow your nose with two fingers and something falls to the ground, tread on it. The use of the handkerchief is known but not yet widely disseminated, even in the upper class for which Erasmus primarily writes.

Two centuries later, the situation is almost reversed. The use of the handkerchief has become general, at least among people who lay claim to "good behavior." But the use of the hands has by no means disappeared. Seen from above, it has become "ill-mannered," or at any rate common and vulgar. One reads with amusement La Salle's gradations between *vilain*, for certain very coarse ways of blowing the nose with the hand, and *très contraire à la bienséance*, for the better manner of doing so with two fingers (Examples H, J, K, L).

Once the handkerchief begins to come into use, there constantly recurs a prohibition on a new form of "bad manners" that emerges at the same time as the new practice—the prohibition on looking into one's handkerchief when one has used it (Examples F, H, I, K, L). It almost seems as if inclinations which have been subjected to a certain control and restraint by the introduction of the handkerchief are seeking a new outlet in this way. At any rate, an instinctual tendency which today appears at most in the unconscious, in dreams, in the sphere of secrecy, or more consciously only behind the scenes, the interest in bodily secretions, here shows itself at an earlier stage of the historical process more clearly and openly, and so in a form in which today it is only "normally" visible in children.

In the later edition of La Salle, as in other cases, the major part of the very detailed precepts from the earlier one are omitted. The use of the handkerchief has become more general and self-evident. It is no longer necessary to be so explicit. Moreover, there is less and less inclination to speak about these details that La Salle originally discussed straightforwardly and at length without embarrassment. More stress, on the other hand, is laid on children's bad habit of putting the fingers in the nose. And, as with other childish habits, the medical warning now appears alongside or in place of the social one as an instrument of conditioning, in the reference to the injury that can be done by doing "such a thing" too often. This is an expression of a change in the manner of conditioning that has already been considered from other aspects. Up to this time, habits are almost always judged expressly in their relation to other people, and they are forbidden, at least in the secular upper class, because they may be troublesome or embarrassing to others, or because they betray a "lack of respect." Now habits are condemned more and more as such, not in regard to others. In this way, socially undesirable impulses or inclinations are more radically repressed. They are associated with embarrassment, fear, shame, or guilt, even when one is alone. Much of what we call "morality" or "moral" reasons has the same function as "hygiene" or "hygienic" reasons: to condition children to a certain social standard. Molding by such means aims at making socially desirable behavior automatic, a matter of self-control, causing it to appear in the consciousness of the individual as the result of his own free will, and in the interests of his own health or human dignity. And it is only with the advent of this way of consolidating habits, or conditioning, which gains predominance with the rise of the middle classes, that conflict between the socially inadmissible impulses and tendencies, on the one hand, and the pattern of social demands anchored in the individual, on the other, takes on the sharply defined form central to the psychological theories of modern times—above all, to psychoanalysis. It may be that there have always been "neuroses." But the "neuroses" we see about us today are a specific historical form of psychic conflict which needs psychogenetic and sociogenetic elucidation.

3. An indication of the mechanisms of repression may already be contained in the two verses quoted from Bonvicino da Riva (Example A). The difference between what is exited of knights and lords, on the one hand, and of the *donizelli*, pages, or servants, on the other, calls to mind a much-documented social phenomenon. The masters find the sight of the bodily functions of their servants distasteful; they compel them, the social inferiors in their immediate surroundings, to control and restrain these functions in a way that they do not at first impose on themselves. The verse addressed to the masters says simply: If you blow your nose, turn round so that nothing falls on the table. There is no mention of using a cloth. Should we believe that the use of cloths for cleaning the nose was already taken so much for granted in this society that it was no longer thought necessary to mention it in a book on manners? That is highly

improbable. The servants, on the other hand, are expressly instructed to use not their fingers but their foot bandages if they have to blow their noses. To be sure, this interpretation of the two verses cannot be considered absolutely certain. But the fact can be frequently demonstrated that functions are found distasteful and disrespectful in inferiors which superiors are not ashamed of in themselves. This fact takes on special significance with the transformation of society under absolutism, and therefore at absolutist courts, when the upper class, the aristocracy as a whole, has become, with degrees of hierarchy, a subservient and socially dependent class. This at first sight highly paradoxical phenomenon of an upper class that is socially extremely dependent will be discussed later in another context. Here we can only point out that this social dependence and its structure have decisive importance for the structure and pattern of affect restrictions. The examples contain numerous indications of how these restrictions are intensified with the growing dependence of the upper class. It is no accident that the first "peak of refinement" or "delicacy" in the manner of blowing the nose—and not only here—comes in the phase when the dependence and subservience of the aristocratic upper class is at its height, the period of Louis XIV (Examples H and I).

The dependence of the upper class also explains the dual aspect which the behavior patterns and instruments of civilization have at least in this formative stage. They express a certain measure of compulsion and renunciation, but they also immediately become a weapon against social inferiors, a means of distinction. Handkerchief, fork, plates, and all their related implements are at first luxury articles with a particular social prestige value (Example G).

The social dependence in which the succeeding upper class, the bourgeoisie, lives, is of a different kind, to be sure, from that of the court aristocracy, but tends to be greater and more compelling.

In general, we scarcely realize today what a unique and astonishing phenomenon a "working" upper class is. Why does it work? Why submit itself to this compulsion even though it is the "ruling" class and is therefore not commanded to do so? The question demands a more detailed answer than is possible in this context. What is clear, however, is the parallel to what has been said on the change in the instruments and forms of conditioning. During the stage of the court aristocracy, the restraint imposed on inclinations and emotions is based primarily on consideration and respect due to others and above all to social superiors. In the subsequent stage, renunciation and restraint of impulses is compelled far less by particular persons; expressed provisionally and approximately, it is now, more directly than before, the less visible and more impersonal compulsions of social interdependence, the division of labor, the market, and competition that impose restraint and control on the impulses and emotions. It is these pressures, and the corresponding manner of explanation and conditioning mentioned above, which make it appear that socially desirable behavior is voluntarily produced by the individual himself, on his own initiative. This applies to the regulation and restraint of drives necessary for "work"; it also applies to the whole pattern according to which drives are modeled in bourgeois industrial societies. The pattern of affect control, of what must and what must not be restrained, regulated, and transformed, is certainly not the same in this stage as in the preceding one of the court aristocracy. In keeping with its different interdependencies, bourgeois society applies stronger restrictions to certain impulses, while in the case of others aristocratic restrictions are simply continued and transformed to suit the changed situation. In addition, more clearly distinct national patterns of affect control are formed from the various elements. In both cases, in aristocratic court society as well as in the bourgeois societies of the nineteenth and twentieth centuries, the upper classes are socially constrained to a particularly high degree. The central role played by this increasing dependency of the upper classes as a motor of civilization will be demonstrated later.

VII

On Spitting

Examples

Middle Ages

A

From *Stans puer in mensam*:[70]

   27 Do not spit over or on the table.

   37 Do not spit into the bowl when washing your hands.

B

From a *Contenence de table*:[71]

   29 Do not spit on the table.

   51 Do not spit into the basin when you wash your hands, but beside it.

C

From *The Book of Curtesye*:[72]

   85 If thou spitt over the borde, or elles opon,
      thou schalle be holden an uncurtayse mon.

133 After mete when thou shall wasshe,
    spitt not in basyn, ne water thou dasshe.

D

From Zarncke, *Der deutsche Cato*, p. 137:

276 Do not spit across the table in the manner of hunters.

E

1530

From *De civilitate morum puerilium*, by Erasmus:

Turn away when spitting, lest your saliva fall on someone. If anything purulent falls to the ground, it should be trodden upon, lest it nauseate someone. If you are not at liberty to do this, catch the sputum in a small cloth. It is unmannerly to suck back saliva, as equally are those whom we see spitting at every third word not from necessity but from habit.

F

1558

From *Galateo*, by Della Casa, quoted from the five-language edition (Geneva, 1609), p. 570:

It is also unseemly for someone sitting at table to scratch himself. At such a time and place you should also abstain as far as possible from spitting, and if it cannot be completely avoided it should be done politely and unnoticed.

    I have often heard that whole peoples have sometimes lived so moderately and conducted themselves so honorably that they found spitting quite unnecessary. Why, therefore, should not we too be able to refrain from it just for a short time? [That is, during meals; the restriction on the habit applied only to mealtimes.]

G

1672

From Courtin, *Nouveau traité de civilité*, p. 273:

The custom we have just mentioned does not mean that most laws of this kind are immutable. And just as there are many that have already changed, I have no doubt that many of these will likewise change in the future.

    Formerly, for example, it was permitted to spit on the ground before people of rank, and was sufficient to put one's foot on the sputum. Today that is an indecency.

In the old days you could yawn, provided you did not speak while doing so; today, a person of rank would be shocked by this.

H

1714
From an anonymous *Civilité française* (Liège, 1714), pp. 67, 41:

Frequent spitting is disagreeable. When it is necessary you should conceal it as much as possible, and avoid soiling either persons or their clothes, no matter who they are, nor even the embers beside the fire. And wherever you spit, you should put your foot on the saliva.
At the houses of the great, one spits into one's handkerchief. . . .
It ill becomes you to spit out of the window or onto the fire.
Do not spit so far that you have to look for the saliva to put your foot on it.

I

1729
From La Salle, *Les Règles de la bienséance et de la civilité chrétienne* (Rouen, 1729), p. 35:

You should not abstain from spitting, and it is very ill-mannered to swallow what should be spat. This can nauseate others.
Nevertheless, you should not become accustomed to spitting too often, and without need. This is not only unmannerly, but disgusts and annoys everyone. *When you are with well-born people*, and when you are in places that are kept clean, it is polite to spit into your handkerchief while turning slightly aside.
It is even good manners for everyone to get used to spitting into a handkerchief when in the houses of the great and in all places with waxed or parquet floors. But it is far more necessary to acquire the habit of doing so when in church, as far as is possible. . . . It often happens, however, that no kitchen or even stable floor is dirtier . . . than that of the church.
After spitting into your handkerchief, you should fold it at once, without looking at it, and put it into your pocket. You should take great care never to spit on your clothes, or those of others. . . . If you notice saliva on the ground, you should immediately put your foot adroitly on it. If you notice any on someone's coat, it is not polite to make it known; you should instruct a servant to remove it. If no servant is present, you should remove it yourself without being noticed. For good breeding consists in not bringing to people's attention anything that might offend or confuse them.

J

1774
From La Salle, *Les Règles de la bienséance et de la civilité chrétienne* (1774 ed.), p. 20.

In this edition the chapter "On Yawning, Spitting, and Coughing," which covers four pages in the earlier editions, has shrunk to one page:

> In church, in the houses of the great, and in all places where cleanliness reigns, you should spit into your handkerchief. It is an unpardonably gross habit of children to spit in the faces of their playmates. Such bad manners cannot be punished too severely; nor are those who spit out of windows, on walls and on furniture to be excused. . . .

K
1859
From *The Habits of Good Society*, p. 256:

> Spitting is at all times a disgusting habit. I need say nothing more than—never indulge in it. Besides being coarse and atrocious, *it is very bad for the health*.

L
1910
From Cabanès, *Moeurs intimes*, p. 264:

> Have you noticed that today we relegate to some discreet corner what our fathers did not hesitate to display quite openly?
>
> Thus a certain intimate article of furniture had a place of honor . . . no one thought of concealing it from view.
>
> The same is true of another piece of furniture no longer found in modern households, whose disappearance some will perhaps regret in this age of "bacillophobia": I am referring to the spittoon.

Comments on the Quotations on Spitting

1. Like the other groups of examples, the series of quotations about spitting shows very clearly that, since the Middle Ages, behavior has changed in a particular direction. In the case of spitting, the movement is unmistakably of the kind that we call "progress." Frequent spitting is even today one of the experiences that many Europeans find particularly unpleasant when traveling in the East or in Africa, together with the lack of "cleanliness." If they started out with idealized preconceptions, they call the experience disappointing, and find their feelings on the "progress" of Western civilization confirmed. No more than four centuries ago, this custom was no less widespread and commonplace in the West, as the examples show. Taken together, they give a particularly clear demonstration of the way in which the civilizing process took place.

2. The examples show a movement with the following stages: The Latin as well as the English, French, and German guides to table manners bear witness to the

fact that in the Middle Ages it was not only a custom but also clearly a generally felt need to spit frequently. It is also entirely commonplace in the courts of the feudal lords. The only major restraint imposed is that one should not spit on or over the table but under it. Nor should one spit into the washbasin when cleaning mouth or hands, but beside it. These prohibitions are repeated in so stereotyped a fashion in the *courtois* codes of manners that one can imagine the frequency of this instance of "bad manners." The pressure of medieval society on this practice never becomes so strong, nor the conditioning so compelling, that it disappears from social life. Here again we see the difference between social control in the medieval and the subsequent stages.

In the sixteenth century, social pressure grows stronger. It is demanded that sputum be trodden upon—at least if it contains purulence, says Erasmus, who here as always marks the transitional situation. And here again the use of a cloth is mentioned as a possible, not a necessary, way of controlling this habit, which is slowly becoming more distasteful.

The next step is shown clearly by Courtin's comment of 1672: "Formerly . . . it was permitted to spit on the ground before people of rank, and was sufficient to put one's foot on the sputum. Today that is an indecency."

Similarly, we find in the *Civilité* of 1714, intended for a wider audience: "Conceal it as much as possible, and avoid soiling either persons or their clothes. . . . At the houses of the great, one spits into one's handkerchief."

In 1729, La Salle extends the same precept to all places "that are kept clean." And he adds that in church, too, people ought to get used to using their handkerchiefs and not the floor.

By 1774 the whole practice, and even speaking about it, had become considerably more distasteful. By 1859 "spitting is at all times a disgusting habit." All the same, at least within the house, the spittoon, as a technical implement for controlling this habit in keeping with the advancing standard of delicacy, still has considerable importance in the nineteenth century. Cabanès, in 1910, reminds us that, like other implements (cf. Example L), it has slowly evolved from a prestige object to a private utensil.

Gradually this utensil too becomes dispensable. In large sections of Western society, even the need to spit from time to time seems to have disappeared completely. A standard of delicacy and restraint similar to that which Della Casa knew only from his reading of ancient writers, where "whole peoples . . . lived so moderately and . . . so honorably that they found spitting quite unnecessary" (Example F), has been attained once more.

3. Taboos and restrictions of various kinds surround the ejection of saliva, like other natural functions, in very many societies, both "primitive" and "civilized." What distinguishes them is the fact that in the former they are always maintained by fear of other beings, even if only imaginary ones—that is, by external constraints—whereas in the latter these are transformed more or less completely

into internal constraints. The prohibited tendencies (e.g., the tendency to spit) partly disappear from consciousness under the pressure of this internal restraint or, as it may also be called, the superego and the "habit of foresight." What remains behind in consciousness as the motivation of anxiety is some long-term consideration. So in our time the fear of spitting, and the feelings of shame and repugnance in which it is expressed, are concentrated about the more precisely defined and logically comprehensible idea of certain illnesses and their "causes," rather than around the image of magical influences, gods, spirits, or demons. But the series of examples also shows very clearly that rational understanding of the origins of certain diseases, of the danger of sputum as a carrier of illness, is neither the primary cause of fear and repugnance nor the motor of civilization, the driving force of the changes in behavior with regard to spitting.

At first, and for a long period, the retention of spittle is expressly discouraged. To suck back saliva is "unmannerly," says Erasmus (Example E). And as late as 1729, La Salle says: "You should not abstain from spitting" (Example I). For centuries there is not the faintest indication of "hygienic reasons" for the prohibitions and restrictions with which the tendency to spit is surrounded. Rational understanding of the "danger" of saliva is attained only at a very late stage of the change in behavior, and thus in a sense retrospectively, in the nineteenth century. And even then, the reference to what is indelicate and disgusting in such behavior still appears separately, alongside the reference to its ill effects on health: "Besides being coarse and atrocious, it is very bad for the health," Example K says of spitting.

It is well to establish once and for all that something which we know to be harmful to health by no means necessarily arouses feelings of distaste or shame. And conversely, something that arouses these feelings need not be at all detrimental to health. Someone who eats noisily or with his hands nowadays arouses feelings of extreme distaste without there being the slightest fear for his health. But neither the thought of someone reading by bad light nor the idea of poison gas, for example, arouses remotely similar feelings of distaste or shame, although the harmful consequences for health are obvious. Thus, disgust at the ejection of saliva intensifies, and the taboos surrounding it increase, long before people have a clear idea of the transmission of certain germs by saliva. What first arouses and increases the distasteful feelings and restrictions is a transformation of human relationships and dependencies. "Earlier it was permitted to yawn or spit openly; today, a person of rank would be shocked by it," Example G says, in effect. That is the kind of reason that people first give for increased restraint. Motivation from social consideration exists long before motivation from scientific insight. The king requires this restraint as a "mark of respect" from his courtiers. In court circles this sign of their dependence, the growing compulsion to be restrained and self-controlled, becomes also a "mark of distinction" that is immediately imitated below and disseminated with the rise of broader classes.

And here, as in the preceding civilization-curves, the admonition "That is not done," with which restraint, fear, shame, and repugnance are inculcated, is connected only very late, as a result of a certain "democratization," to a scientific theory, to an argument that applies to all men equally, regardless of their rank and status. The primary impulse for this slow repression of an inclination that was formerly strong and widespread does not come from rational understanding of the causes of illness, but—as will be discussed in more detail later—from changes in the way people live together, in the structure of society.

4. The modification of the manner of spitting, and finally the more or less complete elimination of the need for it, is a good example of the malleability of psychic life. It may be that this need has been compensated by others (e.g., the need to smoke) or weakened by certain changes of diet. But it is certain that the degree of suppression which has been possible in this case is not possible with regard to many other drives. The inclination to spit, like that of looking at the sputum, mentioned in the examples, is replaceable; it now manifests itself only in children or in dream analyses, and its suppression is seen in the specific laughter that overcomes us when "such things" are spoken of openly.

Other needs are not replaceable or malleable to the same extent. And this raises the question of the limit of the transformability of the human personality. Without doubt, it is bound to certain regularities that may be called "natural." The historical process modifies it within these limits. The degree to which human life and behavior can be molded by historical processes remains to be determined in detail. At any rate, all this shows once again how natural and historical processes interact almost inseparably. The formation of feelings of shame and revulsion and advances in the threshold of delicacy are both at once natural and historical processes. These forms of feeling are manifestations of human nature under specific social conditions, and they react in their turn on the sociohistorical process as one of its elements.

It is difficult to see whether the radical contraposition of "civilization" and "nature" is more than an expression of the tensions of the "civilized" psyche itself, of a specific imbalance within psychic life produced in the recent stage of Western civilization. At any rate, the psychic life of "primitive" peoples is no less historically (i.e., socially) stamped than that of "civilized" peoples, even if the former are scarcely aware of their own history. There is no zero point in the historicity of human development, just as there is none in the sociality, the social interdependence among men. In both "primitive" and "civilized" peoples, there are socially induced prohibitions and restrictions, together with their psychic counterparts, socially induced anxieties, pleasure and displeasure, distaste and delight. At the least, therefore, it is not very clear what is meant when the so-called primitive standard is opposed as "natural" to the "civilized" as social and historical. So far as the psychical functions of men are concerned, natural and historical processes work indissolubly together.

VIII

On Behavior in the Bedroom

Examples

A

Fifteenth century

From *Stans puer in mensam*, an English book of table manners from the period 1463–1483:

> 215 And if that it forten so by
> > nyght or Any tyme
>
> That you schall lye with Any man
> > that is better than you
>
> Spyre hym what syde of the bedd
> > that most best will ples hym,
>
> And lye you on thi tother syde,
> > for that is thi prow;
>
> Ne go you not to bede before bot
> > thi better cause the,
>
> For that is no curtasy, thus seys
> > doctour paler.

> 223 And when you arte in thi bed,
> > this is curtasy,
>
> Stryght downe that you lye with
> > fote and hond.
>
> When ze have talkyd what ze
> > wyll, byd hym gode nyght in hye
>
> For that is gret curtasy so schall
> > thou understand.*

Let your better choose which side of the bed he'll lie on; don't go to bed first, till he asks you to (says Dr. Paler).

When you're both in bed, lie straight, and say "Good Night" when you've done your chat.

B

1530

From *De civilitate morum puerilium*, by Erasmus, ch. 12, "On the Bedchamber":

---

* To facilitate comprehension, the old spelling is not reproduced exactly. The philologically accurate text can be found in *A Booke of Precedence*, p. 63.

When you undress, when you get up, be mindful of modesty, and take care not to expose to the eyes of others anything that morality and nature require to be concealed.

If you share abed with a comrade, lie quietly; do not toss with your body, for this can lay yourself bare or inconvenience your companion by pulling away the blankets.

C

1555

From *Des bonnes moeurs et honnestes contenances*, by Pierre Broë (Lyons, 1555):

If you share abed with another man, keep still.

Take care not to annoy him or expose yourself by abrupt movements.

And if he is asleep, see that you do not wake him.

D

1729

From La Salle, *Les Règles de la bienséance et de la civilité chrétienne* (Rouen, 1729), p. 55:

You ought . . . neither to undress nor go to bed in the presence of any other person. Above all, unless you are married, you should not go to bed in the presence of anyone of the other sex.

It is still less permissible for people of different sexes to sleep in the same bed, unless they are very young children. . . .

If you are forced by unavoidable necessity to share a bed with another person of the same sex on a journey, it is not proper to lie so near him that you disturb or even touch him; and it is still less decent to put your legs between those of the other. . . .

It is also very improper and impolite to amuse yourself with talk and chatter. . . .

When you get up you should not leave the bed uncovered, nor put your nightcap on a chair or anywhere else where it can be seen.

E

1774

From La Salle, *Les Règles de la bienséance et de la civilité chrétienne* (1774 ed.) p.31:

It is a strange abuse to make two people of different sex sleep in the same room. And if necessity demands it, you should make sure that the beds are apart, and that modesty does not suffer in any way from this commingling. Only extreme indigence can excuse this practice. . . .

If you are forced to share a bed with a person of the same sex, which seldom happens, you should maintain a strict and vigilant modesty. . . .

When you have awakened and had sufficient time to rest, you should get out of bed with fitting modesty and never stay in bed holding conversations or concerning yourself with other matters . . . nothing more clearly indicates indolence and frivolity; the bed is intended for bodily rest and for nothing else.

Comments on the Examples

1. The bedroom has become one of the most "private" and "intimate" areas of human life. Like most other bodily functions, sleeping has been increasingly shifted behind the scenes of social life. The nuclear family remains as the only legitimate, socially sanctioned enclave for this and many other human functions. Its visible and invisible walls withdraw the most "private," "intimate," irrepressibly "animal" aspects of human existence from the sight of others.

In medieval society this function had not been thus privatized and separated from the rest of social life. It was quite normal to receive visitors in rooms with beds, and the beds themselves had a prestige value related to their opulence. It was very common for many people to spend the night in one room: in the upper class, the master with his servants, the mistress with her maid or maids; in other classes, even men and women in the same room,[73] and often guests staying overnight.[74]

2. Those who did not sleep in their clothes undressed completely. In general, people slept naked in lay society, and in monastic orders either fully dressed or fully undressed according to the strictness of the rules. The rule of St. Benedict—dating back at least to the sixth century—required members of the order to sleep in their clothes and even to keep their belts on.[75] In the twelfth century, when their order became more prosperous and powerful and the ascetic constraints less severe, the Cluniac monks were permitted to sleep without clothes. The Cistercians, when striving for reform, returned to the old Benedictine rule. Special nightclothes are never mentioned in the monastic rules of this period, still less in the documents, epics, or illustrations left behind by secular society. This is also true for women. If anything, it was unusual to keep on clothing in bed. It aroused suspicion that one might have some bodily defect—for what other reason should the body be hidden?—and in fact this usually was the case. In the *Roman de la violette*, for example, we hear the servant ask her mistress in surprise why she is going to bed in her chemise, and the latter explains it is because of a mark on her body.[76]

This unconcern in showing the naked body, and the position of the shame frontier represented by it, are seen particularly clearly in bathing manners. It has been noted with surprise in later ages that knights were waited on in their baths by women; likewise, their night drink was often brought to their beds by women. It seems to have been common practice, at least in the towns, to undress at home before going to the bathhouse. "How often," says an observer, "the father, wearing nothing but his breeches, with his naked wife and children, runs through the streets from his house to the baths. . . . How many times have I seen girls of ten, twelve, fourteen, sixteen, and eighteen years entirely naked except for a short smock, often torn, and a ragged bathing gown at front and back! With this open at the feet and with their hands held decorously behind them, running from their houses through the long streets at midday to the baths. How many completely naked boys of ten, twelve, fourteen, and sixteen run beside them. . . ."[77]

This unconcern disappears slowly in the sixteenth and more rapidly in the seventeenth, eighteenth, and nineteenth centuries, first in the upper classes and much more slowly in the lower. Up to then, the whole mode of life, with its greater closeness of individuals, made the sight of the naked body, at least in the proper place, incomparably more commonplace than in the first stages of the modern age. "We reach the surprising conclusion," it has been said with reference to Germany, "that . . . the sight of total nakedness was the everyday rule up to the sixteenth century. Everyone undressed completely each evening before going to bed, and likewise no clothing was worn in the steambaths."[78] And this certainly applies not only to Germany. People had a less inhibited—one might say a more childish—attitude toward the body, and to many of its functions. Sleeping customs show this no less than bathing habits.

3. A special nightdress slowly came into use at roughly the same time as the fork and handkerchief. Like the other "implements of civilization," it made its way through Europe quite gradually. And like them it is a symbol of the decisive change taking place at this time in human beings. Sensitivity toward everything that came into contact with the body increased. Shame became attached to behavior that had previously been free of such feelings. The psychological process which is already described in the Bible by—"and they saw that they were naked and were ashamed"—that is, an advance of the shame frontier, a thrust toward greater restraint—is repeated here, as so often in the course of history. The unconcern in showing oneself naked disappears, as does that in performing bodily functions before others. And as this sight becomes less commonplace in social life, the depiction of the naked body in art takes on a new significance. More than hitherto it becomes a dream image, an emblem of wish-fulfillment. To use Schiller's terms it becomes "sentimental," as against the "naïve" form of earlier phases.

In the courtly society of France—where getting up and going to bed, at least in the case of great lords and ladies, is incorporated directly into social life—nightdress, like every other form of clothing appearing in the communal life of man, takes on representational functions as it develops. This changes when, with the rise of broader classes, getting up and going to bed become intimate and are displaced from social life into the interior of the nuclear family.

The generations following World War I, in their books on etiquette, look back with a certain irony—and not without a faint shudder—at this period, when the exclusion of such functions as sleeping, undressing, and dressing was enforced with special severity, the mere mention of them being blocked by relatively heavy prohibitions. An English book on manners of 1936 says, perhaps with slight exaggeration, but certainly not entirely without justification: "During the Genteel Era before the War, camping was the only way by which respectable writers might approach the subject of sleep. In those days ladies and gentlemen did not go to bed at night—they retired. How they did it was nobody's business. An author who thought differently would have found himself excluded from the circulating library."[79] Here, too, there has been a certain reaction and relaxation since the war. It is clearly connected with the growing mobility of society, with the spread of sport, hiking, and travel, and also with the relatively early separation of young people from the family community. The transition from the nightshirt to pajamas—that is, to a more "socially presentable" sleeping costume—is a symptom of this. This change is not, as is sometimes supposed, simply a retrogressive movement, a recession of the feelings of shame or delicacy, or a release and decontrol of instinctual urges, but the development of a form that fits both our advanced standard of delicacy and the specific situation in which present-day social life places the individual. Sleep is no longer so intimate and segregated as in the preceding stage. There are more situations in which people are exposed to the sight of strangers sleeping, undressing, or dressing. As a result, nightclothes (like underwear) have been developed and transformed in such a way that the wearer need not be "ashamed" when seen in such situations by others. The nightclothes of the preceding phase aroused feelings of shame and embarrassment precisely because they were relatively formless. They were not intended to be seen by people outside the family circle. On the one hand, the nightshirt of the nineteenth century marks an epoch in which shame and embarrassment with regard to the exposure of one's own body were so advanced and internalized that bodily forms had to be entirely covered even when alone or in the closest family circle; on the other hand, it characterizes an epoch in which the "intimate" and "private" sphere, because it was so sharply severed from the rest of social life, had not to any great extent been socially articulated and patterned. This peculiar combination of strongly internalized, compulsive feelings of delicacy, or morality, with a lack of social patterning with respect to the "spheres of intimacy" is characteristic of nineteenth-century society and not a little of our own.[80]

4. The examples give a rough idea of how sleep, becoming slowly more intimate and private, is separated from most other social relations, and how the precepts given to young people take on a specific moralistic undertone with the advance of feelings of shame. In the medieval quotation (Example A) the restraint demanded of young people is explained by consideration due to others, respect for social superiors. It says, in effect, "If you share your bed with a better man, ask

him which side he prefers, and do not go to bed before he invites you, for that is not courteous." And in the French imitation of Johannes Sulpicius by Pierre Broë (Example C), the same attitude prevails: "Do not annoy your neighbor when he has fallen asleep; see that you do not wake him up, etc." In Erasmus we begin to hear a moral demand, which requires certain behavior not out of consideration for others but for its own sake: "When you undress, when you get up, be mindful of modesty." But the idea of social custom, of consideration for others, is still predominant. The contrast to the later period is particularly clear if we remember that these precepts, even those of Dr. Paler (Example A), were clearly directed to people who went to bed undressed. That strangers should sleep in the same bed appears, to judge by the manner in which the question is discussed, neither unusual nor in any way improper even at the time of Erasmus.

In the quotations from the eighteenth century this tendency is not continued in a straight line, partly because it is no longer confined predominantly to the upper class. But in the meantime, even in other classes, it has clearly become less commonplace for a young person to share his bed with another: "If you are forced by unavoidable necessity to share a bed with another person . . . on a journey, it is not proper to lie so near him that you disturb or even touch him," La Salle writes (Example D). And: "You ought neither to undress nor go to bed in the presence of any other person."

In the 1774 edition, details are again avoided wherever possible. And the tone is appreciably stronger. "If you are forced to share a bed with a person of the same sex, which seldom happens, you should maintain a strict and vigilant modesty" (Example E). This is the tone of moral injunction. Even to give a reason has become distasteful to the adult. The child is made by the threatening tone to associate this situation with danger. The more "natural" the standard of delicacy and shame appears to adults and the more the civilized restraint of instinctual urges is taken for granted, the more incomprehensible it becomes to adults that children do not have this delicacy and shame by "nature." The children necessarily touch again and again on the adult threshold of delicacy, and—since they are not yet adapted—they infringe the taboos of society, cross the adult shame frontier, and penetrate emotional danger zones which the adult himself can only control with difficulty. In this situation the adult does not explain the demand he makes on behavior. He is unable to do so adequately. He is so conditioned that he conforms to the social standard more or less automatically. Any other behavior, any breach of the prohibitions or restraints prevailing in his society means danger, and a devaluation of the restraints imposed on himself. And the peculiarly emotional undertone so often associated with moral demands, the aggressive and threatening severity with which they are frequently upheld, reflects the danger in which any breach of the prohibitions places the unstable balance of all those for whom the standard behavior of society has become more or less "second nature." These attitudes are symptoms of the anxiety aroused in adults whenever the structure of their own instinctual life, and with it their own social existence and the social order in which it is anchored, is even remotely threatened.

A whole series of specific conflicts—above all, those between parents (usually ill-prepared for conditioning) and their children, conflicts arising with the advance of the shame-frontier and the growing distance between adults and children, and therefore largely founded on the structure of civilized society itself—are explained by this situation. The situation itself has been understood only relatively recently by society, first of all by small groups of professional educators. And only now, in the age that has been called the "century of the child," is the realization that, in view of the increased distance between them, children cannot behave like adults slowly penetrating the family circle with appropriate educational advice and instructions. In the long preceding period, the more severe attitude prevailed that morality and respect for taboos should be present in children from the first. This attitude certainly cannot be said to have disappeared today.

The examples on behavior in the bedroom give, for a limited segment, a certain impression of how late it really was that the tendency to adopt such attitudes reached its full development in secular education.

The line followed by this development scarcely needs further elucidation. Here, too, in much the same way as with eating, the wall between people, the reserve, the emotional barrier erected by conditioning between one body and another, grows continuously. To share a bed with people outside the family circle, with strangers, is made more and more embarrassing. Unless necessity dictates otherwise, it becomes usual even within the family for each person to have his own bed and finally—in the middle and upper classes—his own bedroom. Children are trained early in this isolation from others, with all the habits and experiences that this brings with it. Only if we see how natural it seemed in the Middle Ages for strangers and for children and adults to share a bed can we appreciate what a fundamental change in interpersonal relationships and behavior is expressed in our manner of living. And we recognize how far from self-evident it is that bed and body should form such psychological danger zones as they do in the most recent phase of civilization.

IX

Changes in Attitude Toward Relations Between the Sexes

1. The feeling of shame surrounding human sexual relations has increased and changed considerably in the process of civilization.[81] This manifests itself

particularly clearly in the difficulty experienced by adults in the later stages of civilization in talking about these relations to children. But today this difficulty appears almost natural. It seems to be explained almost by biological reasons alone that a child knows nothing of the relations of the sexes, and that it is an extremely delicate and difficult task to enlighten growing girls and boys about themselves and what goes on around them. The extent to which this situation, far from being self-evident, is a further result of the civilizing process is only perceived if the behavior of people in a different stage is observed. The fate of Erasmus's renowned *Colloquies* is a good example.

Erasmus discovered that one of the works of his youth had been published without his permission in a corrupt form, with additions by others and partly in a bad style. He revised it and published it himself under a new title in 1522, calling it *Familiarum colloquiorum formulae non tantum ad linguam puerilem expoliandam, verum etiam ad vitam instituendam.*

He worked on this text, augmenting and improving it, until shortly before his death. It became what he had desired, not only a book from which boys could learn a good Latin style, but one which could serve, as he says in the title, to introduce them to life. The *Colloquies* became one of the most famous and widely read works of their time. As his treatise *De civilitate morum puerilium* did later, they went through numerous editions and translations. And like it, they became a schoolbook, a standard work from which boys were educated. Hardly anything gives a more immediate impression of the change in Western society in the process of civilization than the criticism to which this work was subjected by those who still found themselves obliged to concern themselves with it in the nineteenth century. An influential German pedagogue, Von Raumer, comments on it as follows in his *Geschichte der Pädagogik* (History of pedagogy):[82]

> How could such a book be introduced in countless schools? What had boys to do with these satyrs? Reform is a matter for mature men. What sense were boys supposed to make of dialogues on so many subjects of which they understand nothing; conversations in which teachers are ridiculed, or between two women about their husbands, between a suitor and a girl he is wooing, or the colloquy "Adolescentis et Scorti" (The young man and the harlot). This last dialogue recalls Schiller's distich entitled "Kunstgriff" (The knack): "If you would please both the worldly and godly alike, paint them the joys of the flesh, but paint them the devil as well." Erasmus here paints fleshly lust in the basest way and then adds something which is supposed to edify. Such a book is recommended by the Doctor Theologiae to an eight-year-old boy, that he might be improved by reading it.

The work is indeed dedicated to the young son of Erasmus's publisher, and the father clearly felt no qualms at printing it.

2. The book met with harsh criticism as soon as it appeared. But this was not directed chiefly at its moral qualities. The primary target was the "intellectual,"

the man who was neither an orthodox Protestant nor an orthodox Catholic. The Catholic Church, above all, fought against the *Colloquies*, which certainly contain occasional virulent attacks on Church institutions and orders, and soon placed it on the Index.

But against this must be set the extraordinary success of the *Colloquies* and, above all, their introduction as a schoolbook. "From 1526 on," says Huizinga in his *Erasmus* (London, 1924, p. 199), "there was for two centuries an almost uninterrupted stream of editions and translations."

In this period, therefore, Erasmus's treatise must have remained a kind of standard work for a very considerable number of people. How is the difference between its viewpoint and that of the nineteenth-century critic to be understood?

In this work Erasmus does indeed speak of many things which with the advance of civilization have been increasingly concealed from the eyes of children, and which in the nineteenth century would under no circumstances have been used as reading matter for children in the way Erasmus desired and expressly affirmed in the dedication to his six- or eight-year-old godson. As the nineteenth-century critic stresses, Erasmus presents in the dialogues a young man wooing a girl. He shows a woman complaining about the bad behavior of her husband. And there is even a conversation between a young man and a prostitute.

Nevertheless, these dialogues bear witness, in exactly the same way as *De civilitate morum puerilium*, to Erasmus's delicacy in all questions relating to the regulation of instinctual life, even if they do not entirely correspond to our own standard. They even represent, measured by the standard of medieval secular society, and even by that of the secular society of his own time, a very considerable shift in the direction of the kind of restraint of instinctual urges which the nineteenth century was to justify above all in the form of morality.

Certainly, the young man who woos the girl in the colloquy "Proci et puellae" (Courtship) expresses very openly what he wants of her. He speaks of his love for her. When she resists, he tells her that she has drawn his soul half out of his body. He tells her that it is permissible and right to conceive children. He asks her to imagine how fine it will be when he as king and she as queen rule over their children and servants. (This idea shows very clearly how the lesser psychological distance between adults and children very often went hand in hand with a greater social distance.) Finally the girl gives way to his suit. She agrees to become his wife. But she preserves, as she says, the honor of her maidenhood. She keeps it for him, she says. She even refuses him a kiss. But when he does not desist from asking for one, she laughingly tells him that as she has, in his own words, drawn his soul half out of his body, so that he is almost dead, she is afraid that with a kiss she might draw his soul completely out of his body and kill him.

3. As has been mentioned, Erasmus was occasionally reproached by the Church, even in his own lifetime, with the "immorality" of the *Colloquies*. But one should not be misled by this into drawing false conclusions about the actual

standard, particularly of secular society. A treatise directed against Erasmus's *Colloquies* from a consciously Catholic position, about which more will be said later, does not differ in the least from the *Colloquies* so far as unveiled references to sexual matters are concerned. Its author, too, was a humanist. The novelty of the humanists' writings, and particularly of those of Erasmus, is precisely that they do not conform to the standard of clerical society but are written from the standpoint of, and for, secular society.

The humanists were representatives of a movement which sought to release the Latin language from its confinement within the ecclesiastical tradition and sphere, and make it a language of secular society, at least of the secular upper class. Not the least important sign of the change in the structure of Western society, which has already been seen from so many other aspects in this study, is the fact that its secular constituents now feel an increasing need for a secular, scholarly literature. The humanists are the executors of this change, the functionaries of this need of the secular upper class. In their works the written word once again draws close to worldly social life. Experiences from this life find direct access to scholarly literature. This, too, is a line in the great movement of "civilization." And it is here that one of the keys to the "revival" of antiquity will have to be sought.

Erasmus once gave very trenchant expression to this process precisely in defending the *Colloquies*: "As Socrates brought philosophy from heaven to earth, so I have led philosophy to games and banquets," he says in the notes *De utilitate colloquiorum* that he appended to the *Colloquies* (1655 ed., p. 668). For this reason these writings may be correctly regarded as representing the standard of behavior of secular society, no matter how much their particular demands for a restraint of instincts and moderation of behavior may have transcended this standard and, represented in anticipation of the future, an ideal.

In *De utilitate colloquiorum*, Erasmus says with regard to the dialogue "Proci et puellae" mentioned above: "I wish that all suitors were like the one I depict and conversed in no other way when entering marriage."

What appears to the nineteenth-century observer as the "basest depiction of lust," what even by the present standard of shame must be veiled in silence particularly before children, appears to Erasmus and his contemporaries who help to disseminate this work as a model conversation, ideally suited to set an example for the young, and still largely an ideal when compared with what was actually going on around them.[63]

4. The case is similar with the other dialogues mentioned by Von Raumer in his polemic. The woman who complains about her husband is instructed that she will have to change her own behavior, then her husband's will change. And the conversation of the young man with the prostitute ends with his rejection of her disreputable mode of life. One must hear this conversation oneself to understand what Erasmus wishes to set up as an example for boys. The girl, Lucretia, has not

seen the youth, Sophronius, for a long time. And she clearly invites him to do what he has come to the house to do. But he asks whether she is sure that they cannot be seen, whether she has not a darker room. And when she leads him to a darker room he again has scruples. Is she really sure that no one can see them? "No one can see or hear us, not even a fly," she says. "Why do you hesitate?" But the young man asks: "Not even God? Not even the angels?"* And then he begins to convert her with all the arts of dialectics. He asks whether she has many enemies, whether it would not please her to annoy her enemies. Would she not annoy her enemies by giving up her life in this house and becoming an honorable woman? And finally he convinces her. He will secretly take a room for her in the house of a respectable woman, he will find a pretext for her to leave the house unseen. And at first he will look after her.

However "immoral" the presentation of such a situation (in a "children's book," of all places) must appear to an observer from a later period, it is not difficult to understand that from the standpoint of a different social standard and a different structure of feelings it could appear highly "moral" and exemplary.

The same line of development, the same difference in standards, could be demonstrated by any number of examples. The observer of the nineteenth and, to some extent, even of the twentieth century confronts the models and conditioning precepts of the past with a certain helplessness. And until we come to see that our own threshold of repugnance, our own structure of feelings, have developed—in a structured process—and are continuing to develop, it remains indeed almost incomprehensible from the present standpoint how such dialogues could be included in a schoolbook or deliberately produced as reading matter for children. But this is precisely why our own standard, including our attitude to children, should be understood as something which has developed.

More orthodox men than Erasmus did the same as he. To replace the *Colloquies*, which were suspected of heresy, other dialogues were written, as already

---

* The text of this excerpt from the dialogue is as follows:

SOPHRONIUS: Nondum hic locus mihi videtur satis secretus.
LUCRETIA: Unde iste novus pudor? Est mihi museion,[84] ubi repono mundum meum, locus adeo obscurus, ut vix ego te visura sim, aut te me.
SOPH.: Circumspice rimas omnes.
LUC.: Ne musca quidem, mea lux. Quid cunctaris?
SOPH.: Fallemus heic oculos Dei?
LUC.: Nequaquam: ille perspicit omnia.
SOPH.: Et angelorum?

SOPH: This place doesn't seem secret enough to me. LUC.: How come you're so bashful all at once? Well, come to my private dressing room. It's so dark we shall scarcely see each other there. SOPH.: Examine every chink. LUC.: There's not a single chink. SOPH.: Is there nobody near to hear us? LUC.: Not so much as a fly, my dearest. Why are you hesitating? SOPH.: Can we escape the eye of God here? LUC.: Of course not; he sees everything. SOPH.: And the angels?

mentioned, by a strict Catholic. They bear the title *Johannis Morisoti medici colloquiorum libri quatuor, ad Constantinum filium* (Basel, 1549). They are likewise written as a schoolbook for boys, since, as the author Morisotus says, one is often uncertain, in Erasmus's *Colloquies*, "whether one is listening to a Christian or a heathen." And in later evaluations of this opposing work from a strictly Catholic camp the same phenomenon appears.[85] It will suffice to introduce the work as it is reflected in a judgment from 1911:[86]

> In Morisotus girls, maidens, and women play a still greater role than in Erasmus. In a large number of dialogues they are the sole speakers, and their conversations, which even in the first and second books are by no means always quite harmless, often revolve in the last two.[87] . . . around such risky matters that we can only shake our heads and ask: Did the stem Morisotus write this for his son? Could he be so sure that the boy would really only read and study the later books when he had reached the age for which they were intended? Admittedly, we should not forget that the sixteenth century knew little of prudery, and frequently enough presented its scholars with material in their exercise books that our pedagogues would gladly do without. But another question! How did Morisotus imagine the use of such dialogues in practice? Boys, youths, and men could never use as a model for bin such a conversation in which there are only female speakers. Therefore Morisotus, no better than the despised Erasmus, has lost sight of the didactic purpose of the book.

The question is not difficult to answer.

5. Erasmus himself never "lost sight of his didactic purpose." His commentary *De utilitate colloquiorum* shows this quite unequivocally. In it he makes explicit what kind of didactic purpose was attached to his "conversations" or, more exactly, what he wanted to convey to the young man. On the conversation of the young man with the harlot, for example, he says: "What could I have said that would have been more effective in bringing home to the young man the need for modesty, and in bringing girls out of such dangerous and infamous houses?" No, he never lost sight of his pedagogical purpose; he merely has a different standard of shame. He wants to show the young man the world as in a mirror; he wants to teach him what must be avoided and what is conducive to a tranquil life: "In senili colloquio quam multa velut in speculo exhibentur, quae, vel fugienda sunt in vita, vel vitam reddunt tranquillam!"

The same intention undoubtedly also underlies the conversations of Morisotus; and a similar attitude appears in many other educational writings of the time. They all set out to "introduce the boy to life," as Erasmus puts it.[88] But by this they meant the life of adults. In later periods there is an increasing tendency to tell and show children how they ought and ought not to behave. Here they are shown, by introducing them to life, how adults ought and ought not to behave. This is the difference. And one did not behave here in this way, there in that, as a result of theoretical reflection. For Erasmus and his contemporaries it was a matter of course to speak to children in this way. Even though subservient and socially dependent, boys lived very early in the same social sphere as adults. And adults did not impose upon themselves either in action or in words the same restraint with regard to the sexual life as later. In keeping with the different state of restraint of feelings produced in the individual by the structure of interpersonal relations, the idea of strictly concealing these drives in secrecy and intimacy was largely alien to adults themselves. All this made the distance between the behavioral and emotional standards of adults and children smaller from the outset. We see again and again how important it is for an understanding of the earlier psychic constitution and our own to observe the increase of this distance, the gradual formation of the peculiar segregated area in which people gradually come to spend the first twelve, fifteen, and now almost twenty years of their lives. Human biological development in earlier times will not have taken a very different course from today. Only in relation to this social change can we better understand the whole problem of "growing up" as it appears today, and with it such particular problems as the "infantile residues" in the personality structure of grown-ups. The more pronounced difference between the dress of children and adults in our time is only a particularly visible expression of this development. It, too, was minimal at Erasmus's time and for a long period thereafter.

6. To an observer from modern times, it seems surprising that Erasmus in his *Colloquies* should speak at all to a child of prostitutes and the houses in which they live. In our phase of civilization it seems immoral even to acknowledge the existence of such institutions in a schoolbook. They certainly exist as enclaves even in the society of the nineteenth and twentieth centuries. But the fear and shame with which the sexual area of instinctual life, like many others, is surrounded from the earliest years, the "conspiracy of silence" observed on such matters in social discourse, are as good as complete. The mere mention of such opinions and institutions in social life is forbidden, and references to them in the presence of children are a crime soiling the childish soul, or at least a very grave error of conditioning.

In Erasmus's time it was taken equally for granted that children knew of the existence of these institutions. No one concealed them. At most they were warned about them. Erasmus does just that. If we read only the pedagogical books of the time, the mention of such social institutions can certainly appear as an idea emanating from an individual. If we see how the children actually lived with adults, and how scanty was the wall of secrecy between adults themselves and therefore also between adults and children, we comprehend that conversations like those of Erasmus and Morisotus relate directly to the standard of their times. They could reckon with the fact that children knew about all this; it was taken for granted. They saw it as their task as educators to show children how they ought to conduct themselves in the face of such institutions.

It may not seem to amount to very much to say that such houses were spoken about quite openly at the universities. All the same, people generally went to university a good deal younger than today. And it illustrates the theme of this whole chapter to point out that the prostitute was a topic even of comic public speeches at universities. In 1500 a master of arts at Heidelberg spoke "De fide meretricum in suos amatores" (On the fidelity of courtesans to their paramours), another "De fide concubinarum" (On the fidelity of concubines), a third "On the monopoly of the guild of swine," or "De generibus ebriosorum et ebrietate vitanda."[89]

And exactly the same phenomenon is apparent in many sermons of the time; there is no indication that children were excluded from them. This form of extramarital relationship was certainly disapproved in ecclesiastical and many secular circles. But the social prohibition was not yet imprinted as a self restraint in the individual to the extent that it was embarrassing even to speak about it in public. Society had not yet outlawed every utterance that showed that one knew anything about such things.

This difference becomes even clearer if one considers the position of venal women in medieval towns. As is the case today in many societies outside Europe, they have their own very definite place in the public life of the medieval town. There were towns in which they ran races on festival days. They were frequently sent to welcome distinguished visitors. In 1438, for example, the protocols of the city accounts of Vienna read: "For the wine for the common women 96 Kreutzers. Item, for the women who went to meet the king, 96 Kreutzers for wine."[91] Or the mayor and council give distinguished visitors free access to the brothel. In 1434 the Emperor Sigismund publicly thanks the city magistrate of Bern for putting the brothel freely at the disposal of himself and his attendants for three days.[92] This, like a banquet, formed part of the hospitality offered to highranking guests.

The venal women form within city life a corporation with certain rights and obligations, like any other professional body. And like any other professional group, they occasionally defend themselves against unfair competition. In 1500, for example, a number of them go to the mayor of a German town and complain about another house in which the profession to which their house has the sole public rights is practiced. The mayor gives them permission to enter this house; they smash everything and beat the landlady. On another occasion they drag a competitor from her house and force her to live in theirs.

In a word, their social position was similar to that of the executioner, lowly and despised, but entirely public and not surrounded with secrecy. This form of extramarital relationship between man and woman had not yet been removed "beheld the scenes."

7. To a certain extent, this also applies to sexual relations in general, even marital ones. Wedding customs alone give us an idea of this. The procession into the bridal chamber was led by the best men. The bride was undressed by the

bridesmaids; she had to take off all finery. The bridal bed had to be mounted in the presence of witnesses if the marriage was to be valid. They were "laid together."[93] "Once in bed you are rightly wed," the saying went. In the later Middle Ages this custom gradually changed to the extent that the couple was allowed to lie on the bed in their clothes. No doubt these customs varied somewhat between classes and countries. All the same, the old form was retained in Lübeck, for example, up to the first decade of the seventeenth century. Even in the absolutist society of France, bride and bridegroom were taken to bed by the guests, undressed, and given their nightdress. All this is symptomatic of a different standard of shame concerning the relations of the sexes. And through these examples one gains a clearer perception of the specific standard of shame which slowly becomes predominant in the nineteenth and twentieth centuries. In this period, even among adults, everything pertaining to sexual life is concealed to a high degree and dismissed behind the scenes. This is why it is possible, and also necessary, to conceal this side of life for a long period from children. In the preceding phases the relations between the sexes, together with the institutions embracing them, are far more directly incorporated into public life. Hence it is more natural for children to be familiar with this side of life from an early age. From the point of view of conditioning, there is no need to burden this sphere with taboos and secrecy to the extent that becomes necessary in the later stage of civilization, with its different standard of behavior.

In aristocratic court society, sexual life was certainly a good deal more concealed than in medieval society. What the observer from a bourgeois-industrial society often interprets as the "frivolity" of court society is nothing other than this shift toward concealment. Nevertheless, measured by the standard of control of the impulses in bourgeois society itself, the concealment and segregation of sexuality in social life, as in consciousness, was relatively slight in this phase. Here, too, the judgment of later phases is often misled because standards, one's own and that of the court aristocracy, are viewed as absolute rather than as inseparable opposites, and because one's own standard is made the measure of all others.

In this society, too, the relative openness with which the natural stages in a process of development, functions are referred to among adults is matched by a greater freedom of speech and action in the presence of children. There are numerous examples of this. To take a particularly illustrative one, there lives at the court in the seventeenth century a little Mlle. de Bouillon who is six years old. The ladies of the court are wont to converse with her, and one day they play a joke on her: they try to persuade the young lady she is pregnant. The little girl denies it. She defends herself. It is absolutely impossible, she says, and they argue back and forth. But then one day on waking up she finds a newborn child in her bed. She is amazed; and she says in her innocence, "So this has happened only to the Holy Virgin and me; for I did not feel any pain." Her words are passed round, and now the little affair becomes a diversion for the whole court. The child receives visits, as is customary on such occasions. The Queen herself comes to console her and to offer herself as godmother to the baby. And the game goes further: the little girl is press to say who is the father of the child. Finally, after a period of strenuous reflection, she reaches the conclusion that it can only be the King or the Count de Guiche, since they are the only two men who have given her a kiss.[95] Nobody takes this joke amiss. It falls entirely within the existing standard. No one sees in it a danger to the adaptation of the child to this standard, or to her spiritual purity, and it is clearly not seen as in any way contradicting her religious education.

8. Only very gradually, subsequently, does a stronger association of sexuality with shame and embarrassment, and a corresponding restraint of behavior, spread more or less evenly over the whole of society. And only when the distance between adults and children grows does "sexual enlightenment" become an "acute problem."

Above, the criticism of Erasmus's *Colloquies* by the well-known pedagogue Von Raumer was quoted. The picture of this whole curve of development becomes even more distinct if we see how the problem of sexual education, the adaptation of the child to the standard of his own society, posed itself to this educator. In 1857, Von Raumer published a short work called *The Education of Girls*. What he prescribes in it (p. 72) as a model behavior for adults in answering the sexual questions of their children was certainly not the only possible form of behavior at his time; nevertheless, it is highly characteristic of the standard of the nineteenth century, in the instruction of both girls and boys:

> Some mothers are of the opinion, fundamentally perverse in my view, that daughters should be given insight into all family circumstances, even into the relations of the sexes, and initiated into things that will fall to their lot in the event that they should marry. Following the example of Rousseau, this view degenerated to the coarsest and most repulsive caricature in the philanthropist of Dessau. Other mothers exaggerate in the opposite direction by telling girls things which, as soon as they grow older, must reveal themselves as totally false. As in all other cases, this is reprehensible. *These things should not be touched upon at all in the presence of children*, least of all in a secretive way which is liable to arouse curiosity. Children should be left for as long as is at all possible in the belief that an angel brings the mother her little children. This legend, customary in some regions, is far better than the story of the stork common elsewhere. Children, if they really grow up under their mother's eyes, will seldom ask forward questions on this point . . . not even if the mother is prevented by a childbirth from having them about her. . . . If girls should later ask how little children really come into the world, they should be told that the good Lord gives the mother her child, who has a guardian angel in heaven who certainly played an invisible part in bringing us this great joy. "You do not need to know nor could you understand how God gives children." Girls must be satisfied with such answers in a hundred cases, and it is the mother's task to occupy her daughters' thoughts so incessantly with the good and beautiful that they are left no time

to brood on such matters. . . . A mother . . . ought only once to say seriously: "It would not be good for you to know such a thing, and you should take care not to listen to anything said about it." A truly well-brought-up girl will from then on feel shame at hearing things of this kind spoken of.

Between the manner of speaking about sexual relations represented by Erasmus and that represented here by Von Raumer, a civilization-curve is visible similar to that shown in more detail in the expression of other impulses. In the civilizing process, sexuality too is increasingly removed behind the scenes of social life and enclosed in a particular enclave, the nuclear family. Likewise, the relations between the sexes are isolated, placed behind walls in consciousness. An aura of embarrassment, the expression of a sociogenetic fear, surrounds this sphere of life. Even among adults it is referred to officially only with caution and circumlocutions. And with children, particularly girls, such things are, as far as possible, not referred to at all. Von Raumer gives no reason why one ought not to speak of them with children. He could have said it is desirable to preserve the spiritual purity of girls for as long as possible. But even this reason is only another expression of how far the gradual submergence of these impulses in shame and embarrassment has advanced by this time. It is now as natural not to speak of these matters as it was to speak of them in Erasmus's time. And the fact that both the witnesses invoked here, Erasmus and Von Raumer, were serious Christians who took their authority from God further underlines the difference.

It is clearly not "rational" motives that underlie the model put forward by Von Raumer. Considered rationally, the problem confronting him seems unsolved, and what he says appears contradictory. He does not explain how and when the young girl should be made to understand what is happening and will happen to her. The primary concern is the necessity of instilling "modesty" (i e., feelings of shame, fear, embarrassment, and guilt) or, more precisely, behavior conforming to the social standard. And one feels how infinitely difficult it is for the educator himself to overcome the resistance of the shame and embarrassment which surround this sphere for him. One detects something of the deep confusion in which this social development has placed the individual; the only advice that the educator is able to give mothers is to avoid contact with these things wherever possible. What is involved here is not the lack of insight or the inhibition of a particular person; it is a social, not an individual problem. Only gradually, as if through insight gained retrospectively, were better methods evolved for adapting the child to the high degree of sexual restraint, to the control, transformation, and inhibition of these drives that were indispensable for life in this society.

Von Raumer himself sees in a sense that this area of life ought not to be surrounded with an aura of secrecy "which is liable to arouse curiosity." But as this has become a "secret" area in his society, he cannot escape the necessity of secrecy in his own precepts: "A mother . . . ought only once to say seriously: 'It would not be good for you to know such a thing. . . .' " Neither "rational" motives nor practical reasons primarily determine this attitude, but rather the shame of adults themselves, which has become compulsive. It is the social prohibitions and resistances within themselves, their own superego, that makes them keep silent.

For Erasmus and his contemporaries, as we have seen, the problem is not that of enlightening the child on the relations of man and woman. Children find out about this of their own accord through the kind of social institutions and social life in which they grow up. As the reserve of adults is less, so too is the discrepancy between what is permitted openly and what takes place behind the scenes. Here the chief task of the educator is to guide the child, within what he already knows, in the correct direction—or, more precisely, the direction desired by the educator. This is what Erasmus seeks to do through conversations like that of the girl with her suitor or the youth with the prostitute. And the success of the book shows that Erasmus struck the right note for many of his contemporaries.

As in the course of the civilizing process the sexual drive, like many others, is subjected to ever stricter control and transformation, the problem it poses changes. The pressure placed on adults to privatize all their impulses (particularly sexual ones), the "conspiracy of silence," the socially generated restrictions on speech, the emotionally charged character of most words relating to sexual urges—all this builds a thick wall of secrecy around the adolescent. What makes sexual enlightenment—the breaching of this wall, which will one day be necessary—so difficult is not only the need to make the adolescent conform to the same standard of instinctual restraint and control as the adult. It is, above all, the personality structure of the adults themselves that makes speaking about these secret things difficult. Very often adults have neither the tone nor the words. The "dirty" words they know are out of the question. The medical words are unfamiliar to many. Theoretical considerations in themselves do not help. It is the sociogenetic repressions in them that resist speech. Hence the advice given by Von Raumer to speak on these matters as little as possible. And this situation is further exacerbated by the fact that the tasks of conditioning and "enlightenment" fall more and more exclusively to parents. The manifold love relationships between mother, father, and child tend to increase resistance to speaking about these questions, not only on the part of the child but also on that of the father or mother.

It is clear from this how the question of childhood is to be posed. The psychological problems of growing people cannot be understood if the individual is regarded as developing uniformly in all historical epochs. The problems relating to the child's consciousness and instinctual urges vary with the nature of the relations of children to adults. These relations have in each society a specific form corresponding to the peculiarities of its structure. They are different in chivalrous society from those in urban bourgeois society; they are different in the whole secular society of the Middle Ages from those of modern times. Therefore, the problems arising from the adaptation and molding of adolescents to the standard of adults—for example, the specific problems of puberty in our civilized society—can only be understood in relation to the historical phase, the structure of society as a whole, which demands and maintains this standard of adult behavior and this special form of relationship between adults and children.

9. A civilizing process analogous to that of "sexual enlightenment" could be shown in relation to marriage and its development in Western society. That monogamous marriage is the predominant institution regulating sexual relations in the West is undoubtedly correct in general terms. Nevertheless, the actual control and molding of sexual relations changes considerably in the course of Western history. The Church certainly fought early for monogamous marriage. But marriage takes on this strict form as a social institution binding on both sexes only at a late stage, when drives and impulses come under firmer and stricter control. For only then are extramarital relationships for men really ostracized socially, or at least subjected to absolute secrecy. In earlier phases, depending on the balance of social power between the sexes, extramarital relationships for men and sometimes also for women were taken more or less for granted by secular society. Up to the sixteenth century we hear often enough that in the families of the most honorable citizens the legitimate and illegitimate children of the husband are brought up together; nor is any secret made of the difference before the children themselves. The man was not yet forced socially to feel ashamed of his extramarital relationships. Despite all the countervailing tendencies that undoubtedly already exist, it is very often taken for granted that the bastard children are a part of the family, that the father should provide for their future and, in the case of daughters, arrange an honorable wedding. But no doubt this led more than once to serious "misunderstanding"[96] between the married couples.

The situation of the illegitimate child is not always and everywhere the same throughout the Middle Ages. For a long time, nevertheless, there is no trace of the tendency toward secrecy which corresponds later, in professional-bourgeois society, to the tendency toward a stricter confinement of sexuality to the relationship of one man to one woman, to the stricter control of sexual impulses, and to the stronger pressure of social prohibitions. Here, too, the demands of the Church cannot be taken as a measure of the real standard of secular society. In reality, if not always in law, the situation of the illegitimate children in a family differed from that of the legitimate children only in that the former did not inherit the status of the father nor in general his wealth, or at least not the same part of it as the legitimate children. That people in the upper class often called themselves "bastard" expressly and proudly is well enough known.[97]

Marriage in the absolutist court societies of the seventeenth and eighteenth centuries derives its special character from the fact that, through the structure of these societies, the dominance of the husband over the wife is broken for the first time. The social power of the wife is almost equal to that of the husband. Social opinion is determined to a high degree by women. And whereas society had hitherto acknowledged only the extramarital relationships of men, regarding those of the socially "weaker sex" as more or less reprehensible, the extramarital relationships of women now appear, in keeping with the transformation of balance of social power between the sexes, as legitimate within certain limits.

It remains to be shown in more detail how decisive this first increase in power changes or, if one likes, this first wave of emancipation of women in absolutist court society was for the civilizing process, for the advance of the frontier of shame and embarrassment and for the strengthening of social control over the individual. Just as the increased power changes, the social ascent of other social groups necessitated new forms of drive control for all at a level midway between those previously imposed on the rulers and the ruled respectively, so this strengthening of the social position of women signified (to express the point schematically) a decrease in the restrictions on their drives for women and an increase in the restrictions on their drives for men. At the same time, it forced both men and women to adopt a new and a stricter self-discipline in their relations with one another.

In the famous novel *La Princesse de Clèves*, by Madame de la Fayette, the Princess's husband, who knows his wife to be in love with the Duc de Nemours, says: "I shall trust only in you; it is the path my heart counsels me to take, and also my reason. With a temperament like yours, *by leaving you your liberty I set you narrower limits* than I could enforce."[98]

This is an example of the pressure toward self-discipline imposed on the sexes by this situation. The husband knows that he cannot hold his wife by force. He does not rant or expostulate because his wife loves another, nor does he appeal to his rights as a husband. Public opinion would support none of this. He restrains himself. But in doing so he expects from her the same self-discipline as he imposes on himself. This is a very characteristic example of the new constellation that comes into being with the diminishment of social inequality between the sexes. Fundamentally, it is not the individual husband who gives his wife this freedom. It is founded in the structure of society itself. But it also demands a new kind of behavior. It produces very specific conflicts. And there are certainly enough women in this society who make use of this freedom. There is plentiful evidence that in this courtly aristocracy the restriction of sexual relationships to marriage was very often regarded as bourgeois and socially unsuitable. Nevertheless, all this gives an idea of how directly a specific kind of freedom corresponds to particular forms and stages of social interdependence among human beings.

The nondynamic linguistic forms to which we are still bound today oppose freedom and constraint like heaven and hell. From a short-term point of view, this thinking in absolute opposites is often reasonably adequate. For someone in prison the world outside the prison walls is a world of freedom. But considered more precisely, there is, contrary to what antitheses such as this one suggest, no such thing as "absolute" freedom, if this means a total independence and absence of social constraint. There is a liberation from one form of constraint that is oppressive or intolerable to another which is less burdensome. Thus the civilizing process, despite the transformation and increased constraint that it imposes on the emotions, goes hand in hand with liberations of the most diverse kinds. The form of marriage at the absolutist courts, symbolized by the same arrangement of living rooms and bedrooms for men and women in the mansions of the court aristocracy, is one of many examples of this. The woman was more free from external constraints than in feudal society. But the inner constraint which she had to impose on herself in accordance with the form of integration and the code of behavior of court society, and which stemmed from the same structural features of this society as her "liberation," had increased for women as for men in comparison to chivalrous society.

The case is similar if the bourgeois form of marriage of the nineteenth century is compared with that of the court aristocracy of the seventeenth and eighteenth centuries. In this later period the bourgeoisie as a whole is freed from the pressures of an absolutist estate society. Both bourgeois men and bourgeois women are now relieved of the external constraints to which they were subjected as second-rate people in the hierarchy of estates. But the intertwinement of trade and money, the growth of which had given them the social power to liberate themselves, has increased. In this respect, the social constraints on the individual are also stronger than before. The pattern of self-restraint imposed on the people of bourgeois society through their occupational work is in many respects different from the pattern imposed on the emotional life by the functions of court society. For many aspects of the "emotional economy", bourgeois functions—above all, business life—demand and produce greater self-restraint than courtly functions. Why the occupational work that became a general way of life with the rise of the bourgeoisie should necessitate a particularly strict disciplining of sexuality is a question in its own right. The connections between the personality structure and the social structure of the nineteenth century cannot be considered here. However, by the standard of bourgeois society, the control of sexuality and the form of marriage prevalent in court society appear extremely lax. Social opinion now severely condemns all extramarital relations between the sexes, though here, unlike the situation in court society, the social power of the husband is again greater than that of the wife, so that violation of the taboo on extramarital relationships by the husband is usually judged more leniently than the same offense by women. But both breaches must now be entirely excluded from official social life. Unlike those in court society, they must be removed strictly behind the scenes, banished to the realm of secrecy. This is only one of many examples of the increase in reserve and self-restraint which the individual now has to impose on himself.

10. The civilizing process does not follow a straight line. The general trend of change can be determined, as has been done here. On a smaller scale there are the most diverse crisscross movements, shifts and spurts in this or that direction. But if we consider the movement over large time spans, we see clearly how the compulsions arising directly from the threat of weapons and physical force gradually diminish, and how those forms of dependency which lead to the regulation of the affects in the form of self-control, gradually increase. This change appears at its most rectilinear if we observe the men of the upper class of the time—that is, the class composed first of warriors or knights, then of courtiers, and then of professional bourgeois. If the whole many-layered fabric of historical development is considered, however, the movement is seen to be infinitely more complex. In each phase there are numerous fluctuations, frequent advances or recessions of the inward and outward constraints. An observation of such fluctuations, particularly those chose to us in time, can easily obscure the general trend. One such fluctuation is present today in the memories of all: in the period following World War I, as compared to the prewar period, a "relaxation of morals" appears to have occurred. A number of constraints imposed on behavior before the war have weakened or disappeared entirely. Many things forbidden earlier are now permitted. And, seen at close quarters, the movement seems to be proceeding in the direction opposite to that shown here; it seems to lead to a relaxation of the constraints imposed on the individual by social life. But on closer examination it is not difficult to perceive that this is merely a very slight recession, one of the fluctuations that constantly arise from the complexity of the historical movement within each phase of the total process.

One example is bathing manners. It would have meant social ostracism in the nineteenth century for a woman to wear in public one of the bathing costumes commonplace today. But this change, and with it the whole spread of sports for men and women, presupposes a very high standard of drive control. Only in a society in which a high degree of restraint is taken for granted, and in which women are, like men, absolutely sure that each individual is curbed by self-control and a strict code of etiquette, can bathing and sporting customs having this relative degree of freedom develop. It is a relaxation which remains within the framework of a particular "civilized" standard of behavior involving a very high degree of automatic constraint and affect transformation, conditioned to become a habit.

At the same time, however, we also find in our own time the precursors of a shift toward the cultivation of new and stricter constraints. In a number of societies there are attempts to establish a social regulation and management of the emotions far stronger and more conscious than the standard prevalent hitherto, a pattern of molding that imposes renunciations and transformation of drives on the individual with vast consequences for human life which are scarcely foreseeable as yet.

11. Regardless, therefore, of how much the tendencies may crisscross, advance and recede, relax or tighten on a small scale, the direction of the main movement—as far as it is visible up to now—is the same for all kinds of behavior. The process of civilization of the sex drive, seen on a large scale, runs parallel to those of other drives, no matter what sociogenetic differences of detail may always be present. Here, too, measured in terms of the standards of the men of successive ruling classes, control grows ever stricter. The instinct is slowly but progressively suppressed from the public life of society. The reserve that must be exercised in speaking of it also increases.[99] And this restraint, like all others, is enforced less and less by direct physical force. It is cultivated in the individual from an early age as habitual self-restraint by the structure of social life, by the pressure of social institutions in general, and by certain executive organs of society (above all, the family) in particular. Thereby the social commands and prohibitions become increasingly a part of the self, a strictly regulated superego.

Like many other drives, sexuality is confined more and more exclusively, for both women and men, to a particular enclave, socially legitimized marriage. Social tolerance of other relationships, for both husband and wife, which was by no means lacking earlier, is suppressed increasingly, if with fluctuations. Every violation of these restrictions, and everything conducive to one, is therefore relegated to the realm of secrecy, of what may not be mentioned without loss of prestige or social position.

And just as the nuclear family only very gradually became, so exclusively, the only legitimate enclave of sexuality and of all intimate functions for men and women, so it was only at a late stage that it became the primary organ for cultivating the socially required control over impulses and behavior in young people. Before this degree of restraint and intimacy was reached, and until the separation of instinctual life from public view was strictly enforced, the task of early conditioning did not fall so heavily on father and mother. All the people with whom the child came into contact—and when intimization was less advanced and the interior of the house less isolated, they were often quite numerous—played a part. In addition, the family itself was usually larger and—in the upper classes—the servants more numerous in earlier times. People in general spoke more openly about the various aspects of instinctual life, and gave way more freely to their own impulses in speech and act. The shame associated with sexuality was less. This is what makes Erasmus's educational work quoted above so difficult for pedagogues of a later phase to understand. And so conditioning, the reproduction of social habits in the child, did not take place so exclusively behind closed doors, as it were, but far more directly in the presence of other people. A by no means untypical picture of this kind of conditioning in the upper class can be found, for example, in the diary of the doctor Jean

Héroard, which records day by day and almost hour by hour the childhood of Louis XIII, what he did and said as he grew up.

It is not without a touch of paradox that the greater the transformation, control, restraint, and concealment of drives and impulses that is demanded of the individual by society, and therefore the more difficult the conditioning of the young becomes, the more the task of first instilling socially required habits is concentrated within the nuclear family, on the father and mother. The mechanism of conditioning, however, is still scarcely different than in earlier times. For it does not involve a closer supervision of the task, or more exact planning that takes account of the special circumstances of the child, but is effected primarily by automatic means and to some extent through reflexes. The socially patterned constellation of habits and impulses of the parents gives rise to a constellation of habits and impulses in the child; these may operate either in the same direction or in one entirely different from that desired or expected by the parents on the basis of their own conditioning. The interrelation of the habits of parents and children, through which the instinctive life of the child is slowly molded, is thus determined by nothing less than by "reason." Behavior and words associated by the parent with shame and repugnance are very soon associated in the same way by the children, through the parents' expressions of displeasure, their more or less gentle pressure; in this way the social standard of shame and repugnance is gradually reproduced in the children. But such a standard forms at the same time the basis and framework of the most diverse individual drive formations. How the growing personality is fashioned in particular cases by this incessant social interaction between the parents' and children's feelings, habits, and reactions is at present largely unforeseeable and incalculable to parents.

12. The tendency of the civilizing process to make all bodily functions more intimate, to enclose them in particular enclaves, to put them "behind closed doors," has diverse consequences. One of the most important, which has already been observed in connection with various other forms of drives, is seen particularly clearly in the case of the development of civilizing restraints on sexuality. It is the peculiar division in man which becomes more pronounced the more sharply those aspects of human life that may be displayed in social life are divided from those that may not, and which must remain "intimate" or "secret." Sexuality, like all the other natural human functions, is a phenomenon known to everyone and a part of each human life. We have seen how all these functions are gradually charged with sociogenetic shame and embarrassment, so that the mere mention of them in society is increasingly restricted by a multitude of controls and prohibitions. More and more, people keep the functions themselves, and all reminders of them, concealed from one another. Where this is not possible—as in marriage, for example—shame, embarrassment, fear, and all the other emotions associated with these driving forces of human life are mastered by a precisely

regulated social ritual and by certain concealing formulas that preserve the standard of shame. In other words, with the advance of civilization the lives of human beings are increasingly split between an intimate and a public sphere, between secret and public behavior. And this split is taken so much for granted, becomes so compulsive a habit, that it is hardly perceived in consciousness.

In conjunction with this growing division of behavior into what is and what is not publicly permitted, the personality structure is also transformed. The prohibitions supported by social sanctions are reproduced in the individual as self-controls. The pressure to restrain his impulses and the sociogenetic shame surrounding them—these are turned so completely into habits that we cannot resist them even when alone, in the intimate sphere. Pleasure promising drives and pleasure denying taboos and prohibitions, socially generated feelings of shame and repugnance, come to battle within him. This, as has been mentioned, is clearly the state of affairs which Freud tries to express by concepts such as the "superego" and the "unconscious" or, as it is not unfruitfully called in everyday speech, the "subconscious." But however it is expressed, the social code of conduct so imprints itself in one form or another on the human being that it becomes a constituent element of his individual self. And this element, the superego, like the personality structure of the individual as a whole, necessarily changes constantly with the social code of behavior and the structure of society. The pronounced division in the "ego" or consciousness characteristic of man in our phase of civilization, which finds expression in such terms as "superego" and "unconscious," corresponds to the specific split in the behavior which civilized society demands of its members. It matches the degree of regulation and restraint imposed on the expression of drives and impulses. Tendencies in this direction may develop in any form of human society, even in those which we call "primitive." But the strength attained in societies such as ours by this differentiation and the form in which it appears are reflections of a particular historical development, the results of a civilizing process.

This is what is meant when we refer here to the continuous correspondence between the social structure and the structure of the personality, of the individual self.

X

On Changes in Aggressiveness

The affect structure of man is a whole. We may call particular instincts by different names according to their different directions and functions, we may speak of hunger and the need to spit, of the sexual drive and of aggressive impulses, but in life these different instincts are no more separable than the heart from the stomach or the blood in the brain from the blood in the genitalia. They complement and in part supersede each other, transform themselves within certain limits and compensate for each other; a disturbance here manifests itself there. In short, they form a kind of circuit in the human being, a partial system within the total system of the organism. Their structure is still opaque in many respects, but their socially imprinted form is of decisive importance for the functioning of a society as of the individuals within it.

The manner in which impulses or emotional manifestations are spoken of today sometimes leads one to surmise that we have within us a whole bundle of different drives. A "death instinct" or a "self-assertive drive" are referred to as if they were different chemical substances. This is not to deny that observations of these different instincts in the individual may be extremely fruitful and instructive. But the categories by which these observations are classified must remain powerless in the face of their living objects if they fail to express the unity and totality of instinctual life, and the connection of each particular instinctual tendency to this totality. Accordingly, aggressiveness, which will be the subject of this chapter, is not a separable species of instinct. At most, one may speak of the "aggressive impulse" only if one remains aware that it refers to a particular instinctual function within the totality of an organism, and that changes in this function indicate changes in the personality structure as a whole.

1. The standard of aggressiveness, its tone and intensity, is not at present exactly uniform among the different nations of the West. But these differences, which from close up often appear quite considerable, disappear if the aggressiveness of the "civilized" nations is compared to that of societies at a different stage of affect control. Compared to the battle fury of Abyssinian warriors—admittedly powerless against the technical apparatus of the civilized army—or to the frenzy of the different tribes at the time of the Great Migrations, the aggressiveness of even the most warlike nations of the civilized world appears subdued. Like all other instincts, it is bound, even in directly warlike actions, by the advanced state of the division of functions, and by the resulting greater dependence of individuals on each other and on the technical apparatus. It is confined and tamed by innumerable rules and prohibitions that have become self-constraints. It is as much transformed, "refined," "civilized," as all the other forms of pleasure, and its immediate and uncontrolled violence appears only in dreams or in isolated outbursts that we account for as pathological.

In this area of the affects, the theater of the hostile collisions between men, the same historical transformations has taken place as in all others. No matter at what point the Middle Ages stand in this transformation, it will again suffice here to take the standard of their secular ruling class, the warriors, as a starting point, to illustrate the overall pattern of this development. The release of the affects in battle in the Middle Ages was no longer, perhaps, quite so uninhibited as in the early period of the Great Migrations. But it was open and uninhabited enough compared to the standard of modern times. In the latter, cruelty and joy in the destruction and torment of others, like the proof of physical superiority, are placed under an increasingly strong social control anchored in the state organization. All these forms of pleasure, limited by threats of displeasure, gradually come to express themselves only indirectly, in a "refined" form. And only at times of social upheaval or where social control is looser (e.g., in colonial regions) do they break out more directly, uninhibitedly, less impeded by shame and repugnance.

2. Life in medieval society tended in the opposite direction. Rapine, battle, hunting of men and animals—all these were vital necessities which, in accordance with the structure of society, were visible to all. And thus, for the mighty and strong, they formed part of the pleasures of life.

"I tell you," says a war hymn attributed to the minstrel Bertran de Born,[100] "that neither eating, drinking, nor sleep has as much savor for me as to hear the cry 'Forwards!' from both sides, and horses without riders shying and whinnying, and the cry 'Help! Help!', and to see the small and the great fall to the grass at the ditches and the dead pierced by the wood of the lances decked with banners."

Even the literary formulation gives an impression of the original savagery of feeling. In another place Bertran de Born sings: "The pleasant season is drawing nigh when our ships shall land, when King Richard shall come, merry and proud as he never was before. Now we shall see gold and silver spent; the newly built stonework will crack to the heart's desire, walls crumble, towers topple and collapse, our enemies taste prison and chains. I love the melee of blue and vermilion shields, the many-colored ensigns and the banners, the tents and rich pavilions spread out on the plain, the breaking lances, the pierced shields, the gleaming helmets that are split, the blows given and received."

War, one of the *chansons de geste* declares, is to descend as the stronger on the enemy, to hack down his vines, uproot his trees, lay waste his land, take his castles by storm, fill in his wells, and kill his people. . . .

A particular pleasure is taken in mutilating prisoners: "By my troth," says the king in the same *chanson*, "I laugh at what you say, I care not a fig for your threats, I shall shame every knight I have taken, cut off his nose or his ears. If he is a sergeant or a merchant he will lose a foot or an arm."[101]

Such things are not only said in song. These epics are an integral part of social life. And they express the feelings of the listeners for whom they are intended far more directly than most of our literature. They may exaggerate in detail. Even in the age of chivalry money already had, on occasions, some power to subdue and transform the affects. Usually only the poor and lowly, for whom no considerable ransom could be expected, were mutilated, and the knights who commanded ransoms were spared. The chronicles which directly document social life bear ample witness to these attitudes.

They were mostly written by clerics. The value judgments they contain are therefore often those of the weaker group threatened by the warrior class. Nevertheless, the picture they transmit to us is quite genuine. "He spends his life," we read of a knight, "in plundering, destroying churches, falling upon pilgrims, oppressing widows and orphans. He takes particular pleasure in mutilating the innocent. In a single monastery, that of the black monks of Sarlat, there are 150 men and women whose hands he has cut off or whose eyes he has put out. And his wife is just as cruel. She helps him with his executions. It even gives her pleasure to torture the poor women. She had their breasts hacked off or their nails torn off so that they were incapable of work."[102]

Such affective outbursts may still occur as exceptional phenomena, as a "pathological" degeneration, in later phases of social development. But here no punitive social power existed. The only threat, the only danger that could instill fear was that of being overpowered in battle by a stronger opponent. Leaving aside a small elite, rapine, pillage, and murder were standard practice in the warrior society of this time, as is noted by Luchaire, the historian of thirteenth-century French society. There is little evidence that things were different in other countries or in the centuries that followed. Outbursts of cruelty did not exclude one from social life. They were not outlawed. The pleasure in killing and torturing others was great, and it was a socially permitted pleasure. To a certain extent, the social structure even pushed its members in this direction, making it seem necessary and practically advantageous to behave in this way.

What, for example, ought to be done with prisoners? There was little money in this society. With regard to prisoners who could pay and who, moreover, were members of one's own class, one exercised some degree of restraint. But the others? To keep them meant to feed them. To return them meant to enhance the wealth and fighting power of the enemy. For subjects (i.e., working, serving, and fighting hands) were a part of the wealth of the ruling class of that time. So prisoners were killed or sent back so mutilated that they were unfitted for war service and work. The same applied to destroying fields, filling in wells, and cutting down trees. In a predominantly agrarian society, in which immobile possessions represented the major part of property, this too served to weaken the enemy. The stronger affectivity of behavior was to a certain degree socially necessary. People behaved in a socially useful way and took pleasure in doing so. And it is entirely in keeping with the lesser degree of social control and constraint of instinctual life that this joy in destruction could sometimes give way, through a sudden identification with the victim, and doubtless also as an expression of the fear and guilt produced by the permanent precariousness of this life; to extremes of pity. The victor of today was defeated tomorrow by some accident, captured, and imperiled. In the midst of this perpetual rising and falling, this alternation of the human hunts of wartime with the animal hunts or tournaments that were the diversions of "peacetime," little could be predicted. The future was relatively uncertain even for those who had fled the "world"; only God and the loyalty of a few people who held together had any permanence. Fear reigned everywhere; one had to be on one's guard all the time. And just as people's fate could change abruptly, so their joy could turn into fear and this fear, in its turn, could give way, equally abruptly, to submission to some new pleasure.

The majority of the secular ruling class of the Middle Ages led the life of leaders of armed bands. This formed the taste and habits of individuals. Reports left to us by that society yield, by and large, a picture similar to those of feudal societies in our own times; and they show a comparable standard of behavior. Only a small elite, of which more will be said later, stood out to some extent from this norm.

The warrior of the Middle Ages not only loved battle, he lived in it. He spent his youth preparing for battle. When he came of age he was knighted, and waged war as long as his strength permitted, into old age. His life had no other function. His dwelling place was a watchtower, a fortress, at once a weapon of attack and defense. If by accident, by exception, he lived in peace, he needed at least the illusion of war. He fought in tournaments, and these tournaments often differed little from real battles. [103]

"For the society of that time war was the normal state," says Luchaire of the thirteenth century. And Huizinga says of the fourteenth and fifteenth centuries: "The chronic form which war was wont to take, the continuous disruption of town and country by every kind of dangerous rabble, the permanent threat of harsh and unreliable law enforcement . . . nourished a feeling of universal uncertainty." [104]

In the fifteenth century, as in the ninth or thirteenth, the knight still gives expression to his joy in war, even if it is no longer so open and intact as earlier.

"War is a joyous thing." [105] It is Jean de Bueil who says this. He has fallen into disfavor with the king. And now he dictates to his servant his life story. This is in the year 1465. It is no longer the completely free, independent knight who speaks, the little king in his domain. It is someone who is himself in service: "War is a joyous thing. We love each other so much in war. If we see that our cause is just and our kinsmen fight boldly, tears come to our eyes. A sweet joy rises in our hearts, in the feeling of our honest loyalty to each other; and seeing our friend so bravely exposing his body to danger in order to keep and fulfill the commandment of our Creator, we resolve to go forward and die or live with him and never leave him on account of love. This brings such delight that anyone who has not felt it cannot say how wonderful it is. Do you think that someone who feels this is afraid of death? Not in the least! He is so strengthened, so delighted, that he does not know where he is. Truly he fears nothing in the world!"

This is the joy of battle, certainly, but it is no longer the direct pleasure in the human hunt, in the flashing of swords, in the neighing of steeds, in the fear and death of the enemy—how fine it is to hear them cry "Help, help!" or see them lying with their bodies torn open![106] Now the pleasure lies in the closeness to one's friends, the enthusiasm for a just cause, and more than earlier we find the joy of battle serving as an intoxicant to overcome fear.

Very simple and powerful feelings speak here. One kills, gives oneself up wholly to the fight, sees one's friend fight. One fights at his side. One forgets where one is. One forgets death itself. It is splendid. What more?

3. There is abundant evidence that the attitude toward life and death in the secular upper class of the Middle Ages by no means always accords with the attitude prevalent in the books of the ecclesiastical upper class, which we usually consider "typical" of the Middle Ages. For the clerical upper class, or at least for its spokesmen, the conduct of life is determined by the thought of death and of what comes after, the next world.

In the secular upper class this is by no means so exclusively the case. However frequent moods and phases of this kind may be in the life of every knight, there is recurrent evidence of a quite different attitude. Again and again we hear an admonition that does not quite accord with the standard picture of the Middle Ages today: do not let your life be governed by the thought of death. Love the joys of this life.

"Nul courtois ne doit blâmer joie, mais toujours joie aimer." (No *courtois* man should revile joy, he should love joy.)[107] This is a command of *courtoisie* from a romance of the early thirteenth century. Or from a rather later period: "A young man should be gay and lead a joyous life. It does not befit a young man to be mournful and pensive."[108] In these statements the chivalrous people, who certainly did not need to be "pensive," clearly contrast themselves to the clerics, who no doubt were frequently "mournful and pensive."

This far from life-denying attitude is expressed particularly earnestly and explicitly with regard to death in some verses in the *Distiche Catonis*, which were passed from generation to generation throughout the Middle Ages. That life is uncertain is one of the fundamental themes which recur in these verses:[109]

To us all a hard uncertain life is given.

But this does not lead to the conclusion that one should think of death and what comes afterward, but rather:

If you fear death you will live in misery.

Or in another place, expressed with particular clarity and beauty:[110]

We well know that death shall come
and our future is unknown:
stealthy as a thief he comes,
and body and soul he does part.

So be of trust and confidence:
be not too much afraid of death,
for if you fear him overmuch
joy you nevermore shall touch.

Nothing of the next life. He who allows his life to be determined by thoughts of death no longer has joy in life. Certainly, the knights felt themselves strongly to be Christians, and their lives were permeated by the traditional ideas and rituals of the Christian faith; but Christianity was linked in their minds, in accordance with their different social and psychological situation, with an entirely different scale of values from that existing in the minds of the clerics who wrote and read books. Their faith had a markedly different tenor and tone. It did not prevent them from savoring to the full the joys of the world; it did not hinder them from killing and plundering. This was part of their social function, an attribute of their class, a source of pride. Not to fear death was a vital necessity for the knight. He had to fight. The structure and tensions of this society made this an inescapable condition for the individual.

4. But in medieval society this permanent readiness to fight, weapon in hand, was a vital necessity not only for the warriors, the knightly upper class. The life of the burghers in the towns was characterized by greater and lesser feuds to a far higher degree than in later times; here, too, belligerence, hatred, and joy in tormenting others were more uninhibited than in the subsequent phase.

With the slow rise of a Third Estate, the tensions in medieval society were increased. And it was not only the weapon of money that carried the burgher upward. Robbery, fighting, pillage, family feuds—all this played a hardly less important role in the life of the town population than in that of the warrior class itself.

There is—to take one example—the fate of Mathieu d'Escouchy. He is a Picard, and one of the numerous men of the fifteenth century who wrote a "Chronicle."[111] From this "Chronicle" we would suppose him to be a modest man of letters who devoted his time to meticulous historical work. But if we try to find out something of his life from the documents, a totally different picture emerges.[112]

Mathieu d'Escouchy begins his career as magistrate as a councillor, juror, and mayor (prévot) of the town of Péronne between 1440 and 1450. From the beginning we find him in a kind of feud with the family of the procurator of the town, Jean Froment, a feud that is fought out in lawsuits. First it is the procurator who accuses d'Escouchy of forgery and murder, or of "excès et attemptaz." The mayor for his part threatens the widow of his enemy with investigation for magical practices. The woman obtains a mandate compelling d'Escouchy to place the investigation in the hands of the judiciary. The affair comes before the parliament in Paris, and d'Escouchy goes to prison for the first time. We find him under arrest six times subsequently, partly as defendant and once as a prisoner of war. Each time there is a serious criminal case, and more than once he sits in heavy chains. The contest of reciprocal accusations between the Froment and d'Escouchy families is interrupted by a violent clash in which Froment's son wounds d'Escouchy. Both engage cutthroats to take each other's lives. When this lengthy feud passes from our view, it is replaced by new attacks. This time the mayor is wounded by a monk. New accusations, then in 1461 d'Escouchy's removal to Nesle, apparently under suspicion of criminal acts. Yet this does not prevent him from having a successful career. He becomes a bailiff, mayor of Ribemont, procurator to the king at Saint Quintin, and is raised to the nobility. After new woundings, incarcerations, and expiation we find him in war service. He is made a prisoner of war; from a later campaign he returns home crippled. Then he marries, but this does not mean the beginning of a quiet life. We find him transported as a prisoner to Paris "like a criminal and murderer," accused of forging seals, again in feud with a magistrate in Compiègne, brought to an admission of his guilt by torture and denied promotion, condemned, rehabilitated, condemned once again, until the trace of his existence vanishes from the documents.

This is one of innumerable examples. The well-known miniatures from the "book of hours" of the Duc de Berry[113] are another. "People long believed," says its editor, "and some are still convinced today, that the miniatures of the fifteenth century are the work of earnest monks or pious nuns working in the peace of their monasteries. That is possible in certain cases. But, generally speaking, the situation was quite different. It was worldly people, master craftsmen, who executed these beautiful works, and the life of these secular artists was very far from being edifying." We hear repeatedly of actions which by the present standards of society would be branded as criminal and made socially "impossible." For example, the painters accuse each other of theft; then one of them, with his kinsmen, stabs the other to death in the street. And the Duc de Berry, who needs the murderer, must request an amnesty, a *lettre de rémission* for him. Yet another abducts an eight-year-old girl in order to marry her, naturally against the will of her parents. These *lettres de rémission* show us such bloody feuds taking place everywhere, often lasting for many years, and sometimes leading to regular battles in public places. And this applies to knights as much to merchants or craftsmen. As in all other countries with related social forms—for example, Ethiopia or Afghanistan today—the noble has bands of followers who are ready for anything. ". . . During the day he is constantly accompanied by servants and arms bearers in pursuit of his 'feuds.'. . . The *roturiers*, the citizens, cannot afford this luxury, but they have their 'relatives and friends' who come to their help, often in great numbers, equipped with every kind of awesome weapon that the local *coutumes*, the civic ordinances, prohibit in vain. And these burghers, too, when they have to avenge themselves, are *de guerre*, in a state of feud."[114]

The civic authorities sought in vain to pacify these family feuds. The magistrates call people before them, order a cessation of strife, issue commands and decrees. For a time, all is well; then a new feud breaks out, an old one is rekindled. Two *associés* fall out over business; they quarrel, the conflict grows violent; one day they meet in a public place and one of them strikes the other dead.[115] An innkeeper accuses another of stealing his clients; they become mortal enemies. Someone says a few malicious words about another; a family war develops.

Not only among the nobility were there family vengeance, private feuds, vendettas. The fifteenth-century towns are no less rife with wars between families and cliques. The little people, to—the hatters, the tailors, the shepherds—were all quick to draw their knives. "It is well known how violent manners were in the fifteenth century, with what brutality passions were assuaged, despite the fear of hell, despite the restraints of class distinctions and the chivalrous sentiment of honor, *despite the bonhomie and gaiety of social relations.*"[116]

Not that people were always going around with fierce looks, drawn brows, and martial countenances as the clearly visible symbols of their warlike prowess. On the contrary, a moment ago they were joking, now they mock each other, one word leads to another, and suddenly from the midst of laughter they find themselves in the fiercest feud. Much of what appears contradictory to us—the intensity of their piety, the violence of their fear of hell, their guilt feelings, their penitence, the immense outbursts of joy and gaiety, the sudden flaring and the uncontrollable force of their hatred and belligerence—all these, like the rapid changes of mood, are in reality symptoms of the same social and personality structure. The instincts, the emotions were vented more freely, more directly, more openly than later. It is only to us, in whom everything is more subdued, moderate, and calculated, and in whom social taboos are built much more deeply into the fabric of instinctual life as self-restraints, that this unveiled intensity of piety, belligerence, or cruelty appears as contradictory. Religion, the belief in the punishing or rewarding omnipotence of God, never has in itself a "civilizing" or affect-subduing effect. On the contrary, religion is always exactly as "civilized" as the society or class which upholds it. And because emotions are here expressed in a manner that in our own world is generally observed only in children, we call these expressions and forms of behavior "childish."

Wherever one opens the documents of this time, one finds the same: a life where the structure of affects was different from our own, an existence without security, with only minimal thought for the future. Whoever did not love or hate to the utmost in this society, whoever could not stand his ground in the play of passions, could go into a monastery; in worldly life he was just as lost as was, conversely, in later society, and particularly at court, the man who could not curb his passions, could not conceal and "civilize" his affects.

5. In both cases it is the structure of society that demands and generates a specific standard of emotional control. "We," says Luchaire, "with our peaceful

manners and habits, with the care and protection that the modern state lavishes on the property and person of each individual," can scarcely form an idea of this other society.

> At that time the country had disintegrated into provinces, and the inhabitants of each province formed a kind of little nation that abhorred all the others. The provinces were in turn divided into a multitude of feudal estates whose owners fought each other incessantly. Not only the great lords, the barons, but also the smaller lords of the manor lived in desolate isolation and were uninterruptedly occupied in waging war against their "sovereigns," their equals, or their subjects. In addition, there was constant rivalry between town and town, village and village, valley and valley, and constant wars between neighbors that seemed to arise from the very multiplicity of these territorial units.[117]

This description helps to see more precisely something which so far has been stated mainly in general terms, namely, the connection between social structure and personality structure. In this society there is no central power strong enough to compel people to restraint. But if in this or that region the power of a central authority grows, if over a larger or smaller area the people are forced to live in peace with each other, the molding of affects and the standards of the economy of instincts are very gradually changed as well. As will be discussed in more detail later, the reserve and "mutual consideration" of people increase, first in normal everyday social life. And the discharge of affects in physical attack is limited to certain temporal and spatial enclaves. Once the monopoly of physical power has passed to central authorities, not every strong man can afford the pleasure of physical attack. This is now reserved to those few legitimized by the central authority (e g., the police against the criminal), and to larger numbers only in exceptional times of war or revolution, in the socially legitimized struggle against internal or external enemies.

But even these temporal or spatial enclaves within civilized society in which belligerence is allowed freer play—above all, wars between nations—have become more impersonal, and lead less and less to an affective discharge having the immediacy and intensity of the medieval phase. The necessary restraint and transformation of aggression cultivated in the everyday life of civilized society cannot be simply reversed, even in these enclaves. All the same, this could happen more quickly than we might suppose, had not the direct physical combat between a man and his hated adversary given way to a mechanized struggle demanding a strict control of the affects. Even in war in the civilized world, the individual can no longer give free rein to his pleasure, spurred on by the sight of the enemy, but must fight, no matter how he may feel, according to the commands of invisible or only indirectly visible leaders, against a frequently invisible or only indirectly visible enemy. And immense social upheaval and urgency, heightened by carefully concerted propaganda, are needed to reawaken and legitimize in large masses of people the socially outlawed instincts, the joy in killing and destruction that have been repressed from everyday civilized life.

6. Admittedly, these affects do have, in a "refined," rationalized form, their legitimate and exactly defined place in the everyday life of civilized society. And this is very characteristic of the kind of transformation through which the civilization of the affects takes place. For example, belligerence and aggression find socially permitted expression in sporting contests. And they are expressed especially in "spectating" (e.g., at boxing matches), in the imaginary identification with a small number of combatants to whom moderate and precisely regulated scope is granted for the release of such affects. And this living-out of affects in spectating or even in merely listening (e.g., to a radio commentary) is a particularly characteristic feature of civilized society. It partly determines the development of books and the theater, and decisively influences the role of the cinema in our world. This transformation of what manifested itself originally as an active, often aggressive expression of pleasure, into the passive, more ordered pleasure of spectating (i e., a mere pleasure of the eye) is already initiated in education, in conditioning precepts for young people.

In the 1774 edition of La Salle's *Civilité*, for example, we read (p. 23): "Children like to touch clothes and other things that please them with their hands. This urge must be corrected, and they must be taught to touch all they see only with their eyes."

By now this precept is taken almost for granted. It is highly characteristic of civilized man that he is denied by socially instilled self-control from spontaneously touching what he desires, loves, or hates. The whole molding of his gestures—no matter how its pattern may differ among Western nations with regard to particulars—is decisively influenced by this necessity. It has been shown elsewhere how the use of the sense of smell, the tendency to sniff at food or other things, comes to be restricted as something animal-like. Here we see one of the interconnections through which a different sense organ, the eye, takes on a very specific significance in civilized society. In a similar way to the ear, and perhaps even more so, it becomes a mediator of pleasure, precisely because the direct satisfaction of the desire for pleasure has been hemmed in by a multitude of barriers and prohibitions.

But even within this transfer of emotions from direct action to spectating, there is a distinct curve of moderation and "humanization" in the transformation of affects. The boxing match, to mention only one example, represents a strongly tempered form of the impulses of aggressiveness and cruelty, compared with the visual pleasures of earlier stages.

An example from the sixteenth century may serve as an illustration. It has been chosen from a multitude of others because it shows an institution in which the visual satisfaction of the urge to cruelty, the joy in watching pain inflicted, emerges particularly purely, without any rational justification and disguise as punishment or means of discipline.

In Paris during the sixteenth century it was one of the festive pleasures of Midsummer Day to burn alive one or two dozen cats. This ceremony was very famous. The populace assembled. Solemn music was played. Under a kind of scaffold an enormous pyre was erected. Then a sack or basket containing the cats was hung from the scaffold. The sack or basket began to smolder. The cats fell into the fire and were burned to death, while the crowd reveled in their caterwauling. Usually the king and queen were present. Sometimes the king or the dauphin was given the honor of lighting the pyre. And we hear that once, at the special request of King Charles IX, a fox was caught and burned as well.[118]

Certainly, this is not really a worse spectacle than the burning of heretics, or the torturings and public executions of every kind. It only appears worse because the joy in torturing living creatures shows itself so nakedly and purposelessly, without any excuse before reason. The revulsion aroused in us by the mere report of the institution, a reaction which must be taken as "normal" for the present-day standard of affect control, demonstrates once again the long term change of personality structure. At the same time, it enables us to see one aspect of this change particularly clearly: much of what earlier aroused pleasure arouses displeasure today. Now, as then, it is not merely individual feelings that are involved. The cat-burning on Midsummer Day was a social institution, like boxing or horse-racing in present-day society. And in both cases the amusements created by society for itself, are embodiments of a social standard of affects within the framework of which all individual patterns of affect regulation, however varied they may be, are contained; anyone who steps outside the bounds of this social standard is considered "abnormal." Thus, someone who wished to gratify his pleasure in the manner of the sixteenth century by burning cats would be seen today as "abnormal," simply because normal conditioning in our stage of civilization restrains the expression of pleasure in such actions through anxiety instilled in the form of self-control. Here, obviously, the same psychological mechanism is at work on the basis of which the long term change of personality structure has taken place: socially undesirable expressions of instinct and pleasure are threatened and punished with measures that generate and reinforce displeasure and anxiety. In the constant recurrence of displeasure aroused by threats, and in the habituation to this rhythm, the dominant displeasure is compulsorily associated even with behavior which at root may be pleasurable. In this manner, socially aroused displeasure and anxiety—nowadays represented, though by no means always and by no means solely, by the parents—fight with hidden desires. What has been shown here from different angles as an advance in the frontiers of shame, in the threshold of repugnance, in the standards of affect, has probably been set in motion by mechanisms such as these.

It remains to be considered in more detail what change in the social structure actually triggered these psychological mechanisms, what change in external compulsions set in motion this "civilization" of affects and behavior.

XI

Scenes from the Life of a Knight

The question why men's behavior and emotions change is really the same as the question why their forms of life change. In medieval society certain forms of life had been developed, and the individual was bound to live within them, as knight, craftsman, or bondsman. In more recent society different opportunities, different forms of life were prescribed, to which the individual had to adapt. If he was of the nobility he could lead the life of a courtier. But he could no longer, even if he so desired (and many did), lead the less constrained life of a knight. From a particular time on, this function, this way of life was no longer present in the structure of society. Other functions, such as those of the guild craftsmen and the priest, which played an extraordinary part in the medieval phase, largely lost their significance in the total structure of social relations. Why do these functions and forms of life, to which the individual must adapt himself as to more or less fixed molds, change in the course of history? As has been mentioned, this is really the same question as why feelings and emotions, the structure of drives and impulses, and everything connected with them change.

A good deal has been said here on the emotional standards of the medieval upper class. To complement this, and at the same time to provide a link with the question of the causes of the change these standards underwent, we shall now add a short impression of the way in which knights lived, and thus of "social space" which society opened to individuals of noble birth, and within which it also confined them. The picture of this "social space," the image of the knight in general, became clouded in obscurity quite soon after what is called their "decline." Whether the medieval warrior was seen as the "noble knight" (only the grand, beautiful, adventurous, and moving aspects of his life being remembered) or as the "feudal lord," the oppressor of peasants (only the savage, cruel, barbaric aspects of his life being emphasized), the simple picture of the actual life of this class was usually distorted by values and nostalgia from the period of the observer. A few drawings, or at least descriptions of them, may help to restore this picture. Apart from a few writings, the works of sculptors and painters of the period convey particularly strongly the special quality of its atmosphere or, as we may call it, its emotional character, and the way it differs from our own, though only a few works reflect the life of a knight in its real context. One of the few picture books of this kind, admittedly from a relatively late period, between 1475 and 1480, is the sequence of drawings that became known under the not very appropriate title *Medieval House-Book*. The name of the artist who drew them is unknown, but he must have been very familiar with the knightly life of his time; moreover, unlike many of his fellow craftsmen, he must have seen the world with the eyes of a knight and largely identified with their social values. A not insignificant indication of this is his depiction on one sheet of a man of his own craft as the only craftsmen in courtly dress, as is the girl behind him, who places her arm on his shoulder and for whom he clearly expresses his sentiments. Perhaps it is a self-portrait.[119]

These drawings are from the late period of chivalry, the time of Charles the Bold and Maximilian, the last knight. We may conclude from the coats of arms that these two, or knights close to them, are themselves represented in one or another of the pictures. "There is no doubt," it has been said, "that we have . . . Charles the Bold himself or a Burgundian knight from his entourage before us."[120] Perhaps a number of the pictures of tournaments directly depict the jousting following the Feud of Neuss (1475), at the betrothal of Maximilian to Charles the Bold's daughter, Marie of Burgundy. At any rate, those we see before us are already people of the transitional age in which the knightly aristocracy is being gradually replaced by a courtly one. And a good deal that is reminiscent of the courtier is also present in these pictures. Nevertheless, they give, on the whole, a very good idea of the social space of a knight, of how he fills his days, of what he saw around him and how he saw it.

What do we see? Nearly always open country, hardly anything recalling the town. Small villages, fields, trees, meadows, hills, short stretches of river and, frequently, the castle. But there is nothing in these pictures of the nostalgic mood, the "sentimental" attitude to "nature" that slowly becomes perceptible not very long afterward, as the leading nobles have to forgo more and more frequently the relatively unbridled life at their ancestral seats, and are bound increasingly tightly to the semiurban court and to dependence on kings or princes. This is one of the most important differences in emotional tone these pictures convey. In later periods the artist's consciousness sifts the material available to him in a very strict and specific way which directly expresses his taste or, more precisely, his affective structure. "Nature," the open country, shown first of all as merely a background to human figures, takes on a nostalgic glow, as the confinement of the upper class to the towns and courts increases and the rift between town and country life grows more perceptible. Or nature takes on, like the human figures it surrounds in the picture, a sublime, representative character. At any rate, there is a change in the *selection by feeling*, in what appeals to feeling in the representation of nature, and in what is felt as unpleasant or painful. And the same is true of the people depicted. For the public in the absolute court, much that really exists in the country, in "nature," is no longer portrayed. The hill is shown, but not the gallows on it, nor the corpse hanging from the gallows. The field is shown, but no longer the ragged peasant laboriously driving his horses. Just as everything "common" or "vulgar" disappears from courtly language, so it vanishes also from the pictures and drawings intended for the courtly upper class.

In the drawings of the *House-Book*, which give an idea of the structure of feeling of the late medieval upper class, this is not so. Here, all these things—gallows, ragged servants, laboring peasants—are to be seen in drawings as in real life. They are not emphasized in a spirit of protest, in the manner of later times, but shown as something very matter-of-fact, part of one's daily surroundings, like the stork's nest or the church tower. One is no more painful in life than the other, and so is not more painful in the picture. On the contrary, as everywhere in the Middle Ages, it is an inseparable part of the existence of the rich and noble that there also exist peasants and craftsmen working for them, and beggars and cripples with open hands. There is no threat to the noble in this, nor does he identify in any way with them; the spectacle evokes no painful feeling. And often enough the yokel and peasant are even the objects of pleasantries.

The pictures reveal the same attitude. First there is a sequence of drawings showing people under particular constellations. They are not grouped directly around the knight, but they make clear how and what he sees around him. Then comes a series of pages showing how a knight spends his life, his occupations and his pleasures. Measured by later times, they all bear witness to the same standard of repugnance and the same social attitudes.

At the beginning, for example, we see people born under Saturn. In the foreground a poor fellow is disemboweling a dead horse or perhaps cutting off the usable meat. His trousers have slipped down somewhat as he bends; part of his posterior is visible, and a pig behind him is sniffing at it. A frail old woman, half in rags, limps by supported on a crutch. In a small cave beside the road sits a wretch with his hands and feet in the stocks, and beside him a woman with one hand in the stocks, the other in fetters. A farm worker is toiling at a watercourse that vanishes between trees and hills. In the distance we see the farmer and his young son laboriously plowing the hilly field with a horse. Still further back a man in rags is led to the gallows, an armed man with a feather in his cap marching proudly beside him; at his other side a monk in his cowl holds out a large crucifix to him. Behind him ride the knight and two of his men. On the top of the hill stands the gallows with a body hanging from it, and the wheel with a corpse on it. Dark birds fly around; one of them pecks at the corpse.

The gallows is not in the least emphasized. It is there like the stream or a tree; and it is seen in just the same way when the knight goes hunting. A whole company rides past, the lord and lady often on the same horse. The deer vanish into a little wood; a stag seems to be wounded. Further in the background one sees a little village or perhaps the yard of a household—well, mill wheel, windmill, a few buildings. The farmer is seen plowing a field; he looks round at the deer, which are just running across his field. High up to one side is the castle; on the other, smaller hill opposite, wheel and gallows with a body, and birds circling.

The gallows, the symbol of the knight's judicial power, is part of the background of his life. It may not be very important, but at any rate, it is not a particularly painful sight. Sentence, execution, death—all these are immediately present in this life. They, too, have not yet been removed behind the scenes.

And the same is true of the poor and the laborers. "Who would plow our fields for us if you were all lords," asks Berthold von Regensburg in one of his sermons in the thirteenth century. [121] And elsewhere he says even more clearly: I shall tell you Christian folk how Almighty God has ordered Christendom, dividing it into ten kinds of people, "and what kinds of services the lower owe the higher as their rulers. The first three are the highest and most exalted whom Almighty God himself chose and ordained, so that the other seven should all be subject to them and serve them." [122] The same attitude to life is still found in these pictures from the fifteenth century. It is not distasteful, it is part of the natural and unquestioned order of the world that warriors and nobles have leisure to amuse themselves, while the others work for them. There is no identification of man with man. Not even on the horizon of this life is there an idea that all men are "equal." But perhaps for that very reason the sight of the laborers has about it nothing shameful or embarrassing.

A picture of the manor shows the pleasures of the lords. A young lady of the nobility crowns her young friend with a wreath; he draws her to him. Another pair go walking in a close embrace. The old servant woman pulls an angry face at the love games of the young people. Nearby the servants are working. One of them sweeps the yard, another grooms the horse, a third scatters food for the ducks, but the maid waves to him from the window; he turns round, soon he will disappear into the house. Noble ladies at play. Peasant antics behind them. On the roof the stork clatters.

Then there is a small courtyard by a lake. On the bridge stands a young nobleman with his wife. Leaning on the balustrade they watch the servants in the water catching fish and ducks. Three young ladies are in a boat. Rushes, bushes, in the distance the walls of a small town.

Or we see workmen building a house in front of a wooded hill. The lord and lady of the castle look on. Tunnels have been driven into the little hill to quarry stones. Workmen are seen hewing the stones; others cart them away. Nearer to us, men are working on the half-finished building. In the foreground workmen are quarreling; they are about to stab and strike each other down. The lord of the castle stands not far from them. He shows his wife the angry scene; the complete calm of the lord and his wife is placed in sharp contrast to the excited gestures of the disputants. The rabble fight, the lord has nothing to do with it. He lives in another sphere.

It is not the events themselves, which in part are no different today, but above all the fact and the manner of their portrayal that underline the changed emotive condition. The upper classes of later phases did not have such things drawn. Such drawings did not appeal to their feelings. They were not "beautiful." They did not form part of "art." In later periods it is at most among the Dutch (who depict middle-class, specifically uncourtly strata) that we find, for example, in the work of Breughel a standard of repugnance that permits him to bring cripples, peasants, gallows, or people relieving themselves into his pictures. But the standard there is linked with very different social feelings than in these pictures of the late medieval upper class.

Here, it is a matter of course that the laboring classes exist. They are even indispensable figures in the landscape of knightly existence. The lord lives in their midst. It does not shock him to see the servant working beside him, nor does it shock him if the latter amuses himself in his own way. On the contrary, it is an integral part of his self-esteem to have these other people moving about him who are not like him, whose master he is. This feeling is expressed again and again in the drawings. There is scarcely one of them in which *courtois* occupations and gestures are not contrasted to the vulgar ones of the lower classes. Whether he rides, hunts, loves, or dances, whatever the lord does is noble and *courtois*, whatever the servants and peasants do coarse and uncouth. The feelings of the medieval upper class do not yet demand that everything vulgar should be suppressed from life and therefore from pictures. It is gratifying for the nobles to know themselves different from others. *The sight of contrast heightens joy in living*; and we should remember that, in a milder form, something of the pleasure taken in such contrasts is still to be found, for example, in Shakespeare. Wherever one looks at the heritage of the medieval upper class, one finds this same attitude in an unrestrained form. The further interdependence and the division of labor in society advance, the more dependent the upper classes become on the other classes, and the greater, therefore, becomes the social strength of these classes, at least potentially. Even when the upper class is still primarily a warrior class, when it keeps the other classes dependent chiefly through the sword and the monopoly of weapons, some degree of dependence on these other classes is certainly not entirely absent. But it is incomparably less; and less, too—as will be seen in more detail later—is the pressure from below. Accordingly, the sense of mastery of the upper class, its contempt for other classes, is far more open, and the pressure on them to exercise restraint and to control their drives, is far less strong.

Seldom has the matter-of-fact sense of mastery of this class, and its patriarchal contempt of others, been so vividly conveyed as in these drawings. This is expressed not only in the gesture with which the nobleman shows his wife the quarreling craftsmen and the workers in a kind of foundry who are holding their noses to ward off the foul vapors; not only where the lord watches his servants catching fish, or in the repeated depiction of the gallows with a corpse hanging from it; but also in the matter-of-fact and casual way in which the nobler gestures of the knight are juxtaposed to the coarse ones of the people.

There is a picture of a tournament. Musicians play. Fools cut clumsy capers. The noble spectators on their horses, often the lord and lady on the same horse, are conversing. The peasants, the citizens, the doctor, all recognizable by their dress, look on. The two knights, somewhat helpless in their heavy armor, wait at the center. Friends advise them. One of them is just being handed the long lance. Then the herald blows his trumpet. The knights charge at each other with their lances leveled. And in the background, contrasting to the *courtois* occupation of the masters, we see the vulgar pastimes of the people, a horse race accompanied by all kinds of nonsense. A man hangs onto the tail of one of the horses. The rider is furious. The others whip their horses and make off at a somewhat grotesque gallop.

We see a military camp. A circular barricade has been made with the gun carriages. Within it stand resplendent tents with their different coats of arms and banners, among them the imperial banner. At the center, surrounded by his knights, we see the king or even the emperor himself. A messenger on horseback is just bringing him a message. But at the gate of the camp, beggar women sit with their children, wringing their hands, while a man in armor on horseback brings in a fettered prisoner. Further back we see a peasant plowing his field. Outside the rampart, bones lie about, animal skeletons, a dead horse with a crow and a wild dog eating it. Close to a wagon a crouching servant relieves himself.

Or we see knights attacking a village under the sign of Mars. In the foreground, one of the soldiers is stabbing a prostrate peasant; on the right, apparently in a chapel, a second man is stabbed and his possessions are dragged away. On the roof the stork sit peacefully in their nest. Further back a peasant is trying to escape over the fence, but a knight on his horse holds him by the protruding tail of his shirt. A peasant woman cries out, wringing her hands. A peasant in fetters, doleful and wretched, is being beaten over the head by a knight on horseback. Further back horsemen are setting fire to a house; one of them drives off the cattle and strikes at the farmer's wife, who is trying to stop him; above, in the little tower of the village church, the peasants huddle together, and frightened faces look out of the window. In the far distance, on a small hill, stands a fortified monastery; behind the high walls one sees the church roof with a cross on it. Somewhat higher up, on a hill, a castle or another part of the monastery.

These are the ideas suggested to the artist by the sign of the god of war. The picture is wonderfully full of life. As in a number of the other drawings, one feels that something that has been really experienced is before one's eyes. One has this feeling because these pictures are not yet "sentimental," because they do not express the greater restraint of the emotions which from now on, for a long period, caused the art of the upper class to express more and more exclusively its wishful fantasies, and compelled it to suppress everything that conflicted with this advancing standard of repugnance. These pictures simply narrate how the knight sees and feels the world. The sifting of feeling, the grid placed on the affects which admits to the picture what is pleasurable and excludes what is painful or embarrassing, allows many facts to pass unimpeded which later attain expression only when a conscious or unconscious protest against the upper class censoring of drives is being expressed, and are then somewhat overemphasized. Here the peasant is neither pitiable nor a representative of virtue. Nor is he a representative of ugly vice. He is simply miserable and somewhat ridiculous, exactly as the knight sees him. The world centers around the knight. Hungry dogs, begging women, rotting horses, servants crouching against the ramparts, villages in flames, peasants being plundered and killed—all this is as much a part of the landscape of these people as are tournaments and hunts. So God made the world: some are rulers, the others bondsmen. There is nothing embarrassing about all this.

And the same difference in standard of feeling between even this late chivalrous society and the subsequent society of the absolute courts is also shown in the representation of love. There is a picture of people under the sign of Venus. Again we look far into the open country. There are little hills, a meandering river, bushes, and a small wood. In the foreground three or four pairs of young nobles, always a young lord and a young lady together; they walk in a circle to the sound of music, ceremoniously, elegantly, all with the long-toed, fashionable shoes. Their movements are measured and rounded; one noble has a large feather in his hat; others have garlands in their hair. Perhaps we are looking at a kind of slow dance. Behind stand three boys making music; there is a table with fruits and drink and a young fellow leaning against it, who is to serve.

At the opposite side, enclosed by a fence and gate, is a little garden. Trees form a kind of bower, beneath which is an oval bathtub. In it sits a young man, naked, who grabs eagerly at a naked girl who is just climbing into the bath with him. As above, an old female servant who is bringing fruits and drinks surveys the love game of the young people with an angry face. And as the masters arouse themselves in the foreground, so do the servants in the background. One of them falls upon a maid who lies on the ground with her skirts already pulled up. He looks round once more to see whether there is anyone nearby. On the other side, two young fellows of the common people are dancing around, flinging their arms and legs like Morisco dancers; a third plays for them.

Or we see, likewise in the open country, a small stone bathhouse with a small yard in front of it surrounded by a stone wall. We can see a little beyond it. A path is indicated, bushes, a row of trees leading into the distance. In the yard young couples are sitting and walking about; one of them admires the fashionable fountains, others converse, one of the young men with a falcon on his hand. Dogs, a little monkey. Potted plants.

We can see into the bathhouse through a large, open, arched window. Two young men and a girl sit naked in the water, side by side, and talk. A second girl, already undressed, is just opening the door to climb into the water with them. In the large open vault of the bathhouse a boy sits playing something to the bathers on his guitar. Under the arch is a tap from which the water runs. In front of the little house, drinks are placed to cool in a small tub of water. On a table next to it are fruits and a goblet; at the table is a young man, a wreath in his hair and his head supported elegantly on his hands. Above, from the second floor of the bathhouse, a maid and a servant watch the masters enjoying themselves.

In this picture, as one can see, the erotic relation between man and woman is much more open than in the later phase, where it is hinted at in social life, as in pictures, in a way that is comprehensible to all but nevertheless half-concealed. Nakedness is not yet associated with shame to the extent that, to circumvent internal and external social controls, it can only appear in pictures sentimentally, as the costume, so to speak, of the Greeks and Romans.

But neither is the naked body depicted here in the way it sometimes appeared in later times, in "private drawings" passed secretly from hand to hand. These love scenes are anything but "obscene."Love is presented here like anything else in the life of the knight, tournaments, hunts, campaigns, or plunderings. The scenes are not particularly stressed; one does not feel in their representation anything of the violence, the tendency to excite or gratify a wish-fulfillment denied in life, characteristic of everything "obscene." This picture does not come from an oppressed soul; it does not reveal something "secret" by violating taboos. It seems quite carefree. Here, too, the artist drew what he must have seen himself often enough in life. And on account of this unconcern, this matter-of-factness with which, compared to our standard of shame and embarrassment, the relations between the sexes are presented, we call this attitude "naïve." Even in the *House-Book* we occasionally find a joke which is (to our taste) thoroughly coarse, as also in other artists of this phase—for example, Master E. F. and, perhaps copied from him, even in the popularizing "Master with the Banderoles."[123] And the adoption of such motifs by a popularizing copyist, who was possibly even a monk, indicates how different was the social standard of shame. These things are depicted with the same matter-of-factness as some detail of clothing. It is a joke, certainly a coarse one, if we like to call it that, but really no coarser than the joke the artist permits himself when he makes the shirttail of the plundered and fleeing peasant stick out so that the knight can catch hold of it, or when he gives the old servant surveying the love games of the young people an angry expression, as if mocking her for being too old for such dalliance.

All these are expressions of a society in which people gave way to drives and feelings incomparably more easily, quickly, spontaneously, and openly than today, in which the emotions were less restrained and, as a consequence, less evenly regulated and more liable to oscillate more violently between extremes. Within this standard of regulation of the emotions, which is characteristic of the whole secular society of the Middle Ages, of peasants as of knights, there were certainly considerable variations. And the people conforming to this standard were subjected to a large number of drive controls. But these were in a different direction; they were not of the same degree as in later periods, and they did not take the form of a constant, even almost automatic self-control. The kind of integration and interdependence in which these people lived did not compel them to restrain their bodily functions before each other or to curb their aggressive impulses, to the same extent as in the following phase. This applies to everyone. But of course, for the peasants the scope for aggression was more restricted than for the knight—restricted, that is, to his equals. For the knight, by contrast, aggression was less restricted outside his own class than within it, for here it was regulated by the code of chivalry. A socially generated restraint was at times imposed on the peasant by the simple fact that he had not enough to eat. This certainly represents a restriction of drives of the highest degree, which expresses itself in the whole behavior of a human being. But no one paid attention to this, and his social situation scarcely made it necessary for him to impose constraint on himself when blowing his nose or spitting or snatching food at table. In this direction, coercion in the knightly class was stronger. However uniform, therefore, the medieval standard of control of emotions appears in comparison to later developments, it contained considerable differences corresponding to the stratification of secular society itself, not to mention clerical society; these differences remain to be examined in detail. They are visible in these pictures, if the measured and sometimes even affected gestures of the nobles are compared to the clumsy movements of the servants and peasants.

The expressions of feeling of medieval people are, on the whole, more spontaneous and unrestrained than in the following period. But they are not unrestrained or without social molding in any *absolute* sense. In this respect there is no zero point. Man without restrictions is a phantom. Admittedly, the nature, strength, and elaboration of the prohibitions, controls, and dependencies change in a hundred ways, and with them the tension and equilibrium of the emotions, and likewise the degree and kind of gratification that the individual seeks and finds.

Taken together, these pictures give a certain impression of where the knight sought and found gratification. At this time he may already live more frequently at court than earlier. But castle and manor, hill, stream, fields and villages, trees and woods still form the background of his life; they are taken for granted and regarded quite without sentimentality. Here he is at home, and here he is the master. His life is divided essentially between war, tournaments, hunts, and love.

But in the fifteenth century itself, and more so in the sixteenth, this changes. At the semiurban courts of princes and kings, partly from elements of the old nobility and partly from new rising elements, a new aristocracy forms with a new social space, new functions, and accordingly a different emotional structure.

People feel this difference themselves and express it. In 1562 a man named Jean du Peyrat translates Della Casa's book on manners into French. He gives it the title *Galatée ou la maniere et fasson comme le gentilhomme se doit gouverner en toute compagnie* (Galateo, or the manner in which the gentleman should conduct himself in all company). And even in this title the increased compulsion now imposed on the nobles is clearly expressed. But Peyrat himself, in his introduction, explicitly stresses the difference between the demands that life used to make on the knight and those which are now made on the noblemen by life in court:

> The entire virtue and perfection of the gentleman, your lordship, does not consist in correctly spurring a horse, handling a lance, sitting straight in one's armor, using every kind of weapon, behaving modestly among ladies, or in the pursuit of love: for this is another of the exercises attributed to the gentleman. There is, in addition, service at table before kings and princes, the manner of adjusting one's language toward people according to their rank and quality, their glances, gestures, and even the smallest signs or winks they might give.

Here, exactly the same things are enumerated as constituting the customary virtue, perfection, and activities of the noble as in the pictures of the *House-Book*: feats of arms and love. Contrasted to them are the additional perfections and the new sphere of life of the nobleman in the service of a prince. A new constraint, a new, more extensive control and regulation of behavior than the old knightly life made either necessary or possible, is now demanded of the nobleman. These are consequences of the new, increased dependence in which the noble is now placed. He is no longer the relatively free man, the master in his own castle, whose castle is his homeland. He now lives at court. He serves the prince. He waits on him at table. And at court he lives surrounded by people. He must behave toward each of them in exact accordance with their rank and his own. He must learn to adjust his gestures exactly to the different ranks and standing of the people at court, to measure his language exactly, and even to control his eyes exactly. It is a new self-discipline, an incomparably stronger reserve that is imposed on people by this new social space and the new ties of interdependence.

The attitude whose ideal form was expressed by the concept of *courtoisie* is giving way to another expressed more and more by the concept of *civilité*.

The translation of *Galateo* by Jean du Peyrat represents this transitional period linguistically as well. Up to 1530 or 1535 the concept of *courtoisie* predominates more or less exclusively in France. Toward the end of the century the concept of *civilité* slowly gains precedence, without the other being lost. Here, about the year 1562, the two are used together without any noticeable precedence of one or the other. In his dedication Peyrat says: "Let this book, which treats the instruction of a young courtier and gentleman, be protected by him who is as the paragon and mirror of others in *courtesy*, *civility*, good manners, and praiseworthy customs."

The man to whom these words are addressed is that very Henri de Bourbon, Prince of Navarre, whose life most visibly symbolizes this transition from the chivalrous to the courtly man and who, as Henri IV, was to be the direct executor of this change in France, being obliged, often against his will, to compel or even condemn to death those who resisted, those who did not understand that from free lords and knights they were to become dependent servants of the king.[124]

APPENDICES

APPENDICES

Appendix I

Introduction to the 1968 Edition

I

In thinking and theorizing about the structure and controls of human affects nowadays, we are usually content to use as evidence observations from the more developed societies of today. We thus proceed from the tacit assumption that it is possible to construct theories about the affect structures of man in general on the basis of studies of people in a specific society that can be observed here and now—our own. However, there are numerous relatively accessible observations which point to the conclusion that the standard and pattern of affect controls in societies at different stages of development, and even in different strata of the same society, can differ. Whether we are concerned with the development of European countries, which has lasted for centuries, or with the so-called "developing countries" in other parts of the world, we are constantly confronted by observations which give rise to the following question: how and why, in the course of the overall transformations of society which take place over long time spans and in a particular direction—which the term "development" has been adopted—is the affectivity of human behavior and experience, the control of individual affects by external and internal constraints, and in this sense the structure of all forms of human expression altered in a particular direction? Such changes are indicated in everyday speech by such statements as that the people of our own society are more "civilized" than they were earlier, or that those of other societies are more "uncivilized" (or even more "barbaric") than those of our own.

The value judgments contained in such statements are obvious; the facts to which they relate are less so. This is partly because empirical investigations of long-term transformations of personality structures, and especially of affect controls, give rise at the present stage of sociological research to very considerable difficulties. At the forefront of sociological interest at present are relatively short-term processes, and usually only problems relating to a given state of society. Long-term transformations of social structures, and therefore of personality structures as well, have by and large been lost to view.

The present study is concerned with these long-term processes. Understanding of it may be aided by a brief indication of the various kinds of such processes. To begin with, two main directions in the structural changes of societies may be distinguished: those tending toward increased differentiation and integration, and those tending toward decreased differentiation and integration. In addition, there is a third type of social process, in the course of which the structure of a society or of its particular aspects is changed, but without a tendency toward either an increase or a decrease in the level of differentiation and integration. Finally, there are countless changes in a society which do not involve a change in its structure. This account does not do justice to the full complexity of such changes, for there are numerous hybrid forms, and often several types of change, even in opposite directions, can be observed simultaneously in the same society. But for the present, this brief outline of the different types of change suffices to indicate the problems with which this study is concerned.

The History of Manners addresses itself above all to the question of whether the supposition, based on scattered observations, that there are long-term changes in the affect and control structures of people in particular societies—changes which follow one and the same direction over a large number of generations—can be confirmed by reliable evidence and proved to be factually correct. It therefore contains an account of sociological procedures and findings, the best-known counterpart of which in the physical sciences is the experiment and its results. It is concerned with the discovery and elucidation of what actually takes place in the as yet unexplored field of inquiry to which our questions relate: the discovery and definition of factual connections.

The demonstration of a change in human affect and control structures taking place over a large number of generations in the same direction—to state it briefly, the increased tightening and differentiation of controls—gives rise to a further question. Is it possible to relate this long-term change in personality structures with long-term structural changes in society as a whole, which likewise tend in a particular direction, toward a higher level of social differentiation and integration? *State Formation and Civilization* is concerned with these problems.

For these long-term structural changes of society, empirical evidence is likewise lacking. It has therefore been necessary to devote a part of *State Formation and Civilization* to the discovery and elucidation of factual connections in this second area. The question is whether a structural change of society as a whole, tending toward a higher level of differentiation and integration, can be demonstrated with the aid of reliable empirical evidence. This proves possible. The process of the formation of nation states, discussed in *State Formation and Civilization*, is an example of this kind of structural change.

Finally, in *State Formation and Civilization*, in a provisional sketch of a theory of civilization, a model is evolved to show the possible connections between the long-term change in human personality structures toward a consolidation and differentiation of affect controls, and the long-term change in the social structure toward a higher level of differentiation and integration—for example, toward a differentiation and prolongation of the chains of interdependence and a consolidation of "state controls."

II

It can readily be seen that in adopting an approach directed at factual connections and their explanation (that is, an empirical and theoretical approach concerned with long-term structural changes of a specific kind, or "developments"), we take leave of the metaphysical ideas which connect the concept of development either to the notion of a mechanical necessity or to that of a teleological purpose. The concept of civilization, as Part One of *The History of Manners* shows, has often been used in a semimetaphysical sense and has remained highly nebulous until today. Here, the attempt is made to isolate the factual core to which the current prescientific notion of the civilizing process refers. This core consists primarily of the structural change in people toward an increased consolidation and differentiation of their affect controls, and therefore both of their experience (e.g., in the form of an advance in the threshold of shame and revulsion) and of their behavior (e.g., in the differentiation of the implements used at table). The next task posed by the demonstration of such a change in a specific direction over many generations is to provide an explanation. A sketch of one is to be found, as already mentioned, at the end of *State Formation and Civilization*.

But with the aid of such an investigation we likewise take leave of the theories of social change predominant today, which in the course of time have taken the place in sociological inquiry of an earlier one centered on the old, semimetaphysical notion of development. As far as can be seen, these current theories scarcely ever distinguish in an unambiguous way between the different types of social change briefly mentioned earlier. In particular, there is still a lack of theories based on empirical evidence to explain the type of long-term social changes which take the form of a process and, above all, of a development.

When I was working on *The Civilizing Process* it seemed quite clear to me that I was laying the foundation of an undogmatic, empirically based sociological theory of social processes in general and of social development in particular. I believed it quite obvious that the investigation, and the concluding model of the long-term process of state formation to be found in *State Formation and Civilization*, could serve equally as a model of the long-term dynamic of societies in a particular direction, to which the concept of social development refers. I did not believe at that time that it was necessary to point out explicitly that this study was neither of an "evolution" in the nineteenth-century sense of an automatic progress, nor of an unspecific "social change" in the twentieth-century sense. At that time this seemed so obvious that I omitted to mention these theoretical implications explicitly. The introduction to the second edition gives me the opportunity to make good this omission.

III

The comprehensive social development studied and presented here through one of its central manifestations—a wave of advancing integration over several centuries, a process of state formation with the complementary process of advancing differentiation—is a figurational change which, in the to-and-fro of contrary movements, maintains, when surveyed over an extended time span, a constant direction through many generations. This structural change in a specific direction can be demonstrated as a fact, regardless of how it is evaluated. The factual proof is what matters here. The concept of social change by itself does not suffice, as an instrument of research, to take account of such facts. A mere change can be of the kind observable in clouds or smoke rings: now they look like this, now like that. A concept of social change that does not distinguish clearly between changes that relate to the structure of a society and those that do not—and, further, between structural changes without a specific direction and those which follow a particular direction over many generations, e.g., toward greater or lesser complexity—is a very inadequate tool of sociological inquiry.

The situation is similar with a number of other problems dealt with here. When, after several preparatory studies which enabled me both to investigate documentary evidence and to explore the gradually unfolding theoretical problems, the way to a possible solution became clearer, I was made aware that this study brings somewhat nearer to resolution the intractable problem of the connection between individual psychological structures (so-called personality structures) and figurations formed by large numbers of interdependent individuals (social structures). It does so because it approaches both types of structure not as fixed, as usually happens, but as changing, and as interdependent aspects of the same long-term development.

IV

If the various academic disciplines whose subject matter is touched on by this study—including, above all, the discipline of sociology—had already reached the stage of scientific maturity at present enjoyed by many of the natural sciences, it might have been expected that a carefully documented study of long-term processes, such as those of civilization or state formation, with the theoretical proposals developed from it, would be assimilated, either in its entirety or in some of its aspects, after thorough testing and discussion, after critical sifting of all unsuitable or disproved content, to that discipline's stock of empirical and theoretical knowledge. Since the advance of scholarship depends in large measure on interchange and cross-fertilization between numerous colleagues and on the continuous development of the common stock of knowledge, it might have been expected that thirty years later this study would either have become a part of the standard knowledge of the discipline or have been more or less superseded by the work of others and laid to rest.

Instead, I find that a generation later this book still has the character of a pioneering work in a problematic field which today is hardly less in need than it was thirty years ago, of the simultaneous investigation on the empirical and theoretical plane that is to be found here. Understanding of the urgency of the problems discussed here has grown. Everywhere gropings in the direction of these problems are observable. There is no lack of later attempts to solve problems to whose solution the empirical documentation in *The History of Manners* and *State Formation and Civilization* endeavors to contribute. I do not believe these later attempts to have been successful.

To exemplify this, it must suffice to discuss the way in which the man who at present is widely regarded as the leading theoretician of sociology, Talcott Parsons, attempts to pose and solve some of the problems dealt with here. It is characteristic of Parsons's theoretical approach to attempt to dissect analytically into their elementary components, as he once expressed it,[1] the different types of society in his field of observation. He called one particular type of elementary component "pattern variables." These pattern variables include the dichotomy of "affectivity" and "affective neutrality." His conception can best be understood by comparing society to a game of cards: every type of society, in Parsons's view, represents a different "hand." But the cards themselves are always the same; and their number is small, however diverse their faces may be. One of the cards with which the game is played is the polarity between affectivity and affective neutrality. Parsons originally conceived this idea, he tells us, in analysing Tönnies's society types *Gemeinschaft* (community) and *Gesellschaft* (society). "Community," Parsons appears to believe, is characterized by affectivity and "society" by affective neutrality. But in determining the differences between different types of society, and between different types of relationship within one and the same society, he attributes to this "pattern variable" in the card game, as to the others, a wholly general meaning. In the same context, Parsons addresses himself to the problem of the relation of social structure to personality.[2] He indicates that while he had previously seen them merely as closely connected and interacting "human action systems," he can now state with certainty that in a theoretical sense they are different phases or aspects of one and the same fundamental action system. He illustrates this by an example, explaining that what may be considered on the sociological plane as an institutionalization of affective neutrality is essentially the same as what may be regarded on the level of personality as "the imposition of renunciation of immediate gratification in the interests of disciplined organization and the longer-run goals of the personality."

It is perhaps useful for an understanding of this study to compare this later attempt to solve such problems with the earlier one reprinted in unchanged form here. The decisive difference in scientific approach, and in the conception of the objectives of sociological theory, is evident from even this short example of Parsons's treatment of similar problems. What in this book is shown with the aid of extensive empirical documentation to be a process, Parsons, by the static nature of his concepts, reduces retrospectively, and it seems to me quite unnecessarily, to states. Instead of a relatively complex process whereby the affective life of people is gradually moved toward an increased and more even control of affects—but certainly not toward a state of total affective neutrality—Parsons presents a simple opposition between two states, affectivity and affective neutrality, which are supposed to be present to different degrees in different types of society, like different quantities of chemical substances. By reducing to two different states what was shown empirically in *The Civilizing Process* to be a process and interpreted theoretically as such, Parsons deprives himself of the possibility of discovering how the distinguishing peculiarities of different societies to which he refers are actually to be explained. So far as is apparent, he does not even raise the question of explanation. The different states denoted by the antitheses of the "pattern variables" are, it seems, simply given. The subtly articulated structural change toward increased and more even affect control that may be observed in reality disappears in this kind of theorizing. Social phenomena in reality can only be observed as evolving and having evolved; their dissection by means of pairs of concepts which restrict the analysis to two antithetical states represents an unnecessary impoverishment of sociological perception on both empirical and theoretical levels.

Certainly, it is the task of every sociological theory to clarify the characteristics that all possible human societies have in common. The concept of the social process, like many others used in this study, has precisely this function. But the basic categories selected by Parsons seem to me arbitrary to a high degree. Underlying them is the tacit, untested, and seemingly self-evident notion that the objective of every scientific theory is to reduce everything variable to something invariable, and to simplify all complex phenomena by dissecting them into their individual components.

The example of Parsons's theory suggests, however, that theorizing in the field of sociology is complicated rather than simplified by a systematic reduction of social processes to social states, and of complex, heterogeneous phenomena to simpler, seemingly homogeneous components. This kind of reduction and abstraction could be justified as a method of theorizing only if it led unambiguously to a clearer and deeper understanding by men of themselves as societies and as individuals. Instead of this we find that the theories formed by such methods, like the epicycle theory of Ptolemy, require needlessly complicated auxiliary constructions to make them agree with the observable facts. They often appear like dark clouds from which here and there a few rays of light touch the earth.

V

One example of this, which will be discussed more fully later, is Parsons's attempt to develop a theoretical model of the relation between personality structures and social structures. In this undertaking two not very compatible ideas are frequently thoroughly confused: the notion that individual and society—"ego" and "social system"—are two entities existing independently of each other, with the individual regarded as the actual reality and society treated as an epiphenomenon; and the notion that the two are different but inseparable planes of the universe formed by men. Furthermore, concepts like "ego" and "social system" and all those related to them, which refer to men as individuals and as societies, are applied by Parsons—except when he is using psychoanalytical categories—as if the normal condition of both could be considered as an unalterable state. This study cannot be properly understood if the view of what is actually observable in human beings is blocked by such notions. It cannot be understood if we forget that concepts such as "individual" and "society" do not relate to two objects existing separately but to different yet inseparable aspects of the same human beings, and that both aspects (and human beings in general) are normally involved in a structural transformation. Both have the character of processes, and there is not the slightest necessity, in forming theories about human beings, to abstract from this process-character. Indeed, it is indispensable that the concept of process be included in sociological and other theories relating to human beings. As is shown in this book, the relation between individual and social structures can only be clarified if both are investigated as changing, evolving entities. Only then is it possible to develop models of their relationship, as is done here, which are in some agreement with the demonstrable facts. It can be stated with complete certainty that the relation between what is referred to conceptually as the "individual" and as "society" will remain incomprehensible so long as these concepts are used as if they represented two separate bodies, and even bodies normally at rest, which only come into contact with one another afterwards as it were. Without ever saying so clearly and openly, Parsons and all sociologists of the same persuasion undoubtedly envisage those things to which the concepts "individual" and "society" refer as existing separately. Thus—to give only one example—Parsons adopts the notion already developed by Durkheim that the relation between "individual" and "society" is an "interpenetration" of the individual and the social system. However such an "interpenetration" is conceived, what else can this metaphor mean than that we are concerned with two different entities which first exist separately and then subsequently "interpenetrate"?[3]

This makes clear the difference between the two sociological approaches. In this study the possibility of discerning more precisely the connection between individual structures and social structures results from a refusal to abstract from the process of their evolution as from something incidental or "merely historical." For the structures of personality and of society evolve in an indissoluble interrelationship. It can never be said with certainty that the people of a society *are* civilized. But on the basis of systematic investigations referring to demonstrable evidence, it can be said with a high degree of certainty that some groups of people have *become* more civilized, without necessarily implying that it is better or worse, has a positive or negative value, to become more civilized. Such a change in personality structures can, however, be shown without difficulty to be a specific aspect of the development of social structures. This is attempted in what follows.

It is not particularly surprising to encounter in Parsons, and in many other contemporary sociological theoreticians, a tendency to reduce processes to states even when these writers are explicitly concerned with the problem of social change. In keeping with the predominant trend in sociology, Parsons takes as his starting point the hypothesis that every society normally exists in a state of unchanging equilibrium which is homeostatically preserved. It changes, he supposes, when this normal state of social equilibrium is disturbed by, for example, a violation of the social norms, a breach of conformity. Social change thus appears as a phenomenon resulting from the accidental, externally activated malfunction of a normally well-balanced social system. Moreover, the society thus disturbed strives, in Parsons's view, to regain its state of rest. Sooner or later, as he sees it, a different "system" with a different equilibrium is established, which once again maintains itself more or less automatically, despite oscillations, in the given state. In a word, the concept of social change refers here to a transitional state between two normal states of changelessness, brought about by malfunction. Here, too, the difference between the theoretical approaches represented by this study and by Parsons and his school emerges very distinctly.

The present study upholds the idea, based on abundant documentary material, that change is a normal characteristic of society. A structured sequence of continuous change serves here as the frame of reference for investigating states located at particular points in time. In prevailing sociological opinion, conversely, social situations treated as if they normally existed in a state of rest serve as the frame of reference for all change. Thus a society is regarded as a "social system," and a "social system" as a "system in a state of rest." Even when a relatively differentiated, "highly developed" society is involved, the attempt is often made to consider it as at rest and self-contained. It is not regarded as an integral part of the inquiry to ask how and why this highly developed society has developed to this state of differentiation. In keeping with the static frame of reference of the predominant system-theories, social changes, processes, and developments, which include the development of a state or a civilizational process, appear merely as something additional, a mere "historical introduction" the investigation and explanation of which may very well be dispensed with in coming to an understanding of the "social system" and its "structure" and "functions," as they may be observed here and now from a short-term viewpoint. These conceptual tools themselves—including concepts like "structures" and "function," which serve as the badge of the contemporary sociological school of "structural functionalists"—bear the stamp of this specific mode of thinking, which reduces processes to states. Of course, their originators cannot entirely dismiss the idea that the "structures" and "functions" of the social "unit" or its "parts," which they picture as states, move and change. But the problems which thus come into view are reconciled with the static mode of thought by encapsulating them in a special chapter with the title "Social Change," as though the phenomenon were supplementary to the problems of the normally unchanging system. In this way "social change" itself is treated as an attribute of a state of rest. In other words, the basic, state-orientated attitude is reconciled with empirical observations of social change by introducing into the theoretical waxworks of motionless social phenomena a few more equally motionless figures with labels like "social change" or "social process." In this way the problems of social change are in a sense frozen and rendered innocuous to state-oriented sociology. So it happens that the concept of "social development" has almost completely vanished from the sight of contemporary sociological theorists—paradoxically, in a phase of social development when, in actual social life and partly also in empirical sociological research, people are concerning themselves more intensely and consciously than ever before with problems of social development.

VI

In writing an introduction to a book that on both the theoretical and the empirical side is squarely opposed to widespread tendencies in contemporary sociology, one has a certain obligation to tell the reader clearly and unequivocally how and why the problems posed here, and the steps taken to solve them, differ from those of the predominant type of sociology, and particularly from those of theoretical sociology. To do this, one cannot entirely evade the question how it is to be explained that sociology, for whose leading nineteenth-century representatives the problems of long-term social processes were of primordial interest, should in the twentieth century have become a sociology of states to such an extent that the investigation of long-term social processes has as much as disappeared from its research activity. Within the scope of this introduction I cannot presume to discuss this displacement of the center of interest of sociological research, and the radical change in the entire sociological manner of thinking connected with it, with the thoroughness they deserve. But the problem is too important for an understanding of what follows, and beyond that for the further development of sociology, to be passed over in complete silence. I shall therefore confine myself to picking out a few elements from the complex of conditions responsible for this regression in the intellectual apparatus of sociology and the concomitant narrowing of its field of inquiry.

The most obvious reason why awareness of the significance of problems of long-term social change, of the sociogenesis and development of social formations of all kinds has been largely lost to sociologists, and why the concept of development has fallen into disrepute among them, is to be found in the reaction of many sociologists—above all, the leading theoreticians of the twentieth century—to certain aspects of the outstanding sociological theories of the nineteenth century. It has been shown that the theoretical models of long-term social development elaborated in the nineteenth century by men like Comte, Spencer, Marx, Hobhouse, and many others rested in part on hypotheses determined primarily by the political and philosophical ideals of these men and only secondarily by their relation to facts. Later generations had a much larger and constantly increasing supply of facts at their disposal. Reexamination of the classical nineteenth-century theories of development in light of the more comprehensive findings of subsequent generations made many aspects of the earlier process-models appear questionable or at any rate in need of revision. Many of the sociological pioneers' articles of faith were no longer accepted by twentieth-century sociologists. These included, above all, the belief that the development of society is necessarily a development for the better, a movement in the direction of progress. This belief was emphatically rejected by many later sociologists in accordance with their own social experience. They could see more clearly in retrospect that the earlier models of development comprised a mixture of relatively fact-based and of ideological notions.

In a mature discipline one might, first of all, have set about the task of revising and correcting the earlier models of development. One might have tried, in this situation, to ascertain which aspects of the old theories could be used as a basis for further research in light of the more comprehensive factual knowledge now available, and which should find their place as expressions of time-bound political or philosophical prejudice, with a suitable tombstone, in the graveyard of dead doctrines.

Instead, an extremely sharp reaction against the type of sociological theory concerned with long-term social processes set in. The study of the long-term development of society was almost universally decried, and the center of sociological interest moved, in a radical reaction against the older type of theory, to the investigation of data on society conceived as normally existing in a state of rest and equilibrium. Hand in hand with this went the hardening of a collection of stereotyped arguments against the older sociological theories and many of their central concepts, particularly that of social development. As these sociologists did not trouble to distinguish between the fact-based and the ideological elements in the concept of development, the whole discussion of long-term social processes, particularly developmental processes, was henceforth associated with one or another of the nineteenth-century systems of belief, and so, above all, with the notion that social development, whether proceeding in a straight line without conflict or dialectically with conflict, must automatically be a change for the better, a movement in the direction of progress. From then on it appeared almost old-fashioned to occupy oneself with questions of social development. It is sometimes said that generals, in planning strategy for a new war, take the strategy of the old one as their model. To assume without question that concepts like "social development" or "long-term social processes" inevitably include the old idea of progress is to proceed in a similar way.

We find, therefore, in the framework of sociology, an intellectual development involving a radical swing of the pendulum from a one-sided position to an opposite position no less one-sided. A phase in which sociological theorists primarily sought models of long-term social development has been succeeded by one in which they are primarily concerned with models of societies in a state of rest and immutability. If research was once founded on a Heraclitean kind of basic assumption that all is in flux (with the difference that it was taken almost for granted that the flow was in the direction of improvement), it is based now on an Eleatic idea. The Eleatics, it is said, imagined the flight of an arrow as a series of states of rest; actually, it seemed to them, the arrow does not move at all. For at every given moment it is in a particular place. The assumption of many present-day sociological theorists that societies are usually to be found in a state of equilibrium, so that the long-term social development of mankind appears as a chain of static social types, is strongly reminiscent of the Eleatic conception of the flight of an arrow. How can this swing of the pendulum from one extreme to the other in the development of sociology be explained?

At first sight it seems that the decisive reason for the change in the theoretical orientation of sociology is a reaction of scientists protesting in the name of the scientific character of their research against the interference of political and philosophical ideas in the theory of their subject. Exponents of contemporary sociological theories of state are themselves often inclined to this interpretation. On closer examination, however, it is found to be inadequate. The reaction against the sociology of development predominant in the nineteenth century was not directed simply against the primacy of ideals, the dominance of preconceived social doctrines, in the name of scientific objectivity. It was not simply the expression of a concern to pull aside the veil of short-lived notions of what society ought to be, in order to perceive the real dynamics and functioning of society itself. In the last analysis it was a reaction against the primacy of *particular* ideals in sociological theory, in the name of others partly opposed to them. If in the nineteenth century specific conceptions of what ought to be or of what was desired—specific ideological conceptions—led to a central interest in the development of society, in the twentieth century other conceptions of what ought to be or is desirable—other ideological conceptions—led to the pronounced interest among leading sociological theorists in the state of society as it is, to their neglect of problems of the dynamics of social formations, and to their lack of interest in problems of long-term processes and in all the opportunities of explanation that the investigation of such problems provides.

This sharp change in the character of social ideals, encountered here in the development of sociology, is not an isolated phenomenon. It is symptomatic of a more comprehensive change in the ideals predominant in the countries in which the main work of sociology is concentrated. This change points, in turn, to a specific transformation that has been taking place in the nineteenth and twentieth centuries in the internal and external relations of the older, developed industrial states. It must suffice here—as a summary of a more extensive inquiry—to indicate briefly the main outline of this transformation. This will facilitate understanding of sociological studies which, like the present one, give a central place to the investigation of long-term processes. The purpose is not to attack other ideals in the name of one's own, but to seek a better understanding of the structure of such processes themselves and to emancipate the theoretical framework of sociological research from the primacy of social ideals and doctrines. For we can only elicit sociological knowledge which is sufficiently adequate to be of use in solving the acute problems of society if, when posing and solving sociological problems, we cease giving precedence to preconceived notions of what the solutions ought to be over the investigation of what is.

VII

In the industrializing countries of the nineteenth century in which the first great pioneering works of sociology were written, the voices expressing the social beliefs, ideals, hopes, and long-term goals of the rising industrial classes gradually gained the advantage over those seeking to preserve the existing social order in the interests of the established courtly-dynastic, aristocratic, or patrician power elites. It was the former who, in keeping with their situation as the rising classes, had high expectations of a better future. And as their ideal lay not in the present but in the future, they were particularly interested in the dynamics, the development of society. In conjunction with one or another of these rising industrial classes, the sociologists of the time sought confirmation that the development of mankind would move in the direction of their wishes and hopes. They did so by exploring the direction and the driving forces of social development hitherto. In this activity they undoubtedly brought to light a very considerable amount of adequate knowledge on the problems of social development. But it is often very difficult in retrospect to distinguish between specific heteronomous doctrines filled with short-lived, time-bound ideals and those conceptual models which have significance independently of these ideals, solely with regard to verifiable facts.

On the other side, in the nineteenth century, were to be heard the voices of those who for one reason or another opposed the transformation of society through industrialization, whose social faith was oriented toward conservation of the existing heritage, and who held up, against what they took to be the deteriorating present, their ideal of a better past. They represented not only the preindustrial elites of the dynastic states but also broader working groups—above all, those engaged in agriculture and handicrafts, whose traditional livelihoods were being eroded by advancing industrialization. They were the opponents of all those who spoke from the standpoint of the two rising industrial working class, and who, in keeping with the rising situation of these classes, drew their inspiration from a belief in a better future, the progress of mankind. Thus, in the nineteenth century, the chorus of voices was split between those extolling a better past and those celebrating a better future.

Among the sociologists whose image of society was oriented toward progress and a better future are to be found, as we know, spokesmen of the two industrial classes. They include men like Marx and Engels, who identified themselves with the industrial working class; and they include bourgeois sociologists like Comte at the beginning of the nineteenth century or Hobhouse at the end. The spokesmen for the two rising industrial classes took confidence in the thought of the future improvement of the human condition, even if what they envisaged as improvement and progress varied widely depending on their class. It is of no small importance to realize how intense the interest in the problems of social development in the nineteenth century was, and to ask on what this interest was founded, if one is to understand why the belief in progress waned in the twentieth century and why, correspondingly, interest among sociologists in the problems of long-term social development declined.

But to understand this shift it is not sufficient, as has already been indicated, to consider only class figurations, the social relationships within states. The rise of industrial classes within the industrializing states of Europe in the nineteenth century went hand in hand with the continuing rise of these nations themselves. In that century these nations drove each other by constant rivalry to a greater increase of their predominance over less developed nations than ever before. Not only the classes within them but also these state-societies in their totality were rising, expanding social formations.

One might be tempted to attribute the belief in progress in European writing in the centuries preceding the twentieth primarily to the progress in science and technology. But that is an insufficient explanation. How little the experience of scientific and technological progress alone gives rise to an idealization of progress, to a confident faith in the continuous improvement of the human condition, is shown clearly enough by the twentieth century. The actual degree and tempo of progress in science and technology in this century exceed that in the preceding centuries very considerably. Likewise, the standard of living of the masses in the countries of the first wave of industrialization has been higher in the twentieth century than in preceding centuries. The state of health has improved; life expectancy has increased. But in the total chorus of the time, the voices of those who affirm progress as something valuable, who see in the improvement of the condition of men the centerpiece of a social ideal, and who believe confidently in the better future of mankind, have become appreciably fewer than in preceding centuries. On the other side of the choir, the voices of those who cast doubt on all these developments, who see no great promise of a better future for mankind or even for their own nation, and whose central social faith concentrates instead on the present as the highest value, on the conservation of their own nation, on the idealization of its existing social form or even of its past, its heritage and its traditional order, are increasing in the twentieth century and gradually becoming ever louder. In the preceding centuries, in which actual progress was already very palpable yet still slow and relatively limited, the idea of further, future progress had the character of an ideal toward which its adherents were striving and which possessed high value precisely as an ideal. In the twentieth century, when actual progress in science, technology, health, the standard of living, and not least in the reduction of inequality between people exceeds by far, in the older industrial nations, the progress in all previous centuries, progress has ceased for many people to be an ideal. The voices of those who doubt all this actual progress are growing more numerous.

The reasons for this change are manifold. Not all need be considered here. The recurrent wars, the incessant danger of war, and the threat of nuclear and other new scientific weapons certainly contribute to this coincidence of accelerating progress, particularly in the scientific and technical fields, with diminishing confidence in the value of this progress and of progress in general.

But the contempt heaped in the twentieth century on the preceding centuries' "shallow" belief in progress or their notion of a progressive development of human society; the obstructions blocking sociologists' view of problems of long-term social processes; the almost complete disappearance of the concept of social development from sociological texts—these and other symptoms of an extreme swing of the intellectual pendulum are not sufficiently explained by the upheavals of war and related phenomena. To understand them, we must also take account of specific changes in the twentieth century in the overall internal structure and international position of the great industrial nations of the nineteenth century.

Within these nations the representatives of the two industrial classes, the industrial bourgeoisie and the industrial working class, now establish themselves firmly against the earlier dynastic-aristocratic military power elites as the ruling groups in their states. The two industrial classes hold each other in an often precarious and always unstable balance of tensions, with the established working class still in the weaker position, but slowly gaining strength. The rising classes of the nineteenth century, who still had to fight within their states against the traditional dynastic elite, and for whom development, progress, a better future was not only a fact but also an ideal of great emotional significance, have become in the course of the twentieth century the more or less established industrial classes whose representatives are installed institutionally as the ruling or co-ruling groups. Partly as partners, partly as opponents, the representatives of the industrial bourgeoisie and the established industrial working class now form the primary elite in the nations of the first wave of industrialization. Accordingly, alongside class-consciousness and class ideals, and partly as a disguise for them, national consciousness and the ideal of their own nation as the highest value play an increasing role within the two industrial classes—first of all in the industrial bourgeoisie, but increasingly in the industrial working class as well.

Seen as an ideal, however, the nation turns attention to what already exists. Since representatives of the two powerful and populous industrial classes now have access to positions of power in the state, the nation, organized as a state, appears emotionally and ideologically as the highest value in its present condition. Moreover, it appears—emotionally and ideologically—as eternal, immutable in its essential features. Historical changes affect only externals; the people, the nation, so it appears, do not change. The English, German, French, Italian, and all other nations are, for those who constitute them, everlasting. In their "essence" they are always the same, whether we are speaking of the tenth or the twentieth century.

Furthermore, it was not only the two industrial classes within the older industrial nations which changed, once and for all, in the course of the twentieth century. The rise of the European nations and of their offshoots in other parts of the world, which had gone on for centuries, also came slowly to a standstill in our own. To be sure, their actual lead over non-European nations (with few exceptions) at first remained large; for a time it even increased. But the idea had formed and established itself in the age of the unchallenged ascendancy of the European nations, as among all powerful and ruling groups in the world, that the power they were able to wield over other nations was the expression of an eternal mission bestowed on them by God or nature or historical destiny, the expression of a superiority over those less powerful which was founded in their very essence. This idea of their own self-evident superiority, deeply rooted in the self-image of the older industrial nations, has been profoundly shaken by the actual course of development in the twentieth century. The reality-shock suffered when a national ideal collides with social reality has been absorbed by each nation in a different way, according to its own development and the specific nature of its national self-image. For Germany the more comprehensive significance of this collision was first concealed by the more direct shock of the military defeats. But it is indicative both of the solidity of the old national ideals and of the relative autonomy of this development as a whole that even in the victorious countries of the second European-American war there were, at first, immediately after the victory had been won, as far as can be determined, only very few people who realized how radically and fundamentally the military conflicts between two groups of relatively highly developed countries would reduce the power of this class of countries as a whole over the less developed countries, a reduction which had been prepared for some time. As is often the case, this sudden diminution in their power found the previously mighty countries unprepared and bewildered.

The actual opportunities for progress, for a better future, are—leaving aside the regressive possibilities of war—still very great for the older industrial nations. But in relation to their traditional national self-images, in which the idea of their own national civilization or culture is usually ensconced as the highest value of mankind, the future is disappointing. The idea of the unique nature and value of one's own nation often serves as legitimation for that nation's claim to lead all other nations. It is this self-image, this claim to leadership by the older industrial nations, that has been shaken in the second half of the twentieth century by what is still a very limited increase in power among the poorer, previously dependent and partly subjugated preindustrial societies in other parts of the world.[5]

In other words, this reality-shock, insofar as it affects the emotive vale of the present state of a nation in regard to its future possibilities, merely reinforces a tendency already present in national feeling present what the nation is and always has been, its eternal, unalterable heritage, possesses a far greater emotive value, as a means of self-legitimation and as an expression of the national scale of values and the national ideal, than any promise or ideal located in the future. The "national ideal" draws attention away from what changes to the enduring and the immutable.

This aspect of the transformation taking place in the European states, and in a number of closely related non-European states as well, has been matched by specific changes in the realm of ideas and in the modes of thought of intellectuals.

In the eighteenth and nineteenth centuries, philosophers and sociologists who spoke of "society" were usually thinking of "bourgeois society"—that is, aspects of social life that seemed to lie beyond the dynastic and military aspects of the state. In keeping with their situation and their ideals as spokesmen for groups which were by and large excluded from access to the central positions of state power, these men, when talking of society, usually had in mind a human society transcending all state frontiers. With the extensive assumption of state power by representatives of the two industrial classes, and with the corresponding development of national ideals in these two classes and particularly in their representative ruling elites, this conception of society was changed in sociology as well.

In society at large, the various class ideals of the industrial classes increasingly mingle and interpenetrate with national ideals. Certainly, conservative and liberal national ideals show a different nuance of nationalism than do socialist or communist ones. But such nuances influenced only marginally, if at all, the broad outline of the change that took place in the attitude toward state and nation of the established industrial classes, including their political and intellectual spokesmen, when these classes, ceasing to be groups excluded from central state power, became groups truly constituting the nation, whose leaders themselves represented and exercised state power. It accords with this development that many twentieth-century sociologists, when speaking of "society," no longer have in mind (as did their predecessors) a "bourgeois society" or a "human society" beyond the state, but increasingly the somewhat diluted ideal image of a nation-state. Within their general conception of society as something abstracted from the reality of the nation-state, the above-mentioned political and ideological nuances are again to be found. Among the leading sociological theorists of the twentieth century, conservative and liberal as well as socialist and communist shades are to be found in the image of society. Since, in the twentieth century, American sociology has taken over for a time the leading role in the development of theoretical sociology, the dominant type of sociological theory of this period reflects the specific character of its predominant national ideal, within which conservative and liberal features are not so sharply divided, or felt to be so antithetical, as in some European nation-states, particularly Germany.[6]

In sociological discussions, and in philosophical debates as well, the rejection of certain aspects of the sociological theories of the nineteenth century—above all, their orientation toward social development and the concept of progress—is often presented as based solely on the factual inadequacy of these theories. The short survey that has been given here of one of the main structural tendencies of the development of relations within and between the older industrial nations throws into sharper relief certain ideological aspects of this rejection. In accordance with the concept of ideology developed within the Marxian tradition, one might seek to explain the ideological aspects of the neglect of social development, and the preoccupation with the state of social systems, dominant in recent sociological theories solely by reference to the ideals of classes whose hopes, wishes, and ideals are related not to the future but to the conservation of the existing order. But this class-explanation of the social beliefs and ideals implicit in sociological theory is no longer sufficient in the twentieth century. In this period we must also take account of the development of national ideals transcending social classes in order to understand the ideological aspects of sociological theories. The integration of the two industrial classes into a state structure previously ruled by numerically very small preindustrial minorities; the rise of both classes to a position in which their representatives play a more or less dominant role in the state, and in which even the weaker sectors of the industrial workers can no longer be ruled without their consent; and the resulting stronger identification of both classes with the nation—all these factors give special impetus, in the social attitudes of this time, to the belief in one's own nation as one of the highest values in human life. The lengthening and multiplication of chains of interdependence between states, and the heightening of specific tensions and conflicts between states resulting from this, the momentous national wars and the ever-present danger of war—all these factors contribute to the growth of nation-centered patterns of thought.

It is the convergence of these two intrastate and interstate lines of development in the older industrial nations that has weakened the ideal of progress, the orientation of faith and desire toward a better future and therefore also toward an image of the past considered as development. Combined, the two lines of development cause this type of ideal to be replaced by others directed at conserving and defending the existing order. They relate to something that is felt to be immutable and realized in the present—the eternal nation. The voices proclaiming belief in a better future and the progress of mankind as their ideal make way, as the dominant section in the mixed social chorus of the time, for the voices of those who give precedence to the value of what exists and, above all, to the timeless value of their own nations, for which, in the succession of great and small wars, many people have lost their lives. This is—sketched in its main outline—the overall structural development which is reflected in the development of theories of society. Theories which reflect the ideals of rising classes in expanding industrial societies are replaced by theories dominated by the ideals of more or less established classes in highly developed societies whose growth has reached or passed its peak.

As an example of this type of sociological theory, it may suffice to cite one of its representative concepts, that of the "social system," as used by Parsons, but certainly not by him alone. It expresses very clearly the way in which a "society" is now conceived. A "social system" is a society "in equilibrium." Small oscillations of this equilibrium do occur, but normally society exists in a state of rest. All its parts, in this conception, are normally harmoniously attuned to one another. All individuals belonging to it are normally attuned by the same kind of socialization to the same norms. All are normally well-integrated, respect the same values in their actions, fulfill their prescribed roles without difficulty. Conflicts between them do not normally occur; these, like changes in the system, are manifestations of malfunction. In short, the image of society represented theoretically by this concept of the social system reveals itself on closer inspection to be the ideal image of a nation: all the people belonging to it obey the same norms on the basis of the same socialization, uphold the same values, and thus live normally in well-integrated harmony with one another. In the conception of the "social system" that we have before us, in other words, the image of the nation as community can be discerned. It is tacitly assumed that within such a "system" there is a relatively high degree of equality between people, for integration rests on the same socialization of people, on the uniformity of their values and norms throughout the entire system. Such a "system" is therefore a construction abstracted from a democratically conceived nation-state. From whatever side this construction is considered, the distinction between what the nation is and what the nation ought to be is blurred. Just as in the nineteenth-century sociological models of development the desired social process was presented (mingled with realistic observations) as a fact, so in the twentieth-century sociological models of a normally unchanging "social system" the desired ideal of a harmonious integration of all parts of the nation is also presented (mingled with realistic observations) as something that exists, a fact. But in the former case it is the future, in the latter the present, the nation-state existing here and now, that is idealized.

A mixture of "is" and "ought," of factual analyses and normative postulates, relating primarily to a society of a very definite type, a nation-state conceived in broadly egalitarian fashion, thus presents itself as the centerpiece of a theory which claims to be capable of serving as a model for the scientific investigation of societies in all times and places. One need only raise the question of whether and how far such sociological theories—derived primarily from present-day, more or less democratic nation-state societies which presuppose a high degree of integration of people into the "social system" as something both self-evident and desirable, and which therefore, imply a relatively advanced stage of social democratization—are applicable to societies at different stages of development, and which are less centralized and democratized, in order to perceive the weakness of a general theory of society from the church-steeple perspective of the present state of our own society. If such models of a "social system" are tested for their suitability as theoretical tools for the scientific investigation of a society with a high percentage of slaves or unfree subjects, or of feudal or hierarchical states—that is, societies in which not even the same laws apply to all people, not to speak of the same norms and values—it is quickly seen how present-centered these sociological models of systems conceived as states actually are.

What has been illustrated here by the "social" system example could be shown without difficulty to apply to other concepts of dominant contemporary sociology. Concepts like "structure," "norm," "integration," and "role" all represent in their current forms attempts to conceptualize certain aspects of human societies by abstracting from their dynamics, their genesis, their character as a process, their development. The rejection of the nineteenth-century ideological understanding of these dynamic aspects of society that has taken place can therefore be seen not only as a criticism of these ideological aspects in the name of a scientific concern with fact, but above all as a criticism of earlier ideals that no longer correspond to present social conditions and experience and have therefore been rejected in the name of later ideals. This replacement of one ideology by another[7] explains the fact that it is not simply the ideological elements in the nineteenth-century sociological concept of development that have been called into question, but the concept of development itself, the very consideration of problems of long-term social development, of sociogenesis and psychogenesis. In a word, the baby has been thrown out with the bathwater.

The present study, which concerns itself once again with social processes, may be better understood if this development of theoretical sociology is kept in mind. The tendency to condemn the social ideologies of the nineteenth century from the standpoint of those of the twentieth appears to preclude the idea that long-term processes might be the object of investigation without an ideological motive that is, without the author, under the pretense of speaking of what is or was, speaking in reality of what he believes and wishes ought to be. If the present study has any significance at all, this results not least from its opposition to this mingling of what is and what ought to be, of scientific analysis and ideal. It points to the possibility of freeing the study of society from its bondage to social ideologies. This is not to say that an investigation of social problems which excludes political and philosophical ideas means renouncing the possibility of influencing the course of political events through the results of sociological research. The opposite is the case. The usefulness of sociological research as a tool of social practice is increased if the researcher does not deceive himself by projecting what he desires, what he believes ought to be, into his investigation of what is and has been.

VIII

To understand the blockage which the predominant modes of thinking and feeling place in the way of the investigation of long-term changes of social structure and personality structure—and thus in the way of an understanding of this book—it is not enough to trace the development of the image of men as societies, the image of society. It is also necessary to keep in mind the development of the image of men as individuals, the image of the personality. As has been mentioned, one of the peculiarities of the traditional image of man is that people often speak and think of individuals and societies as if these were two phenomena existing separately—of which, moreover, one is often considered "real" and the other "unreal"—instead of two different aspects of the same human being.

This curious aberration of thinking, too, cannot be understood without a glance at its implicit ideological content. The splitting of the image of humanity into an image of man as individual and an image of men as societies has widely ramifying roots. One branch is a very characteristic split in the values and ideals encountered, on close inspection, in all the more developed nation-states, and perhaps most pronounced in nations with a strong liberal tradition. In the development of the value systems of all such nation-states, one finds, on the one hand, a strand which sees society as a whole, the nation, as the highest value; and, on the other, a strand which posits the wholly self-sufficient, free individual, the "closed personality," as the highest value. It is not always easy to harmonize these two "highest values" with one another. There are situations in which the two ideals are plainly irreconcilable. But usually this problem is not squarely faced. People talk with great warmth of the freedom and independence of the individual, and with equal warmth of the freedom and independence of their own nation. The first ideal arouses the expectation that the individual member of a nation-state, despite his community and interdependence with others, can reach his decisions in an entirely self-sufficient way, without regard to others; the second arouses the expectation—fulfilled particularly in war but often enough in peacetime, too—that the individual should and must subordinate everything belonging to him, even his life, to the survival of the "social whole."

This split in the ideals, this contradiction in the ethos by which people are brought up, finds expression in the theories of sociology. Some of these theories take as their starting point the independent, self-sufficient individual as the "true" reality, and therefore as the true object of social science; others start with the independent social totality. Some theories attempt to harmonize the two conceptions, usually without indicating how it is possible to reconcile the idea of an absolutely independent and free individual with that of an equally independent and free "social totality," and often without clearly perceiving the problem. The reflection of this unresolved inner division between the two ideals is seen above all in the theories of sociologists whose national ideal has a conservative-liberal tinge. Max Weber's theoretical work—if not his empirical work—and the theories of his successor Talcott Parsons are examples of this.

It may suffice as illustration to return once more to what has already been said about Parsons's conception of the relation of individual and society, of the "individual actor" and the "social system." One description of their relation is contained in the metaphor of "interpenetration," which shows clearly the important role played by the idea of the separate existence of the two human aspects. The reification of the ideal therefore finds expression in this conceptual edifice not only in the notion of the social system as a specific ideal image of the nation, but also in that of the individual actor, the "ego," as an ideal image of the free individual existing independently of all others. In both cases the theorist's ideal image is changed unawares under his hands into a fact, something that actually exists. For with regard to the image of the individual, too, what in the mind of the theorist ought to be, the image of the absolutely free and independent individual, is treated as if it were the image of what the individual actually is.

Now this is certainly not the place to fathom the reasons for this widely disseminated split in thinking about human beings. But the concern of the present study cannot properly be understood so long as the problems of the civilizing process are approached with the notions of the individual that have just been mentioned. In the course of this process the structures of the individual human being are changed in a particular direction. This is what the concept of "civilization," in the factual sense in which it is used here, actually means. The image current today of the individual as an absolutely independent and self-sufficient being is difficult to reconcile with the facts adduced here. It obstructs understanding of the long-term processes which people undergo on both the individual and social planes. Parsons uses on occasion, to illustrate his image of the personality, the old metaphor of the personality of the human actor as a "black box,"[8] i.e., a closed container "inside" which certain individual processes take place. The metaphor is taken from the toolbox of psychology. It basically means that all that can be observed scientifically in a human being is his behavior. We can observe what the "black box" does. But what goes on inside the box, what is also termed the "soul" or "mind"—the "ghost in the machine," as an English philosopher called it[9]—is not an object of scientific investigation. One cannot avoid, in this context, exploring in more detail an image of the individual which plays a considerable role in the human sciences today and thus also contributes to the neglect of long-term changes in human beings in the course of social development as a subject of research.

The image of the individual as an entirely free, independent being, a "closed personality" who is "inwardly" quite self-sufficient and separate from all other people, has behind it a long tradition in the development of European societies. In classical philosophy this figure comes onto the scene as the epistemological subject. In this role, as *homo philosophicus*, the individual gains knowledge of the world "outside" him in a completely autonomous way. He does not need to learn, to take this knowledge from others. The fact that he came into the world as a child, the whole process of his development to adulthood and as an adult, is neglected as immaterial by this image of man. In the development of mankind it took many thousands of years for people to learn to understand the relations

between natural events, the course of the stars, rain and sun, thunder and
lightning, as manifestations of a blind, impersonal, purely mechanical and
regular sequence of causal connections. But the "closed personality" of *homo
philosophicus* apparently perceives this mechanical and regular causal chain as an
adult simply by opening his eyes, without needing to learn anything about it
from others, and quite independently of the stage of knowledge reached by
society. The process—the individual human being as a process in growing up,
human beings together as a process in the development of mankind—is reduced
in thought to a state. The individual opens his eyes as an adult and not only
recognizes autonomously here and now, without learning from others, what all
these objects are that he perceives; he not only knows immediately what he is to
classify as animate and inanimate, as mineral, vegetable, or animal; but he also
knows directly here and now that they are linked causally in accordance with
natural laws. The question for philosophers is merely whether he gains this
knowledge of causal connections here and now on the basis of his experience—
whether, in other words, these connections are a property of the observable facts
"outside" him—or the connections are something rooted in the nature of human
reason and superadded from "inside" the human being to what flows into him
from "outside" through the sense organs. If we start from this image of man,
from the *homo philosophicus* who was never a child and seemingly came into the
world an adult, there is no way out of the epistemological impasse. Thought
steers helplessly back and forth between the Scylla of positivism and the
Charybdis of apriorism. It does so precisely because what is actually observable as
a process, a development of the social macrocosm within which the development
of the individual microcosm can also be observed, is reduced in thought to a
state, an act of perception taking place here and now. We have here an example of
how closely the inability to conceive long-term social processes (i.e., structured
changes in the figurations formed by large numbers of interdependent human
beings) or to understand the human beings forming such figurations is connected
to a certain type of image of man and of self-perception. People to whom it seems
self-evident that their own self (or their ego, or whatever else it may be called)
exists, as it were, "inside" them, isolated from all the other people and things
"outside," have difficulty assigning significance to all those facts which indicate
that individuals live from the first in interdependence with others. They have
difficulty conceiving people as relatively but not absolutely autonomous and
interdependent individuals forming changeable figurations with one another.
Since the former self-perception seems self-evident to those subscribing to it, they
cannot easily take account of facts which show that this kind of perception is itself
limited to particular societies, that it comes into being in conjunction with
certain kinds of interdependencies, of social bonds between people—in short,
that it is a structural peculiarity of a specific stage in the development of
civilization, corresponding to a specific stage of differentiation and individualiz-

ation of human groups. If one grows up in the midst of such a group, one cannot easily imagine that there could be people who do not experience themselves in this way as entirely self-sufficient individuals cut off from all other beings and things. This kind of self-perception appears as obvious, a symptom of an eternal human state, simply the normal, natural, and universal self-perception of all human beings. The conception of the individual as *homo clausus*, a little world in himself who ultimately exists quite independently of the great world outside, determines the image of man in general. Every other human being is likewise seen as a *homo clausus*; his core, his being, his true self appears likewise as something divided within him by an invisible wall from everything outside, including every other human being.

But the nature of this wall itself is hardly ever considered and never properly explained. Is the body the vessel which holds the true self locked within it? Is the skin the frontier between "inside" and "outside"? What in man is the capsule, and what the encapsulated? The experience of "inside" and "outside" seems so self-evident that such questions are scarcely ever posed; they seem to require no further examination. One is satisfied with the spatial metaphor of "inside" and "outside," but one makes no serious attempt to locate the "inner" in space; and although this omission to investigate one's own presuppositions is hardly appropriate to scientific procedure, this preconceived image of *homo clausus* commands the stage not only in society at large but also in the human sciences. Its derivatives include not only the traditional *homo philosophicus*, the image of man of classical epistemology, but also *homo oeconomicus, homo psychologicus, homo historicus*, and not least *homo sociologicus* in his present-by version. The images of the individual of Descartes, of Max Weber, and of Parsons and many other sociologists are of the same provenance. As philosophers did before them, many sociological theorists today accept this self-perception, and the image of the individual corresponding to it, as the untested basis of their theories. They do not detach themselves from it in order to confront it and call its aptness into question. Consequently, this kind of self-perception and image of the individual often coexists unchanged with attempts to abolish the reduction to states. In Parsons, for example, the static image of the ego, the individual actor, the adult abstracted from the process of growing up, coexists unmediated with the psychoanalytical ideas that he has taken over in his theory—ideas which relate not to the state of adulthood but to the process of becoming adult, to the individual as an open process in indissoluble interdependence with other individuals. As a result, the ideas of social theorists constantly find themselves in blind alleys from which there seems no way out. The individual—or, more precisely, what the present concept of the individual refers to—appears again and again as something existing "outside" society. What the concept of society refers to appears again and again as something existing outside and beyond individuals. One seems to have the choice only between theoretical approaches which present the individual as the truly existent beyond society, the truly "real" (society being seen as an abstraction, something not truly existing), and other theoretical approaches which posit society as a "system," a "social fact *sui generis*," a reality of a peculiar type beyond individuals. At most one can—as is occasionally done in an apparent solution to the problem—juxtapose the two conceptions unconnectedly, that of the individual as *homo clausus*, as ego, as individual beyond society, and that of society as a system outside and beyond individuals. But the incompatibility of these two conceptions is not thereby disposed of. In order to pass beyond this dead end of sociology and the social sciences in general, it is necessary to make clear the inadequacy of both conceptions, that of the individual outside society and, equally, that of a society outside individuals. This is difficult as long as the sense of the encapsulation of the self within itself serves as the untested basis of the image of the individual, and as long as, in conjunction with this, the concepts "individual" and "society" are understood as if they related to unchanging states.

The conceptual trap in which one is continually being caught by these static notions of "individual" and "society" can only be prized open if, as is done here, these notions are developed further, in conjunction with empirical investigations, in such a way that the two concepts are made to refer to processes. But this development is initially blocked by the extraordinary conviction carried in European societies since roughly the Renaissance by the self-perception of human beings in terms of their own isolation, the severance of their own "inside" from everything "outside." In Descartes the perception of the isolation of the individual, who finds himself confronted as a thinking ego within his own head by the entire external world, is somewhat weakened by the idea of God. In contemporary sociology the same basic experience finds theoretical expression in the acting ego, which finds itself confronted with people "outside" as "others." Apart from Leibnizian monadology, there is in this philosophico-sociological tradition scarcely a single approach to the problem that sets out from the basis of a multiplicity of interdependent human beings. Leibniz, who did just that, only managed to do so by bringing his version of *homo clausus*, the "windowless monads," in relation to one another by a metaphysical construction. All the same, monadology represents an early advance in the direction of precisely the kind of model that is urgently in need of further development in sociology today. The decisive step Leibniz took was an act of self-distantiation, which enabled him to entertain the idea that one might experience oneself not as an "ego" confronting all other people and things, but as a being among others. It was characteristic of the prevalent kind of experience in that whole period that the geocentric world-picture of the preceding age was superseded only in the area of inanimate nature by a world-picture demanding from the subject of experience a higher degree of self-detachment, a removal of oneself from the center. In men's reflection on themselves the geocentric world-picture was to a large extent preserved in the egocentric one that replaced it. At the center of the human universe, or so it appeared, stood each single human being as an individual completely independent of all others.

Nothing is more characteristic of the unquestioning way in which even today, in thinking about human beings, the separate individual is taken as the starting point than the fact that one does not speak of *homines sociologiae* or *oeconomicus* when talking of the image of man in the social sciences, but always of the image of the single human being, the *homo sociologicus* or *oeconomicus*. From this conceptual starting point, society presents itself finally as a collection of individuals completely independent of each other, whose true essence is locked within them and who therefore communicate only externally and from the surface. One must call on the help of a metaphysical solution, as Leibniz did, if, starting from windowless, closed, human and extrahuman monads, one is to justify the notion that interdependence and communication between them, or the perception by human beings of interdependence and communications, are possible. Whether we are dealing with human beings in their role as "subject" confronting the "object," or in their role as "individual" confronting "society," in both cases the problem is presented as if an adult human being, completely isolated and self-sufficient—that is, in a form reflecting the prevalent self-perception of people in the modern age crystallized in an objectifying concept—constitutes the frame of reference. What is discussed is his relation to something "outside" himself conceived (like the isolated human being) as a state, to "nature" or to "society." Does this something exist? Or is it only produced by a mental process, or at any rate founded primarily on a mental process?

IX

Let us try to me clear what the problem actually is that is being discussed here. We are not concerned with calling into doubt the authenticity of the self-perception that finds expression in the image of man as *homo clausus* and its many variations. The question is whether this self-perception, and the image of man in which it is usually crystallized quite spontaneously and without reflection, can serve as a reliable starting point for an attempt to gain adequate understanding of human beings—and therefore also of oneself—regardless of whether this attempt is philosophical or sociological. Is it justified—that is the question—to place at the foundation of philosophical theories of perception and knowledge, and of sociological and other theories in the human sciences, as a self-evident assumption incapable of further explanation, the sharp dividing line between what is "inside" man and the "external world," a division which often appears directly given in self-awareness, and furthermore has put down deep roots in European intellectual and linguistic traditions, without a critical and systematic examination of its validity?

This conception has had, for a certain period of human development, an extraordinary persistence. It is found in the writings of all groups whose powers of reflection and whose self-awareness have reached the stage at which people are in a position not only to think but also to be conscious of themselves, and to reflect on themselves, as thinking beings. It is already found in Platonic philosophy and in a number of other schools of philosophy in antiquity. The idea of the "self in a case," as already mentioned, is one of the recurrent *leitmotifs* of modern philosophy, from the thinking subject of Descartes, Leibniz's windowless monads, and the Kantian subject of knowledge (who from his aprioristic shell can never quite break through to the "thing in itself") to the more recent extension of the same basic idea of the entirely self-sufficient individual: beyond the perspective of thought and perception as reified into "understanding" (*Verstand*) and "reason" (*Vernunft*), to the whole "being" of man, his "existence" in the various versions of existentialist philosophy; or to his action as the starting point of the social theory of Max Weber, for example, who—entirely in keeping with the above-mentioned split—made the not wholly successful attempt to distinguish between "social action" and "nonsocial action," i.e., presumably "purely individual action."

But one would gain only a very inadequate idea of the nature of this self-perception and this image of man if they were understood merely as ideas set forth in scholarly writings. The windowlessness of the monads, the problems surrounding *homo clausus*, which a man like Leibniz tries to make at least more bearable by a speculative solution showing the possibility of relationships between monads, is today accepted as self-evident not only by scholars. Expressions of this self-perception are found in a less reflected form in imaginative literature—for example, in Virginia Woolf's lament over the incommunicability of experience as the cause of human solitude. Its expression is found in the concept of "alienation," used more and more frequently within and outside literature in the most diverse variations in recent decades. It would be not uninteresting to ascertain more systematically whether and how far gradations and variations of this type of self-perception extend to the various elite groups and the broader strata of more developed societies. But the examples cited suffice to indicate how persistent and how much taken for granted in the societies of modern Europe is the feeling of people that their own "self," their "true identity," is something locked away "inside" them, severed from all other people and things "outside"—although, as has been mentioned, no one finds it particularly simple to show clearly where and what the tangible walls or barriers are which enclose this inner self as a vessel encloses its contents, and separate it from what is "outside." Are we here concerned, as it often appears, with an eternal, fundamental experience of all human beings accessible to no further explanation, or with a type of self-perception which is characteristic of a certain stage in the development of the figurations formed by people, and of the people forming these figurations?

In the context of this book the discussion of this complex of problems has a twofold significance. On the one hand, the civilizing process cannot be understood so long as one clings to this type of self-perception and regards the image of man as *homo clausus* as self-evident, not open to discussion as a source of problems. On the other hand, the theory of civilization developed in this study offers a procedure for solving these problems. The discussion of this image of man serves in the first place to improve understanding of the ensuing study of the civilizing process. It is possible, however, that one might gain a better understanding of this introductory discussion from the vantage point of the end of the book, from a more comprehensive picture of the civilizing process. It will suffice here to indicate briefly the connection between the problems arising from the concept of *homo clausus* and the civilizing process.

One can gain a clear idea of this connection relatively simply by first looking back at the change in people's self-perception that was influenced by the abandonment of the geocentric world-picture. Often this transition is presented simply as a revision and extension of knowledge about the movements of the stars. But it is obvious that this changed conception of the figurations of the stars would not have been possible had not the prevailing image of man been seriously shaken on its own account, had not people become capable of perceiving themselves in a different light than before. Of primary importance for human beings everywhere is a mode of experience by which they place themselves at the center of public events, not just as individuals but as groups. The geocentric world-picture is the expression of this spontaneous and unreflecting self-centeredness of men, which is still encountered unequivocally today in the ideas of people outside the realm of nature, e.g., in natiocentric sociological modes of thought or those centered on the isolated individual.

The geocentric experience is still accessible to everyone as a plane of perception even today. It merely does not constitute the dominant plane of perception in public thought. When we say, and indeed "see," that the sun rises in the east and goes down in the west, we spontaneously experience ourselves and the earth on which we live as the center of the cosmos, as the frame of reference for the movements of the stars. It was not simply new discoveries, a cumulative increase in knowledge about the objects of human reflection, that were needed to make possible the transition from a geocentric to a heliocentric world-picture. What was needed above all was an increased capacity in men for self-detachment in thought. Scientific modes of thought cannot be developed and become generally accepted unless people renounce their primary, unreflecting, and spontaneous attempt to understand all their experience in terms of its purpose and meaning for themselves. The development that led to more adequate knowledge and increasing control of nature was therefore, considered from one aspect, also a development toward greater self-control by men.

It is not possible to go into more detail here about the connections between the development of the scientific manner of acquiring knowledge of objects, on the one hand, and the development of new attitudes of men toward themselves, new personality structures, and especially shifts in the direction of greater affect control and self-detachment, on the other. Perhaps it will contribute to an understanding of these problems if one recalls the spontaneous, unreflecting self-centeredness of thought that can be observed at any time among children in our own society. A heightened control of the affects, developed in society and learned by the individual, and above all a heightened degree of autonomous affect control, was needed in order for the world-picture centered on the earth and the people living on it to be overcome by one which, like the heliocentric world-picture, agreed better with the observable facts but was at first far less satisfying emotionally; for it removed man from his position at the center of the universe and placed him on one of many planets circling about the center. The transition from an understanding of nature legitimized by a traditional faith to one based on scientific research, and the shift in the direction of greater affect control that this transition involved, thus represents one aspect of the civilizing process examined from other aspects in the following study.

But at that particular stage in the development of these more object-related than self-related conceptual instruments for exploring extra-human nature, it was apparently not possible to include in the investigation, and to reflect upon, this civilizational shift itself, the move toward stronger and more "internalized" self-control that was taking place within man himself. What was happening to human beings as they increased their understanding of nature remained at first inaccessible to scientific insight. It is not a little characteristic of this stage of self-consciousness that the classical theories of knowledge representing it are concerned far more with the problems of the object of knowledge than with the subject of knowledge, with object-perception than with self-perception. But if the latter is not included from the start in posing epistemological problems, then this very posing leads to an impasse of equally inadequate alternatives.

The development of the idea that the earth circles round the sun in a purely mechanical way in accordance with natural laws—that is, in a way not in the least determined by any purpose relating to mankind, and therefore no longer possessing any great emotional significance for men—presupposed and demanded at the same time a development in human beings themselves toward increased emotional control, a greater restraint of their spontaneous feeling that everything they experience and everything that concerns them takes its stamp from them, is the expression of an intention, a destiny, a purpose relating to themselves. Now, in the age that we call "modern," men reach a stage of self-detachment that enables them to conceive of natural processes as an autonomous sphere operating without intention or purpose or destiny in a purely mechanical or causal way, and having a meaning or purpose for themselves only if they are in a position, through objective knowledge, to control it and thereby give it a meaning and a purpose.

But at this stage they are not yet able to detach themselves sufficiently from themselves to make their own self-detachment, their own affect restraint—in short, the conditions of their own role as the subject of the scientific understanding of nature—the object of knowledge and scientific enquiry.

Herein lies one of the keys to the question of why the problem of scientific knowledge took on the form of classical European epistemology today. The detachment of the thinking subject from his objects in the act of cognitive thought, and the affective restraint that is demanded, did not appear to those thinking about it at this stage as an act of distancing but as a distance actually present, as an eternal condition of spatial separation between a mental apparatus apparently locked "inside" man, an "understanding" or "reason," and the objects "outside" and divided from it by an invisible wall.

If we saw earlier how ideals can turn unawares in thought into something actually existing, how "ought" becomes "is," we are here confronted with a reification of a different kind. The act of conceptual distancing from the objects of thought that any more emotionally controlled reflection involves—which scientific observations and thought demand in particular, and which at the same time makes them possible—appears to self-perception at this stage as a distance actually existing between the thinking subject and the objects of his thought. And the greater restraint of affect-charged impulses in the face of the objects of thought and observation, which accompanies every step toward increased conceptual distancing, appears here in people's self-perception as an actually existing cage which separates and excludes the "self" or "reason" or "existence," depending on the point of view, from the world "outside" the individual.

The fact that, and in part the reason why, from the late Middle Ages and the early Renaissance on, there was a particularly strong shift in individual self-control—above all, in self-control acting independently of external agents as a self-activating automatism, revealingly said today to be "internalized"—is presented in more detail from other perspectives in the following study. The transformation of interpersonal external compulsion into individual internal compulsion, which now increasingly takes place, leads to a situation in which many affective impulses cannot be lived out as spontaneously as before. The autonomous individual self-controls produced in this way in social life, such as "rational thought" or the "moral conscience," now interpose themselves more sternly than ever before between spontaneous and emotional impulses, on the one hand, and the skeletal muscles, on the other, preventing the former with greater severity from directly determining the latter (i.e., action) without the permission of these control mechanisms.

That is the core of the structural change and the structural peculiarities of the individual which are reflected in self-perception, from about the Renaissance onward, in the notion of the individual "ego" in its locked case, the "self" divided by an invisible wall from what happens "outside." It is these civilizational self-controls, functioning in part automatically, that are now experienced in individual self-perception as a wall, either between "subject" and "object" or between one's own "self" and other people ("society").

The shift in the direction of greater individualization that took place during the Renaissance is well enough known. This study gives a somewhat more detailed picture of this development in terms of personality structure. At the same time, it points to connections that have not yet been properly clarified. The transition from the experience of nature as landscape standing opposed to the observer, from the experience of nature as a perceptual object separated from its subject as if by an invisible wall; the transition from the intensified self-perception of the individual as an entirely self-sufficient entity independent and cut off from other people and things—these and many other phenomena of the time bear the structural characteristics of the same civilizational shift. They all show marks of the transition to a further stage of self-consciousness at which the inbuilt self-control of the affects grows stronger and reflective detachment greater, while the spontaneity of affective action diminishes, and at which people feel these peculiarities of themselves but do not yet detach themselves sufficiently from them in thought to make themselves the object of investigation.

We thus come somewhat closer to the center of the structure of the individual personality underlying the self-experience of *homo clausus*. If we ask once again what really gives rise to this concept of the individual as encapsulated "inside" himself, severed from everything existing outside him, and what the capsule and the encapsulated really stand for in human terms, we can now see the direction in which the answer must be sought. The firmer, more comprehensive and uniform restraint of the affects characteristic of this civilizational shift, together with the increased internal compulsions that, more implacably than before, prevent all spontaneous impulses from manifesting themselves directly and motorically in action, without the intervention of control mechanisms—these are what is experienced as the capsule, the invisible wall dividing the "inner world" of the individual from the "external world" or, in different versions, the subject of cognition from its object, the "ego" from the "other," the "individual" from "society." What is encapsulated are the restrained instinctual and affective impulses denied direct access to the motor apparatus. They appear in self-perception as what is hidden from all others, and often as the true self, the core of individuality. The term "the inner man" is a convenient metaphor, but it is a metaphor that misleads.

There is good reason for saying that the human brain is situated within the skull and the heart within the rib cage. In these cases we can say clearly what is the container and what is contained, what is located within walls and what outside, and of what the dividing walls consist. But if the same figures of speech are applied to personality structures they become inappropriate. The relation of instinct controls to instinctive impulses, to mention only one example, is not a spatial relationship. The former do not have the form of a vessel containing the latter within it. There are schools of thought that consider the control mechanisms, conscience or reason, as more important, and there are others which attach greater importance to instinctual or emotional impulses. But if we are not disposed to argue about values, if we restrict our efforts to the investigation of what is, we find that there is no structural feature of man that justifies our calling one thing the core of man and another the shell. Strictly speaking, the whole complex of tensions, such as feeling and thought, or spontaneous behavior and controlled behavior, consists of human activities. If instead of the usual substance-concepts like "feeling" and "reason" we use activity-concepts, it is easier to understand that while the image of "outside" and "inside," of the shell of a receptacle containing something inside it, is applicable to the physical aspects of a human being mentioned above, it cannot apply to the structure of the personality, to the living human being as a whole. On this level there is nothing that resembles a container—nothing that could justify metaphors like that of the "inside" of a human being. The intuition of a wall, of something "inside" man separated from the "outside" world, however genuine it may be as an intuition, corresponds to nothing in man having the character of a real wall. One recalls that Goethe once expressed the idea that nature has neither core nor shell and that in her there is neither inside nor outside. This is true of human beings as well.

On the one hand, therefore, the theory of civilization which the following study attempts to develop helps us to see the misleading image of man in what we call the modern age as less self-evident, and to detach ourselves from it, so that work can begin on an image of man oriented less by one's own feelings and the value judgments attached to them than by men as the actual objects of thought and observation. On the other hand, a critique of the modern image of man is needed for an understanding of the civilizing process. For in the course of this process the structure of individual human beings changes; they become "more civilized." And so long as we see the individual human being as by nature a closed container with an outer shell and a core concealed within it, we cannot comprehend how a civilizing process embracing many generations is possible, in the course of which the personality structure of the individual human being changes without the nature of human beings changing.

This must suffice here as an introduction to the reorientation of individual self-consciousness and to the resulting development of the image of man, without which any ability to conceive a civilizing process or a long-term process involving social and personality structures is largely blocked. So long as the concept of the individual is linked with the self-perception of the "ego" in a closed case, we can hardly conceive "society" as anything other than a collection of windowless monads. Concepts like "social structure," "social process," or "social development" then appear at best as artificial products of sociologists, as "ideal-typical" constructions needed by scientists to introduce some order, at least in thought, into what appears in reality to be a completely disordered and structureless accumulation of absolutely independent individual agents.

As can be seen, the actual state of affairs is the exact converse. The notion of individuals deciding, acting, and "existing" in absolute independence of one another is an artificial product of men which is characteristic of a particular stage in the development of their self-perception. It rests partly on a confusion of ideals and facts, and partly on a reification of individual self-control mechanism's—of the severance of individual affective impulses from the motor apparatus, from the direct control of bodily movements and actions.

This self-perception in terms of one's own isolation, of the invisible wall dividing one's own "inner" self from all the people and things "outside," takes on for a large number of people in the course of the modern age the same immediate force of conviction that the movement of the sun around an earth situated at the center of the cosmos possessed in the Middle Ages. Like the geocentric picture of the physical universe earlier, the egocentric image of the social universe is certainly capable of being conquered by a more realistic, if emotionally less appealing picture. The emotion may or may not remain: it is an open question how far the feeling of isolation and alienation is attributable to ineptitude and ignorance in the development of individual self-controls, and how far to structural characteristics of advanced societies. Just as the public predominance of emotionally less appealing images of a physical universe not centered on the earth did not entirely efface the more private self-centered experience of the sun as circling around the earth, the ascendancy of a more objective image of man in public thinking may not necessarily efface the more private ego-centered experience of an invisible wall dividing one's own "inner world" from the world "outside." But it is certainly not impossible to dislodge this experience, and the image of man corresponding to it, from its self-evident acceptance in research in the human sciences. Here and in what follows one can see at least the beginnings of an image of man that agrees better with unhindered observations of human beings, and for this reason facilitates access to problems which, like those of the civilizing process or the state-building process, remain more or less inaccessible from the standpoint of the old image of man, or which, like the problem of the relation of individuals to society, continually give rise from that standpoint to unnecessarily complicated and never entirely convincing solutions.

The image of man as a "closed personality" is here replaced by the image of man as an "open personality" who possesses a greater or lesser degree of relative (but never absolute and total) autonomy vis-à-vis other people and who is, in fact, fundamentally oriented toward and dependent on other people throughout his life. The network of interdependencies among human beings is what binds them together. Such interdependencies are the nexus of what is here called the figuration, a structure of mutually oriented and dependent people. Since people are more or less dependent on each other first by nature and then through social learning, through education, socialization, and socially generated reciprocal needs, they exist, one might venture to say, only as pluralities, only in figurations. That is why, as was stated earlier, it is not particularly fruitful to conceive of men in the image of the individual man. It is more appropriate to envisage an image of numerous interdependent people forming figurations (i.e., groups or societies of different kinds) with each other. Seen from this basic standpoint, the rift in the traditional image of man disappears. The concept of the figuration has been introduced precisely because it expresses what we call "society" more clearly and unambiguously than the existing conceptual tools of sociology, as neither an abstraction of attributes of individuals existing without a society, nor a "system" or "totality" beyond individuals, but the network of interdependencies formed by individuals. It is certainly quite possible to speak of a social system formed of individuals. But the undertones associated with the concept of the social system in contemporary sociology make such an expression seem forced. Furthermore, the concept of the system is prejudiced by the associated notion of immutability.

What is meant by the concept of the figuration can be conveniently explained by reference to social dances. They are, in fact, the simplest example that could be chosen. One should think of a mazurka, a minuet, a polonaise, a tango, or rock'n'roll. The image of the mobile figurations of interdependent people on a dance floor perhaps makes it easier to imagine states, cities, families, and also capitalist, communist, and feudal systems as figurations. By using this concept we can eliminate the antithesis, resting finally on different values and ideals, immanent today in the use of the words "individual" and "society." One can certainly speak of a dance in general, but no one will imagine a dance as a structure outside the individual or as a mere abstraction. The same dance figurations can certainly be danced by different people; but without a plurality of reciprocally oriented and dependent individuals, there is no dance. Like every other social figuration, a dance figuration is relatively independent of the specific individuals forming it here and now, but not of individuals as such. It would be absurd to say that dances are mental constructions abstracted from observations of individuals considered separately. The same applies to all other figurations. Just as the small dance figurations change—becoming now slower, now quicker—so too, gradually or more suddenly, do the large figurations which we call societies. The following study is concerned with such changes. Thus, the starting point of the study of the process of state formation is a figuration made up of numerous relatively small social units existing in free competition with one another. The investigation shows how and why this figuration changes. It demonstrates at the same time that there are explanations which do not have the character of causal explanations. For a change in a figuration is explained partly by the endogenous dynamic of the figuration itself, the immanent tendency of a figuration of freely competing units to form monopolies. The investigation therefore shows how in the course of centuries the original figuration changes into another, in which such great opportunities of monopoly power are linked with a single social position—kingship—that no occupant of any other social position within the network of interdependencies can compete with the monarch. At the same time, it indicates how the personality structures of human beings also change in conjunction with such figurational changes.

Many questions that deserve consideration in an introduction have had to be left aside here; otherwise, the introduction would have become a separate volume. Limited as they are, however, these reflections show perhaps that an understanding of the following study requires a fairly extensive reorientation in the sociological thought and imagination predominant today. To detach oneself from the idea of oneself and of every individual human being as *homo clausus* is certainly not easy. But without detachment from this notion, one cannot possibly understand what is meant when a civilizing process is referred to as a transformation of individual structures. Similarly, it is not easy so to develop one's own imaginative capacity that one is able to think in figurations, and, moreover, in figurations whose normal characteristics include a tendency to change, sometimes even in a specific direction.

In this introduction I have endeavored to discuss some fundamental problems which, had they not been discussed, would have stood in the way of an understanding of this book. The ideas expressed are not all simple, but I have attempted to present them as simply as I could. I hope they may facilitate and deepen the understanding, and perhaps also the pleasure, afforded by this book.

Leicester   N.E.
July, 1968

Appendix II

Foreign Language Originals of the Exemplary Extracts and Verses

Medieval Manners
(p. 48)

"Dem vrumen soltu volgen,
dem boesen wis erbolgen."[8]

"Svee dîn gesinde dich
erzürne, lieber sun, sô sich
daz dir werde iht sô gâch
daz dich geriuve nâch."[9]

"Kein edeler man selbander sol
mit einem leffel sufen niht;
dar zimet hübschen liuten wol,
den dicke unedellich geschiht."[10]

"Sümliche bizent ab der sniten
und stozents in die schüzzel wider
nach geburischen siten;
sülh unzuht legent diu hübschen niden."[11]

"Etlicher ist also gemuot,
swenn er daz bein genagen hat,
daz erz wider in die schüzzel tuot;
daz habet gar fü missetat."[12]

"Der riuspet, swenne er ezzen sol,
und in daz tischlach sniuzet sich,
diu beide ziment niht gar wol,
als ich des kan versehen mich."[13]

"Swer ob tem tische sniuzet sich,
ob er ez ribet an die hant,
der ist ein gouch, versihe ich mich,
dem ist niht besser bekannt."[14]

"Swer snudet als ein wazzerdahs,
so er izzet, als etlicher phliget,
und smatzet als ein Beiersahs,
wie der sich der zuht verwiget."[15]

"Ir sült die kel ouch jucken niht,
so ir ezrt, mit blozer hant;
ob ez aber also geschiht,
so nemet hovelich daz gewant."[16]

"In diu oren grifen niht enzimt
und ougen, als etlicher tuot,
swer den unflat von der nasen nimt,
so er izzet, diu driu sint niht guot."[17]

"ich hoere von sümlichen sagen
(ist daz war, daz zimet übel),
daz si ezzen ungetwagen;
den selben müezen erlamen die knübel."[18]

"man sol ouch ezzen alle frist
mit der hant diu engegen ist;
sitzt der gesell ze der rehten hant,
mit der tenken iz zehant;
man sol sich geren wenden
daz man ezz mit beiden henden."[20]

"Schaffe vor swaz dir sî nöt
daz du iht sitzest schamerôt."[22]

The Problem of the Change in Behavior during the Renaissance
(p. 56)

"Ne mangue mie je te commande,
avant que on serve de viande,
car il sembleroit que tu feusses
trop glout, ou que trop fain eüsses."
....
"Vuiddier et essever memoire
aies ta bouche, quant veulz boire."[32]

On Behavior at Table
(p. 68)

A.

Thirteenth century
Daz ist des tanhausers getiht und ist guod hofzuht.

1   Er dünket mich ein zühtic man,
der alle zuht erkennen kan,
der keine unzuht nie gewan
und im der zühte nie zeran.

2   Der zühte der ist also vil
und sint ze manegen dingen guot;
nu wizzent, der in volgen wil,
daz er vil selten missetuot.

        ....

25   Swenne ir ezzt, so sit gemant,
daz ir vergezzt der armen niht;
so wert ir gote vil wol erkant,
ist daz den wol von iu geschiht.

On v. 25 c.f. the first rule of Bonvicino da Riva:

        La primiera è questa:
        che quando tu è mensa,
        del povero bexognoxo
        imprimamenté inpensa.

From *Ein spruch der ze tische kêrt*:

313   Mit der schüzzel man niht sûfen sol,
mit einem lefel, daz stât wol.

315   Swer sich über die schüzzel habt,
und unsüberlichen snabt
mit dem munde, als ein swin,
der sol bi anderm vihe sîn.

33   Kein edeler man selbander sol
mit einem leffel sufen niht;
daz zimet hübschen liuten wol,
den dicke unedellich geschiht.

37   Mit schüzzeln sufen niemen zimt,
swie des unfuor doch maneger lobe,
der si frevellichen nimt
und in sich giuzet, als er tobe.

41   Und der sich über die shüzzel habet,
so er izzet, als ein swin,

und gar unsuberliche snabet,
und smatzet mit dem munde sin

45   Sümliche bizent ab der sniten
und stozents in die schüzzel wider

319   swer sniubet als ein lahs,
unde smatzet als ein dahs,
und rüsset sô er ezzen sol,
diu driu dinc ziment niemor wol.

In the *Curtesien* of Bonvicino da Riva:

La sedexena apresso con veritae:
No sorbilar dra bocha quando tu mangi con cugial;
Quello fa sicom bestia, chi con cugial sorbilia
Chi doncha à questa usanza, ben fa s'el se dispolia.
                         or

In *The Book of nurture and school of good manners*:

201   And suppe not lowde of thy Pottage
no tyme in all thy lyfe.

On v. 45 c.f. *Ein spruch der ze tische kêrt*:

346   Swer diu bein benagen hât,
und wider in die schüzzel tuot,
dâ sîn die höveschen vor behuot.
                         or

From *Quisquis es in mensa*:

In disco racta non sit bucella redacta.

nach geburischen siten;
sülh unzuht legent die hübschen nider.

49   Etlicher ist also gemuot,
swenn er daz bein genagen hat,
daz erz wider in die schüzzel tuot;
daz habet gar für missetat.

53   Die senf und salsen ezzent gern,
die sulen des vil flizic sin,
daz si den unflat verbern
und stozen niht die vinger drin.

57   Der riuspet, swenne er ezzen sol,
und in daz tischlach sniuzet sich,
diu beide ziment niht gar wol,
als ich des kan versehen mich.

65 Der beide reden und ezzen wil,
    diu zwei werc mit einander tuon,
    und in dem slaf wil reden vil,
    der kan vil selten wol geruon.

69 Ob dem tische lat daz brehten sin,
    so ir ezzet, daz sümliche tuont,
    dar an gedenkent, friunde min,
    daz nie kein site so übele stuont.

    ....

81 Ez dünket mich groz missetat,
    an sweme ich die unzuht sihe,
    der daz ezzen in dem munde hat
    und die wile trinket als ein vihe.

85 Ir sült niht blasen in den tranc,
    des spulgent sümeliche gern;
    daz ist ein ungewizzen danc,
    der unzuht solte man enbern.

94 E daz ir trinkt, so wischt den munt,
    daz if besmalzet niht den tranc;
    diu hovezuht wol zimt alle stunt
    und ist ein hovelich gedanc.

105 Und die sich uf den tisch legent,
    so si ezzent, enstet niht wol;
    wie selten die die helme wegent,
    da man frouwen dienen sol.

109 Ir sült die kel ouch jucken niht,
    so ir ezzt, mit blozer hant;
    ob ez aber also geschiht,
    so nemet hovelich daz gewant.

113 Und jucket da mit, daz zimt baz,
    denn iu diu hant unsuber wirt;
    die zuokapher merkent daz,
    swer sülhe unzuht niht verbirt.

117 Ir sült die zende stüren niht
    mit mezzern, als etlicher tuot,
    und als mit manegem noch geschiht;
    swer des phliget, daz ist niht guot.

125 Swer ob dem tisch des wenet sich,
    daz er die gürtel witer lat,
    so wartent sicherliche uf mich,
    er ist niht visch biz an den grat.

129 Swer ob dem tische sniuzet sich,
    ob er ez ribet an die hant,
    der ist ein gouch, versihe ich mich,
    dem ist niht bezzer zuht bekant.

141   Ich hoere von sümlichen sagen
       (ist daz war, daz zimet übel),
       daz si ezzen ungetwagen;
       den selben müezen erlamen die knübel!

157   In diu oren grifen niht enzimt
       und ougen, als etlicher tuot,
       swer den unflat von der nasen nimt,
       so er izzet, diu driu sint niht guot.

B.

Fifteenth century
From *S'ensuivent les contenances de la table*:

I

Enfant qui veult estre courtoys
Et à toutes gens agreable,
Et principalement à table,
Garde ces rigles en françois.

II

Enfant soil de copper soigneux
Ses ongles, et oster l'ordure,
Car se l'ordure il y endure,
Quant ilz se grate yert roingneux.

III

Enfant d'honneur, lave tes mains
A ton lever, à ton disner,
Et puis au supper sans finer;
Ce sont trois foys à tous le moins.

XII

Enfant, se tu es bien sçavant,
Ne mès pas ta main le premier
Au plat, mais laisse y toucher
Le maistre de l'hostel avant.

XIII

Enfant, gardez que le morseau
Que tu auras mis en ta bouche
Par une fois, jamais n'atouche,
Ne soit remise en ton vaisseau.

XIV

Enfant, ayes en toy remors
De te'n garder, se y as failly,
Et ne presentes à nulluy
Le morseau que tu auras mors.

XV

Enfant, garde toy de maschier
En ta bouche pain ou viande,
Oultre que ton cuer ne demande,
Et puis après le recrascher.

XVII

Enfant, garde qu'en la saliere
Tu ne mettes point tes morseaulx
Pour les saler, ou tu deffaulx,
Car c'est deshonneste maniere.

XXIV

Enfant, soyes tousjours paisible,
Doulx, courtois, bening, amiable,
Entre ceulx qui sierront à table
Et te gardes d'estre noysibles.

XXVI

Enfant, se tu faiz en ton verre
Souppes de vin aucunement,
Boy tout le vin entierement,
ou autrement le gecte à terre.

XXXI

Enfant se tu veulx en ta pence
Trop excessivement bouter
Tu seras constraint à rupter
Et perdre toute contenance.

XXXIV

Enfant garde toy de frotter
Ensamble tes mains, ne tes bras
Ne à la nappe, ne aux draps
A table on ne se doit grater.

C.

1530

From *De civilitate morum puerilium*, by Erasmus of Rotterdam:

Mantile si datur, aut humero sinistro aut bracchio laevo imponito.

Cum honoratioribus accubiturus, capite prexo, pileum relinquito.

A dextris sit poculum et cultellus escarius rite purgatus, ad laevam panis.

Quidam ubi vix bene consederint, mox manus in epulas conjiciunt. Id luporum est . . .

Primus cibum appositum ne attingito, non tantum ob id quod arguit avidum, sed quod interdum cum periculo conjunctum est, dum qui fervidum inexploratum recipit in os, aut expuere cogitur, aut si deglutiat, adurere gulam, utroque ridiculus aeque ac miser.

Aliquantisper morandum, ut puer assuescat affectui temperare.

Digitos in jusculenta immergere, agrestium est: sed cultello fuscinave tollat quod vult, nec id ex toto eligat disco, quod solent liguritores, sed quod forte ante ipsum jacet, sumat.

Quad digitis excipi non potest, quadra excipiendum est.

Si quis e placenta vel artorcrea porrexit aliquid, cochleari aut quadra excipe, aut cochleare porrectum accipe, et inverso in quadram cibo, cochleare reddito.

Si liquidius est quad datur, gustandum sumito et cochleare reddito, sed ad mantile extersum.

Digitos unctos vel ore praelingere, vel ad tunicam, extergere, pariter incivile est: id mappa potius aut mantili faciendum.

D.

1558

From *Galateo*, by Giovanni della Casa, Archbishop of Benevento, quoted from the five-language edition (Geneva, 1609), p. 68:

Was meynstu würde dieser Bischof und seine edle Gesellschaft (il Vescove e la sua nobile brigata) denen gesagt haben, die wir bisweilen sehen wie die Säwe mit dem rüssel in der suppen ligen und ihr gesicht nit einmal auffheben und ihre augen, viel weniger die hände nimmermehr von der speise abwenden, die alle beyde backen auffblasen gleich als ob sie in die Trommete bliesen oder ein fewer auffblasen wolten, die nicht essen sondern fressen und die kost einschlingen, die ihre Hände bey nahe bis an den Elbogen beschmutzen und demnach die servieten also zu richten, dass unflätige küchen oder wischlumpen viel reiner sein möchten.

Dennoch schämen sich diese unfläter nit mit solchen besudelten servieten ohn unterlass den schweiss abzuwischen (der dann von wegen ihrs eilenden und ubermessigen fressens von irem haüpt über die stirn und das angesicht bis auff den hals häufig herunter trüpffet) ja auch wol die Nase so offt es inen gelicht darin zu schneutzen.

E.

1560
From à *Civilité* by C. Calviac:

L'enfant estant assis, s'il ha une serviette devant luy sur son assiette, il la prendra et la mettra sur son bras ou espaule gauche, puis il mettra son pain de costé gauche, le cousteau du costé droit, comme le verre aussi, s'il le veut laisser sur la table, et qu'il ait la commodité de l'y tenir sans offenser personne. Car il pourra advenir qu'on ne sçaurait tenir le verre à table ou du costé droit sans empescher par ce moyen quelqu'un.

Il fault que l'enfant ait la discrétion de cognoistre les circonstances du lieu où il sera.

En mangeant . . . il doit prendre le premier qui luy viendra en main de son tranchoir.

Que s'il y à des sauces, l'enfant y pourra . . . tremper honnestement et sans tourner de l'autre costé après qu'il l'aura tremper de l'un . . .

Il est bien nécessaire à l'enfant qu'il apprenne dès sa jeunesse à despécer un gigot, une perdrix, un lapin et choses semblables.

C'est une chose par trop ords que l'enfant présente une chose après l'avoir rongée, ou celle qu'il ne daigneroit manger, si ce n'est à son serviteur.

Il n'est non plus honneste de tirer par la bouche quelque chose qu'on aura jà mâchée, et la mettre sur le tranchoir; si ce n'est qu'il advienne que quelquefoys il succe la moelle de quelque petit os, comme par manière de passe temps en attendant la desserte, car après l'avoir succé il le doit mettre sur son assiette, comme aussi les os des cerises et des prunes et semblables, pour ce qu'il n'est point bon de les avaler ny de les jecter à terre.

L'enfant ne doit point ronger indécentement les os, comme font les chiens.

Quant l'enfant voudra du sel, il en prendra avec la poincte de son cousteau et non point avec les trois doigs;

Il faut que l'enfant couppe sa chair en menus morceaux sur son tranchoir . . . et ne faut point qu'il porte la viande à la bouche tantost d'une main, tantost de l'autre, comme les petits qui commencent à manger; mais que tousjours il face, avec la main droicte, en prenant honnestement le pain ou la chair avec troys doigs seulement.

Quant à la manière de mâcher, elle est diverse selon les lieux ou pays où on est. Car les Allemans mâchent la bouche close, et trouvent laid de faire autrement. Les Françoys au contraire ouvrent à demy la bouche, et trouvent la procédure des Allemans peu ord. Les Italiens y procèdent fort mollement, et les François plus rondement et en sorte qu'ils trouvent la procédure des Italiens trop délicate et précieuse.

Et ainsi chacune nation ha quelque chose de propre et différent des autres. Pourquoy l'enfant y pourra procéder selon les lieux et coustumes d'iceux où il sera.

Davantage les Allemans usent de culières en mangeant leur potage et toutes les choses liquides, et les Italiens des fourchettes. Et les Françoys de l'un et de l'autre, selon que bon leur semble et qu'ilz en ont la commodité. Les Italiens se plaisent aucunement à avoir chacun son cousteau. Mais les Allemans ont cela en singulière recommandation, et tellement qu'on leur fait grand desplaisir de le prendre devant eux ou de leur demander. Les François au contraire: toute une pleine table de personnes se servont de deux ou trois cousteaux, sans faire difficulté de le demander, ou prendre, ou le bailler s'ilz l'ont. Par quoy, s'il advient que quelqu'un demande son cousteau à l'enfant, il luy doit bailler après l'avoir nettoyé à sa serviette, en tenant la poincte en sa main et présentant le manche à celuy qui le demande: car il seroit deshonneste de la faire autrement.

F.

Between 1640 and 1680
From *Chanson des Marquis de Coulanges*[51]:

> Jadis le potage on mangeoit
> Dans le plat, sans cérémonie,
> Et sa cuillier on essuyoit
> Souvent sur la poule bouillie.
> Dans la fricassée autrefois
> On saussait son pain et ses doigts.
>
> Chacun mange présentement
> Son potage sur son assiette;
> Il faut se servir poliment
> Et de cuillier et de fourchette,
> Et de temps en temps qu'un valet
> Les aille laver au buffet.

G.

1672
From Antoine de Courtin, *Nouveau traité de civilité*:

P. 127. Si chacun prend au plat, il faut bien se garder d'y mettre la main, que les plus qualifiez ne l'y ayent mise les premiers; n'y de prendre ailleurs qu à l'endroit du plat, qui est vis à vis de nous: moins encore doit-on prendre les meilleurs morceaux, quand même on seroit le dernier à prendre.

Il est necessaire aussi d'observer qu'il faut toûjours essuyer vostre cuillere quand, aprés vous en estre servy, vous voulez prendre quelque chose dans un autre plat, y ayant des gens si delicats qu'ils ne voudroient pas manger du potage où vous l'auriez mise, après l'avoir portée à al bouche.

Et même si on est à la table de gens bien propres, il ne suffit pas d'essuyer sa cuillere; il ne faut plus s'en servir, mais en demander une autre. Aussi sert—on à present en bien des lieux des cuilleres dans des plats, qui ne servent que pour prendre du potage et de la sauce.

Il ne faut pas manger le potage au plat, mais en mettre proprement sur son assiette; et s'il estoit trop chaud, il est indecent de souffler à chaque cuillerée; il faut attendre qu'il soit refroidy.

Que si par malheur on s'estoit brûlè, il faut le souffrir si l'on peut patiemment et sans le faire paroître: mais si la brûlure estoit insupportable comme il arrive quelquefois, il faut promptement et avant que les autres s'en apperçoivent, prendre son assiette d'une main, et la porter contre sa bouche, et se couvrant de l'autre main remettre sur l'assiette ce que l'on a dans la bouche, et le donner vistement par derriere à un laquais. La civilité veut que l'on ait de la politesse, mais elle ne pretend pas que l'on soit homicide de soy-même. Il est tres indecent de toucher à quelque chose de gras, à quelque sauce, à quelque syrop etc. avec les doigts, outre que cela en même—temps vous oblige à deux ou trois autres indecences, l'une est d'essuyer frequemment vos mains à vostre serviette, et de la salir comme un torchon de cuisine; en sorte qu'elle fait mal au coeur à ceux qui la voyent porter à la bouche, pour vous essuyer. L'autre est de les essuyer à vostre pain, ce qui est encore tres—malpropre; et la troisième de vous lécher les doigts, ce qui est le comble de l'impropreté.

P. 273 . . . comme il y en a beaucoup (sc. usages) qui ont déja changé, je ne doute pas qu'il n'y en ait plusieurs de celles-cy, qui changeront tout de même à l'avenir.

Autrefois on pouvoit . . . tremper son pain dans la sausse, et il suffisoit pourvu que l'on n'y eût pas encore mordu; maintenant ce seroit une espece de rusticité.

Autrefois on pouvoit tirer de sa bouche ce qu'on ne pouvoit pas manger, et le jetter à terre, pourvu que cela se fist adroitement; et maintenant ce seroit une grande saleté . . .

H.

1717

From *François de Callières, De la science du monde et des connoissances utiles à la conduite de la vie*:

P. 97. En Allemagne et dans les Royaumes du Nord, c'est une civilité et une bienséance pour un Prince de boire le premier à la santé de celui ou de ceux qu'il traite, et de leur faire presenter ensuite le même verre, ou le même gobelet, rempli d'ordinaire de même vin; et ce n'est point parmi eux un manque de politesse de boire dens le même verre, mais une marque de franchise et d'amitié; les femmes boivent aussi les premieres, et donnent ensuite, ou font porter leur verre avec le même vin, dont elles ont bû à la santé de celui à qui elles se sont adressées, sans que cela passe pour une faveur particulière comme parmi nous . . .

Je ne sçaurois approuver (p. 101)—n'en déplaise a Messicurs les Gens du Nort—cette maniere de boire dans le même verre, et moins encore sur le reste des Dames, cela a un air de malpropreté, qui me feroit souhaiter qu'ils témoignassent leur franchise par d'autres marques.

I.

1714

From an anonymous *Civilité française* (Liège, 1714?):

P. 48. Il n'est pas . . . honnéte d'humer sa soupe quand on se serviroit d'ecuelle si ce n'étoit que ce fut dans la famille aprés en avoir pris la plus grande partie avec la cuilliére.

Si le potage est dans un plat portez-y la cuilliére à votre tour sans vous précipiter.

Ne tenez-pas toujours votre couteau à la main comme font les gens de village; il suffit de le prendre lorsque vous voulez vous en servir.

Quand on vous sert de la viande, il n'est pas séant de la prendre avec la main; mais il faut présenter votre assiette de la main gauche en tenant votre fourchette ou votre couteau de la droite.

Il est contre la bienséance de donner à flairer les viandes et il faut se donner bien de garde de les remettre dans le plat après les avoir flairées. Si vous prenez dans un plat commun ne choisissez pas les meilleurs morceaux. Coupez avec le couteau aprés que vous aurez arrêté la viande qui est dans le plat avec la fourchette de laquelle vous vous servirez pour porter sur votre assiette ce que vous aurez coupé, ne prenez donc pas la viande avec la main . . .

Il ne faut pas jetter par terre ni os ni coque d'oeuf ni pelure d'aucun fruit.

Il en est de méme des noyaux que l'on tire plus honnétement de la bouché avcc les deux doigts qu'on ne les crache dans la main.

J.

1729

From La Salle, *Les Règles de la bienséance et de la civilité chrétienne* (Rouen, 1729):

Des choses dont on doit se servir lorsqu'on est à Table (p. 87).

On doit se servir à Table d'une serviette, d'une assiette, d'un couteau, d'une cuillier, et d'une fourchette: il serait tout à fait contre l'honnêteté, de se passer de quelqu'une de toutes ces choses en mangeant.

C'est à la personne la plus qualifée de la compagnie à déplier sa serviette la premiere, et les autres doivent attendre qu'elle ait déplie la sienne, pour déplier la leur. Lorsque les pesonnes sont à peu prés égales, tous la déplient ensemble sans cérémonie.

Il est malhonneste de se servir de sa serviette pour s'essuier le visage; il l'est encore bien plus de s'en frotter les dents et ce serait une faute des plus grossieres contre la Civilité de s'en servir pour se moucher . . . L'usage qu'on peut et qu'on doit faire de sa serviette lorsqu'on est à Table, est de s'en servir pour nettoïer sa bouche, ses lévres et ses doigts quand ils sont gras, pour dégraisser le couteau avant que de couper du Pain, et pour nettoïer la cuiller, et la fourchette après qu'on s'en est servi.

Lorsque les doits sont fort gras, il est á propos de les dégraisser d'abord avec un morceau de pain, qu'il faut ensuite laisser sur l'assiette avant que de les essuïer a sa serviette, afin de ne la pas beaucoup graisser, et de ne la pas rendre malpropre.

Lorsque la cuillier, la fourchette ou le couteau sont sales, ou qu'ils sont gras, il est tres mal honnète de les lecher, et il n'est nullement séant de les essuïer, ou quelqu'autre chose que ce soit, avec la nape, on doit dans ces occasions, et autres semblables, se servir de la serviette et pour ce qui est de la nape, il faut avoir égard de la tenir toújours fort propre, et de n'y laisser tomber, ni eau, ni vin, ni rien qui la puisse salir.

Lorsque l'assiette est sale, on doit bien se garder de la ratisser avec la cuillier, ou la fourchette, pour la rendre nette, ou de nettoïer avec ses doigts son assiette, ou le fond de quelque plat: cela est trés indécent, il faut, ou n'y pas toucher, ou si on a la commodité d'en changer, se la faire déservir, et s'en faire aporter une autre.

Il ne faut pas lorsqu'on est à Table tenir toújours le couteau á la main, il suffit de le prendre lorsqu'on veut s'en servir.

Il est aussi trés incivil de porter un morceau de pain à la bouche aïant le couteau á la main; il l'est encore plus de l'y porter avec la pointe du couteau. Il faut observer la même chose en mangeant des pommes, des poires ou quelques autres fruits.

Il est contre la Bienséance de tenir la fourchette ou la cuillier á plaine main, comme si on tenoit un bàton; mais on doit toújours les tenir entre scs doights.

On ne doit pas se servir de la fourchette pour porter à sa bouche des choses liquides . . . c'est la cuiller qui est destinée pour prendre ces sortes de choses.

Il est de l'honnèteté de se servir toujours de la fourchette pour porter de la viande á sa bouche, car la Bien-séance ne permet pas de toucher avec les doigts à quelque chose de gras, à quelque sauce, ou á quelque sirop; et si quelqu'un le faisoit, il ne pouoit se dispenser de commettre ensuite plusieurs autres incivilitez: comme seroit d'essuïer souvent ses doigts à sa serviette, ce qui la rendroit fort sale et fort malpropre, ou de les essuïer à son pain, ce qui seroit très incivil, ou de lécher ses doigts, ce qui ne peut être permis à une personne bien née et bien élevée.

K.

1774

From La Salle, *Les Règles de la bienséance et de la civilité chrétienne* (1774 ed.) p. 45ff.:

La serviette qui est posée sur l'assiette, étant destinée à préserver les habits des taches ou autres malpropretés inséparables des repas, il faut tellement l'étendre sur soi qu'elle couvre les devants du corps jusques sur les genoux, en allant au-dessous du col et non la passant en dedans du même col. La cuillier, la fourchette et le couteau doivent toujours être placée à la droite.

La cuillier est destinée pour les choses liquides, et la fourchette pour les viandes de consistance.

Lorsque l'une ou l'autre est sale, on peut les nettoyer avec sa serviette, s'il n'est pas possible de se procurer un autre service; il faut éviter de les assuyer avec la nappe, c'est une malpropreté impardonnable.

Quand l'assiette est sale, il faut en demander une autre; ce seroit une grossiéreté révoltante de la nettoyer avec les doigts avec la cuiller, la fourchette et le couteau.

Dans les bonnes tables, les domestiques attentifs changent les assiettes sans qu'on les en avertissent.

Rien n'est plus mal-propre que de se lécher les doigts, de toucher les viandes, et de les porter à la bouche avec la main, de remuer les sauces avec le doigt, ou d'y tremper le pain avec la fourchette pour la sucer.

On ne doit jamais prendre du sei avec les doigts. Il est très ordinaire aux enfants d'entasser morceaux sur morceaux, de retirer même de la bouche ce qu'ils y ont mis et qui est maché, de pousser les morceaux avec les doigts. Rien n'est plus mal honnête. . . . porter les viandes au nez, les flairer, ou les donner à flairer est une autre impolitesse qui attaque le Maître de la table; et s'il arrive que l'on trouve quelque malpropreté dans les aliments, il faut les retirer sans les montrer.

L.

1780?
From an anonymous work, *La Civilité honete pour les enfants* (Caen, n.d.) p. 35:

. . . Après, il mettra sa serviette sur lui, son pain à gauche et son couteau à droite, pour couper la viande sans le rompre. Il se donnera aussi de garde de porter son couteau à sa bouche. Il ne doit point avoir ses mains sur son assiette. . . . il ne doit point non plus s'accouder dessus, car cela n'appartient qu'à des gens malades ou vieux.

Le sage Enfant s'il est avec des Supérieurs mettra le dernier la main au plat . . .

. . . après si c'cst de la viande, la coupera proprement avec son couteau et la mangera avec son pain.

C'est une chose rustique et sale de tirer de sa bouche la viande qu'on a déjà mâchée et la mettre sur son assiette. Aussi ne faut-il jamias remettre dans le plat ce qu'on en a osté.

M.

1786
From a conversation between the poet Delille and Abbé Cosson:

Dernièrement, l'abbé Cosson, professeur de belles lettres au collège Mazarin, me parla d'un dîner où il s'étoit trouvé quelques jours auparavant avec des gens de la cour . . . à Versailles.

Je parie, lui dis-je, que vous avez fait cent incongruités.

—Comment donc, reprit vivement l'abbé Cosson, fort inquiet. Il me semble que j'ai fait la même chose que tout le monde.

—Quelle présomption! Je gage que vous n'avez rien fait comme personne. Mais voyons, je me bornerai au dîner. Et d'abord que fîtes-vous de votre serviette en vous mettant à table?

—De ma serviette? Je fis comme tout le monde; je la déployai, je l'étendis sur moi et l'attachai par un coin à ma boutonnière.

—Eh bien mon cher, vous êtes le seul qui ayez fait cela; on n'étale point sa serviette, on la laisse sur ses genoux. Et comment fîtes-vour pour manger votre soupe?

—Commte tout le monde, je pense. Je pris ma cuiller d'une main et ma fourchette de l'autre . . .

—Votre fourchette, bon Dieu! Personne ne prend de fourchette pour manger sa soupe . . . Mais dites-mois quelque chose de la manière dont vous mangeâtes votre pain.

—Certainement à la manière de tout le monde: je la coupai proprement avec mon couteau.

—Eh, on rompt son pain, on ne le coup pas . . . Avançons. Le café, comment le prîtes-vous?

—Eh, pour le coup, comme tout le monde; il était brûlant, je le versai par petites parties de ma tasse dans ma soucoupe.

—Eh bien, vous fîtes comme ne fit sûrement personne: tout le monde boit son café dans sa tasse, et jamais dans sa soucoupe . . .

Changes in Attitude Toward the Natural Functions
(p. 105)

A.

Fifteenth century

From *S'ensuivent les contenances de la table*:

VIII.

Enfant, prens de regarder peine
Sur le siege où tu te sierras
Se aucune chose y verra
Qui soit deshonnete ou vilaine

B.

From *Ein spruch der ze tische kêrt*[61]:

329   Grîf ouch niht mit blôzer hant
        Dir selben under dîn gewant.

C.

1530

From *De civilitate morum puerilium*, by Erasmus of Rotterdam:

Incivile est eum salutare, qui reddit urinam aut alvum exonerat . . .

Membra quibus natura pudorem addidit retegere citra necessitatem procul abesse debet ab indole liberali. Quin ubi necessitas huc cogit, tamen id quoque decente verecundia faciendum est, etiam si nemo testis adsit. Nunquam emin non adsunt angeli, quibus in pueris gratissimus est pudicitiae comes custosque pudor.

Lotium remorari valetudini perniciosum, secreto reddere verecundum. Sunt qui praecipiant ut puer compressis natibus ventris flatum retineat. Atqui civile non est, dum urbanus videri studes morbum accersere. Si licet secedere, solus id faciat. Sin minus, iuxta vetustissimum proverbium: Tussi crepitum dissimulet. Alioqui cur non eadem opera praecipiunt ne aluum deijciant, quum remorari flatum periculosius sit, quam alvum stringere.

Morbum accersere: Audi Coi senis de crepitu sententiam . . . Si flatus sine crepitu sonituque excernitur optimus. Melius tamen est, ut erumpat eum sonitu quam si condatur retineaturque. Atqui adeo utile hic fuerit devorare pudorem, ut corpus redimas, ut consilio omnium medicorum sic nates comprimas, quemadmodum apud epigrammatarium Aethon, qui quamvis in sacro sibi caverit crepando, tamen compressis natibus Iovem salutat. Parasitica, et illorum qui ad supercilinin stant, vox est; Didici comprimere nates.

Tussi crepitum dissimulare: Tussire se simulant, qui pudoris gratia nolunt crepitum audiri. Lege Chiliades; Tussis pro crepitu.

Quum remorari flap perniciosus sit: Extant Nicarchi versus epigrammatum libro secundo. . . .

quibus pestiferam retenti crepitus vim describit, sed quia omnium manibus teruntur non duxi adscribendos.

D.

1558

From *Galateo*, by Giovanni della Casa, Archbishop of Benevento:

Uber das stehet es einem sittsamen, erbahrn mensch nicht an (Similmente non si conviene a Gentlihuomo costumatè apparecchiarsi alle necessità naturali . . .), dass er sich zu natürlicher notdurft in andrer Leute gegenwertigkeit rüste und vorbereite oder nach dem er solches verrichtet sich in iher gegenwertigkeit widerum nestele und bekleide. So wird auch ein solcher nach seiner aus heimlichen orten wiederkunfft fur ehrliche gesellschaft die hände nicht waschen, nach dem die ursache darumb er sich wäschet der leut gedancken eine unfläterey für die augen stellt. Ist auch eben umb derselbigen ursach willen kein feine gewohnheit, wenn einem auf der Gassen etwas abscheuliches, wie es sich wol bisweilen zuträgt, fürkommet, statim ad comitem se convertat eique illam monstrat.

Multo minus decebit alteri re foetidam, ut olfaciat porrigere, quod nonnunquam facere aliqui solent atque adeo urgere, quum etiam naribus aliorum rem illam grave olentem admovent et inquiunt: Odorare amabo quantopere hoec foeteat; quum potius dicendum esset: Quia foctet, noli odorari.

E.

1570

From the Wernigerode Hofordnung of 1570:

Dass nicht männiglich also unverschämt und ohln alle Scheu, den Bauern gleich, die nicht zu Hofe oder bei einigen ehrbaren, züchtigen Leuten gewesen, vor das Frauenzimmer, Hofstubn und andrer Gemach Thüren oder Fenster seine Nothdurft ausrichte, sondern in jeder sich jederziet und—ort vernünftiger, züchtiger und ehrerbietiger Wort und Geberde erzeige und verhalte.

F.

1589

From the Brunswick Hofordnung of 1589:

Dergleichen dass niemand, der sei auch wer er wolle, unter, nach oder vor den Mahlzeiten, spät oder fruh, die Wendelsteine, Treppen, Gänge and Gemächer mit dem Urin oder anderm Urflath verunreinigen, sondern wegen solcher Nothdurft an gebührliche, verordnete Orte gehen thue.

H.

1694

From the correspondence of the Duchess of Orléans:

L'odeur de la boue est horrible. Paris est un endroit affreux; les rues y ont une si mauvaise odeur qu'on ne peut y tenir; l'extrême chaleur y fait pourrir beaucoup de viande et de poisson et ceci, joint à la foule des gens qui . . . dans les rues, cause une odeur si détestable qu'il n y a pas moyen de la supporter.

I.

1729

From La Salle, *Les Règles de la bienséance et de la civilité chrétienne* (Rouen, 1729), p. 45ff.:

Il est de la Bienséance, et de la pudeur de couvrir toutes les parties du Corps, hors la teste et les mains. On doit éviter avec soin, et autant qu'on le peut, de porter la main nué sur toutes les parties du Corps qui ne sont pas ordinairement découvertes; et si on est obligé de les toucher, il faut que ce soit avec beaucoup de précaution. Il est à propos de s'accoutumer à souffrir plusieurs petites incommoditez sans se tourner, frotter, ni gatter . . .

Il est bien plus contre la Bienséance et l'honnesteté, de toucher, ou de voir en une autre personne, particulierement si elle est de sexe différent, ce que Dieu défend de regarder en soi. Lorsqu'on a besoin d'uriner, il faut toujours se retirer en quelque lieu ècarté: et quelques autres besoins naturels qu'on puisse avoir, il est de la Bienséance (aux Enfants mesmes) de ne les faire que dans des lieux où on ne puisse pas estre aperçú.

It est très incivil de laisser sortir des vens de son Corps, soit par haut, soit par bas, quand mesme ce seroit sans faire aucun bruit, lorsqu'on est en compagnie; et il est honteux et indécent de le faire d'une maniere qu'on puisse estre entendu des autres.

Il n'est jamais séant de parler des parties du Corps qui doivent estre cacheés, ni de certaines nécessitez du Corps ausquelles la Nature nous a assujetti, ni mesme de les nommer.

J.

1731

From Johann Christian Barth, *Die galanthe Ethica*, in welcher gezeiget wird, wie sich ein junger Mensch bey der galanten Welt sowohl durch manierliche Werke als complaisante Worte recommandiren soll. Allen Liebhabern der heutigen Politesse zu sonderbarem Nutzen and Vergnügen ans Licht gestellet. (Dresden and Leipzig, 1731), p. 288:

Gehet man bey einer Person vorbey, welche sich erleichtert, so stellet man sich, als ob man solches nicht gewahr würde, und also ist es auch wider die Höflichkeit, selbige zu begrüssen.

K.

1774

From La Salle, *Les Règles de la bienséance et de la civilité chrétienne*, p. 24:

Il est de la bienséance et de la pudeur de couvrir toutes les parties du corps, hors de la tête et les mains.

Pour les besoins naturels il est de la bienséance (aux enfants même) de n'y satisfaire que dans des lieux ou on ne soit pas apperçu.

Il nest jamais séant de parler des parties do corps qui doivent toujours être cachées, ni de certaines nécessités du corps auxquelles la nature nous a assujettis, ni même de les nommer.

L.

1768

Letter from Madame du Deffand to Madame de Choiseul, 1768:

Je voudrais, chère grand'maman, venir peindre, ainsi qu'au grand-abbé, quelle fut ma surprise, quand hier matin on m'apporte, sur mon lit, un grand sac de votre part. Je me hate de l'ouvrir, j'y fourre la main, j'y trouve des petits pois . . . et puis un vase . . . je le tire bien vite: c'est un pot de chambre. Mais d'une beauté, d'une magnificence telles, que mes gens tout d'une voix disent qu'il en fallait faire one saucière. Le pot de chambre a été en représentation hier toute la soirée et fit l'admiration de tout le monde. Les pois . . . furent mangés sans qu'il en restât un seul.

On Blowing One's Nose
(p. 117)

A.

Thirteenth Century

Bonvesin de la Riva (Bonvicino da Riva) *De le zinquanta cortexie da tavola*:

(a)   La desetena apresso si è:
           quando tu stranude,
           Over ch'el te prende la tosse,
           guarda con tu làvori
           In oltra parte te volze,
           ed è cortexia inpensa,
           Azò che dra sariva no
           zesse sor la mensa.

(b)   Pox la trentena è questa:
           zaschun cortese donzello
           Che se vore mondà lo naxo,
           con li drapi se faza bello;
           Chi mangia over chi menestra,
           no de'sofià con le die;
           Con li drapi da pcy se monda
           vostra cortexia.

B.

From *Ein spruch der ze tische kêrt*:

323   Swer in daz tischlach sniuzet sich,
           daz stât niht wol, sicherlich.

C.

From *S'ensuivent les contenances de la table*:

XXXIII

      Enfant se ton nez est morveux,
      Ne le torche de la main nue,
      De quoy ta viande est tenue.
      Le fait est vilain et honteux.

D.

From A. Cabanès, *Moeurs intimes du temps passé* (Paris, 1910) p. 101:

Au quinzième siècle, on se mouchait encore dans les doigts et les sculpteurs de l'époque n'ont pas craint de reproduire ce geste, passablement réaliste, dans leur monuments.

E.

1530

From *De civilitate morum puerilium*, by Erasmus, ch. 1:

Pileo aut veste emungi, rusticanum, bracchio cubitove, salsamentariorum, nec multo civilius id manu fieri, si mox pituitam vesti illinas. Strophiolis excipere narium recrementa, decorum; idque paulisper averso corpore, si qui adsint honoratiores. Si quid in solum dejectum est emuncto duobus digitis naso, mox pede proterendum est.

[From the scholia:]
Inter mucum et pituitam parum differentiae est, nisi quod mucum crassiores, pituitam fluidas magis sordes interpretantur. Strophium et strophiolum, sudarium et sudariolum, linteum et linteolum confundunt passim Latini scriptores.

G.

1558
From *Galateo*, by Giovanni della Casa:

P. 72: Du solt dein fatzenetlein niemand, überreichen als ob es new gewaschen were . . . (non offerirai il suo mocichino . . .).

P. 44: Es gehöret sich auch nicht, wenn du die nase gewischet hast, dass du das schnuptuch auseinander ziehest und hineinguckest gleich als ob dir perlen und robinen vom gehirn hätte abfallen mögen.

P. 618: . . . Was soll ich dann nun von denen sagen . . . die ihr fatzolet oder wischtüchlein im mund umbhertragen? . . .

G.
From Cabanès, *Moeurs intimes du passé* (Paris 1910):

(a)
P. 103: Martial d'Auvergne, les "Arrêts d'amour":
. . t . à fin qu'elle l'eut en mémoire, il s'advisa de luy faire faire un des plus beaulx et riches mouchoirs, où son nom estoit en lettres entrelacées, le plus gentement du monde, car il estoit attaché à un beau cueur d'or, et franges de menues pensées.

(b)
P. 168: 1594 Henry IV demandait à son valet de chambre combien il avait de chemises et celui-ci répondait: Une douzaine, Sire, encore i en a-t-il de déschirées.—Et de mouchoirs, dit le roi, est-ce pas huit que j'ai?—Il n'i en a pour reste heure que cinq, dist-il. (Lestoil, Journal d'Henci IV.)

"Cinq mouchoirs d'ouvrage d'or, d'argent et soye, prisez cent escuz."

(c)
P. 102: Au seizième siècle, dit Monteil, en France cone partout, le petit peuple se mouche sans mouchoir; mais, dans la bourgeoisie, il est reçu qu'on se mouche avec la manche. Quant aux gens riches, ils portent dans la poche un mouchoir; aussi, dire qu'un homme a de la fortune, on dit qu'il ne se mouche pas avec la manche.

H.

1672
From Antoine de Courtin, *Nouveau traité de civilité*:

P. 134. Se moucher avec son mouchoir à découvert et sans se couvrir de sa serviette, en essuyer la sucur du visage . . . sont des saletez á faire soulever le coeur à tout le monde.

Il faut éviter de bâiller, de se moucher et de cracher. Si on y est obligè en des lieux que l'on tient proprement, il faut le faire dans son mouchoir, en se détournant le visage et se couvrant de sa main gauche, et ne point regarder après dans son mouchoir.

I.

1694

From Ménage, *Dictionnaire étymologique de la langue fançaise*:
Mouchoir à moucher:
Comme ce mot de moucher donne one vilaine image, les dames devroient plutost appeler ce mouchoir, de poche, comme on dit mouchoir de cou, que mouchoir à moucher.

J.

1714

From an anonymous *Civilité française* (Liège, 1714):

P. 41: Gardez-vous bien de vous moucher avec les doigts ou sur la manche comme les enfans, mais servez-vous de votre mouchoir et ne regardez pas dedans après vous être mouché.

K.

1729

From La Salle, *Les Règles de la bienséance et de la civilité chrétienne* (Rouen, 1729):

Du nez et de la maniere de se moucher et d'éternuer (p. 23).

Il est trés mal honneste de foüiller incessament dans les narines avec le doigt, et il est encore bien plus insuportable de porter ensuite dans la bouche ce qu'on a tiré hors des narines . . .

Il est vilain de se moucher avec la main nuë, en la passant dessous le Nez, ou de se moucher sur sa manche, ou sur ses habits. C'est one chose trés contraire à la Bienséance, de se moucher avec deux doigts, et puis jeter l'ordure à terre, et d'essuier ensuite ses doigts avec ses habits; on sçait combien il est mal séant de voir de telles mal-propretés sur des habits, qui doivent toújours être trés propres, quelques pauvres qu'ils soient.

Il y en à quelques-uns qui mettent on doigt contre le Nez, et qui ensuite en soufflant do Nez, poussent à terre l'ordure qui est dedans; ceux qui en usent ainsi sont des gens qui ne sçavent ce que c'est d'honnêtetè.

Il faut toújours se servir de son mouchoir pour se moucher, et jamais d'autre chose, et en le faisant se couvrir ordinairement le Visage de son chapeau.

On doit éviter en se mouchant de faire du bruit avec le Nez . . . Avant que de se moucher, il est indécent d'estre longtems à tirer son mouchoir: c'est manquer de respect à l'égard des personnes avec qui on est, de le déplier en différends endroits, pour voir de quel côté on se mouchera; il faut tirer son mouchoir de sa poche, sans qu'ii paroisse, et se moucher promptement, de manier qu'on ne puisse presque pas ester aperçú des autres.

On doit bien se garder, après qu'on s'est mouché, de regarder dans son mouchoir; mais il est à propos de le plier aussitót, et le remettre dans sa poche.

L.

1774

From La Salle, *Les Règles de la bienséance et de la civilité chrétienne*:

Tout mouvement volontaire do nez, soil avec la main, soit autrement, est indécent et puérile; porter les doigts dans les narines est une malpropreté qui revolte, et en y touchant trop souvent, il arrive, qu'il s'y forme des incommodités, dont on serssent longtemps.

Les enfants sont assez dans l'usage de tomber dans ce défaut; les parents doivent les en corriger avec soin.

Il faut observer, en se mouchant, toutes les regles de la bienséance et de la properté.

M.

1797

From La Mésangère, *Le voyageur de Paris* (1797), vol. 2, p. 95:

On faisait un art de moucher il y a quelques années. L'un imitait le son de la trompette, l'autre le jurement du chat; le point de perfection consistait à ne faire ni trop de bruit ni trop peu.

On Spitting
(p. 125)

Middle Ages

A.

From *Stans puer in mensam* (*The Babees Book* v. 2, p. 32.):

27   nec ultra mensam spueris nec desuper unquam
        nec carnem propriam verres digito neque scalpes

37   Si sapis extra vas expoe quando lavas

B.

From a *Contenence de table* (*The Babees Book* v. 2, p. 7.):

29   Ne craiche par dessus la table,
        Car c'est chose desconvenable

51   Cellui qui courtoisie a ch'er
        Ne doit pas ou bacin crachier,
        Fors quant sa bouche et ses mains leve,
        Ains mette hors, qu'aucun ne greve

D.

From Zarncke, *Der Deutsche Cato*, p. 137:

        Wirff nit nauch pürschem sin
        Die spaichei über den tisch hin

E.

1530

From *De civilitate morum puerilium*, by Erasmus:

Aversus expuito, ne quem conspuas aspergasve. Si quid purulentius in terram rejectum erit, pede, ut dixi, proteratur, ne cui nauseam moveat. Id si non licet, linteolo sputum excipilo. Resorbere salivam, inurbanum est, quemadmodum et illud quod quosdam videmus non ex necessitate, sed ex usu, ad tertium quodque verbum expuere.

F.

1558

From *Galateo*, by Giovanni della Casa:

P. 570: Es stehet auch übel, dass sich einer, da er am Tisch sitzet, krauet: Ja an dem Ort und zu solcher Zeit sol sich einer so viel es müglich auch dess auswerfens enthalten, und so man es ja nicht ganz umbgehen könte, so sol man es doch auff eine höfliche Weise und unvermercket thun.

Ich habe offt gehöret, dass für zeiten ganze völcker so mass gelebet, und sich so dapfer geübet, dass sie des aussprünzens durchaus nit bedürffet haben. Wie solten dann wir uns auch nit eine geringe zeit desselben enthalten können.

G.

1672

From Antoine de Courtin, *Nouveau traité de civilité*:

P. 273: . . . Cet usage dont nous venons de parler ne permet pas que la pluspart de ces sortes de loix soient immuables. Et comme il y en a beaucoup qui ont déja changé, je ne doute pas qu'il n'y en ait plusieurs de celles-cy, qui changeront tout de même à l'avenir.

Autrefois, par exemple, il estoit permis de cracher à terre devant des personnes de qualité, et il suffisoit de mettre le pied dessus; à present c'est une indecence.

Autrefois on pouvoit bâiller et c'estoit assez, pourvu que l'on ne parlast pas en bâillant; à present une personne de qualité s'en choqueroit.

H.

1714

From an anonymous *Civilité fraçnaise* (Liège, 1714):

P. 67: Le cracher frequent est desagréable; quand il est de nécessité on doit le rendre moins visible que l'on peut et faire en sorte qu'on ne crache ni sur les personnes, ni sur les habits de qui que ce soit, ni méme sur les tisons étant auprés du feu. Et en quelque lieu que l'on crache, on doit mettre le pied sur le crachat.

Chez les grand on crache dans son mouchoir.

P. 41: Il est de mauvaise grace de cracher par la fenétre dans la rue ou sur le feu.

Ne crachez point si loin qu'il faille aller chercher le crachat pour mettre le pied dessus.

I.

1729

From La Salle, *les Règles de la bienséance et de la civilité chrétienne* (Rouen, 1729):

P. 35: On ne doit pas s'abstenir de cracher, et c'est une chose trés indécente d'avaler ce qu'on doit cracher; cela est capable de faire mal au coeur aux autres.

Il ne faut pas cependant s'accoútumer à cracher trop souvent, et sans nécessité: cela est non seulement trés malhonnête; mais cela dégoute et incommode tout le monde. Quand on se trouve avec des personnes de qualité et lorsqu'on est dans des lieux au'on tient propres, il est de l'honnêteté de cracher dans son mouchoir, en se tournant un peu de côté.

Il est même de la Bienséance que chacun s'accoútume à cracher dans son mouchoir, lorqu'on est dans les maison des Grands et dans toutes les places qui sont, ou cirées, ou parquetées; mais il est bien plus nécessaire de prendre l'habitude de le faire lorsqu'on est dans l'Eglise autant qu'il est possible . . . cependant il arrive souvent qu'il n'y à point de pavé de Cuisine, ou même d'Ecurie plus sale . . . que celui de l'Eglise . . .

Après avoir craché dans son mouchoir, il faut le plier aussitòt, sans le reagrder, et le mettre dans sa poche. On doit avoir beaucoup d'égard de ne jamais cracher sur ses habits, ni sur ceux des autres . . . Quand on aperçoit à terre quelque gros Crachat, il faut aossitòt mettre adroitement le pied dessus. Si on en remarque sur l'habit de quelqu'un, il n'est pas bien séant de le faire connoistre: mais il faut avertir quelque domestique de aller óter: et s'il n'y en a point, il faut l'óter soi-méme, sans qu'on s'en apercoive: car il est de l'honnèteté de ne rien faire paroitre á l'égard de qui que ce soit, qui lui puisse faire peine: ou lui donner de la confusion.

J.

1774
From La Salle, *Les Règles de la bienséance et de la civilité chrétienne* (1774):

P. 20: Dans l'Eglise, chez les Grands et dans tous les endroits où regnent la propreté, il faut cracher dans son mouchoir. C'est une grossiéreté impardonnable dans les enfants, que celle qu'ils contractent en crachant au visage de leurs camarades: on ne saurait punir trop sévérement ces incivilités; on ne peut pas plus excuser ceux qui crachent par les fenêtres, sur les murailles et sur les meubles . . .

L.

1910
From Augustin Cabanès, *Moeurs intimes*:

P. 264: Avez-vous observé que nous reléguons aujourd'hui dans quelque coin discret ce que nos pères n'hésitaient pas à étaler au grand jour?

Ainsi certain meuble intime occupait une place d'honneur . . . on ne songeait pas à le dérober aux regards.

Il en était de même d'un autre meuble, qui ne fait plus partie du mobilier moderne et dont, par ce temps de "bacillophobie," d'aucuns regretteront peutêtre la disparition: nous voulons parler du crachoir.

On Behavior in the Bedroom
(p. 132)

B.

1530
From *De civilitate morum querilium* (ch. XII de cubiculo) by Erasmus:

Sive cum exuis te, sive cum surgis, memor verecundiae, cave ne quid nudes aliorum oculis quod mos et natura tectum esse voluit.

Si cum sodali lectum habeas communem, quietus jaceto, neque corporis jactatione vel te ipsum nedes, vel sodali detractis palliis sis molestus.

C.

1555

From *Des bonnes moeurs et honnestes contenances*, Lyon, 1555, by Pierre Broe:

> Et quand viendra que tu seras au lit
> Apres soupper pour prendre le délit
> d'humain repos aucques plaisant some
> si auprès de toi est couché quelque home
> Tien doucement tous tes membres à droyt
> Alonge toy, et garde à son endroyt
> de le facher alor aucunement
> pour te mouvoyr ou tourner rudement
> par toy ne soyent ces membres descouvers
> te remuant ou faisant tours divers:
> Et si tu sens qu'il soit ja someillé
> Fay que par toy il ne soyt esueillé.

D.

1729

From La Salle, *les Règles de la bienséance et de la civilité chrétienne* (Rouen, 1729):

P. 55: On doit . . . ne se deshabiller, ni coucher devant personne; l'on doit surtout, à moins qu'on ne soit engagé dans le Mariage, ne pas se coucher devant aucone personne d'autre sexe.

Il est encore bien moins permis à des personnes de sexe différent, de coucher dans un même lit, quand ce ne serait que des Enfants fort jeunes . . .

Lorsque par une nécessité indispensable, on est contraint dans on voïage de coucher avec quelque autre de mesme séxe, il n'est pas bien-séant de s'en aprocher si fort, qu'on puisse non seulement s'incommoder l'un l'autre, mais mesme se toucher; et il l'est encore moins de mettre ses jambes entre celles de la personne avec qui on est couché . . .

Il est aussi trés indécent et peu honnète, de s'amuser á causer, á badiner . . .

Lorsqu'on sort du lit, il ne faut pas le laisser découvert ni mettre son bonnet de nuit sur quelque siége, ou en quelqu'autre endroit d'oú il puisse ètre aperçú.

E.

1774

From La Salle, *Les Règles de la bienséance et de la civilité chrétienne* (1774) p. 31:

C'est on étrange abus de faire coucher des persones de différents sexes dans une même chambre; et si la nécessité y oblige, il faut bien faire ensorte que les lits soient séparés, et que la pudeur ne souffre en rien de ce mélange. Une grande indigence peut seule excuser cet usage . . .

Lorsqu'on se trouve forcé de coucher avec une personne de même sexe, ce qui arrive rarement, il faut s'y tenir dans une modestie sévere et vigilante . . .

Dès que l'on est éveillé, et que l'on a pris un temps suffisant pour le repos, il faut sortir du lit avec la modestie convenable, et ne jamais y rester á tenir des conversations ou vaquer à d'autres affaires . . . rien n'annonce plus sensiblement la paresse et la légéreté; le lit est destiné au repos du corps et non á toute autre chose.

On Changes in the Aggressive Impulse
(p. 156)

"Sint uns allen ist gegeben
ein harte ungewissez leben"

"Wildu vürhten den tôt,
sô muostu leben mit nôt."
"Man weiz wol daz der tôt geschiht,
man weiz ab sîner zuokunft niht:
er kumt geslichen als ein diep
und scheidet leide unde liep.
Doch habe du guote zuoversiht
vürhte den tôt ze sêre niht
vürhtestu in ze sęre
du gewinnest vreude nie mêre."

Notes

Part One

1. Oswald Spengler, *The Decline of the West* (London, 1926), p. 21: "Each Culture has its own new possibilities of self-expression which arise, ripen, decay, and never return. . . . These cultures, sublimated life-essences, grow with the same superb aimlessness as the flowers of the field. They belong, like the plants and the animals, to the living Nature of Goethe, and not to the dead Nature of Newton."

2. The whole question of the evolution of the concepts *Kultur* and *Zivilisation* needs a fuller examination than is possible here, where the problem can only be briefly introduced. Nevertheless, a few notes may support the ideas in the text.

It could be demonstrated that in the course of the nineteenth century, and particularly after 1870, when Germany was both strong in Europe and a rising colonial power, the antithesis between the two words diminished considerably at times, "culture" referring, as it does today in England and to some extent in France, to only a particular area or a higher form of civilization. Thus, for example, Friedrich Jodl, in his *Die Kulturgeschichtschreibung* (Halle, 1878, p. 3), defines "general cultural history" as "the history of civilization" (cf. also ibid., p. 25).

G. F. Kolb, in his *Geschichte der Menschheit und der Cultur* (1843; a later edition is entitled *Cultur-Geschichte der Menschheit*) includes in his concept of culture the idea of progress that is generally excluded from it today. He bases his conception of *Kultur* explicitly on Buckle's concept of *Zivilisation*. But, as Jodl states (*Die Kulturgeschichtschreibung*, p. 36), his ideal "takes its essential features from modern conceptions and demands with regard to political, social, and religious freedom, and could easily be included in a party-political program."

In other words, Kolb is a "progressive," a liberal from the pre-1848 period, a time when the concept of *Kultur* also approached the Western concept of civilization.

All the same, the 1897 edition of Meyer's *Konversationslexikon* still states: "Civilization is the stage through which a barbaric people must pass in order to attain higher *Kultur* in industry, art, science, and attitudes."

However near the German concept of *Kultur* sometimes seems to come to the French and English concept of civilization in such statements, the feeling that *Zivilisation* is a second-rate value in comparison to *Kultur* never entirely disappears in Germany even in this period. It is an expression of Germany's self-assertion against the Western countries which regard themselves as the standard-bearers of civilization, and of the tension between them. Its strength changes with the degree and kind of this tension. The history of the German concepts *Zivilisation* and *Kultur* is very closely interrelated with the history of relations between England, France, and Germany. Its underlying constituents are certain political circumstances which persist throughout many phases of development, emerging in the psychological makeup of Germans as in their concepts—above all, those expressing their self-image.

Cf. also Conrad Hermann, *Philosophie der Geschichte* (1870), in which France is referred to as the country of "civilization," England as that of "material culture," and Germany as that of "ideal *Bildung*." The term "material culture," current in England and France, has virtually disappeared from ordinary German usage, if not quite from scholarly terminology. The concept of *Kultur* has merged completely in ordinary speech with what is here called *ideale Bildung*. The ideals of *Kultur* and *Bildung* were always closely related, although the reference to objective human accomplishments gradually became more prominent in the concept of *Kultur*.

3. On the problem of the intelligentsia, see in particular K. Mannheim, *Ideology and Utopia: An Introduction to the Sociology of Knowledge* (London, 1936). On the same subject, see also K. Mannheim, *Man and Society in an Age of Reconstruction* (London, 1940), and H. Weil, *Die Entstehung des Deutschen Bildungsprinzips* (Bonn, 1930), ch. 5.

4. *Grosses vollständiges Universal-Lexikon aller Wissenschaften und Künste* (Leipzig and Halle; Joh. H. Zedler, 1736). (All italics in the quotation are the author's.) Cf. also the article on "The Courtier":

"A person serving in a respected position at the court of a prince. Court life has always been described on the one hand as dangerous, on account of vacillating princely favor, the many envious parties, secret slanderers, and open enemies, and on the other as depraved, on account of the idleness, lasciviousness, and luxury frequently encountered there.

"There have, however, at all times been courtiers who prudently avoided these pitfalls and vigilantly escaped the temptations to wickedness, and so represented worthy examples of happy and virtuous courtiers. Nonetheless it is not said without reason that "close to Court is close to the Devil.' "

Cf. also the article "Court": "If all subjects were deeply convinced that they honored their princes on account of their inward merits, there would be no need of outward pomp; as it is, however, the great part of their subjects remain attached to externals. A prince remains the same whether he walks alone or attended by a great company; nevertheless, there is no lack of examples where the prince attracted little or no attention when going alone among his subjects, but was received quite differently when acting in accordance with his position. For this reason it is necessary that the prince have servants not only to rule the land but also for outward appearance and for his own service."

Similar ideas were already expressed in the seventeenth century, e.g., in the *Discurs v. d. Höfflichkeit* (1665); cf. E. Cohn, *Gesellschaftsideale und Gesellschaftsroman des 17 Jahrhunderts*, (Berlin, 1921), p. 12. The German contraposition of "outward courtesy" and "inward merit" is as old as German absolutism and as the social weakness of the German bourgeoisie vis-à-vis the courtly circles of this period, a weakness that is to be understood not least in relation to the particular strength of the German bourgeoisie in the preceding phase.

5. Quoted in Aronson, *Lessing et les classics français* (Montpellier, 1935), p. 18.

6. E. de Mauvillon, *Lettres françoises et germaniques* (London, 1740), p. 430.

7. Ibid., p. 427.

8. Ibid., pp. 461–2.

9. Reprinted in the *Deutsche Literatur-denkmale* (Heilbronn, 1883), vol. 16.

10. Cf. Arnold Berney, *Friedrich der Grosse* (Tübingen, 1934), p. 71.

11. Cf. Hettner, *Geschichte der Literatur im 18 Jahrhundert*, vol. 1, p. 10. "It is undeniable that French drama is in its innermost essence court-drama, the drama of etiquette. The prerogative of being a tragic hero is tied to the strictest court etiquette."

12. G. E. Lessing, *Briefe aus dem zweiten Teil der Schriften* (Göschen, 1753); quoted in Aronson, *Lessing*, p. 161.

13. This and the following references are from Lamprecht, *Deutsche Geschichte* (Freiburg, 1906), vol. 8, pt. 1, p. 195.

14. Mauvillon, *Lettres*, pp. 398f.

15. Sophie de la Roche, *Geschichte des Fräulein von Sternheim* (1771; Berlin: Kuno Ridderhoff, 1907).

16. From Herder's *Nachlass*, vol. 3, pp. 67–8.

17. Sophie de la Roche, *Fräulein von Sternheim*, p. 99.

18. Ibid., p. 25.

19. Ibid., p. 90.

20. Caroline von Wolzogen, *Agnes von Lilien* (pub. in Schiller's *Horen*, 1796; pub. as book, 1798). A short fragment is reprinted in *Deutsche National-Literatur* (Berlin and Stuttgart), vol. 137, pt. 2; quotation from p. 375.

21. Ibid., p. 363.

22. Ibid., p. 364.

23. *Grimms Wörterbuch*, article on "Hofleute."

24. Ibid.

25. Brunot, in his *Histoire de la langue française*, cites the use of the word *civilisation* by Turgot. But it does not appear quite certain that Turgot himself used this word. It proved impossible to find it in a search of his works, with one exception: in the table of contents to the editions by Dupont de Nemours and by Schelle. But this table was probably produced not by Turgot but by Dupont de Nemours. If, however, one looks not for the word but for the idea and meaning, sufficient material is indeed to be found in Turgot in 1751. And it is perhaps not idle to point this out as an example of how a certain idea forms in the minds of people from certain experiences, and then gradually a special word becomes associated with this idea, this conceptual area.

It is no accident that in his edition of Turgot, Dupont de Nemours gives as the contents of the section mentioned: "*La civilisation et la nature.*" This section contains the early idea of civilization to which the word was later gradually attached.

An introductory letter to the publisher of the *Lettres d'une péruvienne*, Madame de Graffigny, gives Turgot the opportunity to express his ideas on the relation of the "savage" to the *homme policé* (*Oeuvres de Turgot*, ed. G. Schelle [Paris, 1913], vol. 1, p. 243). The *péruvienne* ought to consider, he says, "the reciprocal advantages of the savage and the *homme policé*. To prefer the savage is a ridiculous declamation. Let her refute it, let her show that the vices we take to be the product of *politesse* are innate to the human heart."

A few years later, Mirabeau was to use the more comprehensive and dynamic term *civilisation* in the same sense as Turgot here uses the term *politesse*, though with the opposite evaluation.

26. On this and subsequent points, see J. Moras, *Ursprung und Entwicklung des Beriffs Zivilisation in Frankreich (1756–1830)*, in *Hamburger Studien zu Volkstum und Kultur der Romanen* (Hamburg, 1930), vol. 6, p. 38.

27. Ibid., p. 37.

28. Ibid., p. 36.

29. Cf. Lavisse, *Histoire de France* (Paris, 1910), vol. 9, pt. 1, p. 23.

30. Cf. Moras, *Ursprung*, p. 50.

31. Baron d'Holbach, *Système sociale ou principes naturels de la morale et de la politique* (London, 1774), vol. 3, p. 113; quoted in Moras, *Ursprung*, p. 50.

32. Baron d'Holbach, *Système*, p. 162.

33. Voltaire, *Siècle de Louis XIV*, in *Oeuvres Complètes* (Paris: Garnier Frères, 1878), vol. 14, pt. 1, p. 516.

Part Two

1. S. R. Wallach, *Das abendländische Gemeinschaftsbewusstsein im Mittelalter* (Leipzig and Berlin, 1928); *Beiträge zur Kultur-geschichte des Mittelalters und der Renaissance*, ed. W. Goetz, vol. 34, pp. 25–29. Here "Latins" refers to Latin Christianity, i.e., the West in general.

2. The *Bibliotheca Erasmiana* (Ghent, 1893) records 130 editions or, more precisely, 131, including the text of 1526 which unfortunately was unavailable to me, so that I am unaware how far it coincides with subsequent editions.

After the *Colloquies*, the *Moriae encomium*, the *Adagia*, and *De duplici copia verborum ac rerum commentarii*, *De civilitate* achieved the highest number of editions of Erasmus's own writings. (For a table of numbers of editions of all works by Erasmus, cf. Mangan, *Life, Character and Influence of Desiderius Erasmus of Rotterdam* [London, 1927], vol. 2, pp. 396ff.) If account is taken of the long series of writings more or less closely related to Erasmus's civility-book, and so of the wide radius of its success, its significance as compared to his other writings must doubtless be estimated still more highly. An idea of the direct impact of his books is given by noting which of them were translated from scholarly language into popular languages. There is as yet no comprehensive analysis of this. According to M. Mann, *Erasme et les débuts de la réforme française* (Paris, 1934), p. 181, the most surprising thing—as far as France is concerned—is "the preponderance of the books of instruction or piety over those of entertainment or satire. The *Praise of Folly*, the *Colloquies* . . . have scarcely any place in this list . . . It was the *Adages*, the *Preparation for Death* and the *Civility in Boys* that attracted translators and that the public demanded." A similar success analysis for German and Dutch regions would probably yield somewhat different results. It may be supposed that the satirical writings had a somewhat greater success there (cf. note 30 below).

The success of the Latin edition of *De civilitate* was certainly considerable. Kirchhoff (in *Leipziger Sortimentshändler im 16 Jahrhundert*; quoted in W. H. Woodward, *Desiderius Erasmus*, [Cambridge, 1904], p. 156, n. 3) ascertains that in the three years 1547, 1551, and 1558 no less than 654 copies of *De civilitate* were in stock, and that no other book by Erasmus was listed in such numbers.

3. Compare the notice on the writings on civility by A. Bonneau in his edition of the *Civilité puérile* (see n. 35 below).

4. Despite its success in his own time, this work has received relatively little attention in the Erasmus literature of more recent times. In view of the book's theme, this is only too understandable. This theme—manners, etiquette, codes of conduct—however informative on the molding of people and their relations, is perhaps of only limited interest for historians of ideas. What Ehrismann says of a *Hofzucht* (Court discipline) in his *Geschichte der deutschen Literatur bis zum Ausgang des Mittelalters*, vol. 6, pt. 2, p. 330, is typical of a scholarly evaluation frequently encountered in this field: "A book of instruction for youths of noble birth. Not raised to the level of a teaching on virtue."

In France, however, books of courtesy from a particular period—the seventeenth century—have received increasing attention for some time, stimulated no doubt by the work of D. Parodie cited in n. 98, and above all by the comprehensive study by M. Magendie, *La politesse mondaine* (Paris, 1925). Similarly, the study by B. Groethuysen, *Origines de l'esprit bourgeois en France* (Paris, 1927), also takes literary products of a more or less average kind as a starting point in tracing a certain line in the changes in people and the modification of the social standard (cf., e.g., pp. 45ff.).

The material used in Part Two of this study is a degree lower, if we may put it that way, than that in the works just mentioned. But perhaps they, too, show the significance this "slight" literature has for an understanding of the great changes in the structure of people and their relations.

5. Reprinted in part in A. Franklin, *La vie privée d'autrefois: les repas*, (Paris, 1889), pp. 164, 166, which has numerous other quotations on this subject.

6. Reprinted in *The Babees Book*, ed. Frederick Furnivall (London, 1868), pt. 2; for further English, Italian, French, and German books of this genre, cf. Early English Text Society, Extra Series, no. 8, ed. F. J. Furnivall (London, 1869), including *A Booke of Precedence* and others. The molding of the young nobleman through service at the house of one of the "great" of his country is expressed particularly clearly in these English books of conditioning. An Italian observer of English customs, writing about the year 1500, remarks that the English probably adopted this practice because one is served better by strangers than by one's own children. "Had they had their own children at home, they would have been obliged to give them the same food as they had prepared for themselves." (See the introduction to *A Fifteenth-Century Courtesy-Book*, ed. R. W. Chambers [London, 1914], p. 6). Nor is it without interest that the Italian observer of about 1500 stresses that "the English, you see, are great epicures."

For a number of further references, see M. and C. H. B. Quennel, *A History of Everyday Things in England* (London, 1931), vol. 1, p. 144.

7. Edited by F. J. Furnivall (see n. 6 above). For information on the German literature of this genre, with references to the corresponding literature in other languages, cf. G. Ehrismann, *Geschichte*, vol. 6, pt. 2 (speech, p. 326; table disciplines, p. 328); P. Merker and W. Stammler, *Reallexikon der deutschen Literaturgeschichte*, vol. 3, entry on table disciplines (P. Merker); and H. Teske, *Thomasin van Zerclaere* (Heidelberg, 1933), pp. 122ff.

8. For the German version used here, see Zarncke, *Der deutsche Cato* (Leipzig 1852).

9. Ibid, p. 39, v. 223.

10. Tannhäuser, *Die Hofzucht*, in *Der Dichter Tannhäuser*, ed. J. Siebert (Halle, 1934), p. 196, vv. 33f.

11. Ibid., vv. 45f.

12. Ibid., vv. 49f.

13. Ibid., vv. 57f.

14. Ibid., vv. 129f.

15. Ibid., vv. 61f.

16. Ibid., vv. 109f.

17. Ibid., vv. 157f.

18. Ibid., vv. 141f.

19. Zarncke, *Der deutsche Cato*, p. 136.

20. Ibid., p. 137, vv. 287f.

21. Ibid., p. 136, vv. 258f.

22. Ibid., vv. 263f.

23. Tannhäuser, *Hofzucht*, vv. 125f.

24. Glixelli, *Les Contenances de table*.

25. *The Babees Book* and *A Booke of Precedence* (see n. 6).

26. Cf. A. von Gleichen Russwurm, *Die gothische Welt* (Stuttgart, 1922), pp. 320ff.

27. See A. Cabanès, *Moeurs intimes din temps passé* (Paris, 1910), 1st series, p. 248.

28. Ibid., p. 252.

29. A. Bömer, *Anstand und Etikette in den Theorien der Humanisten*, in *Neue Jahrbücher für das Klassische Altertum* 14 (Leipzig, 1904).

30. Characteristic of the German burgher way of giving precepts on manners at the end of the Middle Ages and in the Renaissance is the *grobianische Umkehrung* (boorish inversion). The writer ridicules "bad" conduct by appearing to recommend it. Humor and satire, which later gradually recede in the German tradition, or at least become second-rank values, are in this phase of German burgher society notably dominant.

The satirical inversion of precepts can be traced back as a specifically urban, burgher form of instilling manners at least as far as the fifteenth century. The recurrent precept not to fall greedily on the food is heard, for example, in a little poem of this time, "Wie der maister sein nun lernet" (in Zarncke, *Der deutsche Cato*, p. 148):

> Gedenk und merk waz ich dir sag
> wan man dir die kost her trag
> so bis der erst in der schizzel;
> gedenk und scheub in deinen drizzel
> als groz klampen als ain saw.

Remember, when the food is brought in be the first to the dish; stuff large chunks down your throat like a pig.

The precept not to search about for a long time in the common dish recurs here in the following version:

> Bei allem dem daz ich dir ler
> grab in der schizzel hin und her
> nach dem aller besten stuck;
> daz dir gefall, daz selb daz zuck,
> und leg erz auf dein teller drat;
> acht nicht wer daz für übel hat.

What I teach is, dig about for the best piece in the dish; snatch the piece you like best and put it on your plate, and care nothing for those who disapprove.

In Kaspar Scheidt's German translation of the *Grobianus* (Worms, 1551; reprinted in *Neudruck deutscher Literaturwerke des 16 und 17 Jahrhunderts*, nos. 34 and 35 [Halle, 1882], p. 17, vv. 223f.), the instruction to wipe one's nose in good time appears as follows:

> Es ist der brauch in frembden landen
> Als India, wo golt verhanden
> Auch edel gstein und perlin göt
> Dass mans an d'nasen hencken thut.
> Solch gut hat dir das gluck nit bschert
> Drum hor was zu deinr nasen hon:
> Ein wuster kengel rechter leng
> Auss beiden lochern aussher heng,
> Wie lang eisz zapffen an dem hauss,
> Das ziert dein nasen uberausz.

It is the custom in foreign countries where gold, jewels, and pearls are found to hang them on the nose.
As we are less fortunate, hear what you should wear on your nose: a long filthy trickle hanging from both nostrils, like icicles from a house—that would admirably adorn your nose.

> Doch halt in allen dingen moss,
> Dass nit der kengel werd zu gross:
> Darumb hab dir ein solches mess,
> Wenn er dir fleusst biss in das gfress
> Und dir auff beiden lefftzen leit,
> Dann ist die nass zu butsen zeit.
> Auff beide ermel wüsch den rotz,
> Dasz wer es seh vor unlust kotz.

Yet keep a measure in all things, and when the trickle grows too long and runs all over mouth and lips, the time to clean your nose has come.
Wipe the snot on both your sleeves that all who see may vomit with disgust.

Obviously, this account is intended as an instructive deterrent. Inscribed on the title page of the Worms edition of 1551 one reads:

Lisz wol disz buchlin offt und vil
Und thu allzeit das widerspil

Read this booklet often, and always do the opposite.

To elucidate the specifically burgher character of this book, the dedication of the Helbach edition of 1567 may be quoted:
Dedicated "by Wendelin Helbach, the unworthy vicar of Eckhardtschausen, to the honorable and learned gentlemen Adamus Lonicerus, doctor of medicine and city doctor of Frankfurt am Main, and Johannes Cnipius Andronicus, citizen thereof, my gracious lords and good friends."
The long title of the Latin *Grobianus* itself may give a certain basis for assessing the time at which the concept of *civilitas*, in Erasmus's sense and probably in the wake of his book, begins to spread in the Latin-writing German intellectual stratum. In the title of the 1549 *Grobianus*, this word does not yet occur. There we read: "Iron . . . Chlevastes Studiosae Juventuti. . . . In the 1552 edition the same passage contains the word *civilitas*: "Iron episcoptes studiosae iuventuti civilitatem optat." And so it remains until the edition of 1584. To a 1661 edition of the *Grobianus* an extract from Erasmus's *De civilitate morum puerilium* is appended.
Finally, a new translation of the *Grobianus* of 1708 is inscribed: "Written with poetic pen for the discourteous Monsieur Blockhead, and presented for the merriment of all judicious and *civilized* minds." In this translation much is said in a milder tone and in a far more veiled manner. With increasing "civilization," the precepts of a past phase, which for all their satire were meant very seriously, become merely a subject for laughter, which symbolizes both the superiority of the new phase and a slight violation of its taboos.

31. *The Babees Book*, p. 344.

32. Glixelli, *Les Contenances* (Romania), vol. 47, p. 31, vv. 133ff.

33. François de Callières, *De la science du monde et des connoissances utiles à la conduite de la vie* (Brussels, 1717), p. 6.

34. Arthur Denecke, "Beiträge zur Entwicklungsgeschichte des gesellschaftlichen Anstandsgefühls," in *Zeitschrift für Deutsche Kulturgeschichte*, ed. C. Meyer, New Series, vol. 2, no. 2 (Berlin, 1892), p. 175, quotes the following precepts as new in Erasmus: "If up to now we have acquainted ourselves with the ideas on table manners prevalent in the higher circles of the common people, in Erasmus's famous book *De civilitate morum puerilium* we are given precepts for good behavior in a prince. . . . The following lessons are new: If you are given a napkin at table you should lay it over the left shoulder or arm. . . . Erasmus also says: You should sit bareheaded at table, if the custom of the country does not forbid it. You should have your goblet and knife on the right of your plate, the bread on the left. The latter should not be broken but cut. It is improper and also unhealthy to begin the meal by drinking. It is loutish to dip your fingers into the broth. Of a good piece offered to you, take only a part and pass the rest to the person offering it, or the person next to you. Solid foods offered to you should be taken with three fingers or on your plate; liquids offered on a spoon should be taken with the mouth, but the spoon should be wiped before it is returned. If food offered to you is not wholesome, under no circumstances say, "I cannot eat that," but excuse yourself politely. Every man of refinement must be adept at carving every kind of roast meat. You may not throw bones and leavings onto the floor. . . . To eat meat and bread together is healthy. . . . Some people gobble while eating. . . . A youth should speak at table only when necessary. . . . If you are giving a meal

yourself, apologize for its meagerness and, at all costs, do not list the prices of the various ingredients. Everything is offered with the right hand.

"It may be seen that, despite the caution of the educator of princes and despite the refinement of some details, broadly the same spirit is present in these precepts as in the middle-class table disciplines. . . . Similarly, Erasmus's teaching differs primarily from the other social forms of conduct only in the wide scope of the precepts intended for the other circles, since he is concerned at the least to give an account exhaustive for that time."

This quotation complements the earlier considerations to some extent. Unfortunately, Denecke limits his comparison to German table disciplines. To confirm his findings, a comparison would be needed with books of courtesy in French and English, and above all with the behavior-precepts of earlier humanists.

35. Cf. *"La civilité puérile" par Erasme de Rotterdam, précédé d'une notice sur les libres de civilité depuis le siècle par Alcide Bonneau* (Paris, 1877):

"Did Erasmus have models? Obviously, he did not invent *savoir-vivre,* and long before him the general rules had been laid. . . . Nonetheless, Erasmus is the first to have treated the subject in a special and complete manner; none of the authors just quoted had envisaged civility or, if you will, propriety as capable of providing the subject of a separate study. They had formulated precepts here and there, which naturally related to education, morality, fashion, or hygiene. . . ."

A similar observation is made on Giovanni della Casa's *Galateo* (first edition together with other pieces by the author, 1558) in the introduction by I. E. Spingarn (p. xvi) to an edition entitled *Galateo of Manners and Behavior* (London, 1914).

It is perhaps of service to further work to point out that there already existed in English literature in the fifteenth century longer poems (published by the Early Text Society) treating behavior in getting dressed, at church, at table, etc., almost as comprehensively as Erasmus's treatise. It is not impossible that Erasmus knew something of these poems on manners.

What is certain is that the theme of education for boys had a considerable degree of topicality in humanist circles in the years preceding the appearance of Erasmus's little book. Quite apart from the verses *De moribus in mensa servandis* by Johannes Sulpicius, there appeared—to mention only a few—Brunfels's *Disciplina et puerorum institutio* (1525), Hegendorff's *De instituenda vita* (1529), and S. Heyden's *Formulae puerilium colloquiorum* (1528). Cf. Merker and Stammler, *Reallexikon,* entry on table disciplines.

36. Latin table discipline, *Quisquis es in mensa,* V, 18, in Glixelli, *Les Contenances,* p. 29.

37. Caxton's *Book of Curtesye,* Early English Text Society, Extra Series, no. 3, ed. F. J. Furnivall (London, 1868), p. 22.

38. Della Casa, *Galateo,* pt. 1, chs. 1, 5.

39. Caxton's *Book of Curtesye,* p. 45, v. 64.

40. in the American behaviorist literature a number of terms have been precisely defined that, with some modifications, are useful and even indispensable in investigating the past. These include "socializing the child" (cf., e.g. J. B. Watson, *Psychological Care of Infant and Child,* p. 112) and "habit formation" and "conditioning" (cf. Watson, *Psychology from the Standpoint of a Behaviorist,* p. 312).

41. Tannhäuser, *Hofzucht,* pp. 195ff.

42. Zarncke, *Der Deutsche Cato,* pp. 138ff.

43. Cf. *The Babees Book,* p. 76.

46. Ibid., p. 302.

47. Ibid., pt. 2, p. 32.

48. Ibid.

49. Ibid., pt. 2, p. 8.

50. Cf. A. Franklin, *Les Repas,* pp. 194f.

51. Ibid., p. 42.

52. Ibid., p. 283.

53. Dom. Bouhours, *Remarques nouvelles sur la langue française* (Paris, 1676), vol. 1, p. 51.

54. François de Callières, *Du bon et du mauvais usage dans les manières de s'exprimer. Des façons de parler bourgeoises; en quay elles sont differentes de celles de la cour* (Paris, 1694), p. 12: "Then a footman came to inform the lady that Monsieur Thibault the younger was asking to see her. 'Very well,' said the lady. 'But before admitting him I must tell you who M. Thibault is. He is the son of a bourgeois friend of mine in Paris, one of those rich people whose friendship is sometimes useful to people of rank in lending them money. The son is a young man who has studied with the intention of entering a public office, but who needs to be purged of the bad grace and language of the bourgeoisie.' "

55. Andressen and Stephan, *Beiträge zur Geschichte der Gottdorffer Hof- und Staatsverwaltung van 1594–1659* (Kiel, 1928), vol. 1, p. 26 n. 1.

56. Leon Sahler, *Montbéliard à table. Mémoires de la Société d'Emulation de Montbéliard* (Montbèliard, 1907), vol. 34, p. 156.

57. Cf. Andressen and Stephan, *Beiträge*, vol. 1, p. 12.

58. Cf. Platina, *De honesta voluptate et valitudine* (1475), bk. 6, p. 14. The whole "civilizational curve" is clearly visible in a letter to the editor with the title "Obscurities of Ox-Roasting," published by the *Times* of London on May 8, 1937, shortly before the coronation ceremonies, and obviously suggested by the memory of similar festivities in the past: "Being anxious to know, as many must be at such a time as this, how best to roast an ox whole, I made inquiries about the matter at Smithfield Market. But I could only find that nobody at Smithfield knew how I was to obtain, still less to spit, roast, carve and consume an ox whole. . . . The whole matter is very disappointing." On May 14, on the same page of the *Times*, the head chef at Simpsons in the Strand gives instructions for roasting an ox whole, and a picture in the same issue shows the ox on a spit. The debate, which continued for some time in the columns of the *Times*, gives a certain impression of the gradual disappearance of the custom of roasting animals whole, even on occasions when an attempt is being made to preserve traditional forms.

59. Gred Freudenthal, *Gestaltwandel der bürgerlichen und proletarischen Hauswirtschaft mit besonderer Berücksichtigung des Typenwandels von Frau und Familie von 1760 bis zur Gegenwart*, diss. Frankfurt am Main (Würzburg, 1934).

60. See Andressen and Stephan, *Beiträge*, vol. 1, p. 10, which also contains the information that the use of the fork only began to penetrate the upper strata of society in the north at the beginning of the seventeenth century.

61. Cf. Zarncke, *Der deutsche Cato*, p. 138.

62. See Kurt Treusch von Buttlar, "Das tägliche Leben an den deutschen Fürstenhöfen des 16 Jahrhunderts," in *Zeitschrift für Kulturgeschichte* (Weimar, 1897), vol. 4, p. 13 n.

63. Ibid.

64. Cf. *The Babees Book*, p. 295.

65. Quoted in Cabanés, *Moeurs*, p. 292.

66. The best and briefest guide to the subject is A. Franklin, *Les Soins de la toilette* (Paris, 1877), and, above all, the same author's *La Civilité*(Paris, 1908), vol. 2, where a number of instructive quotations are assembled in an appendix. Some of what the writer says must be read critically, however, since he does not always distinguish fully between what is typical of a particular time and what is regarded as exceptional.

67. Mathurin Cordier, *Colloquiorum scholasticorum libri quatuor* (Paris, 1568), bk. 2, colloquium 54 (*Exemplum ad pueros in simplici narratione exercendos*).

68. Some not easily accessible material is to be found in De Laborde, *Le Palais Mazarin* (Paris, 1816). See, for example, n. 337: "Is it necessary to go into details? The almost political role played throughout this epoch [seventeenth century] by the night commode allows us to speak of it without false shame and to say that people were reduced to this utensil and the Provençal *passarès*. One of

Henri IV's mistresses, Madame de Verneuil, wished to have her chamber pot in her bedroom, which would be an impropriety in our day but at that time was no more than a slightly nonchalant liberty."

The important information in these notes also needs careful scrutiny if one is to gain a perspective of the standards of the various classes. One means of tracing these standards would be a precise study of inventories of estators' estates. Regarding the extract on nose-blowing we may note here, for example, that Erasmus left behind—so far as can be ascertained today—the astonishingly high number of thirty-nine handkerchiefs, but only one golden and one silver fork; see *Inventarium über die Hinterlassenschaft des Erasmus*, ed. L. Sieber (Basel, 1889), reprinted in *Zeitschrift für Kulturgeschichte* (Weimar, 1897), vol. 4, pp. 434ff.

A wealth of interesting information is contained in Rabelais's *Gargantua and Pantagruel*. On the subject of "natural functions," for example, see bk. 1, ch. 13.

69. Georg Brandes quotes this passage of the memoirs in his book *Voltaire* (Berlin, n.d.), vol. 1, pp. 340f., and comments on it as follows: "It does not embarrass her to be seen naked by a servant; she did not consider him as a man in relation to herself as a woman."

70. *The Babees Book*, pt. 2, p. 32.

71. Ibid., pt. 2, p. 7.

72. Ibid., p. 301f.

73. Cf. Rudeck, *Geschichte der öffentlichen Sittlichkeit* (Jena, 1887), p. 397.

74. T. Wright, *The Home of Other Days* (London, 1871), p. 269.

75. Otto Zöckler, *Askese und Mönchstum* (Frankfurt, 1897), p. 364.

76. T. Wright, *Home*, p. 269; also Cabanès, *Moeurs intimes*, 2d series, p. 166. See also G. Zappert, *Über das Badewesen in mittelalterlicher und späterer Zeit*, in *Archiv für Kunde österr, Geschichtsquellen* (Vienna, 1859), vol. 21. On the role of the bed in the household, see G. G. Coulton, *Social Life in Britain* (Cambridge, 1919), p. 386, where the scarcity of beds and the unquestioning use of beds by several people is briefly and clearly demonstrated.

77. Quoted in M. Bauer, *Das Liebesleben in der deutschen Vergangenheit* (Berlin, 1924), p. 208.

78. Rudeck, *Geschichre der öffentlichen Sittlichkeit*, p. 399.

79. Dr. Hopton and A. Balliol, *Bed Manners* (London, 1936), p. 93.

80. There is certainly no lack of reactions against pajamas. An American expression of this, of interest particularly for its argumentation, is as follows (from *The People*, July 26, 1936):

"Strong men wear no pyjamas. They wear night-shirts and disdain men who wear such effeminate things as pyjamas. Theodore Roosevelt wore night-shirts. So did Washington, Lincoln, Napoleon, Nero and many other famous men.

"These arguments in favour of the night-shirt as against pyjamas are advanced by Dr. Davis of Ottawa, who has formed a club of night-shirt wearers. The club has a branch in Montreal and a strong group in New York. Its aim is to re-popularise the night-shirt as a sign of real manhood."

This speaks clearly for the spread of the use of pajamas in the relatively short period since the war.

It is still clearer that the use of pajamas by women has been receding again for some time. What replaces them is clearly a derivative of the long evening dress and an expression of the same social tendencies, including a reaction against the "masculinization" of women and a tendency toward sharper social differentiation, as well as the simple need for a certain harmony between evening and night costume. For precisely this reason, a comparison between this new nightdress and that of the past shows particularly clearly what has here been called the undeveloped state of the intimate sphere. This nightdress of our days is far more like a dress and far better formed than the earlier one.

81. M. Ginsberg, *Sociology* (London, 1934), p. 118: "Whether innate tendencies are repressed, sublimated or given full play depends to a large extent upon *the type of family life and the traditions of the larger society.* . . . Consider, for example, the difficulty of determining whether the aversion to incestuous relationships has an instinctive basis, or of disentangling the genetic factors underlying the various forms of sexual jealousy. The inborn tendencies, in short, have a certain *plasticity* and their mode of expression, repression or sublimation is, in varying degrees, socially conditioned."

The present study gives rise to very similar ideas. It attempts, above all in the conclusion to the second volume, to show that the molding of instinctual life, including its compulsive features, is a function of social interdependencies that persist throughout life. These dependencies of the individual vary in structure according to the structure of society. To the variations in this structure correspond the differences in personality structure that can be observed in history.

It might be recalled at this point that related observations are recorded very unambiguously in Montaigne's *Essays* (bk. 1, ch. 23):

> The laws of conscience that we say are born of nature, are born of custom; anyone holding in inner veneration the opinions and manners approved and accepted around him cannot disregard them without remorse or observe them without applause. It seems to me that the power of custom was very well understood by the originator of the fable of the village woman who, having acquired at birth the habit of caressing and carrying about with her a calf, and continuing to do so ever after, was still carrying it, by virtue of custom, when the animal was fully grown. . . . *Usus efficacissimus rerum omnium magister.* . . . Through custom as often as through illness, says Aristotle, women pull out their hair, bite their nails, eat coals and earth, and as much by custom as by nature males consort with males.

Particularly consonant with the findings of the present study is the idea that "remorse," and thus the psychic structure referred to here on Freudian lines, if with a slightly different meaning, as the superego, is imprinted on the individual by the society in which he grows up—in a word, that this superego is sociogenetic.

In this connection it scarcely needs to be said, but is perhaps worth emphasizing explicitly, how much this study owes to the discoveries of Freud and the psychoanalytical school. The connections are obvious to anyone acquainted with psychoanalytical writings, and it did not seem necessary to point them out in particular instances, especially because this could not have been done without lengthy qualifications. Nor have the not inconsiderable differences between the whole approach of Freud and that adopted in this study been stressed explicitly, particularly as the two could perhaps after some discussion be made to agree without undue difficulty. It seemed more important to build a particular intellectual perspective as clearly as possible, without digressing into disputes at every turn.

82. Von Raumer, *Geschichte der Pädagogik* (Stuttgart, 1857), pt. 1, p. 110.

83. On all these questions, cf. Huizinga, *Erasmus* (New York and London, 1924), p. 200: "What Erasmus really demanded of the world and mankind, how he pictured to himself that passionately desired, purified Christian society of good morals, fervent faith, simplicity and moderation, kindliness, toleration and peace—this we can nowhere else find so clearly and well expressed as in the *Colloquia.*"

84. "Museion," says the 1665 edition, is the word for a secret room.

85. The bewilderment of the later observer is no less when he finds himself confronted by morals and customs of the earlier phase which express a different standard of shame. This applies particularly to medieval bathing manners. In the nineteenth century it seems at first completely incomprehensible that medieval people were not ashamed to bathe naked together in large numbers, and often both sexes together.

Alwin Schultz, *Deutsches Leben im XIV und XV Jahrhundert* (Vienna, 1892), pp. 68f., says on this question:

> We possess two interesting pictures of such a bathhouse. *I should like to say in advance that I consider the pictures exaggerated, and that in my view the medieval predilection for coarse, earthy jokes has been accommodated by them.*
> The Breslau miniature shows us a row of bathtubs in each of which a man and a woman sit facing each other. A board laid across the tub serves as a table, and is covered by a pretty cloth on which are fruit, drinks, etc. The men have a headcloth and wear a loincloth, the women are adorned with coiffure, necklace, etc., but are otherwise quite naked. The Leipzig miniature is similar, except

that the tubs are separate; over each of them there is a kind of awning, with curtains that can be drawn. Behavior in these bathhouses was not unduly decorous, and decent women no doubt kept away from them. Usually, however, the sexes were certainly segregated; the city fathers would never have tolerated such an open flouting of all decency.

It is not without interest to see how the affective condition and the standard of repugnance of his own time put into the author's mouth the supposition that "usually . . . the sexes were certainly segregated," even though the historical evidence that he himself produces points rather to the opposite conclusion. Compare to this the matter of fact and simply descriptive attitude toward these differences of standard in P. S. Allen, *The Age of Erasmus* (Oxford, 1914), pp. 204ff.

86. See A. Bömer, *Aus dem Kampf gegen die Colloquia familiara des Erasmus*, in *Archiv für Kulturgeschichte* (Leipzig and Berlin, 1911), vol. 9, pt. 1, p. 32.

87. A. Bömer writes here: "In the last two books, intended for mature and old men." But the whole book is dedicated by Morisotus to his young son; the whole book was conceived as a schoolbook. In it Morisotus discusses the different stages of life. He introduces grown-ups to the child, men and women, young and old alike, so that the child can see and learn to understand them, and see what good and bad behavior are in this world. The notion that certain parts of this work were intended to be read solely by women or solely by old men is clearly put into the mind of the author by his understandable perplexity in face of the idea that all this might once have been intended as reading matter for children.

88. It is of importance for an understanding of this whole question that the age of marriage in this society was lower than that of later times.

"In this period," writes R. Köbner of the late Middle Ages, "man and woman often marry very young. The Church gives them the right to marry as soon as they have reached sexual maturity, and this right was often exercised. Youths marry between 15 and 19, girls between 13 and 15. This custom has always been regarded as a characteristic peculiarity of the society of that time." See R. Köbner, *Die Eheauffassung des ausgehenden Mittelalters*, in *Archiv für Kulturgeschichte*, (Leipzig and Berlin, 1911), vol. 9, no. 2. For copious information and documentation on child marriages, see Early English Text Society, Orig. Series, no. 108, ed. F. J. Furnivall (London, 1897), including *Child-Marriages, Divorces and Ratifications*, etc. There the possible marriageable age is given as fourteen for boys and twelve for girls (p. xix).

89. F. Zarncke, *Die deutsche Universität im Mittelalter* (Leipzig, 1857), Beitrag 1, pp. 49ff.

90. Bauer, *Das Liebesleben*, p. 136.

91. W. Rudeck, *Geschichte der öffentlichen Sittlichkeit in Deutschland* (Jena, 1897), p. 33.

92. Ibid., p. 33.

93. K. Schäfer, "Wie man früher heiratete," *Zeitschrift für deutsche Kulturgeschichte* (Berlin, 1891), vol. 2, no. 1, p. 31.

94. W.Rudeck, p.319.

95. Brienne, *Mémoires*, vol. 2, p. 11; quoted in Laborde, *Palais Mazarin*, n. 522.

96. F. von Bezold, "Ein Kölner Gedenkbuch des Jahrhunderts," in *Aus Mittelalter und Renaissance* (Munich and Berlin, 1918), p. 159.

97. W. Rudeck, p. 171, Allen, *Age of Erasmus*, p. 205; A. Hyma, *The Youth of Erasmus* (University of Michigan Press, 1930), pp. 56f. See also Regnault, *La condition juridique du bâtard au moyen âge* (Pont Audemer, 1922), where, however, the legal rather than the actual position of the bastard is considered. Common law often takes a not very benevolent attitude toward the bastard. It is a question that remains to be investigated whether common law thus expresses the actual social opinion of different strata or only the opinion of a particular stratum.

It is sufficiently known that as late as the seventeenth century, at the French royal court, the legitimate and illegitimate children were brought up together. Louis XIII, for example, hates his half-sister. Even as a child he says the following of his half-brother: "I like my little sister better than [him] because he has not been in mama's belly with me, as she has."

98. D. Parodie, "L'honnęte homme et l'idéal moral du XVIIe et du XVIIIe siècle," *Revue pédagogique* (1921), vol. 78, no. 2, 94ff.

99. Cf., e.g., Peters, "The Institutionalised Sex-Taboo," in Knight, Peters, and Blanchard, *Taboo and Genetics*, p. 181.

A study of 150 girls made by the writer in 1916/17 showed a taboo on thought and discussion among well-bred girls of the following subjects, which they characterise as "indelicate," "polluting" and "things completely outside the knowledge of a lady."
1. Things contrary to custom, often called "wicked" and "immoral."
2. Things "disgusting" such as bodily functions, normal as well as pathological, and all the implications of uncleanliness.
3. Things uncanny, that "make your flesh creep," and things suspicious.
4. Many forms of animal life, which it is a commonplace that girls will fear or which are considered unclean.
5. Sex differences.
6. Age differences.
7. All matters relating to the double standard of morality.
8. All matters connected with marriage, pregnancy, and childbirth.
9. Allusions to any part of the body except head and hands.
10. Politics.
11. Religion.

100. A. Luchaire, *La societé française au temps de Philippe-Auguste* (Paris, 1909), p. 273.

101. Ibid., p. 275.

102. Ibid., p. 272.

103. Ibid., p. 278.

104. I. Huizinga, *Herbst des Mittelalters, Studien über Lebens und Geistesform des 14 und 15 Jahrhunderts in Frankreich und in den Niederlanden* (Munich, 1924), p. 32.

105. From *"Le Jouvencel" Lebensgeschichte des Ritters Jean de Bueil*, ed. Kervyn de Lettenhove, in Chastellian, *Oeuvres*, vol. 8; quoted in Huizinga, *Herbst*, p. 94.

106. See p. xxx.

107. H. Dupin, *La courtoisie au moyen âge* (Paris, 1931), p. 79.

108. Ibid., p. 77.

109. Zarncke, *Der deutsche Cato*, pp. 36f., vv. 167f., 178ff.

110. Ibid., p. 48, vv. 395ff.

111. Huizinga, *Herbst*, pp. 32ff.

112. L. Mirot, *Les d'Orgemont, leur origine, leur fortune, etc.* (Paris, 1913); P. Champion, *François Villon. Sa vie et son temps* (Paris, 1913) vol. 2, pp. 230ff., quoted in Huizinga, *Herbst*, p. 32.

113. P. Durrieu, *Les très belles heures de Notre Dame du Duc Jean de Berry* (Paris, 1922), p. 68.

114. Ch. Petit-Dutaillis, *Documents nouveaux sur les moeurs populaires et le droit de vengeance dans les Pays-Bas au XV siècle* (Paris, 1908), p. 47.

115. Ibid., p. 162.

116. Ibid., p. 5.

117. Luchaire, *La societé française*, pp. 278f.

118. For further details on this, see A. Franklin, *Paris et les Parisiens au seizième siècle* (Paris, 1921), pp. 508f.

119. Th. Bossert mentions in his introduction to the *House-Book* (p. 20) an engraving by the same artist in which he "ridicules the newfangled nobility, the craving of bourgeois for coats of arms and knightly practices." This may point in the same direction.

120. Introduction to *Das Mittelalterliche Hausbuch*, ed. H. T. Bossert and W. Storck (Leipzig, 1912), pp. 27ff.

121. Berthold von Regensburg, *Deutsche Predigten*, ed. Pfeiffer and Strobl, (Vienna, 1862–1880), vol. 1, fourteen, p. 7.

122. Ibid., vol. 1, one hundred forty-one, pp. 24ff.

123. Max Lehrs, *Der Meister mit den Bandrollen* (Dresden, 1886), 26ff.

124. We shall now consider by way of a note a special problem arising from the material on the civilization of behavior which was not included in the text, partly for reasons of space and partly because it did not seem to contribute and essentially new to the understanding of the main our of civilization. Yet this problem deserves some attention. The relation of Western people to *cleanliness*, to *washing* and *bathing*, shows, over a long time span, the same transformational curve as has been examined in the text from many other sides. The impulse toward regular cleaning and constant bodily cleanliness does not derive in the first place from clearly defined hygienic insight, from a clear or, as we say, "rational" understanding of the danger of dirt to health. The relation to washing, too, changes in conjunction with the transformation of human relationships mentioned in the text and to be considered in more detail in the next volume.

At first it is taken for granted that people should clean themselves regularly only out of respect for others, especially social superiors, i.e., for social reasons, under the pressure of more or less perceptible external compulsions. Regular washing is omitted, or limited to the minimum demanded by immediate personal well-being, when such external compulsions are absent, when the social position does not demand it. Today, washing and bodily cleanliness are instilled in the individual from an early age as a kind of automatic habit, so that it gradually more or less disappears from his consciousness that he washes and disciplines himself to constant cleanliness out of regard for others and, at least originally, at the instigation of others, i.e., for reasons of external compulsion. He washes by self-compulsion even if no one else is present who might censure or punish him for not doing so. If he omits to do so, it is today—as it was not earlier—an expression of a not wholly successful conditioning to the existing social standard. The same change in behavior and in affective life that emerged in the investigation of other civilizational curves is seen here also. Social relations are transformed so that compulsions exerted by people on one another are changed into more and more pronounced self-compulsions in the individual; the formation of the superego is consolidated. It is, in a word, that sector of the individual representing the social code, his own superego, which today constrains the individual to wash and clean himself regularly. The mechanism becomes perhaps even clearer if we remember that today many men shave even if there is no social obligation to do so, simply from habit, because they feel discomfited by their superego if they do not, even though such an omission is quite certainly not detrimental to health. Regular washing with soap and water is another such "compulsive action" cultivated in our society by the nature of our conditioning and consolidated in our consciousness by hygienic, "rational" explanations.

It may suffice in this connection to document this change by evidence from another observer. I. E. Spingarn says in the introduction to an English translation of Della Casa's *Galateo* (The Humanist Library, ed. L. Einstein, [London, 1914], vol. 8, p. xxv): "Our concern is only with secular society, and there we find that cleanliness was considered only in so far as it was a social necessity, if indeed then; as an individual necessity or habit it scarcely appears at all. Della Casa's standard of social manners applies here, too: cleanliness was dictated by the need of pleasing others, and not because of any *inner* demand of individual instinct. . . . All this has changed. Personal cleanliness, because of its complete acceptance as an individual necessity has virtually ceased to touch the problem of social manners at any point." The curve of change is expressed here all the more clearly because the observer takes the standard of his own society—the *inner* desire for cleanliness—as given, without asking how and why it emerged from the other standard in the course of history. Today, indeed, it is in general only children who wash and clean themselves only under external pressure and direct compulsion from outside, out of regard for others on whom they depend. In adults, as we have said, this behavior is now gradually becoming a self-compulsion, a personal habit. Formerly, however, it was produced in adults, too, by direct external compulsion. We here meet again with what was earlier called the *fundamental law* of sociogenesis. The history of a society is mirrored in the history of the individual within it. The individual must pass through anew, in abbreviated form, the civilizing process that society as a whole has passed through over many centuries; for he does not come "civilized" into the world.

One further point in this civilization—curve deserves some attention. It appears, from the accounts of a number of observers, as if people in the sixteenth and seventeenth centuries were, if anything, less "clean" than in the preceding centuries. Such observations, when tested, are found to be correct in at least one way; it appears that the use of water as a means of bathing and cleaning declined somewhat in the transition to modern times, at least if life in the upper classes is considered. If the change is examined in this way, a simple explanation presents itself that certainly needs more exact confirmation. It was well enough known at the end of the Middle Ages that one could contract diseases, even fatal ones, in the bathhouses. To understand the effect of such a discovery, one must place oneself within the consciousness of this society, in which causal connections, in this case the nature of the transmission of disease and infection, were still somewhat vague. What could be imprinted on consciousness was the simple fact: water baths are dangerous, one can poison oneself in them. For it was in this way, as a kind of poisoning, that human reason at this time assimilated the mass infections, the plagues that swept through society in numerous waves. We know and understand the terrible fear which seized people in the face of such plagues. It was a fear that could not, as at our stage of social experience, be limited and guided into certain channels by exact knowledge of the causal connections and therefore of the limits of the danger. And it is very possible that at that time the use of water, particularly warm water for bathing purposes, was associated with a relatively indistinct fear of this kind which greatly exaggerated the real danger.

But if in a society at that stage of experience an object or piece of behavior is associated with fear in this way, it can be a long while before this fear and its symbols, the corresponding prohibitions and resistances, recede again. In the course of generations the memory of the original cause of the fear may very well disappear. What remains alive in the consciousness of people is perhaps only a feeling transmitted from one generation to another that danger is connected to the use of water, and a general discomfort, a feeling of distaste for this custom that is constantly socially reinforced. Thus we find in the sixteenth century, for example, pronouncements like this:

> Estuves et bains, je vous en prie
> Fuyès-les, ou vous en mourrés.

Flee sweating-rooms and baths, I beg you, or you will die.

This is said by a doctor, Guillaume Bunel, in 1513, among other pieces of advice against the plague (*Oeuvre excellente et a chascun désirant soy de peste préserver*, reprinted by Ch. J. Richelet [Le Mans, 1836]). We need only observe from our own standpoint how in his advice right and fantastically wrong ideas are mingled together to understand the effects of a fear less limited than our own. And in the seventeenth and even the eighteenth century we still constantly find warnings against the use of water, since it is harmful to the skin or one might catch a cold, among other "reasons." It looks indeed like a slowly ebbing wave of fear; but at the present state of research this is certainly only a hypothesis.

All the same, the hypothesis shows one thing quite clearly: how such phenomena *could* be explained. And it thereby demonstrates a fact that is highly characteristic of the whole civilizing process. This process takes place in conjunction with a progressive limitation of outward dangers, and so with a limitation and channeling of fear of such external dangers. These outward dangers of human life become more calculable, the paths and scope of human fears more regulated. Life sometimes seems to us uncertain enough today, but this bears no comparison with the insecurity of the individual in medieval society. The greater control of sources of fear that is slowly established in the transition to our social structure is indeed one of the most elementary preconditions for the standard of conduct that we express by the concept of "civilization." The armor of civilized conduct would crumble very rapidly if, through a change in society, the degree of insecurity that existed earlier were to break in upon us again, and if danger became as incalculable as it once was. Corresponding fears would soon burst the limits set to them today.

However, one specific form of fear does grow with the increase of civilization: the half-unconscious "inner" fear of a breaching of the restrictions imposed on civilized men.

Some concluding ideas on this subject are to be found at the end of the second volume in the "Sketch of a Theory of Civilization."

Notes on the 1968
Introduction

1. Talcott Parsons, *Essays in Sociological Theory* (Glencoe, 1963), pp. 359f.

2. Ibid., p. 359.

3. T. Parsons, *Social Structure and Personality* (Glencoe, 1963), pp. 82, 258f.

4. The idea that social change should be understood in terms of a change of structure through a malfunction of a normally stable state of social equilibrium is to be found in numerous places in Parsons's work; c.f., for example, T. Parsons and N. J. Smelser, *Economy and Society* (London, 1957), pp. 247f. Similarly, in Robert K. Merton, *Social Theory and Social Structure* (Glencoe, 1959), p. 122, an ideal social state (though one apparently understood as real) in which there are no contradictions and tensions is counterposed to another in which these social phenomena, evaluated as "dysfunctional," exert a pressure toward "change" on a social structure normally free of tension and immutable.

The problem being put forward for discussion here, as can seen, is not identical with the problem traditionally discussed in terms of the concepts "static" and "dynamic." The traditional discussion often involves the question of which method is preferable in examining social phenomena, one limiting the inquiry to a particular time segment or one involving the study of more extended processes. Here, in contrast, it is not the sociological method or even the sociological selection of problems as such which is under discussion, but the conceptions of society, of human figurations, underlying the use of the various methods and types of problem selection. What is said here is not directed against the possibility of sociologically investigating short-term social conditions, this type of problem being an entirely legitimate and indispensable kind of sociological inquiry. What is said here is directed against a certain type of theoretical conception, often but by no means necessarily associated with empirical sociological investigations of states. It is quite certainly possible to undertake empirical investigations of states while using models of social changes, processes, and developments of one kind or another as a theoretical frame of reference. The debate on the relation between "social statics" and "social dynamics" suffers from insufficiently clear differentiation between the empirical investigation of short-term sociological problems and the methods of inquiry appropriate to them, on the one hand, and the theoretical models by which—explicitly or not—one is guided in posing the problems and in presenting the results of the inquiry, on the other. Merton's use of the terms "static" and "dynamic" in the passage cited above shows very clearly this insufficient capacity to differentiate, as when he says that within the framework of a sociological theory of function the gap between statics and dynamics can be bridged by the consideration that discrepancies, tensions, and antitheses are "dysfunctional" in terms of the existing "social system," and therefore signify malfunction, but are "instrumental" from the point of view of change.

5. The tendencies of the European nations to greater unification may certainly derive a good part of their driving force from the consolidation and extension of chains of interdependencies, above all in the economic and military spheres; but it was the shock to the traditional national self-images of the European countries that gave rise in all these nations to a disposition to adapt their own attitudes—hesitantly and tentatively, at least in the beginning—toward greater functional interdependence, despite the natiocentric tradition. The difficulty of this undertaking lies precisely in the fact that, as a result of the natiocentric socialization of children and adults, each of these nations occupies the dominant emotional position among its own people, whereas the larger transnational

formation which is evolving possesses at first only a "rational" but hardly an emotional significance for them.

6. This difference deserves a more extensive comparative investigation than is possible here. But in general terms it can be explained in a few words. It is connected with the kind and extent of the value of preindustrial power elites which pass into the values of the industrial strata and their representatives as they come into power.

In countries like Germany (but also in other countries on the European continent) a type of bourgeois conservatism can be observed which is determined to a very high degree by the values of the preindustrial dynastic-agrarian-military power elites. These values include a very pronounced depreciation of everything that is referred to as the "world of commerce" (i.e., trade and industry) and an unequivocally higher value attached to the state, the "social whole" as against the individual. Wherever such values play a prominent part in the conservatism of industrial classes, they understandably contain a perceptible antiliberal tendency. In this tradition negative feelings are attached to the high estimation of the individual personality and of individual initiative and to the correspondingly lower evaluation of the "state" totality, in other words, to the values of a commercial world pleading for free competition.

In countries where members of the preindustrial agrarian elite kept less emphatically aloof in their practical life and in their values from commercial operations and from all those earning their livelihood by such operations, and where the power of princes and court circles as centers of the state was limited, as in England, or nonexistent, as in America, the rising bourgeois groups, in their gradual ascent to become the dominant class, evolved a type of conservatism which—apparently—was highly compatible with the ideals of nonintervention by the state, of the freedom of the individual, and therefore with specifically liberal values. More will be said in the text about some of the specific difficulties of this liberal-conservative nationalism, this apparently unproblematic simultaneous assertion of the "individual" and of the nation as the highest value.

7. The superseding of an ideology oriented toward the future by one oriented toward the present is sometimes concealed by an intellectual sleight of hand that can be recommended to any sociologist interested in the study of ideologies as a prime example of the subtler kind of ideology formation. The orientation of the various natiocentric ideologies toward the existing order as the highest ideal sometimes produces the result that exponents of such value—particularly but by no means exclusively exponents of their conservative-liberal shades—posit their own attitudes simply as nonideological statements of fact and restrict the concept of ideology to those kinds of ideologies which are directed at changing the existing order, particularly within the state. An example of this conceptual masking of one's own ideology in the development of German society is the well-known ideology of *Realpolitik*. This argument starts from the idea, conceived as a statement of fact, that in international politics every nation actually exploits its potential power in its own national interest in an entirely ruthless and unrestricted way. This apparent statement of fact served to justify a particular natiocentric ideal, a modern version of the Machiavellian ideal, which states that national policy ought to be pursued in the international field without consideration for others, solely in one's own national interest. This ideal of *Realpolitik* is in fact unrealistic because every nation is actually dependent on others.

A similar train of thought is found in more recent times—and, in keeping with American tradition, in a somewhat more moderate form—in a book by an American sociologist, Daniel Bell, bearing the revealing title *The End of Ideology* (New York, 1961). Bell, too, starts from the assumption that the power struggle between organized groups in the pursuit of their own advantage is a fact. He concludes from this fact, much like the advocates of German *Realpolitik*, that the politician, in pursuing the power goals of his own group, ought to intervene without ethical commitment in the power struggles of different groups. At the same time, Bell claims that this program does not have the character of a profession of political faith, of a preconceived value system, i.e., an ideology (ibid., p. 279). He attempts to limit this concept solely to political doctrines directed at changing the existing order. He forgets that it is possible to treat the existing order not only as a simple fact but as a value underpinned by emotions, as an ideal, as something that ought to be. He does not distinguish between a scientific investigation of what is and an ideological defense of what is (as the embodiment of a highly valued ideal). It is quite obvious that Bell's ideal is the state that he describes as a fact.

"Democracy," writes another American sociologist, Seymour Martin Lipset, "is not only or even primarily a means through which different groups can attain their ends or seek the good society; it is the good society itself in operation" (*Political Man*, New York, 1960, p. 403). Lipset later modified this statement to some extent. But this and other pronouncements by leading American sociologists are examples of how little even the most intelligent representatives of American sociology are in a position to withstand the extraordinarily strong pressure toward intellectual conformity in their society, and of how much this situation impairs their critical faculties. As long as this is the case, as long as natiocentric values and ideals dominate the theorizing of leading American sociologists to such a degree, as long as they fail to realize that sociology can no more be conducted from a primarily national point of view than physics, their predominant influence represents a not inconsiderable danger for the worldwide development of sociology. As can be seen, "the end of ideology" is not yet in sight among sociologists.

Incidentally, something similar would probably have to be said about Russian sociology if it had a similarly dominant influence. But as far as I am aware, while there are in the U.S.S.R. a growing number of empirical sociological investigations, there is as yet scarcely a theoretical sociology. This is understandable, for its place is taken in the Soviet Union not so much by the system of Marx and Engels as by a Marxist intellectual edifice raised to the status of a creed. Like the dominant American theory of society, the Russian theory is a natiocentric mental construct. From this side, too, the end of ideology is quite certainly not in sight in sociological theorizing. But that is no reason not to strive to the utmost to bring nearer the end of this continuous self-deception, this constant masking of short-term social ideals as eternally valid sociological theories.

8. T. Parsons, *Societies: Evolutionary and Comparative Perspectives* (Englewood Cliffs, N.J., 1966), p. 20: "This process occurs inside that "black box,' the personality of the actor."

9. Gilbert Ryle, *The Concept of Mind* (London, 1949).

State Formation and Civilization

Translated by Edmund Jephcott
with some notes and revisions by the author

Table of Contents

Acknowledgements

This translation could not have been produced without the aid of my friends. In particular, Professor Johan Goudsblom has spent a great deal of time and effort in comparing the English and German texts to ensure that the exact meaning has been interpreted. Eric Dunning has also throughout made a number of very useful suggestions. The exercise of checking the translation was in itself a most useful one for me as it enabled me to revise the text in minor, but important ways and to add notes which set the work in the context of my later thinking. None of this should be taken as any reflection on the translator, Edmund Jephcott, to whom I owe the greatest debt. My thanks are also due to Johan and Maria Goudsblom for reading the proofs and compiling the index.

The italic in the quotations indicates the author's emphasis.

PART ONE
Feudalization and State Formation

Introduction

I

Survey of Courtly Society

1. The struggles between the nobility, the Church and the princes for their shares in the control and the produce of the land run through the entire Middle Ages. In the course of the twelfth and thirteenth centuries a further group emerges as a partner in this play of forces: the privileged town-dwellers, the "bourgeoisie".

The actual course of this constant struggle, and the power relations among the contestants, vary widely between countries. But the outcome of the conflicts is, in its structure, nearly always the same: in all the larger Continental countries, and at times in England too, the princes or their representatives finally accumulate a concentration of power to which the estates are not equal. The autarky of the majority, and the estates' share of power, are curtailed step by step, while the dictatorial or "absolute" power of a single supreme figure is slowly established, for a greater or lesser period. In France, England and the Habsburg countries this figure is the king, in the German and Italian regions it is the territorial ruler.

2. Numerous studies describe, for example, how the French kings from Philip Augustus to Francis I and Henry IV increase their power, or how the Elector Frederick William pushes aside the regional estates in Brandenburg, and the

Medici the patricians and senate in Florence, or how the Tudors do the same to the nobility and parliament in England. Everywhere it is the individual agents and their various actions that we see, their personal weaknesses and gifts that are described. And it is no doubt fruitful and even indispensable to see history in this way, as a mosaic of individual actions of individual people.

Nevertheless, something else is obviously at work here besides the fortuitous emergence of a series of great princes and the fortuitous victories of numerous individual territorial rulers or kings over numerous individual estates at approximately the same time. It is not without reason that we speak of an *age* of absolutism. What finds expression in this change in the form of political rule is a structural change in Western society as a whole. Not only did individual kings increase their power but, clearly, the social institution of the monarchy or princedom took on new weight in the course of a gradual transformation of the whole of society, a new weight which at the same time gave new power chances to the central rulers.

On the one hand we might enquire how this or that man gained power and how he or his heirs increased or lost this power in the context of "absolutism".

On the other, we may ask on the basis of what social changes the medieval institution of the king or prince took on, in certain centuries, the character and power referred to by concepts such as "absolutism" or "despotism", and which social structure, which development in human relations, made it possible for the institution to sustain itself in this form for a greater or lesser period of time.

Both approaches work with more or less the same material. But only the second attains to the plane of historical reality on which the civilizing process takes place.

It is by more than a coincidence that in the same centuries in which the king or prince acquires absolutist status, the restraint and moderation of the affects discussed in the previous volume, the "civilizing" of behaviour, is noticeably increased. In the quotations assembled earlier to demonstrate this change in behaviour, it emerged quite clearly how closely this change is linked to the formation of the hierarchical social order with the absolute ruler and, more broadly, his court at its head.

3. For the court, too, the residence of the ruler, took on a new aspect and a new significance in Western society, in a movement that flowed slowly across Europe, to ebb away again, earlier here and later there, at about the time we call the "Renaissance".

In the movements of this period the courts gradually become the actual model and style-setting centres. In the preceding phase they had had to share or even wholly relinquish this function to other centres, according to the prevailing balance of power, now to the Church, now to the towns, now to the courts of the great vassals and knights scattered across the country. From this time on, in German and particularly in Protestant regions, the courts of the central authorities still share their function with the universities turning out the princely bureaucracy, whereas in Romanic and perhaps in all Catholic countries—this latter point remains to be established—the importance of the courts as a social authority, a source of models of behaviour, far exceeds that of the university and all the other social formations of the epoch. The early Renaissance in Florence, characterized by men like Masaccio, Ghiberti, Brunelleschi and Donatello, is not yet an unequivocally courtly style; but the Italian High Renaissance, and more clearly still the Baroque and Rococo, the style of Louis XV and XVI, are courtly, as finally is the "Empire", though in a more transitional way, being already permeated with industrial–bourgeois features.

At the courts a form of society is evolving for which no very specific and unequivocal term exists in German, for the obvious reason that in Germany this type of human bonding never attained central and decisive importance, except at most only in the final, transitional form it had at Weimar. The German concept of "good society", or more simply, of "society" in the sense of *monde*, like the social formation corresponding to it, lacks the sharp definition of the French and English terms. The French speak of *la société polie*. And the French terms *bonne compagnie* or *gens de la Cour* and the English "Society" have similar connotations.

4. The most influential courtly society was formed, as we know, in France. From Paris the same codes of conduct, manners, taste and language spread, for varying periods, to all the other European courts. This happened not only because France was the most powerful country at the time. It was only now made possible because, in a pervasive transformation of European society, similar social formations, characterized by analogous forms of human relations came into being everywhere. The absolutist-courtly aristocracy of other lands adopted from the richest, most powerful and most centralized country of the time the things which fitted their own social needs: refined manners and a language which distinguished them from those of inferior rank. In France they saw, most fruitfully developed, something born of a similar social situation and which matched their own ideals: people who could parade their status, while also observing the subtleties of social intercourse, marking their exact relation to everyone above and below them by their manner of greeting and their choice of words—people of "distinction" and "civility". In taking over French etiquette and Parisian ceremony, the various rulers obtained the desired instruments to express their dignity, to make visible the hierarchy of society, and to make all others, first and foremost the courtly nobility themselves, aware of their dependence.

5. Here, too, it is not enough to see and describe the particular events in different countries in isolation. A new picture emerges, and a new understanding is made possible, if the many individual courts of the West, with their relatively uniform manners, are seen together as communicating organs in European society at large. What slowly begins to form at the end of the Middle Ages is not just one courtly society here and another there. It is a courtly aristocracy embracing

Western Europe with its centre in Paris, its dependencies in all the other courts, and offshoots in all the other circles which claimed to belong to "Society", notably the upper stratum of the bourgeoisie and to some extent even broader layers of the middle class.

The members of this multiform society speak the same language throughout the whole of Europe, first Italian, then French; they read the same books, they have the same taste, the same manners and—with differences of degree—the same style of living. Notwithstanding their many political differences and even the many wars they wage against each other, they orientate themselves fairly unanimously, over greater or lesser periods, towards the centre at Paris. And social communication between court and court, i.e. within courtly-aristocratic society, remains for a long time closer than between courtly society and other strata in the same country; one expression of this is their common language. Then, from about the middle of the eighteenth century, earlier in one country and somewhat later in another, but always in conjunction with the rise of the middle classes and the gradual displacement of the social and political centre of gravity from the court to the various national bourgeois societies, the ties between the courtly-aristocratic societies of different nations are slowly loosened even if they are never entirely broken. The French language gives way, not without violent struggles, to the bourgeois, national languages even in the upper class. And courtly society itself becomes increasingly differentiated in the same way as bourgeois societies, particularly when the old aristocratic society loses its centre once and for all in the French Revolution. The national form of integration displaces that based on social estate.

6. In seeking the social traditions which provide the common basis and deeper unity of the various national traditions in the West, we should think not only of the Christian Church, the common Roman–Latin heritage, but also of this last great pre-national social formation which, already partly in the shadow of the national divergences within Western society, rose above the lower and middle strata in different linguistic areas. Here were created the models of more pacified social intercourse which more or less all classes needed, following the transformation of European society at the end of the Middle Ages; here the coarser habits, the wilder, more uninhibited customs of medieval society with its warrior upper class, the corollaries of an uncertain, constantly threatened life, were "softened", "polished" and "civilized". The pressure of court life, the vying for the favour of the prince or the "great"; then, more generally, the necessity to distinguish oneself from others and to fight for opportunities with relatively peaceful means, through intrigue and diplomacy, enforced a constraint on the affects, a self-discipline and self-control, a peculiarly courtly rationality, which at first made the courtier appear to the opposing bourgeoisie of the eighteenth century, above all in Germany but also in England, as the epitome of the man of reason.

And here, in this pre-national, courtly-aristocratic society, a part of those commands and prohibitions were fashioned or at least prepared that are perceptible even today, national differences notwithstanding, as something common to the West. Partly from them the Western peoples, despite all their differences, have taken the common stamp of a specific civilization.

That the gradual formation of this absolutist-courtly society was accompanied by a transformation of the drive-economy and conduct of the upper class in the direction of "civilization", has been shown by a series of examples. It has also been indicated how closely this increased restraint and regulation of elementary urges is bound up with increased social constraint, the growing dependence of the nobility on the central lord, the king or prince.

How did this increased constraint and dependence come about? How was an upper class of relatively independent warriors or knights supplanted by a more or less pacified upper class of courtiers? Why was the influence of the estates progressively reduced in the course of the Middle Ages and the early modern period, and why, sooner or later, was the dictatorial "absolute" rule of a single figure, and with it the compulsion of courtly etiquette, the pacification of larger or smaller territories from a single centre, established for a greater or lesser period of time in all the countries of Europe? The sociogenesis of absolutism indeed occupies a key position in the overall process of civilization. The civilizing of conduct and the corresponding transformation of human consciousness and libidinal make-up cannot be understood without tracing the process of state-formation, and within it the advancing centralization of society which first finds particularly visible expression in the absolutist form of rule.

II

A Prospective Glance at the Sociogenesis of Absolutism

1. A few of the most important mechanisms which, towards the end of the Middle Ages, gradually gave increasing power chances to the central authority of a territory, can be quite briefly described at this preliminary stage. They are broadly similar in all the larger countries of the West and are particularly clearly seen in the development of the French monarchy.

The gradual increase of the money sector of the economy at the expense of the barter sector in a given region in the Middle Ages had very different consequences for the majority of the warrior nobility on the one hand, and for the king or prince on the other. The more money that came into circulation in a region, the greater the increase in prices. All classes whose revenue did not increase at the same rate, all those on a fixed income, were thus placed at a disadvantage, above all the feudal lords who received fixed rents from their estates.

The social functions whose income increased with these new opportunities were placed at an advantage. They included certain sections of the bourgeoisie, but above all the king, the central ruler. For the taxation apparatus gave him a share of the increasing wealth; a part of all the earnings in his area of rule came to him, and his income consequently increased to an extraordinary degree with the growing circulation of money.

As is always the case, this functional mechanism was only very gradually and, so to speak, retrospectively exploited consciously by the interested parties, being adopted at a relatively late stage by rulers as a principle of domestic politics. Its first result was a more or less automatic and constant increase in the income of the central lord. This is one of the preconditions on the basis of which the institution of kingship gradually gained its absolute or uncircumscribed character.

2. As the financial opportunities open to the central function grew, so too did its military potential. The man who had at his disposal the taxes of an entire country was in a position to hire more warriors than any other; by the same token he grew less dependent on the war services which the feudal vassal was obliged to render in exchange for the land with which he was invested.

This too is a process which, like all the others, begins very early but only gradually leads to the formation of definite institutions. Even William the Conqueror went to England with an army consisting only partly of vassals, the rest being paid knights. Between that time and the establishment of standing armies by the central lords, centuries intervened. A prerequisite for such armies, apart from the growing revenue from taxes, was surplus manpower—the discrepancy between the number of people and the number and profitability of jobs available in a particular society which we know today as "unemployment". Areas suffering from surpluses of this kind, e.g. Switzerland and parts of Germany, supplied mercenaries to anyone who could afford them. Much later, Frederick the Great's recruiting tactics show the solutions open to a prince when the manpower available in his territory is not sufficient for his military purposes. The military supremacy that went hand in hand with financial superiority was, therefore, the second decisive prerequisite enabling the central power of a region to take on "absolute" character.

A transformation of military techniques followed and reinforced this development. Through the slow development of firearms the mass of common foot-soldiers became militarily superior to the numerically limited nobles fighting on horseback. This too was to the advantage of the central authority.

The king, who in the France of the early Capetian period, for example, was not much more than a baron, one territorial lord among others of equal power, and sometimes even less powerful than others, gained from his increasing revenues the possibility of military supremacy over all the forces in his country. Which noble family managed in particular cases to win the crown and thus gain access to these power chances depended on a wide range of factors including the personal talents of individuals and often chance. The growth of the financial and military power chances that gradually attached themselves to the monarchy was independent of the will or talents of individuals; it followed a strict regularity that is encountered wherever social processes are observed.

And this increase in the power chances of the central function was therefore the precondition for the pacification of a given territory, greater or smaller as the case may be, from a single centre.

3. The two series of developments which acted to the advantage of a strong central authority were in all ways detrimental to the old medieval warrior estate. They had no direct connection with the growing money sector of the economy. They could scarcely derive any direct profit from the new opportunities of income that offered themselves. They felt only the devaluation, the rise in prices.

It has been calculated that a fortune of 22,000 francs in the year 1200 was worth 16,000 francs in 1300, 7,500 francs in 1400, and 6,500 in 1500. In the sixteenth century this movement accelerated; the value of the sum fell to 2,500 francs, and the case was similar in the whole of Europe.[1]

A movement originating far back in the Middle Ages underwent an extraordinary acceleration in the sixteenth century. From the reign of Francis I up to the year 1610 alone, the French pound was devalued in approximately the ratio 5 to 1. The importance of this developmental curve for the transformation of society was greater than can be stated in a few words. While money circulation grew and commercial activity developed, while bourgeois classes and the revenue of the central authority rose, the income of the entire remaining nobility fell. Some of the knights were reduced to a wretched existence, others took by robbery and violence what was no longer available by peaceful means, others again kept themselves above water for as long as possible by slowly selling off their estates; and finally a good part of the nobility, forced by these circumstances and attracted by the new opportunities, entered the service of the kings or princes who could pay. These were the economic options open to a warrior class that was not connected to the growth in money circulation and the trade network.

4. How the development of war technology operated to the nobility's disadvantage has already been mentioned: the infantry, the despised foot-soldiers, became more important in battle than the cavalry. Not only the military superiority of the medieval warrior estate was thereby broken, but also its monopoly over weapons. A situation where the nobles alone were warriors or, conversely, all warriors were nobles, began to turn into one where the noble was at best an officer of plebeian troops who had to be paid. The monopoly control of weapons and military power passed from the whole noble estate into the hands of a single member, the prince or king who, supported by the tax income of the whole region, could afford the largest army. Thereby the majority of the nobility

were changed from relatively free warriors or knights into paid warriors or officers in the service of the central lord.

These are a few of the most important lines of this structural transformation.

5. There was another as well. The nobility lost social power with the increase in the money sector of the economy, while bourgeois classes gained it. But in general neither of the two estates proved strong enough to gain the upper hand over the other for a prolonged period. Constant tensions everywhere erupted in periodic struggles. The battle fronts were complicated and varied widely from case to case. There were occasional alliances between groups within the nobility and groups within the bourgeoisie; there were transitional forms and even fusions between sub-groups from the two estates. But however that may be, both the rise and the absolute power of the central institution always depended on the continued existence of this tension between the nobility and the bourgeoisie. One of the structural preconditions for the absolute monarchy or princedom was that neither of the estates nor any group within them should gain the upper hand. The representatives of the absolute central authority therefore had to be constantly on the alert to ensure that this unstable equilibrium was maintained within their territory. Where the balance was lost, where one group or class became too strong, or where aristocratic and upper bourgeois groups even temporarily allied, the supremacy of the central power was seriously threatened or—as in England—doomed. Thus we often observe among rulers that while one protects and promotes the bourgeoisie because the nobility seems too powerful and therefore dangerous, the next inclines towards the nobility, this having grown too weak or the bourgeoisie too refractory, without the other side being ever quite neglected. The absolute rulers were obliged, whether they were entirely conscious of it or not, to manipulate this social mechanism that they had not created. Their social existence depended on its survival and functioning. They too were bound to the social regularity with which they had to live. This regularity and the social structure corresponding to it emerged sooner or later with numerous modifications in almost every country of the West. But it takes on clear delineation only if observed in the process of emergence through a concrete example. The development in France, the country in which this process, from a particular moment on, takes place in the most direct form, will serve here as an example.

Chapter One

Dynamics
of Feudalization

I

Introduction

1. If we compare France, England and the German Empire at the middle of the seventeenth century in terms of the power of their central authorities, the king of France appears particularly strong beside the English king and even more so beside the German emperor. This constellation is the outcome of a very long development.

At the end of the Carolingian and the beginning of the Capetian period the situation is almost the reverse. At that time the central power of the German emperors was strong as compared to the French kings. And England had yet to undergo its decisive unification and reorganization by the Normans.

In the German empire the power of the central authority crumbles persistently—though with occasional interruptions— from this time on.

In England, from Norman times on, periods of strong royal power alternate with the preponderance of the estates or parliament.

In France, from about the beginning of the twelfth century, the king's power grows—again with interruptions—fairly steadily. A continuous line leads from the Capetians through the Valois to the Bourbons.

Nothing entitles us to presuppose that these differences follow any kind of compulsion. Very slowly the different regions of the three countries merge into national units. At first, as long as the integration of those areas which are later to become "France", "Germany", "Italy" and "England" is relatively slight, they do not weigh very heavily as social organisms in the balance of historical forces. And the main developmental curves in the history of these nations are in this phase incomparably more strongly influenced by the fortunes and misfortunes of individuals, by personal qualities, by sympathies and antipathies or "accidents", than later when "England", "Germany" or "France" have become social formations with a quite specific structure and a momentum and regularity of their own. At first the historical lines of development are co-determined very strongly by factors which, from the viewpoint of the later unit, have no inherent necessity.[2] Then, gradually, with the increasing interdependence of larger areas and populations, a pattern slowly emerges which, according to circumstance, either limits or opens opportunities to the whims and interests of powerful individuals or even of particular groups. Then, but only then, do the inherent developmental dynamics of these social units override chance or at least mark it with their stamp.

2. Nothing entitles us to presuppose any compelling necessity determining that it was the duchy of Francia, the "Isle de France", about which a nation would crystallize. Culturally, and also politically, the southern regions of France had much stronger ties with those of northern Spain and the bordering Italian regions than with the area around Paris. There was always a very considerable difference between the old, more Celto–Romanic regions of Provence, the *langue d'oc*, and the *langue d'oïl* parts, that is, regions with a stronger Frankish influence, above all those to the north of the Loire, together with Poitou, Berry, Bourgogne, Saintonge and Franche-Comté.[3]

Moreover, the eastern frontiers established by the Treaty of Verdun (843) and then by the Treaty of Meerssen (870) for the western Frankish empire, were very different from the borders between what gradually emerged as "France" and "Germany" or "Italy".

The Treaty of Verdun fixed as the eastern frontier of the western Frankish empire a line leading from the present Gulf of Lions in the south, and approaching the western side of the Rhône, in an approximately northerly direction as far as Flanders. Lorraine and Burgundy—except for the duchy west of the Saône—, and therefore also Arles, Lyons, Trier and Metz thus lay outside the borders of the western Frankish empire, while to the south the county of Barcelona was still within its frontiers.[4]

The Treaty of Meerssen made the Rhône the direct frontier in the south between the western and the eastern Frankish empires; then the frontier followed the Isère and, further north, the Moselle. Trier and Metz thus became frontier towns, as, to the north, did Meerssen, the place from which the treaty took its name. And the frontier finally ended north of the Rhine estuary in the region of southern Friesland.

But what such frontiers separated were neither states, nor peoples or nations, if by that we mean social formations that are in any sense unified and stable. At most they were states, peoples, nations in the making. The most striking feature of all the larger territories in this phase is their low level of cohesion, the strength of the centrifugal forces tending to disintegrate them.

What is the nature of these centrifugal forces? What peculiarity of the structure of these territories gives such forces their particular strength? And what change in the structure of society, from the fifteenth, sixteenth or seventeenth century onwards, finally gives the central authorities preponderance over all the centrifugal forces, and thus confers on the territories a greater stability?

II

Centralizing and Decentralizing Forces in the Medieval Power Figuration

3. The immense empire of Charlemagne had been brought together by conquest. Certainly the basic, though not the only function of his immediate predecessors, and more so of Charlemagne himself, was that of army leader, victorious in conquest and defence. This was the foundation of his royal power, his renown, his social strength.

As army leader Charlemagne had control of the land he conquered and defended. As victorious prince he rewarded the warriors who followed him with land. And by virtue of this authority he held them together even though their estates were scattered across the country.

The emperor and king could not supervise the whole empire alone. He sent trusted friends and servants into the country to uphold the law in his stead, to ensure the payment of tributes and the performance of services, and to punish resistance. He did not pay for their services in money; this was certainly not entirely lacking in this phase, but existed to only a very limited extent. Needs were supplied for the most part directly from the land, the fields, the forests and the stables, produce being worked up within the household. The earls or dukes, or whatever the representatives of the central authority were called, also fed themselves and their retinue from the land with which the central authority had invested them. In keeping with the economic structure, the apparatus for ruling in this phase of society was unlike that of "states" in a later stage. Most of the "officials", it has been said of this phase, "were farmers who had 'official' duties only for certain set periods or in the case of unforeseen events, and so were most directly comparable to landowners having police and judicial powers".[5] With this legal and law-enforcing role they combined military functions; they were warriors, commanders of a warlike following and of all the other landowners in the area the king had given them, should it be threatened by an external enemy. In a word, all ruling functions were drawn together in their hands.

But this peculiar power figuration—a measure of the division of labour and differentiation in this phase—again and again led to characteristic tensions arising from the nature of its structure. It generated certain typical sequences of events which—with certain modifications—were repeated over and again.

4. Whoever was once entrusted by the central lord with the functions of ruling in a particular area and was thus in effect the lord of this area, no longer depended on the central lord to sustain and protect himself and his dependants, at least as long as he was threatened by no stronger external foe. At the first opportunity, therefore, as soon as the central power showed the slightest sign of weakness, the local ruler or his descendants sought to demonstrate their right and ability to rule the district entrusted to them, and their independence of the central authority.

Over many centuries the same patterns and trends show themselves over and again in this apparatus for ruling. The rulers over parts of the central lord's territory, the local dukes or chieftains, are at all times a danger to the central power. Conquering princes and kings, being strong as army leaders and protectors against external foes, strive, successfully at first, to confront this danger within the area they control. Where possible they replace the existing local rulers with their own friends, relations or servants. Within a short time, often within a generation, the same thing happens again. The erstwhile representatives of the central ruler do their best to take over the area entrusted to them, as if it were the hereditary property of their family.

Now it is the *comes palatii*, once the overseers of the royal palace, who want to become the independent rulers of a region; now it is the margraves, dukes, counts, barons or officials of the king. In repeated waves the kings, strengthened by conquests, send their trusted friends, relations and servants into the country as their envoys, while the previous envoys or their descendants fight just as regularly to establish the hereditary nature and the factual independence of their region, which was originally a kind of fief.

On the one hand the kings were forced to delegate power over part of their territory to other individuals. The state of military, economic and transport arrangements at that time left them no choice. Society offered them no sources of money taxes sufficient for them to keep a paid army or paid official delegates in remote regions. To pay or reward them they could only allocate them land—in amounts large enough to ensure that they were actually stronger than all the other warriors or landowners in the area.

On the other hand the vassals representing the central power were restrained by no oath of allegiance or loyalty from asserting the independence of their area as soon as the relative power positions of the central ruler and his delegates shifted in favour of the latter. These territorial lords or local princes in effect own the land once controlled by the king. Except when threatened from outside, they no longer need the king. They withdraw themselves from his power. When they need the king as military leader, the movement is reversed and the game starts all over again, assuming the central lord is victorious in the war. Then, through the power and threat emanating from his sword, he regains actual control over the whole territory and can distribute it anew. This is one of the recurring processes in the development of Western society in the early Middle Ages and sometimes, in somewhat modified form, in later periods too.

5. Examples of such processes are to be found even today outside Europe, in regions with a similar social structure. The development of Abyssinia shows such configurations in abundance, though they have latterly been somewhat modified by the inflow of money and other institutions from Europe. But the rise of Ras Tafari to the position of central ruler or emperor of the whole country was made possible only by the military subjugation of the most powerful territorial lords; and the unexpectedly quick collapse of opposition to Italy is explained not least by the fact that in this feudal and predominantly agrarian region, the centrifugal tendencies of the individual territories were multiplied as soon as the central ruler failed to fulfil his most important task, that of resisting the external enemy, thus showing himself "weak".

In European history traces of this mechanism are to be found as early as the Merovingian epoch. Here, already, are present "the beginnings of a development which changed the higher imperial offices into hereditary forms of rule".[6] Even to this period the principle applies that: "The greater the actual economic and social power of these officials became, the less could the monarchy contemplate transferring the office outside the family on the death of its incumbent."[7] In other words, large parts of the territory passed from the control of the central lord to that of the local rulers.

Sequences of this kind emerge more clearly in the Carolingian period. Charlemagne, much like the emperor of Abyssinia, replaces the old local dukes wherever he can by his own "officials", the counts. When, within Charlemagne's lifetime, these counts show their self-will and their effective control over the territory entrusted to them, he despatches a new wave of people from his entourage as royal envoys, *musi dominici*, to supervise them. Under Louis the Pious the function of count already begins to become hereditary. Charlemagne's successors are no longer able "to escape factual recognition of the claim to hereditariness".[8] And the royal envoys themselves lose their function. Louis the Pious is forced to withdraw the *missi dominici*. Under this king who lacked the military renown of Charlemagne, the centrifugal tendencies within the imperial and social organization emerge very clearly. They reach a first peak under Charles III, who in 887 can no longer protect Paris from his external enemies, the Danish Normans, by the power of the sword, and scarcely by the power of money. It is characteristic of this tendency that with the end of the direct line of the Carolingians, the crown goes first to Arnulf of Carinthia, the bastard son of

Karlmann, nephew of Charles the Fat. Arnulf had proved his worth as a military leader in the border conflicts with the invading foreign tribes. When he leads the Bavarians against the weak central ruler, he quickly gains the recognition of other tribes, the eastern Franks, the Thuringians, the Saxons and the Swabians. As army leader in the original sense, he is raised to the kingship by the warrior nobility of the German tribes.[9] Once again it is shown very clearly from where the function of kingship in this society derives its power and legitimation. In 891 he succeeds in repelling the Normans at Louvain on the Dyle. But when, confronted by a new threat, he hesitates only slightly to lead his army into battle, the reaction is immediate. At once centrifugal forces gain the upper hand in his weakly unified domain: "Illo diu morante, multi reguli in Europa vel regno Karoli sui patruelis excrevere," says a writer of the time.[10] Everywhere in Europe little kings grew up when he hesitated for a time to fight. This illustrates in one sentence the social regularities which set their stamp on the development of European society in this phase.

The movement is once again reversed under the first Saxon emperors. The fact that rule over the entire empire fell to the Saxon dukes again shows what was the most important function of the central ruler in this society. The Saxons were particularly exposed to pressure from the non-German tribes pushing across from the east. The first task of their dukes was to protect their own tribal territory. But in so doing they also defended the land of the other German tribes. In 924 Henry I manages to conclude at least a truce with the Hungarians; in 928 he himself advances as far as Brandenburg; in 929 he founds the frontier fortress at Meissen; in 933 he defeats the Hungarians at Riade, but without destroying them or really averting the danger; and in 934 in Schleswig he succeeds in restoring the northern frontiers against the Danes.[11] All this he does primarily as a Saxon duke. These are victories of the Saxons over peoples threatening their frontiers and territory. But in fighting and conquering on their own frontiers, the Saxon dukes gain the military power and reputation that are needed to oppose the centrifugal tendencies within the empire. Through external victory they lay the foundation of a strengthened internal central power.

Henry I had by and large maintained and consolidated the frontiers, at least to the north. As soon as he dies the Wends revoke their peace with the Saxons. Henry's son Otto drives them back. In the following years 937 and 938 the Hungarians advance again and are likewise repelled. Then begins a new and more powerful expansion. In 940 the German territory is extended to the Oder region. And, as always, as in the present day, the conquest of new lands is followed by the ecclesiastical organization which—then much more strongly than now——serves to secure military domination.

The same thing happens in the south-east. In 955—still on German territory—the Hungarians are defeated at Augsburg and so driven out more or less finally. As a barrier against them the Eastern Marches, embryo of the later

Austria, are established with their frontier roughly in the region of Pressburg. To the east, in the central Danube area, the Hungarians slowly begin to settle permanently.

Otto's military successes are matched by his power inside the empire. Wherever he can he tries to replace the descendants of lords installed by earlier emperors, who now oppose him as hereditary local leaders, with his own relations and friends. Swabia goes to his son Ludolph, Bavaria to his brother Henry, Lorraine to his son-in-law Conrad, whose son Otto is given Swabia when Ludolph rebels.

At the same time he seeks—more consciously, it seems, than his predecessors—to counteract the mechanisms which constantly weaken centralism. He does this on the one hand by limiting the powers of the local rulers he installs. On the other hand he and, more resolutely still, his successors, oppose these mechanisms by installing clerics as rulers over regions. Bishops are given the secular office of count. This appointment of high ecclesiastics without heirs was intended to put a stop to the tendency of functionaries of the central authority to turn into a "hereditary, landowning aristocracy" with strong desires for independence.

In the long run, however, these measures intended to counter decentralizing forces only reinforced them. They led finally to the conversion of clerical rulers into princes, worldly powers. The preponderance of centrifugal tendencies over centripetal ones that was rooted in the structure of this society emerged yet again. In the course of time the spiritual authorities showed themselves no less concerned for the preservation of their independent hegemony over the territory entrusted to them than the secular. It was now in their interests too that the central authority should not grow too strong. And this convergence of the interests of high ecclesiastical and secular dignitaries was a main contributory factor in keeping the actual power of the central authority of the German Empire low for many centuries, while the power and independence of the territorial rulers increased—the inverse of what happened in France. There the leading ecclesiastics hardly ever became great worldly rulers. The bishops, part of whose possessions were scattered among the lands of the various territorial lords, remained interested in preserving a strong central authority for their own security. These parallel interests of church and monarchy, extending over a considerable period, were not the least of the factors which, in France, gave the central power preponderance over centrifugal tendencies at a relatively early stage. Early on, however, by the same process, the western Frankish empire disintegrated even more rapidly and radically than the eastern one.

6. The last, western Frankish, Carolingians were by all accounts[12] courageous and clear-thinking men, some of them gifted with outstanding qualities. But they were contending with a situation that gave the central ruler little chance, and one which shows particularly clearly how easily, in this social structure, the centre of gravity could shift to the disadvantage of the central ruler.

Leaving aside his role as army leader, conqueror and distributor of new lands, the basis of the social power of the central lord consisted of his family possessions, the land he controlled directly and from which he had to support his servants, his court and his armed retainers. In this respect the central lord was no better off than any other territorial ruler. But the personal territory of the western Frankish Carolingians had in the course of long struggles been largely given away in exchange for services rendered. To obtain and reward support, their forefathers had had to distribute land. Each time this happened—without new conquests-—their own possessions were reduced. This left the sons in a still more precarious position. All new help meant new losses of land. In the end the heirs had very little left to distribute. The retainers they were able to feed and pay became fewer and fewer. We find the last of the western Frankish Carolingians in a sometimes desperate position. To be sure, their vassals were obliged to follow them to war; but if they had no personal interest in doing so, only the open or concealed pressure of a militarily powerful liege lord could induce them to meet this obligation. The fewer vassals followed the king, the less threatening his power became and so the fewer vassals followed him. With military power as with land, therefore, these social mechanisms, once set in motion, progressively weakened the position of the Carolingian kings.

Louis IV, a brave man fighting desperately for survival, is sometimes called "le roi de Monloon", the king of Laon. Of all the family possessions of the Carolingians, little is left to him except the fortress at Laon. At times the last sons of the house have hardly any troops to fight their wars, just as they have hardly any land to support and pay their followers: "The time arrived when the descendant of Charlemagne, surrounded by landowners who were the masters of their domains, found no other means of keeping men in his service than by handing out territory to them with concessions of immunity, that is, attaching them to him by making them more and more independent, and continuing to reign by abdicating more and more."[13] Thus the function of the monarchy goes irremediably downhill, and whatever its occupants do to improve their position in the end turns against them.

7. The former territory of the western Frankish Carolingians, the embryo of what was to become France, had at that time disintegrated into a number of separately ruled areas. After a prolonged struggle between various territorial rulers of roughly equal strength, a kind of equilibrium had been established. When the direct line of the Carolingians becomes extinct, the chieftains and territorial lords elect the one of their number whose house has outdone the others in the fight against the hostile Normans, and has thus long been the strongest rival of the weakening monarchy. In a similar way in the eastern Frankish regions, with the end of the Carolingians, the local princes who had successfully defended the country against the invading peoples from the east and north, Slavs, Hungarians and Danes, that is, the dukes of Saxony, are made kings.

This had been preceded by a protracted struggle between the house of Francia and the last, western Frankish Carolingians.

When the crown went to the former in the person of Hugh Capet, they were themselves already somewhat weakened by a process similar to the one that had brought down the Carolingians. The dukes of Francia too had had to form alliances, and obtain services in exchange for land and rights. The territory of the Norman dukes who had settled and become Christianized in the meantime, the duchies of Aquitaine and Burgundy, the counties of Anjou and Flanders, Vermandois and Champagne, was scarcely smaller, and in some respects more important, than the family territory of the new royal house of Francia. And it was family power and territory that counted. The power available to the king through his family possessions was the real basis of his royal power. If his family possessions were no greater than those of other territorial rulers, then his power was no greater either. It was only from the family possessions and territory that he drew regular income. From other territories he drew, at the most, ecclesiastical dues. What he received beyond that in his capacity as "king" was minimal. Moreover, the factor which in the German territories constantly restored the preponderance of the centralizing royal function over the centrifugal tendencies of the territorial rulers, their function as military leaders in the struggle against external enemies and in the conquest of new land, ceased at a relatively early stage to be of importance in the western Frankish area. And this is one of the decisive reasons why the disintegration of the royal domain into independent territories occurred earlier here and, at first, in a more radical form. The eastern Frankish region was exposed for far longer to attack and threat by foreign tribes. Hence the kings not only constantly re-emerged as leaders in wars fought in common by a number of tribes to protect their lands, but they also had the opportunity of invading and conquering new lands, which they then distributed. So they were at first able to keep a relatively large number of retainers and vassals dependent on them.

In contrast, the western Frankish area, since the Normans had settled, had scarcely been threatened by outside tribes. In addition, there was no possibility of conquering new lands directly outside its borders, unlike the situation in the eastern Frankish region. This accelerated its disintegration. The prime factors giving the king preponderance over the centrifugal forces, defence and conquest, were lacking. Since there was virtually nothing else in the social structure that made the various regions dependent on a central ruler, the latter's domain was in fact reduced to little more than his own territory.

This so-called sovereign is a mere baron who owns a number of counties on the banks of the Seine and the Loire that amount to scarcely four or five present-day *départements*. The royal domain just manages to sustain his theoretical majesty. It is neither the largest nor the richest of the territories making up the France of today. The king is less powerful than some of hIs major vassals. And like them he lives on the income from his estates, duties from his peasants, the work of his bondsmen and the "voluntary gifts" from the abbeys and bishoprics in his territory. [14]

Soon after the crowning of Hugh Capet the weakening not of the individual kings but of the royal function itself, and with it the disintegration of the royal territories, begins slowly and steadily to increase. The first Capetians still travel throughout the whole country with their courts. The places where the royal decrees are signed give us an idea of the way in which they journeyed back and forth. They still sit in judgement at the seats of major vassals. Even in southern France they have a certain traditional influence.

At the beginning of the twelfth century the wholly hereditary and independent nature of the various territories previously subject to the king is an accomplished fact. The fifth of the Capetians, Louis the Fat (1108–37), a brave and belligerent lord and no weakling, has little say outside his own territory. The royal decrees show that he hardly ever travels outside the borders of his own duchy. [15] He lives within his own domain. He no longer holds court in the lands of his great vassals. They hardly ever appear at the royal court. The exchange of friendly visits grows more infrequent, correspondence with other parts of the kingdom, particularly in the south, more sparse. France at the beginning of the twelfth century is at best a union of independent territories, a loose federation of greater and lesser domains between which a kind of balance has provisionally been established.

8. Within the German Empire, after a century filled with wars between the wearers of the royal and imperial crown and the families of powerful dukes, one of the latter, the house of Swabia, succeeds in the twelfth century in again subjugating the others and, for a time, bringing together the necessary means of power in the central authority.

But from the end of the twelfth century onwards the social centre of gravity moves ever more clearly and inevitably towards the territorial rulers in Germany too. However, while in the immense area of the German "Imperium Romanum" or "Sacrum Imperium", as it was later called, the territorial estates are consolidating themselves to the point that they can now for centuries prevent the formation of a strong central power and so the integration of the whole area, in the smaller area of France the extreme disintegration of the end of the twelfth century now begins gradually and—some setbacks notwithstanding—fairly steadily to give way to a restoration of the central authority and the slow reintegration of larger and larger regions around one centre.

The scene of this radical disintegration must be envisaged as in a way the starting point if we are to understand how the smaller areas join together to form a stronger unit, and by which social processes were formed the central organs of the larger units of rule that we designate by the concept of "absolutism"—the ruling apparatus which forms the skeleton of modern states. The relative stability of the central authority and the central institutions in the phase we call the "Age of Absolutism" contrasts sharply with the instability of the central authority in the preceding "feudal" phase.

What was it in the structure of society that favoured centralization in the later phase but strengthened the forces opposing centralization in the earlier one?

This question takes us to the centre of the dynamics of social processes, of the changes in human interweaving and interdependence in conjunction with which conduct and drive structure were altered in the direction of "civilization".

9. What constantly gave the decentralizing forces in medieval, particularly early medieval, society their preponderance over the centralizing tendencies is not difficult to see, and has been emphasized by historians of that epoch in a variety of ways. Hampe, for example, in his account of the European High Middle Ages, writes:

> The feudalization of states everywhere forced rulers to provide their army leaders and officials with land. If they were to avoid being impoverished in the process, and to make use of the military services of their vassals, they were virtually driven to attempts at military expansion, generally at the expense of the power vacuums around them. At that time it was not economically possible to avoid this necessity by constructing a bureaucracy on the modern pattern.[16]

This quotation implicitly shows the essential nature of both the centrifugal forces and the mechanisms in which the monarchy was embroiled in that society, provided that "feudalization" is not understood as an external "cause" of all these changes. The various elements in this dilemma: the necessity of providing warriors and officials with land, the unavoidable diminution of the royal possessions unless new campaigns of conquest took place, the tendency of the central authority to weaken in times of peace—all these are parts of the great process of "feudalization". The quotation also indicates how indissolubly this specific form of rule and its apparatus of government were bound to a particular economic structure.

To make this explicit: as long as barter relationships predominated in society, the formation of a tightly centralized bureaucracy and a stable apparatus of government working primarily with peaceful means and directed constantly from the centre, was scarcely possible. The imminent tendencies we have described—conqueror-king, envoys sent by the central authority to administer the country, independence of these envoys or their descendents as territorial rulers and their struggle against the central power—correspond to certain forms of economic relationship. If in a society the production from a small or large piece of land was sufficient to satisfy all the essential everyday needs of its inhabitants from clothing to food and household implements, if the division of labour and the exchange of products over longer distances were undeveloped, and if accordingly—all these are different aspects of the same form of integration—roads were bad and the means of transportation undeveloped, then the interdependence of different regions was also slight. Only when this interdependence grows considerably can relatively stable central institutions for a number of larger areas be formed. Before this the social structure simply offers no basis for them.

A historian of the period writes: "We can scarcely imagine how difficult it was, given medieval transportation conditions, to rule and administer an extensive empire."[17]

Charlemagne, too, supported himself and his court essentially from the produce of his old family estate scattered between the Rhine, the Maas and the Moselle. Each "Palatium" or manor—in Dopsch's convincing account[18]—was associated with a number of households and villages in the vicinity. The emperor and king moved from manor to manor in this relatively small area, supporting himself and his followers on the revenue from the surrounding households and villages. Trade over long distances was never entirely lacking even at this time; but it was essentially a trade in luxury goods, at any rate not in articles of daily use. Even wine was not, in general, transported over long distances. Anyone who wanted to drink wine had to produce it in his own district, and only his nearest neighbours could obtain any surplus through exchange. This is why there were in the Middle Ages vineyards in regions where wine is no longer cultivated today, the grapes being too sour or their plantations "uneconomic", for example in Flanders or Normandy. Conversely, regions like Burgundy which are for us synonymous with viniculture, were not nearly as specialized in winemaking as they later became. There, too, every farmer and estate had to be, up to a certain point, "autarkic". As late as the seventeenth century there were only eleven parishes in Burgundy where everyone was a wine-grower.[19] Thus slowly do the various districts become interconnected, are communications developed, are the division of labour and the integration of larger areas and populations increased; and increased correspondingly is the need for a means of exchange and units of calculation having the same value over large areas: money.

To understand the civilizing process it is particularly important to have a clear and vivid conception of these social processes, of what is meant by "barter or domestic economy", "money economy", "interdependence of large populations", "change in the social dependence of the individual", "increasing division of functions", and so on. Such concepts too easily become verbal fetishes which have lost all pictorial quality and thus, really, all clarity. The purpose of this necessarily brief account is to give a concrete perception of the social relationships referred to here by the concept of the "barter economy". What it indicates is a quite specific way in which people are bound together and dependent on each other. It refers to a society in which the transfer of goods from the man who gets them from the soil or nature to the man who uses them takes place directly, that is without or almost without intermediaries, and where they are worked up at the house of one or the other, which may well be the same. This transfer very gradually becomes more differentiated. More and more people slowly interpose themselves as functionaries of processing and distribution in the passage of the goods from the primary producer to the final consumer. How and, above all, why this happens, what is the motive power behind this prolongation of the chains, is a question in itself. At any rate money is nothing other than an instrument which is needed and with which society provides itself when these chains grow longer, when work and distribution are differentiated, and which under certain circumstances tends to reinforce this differentiation. If the terms "barter economy" and "money economy" are used, it can easily appear as if an absolute antithesis exists between these two economic forms, and such an imagined antithesis has unleashed many a dispute. In the actual social process the chains between production and consumption change and differentiate very gradually, not to mention the fact that in some sectors of Western society economic communication over long distances and thus the use of money never entirely ceased. Thus, very gradually, the money sector of the economy increases again, as do the differentiation of social functions, the interdependence of different regions, and the dependence of large populations on one another; all these are different aspects of the same social process. And so too the change in the form and apparatus for ruling that has been discussed is nothing other than a further aspect of this process. The structure of the central organs corresponds to the structure of the division and interweaving of functions. The strength of the centrifugal tendencies towards local *political autarky* within societies based predominantly on a barter economy corresponds to the degree of local *economic autarky*.

10. Two phases can generally be distinguished in the development of such predominantly agrarian warrior societies, phases which may occur once only or alternate frequently: the phase of the belligerent expansionist central lords and that of the conserving rulers who win no new land. In the first phase the central authority is strong. The primary social function of the central lord in this society manifests itself directly, that of the army leader. When over a long period the royal house does not manifest itself in this belligerent role, when the king is either not needed as army leader or has no success as such, the secondary functions lapse as well, for example that of the highest arbitrator or judge of the whole region, and the ruler has at bottom no more than his title to distinguish him from other territorial lords.

In the second phase, when the frontiers are not threatened and the conquest of new land is impossible for one reason or another, centrifugal forces necessarily gain the upper hand. Though the conquering king has actually controlled the entire country, in times of relative peace it increasingly slips away from his authority. Anyone with a piece of land regards himself as its first ruler. This reflects his actual dependence on the central lord which in more peaceful times is minimal.

At this stage, when the economic interdependence and integration of large areas is lacking or only beginning, a noneconomic form of integration appears all the more strongly: military integration, alliance to repel a common foe. Beside a traditional sense of community with its strongest support in the common faith and its most important promoters in the clergy—but which never prevents disintegration, nor of itself brings about an alliance, merely strengthening and guiding it in certain directions—the urge to conquer and the necessity of resisting conquest is the most fundamental factor binding together people in regions lying relatively far apart. For this very reason every such alliance in this society is, compared with later periods, highly unstable, and the preponderance of decentralizing forces very great.

The two phases of this agrarian society, the phases of conquering and of conserving rulers, or merely spurts in one direction or the other, may alternate, as has been noted. And this is what actually happened in the history of Western countries. But the examples of German and French development also show that despite all the countervailing movements in the periods of conquering rulers, the tendency for the larger dominions to disintegrate and for land to pass from the control of the central lord to that of his erstwhile vassals proceeds, up to a certain time, continuously.

Why? Had the external threat to the former Carolingian Empire, which really constituted the West at that time, abated? Were there yet other causes for this progressive decentralization of the Carolingian Empire?

The question of the motive forces of this process may take on new significance if seen in relation to a familiar concept. This gradual decentralization of government and territory, this transition of the land from the control of the conquering central ruler to that of the warrior caste as a whole is nothing other than the process known as "feudalization".

III

The Increase in Population after the Migration of Peoples

11. For some time, understanding of the problem of feudalization has been undergoing a pronounced change which perhaps merits more explicit emphasis than it has received hitherto. As with social processes in general, the older mode of historical research has failed to come properly to grips with the process of feudalization in the West. The tendency to think in terms of isolated causes, to look for individual creators of social transformations, or at most to see only the legal aspect of social institutions and to seek the examples on which they were modelled by this or that agent—all this has made these processes and institutions

as inaccessible to our thought as natural processes were earlier to scholastic thinkers.

More recently historians have begun to break through to a new way of posing the question. Increasingly, historians concerned with the origins of feudalism are emphasizing that this is neither a deliberate creation of individuals, nor does it consist of institutions that can be simply explained by earlier ones. Dopsch, for example, says of feudalization: "We are concerned here with institutions that were not called into being deliberately and intentionally by states or the bearers of state power in order to realize certain political ends."[20]

And Calmette formulates still more clearly this approach to the social processes of history:

> However different the feudal system is from the preceding one, it results directly from it. No revolution, no individual will has produced it. It is part of a long evolution. Feudality belongs to the category of what might be called the "natural occurrences" or "natural facts" of history. Its formation was determined by quasi-mechanical forces and proceeded step by step.[21]

Elsewhere in his study *La société féodale* he says:

> To be sure, knowledge of antecedents, that is, of similar phenomena preceding a given phenomenon, is interesting and instructive to historians, and we shall not ignore it. But these "antecedents" are not the only factors involved and perhaps not the most important. The main thing is not to know where the "feudal element" comes from, whether its origins are to be sought in Rome or among the Germans, but why this element has taken on its "feudal" character. If these foundations became what they were, they owe this to an evolution whose secret neither Rome nor the Germans can tell us . . . its formation is the result of forces that can only be compared with geological ones.[22]

The use of images from the realm of nature or technology is unavoidable as long as our language has not developed a clear, special vocabulary for socio-historical processes. Why images are provisionally sought in these realms is readily explained: for the time being they express adequately the compulsive nature of social processes in history. And however much one may thereby expose oneself to misunderstanding, as if social processes and their compulsions, originating in the interrelationships of men, were really of the same nature as, for example, the course of the earth about the sun or the action of a lever in a machine, the endeavour to find a new, structural manner of posing historical questions reveals itself very clearly in such formulations. The relation of later institutions to similar institutions in an earlier phase is always of significance. But here the decisive historical question is why institutions, and also people's conduct and affective make-up *change*, and why they change in this particular way. We are concerned with the strict order of socio-historical *transformations*.

And perhaps it is not easy even today to understand that these transformations are not to be explained by something that itself remains unchanged, and still less easy to realize that in history no isolated fact ever brings about any transformation by itself, but only in combination with others.

Finally, these transformations remain inexplicable as long as explanation is limited to the ideas of individuals written down in books. When enquiring into social processes one must look at the web of human relationships, at society itself, to find the compulsions that keep them in motion, and give them their particular form and their particular direction. This applies to the process of feudalization as to the process of increasing division of labour; it applies to countless other processes represented in our conceptual apparatus by words without process-character, which stress particular institutions formed by the process in question, for example, the concepts of "absolutism", "capitalism", "barter economy", "money economy" and so on. All these point beyond themselves to changes in the structure of human relationships which clearly are not planned by individuals and to which individuals were subjected whether willingly or not. And this applies finally to changes in the make-up of people themselves, to the civilizing process.

12. One of the most important motors of change in the structure of human relationships, and of the institutions corresponding to them, is the increase or decrease of population. It too cannot be isolated from the whole dynamic web of human relationships. It is not, as prevalent habits of thought incline us to assume, in itself the "first cause" of socio-historical movement. But amidst the intertwining factors of change this is an important element that should never be neglected. It also shows particularly clearly the compelling nature of these social forces. It remains to be established what role factors of this kind played in the phase under discussion. It may help understanding of them to recall briefly the last movements in the migration of peoples.

Up to the eighth and ninth centuries tribes migrating from the east, north and south push in recurrent spurts into the already populated areas of Europe. This is the last and biggest wave in a movement that has gone on over a long period. What we see of it are small episodes: the irruption of Hellenic "barbarians" into the populated areas of Asia Minor and the Balkan peninsula, the penetration by the Italian "barbarians" of the neighbouring western peninsula, the advance of the Celtic "barbarians" into the territory of the former who have now in their turn become to some extent "civilized" and whose land has become a centre of "ancient culture", and the definitive settling of these Celtic tribes to the west and partly to the north of them.

Finally the German tribes overrun a large part of the Celts' territory, which in the meantime has likewise given rise to an "older culture". The Germans in their turn defend this "cultured" land they have conquered against new waves of peoples advancing from all sides.

Shortly after the death of Mohammed in 632 the Arabs are set in motion.[23] By

713 they have conquered the whole of Spain with the exception of the Asturian mountains. Towards the middle of the eighth century this wave comes to a standstill at the southern frontier of the Frankish empire, as Celtic waves had earlier done before the gates of Rome.

From the east Slavonic tribes advance against the Frankish empire. By the end of the eighth century they have reached the Elbe.

> If in the year 800 a political prophet had possessed a map of Europe as we can now reconstruct it, he might well have been misled into predicting that the whole eastern half of the Continent from the Danish peninsula to the Peloponnese was destined to become a Slavonic Empire or at least a powerful group of Slavonic countries. From the Elbe estuary to the Ionian sea ran an unbroken line of Slavonic peoples . . . this seems to mark the frontier of Germanic territory.[24]

Their movement comes to a standstill somewhat later than that of the Arabs. Then the struggle remains long undecided. The frontier between Germanic and Slavonic tribes now moves somewhat forward, now back again. By and large the Slavonic wave is held at the Elbe from about 800 onwards.

What may be called the "originally settled territory" of the west had thus, under the rule and leadership of Germanic tribes, preserved its frontier against the migrating tribes. Representatives of earlier waves defend it against those following, the last waves of migration that pass across Europe. These, prevented from advancing further, slowly settle outside the borders of the Frankish empire. And so a fringe of populated regions forms about the latter in large areas in the interior of Europe. Previously nomadic tribes take possession of the land. The great migrations slowly come to rest, and the renewed intrusions of migrating peoples that occur from time to time, by the Hungarians and finally the Turks, founder sooner or later on the superior defensive techniques and the strength of those already in possession.

13. A new situation had been created. There were no longer any empty spaces in Europe. There was virtually no usable land—usable in terms of the agricultural techniques then available—that had not been pre-empted. By and large Europe, and above all its large interior regions, was now more completely populated than ever before, even if incomparably less densely than in the centuries that followed. And there is every indication that population increased to the same extent as the upheavals accompanying the great migrations abated. This changed the whole system of tensions between and within the various peoples.

In late antiquity the population of the "old cultural regions" diminishes more or less rapidly. In consequence the social institutions corresponding to relatively large and dense populations disappear also. The use of money within a society, for example, is bound up with a certain level of population density. It is an essential prerequisite for the differentiation of work and the formation of markets. If the population falls below a certain level—for whatever reasons—the markets automatically empty. The chains between the man producing a commodity from nature and its consumer grow shorter. Money loses its instrumental function. This was the direction of development at the end of antiquity. The urban sector of society grows smaller. The agrarian character of society increases. This development took place the more easily as the division of labour in antiquity was never remotely as great as, for example, in our own society. A proportion of urban households were always to a degree directly supplied, independently of commercial or manufacturing intermediaries, by the great slave estates. And as the overland transportation of goods over long distances was always extremely difficult, given the state of technology in antiquity, long-distance trade was essentially confined to waterborne transport. Large markets and towns and vigorous monetary activity developed in proximity to water. Inland areas always preserved a predominantly domestic type of economy. Even for the urban population, the autarkic household and economic self-sufficiency never declined to the extent that they have in modern Western society. With the fall in population this aspect of the social structure of antiquity regained prominence.

With the end of the migration of peoples, this movement was once again reversed. The influx and subsequent settling of so many new tribes provided the basis for a new and more comprehensive population of the whole European area. In the Carolingian period this population still had an almost completely domestic economy, perhaps even more so than in the Merovingian period.[25] One indication of this may be that the political centre moved still further inland, where hitherto—owing to the difficulties of overland transport—the political centres preceding those of the medieval West had never been situated, with few exceptions such as the Hittite Empire. We may assume that the population was beginning to increase very slowly in this period. We already hear of forest clearance, and that is always a sign that land is growing scarce, the density of population rising. But these are certainly only the initial stages. The migrations of peoples have not yet entirely abated. Only from the ninth century onwards do the signs of a more rapidly increasing population multiply. And not very long afterwards there are already indications of overpopulation here and there in the former Carolingian regions.

Fall in population at the end of antiquity, slow rise once more under different circumstances in the aftermath of the migrations of peoples: a brief retrospective summary must be enough to recall to mind the curve of this movement.

14. Phases of perceptible overpopulation alternate in European history with those of lower internal pressure. But the term "overpopulation" needs explaining. It is not a product of the absolute number of people inhabiting a certain area. In a heavily industrialized society with intensive utilization of the land, highly developed long-distance trade and a government favouring the industrial against the agrarian sector through import and export duties, a number of people can live

more or less tolerably which, in a barter economy with extensive agricultural methods and little long-distance trade, would constitute overpopulation with all its typical symptoms. "Overpopulation" is therefore first of all a term for growth of population in a particular area to a point where, in the given social structure, the satisfaction of basic needs is possible for fewer and fewer people. We thus encounter "overpopulation" only relative to certain social forms and a certain set of needs, a social overpopulation.

Its symptoms in societies which have attained a certain degree of differentiation are, broadly speaking, always the same: increased tension within society; greater self-encapsulation by those who "have", i.e., in a predominantly barter economy, those who "have land", over against those who "have not", or at any rate not enough to support themselves in a manner conforming with their standards; and often, increased self-encapsulation, among the "haves", of those who have more than the rest; a more pronounced cohesion of people in the same social situation to resist pressure from those outside it or, inversely, to seize opportunities monopolized by others. In addition, increased pressure on neighbouring areas with lower population or weaker defences, and finally, an increase in emigration and in the tendency to conquer or at least settle in new lands.

It is difficult to say whether available sources can give an exact picture of population growth in Europe in the centuries following the migrations, and particularly of differences in population density between different regions. But one thing is certain: as the migrations slowly come to a standstill, once the major struggles among the different tribes have come to an end, one after another all the symptoms of such "social overpopulation" show themselves—a rapid growth of population accompanied by the transformation of social institutions.

15. The symptoms of increasing population pressure first appear clearly in the western Frankish empire. Here, about the ninth century, the threat from foreign tribes slowly recedes, unlike the situation in the eastern Frankish empire. In the part of the empire named after them the Normans have grown peaceable. With the help of the western Frankish Church, they rapidly absorb the language and the whole tradition about them, in which Gallo–Romanic and Frankish elements are mingled. They add new elements of their own. In particular, they bring about important advances in the administrative structure within the territorial framework. From now on they play a decisive part as one of the leading tribes in the federation of western Frankish territories.

The Arabs and Saracens cause occasional unrest on the Mediterranean coast, but by and large they too, from the ninth century on, scarcely represent a threat to the survival of this empire.

To the east of France lies the German "Imperium" which under the Saxon emperors has again grown powerful. With minor exceptions the frontier between it and the western Frankish empire scarcely moves from the tenth to the first quarter of the thirteenth century.[26] In 925 Lotharingia is won back from the empire, and in 1034 Burgundy. Apart from this, tension along this line is not high until 1226. The empire's expansionist tendencies are directed essentially to the east.

The external threat to the western Frankish empire is therefore relatively slight. Equally slight, however, are the possibilities of expanding beyond the existing frontiers. The east in particular is blocked both by the population density and the military strength of the empire.

But within this area, now that the external threat has diminished, population begins to increase markedly. It grows so strongly after the ninth century that by the beginning of the fourteenth century it is probably almost as large as at the beginning of the eighteenth.[27]

This movement certainly did not proceed in a straight line, but there is an abundance of evidence to show that, by and large, population increased steadily; this evidence has to be seen as a whole if the strength of the overall movement, and the meaning of each individual piece of evidence within it, are to be understood.

From the end of the tenth century onwards, and more so in the eleventh, the pressure on land, the desire for new land and greater productivity from the old, are more and more visible in the western Frankish region.

As mentioned, forests were already cleared in the Carolingian period and no doubt earlier too. But in the eleventh century the tempo and extent of the clearance accelerate. Woods are felled and marshlands made arable as far as the technology of the time permitted. The period from about 1050 to about 1300 is the great age of deforestation, of the internal conquest of new land, in France.[28] About 1300 this movement slows down again.

IV

Some Observations on the Sociogenesis
of the Crusades

16. The great onslaught from outside has subsided. The earth is fruitful. Population grows. Land, the most important means of production, the epitome of property and wealth in this society, becomes scarce. Deforestation, the opening up of new land within, is not nearly sufficient to offset this scarcity. New land must be sought outside the frontiers. Hand in hand with internal colonization goes the external conquest of new territory elsewhere. By the beginning of the eleventh century Norman knights are going to southern Italy to hire themselves out as warriors to individual princes.[29] In 1029 one of them is enfeoffed for his services with a small piece of land on the northern boundary of the duchy of

Naples. Others follow, among them other sons of a minor Norman lord, Tancrède de Hauteville. He has twelve sons in all; how are they to be sustained to a fitting standard on their father's land? Eight of them therefore go to southern Italy, and there obtain in time what is denied to them at home: control of a piece of land. One of them, Robert Guiscard, gradually becomes the acknowledged leader of the Norman warriors. He unites the scattered estates or territories that individuals have won for themselves. From 1060 onwards they begin under his leadership to advance into Sicily. By Robert Guiscard's death in 1085 the Saracens have been pushed back into the south-west corner of the island. All the rest is in Norman hands and forms a new Norman feudal empire.

None of this had actually been planned. At the outset we have the population pressure and the blocked opportunities at home, the emigration of individuals whose success attracts others; at the end we have an empire.

Something similar happens in Spain. In the tenth century French knights go to the aid of the Spanish princes in their struggles against the Arabs. As mentioned, the western Frankish area, unlike the eastern, does not border on an extensive area open to colonization and peopled by largely disunited tribes. To the east the empire prevents further expansion. The Iberian peninsula is the only direct way out. Up to the middle of the eleventh century only individuals or small bands cross the mountains; then, they gradually become armies. The Arabs, split internally, offer slight, sporadic resistance. In 1085 Toledo is taken, and in 1094 Valencia under the leadership of El Cid, only to be lost shortly afterwards. The struggle is waged back and forth. In 1095 a French count is invested with the reconquered territory of Portugal. But it is only in 1147, with the aid of members of the Second Crusade, that his son finally succeeds in gaining control of Lisbon and there to some degree stabilizing his rule as a feudal king.

Apart from Spain, the only possibility of gaining new land near France lay across the Channel. Even in the first half of the eleventh century individual Norman knights had struck out in this direction. Then in 1066 the Norman Duke with an army of Norman and French knights crosses to the island, seizes power and redistributes the land. The possibilities of expansion, the prospects of new land in the vicinity of France, grow more and more restricted. Eyes are cast further afield.

In 1095, before the great feudal lords begin to move, a band led by the knight Walter Habenichts, or Gautier Senzavoir, sets out for Jerusalem; it perishes in Asia Minor. In 1097 a mighty army under the leadership of Norman and French territorial lords advances into the Holy Land. The Crusaders first have themselves invested by the Eastern Roman Emperor with the lands to be conquered, then advance further, conquer Jerusalem and found new feudal dominions.

There is no reason to assume that without the guidance of the Church and the religious link with the Holy Land, this expansion would have been directed to precisely that place. But nor is it probable that without the social pressure first within the western Frankish region and then in all the other regions of Latin Christendom, the Crusades would have taken place.

The tensions within this society were not only manifested in desire for land and bread. They exerted mental pressure upon the whole person. The social pressure supplied the motive force as a generator supplies current. It set people in motion. The Church steered this pre-existing force. It embraced the general distress and gave it a hope and a goal outside France. It gave the struggle for new land an overarching meaning and justification. It turned this into a struggle for the Christian faith.

17. The Crusades are a specific form of the first great movement of expansion and colonization by the Christian West. During the migrations of peoples, in which for centuries tribes from the east and north-east had been driven in a western and south-western direction, the utilizable areas of Europe had been filled up with people to the furthest frontiers, the British Isles. Now the migrations had stopped. The mild climate, fertile soil and unfettered drives favoured rapid multiplication. The land grew too small. The human wave had trapped itself in a cul-de-sac, and from this confinement it strained back towards the east, both in the Crusades and within Europe itself, where the German-populated area slowly spread, through heavy conflicts, further and further east beyond the Elbe to the Oder, then to the Vistula estuary, and finally Prussia and the Baltic lands, even if it was only German knights, not German farmers, who succeeded in migrating so far.

But precisely this last fact shows very clearly one of the peculiarities distinguishing this first phase of social overpopulation and expansion from later ones. In general, with the advance of the civilizing process, and the concomitant constraint and regulation of human drives—and they always advance further, for reasons to be discussed later, in the upper than in the lower classes—the birthrate slowly declines, usually less rapidly in the lower than in the upper strata. This difference between the average birthrate of the upper and lower classes is often highly significant for the maintenance of the standard of the former.

This first phase of rapid population growth in the Christian West is distinguished from the later ones, however, by the fact that in it the ruling stratum, the warrior class or nobility, increases hardly less rapidly than the stratum of bondsmen, tenants and peasants, in short, of those who directly work the land. The struggle for the available opportunities which, with the growth of population, necessarily shrink for each individual; the incessant feuds that these tensions unleashed; the high rate of infant mortality, illness and plague: all that may have eliminated a part of the human surplus. And it is possible that the relatively unprotected peasantry were harder hit than the warriors. Moreover, the freedom of movement of the former group was so limited and, above all, communications between different regions were so difficult, that the surplus labour power could not be quickly and evenly distributed. Thus in one area shortage of labour might result from feuds and pillage, plagues, the opening up of new land or the flight of serfs, while a surplus was accumulating in others. And in fact we have, for the same period, clear evidence of an excess of bondsmen in one area, and of efforts in others to attract free tenants, *hospites*[30]—that is, rulers offering labourers improved conditions.

Be that as it may, what is above all characteristic of the processes operating here is that not only was a "reserve army" of bondsmen or serfs forming in this society, but also a "reserve army" of the *upper class*, of knights without property, or without enough to maintain their standards. Only in this way can the nature of this first Western expansionist phase be understood. Peasants, the sons of bondsmen, were certainly involved in one way or another in the struggles for colonization, but the main impulse came from the knights' shortage of land. New land could only be conquered by the sword. The knights opened a way by force of arms; they took the lead and formed the bulk of the armies. The surplus population in the upper class gave this first period of expansion and colonization its special stamp.

The rift between those who had land and those who had none or too little, runs right through this society. On the one hand are the land-monopolists—warrior families, noble houses and landowners in the first place, but also peasants, bondsmen, serfs, *hospites*, who occupy a piece of land that supports them, however meagerly. On the other hand are those from both classes who have been deprived of land. Those from the lower classes—displaced by the shortage of opportunities or the oppression of their masters—play a part in the emigration or colonization, but above all they provide the population of the growing towns. Those from the warrior class, in short the "younger sons", whose inheritance is too small either for their demands or for their mere sustenance, the "have-nots" among the knights, appear down the centuries wearing the most disparate social masks: as Crusaders, as robber-leaders, as mercenaries in the service of great lords; finally they form the basis of the first standing armies.

18. The often-quoted dictum: "No land without a lord", is not only a basic legal principle. It is also a social watchword of the warrior class. It expresses the knights' need to take possession of every scrap of usable land. Sooner or later this has come about in all the regions of Latin Christendom. Every available piece of land is in firm ownership. But the demand for land continues and even increases. The chances of satisfying it diminish. The pressure for expansion rises, as does the tension within society. But the specific dynamic which is thus imparted to society as a whole does not emanate solely from the malcontents; it is necessarily communicated also to those rich in land. In the poor, debt-ridden, declining knights the social pressure manifests itself as a simple desire for a piece of land and labourers to support them in keeping with their standards. In the richer warriors, the greater landowners and territorial lords, it is expressed likewise as an urge for new land. But what lower down was a simple desire for a means of

subsistence appropriate to one's class, is higher up a drive for enlarged dominion, for "more" land and so more social power as well. This craving for enlarged property among the richer landowners, above all those of the first rank, the counts, dukes and kings, sprang not only from the personal ambition of individuals. We have already seen by the example of the western Frankish Carolingians, and also the first Capetians, how unremittingly, unless there was a possibility of conquering new land, even royal houses were forced into decline by a compelling social process centred on the ownership and distribution of land. And if, throughout this whole phase of outward and inward expansion, we see not only poor knights but also many rich ones striving after new land to increase their family power, this is no more than a sign of how strongly the structure and situation of this society imposed the same striving on all strata, whether simply to own land in the case of the dispossessed, or to own "more" land in the case of the rich.

It has been thought that this craving for "more" property, the acquisitive urge, is a specific characteristic of "capitalism" and thus of modern times. In this view medieval society was distinguished by contentment with the income appropriate to one's social standing.

Within certain limits this is no doubt correct, if the striving for "more" is understood as applying to money alone. But for a long period of the Middle Ages it was not ownership of money but of land which constituted the essential form of ownership. The acquisitive urge thus necessarily has a different form and a different direction. It demands different modes of conduct to those of a society with a money and market economy. It may be true it is only in modern times that there develops a class specializing in trade, with a desire to earn ever-increasing amounts of *money* through uninterrupted toil. The social structures which, in the predominantly barter economy of the Middle Ages, lead to a desire for ever-increasing means of production—and it is structural features that are important in both cases—are less easy to perceive, because land not money is desired. In addition, political and military functions have not yet been differentiated from economic ones as they have gradually become in modern society. Military action, and political and economic striving, are largely identical, and the urge to increase wealth in the form of land comes to the same thing as extending territorial sovereignty and increasing military power. The richest man in a particular area, i.e. the one with most land, is as a direct result the most powerful militarily, with the largest retinue; he is at once army leader and ruler.

Precisely because the relationship between one estate owner and another in that society was analogous to that between states today, the acquisition of new land by one neighbour represented a direct or indirect threat to the others. It meant, as today, a shift of equilibrium in what was usually a very labile system of power balances in which rulers were always potential allies and potential enemies of one another. This, therefore, is the simple mechanism which, in this phase of internal and external expansion, kept the richer and more powerful knights in motion no less than the poorer ones, each being constantly on guard against expansion by others, and constantly seeking to enlarge his own possessions. When a society has once been put in such a state of flux by the blockage of territorial expansion and population pressure, anyone who declines to compete, merely conserving his property while others strive for increase, necessarily ends up "smaller" and weaker than the others, and is in ever-increasing danger of succumbing to them at the first opportunity. The rich knights and territorial lords of that time did not view the matter quite so theoretically and generally as we have put it here; but they did see quite concretely how powerless they were when their neighbours were richer in land than they, or when others around them won new land and sovereignty. This could be shown in more detail in relation to the Crusade leaders, for example Godefroi de Bouillon, who sells and mortgages his domestic possessions to seek larger ones far away, and in fact finds a kingdom. In a later period this could be shown by the example of the Habsburgs, who even as emperors were possessed by the idea of extending their "family power", and were in fact, even as emperors, completely impotent without the support of their own family power. Indeed, it was precisely because of his poverty and powerlessness that the first emperor from the family was selected for this position by mighty lords jealous of their power. It could be illustrated particularly clearly by the importance which the conquest of England by the Norman Duke had for the development of the western Frankish empire. In fact, this growth in the power of one territorial ruler meant a total displacement of equilibrium within the alliance of territorial rulers comprising this empire. The Norman Duke who, in his own territory, Normandy, was himself no less affected by centrifugal forces than any other territorial ruler, did not conquer England for the Normans as a whole but solely to increase his own family power. And the redistribution of English soil to the warriors who came with him was expressly designed to counter centrifugal forces in his new domain by preventing the formation of large territorial dominions on English soil. That he had to allot land to his knights was dictated by the necessity of ruling and administering it; but he avoided allocating a large self-contained area to any individual. Even to the great lords who could demand the produce of large areas for their maintenance, he assigned lands dispersed throughout the country.[31]

At the same time he had automatically risen, with this conquest, to be the most powerful territorial ruler in the western Frankish empire. Sooner or later there must be a confrontation between his house and that of the dukes of Francia, who held the kingship—a confrontation in which the crown itself was at stake. And it is known how greatly developments in subsequent centuries were determined by this struggle between the dukes of Francia and Normandy, how the rulers of the Isle de France slowly restored the balance of power by the acquisition of new territories, and how these struggles on both sides of the Channel finally gave rise to two different dominions and two different nations.

But this is certainly only one of many examples of the compelling processes in this dynamic phase of the Middle Ages, which impelled both rich and poor knights to seek new land.

V

The Internal Expansion of Society: The Formation of New Social Organs and Instruments

19. The driving force of this social expansion, the disproportion between rising population and land in fixed ownership, drove a large part of the ruling class to conquer new territory. This outlet was largely blocked to people of the lower classes, the workers. The pressures arising from the land shortage here led mainly in a different direction, to the differentiation of work. The bondsmen driven from the land comprised, as we have mentioned, material for the growing settlements of artisans which slowly crystallized around favourably situated feudal seats, the evolving towns.

Somewhat larger agglomerations of people—the word "town" perhaps gives the wrong impression—are already to be found in the society of the ninth century which operated a barter economy. But these were not the communities which "lived by crafts and trade instead of labour on the land, or had any special rights and institutions".[32] They were fortresses and at the same time centres of the agricultural administration of great lords. The towns of earlier periods had themselves lost their unity. They were juxtaposed pieces, groups often belonging to different knights and different dominions, some secular, others ecclesiastical, each leading its own independent economic life. The sole framework for economic activity was the estate, the domain of the territorial lord. Production and consumption took place at essentially the same place.[33]

But in the eleventh century these formations began to grow. Here too, as usually happened with knightly expansion but was now happening among bondsmen, it was at first unorganized individuals, surplus labourers, who were driven to such centres. And the attitude of rulers to the newcomers, who in each case had just left a different estate, was not always the same.[34] Sometimes they gave them a modicum of freedom; but mostly they expected and demanded the same services and tributes as from their own bondsmen and tenants. But the accumulation of such people changed the power relationship between the lord and the lower class. The newcomers gained strength through numbers and gradually obtained new rights in bloody and often protracted struggles. These struggles broke out earliest in Italy, somewhat later in Flanders: in 1030 in Cremona, in 1057 in Milan, in 1069 at Le Mans, in 1077 at Cambrai, in 1080 at Saint-

Quentin, in 1099 in Beauvais, in 1108–9 in Noyon, in 1112 in Laon, in 1127 in Saint-Omer. These dates, together with those of the knights' expansion, give a general impression of the internal tensions which kept society in motion in this phase. These are the first struggles for liberation by working town-dwellers. That they were able, after some defeats, in their struggles with the warrior class in the most different areas of Europe, to secure rights of their own, first a limited and then a substantial degree of freedom, shows how great was the opportunity that social development placed in their hands. And this peculiar fact, the slow rise of lower, working, urban strata to political autonomy and finally—first in the form of the professional middle classes—to political leadership, provides the key to almost all the structural peculiarities distinguishing Western societies from those of the Orient, and giving them their specific stamp.

At the beginning of the eleventh century there are, essentially, only two classes of free people, the warriors or nobles and the clergy; below them exist only bondsmen and serfs. There are "those who pray, those who fight, those who work".[35]

By about 1200, that is to say, in the course of two centuries or even only one and a half—for like forest clearance and colonial expansion this movement too accelerates after 1050—a large number of artisan settlements or communes have secured rights and jurisdiction, privileges and autonomy. A third class of free men joins the other two. Society expands, under the pressure of land shortage and population increase, not only extensively but intensively as well; it becomes differentiated, generates new cells, forms new organs, the towns.

20. But with the increasing differentiation of work, with the new, larger markets that now form, with the slow process of exchange over longer distances, grows the need for mobile and unified means of exchange.

When the bondsman or small tenant brings his tribute direct to his lord, when the chain between producer and consumer is short and without intermediaries, society needs no unit of calculation, no means of exchange to which all other exchanged objects can be related as to a common measure. But now, with the gradual severance of craftsmen from the economic unit of the household, with the formation of an economically independent artisanry and the exchange of products through several hands and down longer chains, the network of exchange—acts becomes complicated. A unified object of exchange is needed. When the differentiation of labour and exchange grows more complex and more active, more money is needed. Money is indeed an incarnation of the social fabric, a symbol of the network of exchange-acts and human chains through which a commodity passes on its way from its natural state to consumption. It is only needed when extended chains of exchange form within society, that is to say, at a certain level of population density and a high level of social interdependence and differentiation.

It would take us too far afield to explore here the question of the gradual recession of the money economy in many areas in late antiquity and its resurgence from about the eleventh century onwards; but one observation on the question is necessary in connection with the foregoing.

It must be pointed out that money never went completely out of use in the older inhabited area of Europe. Over this whole period there were enclaves of money economy within the barter economy, and in addition, outside the Carolingian area there were large regions of the old Roman Empire where money traffic never receded to the same extent as it did here. One can, therefore, always and very rightly ask about the "antecedents" of the money economy in the Christian West, the enclaves in which it never disappears. One can ask: where did the money economy originate? From whom was the use of money relearned? This kind of enquiry is not without value; for it is difficult to imagine that this instrument should have returned to use so relatively quickly had it not been so far developed in other, preceding or neighbouring civilizations, or if it had never been known.

But the essential aspect of the question concerning the revival of money traffic in the West is not answered in this way. The question remains why Western society needed relatively little money over a long stretch of its development, and why the need and use of money, with all the consequent transformations of society, gradually increased once more. Here again the enquiry must be directed toward the *moving*, the *changing* factors. And this question is not answered by examining the origins of money and the antecedents of the money economy. It is answered only by examining the actual social processes which, after the slow ebb of money traffic in declining antiquity, once again brought forth the new human relationships, the new forms of integration and interdependence, which caused the need for money to increase again: the cellular structure of society is differentiated. *One* expression of this was the revival in the use of money. That it was not only internal expansion but also migration and colonization which—through the mobilization of property, the awakening of new needs, the establishment of trade relations over longer distances—played an important part in this revival is immediately evident. Each individual movement in the whole interplay of processes reacts on the others, either obstructing or reinforcing them, and the web of movements and tensions is from now on considerably complicated by the social differentiation. Single factors cannot be absolutely isolated. But without the differentiation within society itself, without the passing of the land into fixed ownership, without the sharp increase in population, without the formation of independent communities of artisans and tradesmen, the need for money within society would never have risen so sharply, nor the money sector of the economy have grown so rapidly. Money, the decrease or increase of its use, cannot be understood by itself, but only from the standpoint of the structure of human relationships. It is here, in the changed form of human integration, that the prime movers of this transformation are to be sought; of course, when the use of money had once begun to grow, it helped in its turn to propel this whole movement—population increase, differentiation, growth of towns—still further, up to a certain point of saturation.

"The beginning of the eleventh century is still characterized by the absence of large-scale money transactions. Wealth is to a large extent immobilized in the hands of the Church and the secular territorial lords."[36]

Then the need for mobile means of exchange gradually increases. The existing coinage is no longer sufficient. First of all people make do with plate and ornaments in precious metal that are weighed to provide a unit of calculation; horses too can serve as measures of value; new money is minted to meet the growing demand, that is to say: pieces of precious metal of a certain weight gauged by authorities. And probably, with the growing need for mobile means of exchange, the process was repeated on various levels; perhaps exchange by barter, when the supply of coinage no longer met the increased demand, repeatedly gained new ground. Slowly the increasing differentiation and interweaving of human actions, the growing volume of trade and exchange, pushes up the volume of coinage and then the reverse takes place. In between, disproportions continually arise.

By the second half of the thirteenth century, at least in Flanders, and somewhat earlier or later in other regions, mobile wealth is very considerable. It circulates fairly rapidly "thanks to a series of instruments that have been created in the meantime":[37] gold coinage minted within the country—hitherto even in France, as in Abyssinia to the present day, no gold coinage had been minted; what was in use, and stored in the treasuries, was Byzantine gold coin—together with small money, the letter of exchange and measurement—all these are symbols of how the invisible network of chains of exchange was growing more and more dense.

21. But how could exchange relations between different areas, and differentiation of work extending beyond the local region be established, if transport was inadequate, if society was incapable of moving heavy loads over long distances?

Examples from the Carolingian period have already shown how the king had to travel with his court from one imperial palace to another in order to consume the products of his estates on the spot. No matter how small this court may have been in comparison to those of the early absolutist phase, it was so difficult to move the quantities of goods that were needed for its sustenance that the people had to move to the goods instead.

But in the same period when population, the towns, interdependence and its instruments, were growing more and more perceptibly, transport too was developing.

In antiquity the harness of horses, as of all other beasts of burden, was little suited to the transportation of heavy loads over long distances. It is open to question what distances and loads it could cope with, but clearly this mode of conveyance was sufficient for the structure and needs of the inland economy of antiquity. Throughout the whole of that period land transport remained extraordinarily expensive,[38] slow and difficult, in comparison to waterborne transport. Virtually all major centres of trade were situated on the coast or on navigable rivers. And this centralization of transport about the waterways is very characteristic of the structure of the society of antiquity. Here, on the waterways and above all on the seacoasts, arose rich and sometimes very densely populated urban centres whose need for food and luxury articles was often met from very remote parts, and which formed central links in the highly differentiated chains of an extensive exchange traffic. In the enormous hinterlands, which by and large were open only to overland transport, that is, in by far the largest part of the Roman Empire, the population met their primary needs directly from the produce of their immediate environment. Here, short exchange chains predominated, in other words, what can be roughly called a "barter economy"; very little money circulated, and the purchasing power of this barter sector of the ancient economy was too low for the acquisition of luxury articles. The contrast between the small urban sector and the vast inland areas was thus very great. Like thin nerve strands the larger urban settlements along the waterways were embedded in the rural districts, drawing off their strength and the products of their labour until, with the decline of the centralized government, and partly through the active struggle of rural elements against the urban rulers, the agrarian sector freed itself from the domination of the towns. Then this narrow, more differentiated urban sector, with its extensive interdependencies, fell into decay, to be obliterated by a somewhat altered form of short, regionally limited exchange chains and barter-economy institutions. In this dominant urban sector of ancient society, however, there was clearly no need to develop overland transport further. Everything that its own country could not supply or only at a high transportation cost, could be more easily obtained from overseas.

But now, in the Carolingian period, the chief waterway of the ancient world, the Mediterranean, was closed, primarily through Arab expansion, to a large number of peoples. Overland transport and internal connections took on an entirely new significance. This generated a pressure for land transport to be developed to promote interdependence and exchange. And if subsequently, as in antiquity, sea connections such as those between Venice and Byzantium, the Flemish cities and England, again played a decisive part in the rise of the West, the specific character of Western development is no less determined by the fact that to the network of sea routes was attached an increasingly dense network of overland connections, and that major inland centres of trade were also gradually developed. The development of land transport beyond the level it had attained in the ancient world is a particularly clear illustration of this growing differentiation and interdependence of societies throughout the inland areas of Europe.

The use of the horse for haulage was, as has been mentioned, not very highly developed in the Roman world. The harness ran across the throat.[39] This was perhaps useful to the rider in guiding his horse. The thrown-back head, the "proud" posture of the horse frequently seen in ancient reliefs is connected with this mode of harnessing. But it makes the horse or mule fairly unusable for haulage, particularly of heavy loads, which necessarily constrict its throat.

The case is similar with the shoeing of animals. The ancients lacked the nailed iron horseshoe without which the full power of the horse cannot be exploited.

Both states of affairs slowly change from the tenth century onwards. In the same phase when the tempo of forest clearance is gradually increased, when society is differentiated and urban markets are formed, when money comes increasingly into use as a symbol of this interdependence, land transport too, in the form of devices for the exploitation of animal labour power, makes decisive progress. And this improvement, insignificant as it may appear to us today, had at that time scarcely less importance than the development of machine technology in a later age.

"In a mighty constructive effort", it has been said,[40] the scope of use of animal labour is slowly extended in the course of the eleventh and twelfth centuries. The main load in haulage is transferred from the throat to the shoulders. The horseshoe appears. And in the thirteenth century the modern haulage technique for both horses and oxen is created in principle. The foundation for the overland transport of heavy loads over long distances has been laid. In the same period the wheeled cart appears and the beginnings of metalled roads. With the development of transport technology, the water-mill takes on an importance it had lacked in antiquity. It was now profitable to transport grain to it over quite long distances.[41] That too was a step on the way to differentiation and interdependence, to the severance of functions from the closed sphere of the estate.

VI

Some New Elements in the Structure of Medieval Society as Compared with Antiquity

22. The change in drive-control and conduct that we call "civilization" is very closely related to the growing interweaving and interdependence of people. In the few examples that it has been possible to give here, this interweaving can be seen as it were in the process of becoming. And even here, at this relatively early phase, the nature of the social fabric in the West is in certain respects different from that of antiquity. As the cellular structure of society began once again to become differentiated, whatever institutions the preceding stage of high

differentiation had left behind were used in many ways. But the conditions under which this renewed differentiation took place, and thus the nature and direction of the differentiation itself, diverged in certain respects from those of the earlier period.

People have spoken of a "renaissance of trade" in the eleventh or twelfth centuries. If this means that institutions of antiquity were now to a certain extent revived, it is certainly correct. Without the heritage of antiquity, the problems confronting society in the course of this development could certainly not have been successfully overcome in this way. In this respect it was a construction on earlier foundations. But the driving force of the movement did not reside in "learning from antiquity". It lay within the society itself, in its own inherent dynamics, in the conditions under which people had to accommodate themselves to one another. These conditions were no longer the same as in antiquity. There is a very widespread conception that the West only really regained and then surpassed the level attained by antiquity in the Renaissance. But whether or not we are here concerned with a "surpassing", with "progress", structural features and developmental tendencies departing from those of antiquity are visible not only in the Renaissance but already—at least to a certain extent—in the early phase of expansion and growth that has been discussed here.

Two such structural differences will be mentioned. Western society lacked the cheap labour of prisoners-of-war, slaves. Or when they were available—and they were not in fact entirely lacking—they no longer played any very significant part in the overall structure of society. This gave social development a new direction from the outset.

No less important was another circumstance that has already been mentioned. Resettlement did not take place as previously about a sea, or as exclusively along waterways, but very largely in inland areas by land transport routes. Both these circumstances, often in close interaction, confronted Western society from the start with problems that ancient society had not needed to solve and which guided social development into new paths. The fact that slaves played only a minor role in the working of estates may be explained by the absence of large slave reservoirs or by the sufficiency of the indigenous population of bondsmen for the needs of the warrior class. However that may be, the insignificance of slave labour is matched by the absence of the typical social patterns of a slave economy. And it is only against the background of these different patterns that the special nature of the Western structure can be fully appreciated. Not only do the division of labour, the interweaving of people, the mutual dependence of upper and lower classes, and concomitantly, the drive economy of both classes, develop differently in a slave society than in one with more or less free labour, but also the social tensions and even the functions of money are not the same, to say nothing of the importance of free labour for the development of work-techniques.

It must be enough here to contrast to the specific processes of Western civilization a brief summary of the different processes operating in a society with highly developed slave markets. These are no less compelling in the latter than in the former. In a *résumé* of present-day research, the mechanisms of a society based on slave labour have been summarized as follows:

> . . . slave-labour interferes with the work of production by free-labour. It interferes in three ways: it causes the withdrawal of a number of men from production to supervision and national defence; it diffuses a general sentiment against manual labour and any form of concentrated activity; and more especially it drives free labourers out of the occupations in which the slaves are engaged. Just as, by Gresham's law, bad coins drive out good, so it has been found by experience that, in any given occupation or range of occupations, slave-labour drives out free; so that it is even difficult to find recruits for the higher branches of an occupation if it is necessary for them to acquire skill by serving an apprenticeship side-by-side with slaves in the lower.
>
> This leads to grave consequences; for the men driven out of these occupations are not themselves rich enough to live on the labour of slaves. They therefore tend to form an intermediate class of idlers who pick up a living as best they can—the class known to modern economists as "poor whites" or "white trash" and to students of Roman history as "clientes" or "faex Romuli". Such a class tends to emphasize both the social unrest and the military and aggressive character of a slave—state. . . .
>
> A slave society is therefore a society divided sharply into three classes: masters, poor whites and slaves; and the middle class is an idle class, living on the community or on warfare, or on the upper.
>
> But there is still another result. The general sentiment against productive work leads to a state of affairs in which the slaves tend to be the only producers and the occupations in which they engage the only industries of the country. In other words, the community will rely for its wealth upon occupations which themselves admit of no change or adaptation to circumstances, and which, unless they supply deficiencies of labour by breeding, are in perpetual need of capital. But this capital cannot be found elsewhere in the community. It must therefore be sought abroad: and a slave community will tend, either to engage in aggressive warfare, or to become indebted for capital to neighbours with a free-labour system. . . .[42]

The use of slaves tends to disincline free men from work as an unworthy occupation. Alongside the non-working upper class of slave-owners a *non-working middle class* forms. By the use of slaves society is bound to a relatively simple work structure, embodying techniques that can be operated by slaves and which for this reason is relatively inaccessible to change, improvement or adaptation to new situations. The reproduction of capital is tied to the reproduction of slaves, and thus directly or indirectly to the success of military campaigns, to the output of the slave reservoirs, and is never calculable to the same degree as in a society in which it is not whole people who are bought for their lifetime but particular work services of people who are socially more or less free.

It is only against this background that we can understand the importance for the whole development of Western society of the fact that, during the slow growth of population in the Middle Ages, slaves were absent or played only a minor part. From the start society was therefore set on a different course than in Roman antiquity.[43] It was subjected to different regularities. The urban revolutions of the eleventh and twelfth centuries, the gradual liberation of the workers displaced from the land—the burghers—from the power of the feudal lord, is a first expression of this. From this a line of descent leads to the gradual transformation of the West into a society where more and more people earn a living through occupational work. The very small part played by slave imports and slave labour gives the workers, even as the lower class, considerable social weight. The further the interdependence of people proceeds and the more, therefore, land and its produce are drawn within the circulation of trade and money, the more dependent the non-working upper classes, warriors or nobility, become on the working lower and middle classes and the more the latter gain in social power. The rise of bourgeois classes to the upper class is an expression of this pattern. In exactly the opposite way to that in which, in the ancient slave society, urban freemen were driven away from labour, in Western society, as a result of the work of freemen, the growing interdependence of all finally drew even members of the previously non-working upper classes more and more within the division of labour. And even the technical development of the West, the evolution of money to that specific form of "capital" which is characteristic of the West, presupposes the absence of slave labour and the development of free work.

23. The above is a brief sketch of one example of the specifically Western developments that run through the Middle Ages to modern times.

Hardly less significant was the fact that settlement in the Middle Ages did not take place around a sea. The earlier waves of migrating peoples had, as already mentioned, given rise to concentrated trade networks and to the integration of large areas in Europe, only along riverbanks and above all in coastal regions of the Mediterranean. This applies to Greece and above all to Rome. The Roman dominion slowly spread out around the Mediterranean basin and finally enclosed it on all sides. "Its outermost frontiers on the Rhine, the Danube, the Euphrates, and the Sahara formed an enormous defensive circle securing the coastal perimeter. Undoubtedly the sea was for the Roman Empire the basis both of its political and its economic unity."[44]

The German tribes too first drove from all sides towards the Mediterranean, and founded their first empires throughout the areas of the Roman Empire surrounding the sea, which the Romans had called "mare nostrum'.[45] The Franks did not get so far; they found all the coastal regions already occupied. They tried to break through by force. All these changes and struggles may well have begun to upset and loosen the communications encircling the Mediterranean. But of course the old importance of the Mediterranean as a means of transport and communication, as the basis and centre of all higher cultural development on

European soil, was more thoroughly destroyed by the invasion of the Arabs. It was only this that finally ruptured the weakened connecting threads. The Roman sea becomes in good part an Arab one. "The bond uniting eastern and western Europe, the Byzantine Empire and the German Empires in the West, is sundered. The consequence of the Islamic invasion . . . was to place these Empires in circumstances which had never previously existed since the beginning of history."[46] To put it somewhat differently: at least in the inland parts of Europe, away from the major river valleys and the few military roads, no highly differentiated society and therefore no differentiated production system had so far developed.

It is still difficult to decide whether the Arab invasion alone created the conditions for a development concentrated inland. The filling up of the European lands by tribes during the migration of peoples may also have played its part. But at any rate this temporary constriction of the hitherto main transport arteries had a decisive effect on the direction taken by the development of western and central European society.

In the Carolingian period a powerful territory was grouped for the first time around a centre situated far inland. Society was confronted by the task of developing inland communications more fully. When, in the course of centuries, it succeeded in doing so, the heritage of antiquity was placed under new conditions in this second way. The foundation was laid for formations unknown in antiquity. It is from this aspect that certain differences between the units of integration in antiquity and those which slowly form in the West are to be understood. States, nations, or whatever we call these entities, are now to a large extent collections of people grouped around inland centres or capitals and connected by inland arteries.

If, subsequently, these Western centres not only colonized the coast or riverbanks, but also large inland regions, if indeed large stretches of the earth were occupied and settled by Western nations, the preconditions for this lay in the evolution of inland forms of communication, which were not tied to slave labour, within the mother countries themselves. The beginnings of this course of development, too, are to be found in the Middle Ages.

And if, finally, even the inland agrarian sector of society is today integrated into the complex division of labour and the extensive exchange networks as never before, the origins of this development are likewise to be sought there. No one can say today that Western society, once set on this course, necessarily had to continue on it. A whole constellation of levers that can not yet be clearly disentangled, contributed to maintaining and stabilizing it on this course. But it is important to recognize that this society entered at this very early stage on a path on which it has remained up to modern times. One can readily imagine that, viewing the development of this whole period of human society, the medieval and modern periods together, later ages will see them as a single unified epoch, a great "Middle Age". And it is scarcely less important to observe that the Middle Ages in the narrower sense of the word were not the static period, the "petrified forest", which they are often taken to be, but that they contained highly dynamic phases and sectors moving in precisely the direction in which the modern age continued, stages of expansion, of advancing division of labour, of social transformation and revolution, of the improvement of the instruments of labour. Alongside these, admittedly, were sectors and phases in which institutions and ideas became more rigid and to a degree "petrified". But even this alternation of expanding phases and sectors with others where conservation is more important than growth and development, is by no means alien to modern times, even if the pace of social development and of this alternation has increased sharply since the Middle Ages.

VII

On the Sociogenesis of Feudalism

24. Processes of social expansion have their limits. Sooner or later they come to a halt. So, too, the movement of expansion that began about the eleventh century gradually reached a standstill. It became increasingly difficult for the western Frankish knights to open up new land by forest clearance. Land outside their frontiers was obtainable, if at all, only by heavy fighting. The colonization of the eastern Mediterranean coastal regions petered out after these first successes. But the warrior population continued to increase. The drives and affects of this ruling class were less restrained by social dependencies and civilizing processes than in subsequent upper classes. The dominance of women by men was still unimpaired. "On every page in the chronicles of this time knights, barons and great lords are mentioned who have eight, ten, twelve or even more male children."[47] The so-called "feudal system" that emerged more clearly in the twelfth century and was more or less established in the thirteenth, is nothing other than the concluding form of this movement of expansion in the agrarian sector of society. In the urban sector this movement persists somewhat longer in a different form, until it finally finds its definitive form in the closed guild system. It becomes increasingly difficult for all those warriors within society who do not already have a piece of land and possessions to obtain them, and for families with small possessions to enlarge them. Property relations are ossified. It grows more and more difficult to rise in society. And accordingly class differences between warriors are hardened. A hierarchy within the nobility corresponding to the differing magnitude of land ownership emerges more and more clearly. And the various titles that earlier had designated positions within service to the ruler, much as civil service grades do today, take on a new and increasingly fixed meaning: they are linked to the name of a particular house as an expression of the size of its estates and thus of its

military power. The dukedoms are descended from the royal servants once sent to represent the king in a territory; they gradually become more or less independent liege lords over this whole territory and possessors of a more or less expensive unenfeoffed family property within it. The case is similar with counts. The viscounts are descendants of a man whom a count has placed as his delegate over a particular smaller region and who now controls this land as his hereditary possession. The "seigneurs" or "sires" are descendants of a man whom a count has earlier installed as guardian of one of his castles or mansions, or who may have built himself a castle in the small area he had been appointed to superintend.[48] Now the castle and land around it have become the hereditary possession of his family in turn. Everyone holds on to what they have. They relinquish nothing to those above them. And there is no room for anyone from below. The land is allocated. A society expanding internally and externally, in which social betterment, the acquisition of land or more land is not too difficult for a warrior, that is, a society with relatively open positions or opportunities, has become within a few generations a society in which most positions are more or less closed.

25. Transitions from phases with large possibilities of social improvement and expansion to those offering diminished satisfaction to these needs, in which the relatively deprived are sealed off and thus more strongly united with those in the same predicament—processes of this sort recur frequently in history. We are ourselves now in the midst of such a transformation, modified by the peculiar elasticity of industrial society which is able to open up new sectors when old ones are closed, and by the different levels of development of interdependent regions. But, taken as a whole, the situation is not only that each crisis marks a shift in one direction and each boom a shift in another: the overall trend of society points increasingly clearly towards a system with closed opportunities.

Such periods can be recognized from afar by a certain despondency of mind, at least among the deprived, by a hardening of social forms, by attempts to break them from below and, as already mentioned, by the stronger cohesion of those occupying the same position in the hierarchy.

The particular pattern of this process, however, is different in a barter economy than in a money society, though no less strict. What above all seems incomprehensible to the later observer in the process of feudalization, is the fact that neither kings nor dukes nor all the ranks below them were able to prevent their servants becoming independent owners of the fief. But precisely the universality of this fact shows the strength of the social regularity at work. We have already sketched the pressures which brought about the slow decline of the royal house in a warrior society with a barter economy, once the crown no longer succeeded in expanding, that is, in conquering new lands. Analogous processes were at work, once the possibility of expansion and the external threat had diminished, throughout the warrior society. This is the typical pattern of a society built up on land ownership, in which trade does not play a major part, in which each estate is more or less autarkic, and in which military alliance for defence or attack is the primary form of integration of large regions.

In the tribal unit the warriors live relatively close together. Then they slowly spread throughout the whole country. Their number grows. But with increase and dispersal across a large region the individual loses the protection once offered by the tribe. Single families ensconced in their estates and castles and often separated by long distances, the individual warriors ruling these families and a retinue of bondsmen and serfs, are now more isolated than before. Gradually new relationships are established between the warriors, as a function of the increased numbers and distance, the greater isolation of the individual and the intrinsic tendencies of land ownership.

With the gradual dissolution of the tribal units and the merging of Germanic warriors with members of the Gallo–Romanic upper class, with the dispersion of warriors over large areas, the individual has no other way of defending himself against those socially more powerful, than by placing himself in the protection of one of them. They in their turn have no other way of protecting themselves against others with similarly large estates and military power, than with the aid of warriors to whom they give land or whose land they protect in exchange for military services.

Individual dependencies are established. One warrior enters an alliance with another under oath. The higher-ranking partner with the greater area of land—the two go hand in hand—is the "liege lord", the weaker partner the "vassal". The latter in turn can, if circumstances so require, take still weaker warriors under his protection in exchange for services. The contracting of such individual alliances is at first the only form in which people can protect themselves from one another.

The "feudal system" stands in strange contrast to the tribal constitution. With the latter's dissolution new groupings and new forms of integration are necessarily set up. There is a strong tendency towards individualization, reinforced by the mobility and expansion of society. This is an *individualization relative to the tribal unit*, and in part relative to the family unit too, just as there will later be movements or individualization relative to the feudal unit, the guild unit, the class unit, and, again and again, to the family unit. And the feudal oath is nothing other than the sealing of a protective alliance between individual warriors, the sacral confirmation of the individual relationship between the warrior giving land and protection and the other giving services. In the first stage of the movement the king stands on one side. As the conqueror he controls the whole area and performs no services; he merely allocates land. The bondsman is at the other extreme of the pyramid; he controls no land and merely performs services or—what comes to the same thing—pays dues. All the degrees between them have at first a double face. They have land and protection to distribute below them and services to perform above them. But this network of dependencies, the need of those higher up for services, particularly military, and of those lower down for land or protection, harboured tensions that led to quite specific shifts. The process of feudalization is none other than one such compulsive shift in this network of dependencies. At a particular phase everywhere in the West the dependence of those above on services is greater than that of their vassals on protection. This reinforces the centrifugal forces in this society in which each piece of land supports its owner. This is the simple structure of those processes in the course of which, throughout the whole hierarchy of warrior society, the former servants over and again become the independent owners of the land entrusted to them, and titles deriving from service become simple designations of rank according to size of property and military power.

26. These shifts and their mechanisms would not in themselves be difficult to understand if the later observer did not constantly project his own idea of "law" and "justice" upon the relations between the warriors of feudal society. So compulsive are the habits of thinking of our own society that the observer involuntarily asks why the kings, dukes and counts tolerated this usurpation of sovereignty over the land which they had originally controlled. Why did they not assert their "legal rights"?

But we are not concerned here with what are called "legal questions" in a more complex society. It is a prerequisite for understanding feudal society not to regard one's own "legal forms" as law in an absolute sense. Legal forms correspond at all times to the structure of society. The crystallization of general legal norms set down in writing, an integral part of property relations in industrial society, presupposes a very high degree of social integration and the formation of central institutions able to give one and the same law universal validity throughout the area they control and strong enough to enforce respect for written agreements. The power which backs up legal titles and property claims in modern times is no longer directly visible. In proportion to the individual it is so great, its existence and the threat emanating from it are so self-evident, that it is very seldom put to the test. This is why there is such a strong tendency to regard this law as something self-explanatory, as if it had come down from heaven, an absolute "right" that would exist even without the support of this power structure, or if the power structure were different.

The chains mediating between the legal system and the power structure have today grown longer, in keeping with the greater complexity of society. And as the legal system often *operates* independently of the power structure, though never completely so, it is easy to overlook the fact that the law is here, as in any society, a function and symbol of the social structure or—what comes to the same thing—the balance of social power.[49]

In feudal society this was less concealed. The interdependence of people and regions was less. There was no stable power structure stretching across the whole region. Property relations were regulated directly according to the degree of mutual dependence and actual social power.*

There is in industrial society a kind of relationship which can in a certain sense be compared to the relationship between the warriors or liege lords in feudal society, and through which the pattern of this relationship can be clarified. It is the relation between states. Here, too, the decisive factor is quite nakedly social power, in which military power plays a relatively major part alongside the interdependencies arising from the economic structure. This military power is in its turn, however, much as in feudal society, largely determined by the size and productivity of a territory and the number and work potential of the people it can support.

There is no law governing the relations between states of the kind that is valid

* *Note on the concept of social power.* The "social power" of a person or group is a complex phenomenon. As regards the individual it is never exactly identical with his individual physical strength and, as regards groups, with their sum of individual strength. But physical strength and skill can under some conditions be an important element in social power. It depends on the total structure of society and the place of the individuals in it, to what extent physical strength contributes to social power. The latter varies in its structure as much as does society itself. In industrial society, for example, extreme social power in an individual can go together with low physical strength, although there can be phases in its development when bodily strength again takes on increased importance for everyone as an ingredient of social power.

In the feudal warrior society considerable physical strength is an indispensable element in social power, but by no means its sole determinant. Simplifying somewhat, one can say that the social power potential of a man in feudal society is exactly equal to the size and productivity of the land and the labour force he controls. His physical strength is undoubtedly an important element in his ability to control it. Anyone who is unable to fight like a warrior and commit his own body to attack and defence has in the long run little chance of owning anything in this society. But anyone who once controls a large piece of land in this society possesses, as monopolist of the most important means of production, a degree of social power, that is to say a quantity of opportunities, transcending his individual personal strength. To others dependent on it he can give land, taking their services in exchange. That his social power equals the size and productivity of the land he actually controls also means that his social power is as great as his following, his army, his military power.

But equally, it is obvious from this that he is dependent on services to maintain and defend his land. This dependence on followers of varying grades is an important element in the latters' social power. When this, his dependence on services, grew, his social power was reduced; when the need and demand for land grew among the propertyless, the social power of those controlling land was increased. The social power of an individual or group can be completely expressed only in proportions. The above is a simple example.

To investigate what constitutes "social power" in more detail is a task in itself. Its importance for understanding social processes in the past and present scarcely needs stating. "Political power", too, is nothing but a certain form of social power. One can therefore understand neither the behaviour nor the destinies of people, groups, social classes or states unless one finds out their actual social power regardless of what they themselves say or believe. Political life itself would lose some of its hazardousness and mystery if the structure of social power relationships between all countries were publicly analysed. To evolve more exact methods of doing so remains one of the many sociological tasks of the future.

within them. There is no all-embracing power apparatus that could back up such an international law. The existence of an international law without a corresponding power structure cannot conceal the fact that in the long run the relationships between nations are governed solely by their relative social power, and that any shift in the latter, any increase in the power of a country within the various figurations of states in different parts of the world and now—with growing interdependence—within world society as a whole, means an automatic reduction of the social power of other countries.

And here too the tension between the "haves" and "have-nots", between those who do and those who do not have enough land or means of production to meet their needs and their standards, automatically increases the more world-wide bourgeois society approaches the state of a "system with closed opportunities".

The analogy that exists between the relationships among individual lords in feudal society and among states in the industrial world, is more than fortuitous. It has its basis in the developmental curve of Western society itself. In the course of this development, with its growing interdependence, relationships of an analogous kind are established, among them legal forms, at first between relatively small territorial units and then at higher and higher levels of magnitude and integration, even if the transition to groups of a different order of size does represent a certain qualitative change.

It will be shown later what importance the process which we have begun to delineate here, i.e. the establishment of increasingly large, internally pacified but externally belligerent units of integration, had for the change of the pattern of drive control and the social standard of conduct—for the civilizing process.

The relations of these individual feudal lords to one another did indeed resemble those of present-day states. Economic interdependence, exchange, the division of labour between individual estates was, to be sure, incomparably less developed in the tenth and eleventh centuries than between modern states, and so the economic dependence between warriors was correspondingly less. All the more decisive in their relationships, therefore, was their military potential, the size of their following and the land they controlled. It can be observed over and over again that in this society no oath of allegiance or contract—as is the case between states today—could in the long run withstand changes in social power. The fealty of vassals was in the end regulated very exactly by the actual degree of dependence between the parties, by the interplay of supply and demand between those giving land and protection in exchange for services on the one hand and those needing them on the other. When expansion, when the conquest or opening up of new land grew more difficult, the greater opportunities were first of all on the side of those who rendered services and received land. This is the background of the first of the shifts which now take place in this society, the self-enfranchisement of the servants.

Land, in this society, is always the "property" of the man actually controlling it, really exercising rights of possession and strong enough to defend what he possesses. For this reason the man with land to invest in exchange for services always starts off at a disadvantage to the man who receives it. The "liege lord" has the "right" to the invested land, to be sure, but the vassal actually controls it. The only thing making the vassal dependent on the liege lord, once he has the land, is the latter's protection in the widest sense of the word. But protection is not always needed. Just as the kings of feudal society are always strong when their vassals need their protection and leadership when threatened by external foes, and above all when they have freshly conquered lands to distribute, but are weak when their vassals are not threatened and no new territory is expected, so too the liege lords of lesser magnitude are weak when those to whom they have entrusted land do not happen to need their protection.

The liege lord at any given level can compel one or other of his vassals to fulfil his obligations, and drive him by force from his land. But he cannot do this to all, or even to many. For, as there can be no thought of arming bondsmen, he needs the services of one warrior to expel another, or he needs new land to reward new services. But for his conquests he needs new services. In this way the western Frankish territory disintegrated in the tenth and eleventh centuries into a multitude of smaller and smaller dominions. Every baron, every viscount, every seigneur controlled his estate or estates from his castle or castles, like a ruler over his state. The power of the nominal liege lords, the more central authorities, is slight. The compelling mechanisms of supply and demand, which make the vassal actually controlling the land generally less dependent on the protection of his liege lord than the latter on his services, have done their work. The disintegration of property, the passing of land from the control of the king to the various gradations of the warrior society as a whole—and this and nothing else is "feudalization"—has reached its utmost limit. But the system of social tensions that is established with this mighty disintegration, contains at the same time the driving forces of a counterthrust, a new centralization.

VIII

On the Sociogenesis of *Minnesang* and Courtly Forms of Conduct

27. Two phases can be distinguished in the process of feudalization: the one of extreme disintegration just discussed, and then a phase in which this movement begins to be reversed and the first, still loose, forms of reintegration on a somewhat large scale emerge. Thus begins, if we take this state of extreme disintegration as the starting point, a long historical process in the course of

which ever larger areas and numbers of people become interdependent and finally tightly organized in integrated units.

> In the tenth and eleventh centuries this fragmentation continues. It seems that no one will hold on to a portion of rule big enough to enable him to exert any effective action. Fiefs, the chances of ruling, and rights are split up more and more . . . from top to bottom, throughout the whole hierarchy, all authority is heading towards dis-integration.
>
> Then, in the eleventh and especially the twelfth century, a reaction sets in. A phenomenon occurs that has been repeated in history several times in different forms. The liege lords who are better placed and have the greatest chances, sequestrate the feudal movement. They give feudal law, that has begun to become fixed, a new turn. They fix it to the disadvantage of their vassals. Their efforts are favoured by certain large historical connections . . . and this reaction serves in the first place to consolidate the situation just reached.[50]

After the gradual transition of the warrior society from a more mobile phase with relatively large opportunities for expansion and social betterment for the individual, to a phase with increasingly closed positions, in which everyone tries to retain and consolidate what he has, power once again shifts among the warriors scattered across the land and ensconced like *reguli* (like little kings) in their castles. The few richer and larger lords gain in social power relative to the many smaller ones.

The monopoly mechanism which thus slowly begins to operate will be discussed in more detail later. Here we shall refer to only one of the factors that from now on act more and more decisively in favour of the few greater warriors at the expense of the many lesser ones: the importance of slowly proceeding commercialization. The network of dependencies, the interplay of supply of and demand for land, protection and services in the less differentiated society of the tenth and even the eleventh century, is simple in its structure. Slowly in the eleventh, and more quickly in the twelfth century, the network grows complex. At the present stage of research it is difficult to determine accurately the growth of trade and money circulating at this time. This alone would provide a possibility of really measuring the changes in social power relations. Suffice it to say that the differentiation of work, and the market and money sector of society, are growing, even though the barter form of economy continues to predominate as it will for a long time; and this growth in trade and money circulation benefits the few rich lords very much more than the many small ones. These continue by and large to live on their estates as they have done up to now. They consume directly what their estates produce, and their involvement in the network of trade and exchange-relationships is minimal. The former, by contrast, not only enter the network of trade relations through the surplus produce of their estates; the growing settlements of artisans and traders, the towns, generally attach themselves to the fortresses and administrative centres of the great dominions, and however uncertain relations between the great lords and the communes within their territory may still be, however much they waver between mistrust, hostility, open struggle and peaceful agreement, in the end they too, and the duties flowing from them, strengthen the great lords as compared to the small ones. They offer them opportunities of escaping the perpetual cycle of land investiture in exchange for services, and subsequent appropriation of the land by the vassal—opportunities that counteract the centrifugal forces. At the courts of the great lords, by virtue of their direct or indirect involvement in the trade network, whether through raw materials or in coined or uncoined precious metal, a wealth accumulates that the majority of lesser lords lack. And these opportunities are supplemented by a growing demand for opportunities from below, a growing supply of services by the less favoured warriors and others driven from the land. The smaller society's possibilities of expansion become, the larger grows the reserve army from all classes, including the upper class. Very many from this class are well content if they can simply find lodging, clothing and food at the courts of the great lords through performing some function. And if ever, by the grace of a great lord, they receive a piece of land, a fief, this is a special stroke of fortune. The story of Walther von der Vogelweide, well known in Germany, is typical in this respect of the lives of many men in France as well. And, realizing the underlying social necessities, we can guess what humiliations, vain supplications and disappointments may have lain behind Walther's exclamation: "I have my fief!"

28. The courts of the greater feudal lords, the kings, dukes, counts and higher barons or, to use a more general term, the territorial lords, thus attract, by virtue of the growing opportunities in their chambers, a growing number of people. Quite analogous processes will take place again some centuries later at a higher level of integration, at the courts of the absolute princes and kings. But by that time the interweaving of social functions, the development of trade and money circulation are so great, that a regular income through taxation from the whole dominion and a standing army of peasants' and burghers' sons with noble officers financed by the absolute ruler from these taxes, can totally paralyse the centrifugal forces, the landed aristocracy's desire for independence, through the whole country. Here, in the twelfth century, integration, the network of trade and communications, is not remotely so far developed. In areas the size of a kingdom it is still quite impossible to oppose the centrifugal forces continuously. Even in territories the size of a duchy or a county it is still very difficult, usually only after hard fighting, to restrain vassals who wish to withdraw their land from the control of a liege lord. The increase in social power falls firstly to the richer feudal lords on account of the size of their family property, their unenfieffed land. In this respect the bearers of the crown are no different from the other major feudal lords. The opportunities that they all derive, through their large holding

of land, from trade and finance, give them a superiority, including military superiority, over the smaller self-sufficient knights, first of all within the limits of one territory. Here, even with the poor travelling conditions of the time, access by the central authority is no longer very difficult. All this converges at this stage of development to give the rulers of medium-sized territories, smaller than kingdoms or "states" in the later sense of this word, and larger than the bulk of the knightly estates, a special social significance.

But this is by no means to say that at that stage a really stable governmental and administrative apparatus could be established even within a territory of this size. The interdependence of regions and the permeation of the country by money had not yet advanced remotely far enough to permit the highest and richest feudal lord of a region to establish a bureaucracy paid exclusively or even primarily in money, and thus a more strict centralization. A whole series of struggles was needed, struggles that were constantly rekindled, before the dukes, kings and counts could assert their social power even within their own territory. And whatever the outcome of these battles, the vassals, the smaller and medium knights, still retained the rights and functions of rule within their estates; here they continued to hold sway like little kings. But while the courts of the great feudal lords became more populated, while their chambers filled and goods began to pass in and out, the bulk of the small knights continued to lead their self-sufficient and often very restricted lives. They took from the peasants whatever was to be got out of them; they fed as best they could a few servants and their numerous sons and daughters; they feuded incessantly with each other; and the only way in which these small knights could get hold of more than the produce of their own fields was by plundering the fields of others, above all the domains of abbeys and monasteries, and then gradually, as money circulation and so the need for money grew, by pillaging towns and convoys of goods, and ransoming prisoners of war. War, rapine, armed attack and plunder constituted a regular form of income for the warriors in the barter economy, and moreover, the only one open to them. And the more wretchedly they lived, the more dependent they were on this form of income.

The slowly increasing commercialization and monetarization therefore favoured the few large landowners and feudal lords rather than the mass of the small. But the superiority of the kings, dukes or counts was not remotely as great as later, in the age of absolutism.

29. Analogous shifts, as already mentioned, have often taken place in the course of history. The increasing differentiation between the upper middle class and the petty-bourgeois classes is probably most familiar to the twentieth-century observer. Here too, after a period of free competition with relatively good possibilities of social improvement and enrichment even for small and medium property owners, the preponderance within the bourgeoisie is gradually shifting to the disadvantage of the economically weaker and in favour of the economically

stronger group. Anyone with small or medium-sized property, leaving aside a few growth areas, finds it increasingly difficult to attain major wealth. The direct or indirect dependence of the small and middle-sized on the great is growing, and while the opportunities of the former diminish, those of the latter almost automatically increase.

Something similar took place in the western Frankish knightly society of the late eleventh and twelfth centuries. The possibilities for expansion of the agrarian sector of society, predominantly a barter economy, were as good as exhausted. The division of labour, the commercial sector of society, was—despite many reverses—still spreading, in the grip of growth. The bulk of the knightly landowners profited but little from this expansion. The few great landlords had a part in it and profited. In this way a differentiation took place within feudal knightly society itself that was not without consequences for attitudes and styles of life.

> Feudal society as a whole [says Luchaire in his incomparable study of society in the age of Philip Augustus][51] has, with the exception of an élite . . . scarcely altered its habits and manners since the ninth century. Almost everywhere the lord of the manor remains a brutal and rapacious cutthroat; he goes to war, fights at tournaments, spends his peacetime hunting, ruins himself with extravagance, oppresses the peasants, practises extortion on his neighbours and plunders the property of the church.

The classes influenced by the slowly increasing division of labour and monetarization are in flux; the others remain stationary and are drawn only resistingly and, as it were, passively into the current of forces of change. It is no doubt never quite correct to say that this or that class is "without history". But what can be said is this: the living conditions of the lesser landlords or knights change only very slowly. They play no direct or active part in the exchange network, the money flow, the quicker movement that passes with it through society. And when they feel the shocks and convulsions of these social movements, it is practically always in a form detrimental to them. All these things are disruptions which the landlords like the peasants usually fail to understand and often detest, until they are actually driven by them more or less violently from their autarkic base into the classes with a faster current. They eat what their land, their stables and the work of their bondsmen yield. In this nothing is changed. If supplies are short or more is wanted, it is taken by force, through pillage and plunder. This is a simple, clearly visible and independent existence; here the knights, and very much later the peasants too, are and remain in a certain sense always the lords of their land. Taxes, trade, money, the rise and fall of market prices, all these are alien and often hostile phenomena from a different world.

The barter sector of society which, in the Middle Ages and for long after, comprises the great majority of people, is certainly not entirely untouched even at this early stage by the social and historical movement. But despite all the upheavals, the pace of real changes in it is, compared to that in other strata, very small. It is not "without history"; but in it, for a very large number of people in the Middle Ages and for a smaller number even in recent times, the same living conditions are constantly reproduced. Here, uninterruptedly, production and consumption are carried on predominantly in the same place within the framework of the same economic unit; the supra-local integration in other regions of society is traceable only late and indirectly. The division of labour and work techniques which, in the commercialized sector, advance more quickly, here are only slowly changed.

It is only much later, therefore, that the personalities of men are here subjected to the peculiar compulsions, the stricter controls and restraints which arise from the money network and the greater division of functions, with its increasing number of visible and invisible dependencies. Feeling and conduct undergo far more hesitantly a civilizing process.

As already stated, in the Middle Ages and long after, this agrarian barter sector of the economy with its low division of labour, its low integration beyond the local level and its high capacity to resist change, contains by far the largest portion of the population. If we are really to understand the civilizing process we must remain aware of this polyphony of history, the pace of change slow in one class, more rapid in another, and the proportion between them. The rulers of this large, ponderous, agrarian sector of the medieval world, the knights, are for the most part scarcely bound in their conduct and passions by money chains. Most of them know only one means of livelihood—thus only one direct dependence—the sword. It is at most the danger of being physically overpowered, a military threat from a visibly superior enemy, that is to say direct, physical, external compulsion, that can induce them to restraint. Otherwise their affects have rather free and unfettered play in all the terrors and joys of life. Their time—and time, like money, is a function of social interdependence—is only very slightly subject to the continuous division and regulation imposed by dependence on others. The same applies to their drives. People are wild, cruel, prone to violent outbreaks and abandoned to the joy of the moment. They can afford to be. There is little in their situation to compel them to impose restraint upon themselves. Little in their conditioning forces them to develop what might be called a strict and stable super-ego, as a function of dependence and compulsions stemming from others transformed into self-restraints.

Towards the end of the Middle Ages, to be sure, a rather larger number of knights has been drawn within the sphere of influence of the great feudal courts. The examples from the life of a knight given earlier in connection with a series of pictures (cf. page 168ff.) come from this circle. But the bulk of the knights still live at this stage in much the same way as they had in the ninth or tenth century. Indeed, a gradually dwindling number of lords of the manor continued to lead a similar life long after the Middle Ages. And if we can believe a poetess, George Sand—and she expressly confirms the historical authenticity of what she says—there were still a few people leading these untamed feudal lives in provincial corners of France right up to the French Revolution, by now doubly savage, fearful and cruel as a result of their outsider situation. She describes life in one of these last castles, that have by now taken on the character of robbers' caves less because they had changed than because society around them had done so, in her short story "Mauprat".

> My grandfather [says the hero of the story] was from then on, with his eight sons, the last debris our province had conserved of that race of petty feudal tyrants by which France had been covered and infested for so many centuries. Civilization, which was striding rapidly towards the great revolutionary upheavals, was increasingly stamping out these exactions and this organized brigandage. The light of education, a kind of good taste which was the distant reflection of a gallant court, and perhaps a presentiment of a close and terrible awakening of the people, penetrated the castles and even the semi-rustic manors of the down-at-heel gentry.

We would need to quote whole sections of this description to show how modes of conduct that in the tenth, eleventh and twelfth centuries were characteristic of the major part of the upper class, are still to be found among isolated outsiders thanks to their similar conditions of life. Still present among them is the low degree of regular drive-control. Still lacking is the transformation of elementary urges into the many kinds of refined pleasure known to society around them. There is mistrust towards women, who are essentially objects of sensual satisfaction, delight in plundering and rape, desire to acknowledge no master, servility among the peasants on whom they live, and behind all this the impalpable pressures that cannot be met with weapons or physical violence: debt, the cramped, impoverished mode of life contrasting sharply with their large aspirations, and mistrust of money whether in the hands of the masters or the peasants:

> Mauprat did not ask for money. Monetary values are what the peasant of these lands obtains with greatest difficulty and parts with most reluctantly. *"Money is dear"*, is one of his proverbs, because money represents for him something other than physical work. *It is a commerce with things and people from outside, an effort of foresight or circumspection, a market, a sort of intellectual struggle*, which jolts him out of his apathetic habits, in a word of mental effort; and to him this is the most painful and disturbing thing of all.

Here we still find enclaves of a predominantly barter economy within a large fabric woven of trade relations and the division of labour. Even here, no one can quite resist being drawn into the current of circulating money. Primarily taxes, but also the need to buy certain things one cannot produce oneself, force people in this direction. But the peculiarly opaque nature of the control and foresight, the restraint of inclination beyond what is required by necessary physical work, that any involvement in money chains imposes on people, remains in these enclaves a detested and uncomprehended kind of compulsion.

This quotation refers to masters and peasants at the end of the eighteenth century. It serves to illustrate once more the slow pace of change in this sector of society, and something of the attitudes of people within it.

30. From the broad landscape of the barter economy with its innumerable castles and its many greater and smaller dominions, therefore, there slowly emerged in France during the eleventh, and more clearly during the twelfth century, two new kinds of social organ, two new forms of settlement or integration, that marked an increase in the division of labour and in the interdependence of people: the courts of the greater feudal lords, and the towns. These two institutions are very closely connected in their sociogenesis, however mistrustful and hostile their members may often have been towards one another.

This should not be misunderstood. It is not as if the undifferentiated sector of the barter economy is confronted at one stroke with more differentiated forms of settlement in which rather larger numbers of people can be supported directly or indirectly on the basis of exchange and the division of labour. Infinitely slowly new, economically autonomous stations are built into the path of goods from the natural state to consumption. And so, step by step, towns and larger feudal courts grow out of the form of economic activity that survives on the small estates. In the twelfth century and long after it neither the urban settlements nor the great feudal courts are remotely as divided from the barter economy as the cities of the nineteenth century were from the so-called open country. On the contrary, urban and rural production are still intimately connected. The few great feudal courts are, to be sure, attached to the trade network and the market through their surplus produce, through the duties flowing into them, and also through an increased demand for luxury goods; but the major part of their everyday needs is still met directly by the produce of their own domains. In this sense they too still operate a predominantly barter economy. Admittedly, the very size of their domains brings about a differentiation of operations within them. Much as in antiquity the great slave estates work in part for the market and in part for the direct needs of the ruling household and in this sense still represent a more differentiated kind of non-market economy, so too do these great feudal estates. This may apply to some extent to the more simple work carried out within them, but it applies above all to the organization of the estate. The domain of the great feudal lord hardly ever forms a single, powerful complex on a self-contained piece of land. The estates have often been acquired very gradually by very different means, conquests, inheritance, gift or marriage. They are usually scattered in different regions of a territory and are therefore not as easy to supervise as a small property. A central apparatus is needed, people to superintend incoming and outgoing goods, to keep accounts, however primitive they may at first be, people who both check the income from duties and administrate the territories. "The small feudal estate was from an intellectual point of view a rudimentary organ, particularly when the master could neither write nor read."[52] The courts of the great and rich feudal lords first attract a staff of educated clerics for administrative purposes. But through the opportunities opening to them at this time the great feudal lords are, as we have mentioned, the richest and most powerful men in their region, and with the possibility grows the desire to express this position by the splendour of their courts. They are not only richer than the other knights but also, to begin with, richer than any burgher. For this reason the great feudal courts have far more cultural significance than the towns at this time. In the competition between the territorial rulers, they become the places to show off the power and wealth of their lords. The latter therefore gather scribes around them not only for administrative purposes but also to chronicle their deeds and destinies. They are bountiful towards minstrels who sing the praises of themselves and their ladies. The great courts become "potential centres of literary patronage" and "potential centres of historiography".[53] As yet there is no book market. And within the framework of secular society, for anyone who has specialized in writing and composing and has to live by it, whether or not he is a cleric, court patronage is the only means of livelihood.[54]

Here, as always in history, higher and more refined forms of poetry develop from simpler ones in conjunction with a differentiation of society, with the formation of richer and more refined social circles. The poet does not work as a wholly self-sufficient individual writing for an anonymous public of which he knows at the most a few representatives. He creates and writes for people he knows through daily contact. And the conviviality, the forms of relationship and behaviour, the atmosphere of his social circle as well as his place within it, find expression in his words.

Players travel from castle to castle. Some are singers, many are merely clowns and fools in the simplest sense of the word. And as such they are to be found too in the castles of the simpler and smaller knights. But they visit them only in passing; there is no room here, no interest and often no means to feed and pay a player for any length of time. These are only available at the few larger courts. And by "players" we must understand a whole range of functions from the simple jester and fool to the *minnesänger* and troubadour. The function is differentiated with the public. The greatest, richest—which is to say the highest-ranking—lords were able to attract the best performers to their courts. More people were gathered there; there was a possibility of more refined conviviality and entertainment, so that the tone of poetry was also refined. The idea that "the higher the lord and lady, the higher and better the bard" was frequently uttered at the time.[55] It was taken for granted. Frequently, not one but several singers lived at the great feudal courts. "The higher the personal qualities and rank of a princess, the more brilliant her court, the more poets she gathered in her service."[56] Matching the power struggle between the great feudal lords was a constant struggle for prestige. The poet, like the historian, was one of its instruments. Thus a *minnesänger*'s change of service from one lord to another could often mean a complete change in the political convictions he expressed.[57] It has been rightly said of the *minnesang*: "In meaning and purpose it was a political panegyric in the form of a personal homage."[58]

31. Retrospectively, *minnesang* can easily appear an expression of knightly society in general. This interpretation has been reinforced by the fact that, with the decline of knightly functions and the growing subservience of the noble upper class with the rise of absolutism, the image of free, unfettered knightly society took on a nostalgic aura. But it is difficult to conceive that *minnesang*, especially in its more delicate tones—and it is not always delicate—springs from the same life as the coarse and unbridled behaviour that was proper to the bulk of knights. It has already been stressed that *minnesang* was actually "very contradictory to the knightly mentality".[59] The whole landscape, with its incipient differentiation, must be kept in view if this contradiction is to be resolved and the human attitude expressed in troubadour poetry understood.

There are three forms of knightly existence which, with many intermediate stages, begin to be distinguishable in the eleventh and twelfth centuries. There are the smaller knights, rulers over one or more not very large estates; there are the great, rich knights, the territorial rulers, few in number compared to the former, and finally the knights without land or with very little, who place themselves in the service of greater ones. It is mainly, though not exclusively, from this last group that the knightly, noble *minnesänger* come. Singing and composing in the service of a great lord and a noble lady is one of the ways open to those driven from the land, whether from the upper class or from the urban–rural lower class. Former members of both groups are to be found as troubadours at the great feudal courts. And even though a great feudal lord may occasionally involve himself in singing and composing, nevertheless troubadour poetry and service are stamped by the dependent status of their practitioners within a rich social life that was slowly taking on more definite forms. The human relationships and compulsions established here are not as strict and continuous, or as inescapable, as they later become at the larger absolutist courts which are far more thoroughly formed by money relationships. But they already act in the direction of stricter drive-control. Within the restricted court circle, and encouraged above all by the presence of the lady, more peaceful forms of conduct become obligatory. Certainly, this should not be exaggerated; pacification is not nearly so far advanced as later when the absolute monarch could even prohibit duelling. The sword still hangs loosely, and war and feud are close at hand. But the moderation of passions, sublimation, is unmistakable and inevitable in feudal court society. Both the knightly and the bourgeois singers are socially dependent; and their subordinate status forms the basis of their song, their attitudes and their affective and emotional mould.

> If the court singer wished to secure respect and regard for his art and his person, he could only raise himself permanently above the travelling player by being taken into the service of a prince or princess. Minnesongs addressed to a distant mistress whom he has not yet visited, had no other purpose than to express readiness and desire to serve at the court of the addressee. That was and remains by the nature of things the real goal of all who had to gain their livelihood from their art, for men of low origin as for younger, non-inheriting sons of noble houses. . . .
>
> In Walther von der Vogelweide's conditions of service we can, as has been clearly demonstrated by Konrad Burdach, observe a typical example of the life of a Minnesänger. King Philip had taken Walther "to himself": this was the usual expression for entry to ministerial service. It was a service without payment or security of tenure lasting from four months to a year. When this time elapsed he could seek a new master with the permission of the old. Walther received no fief from Philip, nor from Dietrich of Meissen, nor from Otto IV or Hermann of Thuringia, to whose household he once belonged. Likewise his service to Bishop Wolfgar of Ellenbrechtskirchen was brief. Then, finally, Friedrich II, a connoisseur of art and a poet himself, granted him a salary that secured him a living. A fief of land or office (only later of money) was, in the barter economy of the feudal age, the highest honour for services rendered, and the ultimate goal. Seldom was it granted to court singers either in France or Germany. They usually had to be content to serve as court poets entertaining society and receiving board and lodging in exchange, and as a special honour . . . the dress needed for court service.[60]

32. The particular structuring of affects expressed in the *minnesang* is inseparable from the social position of the *minnesänger*. The knights of the ninth and tenth centuries, and the majority of knights even later, did not behave particularly delicately towards their own wives, or with women of lower rank in general. The women in the castles were always directly exposed to the rough advances of the stronger man. They could defend themselves by ruse, but here the man ruled. And relations between the sexes were regulated, as in every warrior society with more or less pronounced male rule, by power, and often by open or veiled struggles, that each waged with his own means.

We hear from time to time of women who by temperament and inclination differed little from men. The lady of the castle is in this case a "virago" with a violent temper, lively passions, subjected from her youth to all manner of physical exercise, and taking part in all the pleasures and dangers of the knights around her.[61] But often enough we hear of the other side, of a warrior, whether a king or a simple seigneur, beating his wife. It seems almost an established habit for the knight, flying into a rage, to punch his wife on the nose till blood flows:

"The king hears this and anger rises into his face: raising his fist he strikes her on the nose so hard that he drew four drops of blood. And the lady says: 'Most humble thanks. When it shall please you, you may do it again.' "

"One could quote other scenes of the same kind", says Luchaire.[62] "Always the blow on the nose with the fist." Moreover a knight is often censured for taking advice from his wife.

"Lady, go into the shade," the knight says for example, "and eat and drink with your retinue in your painted and guilded chambers, busy yourself hanging silk: that is your job. Mine is to strike with the sword of steel."

> The conclusion might be drawn [to quote Luchaire again] that even in the epoch of Philip Augustus the courtly, courteous attitude towards women was only exceptionally found in feudal circles. In the great majority of domains the old, less respectful, brutal tendency still prevailed, transmitted and, perhaps, exaggerated in the majority of the "chansons de geste". One should not be misled by the love theories of the Provençal Troubadours and a few "Trouvères" from Flanders and the Champagne: the feelings they expressed were, we believe, those of an élite, a very small minority. . . .[63]

The differentiation between the bulk of smaller and medium knightly courts and the few large ones more closely attached to the slowly developing network of trade and money, brings with it, as can be seen, a differentiation of behaviour too. No doubt this behaviour was not in such stark contrast as it may first appear from these reconstructions. Here, too, there may have been transitional forms and mutual influences. But by and large it can be said that a more peaceable social life formed about the lady of the court only in these few large courts. Only here did the singers have a chance of finding service of any length, and only here was established that peculiar attitude of the serving man towards the lady of the court that finds its expression in *minnesang*.

The difference between the attitude and feelings expressed in *minnesang* and the more brutal ones prevalent in the *chansons de geste*, for which history provides ample documentation, derives, in other words, from two different kinds of relation between man and woman, corresponding to two different classes in feudal society. These two modes of conduct therefore arise with the shift in the centre of gravity of society already discussed. In a society of landed nobility dispersed fairly loosely across the country in their castles and estates, the likelihood of a preponderance of the man over the woman and thus of a more or less unconcealed male dominance, is very great. And wherever a warrior class or a class of landed gentry has strongly influenced the overall behaviour of society, traces of male dominance, forms of purely male social life with its specific eroticism and a certain eclipse of women, are to be found more or less clearly in its tradition.

Relationships of this kind predominated in medieval warrior society. Characteristic of them is a particular kind of mistrust between the sexes, reflecting the great difference in the form and scope of the lives they each lead, and the spiritual estrangement which arises as a result. As in later times—as long as women are excluded from professional life—the men of the Middle Ages, when women were generally excluded from the central sphere of male life, military action, spend most of their time among themselves. And their superiority is matched by a more or less explicit contempt of man for woman: "Go to your ornamented chambers, lady, our business is war." That is entirely typical. The woman belongs in her own special room. And this attitude, like the social basis which produced it, persists for a very long time. Its traces are to be found in French literature as late as the sixteenth century, for precisely as long as the upper class is primarily a military and landed aristocracy.[64] Then this attitude disappears from literature, which by now in France is almost exclusively controlled and modelled by courtly people, but certainly not from the life of the landed nobility itself.

The great absolutist courts are the places in European history in which the most complete equality between the spheres of life of men and women, and also of their behaviour, has so far been achieved. It would take us too far afield here to show why even the great feudal courts of the twelfth century, and incomparably more so the absolutist courts, offered women special opportunities to overcome male dominance and attain equal status with men. It has been pointed out, for example, that in southern France women could at an early stage become liege ladies, own property and play a political role; and it has been surmised that this fact favoured the development of *minnesang*.[65] But to qualify this it has also been emphasized that "the succession to the throne by daughters was only possible if the male relations, the liege lord and the neighbours did not prevent the lady from taking up her inheritance".[66] In fact even in the narrow stratum of great feudal lords, the superiority of man over woman resulting from his warrior function is always perceptible. Within the great feudal courts, however, the military function of the men receded to some extent. Here, for the first time in secular society, a large number of people, including men, lived together in constant close contact in a hierarchical structure, under the eyes of the central person, the territorial lord. This fact alone enforced a certain restraint on all dependents. An abundance of unwarlike administrative and clerical work had to be done. All this created a somewhat more peaceful atmosphere. As happens wherever men are forced to renounce physical violence, the social importance of women increased. Within the great feudal courts a common sphere of life and a common social life for men and women were established.

To be sure, male dominance was by no means broken as it sometimes was later in the absolutist courts. For the master of the court, his function as knight and military leader was still the primary one; his education too was that of a warrior centred upon the wielding of arms. For just this reason the women surpassed him in the sphere of peaceful society. As so often in the history of the West it was not men but women of high class who were first liberated for intellectual development, for reading. The wealth of the great courts gave the woman the possibility of filling her leisure time and pursuing such luxury interests. She could attract poets, singers and learned clerics. And so it was about women that the first circles of peaceful intellectual activity were established. "In aristocratic circles in the twelfth century the education of women was on average more refined than that of men."[67] This certainly refers only to the man of the same status, the husband. The wife's relationship to him was not yet very different from that customary in warrior society. It was more moderate and somewhat more refined than in the case of the small knights; but the compulsion the man placed on himself, as compared with that he placed on his own wife, was in general not great. Here too the man was quite unmistakably the ruler.

33. It is not this relationship of husband to wife that underlies troubadour poetry and *minnesang*, but the relationship of a socially inferior man to a high-ranking woman. And it is only in these courts rich and powerful enough to generate such relationships that *minnesang* is to be found. But compared to the knighthood as a whole they represent a narrow stratum, an "élite".

The connection between the structure of relationships in society at large and the personality structure of people emerges very clearly here. In the greater part of feudal society, where the man ruled and the dependence of women was unconcealed and almost unrestricted, nothing compels the man to constrain his drives and to impose control on them. There is little talk of "love" in this warrior society. And one has the impression that a man in love would have appeared ridiculous among these warriors. Women are generally regarded by these men as inferior beings. There are enough of them available. They serve to gratify drives in their simplest form. Women are given to man "for his necessity and delectation". So it was once expressed at a later time; but this is exactly in keeping with the behaviours of warriors earlier. What they sought of women is physical pleasure; apart from this, "there is scarcely a man with the patience to endure his wife".[68]

The pressures on the libidinal life of women are throughout Western history, with the exception of the great absolutist courts, considerably heavier than on men of equal birth. The fact that women in high positions in this warrior society, and thus with a certain degree of freedom, always found it easier to control, refine and fruitfully transform their affects than did the men of equal status, may reflect habituation and early conditioning in this direction. Even in relation to the man of outwardly equal social status, she is a dependent, socially inferior being.

Accordingly it is only the relation of a socially inferior and dependent man to a woman of higher rank that leads to the restraint, renunciation and the consequent transformation of drives. It is no accident that in this human situation what we call "lyric poetry" evolves as a social and not merely as an individual event;* and—likewise as a social event—that transformation of pleasure, that shade of feeling, that sublimation and refinement of the affects that we call "love" comes into being. Not as exceptions but in a socially institutionalized form, contacts between man and woman arise which 'make it impossible even for the strong man simply to take the woman when he pleases; which make the woman unattainable or attainable only with difficulty; and perhaps, because she is higher placed and difficult to attain, particularly desirable. This is the situation, this the emotional setting of *minnesang*, in which henceforth down the centuries lovers recognize something of their own feelings.

No doubt a large number of songs by troubadours and *minnesänger* are essentially expressions of feudal courtly conventions, ornaments of social life and a mere part of the social game. There may have been many troubadours whose inner relationship to their lady was not quite so consuming, and who indemnify themselves with other, more attainable women. But neither this convention nor its expression could have arisen had genuine experiences and feelings of this kind been absent. They have a core of authentic feeling and real experience. Such tones cannot be simply thought out or invented. Some loved, and some had the strength and greatness to express their love in words; it is not even difficult to say in which poems feeling and experience are genuine and in which they are more or less conventional. Some must first have found words and tones for their feelings, in order that others might play with them and give rise to a convention. "The good poets, undoubtedly, mix their own truth into even these poems of infatuation. From the fullness of their lives flowed the substance of their songs."[69]

34. The literary sources and precursors of *minnesang* have often been investigated. Its relationship with religious poetry addressed to the Virgin and

---

* In the German text I am speaking here of social and individual *phenomena*. At the time of writing this book my awareness of the ambiguities inherent in the term 'phenomenon", especially of its near solipsistic undertones, was not yet sufficiently sharpened to avoid its use. In the English translation, however, it seemed preferable to replace it by expressions such as "events", "data", etc. It is, of course, highly significant for the influence which phenomenalistic types of philosophy have had not only on academic but also on non-academic linguistic usages that the term "phenomenon" has become the most common unspecific expression for data or events of all sorts. One may not be aware of it that it is tainted by the solipsistic doubt as to whether such data really exist, such events really occur. One can easily overlook that the term "phenomenon" carries with it the notion that the data to which it refers may be only appearances, conjured up by the constitution of the human subject. But whether or not one is conscious of the philosophical heritage represented by this concept, its continued reinforces again and again the apparitionist tendencies of our age. It is better to look for expressions less woolly and less affected by this philosophical tradition. I felt that I owe my readers an explanation for the innocent use of this term in the German and its omission in the English edition. [*Author's note to the translation.*]

with the Latin lyric of the Wandering Scholars has, probably correctly, been pointed out.[70]

But the emergence and essence of *minnesang* cannot be understood only in terms of literary antecedents. These earlier forms contained many different possibilities of development. Why did the manner in which people sought to express themselves change? To put the question quite simply: why did not these two forms of religious and secular lyric remain society's predominant forms of expression? Why were formal and emotional elements taken from them and fashioned into something new? Why did this new genre take on just that form which we know as *minnesang*? History has its continuity: wittingly or not, those coming later start with what already exists and develop it further. But what are the dynamics of this movement, the shaping forces of historical change? That is the question here. The investigation of sources and antecedents is doubtless of importance for understanding *minnesang*, but without sociogenetic and psychogenetic study its origins, its feudal connections, remain obscure. *Minnesang* as a supra-individual event, as a social function in relation to feudal society as a whole, cannot be understood, any more than its specific form and typical content, unless one is aware of the actual situation and relationship of the people who express themselves in it, and the genesis of this situation. This special question demands more space than is available here, where the main interest concerns movements and connections on a larger scale. If a more precise line of enquiry for analysing a specific institution such as *minnesang* within this context has now been indicated, and some of the main outlines of its socio- and psychogenetic conditions sketched, that is all that is necessary for the purposes of this study.

35. Great historical changes have a strict regularity of their own. It often appears from present-day studies as if particular social formations whose history constitutes history as such, follow each other at random like the cloud-shapes in the mind of Peer Gynt; now they look like a horse, now like a bear, now society looks Romanic or Gothic, and now Baroque.

What has been shown here are a few basic interdependent trends that led to the shaping of society in the form of the "feudal system", and finally to the kind of relationship expressed in *minnesang*. One of these trends is the more rapid growth of population after the migration of peoples, closely connected with the consolidation of property relationships, the formation of a human surplus, among the nobility as in the class of bondsmen or serfs, and the pressure on these displaced persons from both groups to find new services.

Connected with this too is the slow insertion of discrete stations in the passage of goods from production to consumption, the growth of demand for unified, mobile means of exchange, the shift of the centre of gravity within feudal society in favour of the few great lords at the expense of the many small, the formation of large feudal courts at the centre of regions the size of a territory, where knightly-feudal traits combine with courtly ones in a peculiar unity, as barter and money relations do in this society as a whole.

Again, there is the great feudal lords' need of prestige and display in the more or less violent struggles between them; to their desire to distinguish themselves from lesser knights. And as an expression of all this; poets and singers who praise the lords and ladies, putting into words the interests and political opinions of the lord and the taste and beauty of the lady, become a more or less firmly established social institution.

Likewise one can observe, only in this small upper stratum of knightly society, a first form of emancipation, of greater freedom of movement, for women—very slight, to be sure, when compared to the freedom of women at the great absolutist courts—more continuous contacts between the lady of the court, the woman of high rank, and the troubadour, the man of lower rank and dependent, whether or not he be a knight; the impossibility or difficulty of attaining the desired woman, the self-restraint imposed on the dependent man, the need for circumspection and a certain, still very muted, regulation and transformation of his elementary drives and needs; and finally the expression of such scarcely realizable wishes in the language of dreams, in poetry.

The beauty of one poem and the empty conventionality of another, the greatness of this *minnesänger* and the triviality of that, are facts in their own right. *Minnesang* as a social institution, however, the framework in which the individual develops—and this alone concerns us here—evolves directly from this interplay of social processes.

36. In this very situation, that is, at the great feudal courts, there emerge at the same time a more rigid convention in behaviour, a certain moderation of the affects, and a regulation of manners. It is that standard of manners, that convention of behaviour, that polishing of conduct to which this society itself gave the name of *courtoisie*, and we get a fully rounded picture of it only if we incorporate what was said in Volume One about *courtois* conduct into the account of feudal courts given in the present one.

Precepts of *courtois* society were given earlier, at the beginnings of various series of examples illustrating the civilization of conduct and sentiment. The sociogenesis of the great feudal courts is at the same time the sociogenesis of *courtois* conduct. *Courtoisie*, too, is a form of conduct that doubtless first developed among the more socially dependent members of this knightly-courtly upper class.[71] However that may be, one thing re-emerges here very clearly: this *courtois* standard of conduct is in no sense a beginning. It is not an example of how people behave when their affects have free, "natural" play unfettered by society, that is to say, by the relations between people. Such a condition of totally uncontrolled drives, of an absolute "beginning" simply does not exist. The relatively great licence for acting out instinctual and affective impulses characteristic of men in the *courtois* upper classes—great in comparison with the later secular upper classes in the West—corresponds exactly to the form of integration, the degree and kind of mutual dependence in which people live together here. The division of labour is less developed than in the phases when the stricter absolutist system of rule was developed; the trade network is smaller and so the number of people who can be sustained in one place is less. And whatever the form of individual dependencies may be, the social web of dependencies that intersect within the individual is here much coarser and less extensive than in societies with greater division of labour, where more people live continuously in close proximity in a more exactly ordered system. And, consequently, the control and restraint on the individual's drives and affects is here less strict, continuous and uniform. Nevertheless, it is already considerably greater at the larger feudal courts than at the small or in the warrior society at large, where the interdependence of people is much less extensive and complex, the network of individuals much more loosely woven, and where the strongest functional dependence between people is still that of war and violence. Compared to the behaviour and affective life to be found here, *courtoisie* already represents a refinement, a mark of distinction. And the polemics contained in fairly unchanging form in the many medieval precepts on manners—avoid this and refrain from that—refer more or less directly to the behaviour practised by the bulk of the knights, which changed as slowly and slightly between the ninth or tenth centuries and the sixteenth as did their conditions of life.

37. At the present stage of development we still lack linguistic instruments which do justice to the nature and direction of all these intertwining processes. It is an imprecise and provisional aid to understanding to say that the restraints imposed upon men and their drives became "greater", integration "closer", or interdependence "stronger", just as it does not quite do justice to socio-historical reality to say that one thing belongs to a "barter economy", and another to a "money economy", or, to repeat the form of expression chosen here, that "the money-sector of the economy grew". By how much did it "grow", degree by degree? In what way did the restraints become "greater", integration "closer", interdependence "more pronounced"? Our concepts are too coarse; they adhere too much to the image of material substances. In all this we are not concerned merely with gradations, with "more" or "less". Each "increase" in restraints and interdependencies is an expression of the fact that the ties between people, the way they depend on one another, are changing, and changing qualitatively. This is what is meant by differences in social structure. And with the dynamic network of dependencies into which a human life is woven, the drives and behaviour of people take on a *different* form. This is what is meant by differences in personality structure and in social standards of conduct. The fact that such qualitative changes are sometimes, despite all the fluctuations within the movement, changes in one and the same direction over long periods, that is, continuous, directed processes rather than a random sequence, permits and indeed causes us to speak in comparative terms when discussing different phases. That is not to say

that the direction in which these processes move is towards improvement, "progress", or towards the opposite, "retrogression". But nor is it to say that they involve merely quantitative changes. Here, as so often in history, we are concerned with structural changes that are most easily, visibly, but perhaps most superficially grasped in their quantitative aspect.

We see the following movement: first one castle stands against another, then territory against territory, then state against state, and appearing on the historical horizon today are the first signs of struggles for an integration of regions and masses of people on a still larger scale. We may surmise that with continuing integration even larger units will gradually be assembled under a stable government and internally pacified, and that they in their turn will turn their weapons outwards against human aggregates of the same size until, with a further integration, a still greater reduction of distances, they too gradually grow together and world society is pacified. This may take centuries or millennia; however that may be, the growth of units of integration and rule is always at the same time an expression of structural changes in society, that is to say, in human relationships. Whenever the centre of gravity of society moves towards units of integration of a new order of magnitude—and in the shift that first favoured large feudal lords at the expense of small and middle-sized ones, then kings against the great feudal or territorial lords, a displacement in this direction is expressed —whenever such changes occur they do so in conjunction with social functions that have grown more differentiated, and with chains of organized social action, whether military or economic, that have lengthened. Each time, the network of dependencies intersecting in the individual has grown larger and changed in structure; and each time, in exact correspondence to this structure, the moulding of behaviour and of the whole emotional life, the personality structure, is also changed. The "civilizing" process, seen from the aspects of standards of conduct and drive control, is the same trend which, when seen from the point of view of human relationships, appears as the process of advancing integration, increased differentiation of social functions and interdependence, and the formation of ever-larger units of integration on whose fortunes and movements the individual depends, whether he knows it or not.

It was attempted here to complement the general account of the earliest and least complicated phase of this movement with some illustrative factual evidence; next the further progress of this movement and the mechanisms driving it will be examined. It has been shown how and why, in the early phase of Western history which had a predominantly barter economy, integration and the establishment of stable governments over large empires had little chance. Conquering kings can, it is true, subjugate huge areas through battle and hold them together for a time by respect for their sword. But the structure of society does not yet permit the creation of an apparatus for ruling sufficiently stable to administrate and hold together the empire by relatively peaceful means over long periods of peacetime.

It remains to be shown what social processes make possible the formation of such a more stable government and with it a quite different bonding of individuals.

In the ninth and tenth centuries when, at least in the western Frankish regions, the external threat was small—and when economic integration was slight—the disintegration of the ruler-function reaches extraordinary heights. Each small estate is under its own rule, a "state" in itself, every small knight its independent lord and master. The social landscape comprises a chaotic multitude of governmental and economic units. Each of them is essentially autarkic with little dependence on others, with the exception of a few enclaves—foreign traders, for example, or monasteries and abbeys—which sometimes have links beyond the local level. In the secular ruling stratum integration through aggressive or defensive conflict is the fundamental form. There is not much to constrain members of this ruling stratum to control their affects in any continuous way. This is a "society" in the broader sense of the word which refers to every possible form of human integration. It is not yet a "society" in the narrower sense of a more continuous, relatively close and uniform integration of people with a greater constraint on violence, at least within its confines. The early form of such a "society" in the narrower sense slowly emerges at the great feudal courts. Here, where there is a larger confluence of goods, owing to the amounts produced and the attachment of these courts to the trade network, and where more people congregate in search of service, a sizeable number of people is obliged to maintain a constantly peaceful intercourse. This demands, particularly towards women of higher rank, a certain control and restraint of behaviour, a more precise moulding of affects and manners.

38. This restraint may not always have been as great as it was in the relation of singer to lady in the *minnesang* convention. The *courtois* precepts on manners give a more accurate picture of the standard of behaviour demanded in everyday life. They also occasionally throw light on the conduct of knights towards women that is not confined to the relation of the minstrel to the lady of the court.

We read in a "motto for men",[72] for example: "Above all, take care to behave well towards women. . . . If a lady asks you to sit beside her, do not sit on her dress, or too near her, and if you wish to speak softly to her, never clutch her with your arms, whatever you have to say."

Judging by the habitual standards of the lesser knights, this amount of consideration for women may have demanded considerable effort. But the restraint is slight, like that in other *courtois* precepts, in comparison to what became customary among courtiers at the court of Louis XIV, for example. This gives an idea of the different levels of interdependence and integration that shape the individual's habits in the two phases. But it also shows that *courtoisie* was indeed a step on the path that leads finally to our own affective and emotional mould, a step in the direction of "civilization".

On the one hand, a loosely integrated secular upper class of warriors, with its symbol, the castle on the autarkic estate; on the other, the more tightly integrated secular upper class of courtiers assembled at the absolutist court, the central organ of the kingdom: these are in a sense the two poles of the field of observation which has been isolated from the far longer and broader movement in order to gain initial access to the sociogenesis of civilizing change. The slow emergence from the castle landscape of the greater feudal courts, the centres of courtoisie, has been shown from a number of aspects. It remains to demonstrate the basic dynamics of the processes by which *one* of the great feudal or territorial lords, the king, gained preponderance over the others, and the opportunity to control a more stable government over a region embracing many territories, a "state". This is also the path that leads from the standard of conduct of *courtoisie* to that of *civilité*.

Chapter Two

On the Sociogenesis of the State

I

The First Stage of the Rising Monarchy: Competition and Monopolization within a Territorial Framework

1. The crown signifies very different things in different phases of social development, even though all its wearers have in common certain actual or nominal central functions, above all that of military leader against external enemies.

At the beginning of the twelfth century the former western Frankish empire, hardly threatened any more by strong external foes, has finally decayed into a collection of discrete dominions:

> The bond that formerly united the "provinces" and the feudal dynasties with the monarchy, is as good as completely ruptured. The last traces of real dominance that permitted Hugh Capet and his son, if not to act in the large regions controlled by his vassals, then at least to appear in them, have disappeared. The feudal groups of the first rank . . . conduct themselves like independent states impervious to the king's influence and more so to his actions. The relations between the great feudal lords and the monarchs are reduced to a minimum. This change is reflected even in the official titles.

The feudal princes of the twelfth century cease calling themselves "comtes du Roi" or "comtes du royaume".[73]

In this situation the "king" does what other great feudal lords do: he concentrates on consolidating his own possessions, increasing his power in the only region still open to him, the duchy of Francia.

Louis VI, king from 1108 to 1137, was preoccupied throughout his life with two tasks: to increase his own direct land ownership within the duchy of Francia—the estates and castles not yet, or only partly, enfeoffed, i.e., his own family property—and, within the same area, to subdue all possible rivals, every warrior who might equal him in power. One task assists the other: from the feudal lords he has subdued or conquered he takes all or part of their property without enfeoffing it to anyone else; thus by small steps he increases his family possessions, the economic and military basis of his power.

2. In this the monarch is, to begin with, no different from a great feudal lord. The means of power at his disposal are so small that medium and even lesser feudal lords—in alliance—can successfully oppose him. Not only has the preponderance of the royal house in the whole kingdom vanished with the decline of his function as the common army leader, and with advancing feudalization; even his monopoly power within his own hereditary territory has become extremely precarious. It is disputed by rival lords or warrior families. In the person of Louis VI, the Capetian house struggles against the houses of Montmorency, Beaumont, Rochefort, Montlhéry, Ferté-Alais, Puiset and many others,[74] just as centuries later the Hohenzollerns in the person of the Great Elector have to contend with the Quitzows and the Rochows. Only the Capetians had much less chance of success. The difference between the military and financial means of the Capetians and their opponents was smaller, given the less developed state of money, taxation and military technique. The Great Elector had already a kind of monopoly control of power within his territory. Louis VI was, leaving aside his support from the ecclesiastical institutions, essentially a great landowner who had to contend with lords with somewhat smaller possessions and military power; and only the victor of these battles could attain a kind of monopoly position within the territory, beyond the competition of other houses.

Only from reading contemporary reports can we judge by how little the military and economic means of the Capetians in this period surpassed those of other feudal houses in the duchy of Francia; and how difficult, given the low degree of economic integration, undeveloped transportation and communications, and the limitations of feudal military organization, was the "sovereign's" struggle for monopoly power even within this small area.

For example, there is the fortress of the Montlhéry family commanding the route between the two most important parts of the Capetian domain, the areas around Paris and Orléans. In 1015 the Capetian king Robert had given this land to one of his servants or officials, the "grand forestier", with permission to build a castle on it. From this castle the "grand forestier's" grandson already controlled the surrounding area as an independent lord. This is a typical example of the centrifugal movements that are taking place everywhere in this period.[75] After laborious struggles Louis VI's father finally manages to reach a kind of understanding with the Montlhérys; he marries a bastard son about ten years old to the Montlhéry heiress and thus brings the castle under the control of his house. Shortly before his death he says to his eldest son, Louis VI:

> Guard well that tower of Montlhéry, which by causing me so many torments has aged me before my time, and on account of which I have never enjoyed lasting peace or true repose . . . it was a centre for perfidious people from far and near and disorder came only through it or with its help . . . for . . . Montlhéry being situated between Corbeil on one hand and Châteaufort on the other, each time a conflict arose Paris was cut off, and communication between Paris and Orléans was impossible except by armed force.[76]

Problems of communications of the kind which play no small role between states today, were at that earlier stage of social development no less troublesome on a different scale: in the relations between one feudal lord—whether he wore a crown or not—and others, and in regard to the comparatively microscopic distance between Paris and Orléans: Montlhéry is twenty-four kilometres from Paris.

A good part of Louis VI's reign was taken up by fighting for this fortress, until he finally succeeded in adding Montlhéry to the Capetian possessions. As in all such cases, this meant a military strengthening and economic enrichment of the victorious house. The Montlhéry estate brought in an income of two hundred pounds—a handsome sum for those times—and belonging to it were thirteen direct fiefs and twenty indirect ones depending on these,[77] whose tenants now swelled the military power of the Capetians.

No less protracted and difficult were the other battles Louis VI had to fight. He needed three expeditions in 1111, 1112 and 1118, to break the power of a single knightly family in the Orléans district;[78] and it cost him twenty years to deal with the houses of Rochefort, Ferté-Alais and Puiset, and add their possessions to those of his family. By this time, however, the Capetian domain was so large and well-consolidated that, thanks to the economic and military advantages conferred by such large property, its owners had outstripped all other rivals in Francia, where they now took up a kind of monopoly position.

Four or five centuries later, the monarch has emerged as the monopoly controller of enormous military and financial means flowing from the whole area of the kingdom. Campaigns such as that of Louis VI against other feudal lords within the framework of one territory represent the first step on the way to this later monopoly position of the monarchy. At first the house of the nominal kings is scarcely superior to the feudal houses around it in terms of land ownership and military and economic power. The difference in property among warriors is relatively slight, as therefore is the social difference, no matter with what titles they adorn themselves. Then, through marriage, purchase or conquests, one of these houses accumulates more and more land and thus gains preponderance over its neighbours. The fact that it is the old royal house that succeeds in doing so in Francia may be bound up—apart from the never inconsiderable possessions that made its new start possible—with the personal qualities of its representatives, the support of the church, and a certain traditional prestige. But the same differentiation of property among warriors is taking place at the same time, as has been mentioned, in other territories too. It is the same shift in the centre of gravity of warrior society, favouring the few large knightly families at the expense of the many small and medium ones, that was discussed earlier. In each territory sooner or later one family succeeds, by accumulating land, in attaining a kind of hegemony. That the crown, that Louis the Fat should undertake the same thing looks like an abrogation of the royal function. But given this distribution of social power he has no choice. In this social structure, family property and control of the narrower hereditary area constitutes the most important military and financial basis of even the king's power. By concentrating his forces on the small area of Francia, by creating a hegemony in the restricted space of a territory, Louis VI lays the foundation for the subsequent expansion of his house. He creates a potential centre for the crystallization of the greater area of France, even though we may certainly not assume that he had any prophetic vision of this future. He acts under the direct compulsions of his actual situation. He *must* win Montlhéry if he is not to forfeit communication between parts of his own territory. He *must* subdue the most powerful family in the Orléans region if his power there is not to dwindle. Had the Capetians not succeeded in gaining preponderance in Francia, it would sooner or later—like the other provinces of France—have fallen to another house.

The mechanism leading to hegemony is always the same. In a similar way—through the accumulation of property—a small number of economic enterprises in more recent times slowly outstrip their rivals and compete with each other, until finally one or two of them control and dominate a particular branch of the economy as a monopoly. In a similar way—by accumulating land and thus enlarging their military and financial potential—states in recent times struggle for preponderance in a particular part of the world. But whereas in modern society, with its higher division of functions, this process takes place in a relatively complex way, with a differentiation of the economic and the military and political aspects of hegemony, in the society of Louis VI, with its predominantly barter economy, these aspects remained undivided. The house that rules a territory politically is at the same time by far the richest house in this territory, with the largest area of land; and its political power diminishes if its military power, stemming from the size of its domanial revenues and the number of its bondsmen and retainers, does not exceed that of all the other warrior families within its territory.

Once the preponderance of one house is fairly secure in this small region, the struggle for hegemony in a larger area moves into the foreground—the struggle between the few larger territorial lords for predominance within the kingdom. This is the task confronting the descendants of Louis VI, the next generations of Capetians.

II

Excursus on some Differences in the Paths of Development of England, France and Germany

1. The task implied in the struggle for dominance, i.e. for both centralization and rule, was for a very simple reason different in England and France from that in the German–Roman Empire. The latter formation was very different in size to the other two; geographical and social divergences within it were also much greater. This gave the local, centrifugal forces much greater energy, and made the task of attaining hegemony and thus centralization incomparably more difficult. The ruling house would have needed a far greater territorial area and power than in France or England to master the centrifugal forces of the German–Roman Empire and forge it into a durable whole. There is good reason to suppose that, given the level of division of labour and integration, and the military, transportational and administrative techniques of the time, the task of holding centrifugal tendencies in so vast an area permanently in check was probably insoluble.

2. The scale on which social processes take place is a not unimportant element of their structure. In enquiring why the centralization and integration of France and England was achieved so much earlier and more completely than in the German regions, we should not neglect this point. In this respect the trends of development in the three regions vary very widely.

When the crown of the western Frankish region falls to the Capetians, the area in which the house has real power extends from Paris to Senlis in the north and to Orléans in the south. Twenty-five years previously Otto I had been crowned Roman emperor in Rome. Resistance by other German chieftains he had ruthlessly put down, primarily supported, at first, by the experienced warriors of his own tribal area. At that time Otto's empire stretched roughly from Antwerp and Cambrai in the west, at least (i.e. without the margraviates east of the Elbe) as far as the Elbe, and beyond Brünn and Olmütz to the south-east; it stretched to Schleswig in the north and to Verona and Istria in the south; in addition it included a good part of Italy and for a time Burgundy. What we have here, therefore, is a formation on an entirely different scale, and consequently one fraught by far greater tensions and conflicts of interest, than the western Frankish area, even if we include in the latter the Norman–English colony acquired later. The task confronting the dukes of Francia and Normandy or of the Angevin territory as kings in the struggle for hegemony in this region, was entirely different to that with which every ruler of the German–Roman Empire had to contend. In the former area centralization or integration, despite numerous swerves to one side or the other, proceeded on the whole fairly continuously. In the latter incomparably larger area, one family of territorial rulers after another tried in vain to attain, with the imperial crown, a really stable hegemony over the whole empire. One house after another used up in this fruitless struggle what despite all else continued to be the central source of its income and power—their hereditary or domanial possessions. And after each unsuccessful bid by a new house, decentralization and the consolidation of centrifugal tendencies went a step further.

Shortly before the French monarchy gradually began to regain its strength in the person of Louis VI, the German–Roman Emperor Henry IV collapsed under the combined assaults of the great German territorial lords, the Church, the upper Italian cities and his elder son, that is to say, in face of the most diverse centrifugal forces. This provides a point of comparison with the early period of the French monarchy. Later, when the French King Francis I has his whole kingdom so completely in hand that he no longer needs to call assemblies of the estates and can raise taxes without asking the taxpayers, the Emperor Charles V and his administration have to negotiate even within his own hereditary lands with a whole multitude of local assemblies, before he can muster the duties needed to pay for the court, the army and the administration of the empire. And all this, including income from the overseas colonies, is not nearly enough to meet the cost of running the empire. When Charles V abdicates, the imperial administration is on the verge of bankruptcy. He too has exhausted and ruined himself in trying to rule such an enormous empire torn by such massive centrifugal forces. And it is an indication of the transformation of society in general, and of the royal function in particular, that the Habsburgs are nevertheless able to maintain themselves in power.

3. The mechanism of state-formation—in the modern sense of the word state—has been shown to be, in the European area at the time when society was moving from a barter economy to a money economy, in its main outlines always the same. It will be illustrated in more detail in relation to France. We always find, at least in the history of the great European states, an early phase in which units of the size of a territory play the decisive role within the area later to become a state. These are small, loosely structured dominions such as have arisen in many parts of the world where division of labour and integration are slight, their size corresponding to the limits placed on the organization of rule by the prevalence of

barter relationships in the economy. One example is the feudal territorial dominions within the German–Roman Empire which, with the advance of the money economy, are consolidated to form small kingdoms, duchies or counties; another are areas like the principality of Wales or the kingdom of Scotland, now merged with England in the United Kingdom of Great Britain and Northern Ireland; and a further example is the duchy of Francia, whose development into a more tightly knit feudal dominion has just been discussed.

In its schematic outline, the process taking place *between* the different neighbouring territorial dominions takes a very similar course to the one previously followed *within* a firmly established territory between the individual lords or knights, until one of them attained predominance and a rather more solid territorial dominion was formed. Just as, in one phase, a number of estates placed in competition experience the need to expand if they are not to be subjugated by expanding neighbours, so in the next a group of units one degree larger, duchies or counties, find themselves in the same predicament.

It has already been shown in some detail how, in this society, the internal competition for land is intensified with the growth of population, the consolidation of land-ownership and difficulties of external expansion. It was shown how this drive for land was exerted in the poor knights as a simple desire for a mode of living appropriate to their status, and in the highest and richest as a spur to demand "more" land. For in a society with such competitive pressures, he who does not gain "more" automatically becomes "less". Here again we see the effect of the pressure running through this society from top to bottom: it sets the territorial rulers against one another; and thereby sets the monopoly mechanism in motion. At first the divergences of power are contained, even in this phase, within a framework that allows a considerable number of feudal territorial dominions to remain in contention. Then, after many victories and defeats, some grow stronger through accumulating the means of power, while others are forced out of the struggle. The victorious few fight on and the process of elimination is repeated until finally the decision lies between only two territorial dominions swollen through the defeat and assimilation of others. All the rest—whether they were involved in the struggle or remained neutral—have been reduced by the growth of these two to figures of second or third rank, though they still retain a certain social importance. The other two, however, are approaching a monopoly position; they have outstripped the others; between them lies the issue.

In these "elimination contests", this process of social selection, the personal qualities of individuals and other "accidental" factors such as the late death of one man or a ruling house's lack of male heirs, undoubtedly play a crucial part from time to time in deciding *which* territory triumphs, rises and grows.

The social process itself, however, the fact *that* a society with numerous power and property units of relatively equal size, tends under strong competitive pressures towards an enlargement of a few units and finally towards monopoly, is largely independent of such accidents. They can have an accelerating or retarding effect on the process. But no matter who the monopolist is, that a monopoly will sooner or later be formed has a high degree of probability, at least in the social structures that have existed so far. In the language of exact science this observation would perhaps be called a "law". Strictly speaking, what we have is a relatively precise formulation of a quite simple social mechanism which, once set in motion, proceeds like clockwork. A human figuration in which a relatively large number of units, by virtue of the power at their disposal, are in competition, tends to deviate from this state of equilibrium (many balanced by many; relatively free competition) and to approach a different state in which fewer and fewer units are able to compete; in other words it approaches a situation in which *one* social unit attains through accumulation a monopoly of the contended power chances.

4. The general character of the monopoly mechanism will be discussed in more detail later. It seems necessary to point out at this stage, however, that a mechanism of this kind is at work in the formation of states too, just as it was earlier involved in the formation of the smaller units, the territories, or will be later in the formation of yet larger ones. Only if we have this mechanism in mind can we understand which factors in the history of different countries modify or even impede it. Only in this way can we see with some clarity why the task facing a potential central ruler of the Germano–Roman Empire was incomparably more difficult than that which faced a potential ruler of the western Frankish region. In this empire too, through elimination struggles and the constant accumulation of territory in the hands of the victors, a territorial dominion would have had to emerge strong enough to absorb or eliminate all others. Only in this way could this disparate empire have been centralized. And there was no lack of struggles tending in this direction, not only those between the Welfs and the Hohenstaufens but also between Emperor and Pope, with their special complications. But they all missed their mark. In an area as large and varied as this, the probability of a clearly dominant power emerging was very much less than in smaller areas, especially as at this stage economic integration was lower and effective distances were many times greater than later. In any case, elimination struggles within so large an area would need far longer than in the smaller neighbouring ones.

How, nevertheless, states finally managed to be formed in the Germano–Roman Empire is well known. Among the German territorial dominions—to disregard the analogous process in Italy—a house emerged which, above all through expansion into the German or semi-German colonial region, slowly came into competition with the older Habsburgs: the Hohenzollerns. A struggle for supremacy ensued, leading to victory for the Hohenzollerns, to the formation of an unambiguous supremacy among German territorial rulers and eventually, step by step, to the unification of the German territories under a single apparatus for ruling. But this struggle for supremacy between the two most powerful components of the empire, while leading to greater integration, to the formation of states within them, meant a further step towards the disintegration of the old empire. With their defeat the Habsburg lands left the union. This was in act one of the last stages of the slow and continuous decay of the empire. In the course of centuries more and more parts have crumbled away to become independent dominions. As a whole, the empire was too large and diverse to be other than a hindrance to state-formation.

To reflect on why state-formation in the Germano–Roman Empire was so much more laborious and belated than in its western neighbours certainly helps understanding of the twentieth century. Modern experience of the difference between the longer-established, better balanced and more fully expanded western states, and the recently established states descended from the old empire, states which expanded comparatively late, gives this question topical importance. From a structural point of view it does not seem difficult to answer, at any rate not more so than the complementary question which is scarcely less important for an understanding of historical structures—the question why this colossus, despite its unfavourable structure and unavoidable strength of centrifugal forces within it, held together so long, why the Empire did not founder earlier.

5. As a totality, it did indeed collapse late; but for centuries border areas of the empire—particularly to the west and south—had been crumbling away and going their own way, while incessant colonization and expansion of German settlements in the east to some extent compensated the losses in the west, though only to some extent. Up to the late Middle Ages, and to an extent even later, the empire spread to the west as far as the Maas and the Rhône. If we disregard the irregularities and consider only the general trend of this movement, we have the impression of the empire's constant attrition and diminution, accompanied by a slow shift in the direction of expansion, and a drift of the centre of gravity from west to east. The task remains to demonstrate this trend more exactly than is possible here. But purely in terms of area, the trend is still visible in the most recent changes in German territory proper:

The German Confederation before 1866	630,098 sq. km.
Germany after 1870	540,484 sq. km.
Germany after 1918	471,000 sq. km.

In England, and in France too, the trend is almost the reverse. The traditional institutions first develop in relatively small and restricted areas and then extend their scope. The fate of the central institution, the structure and development of the whole government apparatus in these countries, cannot be understood or the difference between them and the corresponding formations in the states descended from the old empire explained, unless this simple factor, this slow growth from small to larger, is taken into account.

Compared to the Germano–Roman Empire, the island territory that the Norman Duke William conquered in 1066 was quite small. It reminds us roughly of Prussia under the first kings. It comprises, apart from small areas on the northern border with Scotland, present-day England, an area of about 131,764 square kilometres. Wales is only completely united with England at the end of the thirteenth century (England with Wales 151,130 sq. km.). Union with Scotland has existed only since 1603. Such figures are visible but very crude indications of structural differences. They remind us that the formation of the English nation, and then the British, took place within a framework which, compared to that of the great Continental nations, scarcely extended, in its decisive phase, beyond that of a territorial dominion. What William the Conqueror and his immediate successors built up was in fact nothing other than a large territory of the western Frankish empire, and not very different from those which existed at the same time in Francia, Aquitaine or Anjou. The task with which the struggle for supremacy confronted the territorial rulers of this area—through the sheer necessity of expanding to avoid domination by others—this task could not in any way be compared with that facing a potential central ruler of the Continental empire. This is true even of the first phase in which the island territory formed a kind of western Frankish colony, when its Norman or Angevin rulers also controlled considerable territories on the Continent and when they were therefore still struggling for supremacy in the western Frankish area. But it is true above all of the phase when they were thrown back on the island from the Continent, and had to unite it under one government on the basis of England alone. And if the royal function, like the relation of king to estates, took a different form here than in the Continental empire, one of the factors at work, though certainly not the only one, was the relative smallness and also, of course, the isolated position of the area to be united. The likelihood of major regional differentiation was very much less, and the struggle for supremacy between two rivals simpler than between the many factions in the empire. The English parliament, as far as its manner of formation and therefore its structure is concerned, is in no way comparable to the German Imperial Diet, but rather with the regional estates. Much the same is true of all the other institutions. They grow, like England itself, from smaller to larger; the institutions of a feudal territory evolve continuously into those of a state and an empire.

In the British Empire too, however, centrifugal forces immediately begin to act again as soon as territory has been united beyond a certain point. Even with present-day integration and communications this empire is proving dangerously large. Only very experienced and flexible government holds it together with great difficulty. Despite very different preconditions from those of the old German Empire, it still illustrates how a very large empire, brought together by conquest and colonization, finally tends to disintegrate into a number of more or less independent units, or at least to be transformed into a kind of "federal state". Seen thus at close quarters, the mechanism seems almost self-evident.

6. The native region of the Capetians, the duchy of Francia, was smaller than the English territory controlled by the Norman dukes. It was roughly the same size as the Electorate of Brandenburg at the time of the Hohenstaufens. But there, within the framework of the empire, it took five or six centuries for the small colonial area to become a power capable of confronting the old-established territories of the empire. Within the more limited framework of the western Frankish area, the power of such a territory, together with the material and spiritual help given by the Church to the Capetians, was enough to enable the house to begin the struggle for supremacy over larger areas of France at a very early stage.

The area left behind by the western Frankish empire, the basis of the later France, occupied a roughly midway position, as far as its size was concerned, between what was to become England and the Germano–Roman Empire. Regional divergences, and thus centrifugal forces, were less here than in the neighbouring empire and the task of the potential central ruler accordingly less difficult. But the divergences and attendant centrifugal forces were greater than on the British island.[79] In England, however, the very restrictedness of the territory facilitated, under certain circumstances, an alliance of the different estates and, above all, of warriors from the whole territory *against* the central ruler. Furthermore, William the Conqueror's distribution of land favoured contact and common interests among the land-owning class throughout the whole of England, at least as far as relationships to the central ruler were concerned. It remains to be shown how a certain degree of fragmentation and disparateness in a dominion, not enough to permit disintegration but enough to make a direct alliance of the estates throughout the country difficult, strengthens the position of the central ruler.

Thus the chances offered by the former western Frankish region in terms of its size, were not unfavourable to the emergence of a central ruler and the formation of monopoly power.

It remains to be seen in detail how the Capetians took advantage of these opportunities and, in general, by what mechanisms monopoly rule was established in this territory.

III

On the Monopoly Mechanism

1. The society of what we call the modern age is characterized, above all in the West, by a certain level of monopolization. Free use of military weapons is denied

the individual and reserved to a central authority of whatever kind,[80] and likewise the taxation of the property or income of individuals is concentrated in the hands of a central social authority. The financial means thus flowing into this central authority maintain its monopoly of military force, while this in turn maintains the monopoly of taxation. Neither has in any sense precedence over the other; they are two sides of the same monopoly. If one disappears the other automatically follows, though the monopoly rule may sometimes be shaken more strongly on one side than on the other.

Forerunners of such monopoly control of taxes and the army over relatively large territories have previously existed in societies with a less advanced division of functions, mainly as a result of military conquest. It takes a far advanced social division of functions before an enduring, specialized apparatus for administrating the monopoly can emerge. And only when this complex apparatus has evolved does the control over army and taxation take on its full monopoly character. Only then is the military and fiscal monopoly firmly established. From now on social conflicts are not concerned with removing monopoly rule but only with the question of who are to control it, from whom they are to be recruited and how the burdens and benefits of the monopoly are to be distributed. It is only with the emergence of this continuing monopoly of the central authority and this specialized apparatus for ruling that dominions take on the character of "states".

Within them a number of other monopolies crystallize around those already mentioned. But these two are and remain the key monopolies. If they decay, so do all the rest, and with them the "state".

2. The question at issue is how and why this monopoly structure arises.

In the society of the ninth, tenth and eleventh centuries it definitely does not yet exist. From the eleventh century—in the territory of the former western Frankish empire—we see it slowly crystallizing. At first each warrior who controls a piece of land exerts all the functions of rule; these are then gradually monopolized by a central ruler whose power is administered by specialists. Whenever he pleases, he wages wars to gain new land or defend his own. Land-acquisition and the governmental functions going with its possession are, like its military defence, left to "private initiative", to use the language of a later age. And since, with the increasing population of the area, hunger for land is extremely keen, competition for it throughout the country is rife. In this competition both military and economic means are used, in contrast to that of the nineteenth century, for example, which, given the state monopoly of physical violence, is waged solely by economic means.

A reminder of the competitive struggles and the monopolization taking place directly under our own eyes is not without value for an understanding of monopoly mechanisms in earlier stages of society. In addition, consideration of the old in conjunction with the new helps us to see this social development as a whole. The later part of the movement presupposes the earlier, and the centre of both is the accumulation of the most important means of production of the time, or at least control over it, in fewer and fewer hands—earlier the accumulation of land, later that of money.

The mechanism of monopoly formation has already been briefly discussed:[81] in, *in a major social unit*,—so the mechanism may be roughly summarized—*a large number of the smaller social units which, through their interdependence, constitute the larger one, are of roughly equal social power and are thus able to compete freely—unhampered by pre-existing monopolies—for the means to social power, i.e. primarily the means of subsistence and production, the probability is high that some will be victorious and others vanquished, and that gradually, as a result, fewer and fewer will control more and more opportunities, and more and more units will be eliminated from the competition, becoming directly or indirectly dependent on an ever-decreasing number.* The human figuration caught up in this movement will therefore, unless countervailing measures are taken, approach a state in which all opportunities are controlled by a single authority: a system with open opportunities has become a system with closed opportunities.[82]

The general pattern followed by this sequence is very simple: in a social area there are a certain number of people and a certain number of opportunities which are scarce or insufficient in relation to the needs of the people. If we assume that to begin with each of the people in this area fights one other for the available opportunities, the probability that they will maintain this state of equilibrium indefinitely and that no partner will triumph in any of these pairs is extremely small, if this is indeed a free competition uninfluenced by any monopoly power; and the probability that sooner or later individual contestants will overcome their opponents is extremely high. But if some of the contenders are victorious, their opportunities multiply; those of the vanquished decrease. Greater opportunities accumulate in the hands of one group of the original rivals, the others being eliminated from direct competition with them. Assuming that each of the victors now struggles with the others, the process is repeated: once again one group is victorious and gains control of the power chances of the vanquished; a still smaller number of people controls a still greater number of power chances; a still greater number of people are eliminated from the free competition; and the process is repeated until finally, in the extreme case, one individual controls all power chances and all the others are dependent on him.

In historical reality it is certainly not always individual people who become embroiled in this mechanism; frequently it is large associations of people, for example territories or states. The course of events in reality is usually far more complicated than in this schematic pattern, and full of variations. It often happens, for example, that a number of weaker parties combine to bring down an individual who has accumulated too many possibilities and grown too strong. Should they succeed and take over the possibilities of this party, or some of them, they then fight among themselves for predominance. The effect, the shift in power balances, is always the same. In this way, too, an ever-increasing number of power chances tend to accumulate in the hands of an ever-diminishing number of people through a series of elimination contests.

The course and pace of this shift in favour of the few at the expense of the many depend to a large extent on the relation between the supply and demand of opportunities. If we assume that the level of demand and the number of opportunities remain unchanged overall in the course of the movement, the demand for opportunities will increase with the shift in the power relations; the number of the dependents and the degree of their dependence will increase and change in kind. If relatively independent social functions are increasingly replaced by dependent ones in society—for example, free knights by courtly knights and finally courtiers, or relatively independent merchants by dependent merchants and employees—the moulding of affects, the structure of drives and consciousness, in short the whole social personality structure and the social attitudes of people are necessarily changed at the same time. And this applies no less to those who are approaching a monopoly position than to those who have lost the possibility to compete and fallen into direct or indirect dependence.

3. For this process should in no way be understood merely as one whereby fewer and fewer people become "free" and more and more "unfree", although in some phases it appears to answer this description. If the movement is viewed as a whole, we can recognize without difficulty that—at least in highly differentiated societies—dependence undergoes a peculiar qualitative change at a certain stage of the process. The more people are made dependent by the monopoly mechanism, the greater becomes the power of the dependent, not only individually but also collectively, in relation to the one or more monopolists. This happens not only because of the small number of those approaching the monopoly position, but because of their own dependence on ever more dependents in preserving and exploiting the power potential they have monopolized. Whether it is a question of land, soldiers or money in any form, the more that is accumulated by an individual, the less easily can it be supervised by this individual, and the more surely he becomes by his very monopoly dependent on increasing numbers of others, the more he becomes dependent on his dependents. Such changes in power and dependence relationships often take centuries to become perceptible, and centuries more to find expression in lasting institutions. Particular structural properties of society may place endless obstacles in the way of the process, yet its mechanism and trend are unmistakable. The more comprehensive the monopolized power potential, the larger the web of functionaries administering it and the greater the division of labour among them; in short, the more people on whose work or function the monopoly is in any way dependent, the more strongly does this whole field controlled by the monopolist assert its own weight and its own inner regularities. The monopoly ruler can acknowledge this and impose on himself the restraints that his function as the

central ruler of so mighty a formation demands; or he can indulge himself and give his own inclinations precedence over all others. In the latter case the complex social apparatus which has developed along with this private accumulation of power chances will sooner or later lapse into disorder and make its resistance, its autonomous structure, all the more strongly felt. In other words, the more comprehensive a monopoly position becomes and the more highly developed its division of labour, the more clearly and certainly does it move towards a point at which its one or more monopoly rulers become the central functionaries of an apparatus composed of differentiated functions, more powerful than others, perhaps, but scarcely less dependent and fettered. This change may come about almost imperceptibly by small steps and struggles, or through whole groups of dependents asserting their social power over the monopoly rulers by force; in one way or another the power first won through the accumulation of chances in private struggles, tends, from a point marked by an optimal size of possessions, to slip away from the monopoly rulers into the hands of the dependents as a whole, or, to begin with, to groups of dependents, such as the monopoly administration. The privately owned monopoly in the hands of a single individual or family comes under the control of broader social strata, and transforms itself as the central organ of a state into a public monopoly.

The development of what we today call a "national economy" is an illustrative example of this process. The national economy develops from the "private economy" of feudal ruling houses. More precisely, there is at first no distinction between what are later opposed as "public" and "private" income and expenditure. The income of the central rulers derives primarily from their personal family or domanial possessions; expenses for the ruler's court, hunts, clothes or presents are met from this income in exactly the same way as the cost of the relatively small administration, paid soldiers if any, or the building of castles. Then, as more and more land comes together in the hands of one ruling house the management of income and expenditure, the administration and defence of his property become increasingly difficult for the individual to supervise. But even when the direct possessions of the ruling house, its domanial estate, are no longer by any means the most important source of the ruler's income, even when, with the increasing commercialization of society, duties from the whole country flow into the "chambers" of the central ruler and when, with the monopoly of force, the monopoly of land has become at the same time one of duties or taxes, even then the central ruler at first continues to control this revenue as if it were the personal income of his household. He can still decide how much of it should be spent on castles, presents, his kitchen and the court, and how much on keeping the troops and paying the administration. The distribution of the income from the monopolized resources is his prerogative. On closer examination, however, we find that the monopolist's freedom of decision is restricted more and more by the immense human web that his property has gradually become. His dependence on his administrative staff increases and, with it, the influence of the latter; the fixed costs of the monopoly apparatus constantly rise; and at the end of this development the absolute ruler with his apparently unrestricted power is, to an extraordinary degree, governed by and functionally dependent on, the society he rules. His absolute sovereignty is not simply a consequence of his monopoly control of opportunities, but the function of a particular structural peculiarity of society in this phase, of which more will be said later. But however that may be, even the budget of French absolutism still contains no distinction between the "private" and "public" expenditure of the king.

How the transformation into a public monopoly finally finds expression in the budget is well enough known. The wielder of central power, whatever title he may bear, is allocated a sum in the budget like any other functionary; from it the central ruler, king or president, meets the expenses of his household or court; expenditure necessary for the governmental organization of the country is strictly separated from that used by individuals for personal ends. Private monopoly rule has become public monopoly rule, even when in the hands of an individual as the functionary of society.

The same picture emerges if we trace the formation of the governmental apparatus as a whole. It grows out of what might be called the "private" court and domanial administration of the kings or princes. Practically all the organs of state government result from the differentiation of the functions of the royal household, sometimes with the assimilation of organs of autonomous local administration. When this governmental apparatus has finally become the public affair of the state, the household of the central ruler is at most one organ among others and finally hardly even that.

This is one of the most pronounced examples of the way in which private property becomes a public function, and the monopoly of an individual—won in contests of elimination and accumulation over several generations—is finally socialized.

It would take us too far afield to show here what is actually meant by saying that the "private" power of individuals over monopolized resources becomes "public", or "state", or "collective" power. As was said earlier, all these expressions have their full meaning only when applied to societies with extensive division of functions; only in such societies are the activities and functions of each individual directly or indirectly dependent on those of many others, and only here is the weight of these many intertwined actions and interests so great that even the few with monopoly control over immense possibilities cannot escape its pressure.

Social processes involving the monopoly mechanism are to be found in many societies, even those with relatively low division of functions and integration. There, too, every monopoly tends, from a certain degree of accumulation onwards, to escape the control of any single individual and to pass into that of entire social groups, frequently starting with the former government functionaries, the first servants of the monopolists. The process of feudalization is one example of this. It was shown earlier how, in the course of this process, control over relatively large territorial possessions and military power slips away from the monopoly ruler in successive waves, first to his former functionaries or their heirs, then to the warrior class as a whole with its own internal hierarchy. In societies with a lower degree of interdependence between social functions, this shift away from private monopoly control leads either to a kind of "anarchy", a more or less complete decay of the monopoly, or to its appropriation by an oligarchy instead of an individual dynasty. Later, such shifts in favour of the many do not lead to a disintegration of the monopoly, but only to a different form of control over it. Only in the course of a growing social interdependence of all functions does it become possible to wrest monopolies from arbitrary exploitation by a few without causing them to disintegrate. Wherever the division of functions is both high and increasing, the few who, in successive waves, claim monopoly power, sooner or later find themselves in difficulty, at a disadvantage in face of the many, through their need of their services and thus their functional dependence on them. The human web as a whole, with its increasing division of functions, has an inherent tendency that opposes increasingly strongly every private monopolization of resources. The tendency of monopolies, e.g. the monopoly of force or taxation, to turn from "private" into "public" or "state" monopolies, is nothing other than a function of social interdependence. A human web with high and increasing division of functions is impelled by its own collective weight towards a state of equilibrium where the distribution of the advantages and revenues from monopolized opportunities in favour of a few becomes impossible. If it seems self-evident to us today that certain monopolies, above all the key monopoly of government, are "public", held by the state, although this was by no means the case earlier, this marks a step in the same direction. It is entirely possible that obstructions may again and again be placed in the path of such a process by the particular conditions of a society; a particular example of such obstructions was shown earlier in the development of the old Germano–Roman Empire. And wherever a social web exceeds a certain size optimal for that particular monopoly formation, similar breakdowns will occur. But the impulsion of such a human web towards a quite definite structure, in which monopolies are administered to the advantage of the whole figuration, remains perceptible, no matter what factors may repeatedly intrude as countervailing mechanisms to arrest the process in recurrent situations of conflict.

Considered in general terms, therefore, the process of monopoly formation has a very clear structure. In it, free competition has a precisely definable place and a positive function: it is a struggle among many for resources not yet monopolized by any individual or small group. Each social monopoly is preceded by this kind of free elimination contest; each such contest tends towards monopoly.

As against this phase of free competition, monopoly formation means on one hand the closure of direct access to certain resources for increasing numbers of people, and on the other a progressive centralization of the control of these resources. By this centralization, such resources are placed outside the direct competition of the many; in the extreme case they are controlled by a single social entity. The latter, the monopolist, is never in a position to use the profit from his monopoly for himself alone, particularly in a society with a high division of functions. If he has enough social power, he may at first claim the overwhelming part of the monopoly profit for himself, and reward services with the minimum needed for life. But he is obliged, just because he depends on the services and functions of others, to allocate to others a large part of the resources he controls—and an increasingly large part, the larger his accumulated possessions become, and the greater his dependence on others. A new struggle over the allocation of these resources therefore arises among those who depend on them. But whereas in the preceding phase the competition was "free", that is, its outcome depended solely on who proved stronger or weaker at a given time, it now depends on the function or purpose for which the monopolist needs the individual to supervise his dominion. Free competition has been replaced by one that is controlled, or at any rate controllable, from a central position by human agents; and the qualities that promise success in this restricted competition, the selection it operates, the human types it produces, differ in the extreme from those in the preceding phase of free competition.

The difference between the situation of the free feudal nobility and that of the courtly nobility is an example of this. In the former, the social power of the individual house, a function of both its economic and military capacity and of the physical strength and skill of the individual, determines the allocation of resources; and in this free competition the direct use of force is indispensable. In the latter, the allocation of resources is finally determined by the man whose house or whose predecessors have emerged victoriously from the struggle by violence, so that he now possesses the monopoly of force. Owing to this monopoly, the direct use of force is now largely excluded from the competition among the nobility for the opportunities the prince has to allocate. The means of struggle have been refined or sublimated. The restraint of the affects imposed on the individual by his dependence on the monopoly ruler has increased. And individuals now waver between resistance to the compulsion to which they are subjected, hatred of their dependence and unfreedom, nostalgia for free knightly rivalry, on the one hand, and pride in the self-control they have acquired, or delight in the new possibilities of pleasure that it opens, on the other. In brief, this is a new spurt in the civilizing process.

The next step is the seizure of the monopolies of physical force and taxation, with all the other governmental monopolies based on them, by the bourgeoisie. The latter is at this stage a class which, in its totality, controls certain economic opportunities in the manner of an organized monopoly. But these opportunities are still so evenly spread among its members that relatively large numbers of them can compete freely. What this class is struggling with the princes for, and what it finally attains, is not the destruction of monopoly rule. The bourgeoisie do not aspire to re-allocate these monopolies of taxation and military and police power to their own individual members; their members do not want to become landowners each controlling his own military means and his own income from taxes. The existence of a monopoly for raising taxes and exerting physical violence is the basis of their own social existence; it is the precondition for the restriction to economic, non-violent means, of the free competition in which they are engaged with each other for certain economic opportunities.

What they are striving for in the struggle for monopoly rule, and what they finally attain is not, as noted before, a division of the existing monopolies but a different distribution of their burdens and benefits. That control of these monopolies now depends on a whole class instead of an absolute prince is a step in the direction just described; it is a step on that road which leads the opportunities given by this monopoly to be allocated less and less according to the personal favour and interests of individuals, but increasingly according to a more impersonal and precise plan in the interests of many interdependent associates, and finally in the interests of an entire interdependent human figuration.

In other words, through centralization and monopolization, opportunities that previously had to be won by individuals through military or economic force, can now become amenable to planning. From a certain point of development on, the struggle for monopolies no longer aims at their destruction; it is a struggle for control of their yields, for the plan according to which their burdens and benefits are to be divided up, in a word, for the keys to distribution. Distribution itself, the task of the monopoly ruler and administration, changes in this struggle from a relatively private to a public function. Its dependence on all the other functions of the interdependent human network emerges more and more clearly in organizational form. In this entire structure the central functionaries are, like everyone else, dependent. Permanent institutions to control them are formed by a greater or lesser portion of the people dependent on this monopoly apparatus; and control of the monopoly, the filling of its key positions, is itself no longer decided by the vicissitudes of "free" competition, but by regularly recurring elimination contests without force of arms, which are regulated by the monopoly apparatus, and thus by "unfree" competition. In other words, what we are accustomed to call a "democratic regime" is formed. This kind of regime is not—as the mere view of certain economic monopoly processes of our time might make it appear—incompatible with monopolies as such and dependent for its existence on the freest possible competition. On the contrary it presupposes highly organized monopolies, and it can only come into being or survive under certain conditions, in a very specific social structure at a very advanced stage of monopoly formation.

Two main phases can thus be distinguished in the dynamics of a monopoly mechanism, as far as we are at present able to judge. First, the phase of free competition or elimination contests, with a tendency for resources to be accumulated in fewer and fewer and finally in one pair of hands, the phase of monopoly formation; secondly, the phase in which control over the centralized and monopolized resources tends to pass from the hands of an individual to those of ever greater numbers, and finally to become a function of the interdependent human web as a whole, the phase in which a relatively "private" monopoly becomes a public one.

Signs of this second phase are not lacking even in societies with a relatively low division of functions. But, clearly, it can only attain its full development in societies with a very high and rising division of functions.

The overall movement can be reduced to a very simple formula. Its starting point is a situation where a whole class controls unorganized monopoly opportunities and where, accordingly, the distribution of these opportunities among the members of this class is decided by free competition and open force; it is then driven towards a situation where the control of monopoly opportunities and those dependent on them by one class, is centrally organized and secured by institutions; and where the distribution of the yields of monopoly follows a plan that is not exclusively governed by the interests of single individuals or single groups, but is oriented on the overall network of interdependencies binding all participating groups and individuals to each other and on its optimal functioning. For in the long run the subordination of the quest for the optimal functioning of the overall network of interdependencies to the optimation of sectional interests invariably defeats its own end.

So much for the general mechanism of competition and monopoly formation. This schematic generalization takes on its full significance only in conjunction with concrete facts; by them it must prove its worth.

When we talk of "free competition" and "monopoly formation" we usually have present-day facts in mind; we think first of all of a "free competition" for "economic" advantages waged by people or groups within a given framework of rules through the exertion of economic power, and in the course of which some gradually increase their control of economic advantages while destroying, subjecting or restricting the economic existence of others.

But these economic struggles of our day do not only lead before our eyes to a constant restriction of the scope for really "monopoly-free" competition and to the slow formation of monopolistic structures. As has already been indicated, they actually presuppose the secure existence of certain very advanced monopolies. Without the monopoly organization of physical violence and taxation, limited at present to national boundaries, the restriction of this struggle for "economic" advantages to the exertion of "economic" power, and the maintenance of its basic rules, would be impossible over any length of time even within individual states. In other words, the economic struggles and monopolies of modern times occupy a particular position within a larger historical context. And only in relation to this wider context do our general remarks on the mechanism of competition and monopoly take on their full meaning. Only if we bear in mind the sociogenesis of these firmly established "state" monopoly institutions—which during a phase of large—scale expansion and differentiation, no doubt open the "economic sphere" to unrestricted individual competition, and thus to new private monopoly formations—only then can we distinguish more clearly amidst the multitude of particular historical facts the interplay of social mechanisms, the ordered structure of such monopoly formations.

How did these "state" monopoly organizations come to be formed? What kind of struggles gave rise to them?

It must be enough here to follow these processes in the history of the country where they took their course most undeviatingly, and which, partly as a result of this, was for long periods the foremost power in Europe, setting the example for others: France. In so doing we must not shy away from details; otherwise our general model will never take on the wealth of experience without which it remains empty—just as wealth of experience remains chaotic to those unable to perceive order and structures within it.

IV

Early Struggles within the Framework of the Kingdom

1. Within the former western Frankish territory there was a very high probability, in accordance with the inherent tendency of the monopoly mechanism, that sooner or later one of the rival warrior houses would gain predominance and finally a monopoly position; and that in this way the many smaller feudal territories would be welded into a larger unit.

That it would be this particular house, the Capetians, who emerged as victors from the elimination struggles, so becoming the executors of the monopoly mechanism, was at first far less likely, even though a number of factors favouring this house can be readily discerned. It can be said that it was only the course of the Hundred Years' War that conclusively decided whether the descendants of the Capetians or of another house were to become the monopolists or central rulers of the emerging state.

It is not unimportant to bear in mind the difference between these two questions, between the general problem of monopoly and state formation, and the more specific question why this particular house won and retained hegemony. It is with the former rather than the latter that we have been concerned and are still concerned here.

The first shift towards monopoly after the general levelling of property relationships that carries on into the tenth and even the eleventh century, has been sketched above. It involves the formation of a monopoly within the framework of a territory. Within this small area the first elimination contests are fought, and in them the balance first moves in favour of a few and finally of a single contestant. One house—for a house or family is always the social unit that asserts itself, not an individual—wins so much land that the others can no longer match its military and economic strength. As long as there is a possibility of competing with it, the relationship of liege lord to vassal is more or less nominal. With this shift in social power it takes on a new reality. A new dependence of many houses on one is established, even though, in the absence of a highly developed central apparatus, it lacks both the continuity and strength that it later has in the framework of the absolutist regime.

It is characteristic of the rigour with which this monopoly mechanism operates that analogous processes are taking place at approximately the same time in practically all the territories of the western Frankish region. Louis VI, Duke of Francia and in name the King of the whole region, is, as we have pointed out, only the representative of this stage of monopoly formation.

2. If we look at a map of France in the period about 1032, we have a clear impression of the political fragmentation of the region into a multitude of greater and lesser territories.[83] What we have in front of us is certainly not yet the France we know. This emerging France, the former western Frankish region, is bordered to the south-east by the Rhône; Arles and Lyons lie outside it in the kingdom of Burgundy; also outside it to the north lies the region of present-day Toul, Bar le Duc and Verdun, which belong, like the areas around Aachen, Antwerp and, further north, Holland, to the kingdom of Lorraine. The traditional eastern and northern frontier of the former western Frankish region runs deep within present-day France. But neither this frontier of the nominal Capetian empire nor the borders of the smaller political units within it had at that time quite the same function or fixity as present-day state frontiers. Geographical divisions, river valleys and mountain ranges, together with linguistic differences and local traditions, gave the frontiers a certain stability. But as each region, large or small, is the possession of a warrior family, what primarily decides the composition of a territorial unit is the victories and defeats, the marriages, purchases and sales of this family; and the shifts in hegemony over a given area are considerable.

Going from south to north we first see, north of the county of Barcelona, that is, north of the Pyrenees, the duchy of Gascony extending to the region of Bordeaux and the county of Toulouse. Then, to mention only the larger units, come the duchy of Guyenne, i.e. Aquitaine, the county of Anjou, the seat of the second Franco–English royal house, the counties of Maine and Blois, the duchy of Normandy, seat of the first Franco–English royal house, the counties of Troyes, Vermandois and Flanders, and finally, between the Norman dominions—the counties of Blois, Troyes and others—the small domain of the Capetians, the duchy of Francia. It has already been emphasized that this small Capetian dominion did not constitute, any more than other territories, a complete unity in the geopolitical or military sense of the word. It was made up of two or three fairly large adjoining regions, the Isle de France, Berry and the Orléans regions, as well as scattered smaller possessions in Poitou, in the south, and in the most diverse parts of France, that had come into the possession of the Capetians in one way or another.[34]

3. In most of these territories at the time of Louis VI, therefore, a particular house has gained predominance over the others by accumulating land. Conflicts between these princely houses and the smaller nobility within the dominion are constantly flaring up, and tensions between them long remain perceptible.

But the chances of successful resistance by the smaller feudal houses are no longer great. Their dependence on the liege lord or territorial ruler of the time slowly becomes more evident in the course of the eleventh century. The monopoly position of the princely houses within their territories is now only seldom shaken. And what from now on characterizes society more and more is the struggle between these princely houses for predominance in a larger area. People are driven into these conflicts by the same compulsions as in the previous stage: when one neighbour grows larger and thus stronger, the other is threatened with being overpowered by him and made dependent; he must conquer in order not to be subjugated. And though to begin with crusades and wars of expansion to some extent reduce the internal pressure, this grows all the more intense once the chances of outward expansion have diminished. The mechanism of free competition operates from now on within a more confined circle, namely between those warrior families which have become the central houses of territories.

4. The Norman Duke's conquest of England was, as we have mentioned, one of the expansionist campaigns characteristic of this time, one among many. It too bore witness to the general hunger for land that afflicted the growing population, particularly the warriors, whether rich or poor.

But this enrichment of the Norman Duke, this enlargement of his military and financial means, was a grave disturbance to the previous equilibrium between the territorial rulers of France. The full extent of the shift did not become immediately apparent; for the Conqueror needed time to organize his power within his new dominion, and even when this had been done the threat emanating from this aggrandizement of the Norman dukes to other territorial rulers, given the low integration of the western Frankish territories, first made itself felt only in the direct vicinity of Normandy, i.e. in northern France, rather than further south. Felt it was, however, and most directly by the house with the traditional claim to predominance in the area neighbouring Normandy to the east, the house of the dukes of Francia, the Capetians. It is not unlikely that the threat from his stronger neighbour was a powerful factor impelling Louis VI in the direction that he adhered to tenaciously and energetically throughout his life, his urge to consolidate his power and defeat any possible rival within his own territory.

That he, the nominal king and liege lord of the western Frankish region was in fact, in keeping with the size of his possessions, far weaker than his vassal and neighbour, who now as ruler of England likewise wore a crown, was apparent in every conflict between them.

William the Conqueror, because he had recently conquered this island territory, had had the chance to create what was for his time a fairly centralized governmental organization. He distributed the land in a manner intended as far as possible to prevent the formation of houses and families as rich and mighty as his own, that might become rivals. The administration of the English central ruler was the most advanced of its time; even for money revenues there was already a special office.

The army with which William had conquered the island consisted only in part of his feudal retainers, the rest being mercenary knights driven by the same desire for new lands. Only now, after the conquest, was the Norman ruler's treasury large enough to engage paid soldiers; and quite apart from the size of their feudal following, this too gave the island rulers military superiority over their Continental neighbours. Louis the Fat of Francia could not afford this any more than his predecessors. He had been accused of being covetous, seeking by every means at his disposal to take possession of money. In fact it was precisely at this time, as in many periods when money is relatively scarce and the disproportion between what is available and what is needed particularly keenly felt, that an urge or "greed" for money was particularly prominent. But Louis VI did indeed find himself in particularly difficult straits in face of his richer neighbour. In this respect, as in the question of organization, centralization and the elimination of possible internal rivals, the island territory set an example that Continental rulers had to follow if they were not to succumb in the struggle for supremacy.

At the beginning of the twelfth century, therefore, the Capetian house is noticeably weaker than its rival, which controls land and people across the sea. Louis VI is defeated in practically every battle with his English rival, even though the latter does not succeed in penetrating the territory of Francia itself. This is the situation in which the ruler of Francia confines himself to enlarging the basis of his power, his family property, and to breaking the resistance of the smaller feudal lords within or between his territories. In so doing he is preparing his house for that great struggle, for those centuries of conflict for supremacy in the former western Frankish region, in the course of which more and more territories grow together in a single bloc in the hands of a single house, and in which from now on all the other territories in the region and directly or indirectly involved—the struggle for the French crown between the rulers of the Isle de France and the rulers of the English island.

5. The house that takes up the struggle with the Capetians when William the Conqueror's family becomes extinct, is that of the Plantagenets. Their family dominion is Anjou,[85] likewise a region neighbouring Francia. They make their way upwards at about the same time as the Capetians, and in almost the same manner. As in Francia under Philip I, so in neighbouring Anjou under Foulque, the Counts' actual power in relation to their vassals has become very slight. Like Philip's son, Louis VI, the Fat, Foulque's son, Foulque the Young, and his son, Geoffroi Plantagenet, slowly subdue the smaller and medium-sized feudal lords in their domain; and they, too, thus lay the foundation for further expansion.

In England itself, at first, the reverse process takes place, showing the mechanisms of this warrior society from the other side. When Henry I, William of Conqueror's grandson, dies without male heirs, Étienne of Blois, the son of one of William's daughters, lays claim to the English throne. He gains the recognition of the secular feudal lords and the Church; but he is himself no more than a medium-sized, Norman feudal lord. His personal property, the family power on which he must depend, is limited. And thus he is fairly impotent in the face of the other warriors, and also the clergy, of his region. With his accession to the throne, a disintegration of governmental power on the island immediately sets in. The feudal lords build castle upon castle, mint their own money, levy taxes from their own regions; in short, they take over all the powers that hitherto, in keeping with their superior strength, had been a monopoly of the Norman central rulers. Furthermore Étienne of Blois commits a series of blunders, alienating the Church in particular, that a stronger man might perhaps have been able to afford, but not one needing the help of others. This helps his rivals.

These rivals are the counts of Anjou. Geoffroi Plantagenet has married the daughter of the last Norman–English king. And he has the power to back the claim he bases on this marriage. He slowly gains a foothold in Normandy. His son, Henry Plantagenet, unites Maine, Anjou, Touraine and Normandy under his rule. And with this power base he can undertake to reconquer the English dominions of his grandfather as the Norman Duke had done before him. In 1153 he crosses the Channel. In 1154, at the age of twenty-two, he becomes king, and a king who, by virtue both of his military and financial power, and of his personal energy and talent, becomes a strong centralizing force. Two years previously, moreover, he had become, through his marriage with the heiress of Aquitaine, the ruler of this region in southern France. He thus combines with his English lands a territory on the mainland beside which the Capetian domain appears small indeed. The question whether the western Frankish territories are to be integrated around the Isle de France or Anjou is wide open. England itself is conquered territory and to begin with an object of politics rather than a subject.[86] It is—if one will—a semi-colonial part of the loose federation of western Frankish territories.

The distribution of power at that time bears a distant resemblance to that currently existing in the Far East. A small island territory and a dominion many times its size on the Continent are under one rule. The whole southern part of the former Capetian realm belongs to it. The chief southern area not belonging to the Plantagenet dominions is the county of Barcelona. Its rulers are caught up in a similar expansionist movement and have become kings of Aragon, likewise on grounds of marriage. Slowly, and at first almost unnoticed, they disengage themselves from the union of western Frankish territories.

Also outside the Angevin–English dominion in the south—apart from a smaller clerical territory—is the county of Toulouse. Its rulers, like smaller lords north of the Aquitainian region, begin, in face of the threatening supremacy of the Angevin realm, to incline towards the rival power centre, the Capetians. The characteristic power balances which one encounters in figurations such as these tend to determine the conduct of people always in the same way; in the smaller sphere of the western Frankish territorial federation, their operation is little different from that determining the politics of states in modern Europe, for example, and even, incipiently, across the whole globe. As long as no absolutely dominant power has emerged, no power that has unequivocally outgrown all competition and taken up a monopoly position, units of the second rank seek to form a bloc against the one which, by uniting numerous regions, has come closest to the position of supremacy. The formation of one bloc provokes another; and however long this process may oscillate back and forth, the system as a whole tends to consolidate larger and larger regions about a centre, to concentrate real power of decision in ever fewer units and finally at a single centre.

The expansion of the Norman Duke created a bloc which displaced the balance in his favour at first in northern France. The expansion of the house of Anjou built on this and took a step further; the bloc of the Angevin realm called into question the equilibrium of the whole western Frankish region. However loosely connected this bloc may have been, however rudimentary the centralizing government within it, nevertheless the movement by which, under the pressure of the general hunger for land, one house constantly drove another to unite with it or to seek "more" land, manifests itself clearly enough in these formations. Apart from the south, a broad band comprising the whole of western France now belongs to the Plantagenets' dominion. Formerly the king of England was vassal to the Capetian kings on behalf of this mainland area. But "law" counts for little when it is not backed by corresponding social power.

When in 1177 Louis VI's successor, Louis VII of Francia, now an old and weary man, holds a meeting with the representative of the rival house, Henry II, the young King of England, he tells him:

Oh Sire, since the beginning of your reign and earlier you have heaped outrages upon me, trampling underfoot the loyalty you owed me and the homage you have done me; and of all these outrages the gravest and most flagrant is your unjust usurpation of Auvergne which you hold to the detriment of the French Crown. To be sure, old age is on my heels and robs me of the strength to recover this and other lands; but before God, before these Barons of the Realm and our loyal subjects, I publicly protest and uphold the rights of my Crown, most notably to Auvergne, Berry, and Chateauroux, Gisors and the Norman Vexin, beseeching the King of Kings who has given me an heir, to accord to him what he has denied to me.[87]

Vexin—a kind of Norman Alsace-Lorraine—was a contested borderland between the domain of the Capetians and the Norman dominion of the Plantagenets. Further south the frontier between the Capetian and Angevin dominions ran through the Berry region. The Plantagenets were clearly strong enough already to seize parts of the Capetian domain. The struggle for supremacy between Capetians and Plantagenets was in full spate; and the Angevin ruler was still far stronger than the ruler of Francia.

Accordingly, the demands the Capetian makes of his opponent are really very modest; he wants to be given back a few pieces of land that he counts among his own dominions. For the time being he can contemplate nothing more. The glory of the Angevin rule and the paucity of his own he realizes to the full. "We French," he once said, comparing himself with his rival, "have nothing but bread, wine and contentment."

6. But this manner of ruling did not yet possess great stability. It was in fact a "private enterprise"; as such it was subject to the inherent social dynamics of a struggle between freely competing units, which in any given case was much more strongly influenced by the personal capacities of the competitors—their age, their succession and similar personal factors—than were political formations of a later phase, when not only the person of the owner of the monopoly but a certain division of functions, a multiplicity of organized interests and a more stable governmental apparatus, held together larger units.

In 1189 a Capetian again confronts the Plantagenet. Almost all the contested areas have in the meantime been won back to Capetian rule. And now the Plantagenet is an old man, the Capetian younger; he is Louis VII's son, Philip II, surnamed Augustus. Age, as noted above, means much in a society where the incumbent of power is not yet able to delegate military leadership, where very much depends on his personal initiative and where he must attack or defend in person. Henry II, personally a strong ruler who still has the control of his large domains securely in his hands, is now plagued along with age by the rebellions and even the hatred of his eldest son Richard, surnamed Coeur-de-Lion, who sometimes even makes common cause against his father with the rival Capetians.

Exploiting the weakness of his adversary, Philip Augustus took back Auvergne and the parts of Berry mentioned by his father. One month after they faced each other at Tours, Henry II dies at the age of fifty-six.

In 1193—Richard the Lion Heart lies in prison—Philip seizes the long-contested Vexin. His ally is John, the younger brother of the prisoner.

In 1199 Richard dies. He, like his brother and successor John, who is soon to be John Lackland, have squandered much of the basis of their power, the family possessions and treasure of their father. Facing John as his rival, however, is a man who has felt to the quick the whole humiliation and constriction of Capetian power by the growth of the Angevin–English, and whose whole energy, stirred by this experience, is channelled in a single direction: more land, more power. More and yet more. He—like the first Plantagenet before him—is obsessed by this craving. When John Lackland enquires whether he might not have back some of the land lost to Philip for payment, Philip answers by asking if he does not know anyone else willing to sell land; he himself would rather buy more. And at this time Philip is already a man rich in land and power.

Clearly, this is not yet a struggle between states or nations. The whole history of the formation of later monopoly organizations, of nation states, remains incomprehensible until the special character of this preceding social phase of "private initiative" has been understood. This is a struggle between competing or rival houses which, following a general movement of this society, drive each other, first as small and then as larger and larger units, to expand and strive for more possessions.

The Battle of Bouvines in 1214 provisionally decides the issue. John of England and his allies are defeated by Philip Augustus. And as so often in feudal warrior society, defeat in an external battle means an internal weakening as well. Returning home John finds the barons and clergy in revolt, and their demand is the Magna Carta. Conversely, for Philip Augustus the victory in the foreign war strengthens his power within his dominion.

As his father's heir, Philip Augustus took over essentially the small inland district of Paris and Orléans, together with parts of Berry. He added—to mention only his major acquisitions—Normandy, then one of the largest and richest territories in the whole realm; the regions of Anjou, Maine and Touraine; important parts of Poitou and Saintonge; Artois, Valois, Vermandois; the region of Amiens and a large part of the region around Beauvais. "The lord of Paris and Orléans has become the greatest territorial lord in northern France."[88] He has made "the Capetian house the richest family in France".[89] His domain has gained outlets to the sea. In other territories of northern France, in Flanders, Champagne, Burgundy and Brittany, his influence is increasing in proportion to his power. And even in the south he already controls a not inconsiderable area.

This Capetian dominion is still anything but an integrated territory. Between Anjou and the Orléans region lies the domain of the Count of Blois. In the south the coastal districts around Saintes and, further east, Auvergne, are as yet scarcely connected to the northern regions. But the latter, the old family domain together with Normandy and newly conquered areas stretching beyond Arras to the north, constitute purely geographically a fairly self-contained bloc.

Even Philip Augustus did not yet have "France" in our sense in view, and his real dominion was not this France. What he aimed at above all was the territorial, military and economic expansion of his family power and the subjugation of its most dangerous competitors, the Plantagenets. In both these aims he succeeded. On Philip's death the Capetian dominions were roughly four times as large as at his accession. The Plantagenets, by contrast, who had lived hitherto more on the Continent than on the island—and whose administration in England itself was made up as much of Continental Normans and people from their other mainland possessions as of natives of the island—now controlled on the mainland merely a part of the former Aquitaine, the area north of the central and western Pyrenees along the coast as far as the Gironde estuary under the name of the duchy of Guyenne; apart from that there were a few islands in the Norman archipelago. The balance had shifted against them. Their power had decreased. But thanks to their island dominion it was not broken. After a time the balance on the mainland shifted back in their favour. The outcome of this struggle for hegemony in the former western Frankish area remained long undecided. It appears that Philip Augustus regarded as his chief rivals after the Plantagenets the counts of Flanders; and that a new power centre had indeed come into existence there is shown by the whole subsequent history of France. Philip is reputed to have once said that either Francia would become Flemish or Flanders French. He certainly did not lack awareness that in all these conflicts among the lesser territorial houses, what was at issue was supremacy or the loss of independence. But he could still imagine Flanders equally well as Francia as dominating the whole area.

7. Philip Augustus' successors at first hold firm to the course that he has set: they seek to consolidate and further extend the enlarged dominion. No sooner is Philip Augustus dead than the barons of Poitou turn back to the Plantagenets. Louis VIII, Philip Augustus' son, secures this region afresh for his own dominion, as he does Saintonge, Aunis and Languedoc, part of Picardy and the county of Perche. Partly in the form of a religious war, the struggle against the Albigensian heretics, the Capetian house begins to advance south into the sphere of the only great territorial lord in that part who could, beside the Plantagenets, rival the power of the Capetians, the domain of the counts of Toulouse.

The next Capetian, Louis IX, the Saint, has once again to protect his rapidly conglomerated possessions against every kind of internal and external attack. At the same time he goes on building, uniting parts of Languedoc north-east of the Pyrenees, the counties of Mâcon, Clermont and Mortain, and some smaller areas, with his family possessions. Philip III, the Bold, seizes the county of Guines between Calais and Saint-Omer, only to lose it twelve years later to the heirs of the Count. He acquires through purchase or promise of protection every minor possession in his vicinity that offers itself; and he prepares the assimilation of Champagne and the great territory of Toulouse into the dominions of his house.

There is by now in the whole western Frankish area scarcely a single territorial ruler who can, without allies, stand up to the Capetians, with the exception of the Plantagenets. The latter, to be sure, are no less preoccupied than the Capetians with enlarging their sphere of power. On the Continent their rule has once again extended beyond the duchy of Guyenne. Across the sea they have subdued Wales and are in the process of conquering Scotland. They still have possibilities of expansion that do not lead to a direct collision with the Capetians. The latter, too, still have scope for expansion in other directions. At the same time, under Philip the Fair, their dominion is expanding to the frontiers of the Germano–Roman Empire, on one side as far as the Maas, which at that time was usually considered as the natural and—in remembrance of the partition of the Carolingian Empire in 843—the traditional frontier of the western Frankish area; on the other side—further south—it extends as far as the Rhône and the Saône, that is, as far as the regions of Provence, Dauphiné and the county of Burgundy, which likewise do not belong to the traditional confederation of western Frankish territories. Through marriage Philip acquires Champagne and Brie with many annexed areas, some of them in the territory of the Germano–Roman Empire itself. From the Count of Flanders he obtains the dominions of Lille, Douai and Béthune; the county of Chartres and the estate of Beaugency he takes from the counts of Blois. In addition he acquires the counties of Marche and Angoulême, the ecclesiastical properties of Cahors, Mende and Puy, and further south the county of Bigorre and the viscounty of Soule.

His three sons, Louis X, Philip V and Charles IV, die one after the other without leaving a male heir; the family possessions and crown of the Capetians pass to a descendant of a younger son of the house who owns the county of Valois as an apanage.

Up to this point a continuous effort has been made in more or less the same direction throughout generations: to accumulate land. It must be enough here to summarize the results of this effort. Nonetheless, even this summary, even the mere naming of the many lands which step by step were brought together, gives an idea of the perpetual, open or concealed struggle in which the various princely houses were engaged, and in which one of these houses after another, conquered by one more powerful, disappears. Whether or not one fully realizes the meaning of these names, they give an impression of the strength of the impulse emanating from the social situation of the Capetian house, an impulse which passed in the same direction through such widely differing individuals.

At the death of Charles IV, the last Capetian who comes to the throne in direct succession, the great French Capetian dominions—i.e. the complex grouped directly around the duchy of Francia—extend from Normandy in the west to Champagne in the east and to Canche in the north; the Artois region, adjoining this to the north, has been given away as an apanage to a member of the family. Somewhat further south—separated by the apanaged region of Anjou—the county of Poitiers is part of the area directly controlled by the Paris princes; still further south the county of Toulouse belongs to them and parts of the former duchy of Aquitaine. All this already constitutes a mighty complex of lands; but it is not yet a cohesive region. It still has the typical appearance of a territorial family domain, the individual parts of which are held together less by their reciprocal dependence, or through any division of function, than by the person of the owner, through "personal union", and the common administrative centre. The separate identity of each region, the special interests and character of each territory, are still very strongly felt. However, their union under one and the same house and partly under the same administration, does remove a whole series of obstacles in the way of fuller integration. It corresponds to the tendency towards an extension of trade relations, the intensification of links beyond the local level, which is already discernible in small parts of the urban population, even though this tendency does not play remotely the same role as a driving force in the union or expansion of princely houses as it played later, in the nineteenth century, for example, at an entirely different stage in the development of urban bourgeois strata. Here, in the eleventh, twelfth and thirteenth centuries, the struggle for land, the rivalry between an ever-smaller number of warrior families, is the primary impulse behind the formation of larger territories. The initiative lies with the few rising warrior families, the princely houses; under their protection the towns and trade flourish. Both profit from the concentration of power; no doubt they also contribute to it, as will be discussed later. And quite certainly urban strata, once larger regions are united under one rule, play an important part in the consolidation of a territorial union even at this time. Without the help of the human and financial resources flowing to the princes from urban strata and growing commercialization, neither the expansion nor the governmental organization of these centuries would be conceivable. But the significance of towns and commercialization for the integration of larger areas is still mainly indirect, in so far as they are instruments or organs of the princely houses. This integration means first and foremost the conquest of one warrior house by another, that is, the absorption of one by another or at least its subjection, its dependence on the victor.

If the area is regarded from this point of view as it appears at the beginning of the fourteenth century at the extinction of the direct Capetian line, the direction of change is readily perceived. The struggle of lesser and medium warrior houses for land or more land has certainly not stopped; but these feuds no longer play remotely the part they played at the time of Louis VI, not to speak of his predecessors. At that time the lands were distributed relatively evenly among many; to be sure, there were differences between possessions which may have seemed very considerable to contemporaries. But even the possessions and thus the power of the nominal princely houses were so small that a large number of knightly families in their neighbourhood could try their arm with them as rivals for land or power. It was left to the "private initiative" of all these houses to decide how far they participated in this general struggle. Now, in the fourteenth century, these many warrior houses are no longer individually a force to be reckoned with; at most collectively, as a class, they carry a certain social weight. But the real initiative now lies with the very few warrior houses that have emerged for the time being as victors from the preceding conflicts, and have accumulated so much land that all the other houses can no longer challenge them, but act only in dependence on them. To these others, the majority of warriors, the possibility of winning new land on their own initiative in free competition is by and large foreclosed, and with it the chance of rising independently in society. Every warrior house must at most remain on the rung of the social ladder it has reached, unless one or other of its members succeeds in moving higher through the favour of one of the great lords, and thus through dependence on him.

The number of those who are still able to compete independently for land and power in the western Frankish region has steadily diminished. No independent duke or house of Normandy now exists and none of Aquitaine; assimilation or suppression have overtaken—to mention only the very largest—the counties of Champagne, Anjou and Toulouse. There now exist, beside the house of Francia, only four other houses that matter in this region: the duchies of Burgundy and Brittany, the county of Flanders and most powerful of all, the kings of England, dukes of Guyenne and lords of several smaller areas. A warrior society with relatively free competition has become a society where competition is restricted in the manner of a monopoly. And even out of the five great houses that still possess some degree of competitive power, and preserve a certain corresponding independence, two houses again rise as the most powerful, the Capetians and their succession, the kings of France, and the Plantagenets, kings of England. The confrontation between them must decide who will ultimately control monopoly power in the western Frankish region, and where the centre and the boundaries of the monopoly will lie.

V

The Resurgence of Centrifugal Tendencies: The Figuration of the Competing Princes

8. However, the formation of the monopoly of rule is not accomplished by any means as straightforwardly as appears merely from consideration of the accumulation of land. The larger the area becomes that is gradually united and centralized by the Capetians, the more strongly does a countervailing movement

make itself felt; and the stronger, once again, grows the tendency towards decentralization. This tendency is still represented first and foremost by the closest relations and vassals of the monopoly ruler, as in the preceding phase where the barter economy was more intact, and as in the Carolingian period. But the mode of action of the decentralizing social forces has changed considerably. Money, crafts and trade now play an appreciably greater role in society than at that time; groups who concern themselves specially with all this, the burgher class, have taken on a social importance of their own. Transport has developed. All this offers the ruling organization of a large territory opportunities that were lacking earlier. The servants a central ruler sends into the country to administrate and supervise his possessions no longer find it so easy to make themselves independent. Moreover, a growing proportion of these helpers of the central ruler now come from urban strata. The danger of such burghers developing into rivals of the ruler is incomparably less than before, when he had to take some of his aides from the warrior class, and when even bondsmen that he patronized could very rapidly acquire, thanks to the land with which he rewarded their services, the power and social rank of a warrior or noble.

However, a particular social category of people still poses a real threat to the cohesion of very large dominions under single rule, even though their power may have diminished and their mode of action changed. Even under the changed social circumstances, they become over and over again the chief exponents of decentralization. These are the closest family members of the ruler, that is, his uncles, his brothers, his sons or even, though far less so, his sisters or daughters.

A dominion and the monopoly of rule within it are not really, at this time, the possession of a single individual; they are very much a family possession, the property of a warrior house. All the closest relations of this house have and assert a claim to at least parts of this property. This is a claim which the head of the house is, for a long period, less willing or able to refuse, the larger the family possessions grow. It is certainly not a "legal claim" in the later sense of the word. In this society there are hardly more than the rudiments of a general, all-embracing "law" to which even the great warrior rulers are subject. For there is as yet no all-embracing power that could enforce such a law. It is only in conjunction with the formation of monopolies of rule, with the centralization of the ruling functions, that a common legal code is established for large areas. To provide for children is a social obligation that we often find set down in the "Coutumes". Undoubtedly it is only the better-endowed families that can adhere to this custom. For just this reason it carried prestige value. How could the richest house of the land, the royal house, have escaped this prestigious obligation?

The territorial possessions of a house continue to be, if in an increasingly restricted sense, what we would call private property. The head of the house controls it in just as unrestricted a fashion, and perhaps even more freely, than a great landowner controls his property today, or the head of a major family firm its capital, income and branches. Just as the landowner can split off one or other of his estates for the benefit of a younger son or the dowry of a daughter, without asking its tenants whether their new lord is agreeable to them; as the head of the firm can withdraw capital for his daughter's dowry or install his son as director of a subsidiary, without owing his employees the slightest explanation, in the same way the princes of that earlier phase disposed of villages, towns, estates and territories of their realm. And the impulse causing the owner of large properties to provide for his sons and daughters is more or less the same in all these cases. Quite apart from a ruler's possible preference for one of his younger children, to endow them in a fitting manner is necessary for the preservation and public display of the social status of a house; and—at least apparently, at least in a short-term view—it increases the house's chances of gaining power and permanence. That this splitting up of possessions and functions of rule for the benefit of relations very often precisely endangers the power and permanence of the house, is a fact which frequently only enters the consciousness of princes after long and painful experience. In France Louis XIV was really the first to draw the full and ultimate conclusion from such experience. With implacable severity he kept all family relations—even the heir to the throne, as far as this was possible at all—far from all ruling functions and independent positions of power.

9. At the beginning of this line of development, in that early phase when the family possessions of the Capetians were scarcely larger than those of many other warrior families in the land, the danger implicit in any fragmentation of this property is immediately obvious. The direct threat from neighbouring feudal families seldom abates. This causes each family to hold its people together as well as its property. No doubt there are quarrels, fights within the household as everywhere else. But at the same time, all or at least part of the family work constantly to defend or expand the family possessions. The relatively small estates of the royal family, like those of all warrior houses, are essentially autarkic; they lack any larger social importance and have indeed very much the character of a small family enterprise. The brothers and sons, even the mothers and wives of heads of families have a say in the running of the estate which varies with their personal qualities and circumstances. But it hardly occurs to anyone to sever any significant part from the family possessions and hand it over to a member of the family. The younger sons may receive a small estate here and there, or they may marry into a small property; but we also hear of one or other of the younger sons of a royal family leading a fairly penurious existence.

This changes completely as the royal house grows rich. Once the Capetians have become the richest family in the whole territory or indeed the entire country, it is impossible to let the younger sons of the house live like petty knights. The reputation of the royal house demands that all its members, even the younger sons and daughters of the king, receive a fitting endowment, that is to say a sizeable area over which to rule, and from which they can live. In addition, now that the Capetians far surpass most other families in the country in property and wealth, the danger from severing a portion from their possessions is no longer so keenly felt. And so the enlargement of the Capetian dominion is accompanied by the steadily increasing size of the areas passing as apanages to the younger children of the kings. Disintegration sets in on a new basis.

Louis VI, the Fat, gives his son Robert the not very extensive county of Dreux. Philip Augustus, who brought about the family's first great rise from straitened circumstances, holds together his hard-won possessions with a firm hand; the only thing he gives up is a small estate, St Riquier, as his sister's dowry.

Louis VIII, however, lays down in his will that the counties of Artois, Poitiers, Anjou and Maine, that is to say, considerable portions of the family possessions, though never its heartland, shall pass as apanages to his sons.

Louis IX gives his sons Alençon, Perche and Clermont as apanages; Philip III endows a younger son with the county of Valois. But Poitiers, Alençon and Perche return to the Capetian possession when their princely owners die without male heirs.

In 1285 five counties—Dreux, Artois, Anjou, Clermont and Valois—are split off as apanages, and on the death of Charles the Fair in 1328 the number rises to nine.

When Philip of Valois inherits the estates and crown of the Capetians, the apanages of his house, Valois, Anjou and Maine, are reunited with the larger possessions of the ruling family. The county of Chartres returns to the crown estates with the death of another Valois. Philip himself gains a few new smaller dominions as well, among them Montpellier, which he buys from the King of Majorca. Under him, however, it is above all Dauphiné that comes into Capetian hands. Thereby Capetian expansion takes a major step eastwards beyond the traditional frontiers of the western Frankish empire, into the former Lotharingian region—an expansion that Philip the Fair had begun by acquiring the archbishopric of Lyons and through a closer association with the bishoprics of Toul and Verdun.

The manner in which Dauphiné comes into the possession of the Parisian rulers, however, is less characteristic of the relation between the centralizing and decentralizing forces of this period than of the importance of apanages. Dauphiné belongs to the Arlesian or Burgundian realm that arose, following the Lotharingian interregnum, east of the Rhône and the Saône. Its last ruler, Hubert II, bequeathes or, more exactly, sells his possessions to the Capetian heir, following the death of his only son, on a number of conditions. They include the payment of his considerable debts, and also the stipulation that Philip's second son, not his eldest, shall receive Dauphiné. Clearly the Dauphiné's owner wishes to give his land to someone rich enough to pay the sums he needs; by bequeathing it to the ruler of Francia he protects it from becoming a bone of contention for other neighbours after his death, for the Paris kings are strong enough to defend their acquisitions. And this is certainly not the only example of the attraction which the immense power of the Capetians held for weaker neighbours; the need for protection of those less strong is one of the factors that furthers the process of centralization and monopolization once it has reached a certain level.

But at the same time the old ruler whose heir has died clearly wishes to prevent his land, Dauphiné, from losing its independence entirely on passing into French ownership. This is why he demands that his domain shall be given to the king's second son as apanage. This demand obviously implies an expectation that this region shall become a ruling house in its own right and so preserve an independent existence. At that time apanaged regions were indeed beginning to develop more and more clearly in that direction.

Philip of Valois, however, does not abide by this agreement. He gives Dauphiné not to his younger but to his eldest son, John, the heir to the throne, "in recognition", so his nomination declares, "that Dauphiné lies on the frontier, that a good and strong rule in Dauphiné is necessary for the defence and security of the Kingdom, and that if we acted otherwise, great danger to the future of the Kingdom might arise".[90] The danger attending the separation of districts for younger sons is thus fairly clearly perceived at this time; this is attested by a large number of pronouncements. But the need for the king to provide fittingly for his younger sons persists. He withheld Dauphiné from his younger son for security reasons; but in its place he gives him the Orléans region as a duchy and a number of counties as well.

And his eldest son, John the Good, the very man who receives Dauphiné in this way, goes a good deal further once he is king of the entire region on his father's death: he spreads bounty unstintingly. First he gives away two counties, then four viscounties. He endows his second son Louis with Anjou and Maine, his younger son receives the county of Poitiers, then Mâcon. Still larger gifts follow.

10. John the Good came to power in 1350. Under his predecessor, the long latent tension between the two largest powers and the two mightiest warrior houses in the western Frankish region had erupted; in 1337 began the chain of military conflicts known as the "Hundred Years' War". To the Plantagenets, the island rulers, all further expansion on the mainland is blocked; even their existing mainland possessions are under constant threat until they have destroyed Capetian rule and prevented the formation of another leading power on the Continent. Equally, further expansion by the Parisian rulers is very restricted and their position permanently threatened until the island-dwellers are subdued or at least expelled from the mainland. It is the strict compulsion of genuine competition which drives these houses and their dependents against one another, and which—since for a long time neither of the antagonists can decisively defeat the other—makes the struggle so protracted.

To begin with, however, the Paris kings are for a variety of reasons at a disadvantage. John the Good is captured by the English heir, the Prince of Wales, in the Battle of Poitiers in 1356 and sent to England. Immediately the tensions latent in his territory, now ruled as regent by the Dauphin Charles, who is not yet twenty years old, break out: revolution in Paris, peasant revolts, and knights plundering the countryside. The English troops, in alliance with another descendant of the Capetian house, the owner of previously apanaged regions, the King of Navarre, occupy large areas of western France; they even reach the vicinity of Paris. John the Good, to free himself, concludes a treaty with the Plantagenets and their allies handing over to them the whole inland area that Richard the Lion Heart had last controlled at the beginning of the twelfth century. But the States General of the French dominions, summoned in 1356 by the Dauphin, declare that this treaty should be neither approved nor carried out and that the only fitting answer is a well-fought war. And this is without doubt a clear expression of how strong interdependence has become within the great dominion of the Capetian heirs, of the autonomy and self-interest of the ruled that will slowly deprive the monarchy of its private monopoly character. At this stage, however, the development was only beginning. The war is begun anew and the Treaty of Brétigny, by which it is provisionally concluded in 1359, is somewhat more favourable to the Valois than the first concluded by John himself in England. Nevertheless roughly a quarter of what Philip the Fair had possessed has to be relinquished to the Plantagenets, above all Poitou, Saintonge, Aunis, Limousin, Périgord, Quercy, and Bigorre south of the Loire, together with a few other districts making up, with the older English possession Guyenne, the kingdom of Aquitaine; and further north Calais, the counties of Guines, Ponthieu and Montreuil-sur-Mer; in addition, three million golden crowns, instead of the four million demanded by the London treaty, as ransom for the king. But the latter, a worthy and chivalrous man, returns from prison clearly oblivious of the extent of his defeat. His conduct in this situation shows clearly to what extent he is still the sole authority in control of the territory remaining to him, which is one day to become "France", a state and a nation. He feels that his house must now all the more ostentatiously demonstrate its glory. The sense of inferiority resulting from defeat leads him to overemphasize his own prestige. And he considers that the dignity and glory of his house can find no better expression than by all his sons figuring as dukes at the ratification of the peace treaty. One of his first acts after his return from prison is therefore to make duchies from parts of his dominion as apanages for his sons. His eldest is already Duke of Normandy and Dauphin, the next, Louis, he makes Duke of Anjou and Maine; to the next, John, he gives Berry and Auvergne as his duchy; and to the youngest, Philip, Touraine. This is in the year 1360.

A year later, in 1361, the young, fifteen-year-old Duke of Burgundy dies. Two years previously he had married Margaret, the daughter and sole heir of the Count of Flanders; but he dies without leaving children. It is a large region that finds itself without a ruler on the unexpected death of the young Duke; it consists not only of the duchy of Burgundy proper, but also the counties of Boulogne and Auvergne, together with the county of Burgundy, the Franche-Comté and other areas beyond the traditional frontiers of the western Frankish empire. On grounds of somewhat complex family relationships, John the Good claims this whole estate for himself. There is no one to contest it with him and in 1363 he gives it to his youngest son Philip, whom he particularly loves; Philip fought especially bravely at his side in the Battle of Poitiers and accompanied him to prison. This is to be his apanage in place of Touraine, "we being mindful," says the King, "that we are enjoined by nature to give our children enough to allow them to honour the glory of their origin, and that we must be especially generous to those who have particularly merited it".[91]

Both the fact of these apanages and their motivation show unmistakably how far French territorial power still has the character of a family possession in this period; but they also show how this promotes fragmentation. No doubt strong tendencies are already operating in the opposite direction, tendencies restricting the private or domanial character of rule; the groups representing these opposed tendencies at the court will be discussed shortly. The personal character and individual fortunes of John the Good no doubt play a part in his particular propensity for richly endowing all the royal sons for the sake of family prestige. But this tendency clearly owes no less to the heightening of competition that found expression in the Hundred Years' War and which, after the Capetians' defeat, gives rise to a particularly insistent demonstration of the wealth of their heirs. At any rate, under John a specific tendency of large family possessions is merely reinforced, a tendency which, beyond a certain point of growth, none of the preceding representatives of the Capetian house had been able to resist. Its consequences are clear.

When John the Good dies, the existence and occupancy of the central function, despite the debilitation and the defeat, are in no way in doubt. This is an indication of how firmly the power of the central ruler was already founded on social functions other than that of army leader. The Dauphin, a physically weak man, but shrewd and experienced from the trials of his youth, assumes power under the name of Charles V. He is head of all the possessions left to the Capetians by the Treaty of Brétigny, including the apanaged ones. But looking closely at the distribution of power we can see clearly how, beneath the veil of the king's sovereignty, the centrifugal tendencies have gained renewed strength. Once again, a number of territorial formations emerge within the Capetian dominion that aspire more or less obviously to autonomy, and between which there is rivalry. But what gives this rivalry within the western Frankish region its special character is the fact that almost all those involved are descendants of the Capetian house itself. With few exceptions, it is apanaged men or their offspring who now face each other as potential competitors. There are, certainly, other major territorial rulers who are not members of the royal house, or at least not directly. But in the struggle for supremacy they are no longer protagonists of the first order.

The first of these at the time of John the Good is Charles the Bad, King of Navarre. His father, Philip of Evreux, was a grandson of Philip III, a nephew of Philip the Fair and of Charles of Valois; his mother was a granddaughter of Philip the Fair, a daughter of Louis X; in addition he himself is the son-in-law of John the Good. To him belong, besides the Pyrenean territory of Navarre, a number of previously apanaged regions from the Capetian possessions, above all the county of Evreux and parts of the duchy of Normandy. His possessions thus extend dangerously close to Paris itself.

Charles the Bad of Navarre is one of the first proponents of this struggle among apanaged family members of the Capetian house for supremacy in the western Frankish region, and ultimately for the crown. He is the chief mainland ally of the Plantagenets in the first phase of the Hundred Years' War. During this war he is for a time the military commander of Paris (1358); even the burghers of the city, even Étienne Marcel, is temporarily on his side; and his dream of wresting the crown from the other Capetian heir seems close to realization. To this end his membership of the King's family gives him an impetus, powers and claims that others lack.

The Plantagenet with whom he allies himself, Edward III, is likewise, though only from the female line of descent, a close relation of the Capetians. He too is a grandson of Philip III, a nephew of Philip the Fair and of Charles of Valois; his mother is a daughter of Philip the Fair, a niece of Charles of Valois, and he is thus at least as closely related to the Capetians as the French King opposing him, John the Good, the grandson of Charles of Valois.

Adjoining the mainland territory of the Plantagenets to the north are the regions that John the Good had given his younger sons, the territories of Louis, Duke of Anjou, John, Duke of Berry, and of Philip the Bold, Duke of Burgundy, together with the land of Louis, Duke of Bourbon. He, the Duke of Bourbon, is descended from the Capetians through a brother of Philip III, Robert, Count of Clermont, who married Beatrice, the heiress of Bourbon; his mother is a Valois, his sister the wife of Charles V; and he himself is thus on his mother's side an uncle of Charles VI, as the Dukes of Anjou, Burgundy and Berry are on the paternal side. These are the main actors in the struggles of the period of John the Good, Charles V and Charles VI. Apart from the Plantagenets and the Bourbons, they are all owners of apanaged parts of the Capetian inheritance, who are now on their side struggling to increase their family's power and finally to win supremacy.

The balance within these tensions first inclines, under Charles V, to the reigning Valois. When he dies, his son and successor is only twelve years old. Here, as always, circumstances—accidents from the point of view of the whole development—favour certain tendencies already inherent in the structure of society. The youth and weakness of the ruling Valois strengthens the centrifugal forces that have long been gathering, and releases the pent-up pressures.

Charles V had absorbed Dauphiné once and for all into his family possessions; he had recovered the Norman territories of the King of Navarre as well as a number of other apanaged lands like the duchy of Orléans and the county of Auxerre. But on his death there are already seven great feudal lords in the land, descended from St Louis and thus from the Capetian house; at the time they are called "princes des fleurs de lis"; and there are now—apart from a number of smaller and medium lords who have long ceased to play an independent part in the struggles for power[92]—only two major houses besides the Plantagenets whose members are not in direct male line of descent from the Capetian house, the dukes of Brittany and the counts of Flanders. But the Count of Flanders at this time has only one child, a daughter. For her hand and the future ownership of Flanders there arises, after the death of the young Duke of Burgundy to whom she was originally betrothed, an inevitable conflict between the Plantagenets and the Capetian heirs. After much vacillation the hand of the heiress of Flanders finally goes, with the help of the head of the Valois, Charles V, to the latter's younger brother Philip, who through his father's intervention has already become Duke of Burgundy. The marriages of great feudal lords were arranged from what we would today call a purely "business" point of view, for the sake of expansion and success in the territorial competition. Philip the Bold thus unites, after the death of the Count of Flanders, the latter's possessions with Burgundy; and of the great older feudal houses on the mainland only the duchy of Brittany remains. This older stratum, however, has now been replaced by a smaller circle of territorial rulers, stemming from offshoots of the Capetian house, and these are now driven into conflict by the mechanism of territorial competition. The compulsions which—owing to the low degree of integration or division of functions in any society with a barter economy, and particularly a warrior society—threaten the existence of a monopoly of power and possessions over large regions, tending to disintegrate property and reinforce centrifugal tendencies, have begun their work anew. Once again there occurs one of those shifts towards disintegration such as had led centuries earlier to the dissolution of the Carolingian dominions and then to the feudal social order of the twelfth century. Once again people to whom the central ruler has given land from his own large possessions, tend to make themselves independent and become rivals of the weakened central house. But the possibility of entering the competition is now limited to a few descendants of the original central house, a clear indication of how far the structure of human relations has changed in this society, how far this human network has already become, at least in its agrarian sector, a system with closed opportunities.

11. The rivalry between the most powerful "princes des fleurs de lis" erupts

immediately after the death of Charles V in the struggle for the regency and guardianship of the heir to the throne, who is still a minor. Charles V had appointed his brother Louis, Duke of Anjou, as regent, his brother Philip, Duke of Burgundy, and his brother-in-law Louis, Duke of Bourbon, as guardians of his son. This was clearly the only thing he could do to prevent power passing entirely into the hands of a single man. But it is precisely complete power that Louis of Anjou, and Philip as well, are really pursuing. They wish to unite guardianship and regency. And the conflicts between the rival members of the royal house fill the whole reign of Charles VI, who possesses little power of decision and finally succumbs to a kind of madness.

The leading figures in the struggle for supremacy among the King's relations change from time to time. The place of Louis of Anjou as the strongest rival of the Burgundian Duke, for example, is taken at a certain stage in the struggle by the younger brother of Charles VI, Louis, who rules the duchy of Orléans as his apanage. But no matter how the persons change, the network of compulsions impelling them remains the same: again and again two or three people within this, by now, very small circle of competitors come face to face, none of them prepared or able—on pain of annihilation—to allow any of the others to become stronger than himself. These conflicts between relations of the King, however, necessarily become intertwined with the larger conflict of the time, which is still very far from being decided—the struggle with the Plantagenets, whose offshoots likewise become embroiled in similar rivalries by reason of analogous mechanisms.

The situation of these members of the royal house must be visualized: all their life they are second or third. Their feelings tell them often enough that they might be better and stronger monarchs than the man who happens to be the legitimate heir to the crown and the main possessions. Between them and their goal stands often only one person, often only two or three. And there is no lack of examples in history of two or more such people dying in quick succession, opening the way to power to the next in line. But even then, there are often to be hard struggles with their rivals. In this situation the less powerful man hardly ever attains the throne if he belongs to only a secondary line of the family, though he may have the best claim. There are nearly always others who contest his claim; their claim may be worse but they will win if they are stronger. So those next in line to the throne, who already rule apanaged territories of various sizes, are preoccupied with creating and extending their basis of support, increasing their possessions, their income, their power. If they have no direct access to the throne, their rule shall be at least no less rich, mighty and ostentatious than that of their rivals, if possible outshining even the King's, who after all is no more than the greatest among all the rivals or competitors.

This is the situation and attitude of the closest relations of the weak Charles VI, his uncles—not all, but some of them—and also his brother. And with certain changes, with ever-diminishing chances for the second and third in line, this attitude, this situation, these tensions around the throne are transmitted through individuals of the most diverse talents, down to the time when, with Henry of Navarre, a relatively small territorial ruler for the last time becomes King of France; and as we have said, traces of these tendencies are to be found right up to the time of Louis XIV.

The strongest contestant among the *"princes des fleurs de lis"* is Philip the Bold, the youngest son of John the Good. To begin with he has only the duchy of Burgundy as his apanage. Then he unites with it—primarily through his marriage—the counties of Flanders, the Artois region, the county of Nevers and the barony of Doncy. His second son Antoine, Duke of Brabant and Lord of Antwerp, becomes by marriage Duke of Luxembourg. His son marries the heiress of Hainaut. These are the first steps of the Burgundian lords towards expansion in their own right, towards the foundation of a secure realm lying at least in part outside the sphere of the Paris kings, in the territory of present-day Holland.

A similar course of action is adopted by Charles VI's brother, Louis, the strongest rival of Philip the Bold in the struggle for supremacy in France. Both build with considerable haste and determination on their own family power. Louis first receives as apanage the duchy of Orléans, which under Charles V, after the death of his uncle, Philip V of Orléans, had been reunited with the crown possessions.

Then Louis obtains three or four counties and large estates in Champagne. He further acquires by purchase—with the aid of a large dowry from his wife Valentina Visconti—several counties including that of Blois. Finally, through his wife, he owns the county of Asti in Italian territory, and he has the reversion of a number of other Italian territories. The Burgundian expands in the direction of Holland, the Orléans into Italy. Within the former western Frankish territory itself, relations of ownership have been consolidated; the major parts of this region belong either to the London or to the Paris kings; and between them even a "prince des fleurs de lis" can only assert himself, only compete with one or other for supremacy, if he manages in one direction or another to build up a large domestic power of his own. As the earlier elimination struggles within the large area of post-Carolingian feudality had done previously, so now analogous tensions impel members of the far narrower circle of the great Capetian territorial lords to expand their land, to crave incessantly for more possessions. But as means to expansion, marriage, inheritance and purchase now play at least as important a part as war and feud. It is not only the Habsburgs who marry into greatness. Since relatively large property units with correspondingly great military potential have by now formed in this society, individuals, and individual warrior houses who want to rise at this stage, can only hope to survive a military confrontation if they have already gained control over territorial possessions which make them militarily competitive. And this too shows, therefore, how sharply the possibilities of competing in the sphere of major territorial ownership have diminished in this phase, and how the structure of tensions between people necessarily gives rise to the formation of monopolies of rule in regions above a certain order of size.

The Franco–English area at this time is still an interdependent territorial system. Every change in social power to the advantage or disadvantage of one of the rival houses, sooner or later affects the others and thus the equilibrium of the whole system. At any given time one can say with considerable accuracy where the central and where the less central tensions lie; the balance of power and its dynamics, its developmental curve, can be traced fairly precisely. And thus the Hundred Years' War is to be considered not only as the military encounters of a number of ambitious individual princes—although it is that too—but as one of the inevitable discharges within a tension-laden society consisting of territorial possessions of a certain size, as the competitive struggles between rival houses within an interdependent system of dominions with a very unstable equilibrium. The houses of Paris and London, gradually represented by two offshoots of the earlier royal houses, Valois and Lancaster, are, through the size of their possessions and military potential, the two main rivals. Sometimes the aspirations at least of the London rulers—occasionally even those in Paris—go as far as the wish to unite the whole western Frankish area, the mainland territories and the extended island realm, under one rule. Only in the course of these struggles themselves does it become unmistakably clear how great, at this stage of social development, are the resistances to the military conquest, and above all the subsequent internal cohesion, of so large and disparate a territory under the same rule and the same governmental machinery. The question may be raised whether, at this stage of social development, the creation of a central monopoly and the permanent integration of mainland and island territories under London rule would have been possible even if the Valois had been completely defeated by the island kings and their allies. However that may be, it is at any rate the houses of Paris and London that primarily compete for supremacy in the same area, and all the other competitive tensions within this area, above all those between the different branches of the Paris house itself, crystallize about this main tension of the whole territorial system; thus the Burgundian Valois, for example, stand now on one side of this central struggle, now on the other.

But the growth of the division of functions, and of interdependence beyond the local level, not only brings the different units of the enlarged western Frankish territorial society closer together as friend and foe. Less obviously, but unmistakably nevertheless, interdependencies and shifts in the territorial balance begin at this time to be discernible over the larger area of western Europe as a whole. The Franco–English territorial society gradually becomes, in the course of this growing integration, more and more a partial system within the encompassing European one. In the Hundred Years' War this growing interdependence within larger areas, which doubtless was never entirely absent, manifests itself clearly. German and Italian princes already engage their interests and power in the struggle within the Anglo–French sector, even though they as yet play only a peripheral role. This is the first sign of what was to show itself much more fully a few centuries later in the Thirty Years' War; the European Continent as a whole begins to become an interdependent system of countries with its own dynamic equilibrium, within which each shift of power directly or indirectly involves every unit, every country. A few further centuries on, in the 1914–18 war, the first "World War" as it has been called, we can see early signs of how tensions and shifts of balance within the same ever-advancing process of integration now affect units over a far wider area, countries in distant parts of the world. The nature and stages of the monopolization towards which the tensions of this worldwide interweaving are moving, like their possible outcome, the larger units of rule that may arise out of these struggles—all this appears only vaguely to us if it hardly has risen above the horizon of our consciousness at all. But it is scarcely different with the territorial houses and groups of people enmeshed in the Hundred Years' War; there, too, each unit feels only the direct threat that the size or increase of others means for it; for the larger units that slowly come into being in these struggles, France and England, as we call them, are scarcely more present in the consciousness of those forming them than "Europe" as a political unit is for us.

How the individual tensions between rival groups and houses are resolved, how the balance between the main protagonists, the English Lancasters, the French Valois and the Burgundian Valois, tilts now this way and now that, how the English seize a yet larger portion of French land and even the French kingship, and how finally, through the appearance of Joan of Arc, all the forces supporting the French Valois gather themselves in successful resistance and bring back the weak king first to Rheims for his coronation and then as victor to Paris—accounts of all this are readily available elsewhere.

What is decided in this way is the question whether London and the Anglo–Norman island, or Paris and the dominion of the rulers of Francia, are to become the centre of crystallization of the former western Frankish region. The issue is decided in favour of Paris. London's rule is confined to the island. The Hundred Years' War accelerates and makes irreversible the breach between the mainland territory, that really only now becomes "la France", that is, the domain of the rulers of Francia, and the overseas region that previously was nothing but a colonial territory of mainland rulers. The first consequence of this war is thus a disintegration. The islanders, the descendants of the Continental conquerors and the natives, have become a separate society going their own way, forming their own specific institutions of government, and developing their mixed language into a specific entity of a new kind. Neither of the contending rivals has succeeded in gaining and keeping control of the whole area. The French kings and their people have finally lost their claim to the island realm; the English kings' attempt to defeat their Paris rivals and recolonize the mainland has failed. If the people of the island need new land, new areas to colonize, new markets, they must from now on seek them further afield. The English kings are eliminated from the mainland struggles for the French crown. It is a process not unlike that which, centuries later, in the community of German territorial states, ended with the victory of Prussia over Austria. In both cases, as a result of a disintegration, integration was confined to a smaller area and thus made very much easier.

But through the repulsion of the English from the mainland, the elimination of the English kings from the struggle for supremacy there, the tension and balance within this area are altered. As long as the London and Paris kings roughly balance each other, and as long as the contest between them constitutes the main axis of tension, rivalries between the various territorial rulers on the mainland have only secondary importance. They can have considerable influence on whether the main struggle is decided in favour of the Paris or the London rulers; but they cannot directly cause any of the other competitors to take first place.

Now, with the departure of the English, the competition between the various mainland territorial rulers, above all the rivalry between different branches of the Capetian house itself, becomes the dominant tension. The outcome of the Hundred Years' War did not decide, or at any rate not finally, by which of these branches and within which frontiers the integration of the mainland territories of the former western Frankish regions was to be accomplished. In this direction, therefore, the struggles continue.

In the last years of Charles VII there are, besides the Paris house, at least eight other large houses which can pit their weight in the decisive struggles for supremacy. They are the houses of Anjou, Alençon, Armagnac, Bourbon, Burgundy, Brittany, Dreux and Foix. Each of these houses is itself already represented by several branches; the mightiest is the house of Burgundy which, based on Burgundy and Flanders as the core of its family power, is working with great tenacity and single—mindedness to establish a major dominion, related to the earlier Lotharingia, between the empire and France. The rivalry between Burgundy and the Paris kings now forms the main axis of the system of feudal territories from which, with the latter's victory, "France" is finally to emerge. But to begin with, the houses of Bourbon and Brittany are also power-centres of major importance.

With the exception of the latter, the ducal house of Brittany, the members of all the houses named are descendants and relations of people apanaged by the Capetian house, and therefore its offshoots. Seigneurial, post-Carolingian feudality has "contracted", as one writer has put it, to a "princely", a Capetian feudality.[93] From the conflicts of the many great and small warrior houses of the western Frankish region, a single house has emerged victorious. The region has now become, by and large, the monopoly of descendants of the Capetians.

But in the course of generations the family and its accumulated territorial possessions have again become dispersed; and now the different branches of the family are struggling for supremacy. Monopoly formation does not happen in quite such a straight line as appears at first sight. What we have before us here—in the period following the Hundred Years' War—is not yet a complete concentration or centralization of power in one place and in one pair of hands, but a stage on the way to absolute monopoly.

A state of highly restricted competition has been established. For all those who do not belong to a particular family, the chance of acquiring and owning a major dominion, or enlarging their existing one, and thus taking part in further elimination struggles, has become extremely small.

VI

The Last Stages of the Free Competitive Struggle and the Final Monopoly Position of the Victor

12. What here gives the monopolizing process its special character—and what later observers, particularly those of the twentieth century, of course, must bear in mind in looking back—is the fact that social functions which have become separated in recent times were still more or less undifferentiated in that earlier phase. It has already been stressed that the social role of the great feudal lord, or prince, the function of being the richest man, the owner of the largest means of production in his region, is at first completely indistinguishable from that of being the owner of military power and jurisdiction. Functions today represented by different people and groups of people connected through the division of labour, e.g. the functions of great landowner and of head of government, form here, inseparably bound together, a kind of private property. This is partly explained by the fact that in this society, which still had a primarily if diminishingly barter-based economy, land was the most important means of production, whereas in later society it has been supplanted in this role by money, the incarnation of the division of functions. It is explained no less, however, by the fact that in the later phase the key to all monopoly power, the monopoly of physical, of military violence, is a firmly established social institution extending over large areas, whereas in the preceding stage it only slowly develops through centuries of struggle, first of all in the form of a private, family monopoly.

We are accustomed to distinguish two spheres, "economics" and "politics", and two kinds of social function, "economic" and "political" ones. By "economic" we mean the whole network of activities and institutions serving the creation and acquisition of means of consumption and production. But we also take it for granted, in thinking of "economics", that the production and, above all, the acquisition of these means normally takes place without threat or use of physical or military violence. Nothing is less self-evident. For all warrior societies with a barter economy—and not only for them—the sword is a frequent and indispensable instrument for acquiring means of production, and the threat of violence an indispensable means of production. Only when the division of functions is very far advanced; only when, as the result of long struggles, a specialized monopoly administration has formed that exercises the functions of rule as its social property; only when a centralized and public monopoly of force exists over large areas, can competition for means of consumption and production take its course largely without the intervention of physical violence; and only then do the kind of economy and the kind of struggle exist that we are accustomed to designate by the terms "economy" and "competition" in a more specific sense.

The competitive relationship itself is a far more general and all-encompassing social fact than appears when the concept of "competition" is restricted to economic structures[94]—usually those of the nineteenth and twentieth centuries. A situation of competition arises whenever a number of people strive for the same opportunities, when demand exceeds the possibilities of satisfaction, whether these possibilities are controlled by monopolists or not. The particular kind of competition that has been discussed here, so-called "free competition", is characterized by the fact that demand is directed at opportunities not yet controlled by anyone who does not himself belong to the circle of competitors. Such a phase of "free competition" occurs in the history of many societies, if not all. A "free competitive struggle" thus arises also, for example, when land and military opportunities are so evenly distributed among several interdependent parties that none of them has clearly the best chance, the greatest social power. It arises, therefore, in that phase in the relationship between feudal warrior houses or between states, when none of the parties has clearly outgrown the rivalry of others, and when no organized, centralized monopoly of power exists. Likewise, a "free competitive struggle" arises when the financial opportunities of many interdependent people are fairly evenly distributed; in both cases, the struggle is intensified with the growth of population and demand, unless the opportunities grow at the same rate.

The course taken by these free competitive struggles, moreover, is relatively unaffected by the fact that, in one case, they are brought about by the threat and use of physical violence and, in the other, only by the threat of social decline, the loss of economic independence, financial ruin or material distress. In the struggles of the feudal warrior houses, the two forms of violence that we distinguish as physical/military and economic force, acted together more or less as one. These feudal conflicts have, indeed, a functional analogy within modern society both in free economic competition, such as the struggles of a number of firms for supremacy in the same commercial field, and in the struggles of states for predominance within a particular territorial system, conflicts that are resolved by physical violence.

In all these cases what manifests itself as struggles within the sphere not yet monopolized is only one layer of the continuous, general competition for limited opportunities pervading the whole of society. The opportunities open to those engaged in free competition, that is, competition free of monopoly, themselves constitute an unorganized monopoly from which all others are excluded who are unable to compete because they have far smaller resources. These others are thus directly or indirectly dependent on the "free" competitors, and are engaged among themselves in an unfree competition for their limited opportunities. The pressure exerted within the relatively independent section stands in the closest functional relationship to that exerted on all sides by those already dependent on monopolized opportunities.

In feudal as in modern times, free competition for chances not yet centrally organized and monopolized, tends through all its ramifications towards the subjugation and elimination of an ever-increasing number of rivals, who are destroyed as social units or fall into dependence; towards the accumulation of possibilities in the hands of an ever-diminishing number of rivals; towards domination and finally monopoly. Again, the social event of monopolization is not confined to the processes which normally come to mind today when "monopolies" are mentioned. The accumulation of possibilities that can be converted into sums of money or at least expressed as such, represents only one historical shift among many others in the process of monopolization. Functionally similar processes, that is, tendencies towards an overall structure of human relationships in which individuals or groups can by direct or indirect threat of violence, restrict and control the access of others to certain contested possibilities—such processes occur in a variety of forms at very different points in human history.

In the struggles in both these periods, the actual social existence of all the participants is at stake. That is the compulsion behind these struggles. That is what makes such struggles, and their outcome, so inescapable wherever the basic situation of free competition arises. Once a society has embarked on a movement of this kind, each social unit in the sphere not yet monopolized, whether these units are knightly families, economic enterprises, territories or states, is always confronted by the same choice.

Either they can be conquered—whether they choose to struggle or not—which in extreme cases means: imprisonment, violent death or material distress, perhaps starvation, or in the mildest: social decline, loss of independence, absorption by a larger social complex; and thereby the destruction of what gave their lives meaning, value and continuity, even if these things appear to their contemporaries, or to those coming after them, as contrary to their own meaning, social existence and "continuity", and thus as entirely deserving of destruction.

Or they may repel and conquer their nearest rivals. Then their life, their social existence, their striving attains fulfilment; they seize the contested opportunities. The mere preservation of social existence demands, in the situation of free competition, this constant enlargement. Whoever does not rise, falls back. Victory, therefore, means in the first place—whether this is intended or not—dominance of one's closest rivals and their reduction to a position of dependence. The gain of one is here necessarily the other's loss, whether in terms of land, military capacity, money or any other substance of social power. But beyond this, victory sooner or later means confrontation and conflict with a rival of the new size; once again the situation enforces the expansion of one, and the absorption, subjugation, humiliation or destruction of the other. The shift in power relationships, the establishment of domination may be accomplished by open military or economic force, or by peaceful agreement; but however it comes about, all these rivalries are impelled, whether slowly or quickly, through a series of downfalls and aggrandisements, rises and descents, fulfilments and destructions of meaning, in the direction of a new social order, a monopoly order that none of the participants has really intended or foreseen, and which replaces free competition by competition subject to monopoly. And it is only the formation of such monopolies that finally makes it possible to regulate the distribution of opportunities—and thus the conflicts themselves—in which interests of the smooth-functioning collaboration to which people are bound for better or worse.

Alternatives of this kind confront the warrior families of medieval society too. And the resistance of the great feudal lords, and finally of Capetian or princely feudality, to the increase of royal power is to be understood in this sense. The king in Paris is, both in fact and in the minds of the other territorial rulers, one of themselves, not more; he is a rival, and from a certain time on the most powerful, most threatening rival. If he wins, their existence, social if not physical, is destroyed; they lose what in their eyes gives their life meaning and splendour, their independent rule, the control of their family possessions; their honour, their rank, their social standing is at worst annihilated, at best diminished. If they win, centralization, domination, monopoly, the state are for a time obstructed; Burgundy, Anjou, Brittany, and so on, remain for the time being more or less independent dominions. This may appear senseless to some contemporaries, above all the royal officials, and even to us in retrospect; for by virtue of our different state of social integration we tend not to identify with such limited geographical units. For them, the rulers of Burgundy or Brittany and a large number of their dependents, however, it is extremely worthwhile to prevent the formation of an over-mighty central government in Paris, for this means their downfall as independent social units.

But if they win, sooner or later the victors confront each other as rivals; and the ensuing tensions and conflicts cannot end until once again a clearly superior power has emerged. *Just as, in the capitalist society of the nineteenth and, above all, the twentieth century, the general impulsion towards economic monopolization shows itself clearly, regardless of which particular competitor triumphs and outgrows the others; just as, concurrently, an analogous tendency towards the clearer domination that precedes each monopolization, each larger integration, is becoming ever more apparent in the contest of "states", first of all in Europe; in the same way the struggles between medieval warrior houses and later the great feudal and territorial rulers, show a general impulsion towards monopoly formation.* The only difference is that, there, the process takes place in a sphere in which land ownership and rule form an inseparable unity, whereas later—with the increasing use of money–it takes on the combined form of centralization of taxes and of control of all the instruments that serve physical subjugation.

13. It is in an intermediate period between these two stages that, in the second half of the fifteenth century, following the death of Charles VII, the rivalry between the French branch of the Valois, the Burgundian branch together with the remainder of Capetian feudality, and the last representative of the great pre-Capetian feudality, the Duke of Brittany, comes to a head. Once again the centrifugal forces gather themselves for a common assault on the Parisian Valois, Louis XI, whose wealth and power are now particularly dangerous to them all, following the elimination of his chief opponent hitherto, the King of England. And as the centre of gravity inclined ever more threateningly towards the French ruling complex, the Burgundian Valois, Charles the Bold, once stated quite clearly what most of the King's competitors must have felt and desired in the face of this threat to their social existence: "Instead of one king I wish we had six!"[95]

Louis XI himself by no means identifies with his royal task from the first. On the contrary. As crown prince he acts very much in the same way and in the same spirit as the other great Capetian feudal lords who are working for the disintegration of the French territorial complex; and he lives for a time at the court of the strongest rival of the Paris monarchy, the Duke of Burgundy. This is certainly bound up with facts that may be called personal, above all with the peculiar hatred existing between Louis and his father. But it is also further evidence of the specific individualization of the richest house in the land, which in its turn is bound up with the apanaging of each and every prince. Whatever the earlier causes of Louis' hatred for his father may have been, the control of a territory of his own unites his feelings and actions in a common front with his father's other rivals. Even after his accession to the throne, he first thinks of avenging himself on those who had been hostile to him as Dauphin, including many loyal servants of the monarchy, and of rewarding those who had showed friendship for him then, including many opponents of the monarchy. Power is still, to a considerable extent, private property dependent on the personal inclinations of the ruler. But it also has, like any very large possession, a very strict regularity of its own that its wielder cannot contravene without destroying it. Very soon the enemies of the monarchy become the enemies of Louis; those supporting the monarchy become *his* friends and servants. His personal ambitions become one with the traditional ambitions of the central ruler in Paris, and his personal qualities—his curiosity, his almost pathological desire to penetrate all the secrets around him, his cunning, the undeviating violence of his hatred and of his affection, even the naive and intense piety that causes him to woo saints, and especially the patron saints of his enemies, with gifts, as if they were venal human beings—all this now unfolds in the direction in which he is impelled by his social position as ruler of the French territorial possessions; the struggle against centrifugal forces, against the rival feudal lords, becomes the decisive task of his life. And the house of Burgundy, the friends from his time as crown prince, become—as the immanent logic of his royal function demands—his main opponents.

The struggle thus confronting Louis XI is by no means an easy one. At times the Paris government seems on the verge of collapse. But at the end of his reign—partly through the power which his great possessions put at his disposal, partly through the skill with which he wields it, and partly through a number of accidents that come to his aid—his rivals are more or less definitively beaten. In 1476 Charles the Bold of Burgundy is defeated at Granson and Murten by the Swiss, whom Louis has incited to oppose him. In 1477 Charles is killed while attempting to conquer Nancy. Thus the chief rival of the French Valois among the competing Capetian heirs—and, after the elimination of the English, their strongest rival of all—is himself eliminated from the conflict between the western Frankish territorial lords. Charles the Bold leaves an only daughter, Marie; for her hand and inheritance Louis competes with the power which is now gradually emerging in the larger European context as the main rival of the Parisian monarchy, the house of Habsburg. As the elimination contests within the western Frankish area draw to an end with the predominance and monopoly of a single house, rivalry between this victorious house, which now begins to become the centre of the whole country, and powers of a similar magnitude outside the country, move into the foreground. In the competition for Burgundy the Habsburgs win their first victory; with the hand of Maria, Maximillian gains a large part of the Burgundian inheritance. This creates a situation that feeds the rivalry between the Habsburgs and the Paris kings for more than two centuries. However, the duchy of Burgundy itself, and two further direct annexations from Burgundian lands, return to the crown estates of the Valois. The parts of the Burgundian inheritance that are particularly needed to round off French territory are incorporated in it.

There are now only four houses left within the western Frankish region that control territories of any significance. The most powerful or, more exactly, the most important and traditionally most independent, is the house of Brittany. But none of these houses can now match the social power of Paris; the French king's rule has now grown beyond the reach of competition from neighbouring territorial rulers. He takes up a monopoly position among them. Earlier or later, by treaty, violence or accident, they have all become dependent on him and lost their autonomy.

It is—if one will—fortuitous that towards the end of the fifteenth century a Duke of Brittany leaves an only daughter on his death, as the Duke of Burgundy had done before him. The conflict which this accident unleashes shows very exactly the existing constellation of forces. Of the remaining territorial rulers of the old western Frankish area, none is now strong enough to contest the Breton inheritance with the Paris ruler. As with the Burgundian inheritance, the rival for this also comes from outside. Here, too, the question is whether a Habsburg or a Valois shall take Brittany by marriage, whether Charles VIII, the young son of Louis XI, or Maximillian of Habsburg, the Holy Roman Emperor and lord of Burgundy, whose hand has again become free through the death of the Burgundian heiress. As in the case of Burgundy, the Habsburg again succeeds in marrying the young Anne of Brittany, at least provisionally. But after much contention—finally decided by the opinion of the Breton estates—the heiress's hand goes after all to Charles of France. The Habsburgs protest, there is war between the rivals and finally a compromise: the Franche-Comté, which lies outside French territory and does not belong to the traditional western Frankish complex of lands, is ceded to the Habsburgs; in exchange Maximillian recognizes Charles VIII's acquisition of Brittany. And when Charles VIII dies childless, his successor, Louis XII, a Valois from the Orléans branch, promptly has his existing marriage annulled by the Pope and marries the twenty-one-year-old widow of his predecessor, in order to preserve her inheritance, Brittany, for the crown estates which have now become his. When this marriage produces only daughters, the king marries his eldest, who will receive Brittany as heiress to her mother, to the heir-apparent to the throne, the nearest living descendant of the family, Count Francis of Angoulême. The danger that this important territory might fall into the hands of a rival, above all a Habsburg, always leads to the same course of action. And so, under the pressure of the competitive mechanism, the last territory in the western Frankish region that has preserved its autonomy throughout all the elimination struggles, is slowly integrated into the dominion of the Paris king. At first, when the heir to the apanage of Angoulême becomes king under the name of Francis I, Brittany retains a certain autonomy. The independent-mindedness of its Estates remains very much alive; but the military power of a single territory is now far too small to withstand the great dominions now surrounding it. In 1532 the incorporation of Brittany into the French domain is institutionally confirmed. Only the duchy of Alençon, the counties of Nevers and Vendôme, and the dominions of Bourbon and Albret[96] now remain in the former western Frankish region as independent territories, that is, areas not belonging either to the Paris kings or—like Flanders and Artois—to the Habsburgs. Even though some of their rulers, such as the lord of Albret or the house of Bourbon, may still work as best they can to enlarge their dominions, and may still dream of royal crowns,[97] their regions are really no more than enclaves within the dominions of the French kings. The wearers of the crown are now entirely beyond the competition of these other territorial lords. The houses that once existed here have lapsed into dependence or disappeared. Within the former western Frankish region the Paris kings are now finally without rivals; from now on their position takes on more and more clearly the character of an absolute monopoly. But outside the western Frankish region similar processes have been taking place, even though the monopoly process and the elimination struggles have nowhere advanced to the point they have reached in France. All the same, the Habsburgs, too, have now assembled family possessions which, in military and financial potential, far surpass most of the other dominions on the European mainland. What earlier revealed itself through the Burgundian and Breton successions now emerges, from the beginning of the sixteenth century onwards, more and more clearly: the house of the Habsburg emperors and the House of the French kings, represented at this stage by Charles V and Francis I, now stand face to face as rivals on a new scale. Both hold, to slightly varying degrees, monopoly power over a very large area; they are competing for opportunities and supremacy within a large sphere which as yet has no monopoly ruler, and are thus in a situation of "free competition". And accordingly, the rivalry between them now becomes, for a long period, a main axis within a larger evolving European system of tensions.

14. In size the French dominion is considerably smaller than that of the Habsburgs. But it is far more centralized and, above all, self-contained, better protected militarily by "natural frontiers". Its western boundaries are the Channel and the Atlantic; the whole coastal area as far down as Navarre is now in the hands of the French kings. The southern boundary is the Mediterranean; here too the whole coast—with the exception of Roussillon and the Cerdagne—belongs to the French rulers. To the east the Rhône forms the frontier with the county of Nice and the duchy of Savoy; for the time being the frontier projects beyond the Rhône as far as the Alps only in Dauphiné and Provence. North of this, opposite the Franche-Comté, the Rhône and the Saône continue to form the frontier of the kingdom; in its middle and lower parts the Saône is somewhat overstepped. In the north and north-east the frontiers fall further short of those of present-day France; only by taking possession of the archbishoprics of Metz, Toul and Verdun does the kingdom approach the Rhine; but these are for the time being enclaves, outposts within the German Empire; the frontier with it lies only slightly to the west of Verdun and further north, roughly in the region of Sedan;

like the Franche-Comté, Flanders and Artois belong to the Habsburgs. One of the first issues to be decided in the struggle for supremacy against them, is how far the frontier will move in this area. For a considerable period French rule is contained within these limits. Only in the years between 1610 and 1659 are the Artois region, together with the area between France and the three archbishoprics and—a new enclave within the empire—upper and lower Alsace, assimilated to France; only now does France approach the Rhine.[98] A great part of the territory forming France today has now been assembled under a single rule. All that is in question is the extent of this unit's possible expansion, the question whether and where it will finally find "natural", i.e. easily defensible, frontiers within the European system of tensions.

Anyone looking back from within a state, a society with a stable and centralized monopoly of physical violence, a Frenchman living in France or a German in Germany, is apt to take for granted the existence of this monopoly of violence, and the unification of areas of this size and kind, as something natural and useful, to regard them as something consciously planned; and consequently, he tends to observe and evaluate the particular actions which led up to them in terms of their direct use to an order that seems to him self-evident and self-justifying. He is inclined to be less concerned with the actual dilemmas and necessities out of which groups and persons acted formerly, less with their direct plans, wishes and interests, than with the question whether this or that was good or bad for the thing with which he identifies. And, just as if the actors of the past already had before their eyes a prophetic vision of that future which is to him so self-evident and, perhaps, so emphatically affirmed, he praises or condemns these actors, awards them marks according to whether their actions did or did not lead directly to the desired result.

But through such censures, through such expressions of personal satisfaction, through this subjectivistic or partisan view of the past, we usually block our access to the elementary formative regularities and mechanisms, to the real structural history and sociogenesis of historical formations. These formations always develop in the struggle between opposed or, more exactly, in the resolution of ambivalent interests. What finally meets its end in such conflicts or merges into new formations, as the princely dominions merged into the royal ones and royal power into the bourgeois state, is no less indispensable to these new formations than the victorious opponent. Without violent actions, without the motive forces of free competition, there would be no monopoly of force, and thus no pacification, no suppression and control of violence over large areas.

The convolutions of the movement leading to the integration of ever-larger regions around the duchy of Francia as the centre of crystallization, illustrate how much the final integration of the western Frankish area was the outcome of a series of elimination contests in a compelling process of interweavings, and how little it resulted from a prophetic vision or a rigorous plan to which all the individual parties adhered.

"Unquestionably," Henri Hauser once said,[99] "there is always something slightly artificial in placing oneself in an *a posteriori* position and looking at history from back to front, as if the administrative monarchy and the centralized France of Henry II had been destined since the beginning of time to be born and to live within determined limits. . . ."

Only if we are transported for a moment into the landscape of the past, and see the struggles between the many warrior houses, their vital necessities, their immediate goals; only if, in a word, we have the full precariousness of their struggles and their social existence before our eyes, can we understand how probable was the formation of a monopoly within this area, but how uncertain its centre and its boundaries.

To some extent the same is true of the French kings and their representatives as was once said of the American pioneer: "He didn't want all the land; he just wanted the land next to his."[100]

This simple and precise formulation expresses very well how, from the interweaving of countless individual interests and intentions—whether tending in the same direction or in divergent and hostile directions—something comes into being that was planned and intended by none of these individuals, yet has emerged nevertheless from their intentions and actions. And really this is the whole secret of social figurations, their compelling dynamics, their structural regularities, their process character and their development; this is the secret of sociogenesis and of relational dynamics.

The representatives of the French monarchy no doubt possessed, by virtue of their more central position in the later phases of the movement, rather larger intentions and radii of action within the process of integration than the individual American pioneers. But they, too, saw distinctly only the next few steps and the next piece of land that they had to obtain to prevent it going to another, and to prevent a troublesome neighbour or rival from growing stronger than themselves. And if some among them did harbour an image of a larger realm, this image was for a long period rather the shadow of past monopolies, a reflection of the Carolingian and western Frankish monarchies; more a product of memory than of prophecy or a new concept of the future. Here, as always, from the tangle of innumerable individual interests, plans and actions, a single development emerged, a regularity governing the totality of these entangled people and intended by none of them, and giving rise to a formation that none of the actors had really planned, a state: France. For this very reason the understanding of a formation of this kind requires a breakthrough to a still little-known level of reality: to the level of the immanent regularities of social relationships, the field of relational dynamics.

VII

The Distribution of Power Ratios within the Unit of Rule: Their Significance for the Central Authority: The Formation of the "Royal Mechanism"

15. Two main phases have been distinguished in the development of monopolies: the phase of free competition tending to the formation of private monopolies, and the gradual transformation of "private" into "public" monopolies. But on closer consideration this movement does not consist of a simple succession of tendencies. Even though the "opening-up" of monopolies in the course of such change only reaches its full extent and becomes a dominant phenomenon at a late stage, the structures leading up to it have already been present and active in the phase in which, through numerous struggles, the power monopoly slowly emerged in the form of a private possession.

Certainly the French Revolution, for example, represents a massive step on the way to the opening-up of the monopoly of taxation and physical force in France. Here, these monopolies do indeed pass into the power, or at least the institutionally secured control, of broad social classes. The central ruler, whatever title he may bear, and all those exercising monopoly power, become more unequivocally than before functionaries among others within the whole web of a society based on the division of functions. Their functional dependence on the representatives of other social functions has become so great that it is clearly expressed in the organization of society. However, this functional dependence of the monopolies and their incumbents on other functions of society was already present in the preceding phases. It was merely less developed, and for this reason was not expressed in a direct and unconcealed way in the organization and institutional structure of society. And for this reason the power of the monopoly ruler had at first more or less the character of a "private possession".

16. As noted above tendencies towards a kind of "opening-up" of the monopoly of a single family show themselves under certain conditions—namely, when the area it controls or its possessions begin to grow very large—even in societies with a barter economy. What we call "feudalism", what was described above as the action of centrifugal forces, is no more than an expression of such tendencies. They indicate that the functional dependence of a lord on his servants or subjects, that is, on broader strata, is increasing; they lead to the transfer of control of land and military power from the hands of a single warrior family and its head, first to the hierarchy of its closest servants and relations, and then in some cases to the whole warrior society. It has already been pointed out that in

feudal society the "opening-up", as a result of the peculiarities of land-ownership and the instruments of violence, means a dissolution of the centralized—even if only loosely centralized—monopoly; it leads to the transformation of a single large monopoly possession into a number of smaller ones, and so to a decentralized and less organized form of monopoly. As long as land ownership remains the dominant form of ownership, new shifts in this or that direction can take place: the establishment of supremacy within free competition, the assembly of large areas of land and masses of warriors under a single central lord; waves of decentralization under his successors, new struggles in different strata of their servants, their relations or their subjects, new attempts to gain supremacy. And this whole ebb and flow of centralization and decentralization can sometimes —depending on geographical or climatic factors, on particular economic forms, on the kind of animals and plants on which the life of people depends, and always in conjunction with the traditional structure of organized religion—all this can lead to a complex medley of social deposits from the various shifts. The history of other, non-European, feudal societies everywhere follows the same pattern in this respect. But however much this kind of ebb and flow is detectable in the development of France, in comparison with most other societies the movement here follows a relatively straight path.

This rhythm that over and over again threatens the dissolution of the great monopolies of power and possessions is modified and finally broken only to the extent that, with the growing division of functions in society, money rather than land becomes the dominant form of property. Only then is the large centralized monopoly, in passing from the hands of one ruler or a small circle into the control of a larger circle, not broken up into numerous smaller areas as was the case in each advance of feudalization; instead, it slowly becomes, centralized as it is, an instrument of functionally divided society as a whole, and so first and foremost a central organ of what we call the state.

The development of money and exchange, together with the social formations carrying them, stands in a permanent reciprocal relationship to the form and development of monopoly power within a particular area. These two series of developments, constantly intertwining, drive each other upwards. The form and development of power monopolies are influenced on all sides by the differentiation of society, the advance of money use and the formation of classes earning and possessing money. On the other hand, the success of the division of labour itself, the securing of routes and markets over large areas, the standardization of coinage and the whole monetary system, the protection of peaceful production from physical violence and an abundance of other measures of co-ordination and regulation, are highly dependent on the formation of large centralized monopoly institutions. The more, in other words, the work processes and the totality of functions in a society become differentiated, the longer and more complex the chains of individual actions which must interlock for each action to fulfil its social purpose, the more clearly one specific characteristic of the central organ emerges: *its role as supreme co-ordinator and regulator for the functionally differentiated figuration at large.* From a certain degree of functional differentiation onward, the complex web of intertwining human activities simply cannot continue to grow or even to function without co-ordinating organs at a correspondingly high level of organization. Their role is certainly not entirely lacking in the central institutions of more simply organized and less differentiated societies. Even a society as loosely bound together as that of the many autarkic estates of the ninth and tenth centuries needed a supreme co-ordinator under certain conditions. If a powerful enemy threatened from outside, necessitating war, someone was needed to ensure the collaboration of the many knights, to co-ordinate their activity and to take the final decisions. In this situation the interdependence of the many scattered rulers re-emerged more clearly. Each individual was threatened if the whole army failed to co-operate. And as, in this situation, the dependence of all on a central ruler, the king, increased considerably, so too did his importance, his social power—provided he fulfilled his social function, provided he was not beaten. But when the external threat or possibility of expansion lapsed, the dependence of individuals and groups on a supreme co-ordinating and regulating centre was relatively slight. This function only emerges as a permanent, specialized task of the central organ when society as a whole becomes more and more differentiated, when its cellular structure slowly but incessantly forms new functions, new professional groups and classes. Only then do regulating and co-ordinating central organs for maintaining the whole social network become so indispensable that while alterations in the power structure can change their occupants and even their organization, they cannot dissolve them, as happened earlier in the course of feudalization.

17. The formation of particularly stable and specialized central organs for large regions is one of the most prominent features of Western history. As we have said, there are central organs of some sort in every society. But as the differentiation and specialization of social functions have attained a higher level in the West than in any other society on earth—and as they begin to reach this level elsewhere only through an impetus coming from the West—it is in the West that specialized central organs first attain a hitherto unknown degree of stability. However, the central organs and their functionaries do not necessarily gain social power corresponding to their rising importance as supreme social co-ordinators and regulators. One might suppose that, with advancing centralization and the stricter control and supervision of the whole social process by stable authorities, the rift between rulers and ruled would be deepened. The actual course of history shows a different picture. Western history is certainly not lacking in phases when the powers of the central authority are so great and wide that we may speak with some justice of the hegemony of single central rulers. But precisely in the more

recent history of many Western societies there are also phases when, despite their centralization, the control of the centralized institutions themselves is so dispersed that it is difficult to discern clearly who are the rulers and who the ruled. The scope for decision vested in the central functions varies. Sometimes it increases; then the people exercising these functions take on the aspect of "rulers". Sometimes it diminishes, without centralization, or the importance of the central organs as the highest centre of co-ordination and regulation, being reduced. In other words, in the case of the central organs as of all other social formations, two characteristics must be distinguished: *their function within the human network to which they belong, and the social power that is vested in the function.* What we call "rule" is, in a highly differentiated society, no more than the special social power with which certain functions, above all the central functions, endow their occupants in relation to the representatives of other functions. Social power, however, is determined, in the case of the highest central functions of a highly differentiated society, in exactly the same way as with all others: it corresponds—if these functions are not allied to permanent control of individual hereditary monopoly power—solely to the degree of dependence of the various interdependent functions on one another. Growth in the "power" of the central functionaries is, in a society with a high division of functions, an expression of the fact that the dependence of other groups and classes within this society on a supreme organ of co-ordination and regulation is rising; a fall in the latter appears to us as a limitation of the former. Not only the earlier stage in the formation of states which is central to the present study, but also the contemporary history of the Western figuration of states, offers examples enough of such changes in the social power of the central functionaries. They are all sure indications of specific changes in the system of tensions within the society at large. Here again, beneath all the differences between the social structures, we find certain mechanisms of social interweaving which—at least in more complex societies—tend very generally towards either a reduction or an increase in the social power of the central authorities. Whether it is the nobility and the bourgeoisie, or the bourgeoisie and the proletariat, whether, in conjunction with these larger divisions, it is smaller ruling circles, such as competing cliques within a princely court or within the supreme military or party apparatus, that form the two poles of the decisive axis of tension at a given time within society, it is always a quite definite set of social power relationships which strengthens the position of the authority at their centre, and a different set that weakens it.

It is necessary to deal here briefly with the figurational dynamics which determine the power of the central authority. The process of social centralization in the West, particularly in the phase when "states" were formed, remains incomprehensible, like the civilizing process itself, as long as the elementary regularities of figurational dynamics are disregarded as a means of orientation and as a guide to both thought and observation. This "centralization" or state-formation, has been shown in the preceding sections from the point of view of the power-struggle between various princely houses and dominions, i.e. from the point of view of what we would today call the "foreign affairs" of such dominions. Now the complementary problem poses itself; we face the task of tracing the figurational processes *within* one of the units which give the central authority—as compared with the preceding phase—a special power and durability, and thus endow the whole society with the form of an "absolutist state". In historical reality these two processes—shifts in power between classes *within* a unit and displacements in the system of tensions *between* different units—constantly intertwine.

In the course of the struggle between different territorial dominions *one* princely house—as we have shown—slowly outgrows all the others. It thus assumes the function of supreme regulator for a larger unit; but it did not create this function. It appropriates it by virtue of the size of its possessions accumulated in the course of the struggles, and its monopoly control of army and taxes. The function itself derives its form and power from the increasing differentiation of functions within society at large. And from this aspect it seems, at first sight, thoroughly paradoxical that the central ruler in this early phase of state-formation should attain such enormous social power. For, from the end of the Middle Ages onwards, with the rapid advance of the division of functions, the monarchy becomes more and more perceptibly dependent on the other functions. At precisely this time the chains of action based on division of functions take on ever wider scope and ever greater durability. The autonomy of social processes, the central authority's character as a functionary, which gradually receives clearer institutional expression after the French Revolution, are by this time far more prominent than in the Middle Ages. The dependence of the central lords on the revenues from their dominions is a clear indication of this. Beyond doubt, Louis XIV is incomparably more tightly bound to this vast and autonomous network of chains of actions, than, for example, Charlemagne. How, therefore, did the central ruler in this phase have, to begin with, such scope for decision and such social power that we are accustomed to call him an "absolute" ruler?

It was not only the prince's monopoly control of military power which held the other classes within his territory, and especially the powerful leading groups, in check. Owing to a peculiar social constellation, the dependence of precisely these groups on a supreme co-ordinator and regulator of the tension-ridden structure was so great at this phase that, willingly or not, they renounced for a long period the struggle for control and participation in the highest decisions.

This peculiar constellation cannot be understood unless we take account of a special quality of human relationships which was likewise emerging with the increasing division of functions in society: *their open or latent ambivalence*. In the relations between individuals, as well as in those between different functional strata, a specific *duality or even multiplicity of interests* manifests itself more strongly, the broader and denser the network of social interdependence becomes. Here, all people, all groups, estates or classes, are in some way dependent on one another; they are potential friends, allies or partners; and they are at the same time potential opponents, competitors or enemies. In societies with a barter economy there are sometimes unambiguously negative relationships, of pure, unmoderated enmity. When migrant nomads invade a settled region, there need be in their relations with the settlers no trace of mutual functional dependence. Between these groups exists pure enmity to the death. Far greater, too, in such societies, is the chance of a relationship of clear and uncomplicated mutual dependence, unmixed friendships, alliances, relationships of love or service. In the peculiar black-and-white colouring of many medieval books, which often know nothing but good friends or villains, the greater susceptibility of medieval reality to relationships of this kind is clearly expressed. No doubt, at this stage the chains of functional interdependencies are relatively short; hence rapid switches from one extreme to another, an easy changeover from firm friendship into violent enmity also occur more frequently. As social functions and interests become increasingly complex and contradictory, we find more and more frequently in the behaviour and feelings of people a peculiar split, a co-existence of positive and negative elements, a mixture of muted affection and muted dislike in varying proportions and nuances. The possibilities of pure, unambiguous enmity grow fewer; and, more and more perceptibly, every action taken against an opponent also threatens the social existence of its perpetrator; it disturbs the whole mechanism of chains of action of which each is a part. It would take us too far afield to explore in detail this fundamental *ambivalence of interests*, its consequences in political life or psychological make-up, and its sociogenesis in relation to the advancing division of functions. But the little that has already been said shows it to be one of the most important structural characteristics of more highly developed societies, and a chief factor moulding civilized conduct.

Increasingly ambivalent, with the growing division of functions, are the relations between different units of power. The relations between the states of our own time, above all in Europe, offer a clear example of this. Even if integration and the division of functions *between* them have not yet advanced as far as the division of functions *within* them, nevertheless every military exchange so threatens this highly differentiated network of nations as a whole, that in the end the victor himself finds himself in a seriously shaken position. He is no longer able—or willing—to depopulate and devastate the enemy country sufficiently to settle a part of his own population in it. He must, in the interests of victory, destroy as far as possible the industrial power of the enemy, and at the same time, in the interests of his own peace, try within limits to preserve or restore this industrial apparatus. He can win colonial possessions, frontier revisions, export markets, economic or military advantages, in short, a general advance of his power; but just because, in the struggles of highly complex societies, each rival and opponent is at the same time a partner at the production line of the same machinery, every sudden and radical change in one sector of this network inevitably leads to disruption and changes in another. To be sure, the mechanism of competition and monopoly does not for this reason cease to operate. But the inevitable conflicts grow increasingly risky for the whole precarious system of nations. However, through these very tensions and discharges the figuration moves slowly towards a more unequivocal form of hegemony, and towards an integration, perhaps at first of a federative kind, of larger units around specific hegemonial centres.

And the relationship between different social classes *within* a dominion becomes, with the advancing division of functions, more and more ambivalent in the same way. Here, too, within a far more restricted space, groups whose social existence is mutually dependent through the division of functions, are struggling for certain opportunities. They too are at once opponents and partners. There are extreme situations in which the existing organization of a society functions so badly, and the tensions within it grow so large, that a large portion of the people and classes within it "no longer care". In such a situation the negative side of the ambivalent relationships, the opposition of interests, may so gain the upper hand over the positive side, the community of interests arising from the interdependence of functions, that there are violent discharges of tensions, abrupt shifts in the social centre of gravity, and reorganization of society on a changed social basis. Up to this revolutionary situation, the classes bound together by the division of functions are cast back and forth between their split and contradictory interests. They oscillate between the desire to win major advantages over their social opponents and their fear of ruining the whole social apparatus, on the functioning of which their actual social existence depends. And this is the constellation, the form of relationships, that harbours the key to an understanding of the changes in the social power of the central functionaries. If the co-operation of the powerful functional classes gives rise to no special difficulties, if their conflicts of interest are not great enough to conceal from them their mutual dependence and to threaten the functioning of the entire social apparatus, the scope of the central authority is restricted. It tends to increase when the tension between certain leading groups of society grows. And it attains its optimum level when the majority of the various functional classes are still so concerned to preserve their social existence in the established form that they fear any major disturbance of the total apparatus and the concomitant upheaval within their own existence, while at the same time the structural conflict of interests between powerful groups is so great that an ordered voluntary compromise can scarcely be reached, and troublesome social skirmishes without a decisive outcome become a permanent feature of social life. This is most acutely the case in phases when different groups or classes of a society have attained roughly the same power, and hold each other in balance, even though, like the nobility and the bourgeoisie, or the bourgeoisie and the proletariat, they may be institutionally on a quite unequal footing. He who, in this constellation, in a society wearied and disturbed by inconclusive struggles, can attain power over the supreme organs of regulation and control, has the chance of enforcing a compromise between the divided interests in order to preserve the existing social distribution of power. The various interest groups can move neither apart nor together; this makes them dependent on the supreme central co-ordinator for their social existence to a quite different degree than when the interdependent interests are less divergent and direct agreements between them more easily reached. When the situation of the bulk of the various functional classes, or at least their active leading groups, is not yet so bad that they are willing to put their social existence at risk, and they yet feel themselves so threatened by each other, and power is so evenly distributed between them, that each fears the slightest advantage of the other side, they tie each other's hands: this gives the central authority better chances than any other constellation within society. It gives those invested with this authority, whoever they may be, the optimal scope for decision. The variations on this configuration in historical reality are manifold. That it only emerges in a clearly delineated form in more highly differentiated societies, and that in less interdependent societies with lower division of functions it is above all military success and power that form the basis of a strong central authority over large areas, has already been stated. And even in more complex societies, success in war or conflicts with other powers undoubtedly plays a decisive part for strong central authorities. But if for the time being we disregard these external relations of a society and their influence of the internal balance, and ask how a strong central authority is possible in a richly differentiated society, despite the high and evenly distributed interdependence of all functions, we always find ourselves confronted with that specific constellation which can now be stated as a general principle: *the hour of the strong central authority within a highly differentiated society strikes when the ambivalence of interests of the most important functional groups grows so large, and power is distributed so evenly between them, that there can be neither a decisive compromise nor a decisive conflict between them.*

It is a figuration of this kind to which here the term "royal mechanism" is applied. In fact the central authority attains the optimal social power of an "absolute" monarchy in conjunction with such a constellation of social forces. But this balancing mechanism is certainly not only the sociogenetic motive force of a powerful monarchy; we find it in more complex societies as the foundation of every strong one-man rule, whatever its name might be. The man or men at the centre are always balanced on a tension between greater or lesser groups who keep each other in check as interdependent antagonists, as opponents and partners at once. This kind of figuration may appear at first sight extremely fragile. Historical reality shows, however, how compellingly and inescapably it can hold in bondage the individuals who constitute it—until finally the continuous shift of its centre of gravity that accompanies its reproduction through generations makes possible more or less violent changes in the mutual bonds of people, so giving rise to new forms of integration.

18. The regularities of social dynamics place the central ruler and apparatus in a curious situation, the more so the more specialized this apparatus and its organs become. The central ruler and his staff may have reached the top of the central administration as proponents of a particular social formation; or they may be recruited primarily from a certain class of society. But once someone has attained a position in the central apparatus and held on to it for any time, it imposes its own regularities upon him. It distances him in varying degrees from all the other groups and classes of society, even the one which has brought him to power and from which he originates. His specific function gives the central ruler of a differentiated society specific interests. It is his function to superintend the cohesion and security of the whole of society as it exists, and he is thus concerned to balance the interests of the other functional groups. And this task, with which he is simply confronted by daily experience and which conditions his whole view of society—this task itself distances him from all the other groups of functionaries. But he must also, like any other person, be concerned for his own social survival. He must work to ensure that his social power is not reduced, but, if anything, increased. In this sense he, too, is a party within the play of social forces. Insofar as his interests, through the peculiarity of his function, are bound up with the security and smooth functioning of the whole social structure, he must favour some individuals within this structure, he must win battles and enter alliances within it with a view to strengthening his personal position. But in this the interests of the central ruler never become *quite* identical with those of any other class or group. They may sometimes converge with those of one group or another, but if he identifies too strongly with one of them, if the distance between himself and any group diminishes too far, his own social position is sooner or later threatened. For its strength depends, as noted above, on the one hand on the preservation of a certain balance between the different groups, and a certain degree of co-operation and cohesion between the different interests of society; but it also depends on the persistence of sharp and permanent tensions and conflicts of interest between them. The central ruler undermines his own position in using his power and support to make one group clearly superior to others. Dependence on a supreme co-ordinator, and thus his own functional dominance, necessarily shrink when a single group or class of society unequivocally has the upper hand over all others, unless this group is itself torn by internal tensions. And the central ruler's position is no less weakened and undermined if the tensions between the leading groups of society are so reduced that they can settle their differences between themselves and unite in common actions. This is true at least for relatively peaceful times. In time of war, when an external enemy of the whole of society, or at least of its most important groups,

must be repulsed, a reduction of internal tensions can be harmless and useful even to the central ruler.

To put the matter in a few words, the central ruler and his apparatus form within his society a centre of interests of its own. His position often urges an alliance with the second most powerful group rather than identification with the most powerful; and his interest requires both a certain co-operation and a certain tension between society's parts. Thus, his position not only depends on the nature and strength of the ambivalence between the different formations making up society; his relationship to each of these formations is itself ambivalent.

The basic pattern of society that emerges in this way is very simple. The single ruler, the king, is always as an individual incomparably weaker than the whole society whose ruler or first servant he is. If this whole society, or even a considerable part of it, stood together against him, he would be powerless as every individual is powerless in face of pressure from a whole network of interdependent people. The unique position, the abundance of power inhering in a single person as the central ruler of a society is to be explained, as we have said, by the fact that the interests of people in this society are partly alike and partly opposed, that their actions are both adjusted to and contrary to each other's needs; it is explained by the fundamental ambivalence of the social relationships within a complex society. There are conditions in which the positive side of these relationships grows dominant or is at least not smothered by the negative side. But on the way towards dominance of the negative side there are transitional phases in which antagonisms and conflicts of interest grow so strong that the continuing interdependence of actions and interests is obscured to the consciousness of the participants without quite losing its importance. The constellation that thus comes into being has already been described: different parts of society hold each other roughly in balance in terms of social strength; the tensions between them find expression in a chain of major or minor skirmishes; but neither side can conquer or destroy the other; they cannot settle their differences because any strengthening of one side will threaten the social existence of the other; they cannot split wholly apart because their social existence is interdependent. This is a situation that gives the king, the man at the top, the central ruler, optimal power. It shows unmistakably where his specific interests lie. Through this interplay of strong interdependencies and strong antagonisms there arises a social apparatus which might be considered a dangerous invention, at once significant and cruel, were it the work of a single social engineer. Like all social formations in these phases of history, however, this "royal mechanism" which gives a single man extraordinary power as supreme co-ordinator, arises very gradually and unintentionally in the course of social processes.

This apparatus can be brought to mind most vividly and simply by the image of the tug-of-war. Groups, social forces, that hold each other roughly in check, stretch a rope. One side pits itself with all its might against the other; both heave incessantly; but neither side can dislodge the other appreciably from its position. If in this situation of utmost tension between groups pulling the same rope in opposite directions and yet bound together by this rope, there is a man who belongs entirely to neither of the two contending groups, who has the possibility of interposing his individual strength now on the side of one group, now of the other, while taking great care not to allow the tension itself to be reduced or either of the sides to obtain a clear advantage, then he is the one who actually controls this whole tension; the minimal power at the disposal of a single man, who alone could set neither of the groups in motion and quite certainly not both combined, is sufficient, with this arrangement of social forces, to move the whole. The reason why it is sufficient is clear. Within this balanced apparatus enormous forces are latent but bound; without someone to release them they can have no effect. At the touch of a finger an individual releases the forces of one side; he unites himself with the latent forces operating in one direction so that they gain a slight advantage. This enables them to become manifest. This type of social organization represents as it were a power-station which automatically multiplies the smallest effort of the person in control. But an extremely cautious manipulation of this apparatus is called for if it is to function for any length of time without disruption. The man in control is subject to its regularities and compulsions to exactly the same degree as everyone else. His scope for decision is greater than theirs, but he is highly dependent on the structure of the apparatus; his power is anything but absolute.

This is no more than a schematic outline of the arrangement of social forces that gives the central ruler optimal power. But this sketch shows clearly the fundamental structure of his social position. Not by chance, not whenever a strong ruling personality is born, but when a specific social structure provides the opportunity, does the central organ attain that optimal power which usually finds expression in a strong autocracy. The relatively wide scope for decision left open in this way to the central ruler of a large and complex society comes about through his standing in the crossfire of social tensions, so being able to play on the variously directed interests and ambitions counterpoised in his dominion.

Of course, this outline simplifies the actual state of affairs to a certain extent. Equilibrium in the field of tensions making up every society always arises in differentiated human networks through the collaboration and collision of a large number of groups and classes. But the importance of this multi-polar tension for the central ruler's position is no different from that of the bi-polar tension outlined above.

The antagonism between different parts of society certainly does not only take the form of conscious conflict. Plans and consciously adopted goals are far less decisive in producing tensions than anonymous figurational dynamics. To give one example, it is the dynamics of advancing monetarization and commercializ-ation far more than the conscious attacks of bourgeois-urban circles, which push the bulk of the knightly feudal lords downhill at the end of the Middle Ages. But however the antagonisms arising with the advance of the money network may be expressed in the plans and goals of individual people or groups, with them grows the tension between the urban classes who are gaining strength and the functionally weakening lords of the land. With the growth of this network and this tension, however, grows the room to manoeuvre of those who, having won the struggle between initially freely competing units, have become the central rulers of the whole—the kings, until finally, balanced between the bourgeoisie and the nobility, they attain their optimal strength in the form of the absolute monarchy.

19. We asked earlier how it is possible at all for a central authority with absolute power to evolve and survive within a differentiated society, despite the fact that this central ruler is no less dependent on the working of the entire mechanism than the occupants of other positions. The pattern of the royal mechanism provides the answer. It is no longer his military power or the size of his possessions and revenues *alone* that can explain the social power of the central ruler in this phase, even though no central authority can function without these two components. For the central rulers of a complex society to attain such optimal power as they had in the age of absolutism requires, in addition, a special distribution of forces within their society.

In fact the social institution of the monarchy attains its greatest power at that phase in history when a weakening nobility is already forced to compete in many ways with rising bourgeois groups, without either side being able decisively to defeat the other. The quickening monetarization and commercialization of the sixteenth century gives bourgeois groups increased impetus; it appreciably pushes back the bulk of the warrior class, the old nobility. At the end of the social struggles in which this violent transformation of society finds expression, the interdependence between parts of the nobility and parts of the bourgeoisie has grown considerably. The nobility, whose social function and form is itself undergoing a decisive transformation, now has to contend with a third estate, whose members have become, in part, far stronger and more socially ambitious than hitherto. Many families of the old warrior nobility die out, many bourgeois families take on aristocratic character and within a few generations their descendants themselves uphold the interests of the transformed nobility against those of the bourgeoisie, interests which now, in keeping with the closer integration, are more inescapably opposed.

But the objective of this bourgeois class, or at least of its leading groups, is not—like that of substantial parts of the bourgeoisie in 1789—to eliminate the nobility as a social institution. The highest goal of individual bourgeois is, as we have mentioned, to obtain for themselves and their family an aristocratic title with the attendant privileges. The representative leading groups of the bourgeoisie as a whole set out to seize the privileges and prestige of the military nobility; they do not want to remove the nobility as such, but at most to take their place as a new nobility supplanting or merely supplementing the old. Incessantly, this leading group of the third estate, the *noblesse de robe*, emphasize in the seventeenth and above all in the eighteenth century, that their nobility is just as good, important and genuine as that won by the sword. And the rivalry thus expressed certainly does not manifest itself only in words and ideologies. Behind it is a continuous, if more or less concealed and indecisive struggle for power positions and advantages between the representatives of the two estates.

As has been stressed above, it is to block understanding of this social constellation to start from the presupposition that the bourgeoisie of this phase is roughly the same formation as today or at least yesterday—if, in other words, we regard the "independent merchant" as the most typical and socially most important representative of the bourgeoisie. The most representative and socially influential example of the bourgeois in the seventeenth and eighteenth centuries is, at least in the larger Continental countries, the middle-class servant of princes or kings, that is, a man whose nearer or more distant forefathers were indeed craftsmen or merchants, but who himself now occupies a quasi-official position within the governmental apparatus. Before merchant classes themselves form the leading groups of the bourgeoisie, there are at the top of the third estate—to speak in our language—bureaucrats.

The structure and character of official posts varies widely in particular countries. In old France the most weighty representative of the bourgeoisie is a peculiar mixture of *rentier* and official; he is a man who has bought a position in the state service as his personal and, as it were, private property, or, which comes to the same thing, has inherited one from his father. Through this official position he enjoys a number of quite specific privileges; for example, many of these posts carry exemption from taxes; and the capital invested bears interest in the form of fees, a salary or other income which the post brings in.

It is men of this kind, men of the "robe", who during the *ancien régime* represent the bourgeoisie at the assemblies of the estates, and are in general, even outside these assemblies, its spokesmen, the exponents of its interests *vis-à-vis* the other estates and the kings. And whatever social power the third estate possesses is expressed in the demands and political tactics of this leading group. Undoubtedly, the interests of this bourgeois upper class are not always identical with those of the other bourgeois groups. Common to them, however, is one interest above all others: the preservation of their various privileges. For it is not only the social existence of the noble or official which is distinguished by special rights and privileges; the merchant of this time is likewise dependent on them; so, too, are the craft guilds. Whatever these privileges may consist of in particular cases, the bourgeoisie, as far as it carries any social weight, is, up to the second half of the eighteenth century, a social formation characterized and maintained by special rights in exactly the same way as the nobility itself. And here, therefore, we come upon a particular aspect of the machinery by virtue of which this bourgeoisie is never able to deliver a decisive blow against its antagonist, the nobility. It may contest this or that particular privilege of the nobility; but it can and will never eliminate the social institution of privilege as such, which makes the nobility a class apart; for its own social existence, the preservation of which is its main concern, is likewise maintained and protected by privileges. It is only when bourgeois forms of existence no longer based on class privileges emerge more and more in the tissue of society, and when as a result an ever-larger sector of society recognizes these special rights guaranteed or created by the government as a serious impediment to the whole functionally divided network of processes, only then are social forces in existence which can decisively oppose the nobility, which strive to eliminate not only particular noble privileges, but the social institution of noble privileges itself.

But the new bourgeois groups who now oppose privileges as such thereby lay hands, knowingly or otherwise, on the foundation of the old bourgeois formations, the bourgeois estate. Its privileges, its whole organization as an estate, have a social function only as long as a privileged nobility exists in opposition to it. The estates are hostile or, more precisely, ambivalent sibllings, interdependent cells of the same social order. If one is destroyed as an institution, the other automatically falls, and with it the whole order.

In fact, the Revolution of 1789 is not simply a struggle of the bourgeoisie against the nobility. By it the middle-class estate, particularly that of the robe, the privileged officials of the third estate and also those of the old craft guilds, is destroyed no less than the nobility. And this common end illuminates at a stroke the whole social entanglement, the specific constellation of forces of the preceding phase. It illustrates what was said earlier in general terms about the interdependence and ambivalence of the interests of certain social classes, about the balanced mechanism that arises with them, and about the social power of the central authority. The politically relevant parts of the bourgeoisie which did not constitute an estate and emerged very slowly from the earlier one, these older bourgeois groups are bound in their interests, their actions and thoughts, entirely to the existence and the specific equilibrium of an order based on estates. For this reason, in all their conflicts with the nobility and also, of course, with the first estate, the clergy, they are always being caught, like the latter, in the trap of their ambivalent interests. They never dare advance too far in their struggle with the nobility without cutting into their own flesh; any decisive blow against the nobility as an institution would shake the whole state and social structure and thus knock down like skittles the social existence of this privileged bourgeoisie. All the privileged classes are equally concerned not to push the struggle between them too far; they all fear nothing more than a profound upheaval and shift of weight within the social structure as a whole.

But at the same time they cannot entirely avoid conflict with each other; for their interests, parallel in one direction, are diametrically opposed in many others. Social power is so distributed between them and their rivalry so great, that one side feels threatened by the slightest advantage of the other and by anything that might give the other the least superiority of power. Accordingly, there is on the one hand no lack of courteous and even friendly relationships between members of the different groups; but on the other their relations, above all between the leading groups, remain extremely strained throughout the whole of the *ancien régime*. Each fears the other; each observes the other's steps with constant if concealed mistrust. Moreover, this main axis of tension between the nobility and bourgeoisie is embedded in a multitude of others no less ambivalent. The official hierarchy of the secular governmental apparatus is in constant open or latent competition for power and prestige with the clerical hierarchy. The clerics in turn are forever colliding for one reason or another with this or that circle of the nobility. So this multi-polar system of equilibrium constantly gives rise to minor explosions and skirmishes, to social trials of strength in various ideological disguises and for the most diverse and often quite incidental reasons.

The king or his representatives, however, steers and controls this whole mechanism by pitting his weight now in one direction, now another, and his social power is so great precisely because the structural tension between the main groups in the social network is too strong to allow them to reach direct agreement in their affairs and thus to make a determined common stand against the king.

As we know, it was in only one country during this period that bourgeois and noble groups took such a stand successfully against the king—in England. Whatever may be the special structural characteristics of English society that permit the tension between the estates to relax and stable contacts between them to be established—the social constellation which, after considerable tribulations, leads in England to a restriction of the central ruler's powers, makes clear to us once more the different basic constellation which in other countries maintains the social power and the absolutist form of the central authority.

During the sixteenth and even the early seventeenth century, there is no lack, in France too, of attempts by people of the most different social origins to combine against the menacing increase in royal power. They all fail. These civil wars and revolts reveal quite nakedly how strong even in France is the desire among the various estates to restrict the powers of the kings and their representatives. But they show no less clearly how strong are the rivalries and conflicts of interest between these groups, which impede a common pursuit of this objective. Each of them would like to limit the monarchy in its own favour, and each is just strong enough to prevent others from doing so. They all hold each other in check, and so they finally find themselves resigned to their common dependence on a strong king.

There is, in other words, within that great social transformation which makes bourgeois groups functionally stronger and aristocratic ones weaker, a phase when both groups—despite all the tensions both between them and third parties and within themselves—by and large balance each other out in social power. Thus is established for a greater or lesser period that apparatus that was described above as the "royal mechanism": the antitheses between the two main groups are too great to make a decisive compromise between them likely; and the distribution of power, together with their close interdependence, prevents a decisive struggle or the clear predominance of one or the other. So, incapable of uniting, incapable of fighting with all their strength and winning, they must leave to a central ruler all the decisions that they cannot bring about themselves.

This apparatus is formed, as we have said, in a blind, unplanned way in the course of social processes. Whether it is controlled well or badly, however, depends very much on the person exercising the central function. Reference to a few particular historical facts must be enough here to show how the apparatus is formed, and to illustrate what has been said in general terms about the absolutist royal mechanism.

20. In the society of the ninth and tenth centuries there are two classes of free men, the clerics and the warriors. Below them, the mass of the more or less unfree, who are generally excluded from bearing arms, have no active part in social life, even though the existence of society depends on their activities. We have noted that under the special conditions of the western Frankish area, the dependence of the warriors, practically autarkic lords on their estates, on the co-ordinating activity of a central ruler is only slight. The dependence of the clerics on the king, for the most diverse reasons, is far greater. The Church in the western Frankish area never attained major secular power as it did in the empire. Archbishops did not here become dukes. The ecclesiastical peers remain by and large outside the system of competing territorial lords. Thus their centrifugal interests directed at weakening the central ruler are not particularly strong. The possessions of the clerics lie scattered amongst the dominions of secular lords. They are constantly exposed to attacks and encroachment by the latter. The Church therefore desires a central ruler, a king, who has enough power to protect her against secular violence. The feuds, the major and minor wars that are incessantly flaring up across the whole region, are often highly unwelcome to the monks and other clerics who, while certainly more militarily competent and even bellicose than later, at any rate did not live on or for war. These feuds and wars often enough take place at their expense. And over and again priests and abbeys throughout the country, mistreated, injured, deprived of their rights, appeal to the king as judge.

The strong, only occasionally troubled, association between the first Capetian kings and the Church is in no way fortuitous; nor does its cause lie solely in the strong personal faith of these first Capetians. It also expresses an obvious constellation of interests. The dignity of the monarchy in this phase, whatever else it may be, is always an instrument of the priests in their conflict with the warrior class. The royal consecration, anointment and coronation are influenced more and more by Church investiture and ceremony. The monarchy takes on a kind or sacral character; it becomes in a certain sense an ecclesiastical function. That this link, unlike what happens in other societies, does not go beyond these mere beginnings of a merging of worldly and ecclesiastical central authority, and is very soon broken off, results not least from the structure of the Christian Church itself. This Church is older and its organization more firmly established than most secular dominions of the time; and it has its own head, who aspires more and more clearly to combine spiritual pre-eminence with worldly supremacy, a central authority transcending all others. Sooner or later, therefore, a competitive situation arises, a struggle for supremacy between the Pope and the worldly central lord of a given area. This struggle everywhere ends with the Pope being thrown back on his spiritual predominance, with the worldly character of emperor and king re-emerging more clearly, and with the latters' incipient assimilation to the Church hierarchy and ritual regressing without entirely disappearing. But the fact that there are even the beginnings of such an assimilation in the West is worthy of note—especially in comparing historical structures and in explaining differences between social processes in various parts of the world.

The western Frankish kings, for their part, at first collaborate quite closely with the Church, in keeping with the structural regularity governing their function, discussed earlier. They take support for the second strongest group in their conflict with the stronger and more dangerous. They are nominally the liege lords over all warriors. But in the domains of the other great lords they are, to begin with, virtually powerless, and even within their own territory their power is sharply restricted. The close association of royal house and Church turns the monasteries, abbeys and bishoprics in the lands of other territorial lords into bastions of the monarchy; it puts a part of the Church's spiritual influence throughout the country at their disposal. And the kings derive numerous advantages from the writing skills of the clergy, the political and organizational experience of the Church bureaucracy, and not least its finance. It is an open question whether the kings of the early Capetian period receive, over and above the revenues from their own territory, any actual "royal income", that is, duties from the whole western Frankish kingdom. If they have such income, it is hardly a significant addition to what they receive from their own domestic estates. But one thing is certain: they receive duties from Church institutions in regions outside their own territory, for example the income of a vacant diocese or occasional subsidies in extraordinary situations. And if anything gives the traditional royal house an advantage in power over the competing houses, if anything contributes to the fact that in these early elimination struggles beginning within their own territory, the Capetians are the first to begin to rebuild their power, it is this alliance of the nominal central rulers with the

Church. From this alliance above all, in a phase of powerful centrifugal tendencies, spring those social forces which work independently of the individual kings for the continuity of the monarchy, and in the direction of centralization. The importance of the clergy as a motive force of centralization recedes, without entirely disappearing, in proportion as the third estate advances. But even in this phase it is apparent how the tensions between different social groups, beginning with that between the priestly class and the warrior class, benefit the central ruler; but it is clear, too, how he is bound by these tensions, imprisoned by them. The excessive power of the many military lords drives king and Church together, even though minor conflicts between them are not lacking. But the first major difference between king and Church, the first real power struggle between them, occurs only when more abundant human and financial resources are beginning to flow to the king from the bourgeois camp, in the period of Philip Augustus.

21. With the formation of a third estate, the network of tensions becomes more complex and the axis of tension within society moves. Just as in an interdependent system of competing countries or territories, particular tensions become predominant at different times, all the other antagonisms being subordinated to them until one of the main power centres establishes preponderance, similarly there are, within each dominion, certain central tensions about which numerous smaller ones crystallize, and which gradually shift in favour of one side or the other. If these central tensions include, up to the eleventh and twelfth centuries, the ambivalent relationship between the warriors and the clergy, from then on the antagonism between the warriors and the urban–bourgeois groups slowly but steadily moves into the foreground as the central internal tension. With it, and the whole differentiation of society that it expresses, the central ruler gains new importance: the dependence of all parts of society on a supreme co-ordinator grows. The kings who, in the course of the struggles for predominance, detach themselves more and more from the rest of the warrior class as their dominions expand, also distance themselves from the other warriors through their position within the tension between the latter and the urban classes. In this tension they are not by any means unequivocally on the side of the warriors, to whom they belong by origin. Rather, they apply their weight now to one side of the scales, now to the other.

The towns' attainment of communal rights is the first milestone on this road. The kings of this phase, above all Louis VI and VII, like their representatives and all the other feudal lords, regard the growing communes with mistrust and, to say the least, "partial hostility",[101] particularly within their own domain. Only gradually do the kings grasp the uses of these unfamiliar formations. As always, a certain time is needed for them to perceive that the emergence of a third estate within the fabric of society means an immense enlargement of their own scope. But from then on they promote the interests of this third estate with the utmost consistency, as far as these accord with their own. Above all they foster the financial, taxable power of the bourgeoisie. But they emphatically oppose, whenever they have the power to do so, the towns' claims to governmental functions, claims which cannot fail to arise with the growing economic and social power of the urban classes. The rise of the monarchy and that of the bourgeoisie are connected in the closest functional interdependence; partly consciously, partly unwittingly, these two social positions elevate each other; but their relations remain always ambivalent. There is no lack of animosity and conflict between them nor, at first, of occasions when the nobility and bourgeoisie attempt jointly to restrict the sovereign powers of the kings. Throughout the entire Middle Ages, the kings find themselves repeatedly in situations where they have to seek the approval of the assembled representatives of the estates for certain measures; and the course taken by these assemblies, both the smaller regional ones and the larger ones representing broad areas of the kingdom, shows clearly how different the structure of tensions in society still is, despite all its fluctuations, from that existing in the absolutist period. [102] The parliaments of the estates—to use their English name—are able to function, not unlike the party parliaments of bourgeois–industrial society, as long as direct agreement between the representatives of different classes over particular objectives is possible. They function less well the more difficult direct compromise becomes, and the greater the tensions within society; and to the same degree the potential power of the central ruler rises. Given the low degree of monetary and commercial integration in the medieval world, at first neither the interdependence nor the antagonisms between the land-owning warrior class and the urban bourgeois class were such that they needed to hand over the regulation of their relations to the central ruler. Each estate, the knights and the burghers, like the clergy, despite their contacts, live far more within their own confines than later. The different estates do not yet compete so frequently or directly for the same social opportunities; and the leading bourgeois groups are still far from being strong enough to challenge the social pre-eminence of the nobility, the warriors. Only at one point in society do rising bourgeois elements, with the help of the monarchy, gradually displace knights and clergy directly from their positions: within the governmental apparatus, as officials.

22. The functional dependence of the monarchy on what went on in society at large is manifested particularly clearly in the development of the machinery of government, in the splitting-off of all those institutions which first of all were not much more than parts of the royal domestic and domanial administration. When the society of free men consists essentially only of knights and clergy, the government apparatus, too, is made up above all of knights and clergy; the clergy or clerks, as already mentioned, usually being loyal servants and proponents of royal interests, while the feudal lords, even at court and within the royal administration, are often enough rivals of the king, more concerned with developing their own power positions than with consolidating his. Then, as the

warrior class outside the governmental apparatus becomes more complex, as in the course of the elimination struggles major and minor feudal lords are more sharply differentiated, this constellation is mirrored in the structure of a growing governmental machine: clerics and members of minor warrior houses form its staff while major feudal lords find themselves confined to very few positions, for example, as members of the great assembly or the smaller council.

Even in this phase men from the stratum below the warriors and priests are certainly not lacking in the royal administration, even if elements of unfree origin do not play the same role in the development of the French central apparatus as they do in the development of the German. Perhaps that is connected with the fact that in the former case, urban communities, and thus a third estate of freedmen, have risen somewhat earlier to independent significance than in the latter. In France the participation of urban groups in the royal administration rises with the growth of the towns, and as early as the Middle Ages members of these groups gradually permeate the governmental apparatus to an extent that is not reached in the majority of German territories until well into the modern period.

They enter this apparatus by two main routes:[103] first through their growing share of secular posts, that is, positions previously filled by nobles, and secondly through their share of ecclesiastical posts, that is as clerks. The term *clerc* begins slowly to change its meaning from about the end of the twelfth century onwards; its ecclesiastical connotation recedes and it refers more and more to a man who has studied, who can read and write Latin, though it may be that the first stages of an ecclesiastical career are for a time a prerequisite for this. Then, in conjunction with the extension of the administrative apparatus, both the term *clerc* and certain kinds of university study are increasingly secularized. People no longer learn Latin exclusively to become members of the clergy, they also learn it to become officials. To be sure, there are still bourgeois who enter the king's council simply on account of their commercial or organizational competence. But the majority of bourgeois attain the higher regions of government through study, through knowledge of canon and Roman law. Study becomes a normal means of social advancement for the sons of leading urban strata. Bourgeois elements slowly push back the noble and ecclesiastical elements in the government. The class of royal servants, of "officials", becomes—in contrast to the situation in Germany—an exclusively bourgeois formation.

From the time of Philip Augustus onwards at the latest . . . the lawyers, true "knights of law" (*chevaliers ès lois*) appear: they were to take on the task of amalgamating feudal with canon and Roman law to make up monarchic law. . . . A small army of thirty scribes in 1316, 104 or 105 in 1359, about sixty in 1361, these chancellery clerks gained numerous advantages from constantly swelling their ranks in the proximity of the king. The broad mass was to become privileged notaries; the élite (three under Philip the Fair, twelve before 1388, sixteen in 1406, eight in 1413) would give birth to the privy clerks or financial secretaries. . . . The future was theirs. Unlike the grand officers of a palatinate, they had no ancestors, but were themselves to be ancestors.[104]

With the growth of the royal possessions a class of specialists is formed whose social position depends first and foremost on their place in royal service, and whose prestige and interests are largely identical with those of the monarchy and the governmental apparatus. As the Church had done earlier, and still did to some extent, members of the third estate now uphold the interests of the central function. They do so in the most diverse capacities, as scribes and councillors to the king, as tax administrators, as members of the highest courts. And it is they who seek to ensure the continuity of royal policy beyond the life of a particular king and often enough against his personal inclinations. Here too, bourgeois classes elevate the monarchy, and the monarchs elevate the bourgeois classes.

23. With this almost total expulsion of the nobility from the governmental apparatus, the bourgeoisie attains in the course of time a power position which is of the utmost importance to the overall balance of power in society. In France, as already mentioned, it is not, almost till the end of the *ancien régime*, the rich merchants or the guilds who directly represent the bourgeoisie in conflicts with the nobility; it is the bureaucracy in its various formations. The weakening of the social position of the nobility, the strengthening of the bourgeoisie, is most clearly expressed in the fact that the upper bureaucracy lays claim, at least from the beginning of the seventeenth century onwards, to equal social status with the nobility. At this time the interweaving of interests and the tensions between nobility and bourgeoisie have indeed reached a level which secures exceptional power for the central ruler.

This permeation of the central apparatus by sons of the urban bourgeoisie is one of the strands within that process indicating most clearly the close functional interdependence between the rise of the monarchy and of the bourgeoisie. The bourgeois upper stratum, which gradually evolves from the families of the higher "royal servants", attains in the sixteenth and seventeenth centuries such increased social power that the central ruler would have been at its mercy, had it not counterweights in the nobility and clergy, whose resistance neutralizes their strength; and it is not difficult to observe how the kings, above all, Louis XIV, play constantly on this system of tensions. In the preceding phase, however, the nobility and clergy—despite all the ambivalence already inhering in their relationship—are still, at first, far stronger opponents of the central authority than the urban bourgeoisie. For this very reason the bourgeois eager for social advancement are as welcome helpers of the king as they are willing. The kings allow the central apparatus to become a monopoly of people from the third estate, because this is still socially weaker than the first and second estates.

This interdependence between the growth of the power of king and bourgeoisie, and the weakening of nobility and clergy, is seen from a different aspect if we consider the financial connections between the social existence of the various parties. That this shift to the disadvantage of the nobility is to be attributed only in small part to conscious and systematic actions by bourgeois circles has already been stressed. It is, on the one hand, a consequence of the competitive mechanism by which the bulk of the nobility sink into dependence on a single noble house, the royal house, and thus in a sense to the same level as the bourgeoisie. On the other, it is a consequence of advancing monetary integration. Hand in hand with the rise in the volume of money goes a constant devaluation. This increase and devaluation of money accelerates in the sixteenth century to an extraordinary extent. And the nobility who live on the income from their estates, which they cannot increase to keep pace with devaluation, are impoverished.

The religious wars—to mention only this final act—have the same significance for the weakening nobility as civil wars so often have for declining classes: they conceal from them, for a time, the inevitability of their fate. The uproar and unrest, the self-assertion in fighting, the possibility of pillage and the facility of gain, all this encourages the nobility to believe they can maintain their threatened social position and save themselves from downfall and impoverishment. Of the economic upheavals whirling them back and forth, those embroiled in them have scarcely an inkling. They see that money is increasing, prices rising, but they do not understand it. Brantôme, one of the courtly warriors of the period, has captured this mood:

> . . . far from having impoverished France, this (civil) war has positively enriched her, in so far as it has uncovered and placed in full view an infinity of treasures previously hidden underground, where they served no purpose. . . . It has placed them so well in the sun, and turned them into such quantities of good money, that there were more millions of gold to be seen shining in France than there had been millions of silver pounds before, and there appeared more new, subtle silver coins, forged from these fine hidden treasures, than there had been coppers before. . . . And that is not all: the rich merchants, usurers, bankers and other niggards down to the priests, kept their coin locked in their coffers and neither enjoyed it themselves nor lent it except at gross interest and with excessive usury, or by the purchase or mortgage of land, goods or houses at a wretched price; so that the noble who had been impoverished during the foreign wars and had pawned or sold his goods, was at his wits' end, without even the wood to keep himself warm, for these scamps of usurers had pocketed everything—this good civil war restored them to their rightful place. So I have seen gentlemen of high birth who, before the civil war, went about with two horses and a footman, recover to such effect that during and after it they were seen travelling the country with six or seven good horses. . . . *And that is how the honest nobility of France has been restored by the grace or, one might say, by the grease of the good civil war.*[105]

In reality the majority of the French nobility, on their return from this "good" civil war, find themselves debt-ridden and ruined once more. Life grows more

expensive. Creditors, along with rich merchants, usurers and bankers, and above
all high officials, men of the robe, clamour for repayment of the money they have
lent. Wherever they can, they possess themselves of the noble estates, and often
enough the titles too.

The nobles who hold on to their estates very soon find their income no longer
sufficient to cover the increased cost of living:

> The lords who had ceded land to their peasants against duties in cash, continued to
> collect the same revenue but without the same value. What had cost five sous in the past
> cost twenty at the time of Henry III. The nobles grew poor without knowing it.[106]

24. The picture of the distribution of social power that presents itself here is
fairly unambiguous. The change in the social structure which had long been
working against the warrior nobility in favour of bourgeois classes, accelerates in
the sixteenth century. The latter gain in social weight what the former lose.
Antagonisms in society grow. The warrior nobility do not understand the process
forcing them out of their hereditary positions, but they see it embodied in these
men of the third estate with whom they must now compete directly for the same
opportunities, above all for money, but also, through money, for their own land
and even their social pre-eminence. Thereby the equilibrium is slowly established
which gives optimal power to one man, the central ruler.

In the struggles of the sixteenth and seventeenth centuries we come across
bourgeois corporations which have become wealthy, numerous and powerful
enough to confront the warrior nobility's claims to dominance and power with
firm resistance, but neither able nor strong enough to make the warriors, the
military class, directly dependent on them. We find a nobility still strong and
belligerent enough to represent a constant threat to the rising bourgeois classes,
but already too weak, above all economically, to control directly the town-
dwellers and their taxes. The fact that at this time the nobility has already
entirely lost the functions of administration and jurisdiction, these being now in
the hands of bourgeois corporations, contributes in no small way to the nobility's
weakness. Nevertheless, no part of society is yet able to attain a lasting and
decisive preponderance over the others. In this situation the king again and again
appears to each class or corporation as an ally against the threats from other
groups which they cannot master on their own.

Of course, the nobility and bourgeoisie themselves consist of various groups
and strata whose interests do not always run in the same direction. Into the
primary tension between these two classes are woven numerous other tensions,
whether within these groups or between one or other of them and the clergy. But
at the same time all these groups and strata are more or less dependent for their
existence on the others; none is at this stage strong enough to overthrow the
established order as a whole. The leading groups, the only ones which can exert a
certain political influence within the framework of the existing institutions, are

the least disposed to radical change. And this multiplicity of tensions strengthens all the more the potential power of the kings.

Of course, each of these leading groups, the highest nobles, the "great ones" at court, as much as of the bourgeoisie, the parliaments, would like to restrict the royal power in their own favour. Efforts or at least ideas tending in this direction recur throughout the whole of the *ancien regimé*. These social groups with opposed interests and wishes are also divided in their attitude to the monarchy. There is no lack of occasions on which this becomes clear; there are even a number of temporary alliances between noble and urban–bourgeois groups, above all the parliaments, against the representatives of the monarchy. But if anything shows up the difficulty of such direct reconciliation, and the strength of the tensions and rivalries existing between the parties, it is the fate of such occasional alliances.

Take, for example, the *Fronde*. Louis XIV is still a minor. Mazarin is governing. Once more, for the last time for a long period, the most disparate social groups unite to assail royal omnipotence represented by the Minister. Parliaments and broad nobility, urban corporations and men of the high nobility, all try to exploit the monarchy's moment of weakness, the regency of the Queen exercised by the Cardinal. But the picture presented by this rising shows clearly enough how tense are relationships between all these groups. The *Fronde* is a kind of social experiment. It exposes once again the structure of tensions which gives the central authority its strength, but which remains concealed from view as long as this authority is firmly established. No sooner does one of the competing allies seem to gain the slightest advantage than all the others feel threatened, desert the alliance, make common cause with Mazarin against their erstwhile ally, and then partly switch back to his side. Each of these people and groups wants to curtail royal power; but each wants to do it to his own advantage. Each fears that another's power might grow at the same time. Finally—not least thanks to the skill with which Mazarin takes advantage of this mechanism of tensions—the old equilibrium is re-established in favour of the existing royal house. Louis XIV never forgot the lesson of these days; far more consciously and carefully than all his predecessors, he nurtured this equilibrium and maintained the existing social differences and tensions.

25. For a long period of the Middle Ages the urban classes, through their social position, are decidedly weaker than the warrior nobility. In this period the community of interests between the king and the bourgeois section of society is considerable, if not so great that friction and even conflicts between towns and the central ruler are entirely absent. One of the most visible consequences of this community of interests, as we have noted, is the expulsion of the nobility from the monarchy's governmental organization, and its permeation by people of bourgeois origin.

Then, as the relative social power of the nobility diminishes with the advance of monetary integration and monopolization, the kings shift some of their weight back to the side of the nobility. They now secure the existence of the nobility as a privileged class against the bourgeois assault, and they do so to just the degree necessary to preserve the social differences between nobility and bourgeoisie and thus the equilibrium of tensions within the realm. So, for example, they secure for the bulk of the nobility exemption from taxes, which the bourgeoisie would like to see abolished or at least: reduced. But this is certainly not enough to give the economically weak landowners a sufficient basis on which to satisfy their claim to be the upper class and their need to cultivate a demonstratively affluent mode of life. Despite their tax exemption, the mass of the landed nobility lead throughout the *ancien régime* a thoroughly restricted life. They can hardly compete in material prosperity with the upper strata of the bourgeoisie. *Vis-à-vis* the authorities, above all the courts, their position is far from favourable; for the posts in the latter are held by people of bourgeois origin. In addition, the kings, supported by a section of aristocratic opinion, uphold the rule that a noble who engages directly in commerce should renounce both his title and all his noble privileges, at least for the duration of this activity. This rule certainly serves to maintain the existing differences between bourgeoisie and nobility, which the kings no less than the nobles themselves are concerned to preserve. But at the same time it blocks the nobility's only direct access to greater prosperity. Only indirectly, through marriage, can a noble profit from the wealth that stems from commerce and official posts. The nobility would have had nothing of the splendour and social prestige they still enjoyed in the seventeenth and eighteenth centuries; they would unfailingly have succumbed to the increasingly prosperous bourgeoisie and perhaps to a new bourgeois nobility, had they not—or at least a small section of them—obtained with the king's help a new monopoly position at court. This both permitted them a mode of life adequate to their social station, and preserved them from involvement in bourgeois activities. The court offices, the many and various official positions within the royal household, are reserved to the aristocracy. In this way hundreds and finally thousands of nobles find relatively highly paid posts. Royal favour, attested by occasional gifts, is added for good measure; and proximity to the king gives these posts high prestige. And so from the broad mass of the landed aristocracy there arises a stratum of nobles which can counterbalance the upper bourgeoisie in wealth and influence, the courtly nobility. Just as earlier, when the bourgeoisie was weaker than the aristocracy, posts in the royal administration had been made a bourgeois monopoly with the king's help, now that the nobility is weakening, the court positions, likewise with royal assistance, become a preserve of the nobility.

The exclusive filling of court posts by nobles does not happen at one stroke or by the design of a particular king, any more than the reservation of all the other state posts to the bourgeoisie had been earlier.

Under Henry IV, and still under Louis XIII, court positions, like the majority of military appointments and, still more, like administrative and judicial offices, are purchasable and thus the property of their occupant. This is even true of the post of *gouverneur*, the military commanders of particular regions of the kingdom. To be sure, on occasions the occupant of such a post can only exercise his office with the king's approval, and it naturally happens, too, that this or that position is awarded solely through royal favour. But in general the purchase of offices had by this time gained the upper hand over their nomination through favour. And since the majority of the nobility are no match for the upper bourgeoisie in terms of wealth, the third estate, or at least families sprung from it and only recently ennobled, slowly but visibly take over the court and military posts as well. Only the great noble families still have enough revenue, partly thanks to the size of their lands and partly through pensions paid to them by the king, to hold on to positions of this kind in face of such competition.

Nevertheless, a willingness to help the nobility in this situation is quite unmistakable in Henry IV, just as it is in Louis XIII and Richelieu. None of them forgets for a moment that they are themselves aristocrats. Moreover, Henry IV attained the throne at the head of an army of nobles. But apart from the fact that even they are largely impotent in face of the economic processes working against the nobility, the royal function has necessities of its own, and its relation to the nobility is ambivalent. Henry IV, Richelieu and all their successors, in order to secure their own position, are anxious to keep the nobility as far as possible from positions of political influence; but at the same time they are obliged to preserve the nobility as an independent social factor in the internal balance of forces.

The double face of the absolutist court corresponds exactly to this split relationship of king to nobility. This court is at the same time an instrument for controlling the nobility and a means of sustaining it. In this direction it gradually develops.

Even Henry IV takes it for granted that the king lives within an aristocratic circle. But it is not yet his strict policy to demand permanent residence at court of those members of the nobility who wish to remain in royal favour. No doubt he also lacks the means to finance as enormous a court, and to distribute court offices, favours and pensions as lavishly, as Louis XIV was able to do later. At his time, moreover, society is still in an extreme state of flux. Noble families are declining, bourgeois rising. The estates are surviving, but their occupancy is being drastically transformed. The wall dividing the estates is riddled with holes. Personal qualities or lack of them, personal fortune or misfortune, often play as large a part in a family's destiny as its origin in this or that estate. Even the gates to the court and court offices are still fairly wide open to people of bourgeois origin.

This the nobility deplores. It is they who desire and propose that these offices be reserved to them. And not only these offices. They desire a share in many others; they seek to win back their lost positions in the governmental machine. In

1627 they address to Louis XIII, under the title "Requests and Articles for the Restoration of the Nobility", a petition with precise proposals to this effect.[107]

The petition begins by saying that, after divine help and the sword of Henry IV, it is the nobility who are to be thanked for the preservation of the crown at a time when the majority of other classes had been incited to insurrection; yet the nobility were "in the most pitiable state they had ever known . . . crushed by poverty . . . rendered vicious by idleness . . . reduced by oppression almost to despair."

Here, in a few words, a picture of the declining class is sketched. It corresponds closely to reality. Most landed estates are overburdened with debt. Many noble families have lost all their possessions. The youth of the aristocracy is without hope; the unrest and social pressure emanating from these displaced people is felt everywhere in the life of this society. What is to be done?

Among the reasons for this state of affairs, express mention is made of the mistrust which a number of noblemen had aroused in the king through their arrogance and ambition. This had finally led the kings to believe it necessary to reduce the power of such nobles by excluding them from official positions which they had perhaps misused, and by elevating the third estate; so that since that time the nobles had been stripped of their judicial and fiscal duties, and expelled from the king's councils.

Finally, in twenty-two articles, the nobility demand, among other things, the following: in addition to the military command of the various *gouvernements* of the kingdom, the civil and military functions of the royal house—that is, the skeleton of what was later to make the court a sinecure for the nobility—should cease to be purchasable and become reserved to the nobility.

In addition, the nobility demand a certain influence on provincial administration and access for a number of particularly eligible aristocrats to the high courts, the parliaments, at least in an advisory capacity and without emoluments; and they demand, finally, that a third of the membership of the financial and military councils, and other parts of the royal government, should come from their ranks.

Of all these demands, if we disregard a few minor concessions, only one was fulfilled: court posts are closed to the bourgeoisie and reserved to the nobility. All the others, insofar as they involve participation by the nobility, however modest, in government or administration, remain unfulfilled.

In many German territories, nobles seek and receive administrative and judicial offices as well as military ones; at least since the Reformation, they are therefore to be found in the universities.[108] Most of the higher offices of state remain virtually a monopoly of the nobility; elsewhere, nobles and bourgeois normally balance each other *within* many state offices according to a precise formula of allocation.

In the French central government, as we have mentioned, the tension and the constant open or latent struggle between the two estates is expressed in the fact that the whole administration remains a monopoly of the bourgeoisie, while the whole court in the narrower sense, which had always been largely staffed by nobles but was threatened by bourgeoisification when offices were made purchasable, becomes in the seventeenth century once and for all a noble monopoly.

Richelieu, in his will, had recommended that the court should be closed to all those who "have not the good fortune of a noble origin".[109] Louis XIV then restricted access to court offices by bourgeois to the utmost; but even he did not completely close them. Thus, after many preparatory movements in which the social interests of the nobility and the monarchy were, as it were, feeling each other out, the court is given its clear role as an asylum for the nobility on one hand, and a means of controlling and taming the old warrior class on the other. The untrammelled knightly life is gone forever.

For the majority of the nobility, not only are their economic circumstances from now on straitened, but their horizons and scope for action are narrowed. With their meagre revenues they are restricted to their country seats. Escape from this in military campaigns is, to a large extent, blocked. Even in war they no longer fight for themselves as free knights, but as officers in a strict organization. And special luck or connections are needed to escape permanently from the landed nobility to the wider horizons and greater prestige of the noble circle at court.

This smaller part of the nobility finds at court, and in and around Paris, a new, more precarious homeland. Up to the time of Henry IV and Louis XIII it is not difficult for a noble belonging to the court circle to spend time at his country seat or that of another noble. There is, to be sure, a courtly nobility distinct from the broad country gentry; but this society is still relatively decentralized. Louis XIV, having learned his lesson early through the *Fronde*, exploits the nobility's dependence on him to the full. He wants "to unite directly under his eyes all those who are possible leaders of risings, and whose *châteaux* could serve as focal points for rebellion . . . .".[110]

The construction of Versailles corresponds perfectly to both the intertwined tendencies of the monarchy: to provide for and visibly elevate parts of the nobility while controlling and taming them. The king gives liberally, particularly to his favourites. But he demands obedience; he keeps the nobles constantly aware of their dependence on the money and other opportunities he has to distribute.

The King [Saint-Simon records in his *Mémoires*[111]] not only saw that the high nobility were present at his court, he demanded it also of the petty nobles. At his *Lever* and his *Coucher*, at his meals, in his gardens at Versailles, he was always looking about him, noticing everyone. He took it amiss if the most distinguished nobles did not reside permanently at court, and if the others came only seldom, and total disgrace awaited those who showed themselves hardly or not at all. If one of these had a request, the king would say proudly: "I do not know him." And his judgement was irrevocable. He did not mind if a person enjoyed living in the country, but he had to show moderation in this and take precautions before longer absences. Once in my youth when I went to Rouen on some legal business, the king had a minister write to enquire my reasons.

This surveillance of everything that went on is very characteristic of the structure of this monarchy. It shows clearly how strong were the basic tensions which the king had to observe and master in order to maintain his rule, not only within his society but outside it as well. "The art of governing is not at all difficult or unpleasant", Louis XIV once said in his instructions to his heir. "It consists quite simply in knowing the real thoughts of all the princes in Europe, knowing everything that people try to conceal from us, their secrets, and keeping close watch over them."[112]

> The king's curiosity to know what was going on around him [Saint-Simon writes in another place[113]] grew more and more intense; he charged his first valet and the governor of Versailles to enroll a bodyguard. These received the royal livery, were dependent only on those just mentioned, and had the clandestine task of wandering the corridors by day and night, secretly observing and following people, seeing where they went and when they came back, overhearing their conversations and reporting everything exactly.

Hardly anything is as characteristic of the peculiar structure of the society which makes possible a strong autocracy, as this necessity of minutely supervising everything that goes on within the realm. This necessity shows up both the immense tensions and the precariousness of the social apparatus without which the co-ordinating function would not endow the central ruler with so high a power ratio. The tension and equilibrium between the various social groups, and the resulting highly ambivalent attitude of all these groups to the central ruler himself, was certainly not created by any king. But once this constellation had been established, it is vitally important for the ruler to preserve it in all its precariousness. This task demands exact supervision of his subjects.

For good reasons Louis XIV had a particularly watchful eye on people closest to him in rank. The division of labour and the interdependence of everyone, including dependence of the central ruler on the masses, were not yet so advanced that pressure from the common people was the greatest threat to the king, even though popular unrest, above all in Paris, was certainly not without danger; one of the reasons for the removal of his court from Paris to Versailles lies here. But whenever, under Louis' predecessors, dissatisfaction among the masses leads to up-risings, it is members of the royal family or the high nobility who place themselves at their head and use the factions and discontent for their own ambitions. Here, in his closest circle, the monarch's most dangerous rivals are still to be found.

It was shown earlier how, in the course of monopolization, the circle of people able to compete for the chance to rule is gradually reduced to the members of the royal house. Louis XI finally conquered these princely feudal lords and restored their territories to the crown; but in the religious wars different parties are still headed by branches of the royal family. With Henry IV, after the extinction of the main branch, a member of a secondary one again comes to the throne. And the blood princes, the "great ones", the dukes and peers of France, continue to wield considerable power. The basis of this power is fairly clear. It is primarily their position as *Gouverneurs*, military commanders of provinces, and their fortresses. Slowly, with the consolidation of monopoly rule, these possible rivals of the kings take on the character of functionaries in a powerful government apparatus. But they resist this change. The natural brother of Louis XIII, the Duke of Vendôme, Henry IV's bastard son, rises against the central authority at the head of a faction. He is governor of Brittany and believes he has a hereditary right to this province on grounds of marriage. Then it is the governor of Provence from whom the resistance comes, then the governor of Languedoc, the Duke of Montmorency; and even the Huguenot nobility's attempts at resistance have their basis in a similar power position. The army is not yet completely centralized; the commanders of fortresses and captains of strongholds still have a high degree of independence. The governors of provinces regard their purchased and salaried positions as their property. So there are renewed flickerings of centrifugal tendencies in the land. Under Louis XIII they are still perceptible. The king's brother, Gaston, Duke of Orléans, rises, like many royal brothers before him, against the king. He formally renounces friendship for the Cardinal after taking over the leadership of the faction hostile to him, and goes to Orléans to begin his struggle against Richelieu and the King from a strong military position.

Richelieu finally won all these battles, not least with the aid of the bourgeoisie and the superior financial means they put at his disposal. The resisting lords die vanquished, some in prison, some in exile, some in battle; even the king's mother Richelieu lets die abroad.

> The belief that as sons or brothers of the King, or princes of his blood, they may disturb the realm with impunity, is mistaken. It is far more judicious to secure the realm and monarchy than to respect impunity endowed by rank.

So he writes in his memoirs. Louis XIV reaps the benefit of these victories; but a sense of threat from the nobility, particularly the high nobility closest to him, is second nature to him. The lesser nobility he forgives an occasional absence from court if reasons are given. Towards the "great ones" he is implacable. And the court's role as a place of detention emerges particularly clearly in relation to them. "The surest place for a son of France is the heart of the King", he replies when his brother asks him for a governorship and a fortress, a *place de sûreté*. That his eldest son holds separate court at Meudon he views with the utmost displeasure. And when the heir to the throne dies, the king hastily has the furniture of his *château* sold in case the grandson who inherits Meudon should make the same use of it and once again "divide the court".[114]

This fear, says Saint-Simon, was quite groundless. For none of the king's grandsons would have dared to displease him. But when it is a matter of maintaining his prestige and securing his personal rule, the king's severity makes no distinction between his relations and other persons.

Monopoly rule, centred on the monopolies of taxation and physical violence, has thus attained, for this particular stage as the personal monopoly of an individual, its consummate form. It is protected by a fairly efficient organization of surveillance. The land-owning king distributing land or tithes has become a money-owning king distributing salaries: this gives centralization a power and solidity unattained hitherto. The strength of the centrifugal social forces has been finally broken. All possible rivals of the monopoly ruler have been brought into an institutionally secured dependence on him. No longer in free competition but in one restricted by monopoly, only a section of the nobility, the courtly section, competes for the opportunities distributed by the monopoly ruler, and is at the same time under constant pressure from a reserve army of country aristocracy and rising bourgeois elements. The court is the organizational form of this restricted competition.

But even if at this stage the king's personal control of the monopolized opportunities is great, it is anything but unlimited. In the structure of this relatively private monopoly there are already unmistakable elements which will finally lead from personal control of the monopolies to public control by ever-broader sections of society. For Louis XIV the statement: "L'État c'est moi" has, indeed, a measure of truth, whether or not he himself uttered it. Institutionally, the monopoly organization still has to a considerable extent the character of a personal possession. Functionally, however, the monopoly ruler's dependence on other strata, on the entire network of differentiated social functions, is already very great, and is constantly increasing with the advance of the commercial and monetary integration of society. Only the particular situation of society, the peculiar balance of tensions between the rising bourgeois and the declining aristocratic groups, and then between the many major and minor groups throughout the land, gives the central ruler his immense powers of control and decision. The independence with which earlier kings ruled their domains, an expression of lower social interdependence, has vanished. The vast human network that Louis XIV rules has its own momentum and its own centre of gravity which he must respect. It costs immense effort and self-control to preserve the balance of people and groups and, by playing on the tensions, to steer the whole.

The central functionary's ability to govern the whole human network largely in his personal interest is only seriously restricted when the balance on which he is poised tilts sharply in favour of the bourgeoisie, and a new social balance with new axes of tension is established. Only then do personal monopolies begin to become public monopolies in an institutional sense. In a long series of elimination contests, in a gradual centralization of the means of physical violence and taxation, in conjunction with a constantly increasing division of functions and the rise of professional bourgeois classes, French society is organized step by step in the form of a state.

VIII

On the Sociogenesis of the Monopoly of Taxation

26. A certain aspect of this monopolization, and thus of the whole process of state-formation, easily escapes the retrospective observer because he usually has a clearer picture of the later stages, of the results of the process, than of developments lying further back. He can hardly conceive that this absolutist monarchy and centralized government emerged quite gradually from the medieval world as something new and extraordinary in the eyes of its contemporaries. Nevertheless, only an attempt to reconstruct this aspect gives us the possibility of understanding what really happened.

The main outlines of the transformation are clear. From a particular central point it can be described in a few words: *the territorial property of one warrior family, its control of certain lands and its claim to tithes or services of various kinds from the people living on this land, is transformed with the advancing division of functions and in the course of numerous struggles, into a centralized control of military power and of regular duties or taxes over a far larger area.* Within this area no one may now use weapons and fortifications or physical violence of any kind without the central ruler's permission. That is something very novel in a society in which originally a whole class of people could use weapons and physical violence according to their means and their inclinations. And everyone of whom the central ruler requires it is now bound to pay a certain portion of his income or his wealth to the central ruler. This is even more novel, measured by what was customary in medieval society. In the barter economy of that time, where money was relatively rare, demands by princes or kings for money payments—leaving aside certain occasions fixed by tradition—were regarded as something quite unprecedented; such measures were regarded in much the same way as pillaging or the levying of tributes.

"Constituti sunt reditus terrarum, ut ex illis viventes a spoliatione subditorum abstineant";[115] the revenues of the land are intended to prevent those living on them from plundering their subjects, said St Thomas Aquinas. In this he certainly expresses not only the opinion of ecclesiastical circles, even though church institutions are probably particularly exposed to such measures on account of their wealth. The kings themselves do not think very differently, even if, with the general shortage of money, they cannot refrain from repeatedly demanding such compulsory duties. Philip Augustus, for example, arouses so much unrest and opposition through a series of taxes, particularly the contribution for the Crusades in 1188, the famous *dîme saladine*, that in 1189 he declares that no such taxes will ever again be levied. In order, his decree runs, that neither he nor his successors shall ever fall into the same error, he forbids with his royal authority and the whole authority of all the churches and barons of the realm, this damnable effrontery. If anyone, whether the king or anyone else, should attempt "by audacious temperity" to revert to it, he wants them disobeyed.[116] It may be that in the formulation of this decree his pen was guided by agitated notables. But when he is preparing for the Crusade in 1190, he himself expressly orders that in the event of his death during the Crusade, a part of the war treasury shall be distributed among those who have been impoverished by the levies. Duties demanded by the kings in this society with its relative scarcity of money, are indeed something different from taxes in a more commercialized society. No one takes them for granted as a permanent institution; market transactions and the whole level of prices are in no way adjusted to them; they come like a bolt from the blue, ruining large numbers of people. The kings or their representatives, as we can see, are sometimes aware of this. But with the limited revenues they receive directly from their domanial estates, they are constantly faced with the choice of either using all the threats and force at their disposal to raise money by levies, or succumbing to rival powers. All the same, the agitation over the "Saladin tithe" and the opposition it unleashed seem to be long remembered. It is only after seventy-nine years that a king again demands a special tax, an *aide féodale* for his Crusade.

The general belief of kings themselves is that the rulers of a territory and their government should support themselves on the income from their domanial possessions in the narrower sense, that is, on the income from their own estates. To be sure, the kings and a number of other great feudal lords, in the course of monopolization, already rise considerably above the mass of the feudal lords, and we can see in retrospect that new functions are evolving. But these new functions develop only slowly, by small steps and in constant conflict with the representatives of other functions, into solid institutions. For the time being, the king is a great warrior among many other greater or lesser warriors. Like them, he lives on the produce of his estates; but like them he also has a traditional right to raise taxes from the inhabitants of his region on certain extraordinary occasions. Every feudal lord demands and receives certain duties when his daughter is married, when his son is knighted, and to pay his ransom if he is made a prisoner-of-war. These are the original *aides féodales*; and the kings demand them like every other feudal lord. Demands for money over and above these have no basis in custom; this is why they have a similar repute to pillage and extortion.

Then, in about the twelfth and thirteenth centuries, a new form of princely revenue begins to establish itself. In the twelfth century the towns are slowly growing. According to ancient feudal custom, only men of the warrior class, the nobles, are entitled to bear arms; but the burghers have now fought sword in hand for civic freedom or are about to do so; and about the time of Louis VI it becomes customary to enrol the town-dwellers, the "bourgeois", for war duties. Very soon, however, the town-dwellers prefer to offer the territorial lords money instead of war services so that he can hire warriors. They commercialize war service; and to the kings and the other great feudal lords this is not unwelcome. The supply of war services by indigent warriors is usually greater than the purchasing power of the rival feudal lords. So these civic payments for exemption from war service quite quickly become an established custom or an institution. The king's representatives demand from each town community such and such a number of men or the payment of a corresponding sum for a particular campaign, and the towns agree or negotiate a reduction. But even this custom is still seen as only a further form of the feudal *aides* in extraordinary cases; it is called the *aide de l'ost* and these aids are taken together as the "aids in the four cases".

It would take us too far afield to show how the town communities themselves gradually begin to form a kind of internal taxation system for the various communal tasks. Suffice it to say that the king's demands serve to develop this, just as, conversely, the urban taxation institutions that begin to be consolidated about the end of the twelfth century have an importance for the organization of royal taxation that should not be under-estimated. Here, too, the bourgeoisie and the royal house—usually involuntarily—propel each other. But this is certainly not to say that the burghers or any other social class pay willingly and without resistance. As is the case with regular taxation later, no one pays these occasional taxes unless he feels directly or indirectly forced to do so. Both cases indicate exactly the nature of the mutual dependence of groups in society at a given stage and of the prevailing power balances.

The kings do not wish and cannot afford to provoke excessive opposition; the social power of the royal function is clearly not yet strong enough for this. On the other hand, they need for their function and self-assertion, above all to finance the constant struggles with rivals, continual and gradually increasing sums of money that they can only obtain by such *aides*. Their measures change. Under the pressure of this situation the royal representatives grope for one solution after another; they shift the main burden now onto this urban or other class, now that. But in all this twisting and turning the social power of the monarchy is constantly growing, and with this growth, each furthering the other, taxes gradually take on a new character.

In 1292 the king demands a duty of one "denier" in the pound for all wares sold, the duty being payable by both buyer and seller. "An exaction of a kind unheard-of in the French realm"—a chronicler of the time calls it. In Rouen the counting-house of the royal tax-collectors is plundered. Rouen and Paris, the two most important towns in the kingdom, finally buy themselves free for a fixed sum.[117] But this tax remains long in the popular memory under the ominous name *mal-tôte*; and the opposition it arouses remains long in the minds of the royal officials. Accordingly, the king attempts in the following year to raise compulsory loans from the wealthy bourgeois. When this too meets with violent resistance, he reverts in 1295 to the *aide* in its original form; the levy is demanded from all estates, not only the third. One hundredth of the value of all goods is to be paid. But the yield of this tax is clearly not enough. The following year the duty is raised to a fiftieth. And now, of course, the feudal lords also affected by the tax are extremely angry. The king therefore declares himself willing to return to the religious and secular feudal lords a part of the sum he raises from their dominions. He gives them, so to speak, a share of the booty. But this no longer reassures them. Above all, the secular feudal lords, the warriors, feel increasingly threatened in their traditional rights, their independent rule and perhaps even in their whole social existence, by this central governmental apparatus. The king's men are intruding everywhere; they appropriate rights and duties which earlier were the exclusive prerogative of the individual feudal lord. And here, as so often, it is money duties that are the last straw. When, in 1314, shortly before the death of Philip the Fair, high taxes for a campaign in Flanders are once again levied, unrest and discontent, reinforced by the mismanagement of the war, become open resistance. "We cannot tolerate the levying of these 'aides' ", says one of those affected,[118] "we cannot bear them with a quiet conscience; they would cost us our honour, our rights and our freedom." "A new kind of unjustified extortion, of unseemly money-raising, unknown in France and particularly in Paris," another man of the time records, "was used to cover expenses; it was said to be intended for the Flanders war. The servile councils and ministers of the King wanted buyers and sellers to pay six deniers for each pound of the selling price. Nobles and commoners . . . united under oath to maintain their freedom and that of the fatherland."

The unrest is indeed so great and general that towns and feudal lords form an alliance against the king. It is one of those historical experiments from which we can read off the degree of divergence of their interests, the strength of the tension between them. Under the common threat from the fiscal demands of the royal representatives, and the high feelings it arouses on all sides, a league between bourgeoisie and nobility is still possible. Will it last, will it be effective? It has already been pointed out that in other countries, above all in England, on the basis of a different social structure, a rapprochement and concerted action between certain urban and rural classes gradually comes into being which—despite all the tensions and hostility between them—finally contributes in no small way to the curtailment of royal power. The fate of such alliances in France, as can be seen here in embryonic form and far more clearly later, with the growing interdependence of the estates, is very different. The unanimity of the estates does not survive long; the impact of their combined actions is broken by their mutual mistrust. "Anger and discontent bring them together, but their interests admit no unity."[119]

> Il sont lignée deslignée
> Contrefaite et mal alignée

runs a song of the time about the allies. All the same, this violent reaction to wilfully levied taxes leaves a strong impression, not least on the royal officials. Such upheavals within the dominion are not without danger for the struggle with external rivals. The social position of the central ruler is not yet strong enough for him alone to determine the duties and their level; power is still distributed in such a way that he must negotiate on each occasion with the estates whom he is taxing and gain their approval. And as yet the *aides* are no more than occasional and extraordinary payments to assist in a particular concrete purpose. This is only gradually to change in the course of the Hundred Years' War. As war becomes permanent, so also do the duties needed by the central ruler for its conduct.

27. "The struggle facing the monarchy in seeking to establish and develop its fiscal power can only be appreciated if we are aware of the social forces and interests it encountered as obstacles to its designs."[120] This statement does indeed point to the basic feature of the sociogenesis of the taxation monopoly. To be sure, the kings themselves cannot foresee, any more than their adversaries in this struggle, the new institution to which it will give rise. They do not really have any general intention to "increase their fiscal power". To begin with they and their representatives want quite simply to extract as much money as possible from their dominion on one occasion after another, and the tasks and expenses necessitating this are always quite specific and immediate. No single man created taxes or the taxation monopoly; no individual, or series of individuals throughout the century in which this institution was slowly formed, worked towards this goal by any deliberate plan. Taxation, like any other institution, is a product of social interweaving. It arises—as from a parallelogram of forces—from the conflicts of the various social groups and interests, until sooner or later the instrument which has developed in the constant social trials of strength becomes more and more consciously understood by the interested parties and more deliberately constructed into an organization or institution. In this way, in conjunction with a gradual transformation of society and a shift of the power relationships within it, the occasional aids to the lords of estates or territories, levied for specific campaigns or ransom or dowries or the provision of sons, are transformed into regular payments. As the money and trade sector of the economy slowly increases, as a particular house of feudal lords gradually becomes a house of kings over an ever-larger area, the feudal *aide aux quatre cas* turns step by step into taxation.

From 1328 onwards, and more strongly from 1337, this transformation of the extraordinary aid into regular duties accelerates. In 1328 a direct tax for the war with Flanders is again levied in certain parts of the kingdom; in 1335 there is an indirect tax in a number of western towns, a duty on each sale, for equipping a fleet; in 1338 all royal officials have something deducted from their pay; in 1340 the tax on the sale of wares is re-introduced and made general; in 1341 there is an additional tax on the sale of salt, the *gabelle du sel*. In 1344, 1345 and 1346 these indirect taxes continue to be raised. After the Battle of Crécy, the royal officials again try a personal direct tax, and in 1347 and 1348 they revert once more to the indirect form, the tax on sales. All this is to some degree experimental; all these levies are regarded, as we have said, as temporary assistance from society in the conduct of the king's war; they are *les aides sur le fait de la guerre*. The king and his officials declare over and over again that the demands for money will cease with the hostilities.[121] And whenever the estates' representatives have the chance, they underline this; they try to ascertain that the money coming from the *aides* is actually used for military purposes. The kings themselves, however, at least from Charles V on, never adhere very strictly to this demand. They control the funds from the *aides* and continue, when they think it necessary, to meet their own household costs or to reward their favourites from this money. This whole development, this inflow of money to the king's treasury as well as the establishment of a military force paid from this money, slowly but surely leads to an extraordinary strengthening of the central function. Each of the estates, the nobility above all, opposes the central authority's increase in power to the best of its ability. But here, too, their divergence of interests weakens their resistance. They are far too much affected by the war, far too directly interested in a successful repulsion of the English, to be able to refuse the king funds. In addition, the strength of the antagonism between them, together with local differences, not only undermines any common front to limit the king's financial demands or to supervise the use of this income, but prevents a direct organization of the war by the estates. The threat from outside makes the people of this society, which still has relatively little unity and interdependence, particularly dependent on the king as supreme co-ordinator and on his governmental machine. So they have to put up year after year with the levying in the king's name of "extraordinary aids" for a war that does not end.

Finally, after King John is taken prisoner in the Battle of Poitiers, in order to pay the enormous ransom demanded by the English, a tax is levied for the first time not just for one year but for six. Here, as so often, a major but fortuitous event merely accelerates something that had long been prepared in the structure of society. In reality this tax is raised continuously not for six years but for twenty, and we may suppose that by this time a certain adaptation of the market to such payments is taking place. Moreover, apart from this purchase-tax for the king's ransom there are continual taxes for other purposes as well; in 1363 a direct tax to cover the immediate costs of war, in 1367 another to combat pillage by the soldiery, in 1369, on the resumption of war, new direct and indirect taxes including the specially hated house-tax, the *fouage*.

"All these are still, no doubt, feudal 'aides', but generalized, made uniform and levied not only in the king's domain but throughout the kingdom under the supervision of a special, centralized administrative machine."[122] In fact, in this phase of the Hundred Years' War when the *aides* are slowly becoming permanent, there gradually evolve specialized official functions devoted to collecting and legally enforcing these "extraordinary payments", as they are still called. First of all they are represented simply by a few *Généraux sur le fait des finances*, who supervise the army of those responsible for the aides throughout the land. Then, in 1370, there are already two supreme administrators, one of whom specializes in the financial and the other in the legal questions arising from the collection of *aides*. This is the first form of what later, throughout the whole *ancien régime*, remains one of the most important organs of fiscal administration, the *Chambre* or *Cour des Aides*. But here, in the years 1370 to 1380, this institution is still in the process of formation; it lacks a definite form; it is one more attempt in the open or silent struggle in which the different social power-centres are constantly testing each other's strength. And its presence does not, as often happens with solidly established institutions, obliterate the memory of the social conflicts from which it has resulted. Each time the monarchy, meeting resistance in different parts of the population, has to limit its taxation demands, these official functions also recede. Their level and the curve of their growth is a fairly exact indicator of the social strength of the central function and the apparatus for ruling in relation to the nobility, the clergy and the urban classes.

Under Charles V, as has been mentioned, the *aides sur le fait de la guerre* become as permanent as the war itself. They weigh upon a people that is being impoverished in this war by devastation, fire, trade difficulties and not least by continuous raids by troops who want to be fed and feed themselves by force. All the more oppressive are the taxes demanded by the king; and the more strongly their becoming the rule instead of the exception is felt as a contravention of tradition. As long as Charles V is alive all this finds no visible expression. Distress grows unseen, and with it discontent. But it seems that the king is to some extent aware of this growing tension in the country, of the suppressed feelings, particularly against the taxes. He probably realizes the danger to which this mood must give rise if, in his place, in place of an old, experienced king, a child, his son who is still a minor, comes to the throne under the guardianship of rival relations. And perhaps this fear of the future is coupled to pangs of conscience. Certainly the taxes that his government has brought in year after year seem to the king inevitable and indispensable. But even for him, the beneficiary, these taxes clearly still have a tinge of injustice about them. At any rate, a few hours before his death, on 16 September 1380, he signs a decree repealing above all the most oppressive and unpopular tax, the house-tax which weighs equally on rich and poor. How appropriate this decree is to the situation created by the king's death very quickly becomes apparent. The central function weakened, the repressed tensions in the country break out. The competing relations of the dead king, above all Louis of Anjou and Philip the Bold of Burgundy, contest predominance and not least control of the royal treasury. The towns begin to revolt against the taxes. The people put the royal tax-collectors to flight. And the agitation of the lower urban strata is at first not unwelcome to the richer bourgeoisie. The desires of both run parallel. The urban notables who in November 1380 meet representatives of the other estates in Paris, demand the abolition of the royal taxes. Probably the Duke of Anjou, the king's Chancellor, promises to fulfil the demand under this direct pressure. On 16 November 1380 a decree is issued in the king's name by which "henceforth for ever, all 'fouage' impositions, salt taxes, fourths and eights, by which our subjects have been so much aggrieved, all aids and subsidies of any kind which have been imposed on account of the said wars . . .", are abolished.

"The whole financial system of the last ten years, all the conquests made in the years 1358/59 and 1367/68, are sacrificed. The monarchy is thrown back almost a century. It finds itself at almost the same point as at the beginning of the Hundred Years' War."[123]

Like a system of forces that has not yet reached equilibrium, society sways back and forth between the various poles in the struggle for power. It speaks for the social power already possessed by the central government and the royal function at this time, that they are able to make up the lost ground with extraordinary speed, although the king himself is a child and wholly dependent on the administrators and servants of the monarchy. What later manifests itself once more under Charles VIII with particular clarity, emerges fairly clearly even at this time: the opportunities open to the royal function in this structure of French society and in this situation, are already so great that the monarchy can increase its social power even when the king is personally weak or insignificant. The dependence of the groups and classes in this society on a supreme co-ordinator who maintains co-operation between the various social functions and districts, grows with their interdependence, and grows even more under the pressure of military danger. And so, willingly or not, they very quickly restore the means needed to conduct the war to the men who represent their common interests, above all in conflicts with external enemies: the king and his representative. But in so doing they also give the monarchy the means to control them. In 1382/83 the monarchy, i.e. the king together with all the relations, councils and servants who in any way belong to the government machine, is again in a position to dictate to the towns, the chief centres of resistance, the taxes it considers necessary.

The question of taxes is at the centre of the urban risings of 1382. But in the struggle over taxes and the distribution of their burden by the central apparatus, the question of the whole distribution of power, as so often, is tested and decided. The objective of gaining a voice in the raising and distribution of taxes, that is, of supervising from a central position the working of the government machine, is pursued quite consciously by the urban notables of the time, and not only by them. At assemblies, representatives of the other estates sometimes push in the same direction. The horizons of the lower and middle urban classes are generally narrower; what they want above all is release from their oppressive burdens, nothing more. Even in this direction the goals of the various urban groups are not always the same, even if—in their relation to the central apparatus of the country—they are not necessarily mutually hostile. In the smaller circle of the towns themselves matters are very different. Here the interests of the different strata, despite all their interweaving and indeed precisely because of it, are often diametrically opposed.

The urban communities of this time are already highly complex formations. There is in them a privileged upper stratum, the bourgeoisie proper, whose monopoly position is expressed in its control of the civic offices and therefore of finances. There is a middle stratum, a kind of petty bourgeoisie, the less wealthy craftsmen and tradesmen; and finally there is a mass of journeymen and workers, the "people". And here, too, the taxes form the nodal point where both the interdependence and the antitheses emerge particularly clearly. If clear demands are expressed at all, the middle and lower groups seek direct, progressive taxes which each pays according to his means, while the urban upper stratum prefers indirect or flat-rate taxes. As so often, the agitation of the people over taxes and the first wave of unrest are to begin with not unwelcome to the urban upper stratum. It favours this movement as long as it reinforces its own opposition to the monarchy or even to the local feudal lords. But very quickly the insurrection turns against the wealthy town-dwellers themselves. It becomes in part a struggle for urban administration between the ruling bourgeois patriciate and the middle strata, who demand their share in the civic offices as the urban notables demand theirs in the larger sphere of the government of the country. The urban upper strata take flight or defend themselves; and they are usually saved at this stage of the struggle by the arrival of royal troops.

It would take us too far afield to follow these struggles and the risings in different towns in detail. They end with a further shift of power in favour of the central apparatus and the monarchy. The ringleaders of the revolt, particularly those who had refused to pay taxes, are punished by death, others with heavy fines. On the towns as a whole large payments are imposed. In Paris, the fortified royal castles or bastilles are reinforced and new ones built, manned by royal men-at-arms, *gens d'armes*. And urban liberties are restricted. From now on local town administrations are increasingly placed under royal officials until they too are essentially organs of the royal apparatus for ruling. In this way the hierarchy of the central government apparatus, whose occupants are the leading bourgeois, extends from ministerial posts and the highest judicial offices to the positions of mayor and guild-master. And the question of taxes as a whole is decided in the same way. They are now dictated by the central organization.

If we examine the reasons why this trial of strength was so quickly decided in favour of the central function, we again encounter the fact already mentioned so often: it is the antagonisms between the various groups of this society that give the central function its strength. The bourgeois upper class has a tense relationship not only to the secular and clerical feudal lords, but also to the lower urban strata. Here, it is above all the disunity of the urban classes themselves which favours the central ruler. No less important is the fact that as yet scarcely any close association exists between the different towns of the kingdom. There are weak tendencies towards a collaboration of several cities. But integration is not yet nearly close enough to permit concerted action. The different towns still confront each other to some extent like foreign powers; between them too there is more or less intense competition. So the royal representatives first conclude a truce with Paris in order to have a free hand against the towns of Flanders. Thus secured, they break the urban resistance in Flanders; then they break it in Rouen, then in Paris. They defeat each town singly. Not only social but regional fragmentation as well—within certain limits and not excluding a certain degree of interdependence—favours the central function. In face of the combined opposition of all parts of the population, the monarchy would necessarily be defeated. But in face of each individual class or region the central function, drawing its power from the whole country, is the stronger.

Nevertheless, sections of society continue to try to limit or break the growing power of the central function. Each time, in accordance with the same structural regularities, the disturbed balance is restored after a time in the monarch's favour, and each of these trials of strength further advances its power. Taxes paid to the king still disappear now and then or are briefly restricted, but they are always very soon revived. In exactly the same way offices concerned with the administration and collection of taxes vanish and reappear. The history of the *Chambre des Aides*, for example, is full of such upheavals and sudden reversals. There are several successive resurrections between 1370 and 1390. Then again in 1413, 1418, 1425, 1462, 1464 and 1474 it undergoes, as its historian writes, "excesses of life and death, unpredictable resurrections",[124] until finally it becomes a firmly established institution in the royal governmental machine. And while these fluctuations do not, of course, reflect only the great social trials of strength, they nevertheless give a certain picture of the sociogenesis of the royal function, the growth of the monopoly organization in general. They make it clear how little all these functions and formations result from the long-term conscious plans of individuals, and how much they arise by small, tentative steps from a multitude of intertwining and conflicting human efforts and activities.

28. The individual kings themselves are, in the deployment of their personal

power, wholly dependent on the situation in which they find the royal function. This seldom shows itself so clearly as in the case of Charles VII. As an individual he is certainly not especially strong; he is not a great or powerful person. Yet, after the English have been expelled from his territory, during his reign the monarchy grows stronger and stronger. The king now stands before his people as a victorious army leader, however little he may be inclined to this role by personal predisposition. In the war all the financial and human resources of the country have been collected in the hands of the central authority. The centralization of the army, the monopoly control of taxation have advanced a good distance. The external foe has been driven out, but the army, or at least a good part of it, is still present. It gives the king such internal preponderance that resistance to his wishes by the estates is as good as hopeless, particularly as the exhausted population wants one thing above all else: peace. In this situation the king declares in 1436 that the nation has approved the *aides* for an unlimited period, that he has been asked not to assemble the estates in future to decide on taxes; the costs of the journey to the estates' assemblies, he says, place far too heavy a burden on the people.

This justification is, of course, wholly without substance. The measure itself, the suppression of the estates' assemblies, is simply an expression of the social power of the monarchy. This power has become so great that the aides, which during the war have in practice become more or less continuous, can now be openly declared a permanent institution. And this power is already so unquestionable that the king no longer thinks it necessary to agree the amount and kind of taxes with those who pay them. As has been mentioned, the estates still repeatedly attempt to resist. The suppression of their parliament and the dictatorial powers of the kings are not consolidated without a series of trials of strength. But each of these shows yet again, and more and more clearly, how inexorably, in this phase of the advancing differentiation and integration of society, the power of the central function is growing. Again and again it is the military power concentrated in the hands of the central authority which secures and increases his control of taxes, and it is this concentrated control of taxes which makes possible an ever-stronger monopolization of physical and military power. Step by step these two means drive each other upwards until, at a certain point, the total superiority attained by the central function in this process is revealed nakedly to the eyes of its astonished and embittered contemporaries. Here again a voice from that time is better than any description in conveying to us how all this broke upon people as something new, without their knowing how or why.

When, under Charles VII, the central government begins quite openly to announce and collect taxes permanently without the estates' agreement, Juvenal des Ursines, the Archbishop of Rheims, writes a letter to the king. It includes, freely translated, the following:[125]

When your predecessors intended to go to war, it was their custom to assemble the three estates; they invited people from the Church, the nobility and the common people to meet them in one of their good cities. Then they came and explained how things stood and what was needed to resist the enemy and they required that the people took counsel on how the war was to be conducted in order to help the king with taxes decided in this discussion. You yourself always maintained this procedure until you realized that God and Fortune—which is changeable—have so helped you that you feel such discussions to be beneath your dignity. You now impose the "Aides" and other duties, and suffer them to be levied like duties from your domain, without the agreement of your three estates.

Earlier . . . this kingdom could rightly be called "Royaume France", for it used to be free [franc] and had all liberties [franchises et libertés]. Today the people are no more than slaves; wilfully taxed [taillables à voulenté]. If we look at the population of the kingdom we find only a tenth of those who were formerly there. I would not wish to diminish your power, but rather to increase it to the best of my small ability. There is no doubt that a prince, and particularly Your Highness, may in certain cases cut off [tailler] something from your subjects and levy the "Aides", particularly to defend the kingdom and the public cause [chose publique]. But this he must agree in a reasonable manner. His task is not mine. It may be that you are sovereign in matters of justice, and that this is your authority. But as far as domanial revenues are concerned, you have your domain and each private person his [N.B. in other words the king should kindly support himself on his estates and domanial revenues, and not usurp control of the revenues of the whole country]. And today the subjects do not merely have their wool sheared, but their skin, their flesh and blood down to the bones.

In another passage the archbishop gives free rein to his indignation: "He deserves to be stripped of his rule who uses it wilfully and not one half to the advantage of his subjects. . . . Take care, therefore, that the surfeit of money flowing to you from the 'Aides', which you draw from the body, does not destroy your soul. You are also the head of this body. Would it not be great tyranny if the head of a human creature destroyed the heart, the hands, and feet [N.B. probably symbolizing clergy, warriors and common people]."

From now on, and for a long period, it is the subjects who point to the public character of the royal function. Expressions like "public cause", "fatherland" and even "state" are first used generally in opposition to the princes and kings. The central rulers themselves control the monopolized opportunities in this phase, above all the revenue from their dominions—as Juvenal des Ursines says—like private property. And it is in this sense, too, as a reply to the opposition's use of such words as fatherland or state, that we should understand the saying attributed to the king: "I am the state." Amazement at this whole development is not, however, confined to the French. The régime that is emerging in France, the strength and solidity of the central apparatus and function, that subsequently appear, sooner or later, on the basis of analogous structures, in almost every country in Europe, is in the fifteenth century something even more surprising and novel to observers outside France. We need only read reports of Venetian envoys of this time to have an impression of how a foreign observer, who undoubtedly has wide experience in such matters, encounters in France an unknown form of government.

In 1492 Venice sends two envoys to Paris, officially to congratulate Charles VIII on his marriage to Anne of Brittany, but in reality, no doubt, to find out how and where France intends to use her power in Italy, and in general, how things stand in France, what is the financial situation, what kind of people the king and government are, what products are imported and exported, what factions exist; in a word, the envoys have to discover everything worth knowing to enable Venice to take the correct political action. And these embassies, which now gradually change from an occasional to a permanent institution, are themselves a sign of how in this period Europe is slowly becoming interdependent over larger areas.

Accordingly, we find in their report, among other things, an exact depiction of the French finances and of financial procedure in the country. The envoy estimates the king's income at approximately 3,600,000 francs per annum—including "1,400,000 franchi da alcune imposizioni che se solevano metter *estraordinarie* . . . le quali si sono continuate per tal modo che al presente sono fatte *ordinarie*" (1,400,000 francs from impositions which used to be *extraordinary* but have become *ordinary*). The ambassador estimates the king's expenses at 6,600,000 or 7,300,000 francs. The resultant deficit, he reports, is raised in the following way:

> Every year, in January, the directors of the financial administration of each region—that is, those of the royal domain proper, Dauphiné, Languedoc, Brittany and Burgundy—meet to calculate incomes and expenses to meet the needs of the following year. And they *begin* by considering expenses [prima mettono tutta la spesa], and to cover the deficit between the expenses and the expected revenues they fix a general tax for all the provinces of the Kingdom. Of these taxes neither prelates nor nobles pay anything, but only the people. In this way the ordinary revenues and this tax bring in enough to cover the expenditure of the coming year. If, during the year, a war breaks out or there is any other unexpected cause of expenditure, so that the estimates are no longer enough, another tax is levied or stipends are cut so that under all circumstances the necessary sum is obtained.[126]

Up to now a good deal has been said about the formation of the taxation monopoly. Here, in the Venetian envoys' account, we are given a clear picture of its form and functioning at this stage of development. We also find one of the most important structural features of absolutism and—to a certain extent—of the "state" in general: the primacy of expenditure over income. For the individual members of society, particularly in bourgeois society, it becomes more and more a habit and a necessity to determine expenditure strictly by income. In the economy of a social whole, by contrast, expenses are the fixed point; on them income, i.e. the sums demanded from the individual members of society through the tax monopoly, are made dependent. This is another example of how the totality arising from the interdependence of individuals possesses structural characteristics and is subject to regularities different from those of individuals, and not to be understood from the individual's point of view. The only limit set to the financial needs of a central social agency of this time is the taxable capacity of society as a whole, and the social power of individual groups in relation to the controllers of the tax monopoly. Later, when the monopoly administration has come under the control of broader bourgeois strata, the economy of society as a whole is sharply divided from that of the individual people administrating the central monopoly. Society as a whole, the state, can and must continue to make taxes, income, essentially dependent on the socially necessary expenditure; but the kings, the individual central rulers, must now behave like all other individuals; they have precisely fixed stipends and manage their expenses accordingly.

Here, in the first phase of full monopoly, things are different. The royal and public economies are not yet separate. The kings set taxes in accordance with the expenses they consider necessary, whether these are for wars or castles or gifts to their favourites. The key monopolies of rule still have the character of personal monopolies. But what from our point of view is only the first stage on the way to the formation of societal or public monopolies, appears to these Venetian observers of about 1500 as a novelty which they regard with curiosity, as one is apt to consider the unknown manners and customs of strange peoples. Where they come from things are quite different. The power of the supreme Venetian authorities, like that of medieval princes, is restricted to a high degree by the local government of different regions and estates. Venice, too, is the centre of a major dominion. Other municipalities have placed themselves voluntarily or otherwise under its rule. But even in the case of communes subjugated by force, the conditions on which they are incorporated into the Venetian dominion nearly always includes a provision "that no new taxes may be introduced without the agreement of the majority of the council".[127]

In the dispassionate reports of the non-partisan Venetian envoys, the transformation that has taken place in France is perhaps more vividly expressed than in the indignant words of the Archbishop of Rheims.

In 1535 the report of the Venetian envoys contains the following:

Apart from the fact that the king is militarily powerful, he obtains money through his people's obedience. I say that his Majesty usually has an income of two and a half million. I say "usually"; for, if he so wishes, he can increase the taxes on his people. Whatever burdens he places on them, they pay without restriction. But I must say in this regard that the section of the population which bears the major part of his burden is very poor, so that any increase in the burden however small, would be unbearable.

In 1546, finally, the Venetian Ambassador Marino Cavalli gives an exact and detailed report on France in which the peculiarities of the government of that country, as it appears to an impartial contemporary with wide horizons, emerge particularly clearly:

> Many kingdoms are more fertile and richer than France, for example, Hungary and Italy, many are larger and more powerful, for example, Germany and Spain. But none is as united and obedient. I do not believe that her prestige has any other cause than these two things: unity and obedience [unione e obbedienza]. To be sure, freedom is the most cherished gift in the world; but not all are worthy of it. For this reason some peoples are usually born to obey, others to command. If it is the other way round we have a situation like the present one in Germany, or earlier in Spain. The French, however, perhaps feeling unsuited to it, have handed over their freedom and will entirely to the king. So it is enough for him to say: I want such-and-such, I approve such-and-such, I decide such-and-such, and all this is promptly executed as if they had all decided it. Things have gone so far that today one of them who has more wit than the others, says: Earlier their kings had called themselves "reges Francorum", today they can call themselves "reges servorum". So they not only pay the king whatever he demands, but all other capital is likewise open to his grasp.
>
> Charles VII increased this obedience of the people, after he had freed the country from the yoke of the English; and after him Louis XI and Charles VIII, who conquered Naples, did likewise. Louis XII made his own contribution. But the ruling King (Francis I) can boast of having greatly outdone his predecessors: he has his subjects pay extraordinary sums, as much as he wants; he unites new possessions with the Crown Estates without giving anything in return. And if he does give anything away, this is valid only for the lifetime of the giver or of the recipient. And if one or the other lives too long, the whole gift is withdrawn as something due to the Crown. It is true that some are afterwards made permanent. And their practice is the same with regard to the leaders and the various grades of the military. So that if someone enters your service and says he has had such-and-such reward, titles and provisions from the French, Your Serenity will know of what kind these provisions, titles and gifts are. Many never attain them, or on only one occasion in their lives, some remain two, three years without receiving any reward. Your Serenity, who give away quite definite things, but to some extent hereditary ones, should certainly not be influenced by the example of what is done elsewhere. In my judgement the custom of giving only for the duration of a lifetime . . . is excellent. It always gives the king the opportunity of rewarding those who are deserving; and there is always something left to give away. If the gifts were hereditary, we would now have an impoverished Francia and the present kings would have nothing more to give away; but in this way they are served by people of more merit than the heirs of some earlier recipient. Your Serenity might reflect, if France acts in this way, on what other princes ought to do who do not rule such a large country. If we do not carefully consider where these hereditary gifts lead—to the preservation of the family, it is said—it will happen that there are no sufficient rewards left for truly deserving people, or new burdens will have to be placed on the people. Both things are unjust and harmful enough. If gifts are made only for lifetime, then only those who

deserve it are rewarded. Estates circulate and alter a time revert to the fisc. . . . For eighty years new agreements have continually been made with the Crown without giving anything away, through confiscation, reversion on inheritance or purchase. In this way the Crown has absorbed everything, to the extent that there is not a single prince in the whole realm who has an income of 20,000 scudi. Moreover, those who possess incomes and land are not ordinary owners; for the king retains supreme rule by virtue of the appeals, taxes, garrisons and all the other new and extraordinary burdens. The Crown becomes more and more wealthy and unified and attains immense prestige; and that secures it from civil war. For as there are nothing but poor princes, they have neither reason nor the possibility to take action against the king, as the dukes of Brittany, Normandy, Burgundy and many other great lords of Gascony did earlier. And if anyone does anything ill-considered and tries to bring about some change, like the Bourbons, this only gives the king an even earlier opportunity to enrich himself through that man's ruin.[128]

Here, compressed into a single view, we have a summary of the decisive structural features of emergent absolutism. One feudal lord has won predominance over all his competitors, supreme rule over all land. And this control of land is increasingly commercialized or monetarized. The change is expressed on the one hand by the fact that the king possesses a monopoly in collecting and fixing taxes throughout the country, so that he controls by far the largest income. A king owning and distributing land becomes more and more a king owning money and distributing income. This is precisely what enables him to break out of the vicious circle which trapped the rulers of countries with barter economies. He pays no longer for the services he needs, military, courtly or administrative, by giving away parts of his property as the hereditary property of his servants, as is clearly still in part the case in Venice. At most he gives land or salaries for life, and then withdraws them so that the crown possessions are not reduced; and in an increasingly large number of cases he rewards services only with money gifts, with salaries. He centralizes the taxation of the whole country and distributes the inflowing money at his own discretion and in the interests of his rule, so that an immense and ever-growing number of people throughout the country are directly or indirectly dependent on the king's favour, on payments by the royal financial administration. It is the more or less private interests of the kings and their closest servants which veer toward exploitation of their social opportunities in this direction; but what emerges in the conflicts of interest between the various social functions, is the form of social organization which we call the "state". The tax monopoly, together with the monopoly of physical force, are the backbone of this organization. We can understand neither the genesis nor the existence of "states" unless we are aware—even from the example of a single country—how one of these central institutions of the "state" develops step by step in accordance with relational dynamics, as a result of a very specific regularity arising from the structure of interwoven interests and actions. Even at this stage—as we see from the Venetian's report—the central organ of society takes on a hitherto unknown stability and strength because its ruler, thanks to the monetarization of society, no longer needs to pay for services from his own possessions, which without expansion would sooner or later be exhausted, but with sums of money from the regular inflow of taxation. Finally, the peculiarity of money exempts him from the necessity first taken over from the procedure of rewarding with land, of repaying services with a possession to be held for life and hereditary. It makes it possible to reward the service or a number of services by a single payment, by a fee or salary. The numerous and far-reaching consequences of this change must be left aside here. The astonishment of the Venetian envoy is enough to show how this custom, which is now commonplace and taken for granted, appeared then as something new. His account also once again shows particularly clearly why it is only the monetarization of society that makes possible stable central organs: money payment keeps all recipients permanently dependent on the central authority. Only now can the centrifugal tendencies be finally broken.

And it is also from this wider context that we must understand what is happening to the nobility at this time. In the preceding period, when the rest of the nobility were stronger, the king exerted his power as central ruler, within certain limits, in favour of the bourgeoisie. His apparatus for ruling thus became a bastion of the bourgeoisie. Now that, as a result of monetary integration and military centralization, the warriors, the landowners, the nobility are declining further and further, the king begins to pit his weight and the opportunities he has to distribute somewhat more on the side of the nobility. He gives a part of the nobility the possibility of continuing to exist as a stratum elevated above the bourgeoisie. Slowly, after the last fruitless resistance by elements of the estates in the religious wars and then in the *Fronde*, court offices become a privilege and thus a bastion of the nobility. In this way the kings protect the nobility's pre-eminence; they distribute their favour and the money they control in such a way that the balance endangered by the nobility's decline is preserved. But thereby the relatively free warrior nobility of earlier times becomes a nobility in lifelong dependence on, and in the service of, the central ruler. knights become courtiers. And if we ask what social functions these courtiers really have, the answer lies here. We are accustomed to refer to the courtly nobility of the *ancien régime* as a "functionless" class. And indeed, this nobility had no function in terms of the division of labour, and thus in the understanding of the nations of the nineteenth and twentieth centuries. The configuration of functions in the *ancien régime* is different. It is primarily determined by the fact that the central ruler still is to a high degree the personal owner of the power monopoly, that there is not yet any division between the central ruler as a private individual and as a functionary of society. The courtly nobility has no direct function in the division of labour, but it has a function for the king. It is one of the indispensable foundations of his rule. It enables the king to distance himself from the bourgeoisie just as the bourgeoisie enables him to distance himself from the nobility. It is the counterweight to the bourgeoisie in society. That, together with a number of others, is its most important function for the king; without this tension between nobility and bourgeoisie, without this marked difference between the estates, the king would lose the major part of his power. The existence of the courtly aristocracy is indeed an expression of how far monopoly government here is still the personal property of the central ruler, and how far the country's income can still be allocated in the special interests of the central function. The possibility of a kind of planned distribution of national revenue is already created with monopolization. But this possibility of planning is used here to prop up declining strata or functions.

A clear picture of the structure of absolutist society emerges from all this. The secular society of the French *ancien régime* consists, more markedly than that of the nineteenth century, of two sectors: a larger rural agrarian sector, and an urban-bourgeois one which is smaller; but steadily if slowly gaining in economic strength. In both there is a lower stratum, in the latter the urban poor, the mass of journeymen and workers, in the former the peasants. In both there is a lower middle stratum, in the latter the small artisans and probably the lowest officials too, in the former the poorer landed gentry in provincial corners; in both an upper middle stratum, in the latter the wealthy merchants, the high civic officials and even in the provinces the highest judicial and administrative officials, and in the former the more well-off country and provincial aristocracy. In both sectors, finally, there is a leading stratum extending into the court, in the latter the high bureaucracy, the *noblesse de robe*, and the courtly nobility, the élite of the *noblesse d'épée* in the former. In the tensions within and between these sectors, complicated by the tensions and alliances of both with a clergy structured on a similar hierarchy, the king carefully maintains equilibrium. He secures the privileges and social prestige of the nobles against the growing economic strength of bourgeois groups. And, as has been mentioned, he uses part of the social product that he has to distribute by virtue of his control of the financial monopoly to provide for the highest nobility. When, not long before the Revolution, after all attempts at reform have failed, the demand for the abolition of noble privileges moves into the foreground among the watchwords of the opposing bourgeois groups, this implies a demand for a different management of the tax monopoly and tax revenue. The abolition of noble privileges means on the one hand the end of the nobility's exemption from taxes and thus a redistribution of the tax burden; and on the other the elimination or reduction of many court offices, the annihilation of what was—in the eyes of this new professional bourgeoisie—a useless and functionless nobility, and thus a different distribution of tax revenue, no longer in the interests of the king but in those of society at large, or at least, to begin with, of the upper bourgeoisie. Finally, however, the removal of noble privileges means the destruction of the position of the central ruler as the balance maintaining the two estates in their existing order of precedence. The central rulers of the subsequent period are indeed balanced on a different network of tensions. They and their function accordingly have a different character. Only one thing remains the same: even in this new structure of tensions, the power of the central authority is relatively limited as long as the tensions remain relatively low, as long as direct agreement is possible between the representatives of the opposed poles, and it grows in phases when these tensions are growing, as long as none of the competing groups has attained a decisive preponderance.

PART TWO: SYNOPSIS

Towards a Theory
of Civilizing Processes

I

The Social Constraint towards Self-Constraint

What has the organization of society in the form of "states", what have the monopolization and centralization of taxes and physical force over a large area, to do with "civilization"?

The observer of the civilizing process finds himself confronted by a whole tangle of problems. To mention a few of the most important at the outset, there is, first of all, the most general question. We have seen—and the quotations in the first volume served to illustrate this with specific examples—that the civilizing process is a change of human conduct and sentiment in a quite specific direction. But, obviously, individual people did not at some past time intend this change, this "civilization", and gradually realize it by conscious, "rational", purposive measures. Clearly, "civilization" is not, any more than rationalization, a product of human "ratio" or the result of calculated long-term planning. How would it be conceivable that gradual "rationalization" could be founded on pre-existing "rational" behaviour and planning over centuries? Could one really imagine that the civilizing process had been set in motion by people with that long-term perspective, that specific mastery of all short-term affects, considering that this type of long-term perspective and self-mastery already presuppose a long civilizing process?

In fact, nothing in history indicates that this change was brought about "rationally", through any purposive education of individual people or groups. It happened by and large unplanned; but it did not happen, nevertheless, without a specific type of order. It has been shown in detail above how constraints through others from a variety of angles are converted into self-restraints, how the more animalic human activities are progressively thrust behind the scenes of men's communal social life and invested with feelings of shame, how the regulation of the whole instinctual and affective life by steady self-control becomes more and more stable, more even and more all-embracing. All this certainly does not spring from a rational idea conceived centuries ago by individual people and then implanted in one generation after another as the purpose of action and the desired state, until it was fully realized in the "centuries of progress". And yet, though not planned and intended, this transformation is not merely a sequence of unstructured and chaotic changes.

What poses itself here with regard to the civilizing process is nothing other than the general problem of historical change. Taken as a whole this change is not "rationally" planned; but neither is it a random coming and going of orderless patterns. How is this possible? How does it happen at all that formations arise in the human world that no single human being has intended, and which yet are anything but cloud formations without stability or structure?

The preceding study, and particularly those parts of it devoted to the problems of social dynamics, attempts to provide an answer to these questions. It is simple enough: plans and actions, the emotional and rational impulses of individual people, constantly interweave in a friendly or hostile way. *This basic tissue resulting from many single plans and actions of men can give rise to changes and patterns that no individual person has planned or created. From this interdependence of people arises an order sui generis, an order more compelling and stronger than the will and reason of the individual people composing it.*[129] It is this order of interweaving human impulses and strivings, this social order, which determines the course of historical change; it underlies the civilizing process.

This order is neither "rational"—if by "rational" we mean that it has resulted intentionally from the purposive deliberation of individual people; nor "irrational"—if by "irrational" we mean that it has arisen in an incomprehensible way. It has occasionally been identified with the order of "Nature"; it was interpreted by Hegel and some others as a kind of supra-individual "Spirit", and his concept of a "cunning of reason" shows how much he too was preoccupied by the fact that all the planning and actions of people give rise to many things that no one actually intended. But the mental habits which tend to bind us to opposites such as "rational" and "irrational", or "spirit" and "nature", prove inadequate here. In this respect, too, reality is not constructed quite as the conceptual apparatus of a particular standard would have us believe, whatever valuable services it may have performed in its time as a compass to guide us through an unknown world. *The immanent regularities of social figurations are identical neither with regularities of the "mind", of individual reasoning, nor with regularities of what we call "nature", even though functionally all these different dimensions of reality are indissolubly linked to each other.* On its own, however, this general statement about the relative autonomy of social figurations is of little help in their understanding; it remains empty and ambiguous, unless the actual dynamics of social interweaving are directly illustrated by reference to specific and empirically demonstrable changes. Precisely this was one of the tasks to which Part One of *State Formation and Civilization* was devoted. It was attempted there to show what kind of interweaving, of mutual dependence between people, sets in motion, for example, processes of feudalization. It was shown how the compulsion of competitive situations drove a number of feudal lords into conflict, how the circle of competitors was slowly narrowed, and how this led to the monopoly of one and finally—in conjunction with other mechanisms of integration such as processes of increasing capital formation and functional differentiation—to the formation of an absolutist state. This whole reorganization of human relationships went hand in hand with corresponding changes in men's manners, in their personality structure, the provisional result of which is our form of "civilized" conduct and sentiment. The connection between these specific changes in the structure of human relations and the corresponding changes in the structure of the personality will be discussed again shortly. But consideration of these mechanisms of integration is also relevant in a more general way to an understanding of the civilizing process. Only if we see the compelling force with which a particular social structure, a particular form of social intertwining, veers through its tensions to a specific change and so to other forms of intertwining,[130] can we understand how those changes arise in human mentality, in the patterning of the malleable psychological apparatus, which can be observed over and again in human history from earliest times to the present. And only then, therefore, can we understand that the psychological change involved by civilization is subject to a quite specific order and direction, although it was not planned by individual people or produced by "reasonable", purposive measures. Civilization is not "reasonable"; not "rational",[131] any more than it is "irrational". It is set in motion blindly, and kept in motion by the autonomous dynamics of a web of relationships, by specific changes in the way people are bound to live together. But it is by no means impossible that we can make out of it something more "reasonable", something that functions better in terms of our needs and purposes. For it is precisely in conjunction with the civilizing process that the blind dynamics of men intertwining in their deeds and aims gradually leads towards greater scope for planned intervention into both the social and individual structures—intervention based on a growing knowledge of the unplanned dynamics of these structures.

But which specific changes in the way people are bonded to each other mould their personality in a "civilizing" manner? The most general answer to this question too, an answer based on what was said earlier about the changes in Western society, is very simple. From the earliest period of the history of the Occident to the present, social functions have become more and more differentiated under the pressure of competition. The more differentiated they become, the larger grows the number of functions and thus of people on whom the individual constantly depends in all his actions, from the simplest and most commonplace to the more complex and uncommon. As more and more people must attune their conduct to that of others, the web of actions must be organized more and more strictly and accurately, if each individual action is to fulfil its social function. The individual is compelled to regulate his conduct in an increasingly differentiated, more even and more stable manner. That this involves not only a conscious regulation has already been stressed. Precisely this is characteristic of the psychological changes in the course of civilization: the more complex and stable control of conduct is increasingly instilled in the individual from his earliest years as an automatism, a self-compulsion that he cannot resist even if he consciously wishes to. The web of actions grows so complex and extensive, the effort required to behave "correctly" within it becomes so great, that beside the individual's conscious self-control an automatic, blindly functioning apparatus of self-control is firmly established. This seeks to prevent offences to socially acceptable behaviour by a wall of deep-rooted fears, but, just because it operates blindly and by habit, it frequently indirectly produces such collisions with social reality. But whether consciously or unconsciously, the direction of this transformation of conduct in the form of an increasingly differentiated regulation of impulses is determined by the direction of the process of social differentiation, by the progressive division of functions and the growth of the interdependency chains into which, directly or indirectly, every impulse, every move of an individual becomes integrated.

A simple way of picturing the difference between the integration of the individual within a complex society and within a less complex one is to think of their different road systems. These are in a sense spatial functions of a social integration which, in its totality, cannot be expressed merely in terms of concepts derived from the four-dimensional continuum. One should think of the country roads of a simple warrior society with a barter economy, uneven, unmetalled, exposed to damage from wind and rain. With few exceptions, there is very little traffic; the main danger which man here represents for other men is an attack by soldiers or thieves. When people look around them, scanning the trees and hills or the road itself, they do so primarily because they must always be prepared for armed attack, and only secondarily because they have to avoid collision. Life on the main roads of this society demands a constant readiness to fight, and free play of the emotions in defence of one's life or possessions from physical attack. Traffic on the main roads of a big city in the complex society of our time demands a quite different moulding of the psychological apparatus. Here the danger of physical attack is minimal. Cars are rushing in all directions; pedestrians and cyclists are trying to thread their way through the *mêlée* of cars; policemen stand at the main crossroads to regulate the traffic with varying success. But this external control is founded on the assumption that every individual is himself regulating his behaviour with the utmost exactitude in accordance with the necessities of this network. The chief danger that people here represent for others results from someone in this bustle losing his self-control. A constant and highly differentiated regulation of one's own behaviour is needed for the individual to steer his way through traffic. If the strain of such constant self-control becomes too much for an individual, this is enough to put himself and others in mortal danger.

This is, of course, only an image. The tissue of chains of action into which each individual act within this complex society is woven, is far more intricate, and the self-control to which he is accustomed from infancy far more deeply rooted, than this example shows. But at least it gives an impression of how the great formative pressure on the make-up of "civilized" man, his constant and differentiated self-constraint, is connected to the growing differentiation and stabilizing of social functions and the growing multiplicity and variety of activities that continuously have to be attuned to each other.

The pattern of self-constraints, the template by which drives are moulded, certainly varies widely according to the function and position of the individual within this network, and there are even today in different sectors of the Western world variations of intensity and stability in the apparatus of self-constraint that seem at face value very large. At this point a multitude of particular questions are raised, and the sociogenetic method may give access to their answers. But when compared to the psychological make-up of people in less complex societies, these differences and degrees within more complex societies become less significant, and the main line of transformation, which is the primary concern of this study, emerges very clearly: as the social fabric grows more intricate, the sociogenic apparatus of individual self-control also becomes more differentiated, more all-round and more stable.

But the advancing differentiation of social functions is only the first, most general of the social transformations which we observe in enquiring into the change in psychological make-up known as "civilization". Hand in hand with this advancing division of functions goes a total reorganization of the social fabric. It was shown in detail earlier why, when the division of functions is low, the central organs of societies of a certain size are relatively unstable and liable to disintegration. It has been shown how, through specific figurational pressures, centrifugal tendencies, the mechanisms of feudalization, are slowly neutralized and how, step by step, a more stable central organization, a firmer monopolization of physical force, are established. The peculiar stability of the apparatus of mental self-restraint which emerges as a decisive trait built into the habits of every "civilized" human being, stands in the closest relationship to the monopolization of physical force and the growing stability of the central organs of society. Only with the formation of this kind of relatively stable monopolies do societies acquire those characteristics as a result of which the individuals forming them get attuned, from infancy, to a highly regulated and differentiated pattern of self-restraint; only in conjunction with these monopolies does this kind of self-restraint require a higher degree of automaticity, does it become, as it were, "second nature".

When a monopoly of force is formed, pacified social spaces are created which are normally free from acts of violence. The pressures acting on individual people within them are of a different kind than previously. Forms of non-physical violence that always existed, but hitherto had always been mingled or fused with physical force, are now separated from the latter; they persist in a changed form internally within the more pacified societies. They are most visible so far as the standard thinking of our time is concerned as types of economic violence. In reality, however, there is a whole set of means whose monopolization can enable men as groups or as individuals to enforce their will upon others. The monopolization of the means of production, of "economic" means, is only one of those which stand out in fuller relief when the means of physical violence become monopolized, when, in other words, in a more pacified state society the free use of physical force by those who are physically stronger is no longer possible.

In general, the direction in which the behaviour and the affective make-up of people change when the structure of human relationships is transformed in the manner described, is as follows: societies without a stable monopoly of force are always societies in which the division of functions is relatively slight and the chains of action binding individuals together are comparatively short. Conversely, societies with more stable monopolies of force, always first embodied in a large princely or royal court, are societies in which the division of functions is more or less advanced, in which the chains of action binding individuals together are longer and the functional dependencies between people greater. Here the individual is largely protected from sudden attack, the irruption of physical violence into his life. But at the same time he is himself forced to suppress in himself any passionate impulse urging him to attack another physically. And the other forms of compulsion which now prevail in the pacified social spaces pattern the individual's conduct and affective impulses in the same direction. The closer the web of interdependence becomes in which the individual is enmeshed with the advancing division of functions, the larger the social spaces over which this network extends and which become integrated into functional or institutional units—the more threatened is the social existence of the individual who gives way to spontaneous impulses and emotions, the greater is the social advantage of those able to moderate their affects, and the more strongly is each individual constrained from an early age to take account of the effects of his own or other people's actions on a whole series of links in the social chain. The moderation of spontaneous emotions, the tempering of affects, the extension of mental space beyond the moment into the past and future, the habit of connecting events in terms of chains of cause and effect—all these are different aspects of the same transformation of conduct which necessarily takes place with the monopolization of physical violence, and the lengthening of the chains of social action and interdependence. It is a "civilizing" change of behaviour.

The transformation of the nobility from a class of knights into a class of courtiers is an example of this. In the earlier sphere, where violence is an unavoidable and everyday event, and where the individual's chains of dependence are relatively short, because he largely subsists directly from the produce of his own land, a strong and continuous moderation of drives and affects is neither necessary, possible nor useful. The life of the warriors themselves, but also that of all others living in a society with a warrior upper class, is threatened continually and directly by acts of physical violence; thus, measured against life in more pacified zones, it oscillates between extremes. Compared to this other society, it permits the warrior extraordinary freedom in living out his feelings and passions, it allows savage joys, the uninhibited satisfaction of pleasure from women, or of hatred in destroying and tormenting anything hostile. But at the same time it threatens the warrior, if he is defeated, with an extraordinary degree of exposure to the violence and the passions of others, and with such radical subjugation, such extreme forms of physical torment as are later, when physical torture, imprisonment and the radical humiliation of individuals has become the monopoly of a central authority, hardly to be found in normal life. With this monopolization, the physical threat to the individual is slowly depersonalized. It no longer depends quite so directly on momentary affects; it is gradually subjected to increasingly strict rules and laws; and finally, within certain limits and with certain fluctuations, the physical threat when laws are infringed is itself made less severe.

The greater spontaneity of drives and the higher measure of physical threat, that are encountered wherever strong and stable central monopolies have not yet formed are, as can be seen, complementary. In this social structure the victorious have a greater possibility of giving free rein to their drives and affects, but greater too is the direct threat to one man from the affects of another, and more omnipresent the possibility of subjugation and boundless humiliation if one falls into the power of another. This applies not only to the relationship of warrior to warrior, for whom in the course of monetarization and the narrowing of free competition an affect—moderating code of conduct is already slowly forming; within society at large the lesser measure of restraint impinging upon seigneurs initially stands in sharper contrast than later to the confined existence of their female counterparts and to the radical exposure to their whims of dependents, defeated, and bondsmen.

To the structure of this society with its extreme polarization, its continuous uncertainties, corresponds the structure of the individuals who form it and of their conduct. Just as in the relations between man and man danger arises more abruptly, the possibility of victory or liberation more suddenly and incalculably before the individual, so he is also thrown more frequently and directly between pleasure and pain. The social function of the free warrior is indeed scarcely so constructed that dangers are long foreseeable, that the effects of particular actions can be considered three or four links ahead, even though his function is slowly developing in this direction throughout the Middle Ages with the increasing centralization of armies. But for the time being it is the immediate present that provides the impulse. As the momentary situation changes, so do affective expressions; if it brings pleasure this is savoured to the full, without calculation or thought of the possible consequences in the future. If it brings danger, imprisonment, defeat, these too must be suffered more desolately. And the incurable unrest, the perpetual proximity of danger, the whole atmosphere of this unpredictable and insecure life, in which there are at most small and transient islands of more protected existence, often engenders even without external cause, sudden switches from the most exuberant pleasure to the deepest despondency and remorse. The personality, if we may put it thus, is incomparably more ready and accustomed to leap with undiminishing intensity from one extreme to the other, and slight impressions, uncontrollable associations are often enough to induce these immense fluctuations.[132]

As the structure of human relations changes, as monopoly organizations of physical force develop and the individual is held no longer in the sway of constant feuds and wars but rather in the more permanent compulsions of peaceful functions based on the acquisition of money or prestige, affect-expressions too slowly gravitate towards a middle line. The fluctuations in behaviour and affects do not disappear, but are moderated. The peaks and abysses are smaller, the changes less abrupt.

We can see what is changing more clearly from its obverse. Through the formation of monopolies of force, the threat which one man represents for another is subject to stricter control and becomes more calculable. Everyday life is freer of sudden reversals of fortune. Physical violence is confined to barracks; and from this store-house it breaks out only in extreme cases, in times of war or social upheaval, into individual life. As the monopoly of certain specialist groups it is normally excluded from the life of others; and these specialists, the whole monopoly organization of force, now stand guard only in the margin of social life as a control on individual conduct.

Even in this form as a control organization, however, physical violence and the threat emanating from it have a determining influence on individuals in society, whether they know it or not. It is, however, no longer a perpetual insecurity that it brings into the life of the individual, but a peculiar form of security. It no longer throws him, in the swaying fortunes of battle, as the physical victor or vanquished, between mighty outbursts of pleasure and terror; a continuous, uniform pressure is exerted on individual life by the physical violence stored behind the scenes of everyday life, a pressure totally familiar and hardly perceived, conduct and drive economy having been adjusted from earliest youth to this social structure. It is in fact the whole social mould, the code of conduct which changes; and accordingly with it changes, as has been said before, not only this or that specific form of conduct but its whole pattern, the whole structure of the way individuals steer themselves. The monopoly organization of physical violence does not usually constrain the individual by a direct threat. A strongly predictable compulsion or pressure mediated in a variety of ways is constantly exerted on the individual. This operates to a considerable extent through the medium of his own reflection. It is normally only potentially present in society, as an agency of control; the actual compulsion is one that the individual exerts on himself either as a result of his knowledge of the possible consequences of his moves in the game in intertwining activities, or as a result of corresponding gestures of adults which have helped to pattern his own behaviour as a child. The monopolization of physical violence, the concentration of arms and armed men under one authority, makes the use of violence more or less calculable, and forces unarmed men in the pacified social spaces to restrain their own violence through foresight or reflection; in other words it imposes on people a greater or lesser degree of self-control.

This is not to say that every form of self-control was entirely lacking in medieval warrior society or in other societies without a complex and stable monopoly of physical violence. The agency of individual self-control, the super-ego, the conscience or whatever we call it, is instilled, imposed and maintained in such warrior societies only in direct relation to acts of physical violence; its form matches this life in its greater contrasts and more abrupt transitions. Compared to the self-control agency in more pacified societies, it is diffuse, unstable, only a slight barrier to violent emotional outbursts. The fears securing socially "correct" conduct are not yet banished to remotely the same extent from the individual's consciousness into his so-called "inner life". As the decisive danger does not come from failure or relaxation of self-control, but from direct external physical threat, habitual fear predominantly takes the form of fear of external powers. And as this fear is less stable, the control apparatus too is less encompassing, more one-sided or partial. In such a society extreme self-control in enduring pain may be instilled; but this is complemented by what, measured by a different standard, appears as an extreme form of freewheeling of affects in torturing others. Similarly, in certain sectors of medieval society we find extreme forms of asceticism, self-restraint and renunciation, contrasting to a no less extreme indulgence of pleasure in others, and frequently enough we encounter sudden switches from one attitude to the other in the life of an individual person. The restraint the individual here imposes on himself, the struggle against his own flesh, is no less intense and one-sided, no less radical and passionate than its counterpart, the fight against others and the maximum enjoyment of pleasures.

What is established with the monopolization of physical violence in the pacified social spaces is a different type of self-control or self-constraint. It is a more dispassionate self-control. The controlling agency forming itself as part of the individual's personality structure corresponds to the controlling agency forming itself in society at large. The one like the other tends to impose a highly differentiated regulation upon all passionate impulses, upon men's conduct all around. Both—each to a large extent mediated by the other—exert a constant, even pressure to inhibit affective outbursts. They damp down extreme fluctuations in behaviour and emotions. As the monopolization of physical force reduces the fear and terror one man must have for another, but at the same time reduces the possibility of causing others terror, fear or torment, and therefore certain possibilities of pleasurable emotional release, the constant self-control to which the individual is now increasingly accustomed seeks to reduce the contrasts and sudden switches in conduct, and the affective charge of all self-expression.

The pressures operating upon the individual now tend to produce a transformation of the whole drive and affect economy in the direction of a more continuous, stable and even regulation of drives and affects in all areas of conduct, in all sectors of his life.

And it is in exactly the same direction that the unarmed compulsions operate, the constraints without direct physical violence to which the individual is now exposed in the pacified spaces, and of which economic restraints are an instance. They too are less affect-charged, more moderate, stable and less erratic than the constraints exerted by one person on another in a monopoly-free warrior society. And they, too, embodied in the entire spectrum of functions open to the individual in society, induce incessant hindsight and foresight transcending the moment and corresponding to the longer and more complex chains in which each act is now automatically enmeshed. They require the individual incessantly to overcome his momentary affective impulses in keeping with the longer-term effects of his behaviour. Relative to the other standard, they instil a more even self-control encompassing his whole conduct like a tight ring, and a more steady regulation of his drives according to the social norms. Moreover, as always, it is not only the adult functions themselves which immediately produce this tempering of drives and affects; partly automatically, partly quite consciously through their own conduct and habits, adults induce corresponding behaviour-patterns in children. From earliest youth the individual is trained in the constant restraint and foresight that he needs for adult functions. This self-restraint is ingrained so deeply from an early age that, like a kind of relay-station of social standards, an automatic self-supervision of his drives, a more differentiated and more stable "super-ego" develops in him, and a part of the forgotten drive impulses and affect inclinations is no longer directly within reach of the level of consciousness at all.

Earlier, in warrior society, the individual could use physical violence if he was strong and powerful enough; he could openly indulge his inclinations in many directions that have subsequently been closed by social prohibitions. But he paid for this greater opportunity of direct pleasure with a greater chance of direct and open fear. Medieval conceptions of hell give us an idea of how strong this fear between man and man was. Both joy and pain were discharged more openly and freely. But the individual was their prisoner; he was hurled back and forth by his own feelings as by forces of nature. He had less control of his passions; he was more controlled by them.

Later, as the conveyor belts running through his existence grow longer and more complex, the individual learns to control himself more steadily; he is now less a prisoner of his passions than before. But as he is now more tightly bound by his functional dependence on the activities of an every-larger number of people, he is much more restricted in his conduct, in his chances of directly satisfying his drives and passions. Life becomes in a sense less dangerous, but also less emotional or pleasurable, at least as far as the direct release of pleasure is concerned. And for what is lacking in everyday life a substitute is created in dreams, in books and pictures. So, on their way to becoming courtiers, the nobility read novels of chivalry; the bourgeois contemplate violence and erotic passion in films. Physical classes, wars and feuds diminish, and anything recalling them, even the cutting up of dead animals and the use of the knife at table, is banished from view or at least subjected to more and more precise social rules. But at the same time the battlefield is, in a sense, moved within. Part of the tensions and passions that were earlier directly released in the struggle of man and man, must now be worked out within the human being. The more peaceful constraints exerted on him by his relations to others are mirrored within him; an individualized pattern of near-automatic habits is established and consolidated within him, a specific "super-ego", which endeavours to control, transform or suppress his affects in keeping with the social structure. But the drives, the passionate affects, that can no longer directly manifest themselves in the relationships *between* people, often struggle no less violently *within* the individual against this supervising part of himself. And this semi-automatic struggle of the person with himself does not always find a happy resolution; not always does the self-transformation required by life in this society lead to a new balance between drive-satisfaction and drive-control. Often enough it is subject to major or minor disturbances, revolts of one part of the person against the other, or a permanent atrophy, which makes the performance of social functions even more difficult, or impossible. The vertical oscillations, if we may so describe them, the leaps from fear to joy, pleasure to remorse are reduced, while the horizontal fissure running right through the whole person, the tension between "super-ego" and "unconscious"—the wishes and desires that cannot be remembered—increases.

Here too the basic characteristics of these patterns of intertwining, if one pursues not merely their static structures but their sociogenesis, prove to be relatively simple. Through the interdependence of larger groups of people and the exclusion of physical violence from them, a social apparatus is established in which the constraints between people are lastingly transformed into self-constraints. These self-constraints, a function of the perpetual hindsight and foresight instilled in the individual from childhood in accordance with his integration in extensive chains of action, have partly the form of conscious self-control and partly that of automatic habit. They tend towards a more even moderation, a more continuous restraint, a more exact control of drives and affects in accordance with the more differentiated pattern of social interweaving. But depending on the inner pressure, on the condition of society and the position of the individual within it, these constraints also produce peculiar tensions and disturbances in the conduct and drive economy of the individual. In some cases they lead to perpetual restlessness and dissatisfaction, precisely because the person affected can only gratify a part of his inclinations and impulses in modified form, for example in fantasy, in looking-on and overhearing, in daydreams or dreams. And sometimes the habituation to affect-inhibition goes so far—constant feelings of boredom or solitude are examples of this—that the individual is no longer capable of any form of fearless expression of the modified affects, or of direct gratification of the repressed drives. Particular branches of drives are as it were anaesthetized in such cases by the specific structure of the social framework in which the child grows up. Under the pressure of the dangers that their expression incurs in the child's social space, they become surrounded with automatic fears to such an extent that they can remain deaf and unresponsive throughout a whole lifetime. In other cases certain branches of drives may be so diverted by the heavy conflicts which the rough-hewn, affective and passionate nature of the small human being unavoidably encounters on its way to being moulded into a "civilized" being, that their energies can find only an unwanted release through bypasses, in compulsive actions and other symptoms of disturbance. In other cases again, these energies are so transformed that they flow into uncontrollable and eccentric attachments and repulsions, in predilections for this or that peculiar hobby-horse. And in all these cases a permanent, apparently groundless inner unrest shows how many drive energies are dammed up in a form that permits no real satisfaction.

Until now the individual civilizing process, like the social, runs its course by and large blindly. Under the cover of what adults think and plan, the relationships that forms between them and the young has functions and effects in the latter's personalities which they do not intend and of which they scarcely know. Unplanned in that sense are those results of social patterning of individuals to which one habitually refers as "abnormal"; psychological abnormalities which do not result from social patterning but are caused by unalterable hereditary traits need not be considered here. But the psychological make-up which keeps within the social norm and is subjectively more satisfying comes about in an equally unplanned way. It is the same social mould from which emerge both more favourably and more unfavourably structured human beings, the "well-adjusted" as well as the "mal-adjusted", within a very broad spectrum of varieties. The automatically reproduced anxieties which, in the course of each individual civilizing process and in connection with the conflicts that form an integral part of this process, attach themselves to specific drives and affect impulses sometimes lead to a permanent and total paralysis of these impulses, and sometimes only to a moderate regulation with enough scope for their full satisfaction. Under present conditions it is from the point of view of the individuals concerned more a question of their good or bad fortune than that of anybody's planning whether it is the one or the other. In either case it is the web of social relations in which the individual lives during his most impressionable phase, during childhood and youth, which imprints itself upon his unfolding personality where it has its counterpart in the relationship between his controlling agencies, super-ego and ego, and his libidinal impulses. The resulting balance between controlling agencies and drives on a variety of levels determines how an individual person steers himself in his relations with others; it determines that which we call, according to taste, habits, complexes or personality structure. However, there is no end to the intertwining, for although the self-steering of a person, malleable during early childhood, solidifies and hardens as he grows up, it never ceases entirely to be affected by his changing relations with others throughout his life. The learning of self-controls, call them "reason" or "conscience", "ego" or "super-ego", and the consequent curbing of more animalic impulses and affects, in short the civilizing of the human young, is never a process entirely without pain; it always leaves scars. If the person is lucky—and as no one, no parent, no doctor, and no counsellor, is at present able to steer this process in a child according to a clear knowledge of what is best for its future, it is still largely a question of luck—the wounds of the civilizing conflicts incurred during childhood heal; the scars left by them are not too deep. But in less favourable cases the conflicts inherent in the civilizing of young humans—conflicts with others and conflicts within themselves—remain unsolved, or, more precisely, though perhaps buried for a while, open up once more in situations reminiscent of those of childhood; the suffering, transformed into an adult form, repeats itself again and again, and the unsolved conflicts of a person's childhood never cease to disturb his adult relationships. In that way, the interpersonal conflicts of early youth which have patterned the personality structure continue to perturb or even destroy the interpersonal relationships of the grown-up. The resulting tensions may take the form either of contradictions between different self-control automatisms, sunk-in memory traces of former dependencies and needs, or of recurrent struggles between the controlling agencies and the libidinal impulses. In the more fortunate cases, on the other hand, the contradictions between different sections and layers of the controlling agencies, especially of the super-ego structure, are slowly reconciled; the most disruptive conflicts between that structure and the libidinal impulses are slowly contained. They not only disappear from waking consciousness, but are so thoroughly assimilated that, without too heavy a cost in subjective satisfaction, they no longer intrude unintentionally in later interpersonal relationships. In one case the conscious and unconscious self-control always remains diffuse in places and open to the breakthrough of socially unproductive forms of drive energy; in the other this self-control, which even today in juvenile phases is often more like a confusion of overlapping ice-floes than a smooth and firm sheet of ice, slowly becomes more unified and stable in positive correspondence to the structure of society. But as this structure, precisely in our times, is highly mutable, it demands a flexibility of habits and conduct which in most cases has to be paid for by a loss of stability.

Theoretically, therefore, it is not difficult to say in what lies the difference between an individual civilizing process that is considered successful and one that is considered unsuccessful. In the former, after all the pains and conflicts of this process, patterns of conduct well adapted to the framework of adult social functions are finally formed, an adequately functioning set of habits and at the same time—which does not necessarily go hand-in-hand with it—a positive pleasure balance. In the other, either the socially necessary self-control is repeatedly purchased, at a heavy cost in personal satisfaction, by a major effort to overcome opposed libidinal energies, or the control of these energies, renunciation of their satisfaction is not achieved at all; and often enough no positive pleasure balance of any kind is finally possible, because the social commands and prohibitions are represented not only by other people but also by the stricken self, since one part of it forbids and punishes what the other desires.

In reality the result of the individual civilizing process is clearly unfavourable or favourable only in relatively few cases at each end of the scale. The majority of civilized people live midway between these two extremes. Socially positive and negative features, personally gratifying and frustrating tendencies, mingle in them in varying proportions.

The social moulding of individuals in accordance with the structure of the civilizing process of what we now call the West is particularly difficult. In order to be reasonably successful it requires with the structure of Western society, a particularly high differentiation, an especially intensive and stable regulation of drives and affects, of all the more elementary human impulses. It therefore generally takes up more time, particularly in the middle and upper classes, than the social moulding of individuals in less complex societies. Resistance to adaptation to the prevailing standards of civilization, the effort which this adaptation, this profound transformation of the whole personality costs the individual, is always very considerable. And later, therefore, than in less complex societies the individual in the Western world attains with his adult social function the psychological make-up of an adult, the emergence of which by and large marks the conclusion of the individual civilizing process.

But even if in the more differentiated societies of the West the modelling of the individual self-steering apparatus is particularly extensive and intense, processes tending in the same direction, social and individual civilizing processes, most certainly do not occur only there. They are to be found wherever, under competitive pressures, the division of functions makes large numbers of people dependent on one another, wherever a monopolization of physical force permits and imposes a co-operation less charged with emotion, wherever functions are established that demand constant hindsight and foresight in interpreting the actions and intentions of others. What determines the nature and degree of such civilizing spurts is always the extent of interdependencies, the level of the division of functions, and within it, the structure of these functions themselves.

II

Spread of the Pressure for Foresight and Self-Constraint

What lends the civilizing process in the West its special and unique character is the fact that here the division of functions has attained a level, the monopolies of force and taxation a solidity, and interdependence and competition an extent, both in terms of physical space and of numbers of people involved, unequalled in world history.

Hitherto extensive networks of money or trade, with fairly stable monopolies of physical force at their centres, had developed almost exclusively on waterways, that is, above all, on riverbanks and seacoasts. The large areas of the hinterland remained more or less at the level of a barter economy, that is, people remained largely autarkic and their interdependence chains were short, even when a few trade arteries crossed the areas and a few major markets existed. With Western society as its starting point, a network of interdependence has developed which not only encompasses the oceans further than any other in the past, but extends to the furthest arable corners of vast inland regions. Corresponding to this is the necessity for an attunement of human conduct over wider areas, and foresight over longer chains of actions, than ever before. Corresponding to it, too, is the strength of self-control and the permanence of compulsion, affect-inhibition and drive-control, which life at the centres of this network imposes. One of the characteristics which make this connection between the size of and pressure within the network of interdependence on the one hand, and the psychological make-up of the individual on the other particularly clear, is what we call the "tempo"[133] of our time. This "tempo" is in fact nothing other than a manifestation of the multitude of intertwining chains of interdependence which run through every single social function people have to perform, and of the competitive pressure permeating this densely populated network and affecting, directly or indirectly, every single act of individuals. This may show itself in the case of an official or businessman in the profusion of his appointments or meetings, and in that of a worker by the exact timing and duration of each of his movements; in both cases the tempo is an expression of the multitude of interdependent actions, of the length and density of the chains composed by the individual actions, and of the intensity of struggles that keep this whole interdependent network in motion. In both cases a function situated at a junction of so many chains of action demands an exact allocation of time; it makes people accustomed to subordinating momentary inclinations to the overriding necessities of interdependence; it trains them to eliminate all irregularities from behaviour and to achieve permanent self-control. This is why tendencies in the individual so often rebel against social time represented by his own super-ego, and why so many people come into conflict with themselves when they wish to be punctual. From the development of chronometric instruments and the consciousness of time—as from that of money and other instruments of social integration—it is possible to read off with considerable accuracy how the division of functions, and with it the self-control imposed on the individual, advances.

Why, within this network, patterns of affect-control vary in some respects, why, for example, sexuality is surrounded by stronger restrictions in one country than in another, is a question in its own right. But however these differences may arise in particular cases, the general direction of the change in conduct, the "trend" of the movement of civilization, is everywhere the same. It always veers towards a more or less automatic self-control, to the subordination of short-term impulses to the commands of an ingrained long-term view, and to the formation of a more complex and secure "super-ego" agency. And broadly the same, too, is the manner in which this necessity to subordinate momentary affects to more distant goals is propagated; everywhere small leading groups are affected first, and then broader and broader strata of Western society.

It makes a considerable difference whether someone lives in a world with dense and extensive bonds of dependence as a mere passive object of these interdependencies, being affected by distant events without being able to influence or even perceive them—or whether someone has a function in society which demands for its performance a permanent effort of foresight and steady control of conduct. To begin with in Western development it is certain upper- and middle-class functions that require of their incumbents such steadily active self-discipline in long-term interests: courtly functions at the political centres of large societies, and commercial functions at the centres of long-distance trade networks which are under the protection of a fairly stable monopoly of force. But it is one of the peculiarities of social processes in the West that with the extension of interdependence, the necessity for such long-term thinking and the active attunement of individual conduct to some larger entity remote in time and space, spreads to ever-broader sections of society. Even the functions and the whole social situation of the lower social strata demand and make more and more possible a certain foresight, and produce a corresponding transformation or restraint of all those inclinations that promise immediate or short-term satisfactions at the cost of remoter ones. In the past the functions of the lower strata of manual workers were generally involved in the interdependent network only to the extent that their members felt the effect of remote actions and—if they were unpleasant—responded with unrest and rebellion, with short-term affective discharges. But their functions were not so constructed that within themselves the "alien" constraints were constantly converted into "self"-restraints; their daily tasks made them only little capable of restraining their immediate desires and affects in favour of something not tangible here and now. And so such outbursts hardly ever had lasting success.

Here a number of different nexuses are interlocking. Within every large human network there are some sectors which are more central than others. The functions of these central sectors, for example, the higher co-ordinating functions, impose more steady and strict self-control not only because of their central position and the large number of chains of action meeting in them; owing to the large number of actions depending on their incumbents, they carry major social power. What gives Western development its special character is the fact that in its course the dependence of all on all becomes more evenly balanced. To an increasing degree, the complex functioning of Western societies, with their high division of labour, depends on the lower agrarian and urban strata controlling their conduct increasingly through insight into its more long-term and more remote connections. These strata are ceasing to be merely "lower" social strata. The highly differentiated social apparatus becomes so complex, and in some respects so vulnerable, that disturbances, at one point of the inter-dependency chains which pass through all social positions inevitably affect many others, thus threatening the whole social tissue. Established groups engaged in competitive struggles among themselves are at the same time compelled to take into consideration the demands of the broad mass of outsiders. But as the social functions and power of the masses take on greater importance in this way, these functions require and permit greater foresight in their execution. Usually under heavy social pressure, members of the lower strata grow more accustomed to restraining momentary affects, and disciplining their whole conduct from a wider understanding of the total society and their position within it. Thereby their behaviour is forced increasingly in a direction originally confined to the upper strata. Their social power in relation to the latter increases; but at the same time they are increasingly trained to take a long-term view, no matter by whom and on what models their training is conducted. They, too, are increasingly subject to the kind of external compulsions that are transformed into individual self-restraint; in them, too, the horizontal tension between a self-control agency, a "super-ego", and libidinal energies that are now more or less successfully transformed, controlled or suppressed, increases. In this way civilizing structures are constantly expanding within Western society; both upper and lower strata are tending to become a kind of upper stratum and the centre of a network of interdependencies spreading over further and further areas, both populated and unpopulated, of the rest of the world. And only this vision of a comprehensive movement, of the progressive expansion, often in spurts and counter-spurts, of certain functions and patterns of conduct towards more and more outsider groups and outsider regions—only this vision, and the realization that we ourselves are in the midst of this up and down of a civilizing process and its crises, not at its end, places the problem of "civilization" in its proper perspective. If one steps back from the present into the past, what patterns, what structures does one discover in the successive waves of this movement, if one looks not from us to them, but from them to us?

III

Diminishing Contrasts, Increasing Varieties

The civilizing process moves along in a long sequence of spurts and counter-spurts. Again and again a rising outsider stratum or a rising survival unit as a whole, a tribe or a nation state, attains the functions and characteristics of an establishment in relation to other outsider strata or survival units which, on their part, are pressing from below, from their position as oppressed outsiders, against the current establishment. And again and again, as the grouping of people which has risen and has established itself is followed by a still broader, and more populous grouping attempting to emancipate itself, to free itself from oppression, one finds that the latter, if successful, is forced in turn into the position of an established oppressor. The time may well come when the former oppressed groups, freed from oppression, do not become oppressors in turn; but it is not yet in sight.

There are, of course, many unsolved problems raised by this vista. In the present context it may be enough to draw attention to the fact that by and large the lower strata, the oppressed and poorer outsider groups at a given stage of development, tend to follow their drives and affects more directly and spontaneously, that their conduct is less strictly regulated than that of the respective upper strata. The compulsions operating upon the lower strata are predominantly of a direct, physical kind, the threat of physical pain or annihilation by the sword, poverty or hunger. That type of pressure, however, does not induce a stable transformation of constraints through others, or "alien" constraints, into "self"-restraints. A medieval peasant who goes without meat because he is too poor, because beef is reserved for the lord's table, i.e. solely under physical constraint, will give way to his desire for meat whenever he can do so without external danger, unlike the founders of religious orders from the upper strata who deny themselves the enjoyment of meat in consideration of the after-life and the sense of their own sinfulness. A totally destitute person who works for others under constant threat of hunger or in penal servitude, will stop working once the threat of external force ceases, unlike the wealthy merchant who goes on and on working for himself although he probably has enough to live on without this work. He is compelled to do it not by simple need but by the pressure of the competition for power and prestige, because his profession, his elevated status, provide the meaning and justification of his life; and for him constant self-constraint has made work such a habit that the balance of his personality is upset if he is no longer able to work.

It is one of the peculiarities of Western society that in the course of its development this contrast between the situation and code of conduct of the upper and lower strata decreases considerably. Lower-class characteristics are spreading to all classes. The fact that Western society as a whole has gradually become a society where every able person is expected to earn his living through a highly regulated type of work is a symptom of this: earlier, work was an attribute of the lower classes. And at the same time, what used to be distinguishing features of the upper classes are likewise spreading to society at large. The conversion of "alien" social constraints into self-restraints, into a more or less habitual and automatic individual self-regulation of drives and affects—possibly only for people normally protected from external, physical threat by the sword or starvation—is taking place in the West increasingly among the broad masses, too.

Seen at close quarters, where only a small segment of this movement is visible, the differences in social personality structure between the upper and lower classes in the Western world today may still seem considerable. But if the whole sweep of the movement over centuries is perceived, one can see that the sharp contrasts between the behaviour of different social groups—like the contrasts and sudden switches within the behaviour of individuals—are steadily diminishing. The moulding of drives and affects, the forms of conduct, the whole psychological make-up of the lower classes in the more civilized societies, with their growing importance in the entire network of functions, is increasingly approaching that of other groups, beginning with the middle classes. This is the case even though a part of the self-constraints and taboos among the latter, which arise from the urge to "distinguish themselves", the desire for enhanced prestige, may initially be lacking in the former, and even though the type of social dependence of the former does not yet necessitate or permit the same degree of affect-control and steadier foresight as in the upper classes of the same period.

This reduction in the contrasts within society as within individuals, this peculiar commingling of patterns of conduct deriving from initially very different social levels, is highly characteristic of Western society. It is one of the most important peculiarities of the "civilizing process". But this movement of society and civilization certainly does not follow a straight line. Within the overall movement there are repeatedly greater or lesser counter-movements in which the contrasts in society and the fluctuations in the behaviour of individuals, their affective outbreaks, increase again.

What is happening under our eyes, what we generally call the "spread of civilization" in the narrower sense, that is, the spread of our institutions and standards of conduct beyond the West, constitutes, as we have said, the last wave so far within a movement that first took place for several centuries within the

West, and whose trend and characteristic patterns, including science, technology, and other manifestations of a specific type of self-restraint, established themselves here long before the concept of "civilization" existed. From Western society-as a kind of upper class-Western "civilized" patterns of conduct are today spreading over wide areas outside the West, whether through the settlement of Occidentals or through the assimilation of the upper strata of other nations, as models of conduct earlier spread within the West itself from this or that upper stratum, from certain courtly or commercial centres. The course taken by all these expansions is only slightly determined by the plans or desires of those whose patterns of conduct were taken over. The classes supplying the models are even today not simply the free creators or originators of the expansion. This spread of the same patterns of conduct from the "white mother-countries or father-lands" follows the incorporation of the other areas into the network of political and economic interdependencies, into the sphere of elimination struggles between and within the nations of the West. It is not "technology" which is the cause of this change of behaviour; what we call "technology" is itself only *one* of the symbols, one of the last manifestations of that constant foresight imposed by the formation of longer and longer chains of actions and the competition between those bound together by them. "Civilized" forms of conduct spread to these other areas because and to the extent that in them, through their incorporation into the network whose centre the West still constitutes, the structure of their societies and of human relationships in general, is likewise changing. Technology, education—all these are facets of the same overall development. In the areas into which the West has expanded, the social functions with which the individual must comply are increasingly changing in such a way as to induce the same constant foresight and affect-control as in the West itself. Here, too, the transformation of the whole of social existence is the basic condition of the civilization of conduct. For this reason we find in the relation of the West to other parts of the world the beginnings of the reduction in contrasts which is peculiar to every major wave of the civilizing movement.

This recurrent fusion of patterns of conduct of the functionally upper classes with those of the rising classes, is not without significance regarding the curiously ambivalent attitude of the upper classes in this process. The habituation to foresight, and the stricter control of behaviour and the affects to which the upper classes are inclined through their situation and functions, are important instruments of their dominance, as in the case of European colonialism, for example. They serve as marks of distinction and prestige. For just this reason such a society regards offences against the prevailing pattern of drive and affect control, any "letting go" by their members, with greater or lesser disapproval. This disapproval increases when the social power and size of the lower, rising group increase, and concomitantly, the competition for the same opportunities between the upper and lower groups becomes more intense. The effort and foresight which it costs to maintain the position of the upper class is expressed in the internal commerce of its members with each other by the degree of reciprocal supervision they practise on one another, by the severe stigmatization and penalties they impose upon those members who breach the common distinguishing code. The fear arising from the situation of the whole group, from their struggle to preserve their cherished and threatened position, acts directly as a force maintaining the code of conduct, the cultivation of the super-ego in its members. It is converted into individual anxiety, the individual's fear of personal degradation or merely loss of prestige in his own society. And it is this fear of loss of prestige in the eyes of others, instilled as self-compulsion, whether in the form of shame or sense of honour, which assures the habitual reproduction of distinctive conduct, and the strict drive-control underlying it, in individual people.

But while on the one hand these upper classes—and in some respects, as noted above, the Western nations as a whole have an upper-class function—are thus driven to maintain at all costs their special conduct and drive-control as marks of distinction, on the other their situation, together with the structure of the general movement carrying them along, forces them in the long run to reduce more and more these differences in standards of behaviour. The expansion of Western civilization shows this double tendency clearly enough. This civilization is the characteristic conferring distinction and superiority on Occidentals. But at the same time the Western people, under the pressure of their own competitive struggle, bring about in large areas of the world a change in human relationships and functions in line with their own standards. They make large parts of the world dependent on them and at the same time, in keeping with a regularity of functional differentiation that has been observed over and again, become themselves dependent on them. On the one hand they build, through institutions and by the strict regulation of their own behaviour, a wall between themselves and the groups they colonize and whom they consider their inferiors. On the other, with their social forms, they also spread their own style of conduct and institutions in these places. Largely without deliberate intent, they work in a direction which sooner or later leads to a reduction in the differences both of social power and of conduct between colonists and colonized. Even in our day the contrasts are becoming perceptibly less. According to the form of colonization and the position of an area in the large network of differentiated functions, and not least to the region's own history and structure, processes of commingling are beginning to take place in specific areas outside the West similar to those sketched earlier on the example of courtly and bourgeois conduct in different countries within the West itself. In colonial regions too, according to the position and social strength of the various groups, Western standards are spreading downwards and occasionally even upwards from below, if we may adhere to this spatial image, and fusing to form new unique entities, new varieties of civilized conduct. *The contrasts in conduct between the upper and lower groups are reduced with the spread of civilization; the varieties or nuances of civilized conduct are increased.* This incipient transformation of Oriental or African people in the direction of Western standards represents the last wave of the continuing civilizing movement that we are able to observe. But as this wave rises, signs of new and further waves in the same direction can already be seen forming in it; for until now the groups approaching the Western upper class in colonial areas as the lower, rising class, are primarily the upper classes within those nations.

One step further back in history one can observe in the West itself a similar movement: the assimilation of the lower urban and agrarian classes to the standards of civilized conduct, the growing habituation of these groups to foresight, to a more even curbing and more strict control of the affects, and a higher measure of individual self-constraint in their case too. Here too, according to the structure of the history of each country, very diverse varieties of affect-formation emerge within the framework of civilized conduct. In the conduct of workers in England, for example, one can still see traces of the manners of the landed gentry and of merchants within a large trade network, in France the airs of courtiers and a bourgeoisie brought to power by revolution. In the workers too, we find a stricter regulation of conduct, a type of courtesy more informed by tradition in colonial nations which have for a long period had the function of an upper class within a large interdependent network, and less polished control of the affects in nations that achieved colonial expansion late or not at all, because strong monopolies of force and taxation, a centralization of national power—pre-conditions for any lasting colonial expansion—developed later in them than in their competitors.

Further back, in the seventeenth, eighteenth and nineteenth centuries—earlier or later according to the structure of each nation—we find the same pattern in a still smaller circle: the interpenetration of the standards of conduct of the nobility and the bourgeoisie. In accordance with the power-relationship, the product of interpenetration is dominated first by models derived from the situation of the upper class, then by pattern of conduct of the lower, rising classes, until finally an amalgam emerges, a new style of unique character. Here, too, the same dualism in the position of the upper class is visible that can be observed today in the vanguard of "civilization". The courtly nobility, the vanguard of "*civilité*", is gradually compelled to exercise a strict restraint of the affects and an exact moulding of conduct through its increasing integration in a network of interdependencies, represented here by the pincer formed of monarchy and bourgeoisie in which the nobility is trapped. For the courtly nobility, too, the self-restraint imposed on them by their function and situation serves at the same time as a prestige value, a means of distinguishing themselves from the lower groups harrying them, and they do everything within their power to prevent these differences from being effaced. Only the initiated member should know the secrets of good conduct; only within good society should this be learned. Gratian deliberately wrote his treatise on "savoir-vivre", the famous "Hand Oracle", in an obscure style, a courtly princess once explained, [134] so that this knowledge could not be bought by anyone for a few pence; and Courtin does not forget, in the introduction to his treatise on "Civilité", to stress that his manuscript was really written for the private use of a few friends, and that even printed it is intended only for people of good society. But even here the ambivalence of the situation is revealed. Owing to the peculiar form of interdependence in which they lived, the courtly aristocracy could not prevent—indeed, through their contacts with rich bourgeois strata whom they needed for one reason or another, they assisted—the spreading of their manners, their customs, their tastes and their language to other classes. First of all in the seventeenth century, these manners passed to small leading groups of the bourgeoisie—the "Excursus on the Modelling of Speech at Court" gives a vivid example [135]—and then, in the eighteenth century, to broader bourgeois strata; the mass of *civilité*-books that appeared at that time shows this clearly. Here too the force of the current of interweaving as a whole, the tensions and competition leading within it to ever-greater complexity and functional differentiation, to the individual's dependence on an ever-larger number of others, to the rise of broader and broader classes, proved stronger than the barricade the nobility had been seeking to build around themselves.

It is at small functional centres that the foresight, more complex self-discipline, more stable super-ego formation enforced by growing inter-dependence, first becomes noticeable. Then more and more functional circles within the West change in the same direction. Finally, in conjunction with pre-existing forms of civilization, the same transformation of social functions and thus of conduct and the whole personality, begins to take place in countries outside Europe. This is the picture which emerges if we attempt to survey the course followed up to now by the Western civilizing movement in social space as a whole.

IV

The Courtization of Warriors

The courtly society of the seventeenth and eighteenth centuries, and above all the courtly nobility of France that forms its centre, occupies a specific position within this whole movement of interpenetration of the patterns of conduct of ever-wider circles. As noted above, the courtiers did not originate or invent the muting of affects and the more even regulation of conduct. They, like everyone else in this movement, were bending to the constraints of interdependence that were not planned by any individual person or group of persons. But it is in this courtly society that the basic stock of models of conduct is formed which then, fused with others and modified in accordance with the position of the groups carrying them, spread, with the compulsion to exercise foresight, to ever-wider circles of functions. Their special situation makes the people of courtly society, more than any other Western group affected by this movement, specialists in the elaboration and moulding of social conduct. For, unlike all succeeding groups in the position of an established upper class, they have a social function but no profession.

Not only in the Western civilizing process, but in others such as that of eastern Asia, the moulding which behaviour receives at the great courts, the administrative centres of the key monopolies of taxation and physical force, is of equal importance. It is first here, at the seat of the monopoly ruler, that all the threads of a major network of interdependence run together; here, at this particular social nexus, more and longer chains of action intersect than at any other point in the web. Even long-distance trade links, into which urban-commercial centres are interwoven here and there, never prove lasting and stable unless they are protected for a considerable period by strong central authorities. Correspondingly, the provident long-term view, the strict control of conduct which this central organ demands of its functionaries and of the prince himself or his representatives and servants, are greater than at any other point. Ceremony and etiquette give this situation clear expression. So much presses directly and indirectly on the central ruler and his close entourage from the whole dominion, each of his steps, each of his gestures may be of such momentous and far-reaching importance, precisely because the monopolies still have a strongly private and personal character, that without this exact timing, these complex forms of reserve and distance, the tense balance of society on which the peaceful operation of the monopoly administration rests would rapidly lapse into disorder. And, if not always directly, then at least through the persons of the central ruler and his ministers, every movement or upheaval of any significance in the whole dominion reacts on the bulk of the courtiers, on the whole narrower and wider entourage of the prince. Directly or indirectly, the intertwining of all activities with which everyone at court is inevitably confronted, compels him to observe constant vigilance, and to subject everything he says and does to minute scrutiny.

The formation of monopolies of tax and physical force, and of great courts around these monopolies, is certainly no more than one of several interdependent processes of which the civilizing process forms a part. But it certainly provides one of the keys by which we can gain access to the driving forces of these processes. The great royal court stands for a period at the centre of the social networks which set and keep the civilizing of conduct in motion. In tracing the sociogenesis of the court, we find ourselves at the centre of a civilizing transformation that is both particularly pronounced and an indispensable precondition for all subsequent spurts and counter-spurts in the civilizing process. We see how, step by step, a warrior nobility is replaced by a tamed nobility with more muted affects, a courtly nobility. Not only within the Western civilizing process, but as far as we can see within every major civilizing process, one of the most decisive transitions is that of *warriors to courtiers*. But it need scarcely be said that there are widely differing stages and degrees of this transition, this inner pacification of a society. In the West the transformation of the warriors proceeds very gradually from the eleventh or twelfth centuries until it slowly reaches its conclusion in the seventeenth and eighteenth centuries.

How it comes to pass has already been described in detail: first, the wide landscape with its many castles and estates; the degree of integration is slight; the everyday dependence and thus the horizon of the bulk of the warriors, like that of the peasants, is restricted to their immediate district:

"Localism was writ large across the Europe of the early Middle Ages, the localism at first of the tribe and the estate, later shaping itself into those feudal and manorial units upon which medieval society rested. Both politically and socially these units were nearly independent, and the exchange of products and ideas was reduced to a minimum."[136] Then, from the profusion of castles and estates in every region, arise individual houses whose rulers have attained, in many battles and through the growth of their possessions and military power, a position of predominance over the other warriors in a more extended area. Their residences become, as a result of the greater confluence of goods arriving at them, the homes of a larger number of people, "courts" in a new sense of the word. The people who come together here in search of opportunities, always including a number of poorer warriors, are no longer as independent as the free warriors ensconced in their more or less self-sufficient estates; they are all placed in a kind of monopolistically controlled competition. And even here, in a circle of people that is still small compared to the absolutist courts, the co-existence of a number of people whose actions constantly intertwine, compels even the warriors who find themselves thus in closer interdependence to observe some degree of consideration and foresight, a more strict control of conduct and—above all towards the mistress of the house on whom they depend—a greater restraint of the affects, a transformation of the drive economy. The *courtois* code of conduct gives us an idea of the regulation of manners, and the *minnesang*[137] an impression of the drive-control, that become necessary and normal at these major and minor territorial courts. They bear witness to a first spurt in the direction which finally leads to the complete transformation of the nobility into courtiers, and a permanent "civilizing" of their conduct. But the web of interdependence into which the warrior enters at first is not yet very extensive or tight. If he must adopt a certain reserve at court, there are still countless people and situations in respect of which he need observe no special restraint. He may escape the lord and the lady of one court in the hope of finding lodgings at another. The country road is full of sought and unsought encounters which require no very great control of impulses. At court, towards the mistress, he may deny himself violent acts and affective outbursts; but even the *courtois* knight is first and foremost still a warrior, and his life an almost uninterrupted chain of wars, feuds and violence. The more peaceful constraints of social intertwining which tend to impose a profound transformation of drives, do not yet bear constantly and evenly on his life; they intrude only intermittently, are constantly breached by belligerence which neither tolerates nor requires any restraint of the affects. So the self-restraint which the *courtois* knights observe at court is only slightly consolidated into half-unconscious habits, into the almost automatic pattern characteristic of a later stage. The *courtois* precepts—as noted above—are mostly addressed, in the heyday of knightly courtly society, to adults and children alike; conformity to them by adults is never taken so much for granted that one may cease to speak about them. The opposed impulses never disappear from consciousness. The structure of self-constraints, especially the "super-ego", is not yet very strongly or evenly developed.

In addition, one of the main motive forces which later, in absolutist–courtly society, especially consolidates polite manners in the individual and continuously refines them, is as yet still lacking. The rise of urban–bourgeois strata against the nobility is still relatively slight, as therefore is the competitive tension between the two estates. To be sure, at the territorial courts themselves, warriors and town-dwellers sometimes compete for the same opportunities. There are bourgeois as well as noble *minnesänger*; in this respect too the *courtois* court shows incipiently the same structural regularities which later appear, fully developed, in the absolutist court: it brings people of bourgeois and noble origin into constant contact. But later, in the era of fully developed monopolies of rule, the functional integration of nobility and bourgeoisie, and thus the possibility of constant contacts as well as permanent tensions, is already quite highly developed even outside the court. Contacts between bourgeois and warriors such as occur at the *courtois* courts, are still relatively rare. In general, the intertwining of dependencies between bourgeoisie and nobility is still slight compared to the later period. The towns and the feudal lords in their immediate or wider neighbourhood still stand opposed as alien political and social units. How little the division of functions is developed, and how great the relative independence of the different estates still is, is clearly demonstrated by the fact that the spread of customs and ideas between town and town, court and court, monastery and monastery, i.e. relationships within the same social stratum, even over long distances, is often greater than contacts between castle and towns in the same district. [138] This is the social structure which—by way of contrast—we must keep in mind in order to understand the different structure, the different social processes in which gradually an increasing "civilization" of the way the individual steers himself emerges.

Here, as in every society with a barter economy, exchange and thus mutual dependence and integration between different classes is still slight as compared to the following phases. Society's whole mode of life is therefore less uniform. Military potential and property are here extremely closely and directly related. Thus the unarmed peasant lives in an abject condition. He is at the mercy of the armed lord to a degree that no person was exposed to others in the everyday life of later phases, when public or state monopolies of force had developed. The lord and master, on the other hand, the warrior, is functionally so little dependent on his inferiors (though of course not independent of them), he is, through the overwhelming physical threat normally emanating from him, untrammelled in relation to them to an extent which surpasses by far the relative power surplus of any upper class in relation to lower classes at the later stages of social development. Similarly with the standard of living: here, too, the contrast between the highest and lowest classes of this society is extremely great, particularly in the phase when a decreasing number of especially mighty and wealthy lords is emerging from the mass of the warriors. We encounter similar contrasts today in areas where the social structure is nearer to that of Western medieval society than that of the West today, for example in Peru or Saudi Arabia. Members of a small élite have an immense income of which a far larger part than is the case with high incomes in the West today, is used for the personal consumption of its owner, luxuries of his "private life", robes and jewellery, residence and stables, utensils and meals, feasts and other pleasures. The members of the lowest class, the peasants, by contrast, live wretchedly under the constant threat of bad harvests and starvation; even under normal circumstances the produce of their work just suffices to provide them with a subsistence; their standard of living is considerably lower than that of any class in "civilized" societies. And only when these contrasts are reduced, when through the competitive pressure affecting this society from top to bottom the division of functions and interdependence over large areas gradually increases, when the functional dependence of the upper classes grows while the social power and living standards of the lower class rise, only then do we find the constant foresight and self-control in the upper classes, the continuous upward movement of the lower ones, and all the other changes which one can observe in any civilizing spurt encompassing broader strata.

To begin with—at the starting-point of this movement as it were—the warriors live their own lives and the burghers and peasants theirs. Even in spatial proximity the gulf between the estates is deep; customs, gestures, clothes or amusements differ, even if mutual influences are not entirely lacking. On all sides social contrast—or, as people in a more uniform world like to call it, the variety of life—is greater. The upper class, the nobility, does not yet feel any appreciable social pressure from below; even the bourgeoisie scarcely contest their function and prestige. They do not yet need to hold themselves constantly in check and on the alert in order to maintain their position as the upper class. They have their land and their swords: the primary danger for each warrior is other warriors. And so the mutual control the nobles impose on their conduct as a means of class distinction is less, so that from this side too the individual knight is subjected to a lower degree of self-control. He occupies his social position far more securely and as a matter of course than the courtly noble. He does not need to banish coarseness and vulgarity from his life. The thought of the lower classes has nothing disturbing for him; they are not permanently associated with anxiety, and thus there is no social taboo on anything recalling the lower classes in upper-class life, as happened later. No repugnance or embarrassment is aroused by the sight of the lower classes and their behaviour, but a feeling of *contempt*, which is expressed openly, untroubled by any reserve, uninhibited and unsublimated. The "Scenes from the Life of a Knight" included earlier in this study,[139] give a certain impression of this attitude, although the documentation was taken from a later, courtly period of knightly existence.

How the warriors are drawn step by step into the vortex of increasingly stronger and closer interdependencies with other classes and groups, how an increasing part of them falls into functional and finally institutional dependence on others, has already been described in detail from various aspects. These are processes acting in the same direction over centuries: loss of military and economic self-sufficiency by all warriors, and the conversion of a part of them into courtiers.

One can detect the operation of these forces of integration as early as the eleventh and twelfth centuries, when territorial dominions consolidate themselves and a number of people, particularly less favoured knights, are forced to go to the greater and lesser courts to seek service.

Then, slowly, the few great courts of princely feudality rise above all the others; only members of the royal house now have the chance to compete freely with one another. And above all the richest, most brilliant court of this period of competing feudal princes, the Burgundian court, gives an impression of how this transformation of warriors into courtiers gradually advances.

Finally, in the fifteenth and above all the sixteenth century, the whole movement underlying this transformation, the differentiation of functions, the increasing interdependence and integration of ever-larger areas and classes, accelerates. This is seen particularly clearly in the movement of a social instrument the use and changes of which indicate most accurately the degree of division of functions, and the extent and nature of social interdependence: the movement of money. The volume of money grows more quickly, and at a corresponding rate the purchasing power or value of money falls. This movement, too, that is, the devaluation of minted metal, begins, like the transformation of warriors into courtiers, early in the Middle Ages. What is new at the transition from medieval to modern times is not monetarization, the decrease in the purchasing power of minted metal as such, but the pace and extent of this movement. Here, as so often, what first appears as merely a quantitative change, is on closer inspection an expression of qualitative changes, transformations in the structure of human relationships, of society.

Certainly, this accelerating devaluation of money is not by itself the cause of the social changes that emerge more and more clearly at this time; it is part of a larger process, a lever in a more complex system of intertwining trends. Under the pressure of competitive struggles of a particular stage and structure, the demand for money increases at this time; to satisfy it new ways and means are sought and found. But, as was pointed out earlier,[140] this movement has a very different meaning for different sectors of society; precisely this shows how great the functional interdependence of different strata has become. Favoured by this movement are all those groups whose functions permit them to compensate for the falling purchasing power of money by acquiring more money, i.e., above all bourgeois groups and the controllers of the tax monopoly, the kings; disadvantaged are groups of warriors or nobles who have an income which nominally remains the same but in purchasing power constantly diminishes with the accelerating devaluation of money. It is the pull of this movement that in the sixteenth and seventeenth centuries draws more and more warriors to the court and thus into direct dependence on the king, while conversely the kings' tax revenues grow to such an extent that they can maintain an ever-larger number of people at their court.

If one contemplates the past as a kind of aesthetic picture book, if one's gaze is directed above all at changes of "styles", one may easily have the impression that from time to time the tastes or minds of people changed abruptly through a kind of inner mutation: now we have "Gothic people" before us, now "men of the Renaissance", and now "Baroque people". If we try to gain an idea of the structure of the whole network of relationships in which all the individual people of a certain epoch are enmeshed, if we try to follow the changes in the institutions under which they live, or in the functions on which their social existence is based, our impression that at some moment the same mutation suddenly and inexplicably took place in many minds independent of each other, is increasingly dispelled. All these changes take place quite slowly over a considerable period, in small steps and to a large extent noiselessly for ears capable of perceiving only the great events heard far and wide. The explosions in which the existence and attitudes of individual people are changed abruptly and therefore especially perceptibly, are nothing but particular events within these slow and often almost imperceptible social shifts, whose effects are grasped only by comparing different generations, by placing side by side the social destinies of fathers, sons and grandsons. Such is the case with the transformation of the warriors into courtiers, the change whereby an upper class of free knights was replaced by one of courtiers. Even in the last phases of this process, many individuals may still have seen the fulfilment of their existence, of their wishes, affects and talents, in the life of a free knight. But all these talents and affects are now becoming increasingly impossible to put into practice because of the gradual transformation of human relations; the functions that give them scope are disappearing from the fabric of society. And the case is no different, finally, with the absolutist court itself. It too was not suddenly conceived or created at some moment by individuals, but was formed gradually on the basis of a specific transformation of social power-relationships. All individuals are driven by a particular dependence on others into this specific form of relationship. Through their interdependence they hold each other fast within it, and the court is not only generated by this interweaving of dependencies, but creates itself over and again as a form of human relationships outlasting individuals, as a firmly established institution, as long as this particular kind of mutual dependence is continuously renewed on the basis of a particular structure of society at large. Just as, for example, the social institution of a factory is incomprehensible unless we try to explain why the entire social structure continuously generates factories, why people in them are obliged to perform services as employees or workers for an employer, and why the employer is in turn dependent on such services, the social institution of the absolutist court is likewise incomprehensible unless we know the formula of needs, the nature and degree of mutual dependence, by which people of different kinds were bound together in this way. Only thus does the court appear before our eyes as it really was; only thus does it lose the aspect of a fortuitously or arbitrarily created grouping, about which it is neither possible nor necessary to ask the reason for its existence, and takes on meaning as a network of human relationships which, for a period, continuously reproduced itself in this way, because it offered many individual people opportunities of satisfying certain needs generated over and again in their society.

The constellation of needs out of which the "court" constantly reproduced itself as an institution over generations has been shown above: the nobility, or at least parts of it, needed the king because, with advancing monopolization, the function of free warrior was disappearing from society; and because, with increasing monetary integration, the produce from their estates—measured against the standards of the rising bourgeoisie—no longer allowed them more than a mediocre living and frequently not even that, and certainly not a social existence that could maintain the nobility's prestige as the upper class against the growing strength of the bourgeoisie. Under this pressure a part of the nobility—whoever could hope to find a place there—entered the court and thus direct dependence on the king. Only life at court opened to individual nobles within this social space access to economic opportunities and prestige that could in any way satisfy their claims to a demonstratively upper-class existence. Had the nobles been concerned solely or even primarily with economic opportunities, they would not have needed to go to the court; many of them could have acquired wealth more successfully through commercial activity—such as a rich marriage.

But to gain wealth through commercial activity they would have had to renounce their noble rank; they would have degraded themselves in their own eyes and those of other nobles. It was this very distance from the bourgeoisie, their character as nobles, their membership of the upper class of the country, that gave their lives meaning and direction. The desire to preserve their class prestige, to "distinguish" themselves, motivated their actions far more than the desire to accumulate money. They therefore not only remained at court because they were dependent on the king, but they remained dependent on the king because only life amid courtly society could maintain the distance from others and the prestige on which depended their salvation, their existence as members of the upper class, the establishment or the "Society" of the country. No doubt, at least a part of the courtly nobility could not have lived at court had they not been offered many kinds of economic opportunities there. But what they sought were not economic possibilities as such—they were, as noted above, to be had elsewhere—but possibilities of existence that were compatible with the maintenance of their distinguishing prestige, their character as a nobility. And this double bond through the necessity for both money and prestige is to varying degrees characteristic of all upper classes, not only the bearers of "civilité" but also of "civilization". The compulsion that membership of an upper class and the desire to retain it exert on the individual, is no less strong and formative than that arising from the simple necessity of economic subsistence. Motives of both kinds are wound as a double and invisible chain about the individual members of such classes, and the first bond, the craving for prestige and fear of its loss, the struggle against the obliteration of social distinction, is no more to be explained solely by the second, as a masked desire for more money and economic advantages, than it is ever to be found lastingly in classes or families that live under heavy external pressure on the borderline of hunger and destitution. A compulsive desire for social prestige is to be found as the primary motive of action only among members of classes whose income under normal circumstances is substantial and perhaps even growing, and at any rate is appreciably over the hunger threshold. In such classes the impulse to engage in economic activity is no longer the simple necessity of satisfying hunger, but a desire to preserve a certain high, socially expected standard of living and prestige. This explains why, in such elevated classes, affect-control and self-constraint are generally more highly developed than in the lower classes: fear of loss or reduction of social prestige is one of the most powerful motive forces in the transformation from constraints through others into self-restraints. Here, too, as in many other instances, the upper-class characteristics of "good society" are particularly highly developed in the courtly aristocracy of the seventeenth and eighteenth centuries, precisely because, within its framework, money was indispensable and wealth desirable as a means of living, but certainly not, as in the bourgeois world, the basis of prestige as well. Membership of courtly society means to those belonging to it more than wealth; for just this reason they are so entirely and inescapably bound to the court; for just this reason the pressure of courtly life shaping their conduct is so strong. There is no other place where they could live without loss of status; and this is why they are so dependent on the king.

The king for his part is dependent on the aristocracy for a large number of reasons. For his own conviviality he needs a society whose manners he shares; the fact that the people who serve him at table, on going to bed or while hunting belong to the highest nobility of the land, serves his need to be distinguished from all the other groups in the country. But above all he needs the nobility as a counterweight to the bourgeoisie, just as he needs the bourgeoisie to counterbalance the nobility, if his scope to manipulate the key monopolies is not to be reduced. It is the inherent regularities of the "royal mechanism" that place the absolutist ruler in dependence on the nobility. To maintain the nobility as a distinguishing class, and thus to preserve the balance and tension between nobility and bourgeoisie, to allow neither estate to grow too strong or too weak: these are the fundamentals of royal policy.

The nobility—and the bourgeoisie, too—is not only dependent on the king; the king depends on the existence of the nobility. But without doubt the dependence of the individual noble on the king is incomparably greater than that of the king on any individual noble; this is very clearly manifested in the relation between king and nobility at court.

The king is not only the nobility's oppressor, as part of the courtly nobility feel; nor is he only their preserver, as large sections of the bourgeoisie believe; he is both. And the court, therefore, is likewise both: an institution for taming and preserving the nobility. "If a noble," La Bruyère says in a passage on the court, "lives at home in the provinces, he is free, but without support; if he lives at Court, he is protected, but a slave." In many respects this relationship resembles that between a small independent businessman and a high employee in a powerful family concern. At court a part of the nobility find the possibility of living in accordance with their status; but the individual nobles are not now, as the knights were earlier, in free military competition with each other: they are in monopoly-bound competition for the opportunities the monopoly ruler has to allocate. And they not only live under the pressure of this central lord; they are not only subjected to the competitive pressure which they, together with a reserve army of country aristocracy, exert on each other; they are above all under pressure from rising bourgeois strata. With the latters' growing social power the noblemen at court have constantly to contend; they live from the duties and taxes that come primarily from the third estate. The interdependence and integration of different social functions, above all between nobility and bourgeoisie, is very much tighter than in preceding phases. All the more omnipresent, therefore, are the tensions between them. And as the structure of human relationships is changed in this way, as the individual is now embedded in the human network quite differently from before and moulded by the web of his dependencies, so too changes the structure of individual consciousness and affects, of the interplay between drives and drive-controls, between conscious and unconscious levels of the personality. The closer interdependence on every side, the heavy and continuous pressure from all directions, demands and instils a more even self-control, a more stable super-ego and new forms of conduct between people: warriors become courtiers.

Wherever we encounter civilizing processes of any scope, we also find structural similarities within the wider socio-historical context in which these changes in mentality occur. They may take place more or less quickly, they may advance, as here, in a single sweep or in several spurts with strong counter-spurts; but as far as we can see today, a more or less decisive courtization of warriors, whether permanent or transitory, is one of the most elementary social preconditions of every major movement of civilization. And however little importance the social formation of the court may at first sight have for our present life, a certain understanding of the structure of the court is indispensable in comprehending civilizing processes. Some of its structural characteristics may also throw light on the life at centres of power in general.

V

The Muting of Drives: Psychologization and Rationalization

"Life at court", La Bruyère writes,[141] "is a serious, melancholy game, which requires of us that we arrange our pieces and our batteries, have a plan, follow it, foil that of our adversary, sometimes take risks and play on impulse. And after all our measures and meditations we are in check, sometimes checkmate."

At the court, above all at the great absolutist court, there was formed for the first time a kind of society and human relationships having structural characteristics which from now on, over a long stretch of Western history and through many variations, again and again play a decisive part. In the midst of a large populated area which by and large is free of physical violence, a "good society" is formed. But even if the use of physical violence now recedes from human intercourse, if even duelling is now forbidden, people now exert pressure and force on each other in a wide variety of different ways. Life in this circle is in no way peaceful. Very many people are continuously dependent on each other. Competition for prestige and royal favour is intense. "Affaires", disputes over rank and favour, do not cease. If the sword no longer plays so great a role as the means of decision, it is replaced by intrigue, conflicts in which careers and social success are contested with words. They demand and produce other qualities than did the armed struggles that had to be fought out with weapons in one's hand. Continuous reflection, foresight, and calculation, self-control, precise and articulate regulation of one's own effects, knowledge of the whole terrain, human and non-human, in which one acts, become more and more indispensable preconditions of social success.

Every individual belongs to a "clique", a social circle which supports him when necessary; but the groupings change. He enters alliances, if possible with people ranking high at court. But rank at court can change very quickly; he has rivals; he has open and concealed enemies. And the tactics of his struggles, as of his alliances, demand careful consideration. The degree of aloofness or familiarity with everyone must be carefully measured; each greeting, each conversation has a significance over and above what is actually said or done. They indicate the standing of a person; and they contribute to the formation of court opinion on his standing:

"Let a favourite pay close heed to himself: for if he does not keep me waiting as long as usual in his antechamber; if his face is more open, if he frowns less, if he listens to me more willingly and accompanies me a little further when showing me out, I shall think that he is beginning to fall, and I shall be right."[142]

The court is a kind of stock exchange; as in every "good society", an estimate of the "value" of each individual is continuously being formed. But here his value has its real foundation not in the wealth or even the achievements or ability of the individual, but in the favour he enjoys with the king, the influence he has with other mighty ones, his importance in the play of courtly cliques. All this, favour, influence, importance, this whole complex and dangerous game in which physical force and direct affective outbursts are prohibited and a threat to existence, demands of each participant a constant foresight and an exact knowledge of every other, of his position and value in the network of courtly opinion; it exacts precise attunement of his own behaviour to this value. Every mistake, every careless step depresses the value of its perpetrator in courtly opinion; it may threaten his whole position at court.

"A man who knows the court is master of his gestures, of his eyes and his expression; he is deep, impenetrable. He dissimulates the bad turns he does, smiles at his enemies, suppresses his ill-temper, disguises his passions, disavows his heart, acts against his feelings."[143]

The transformation of the nobility in the direction of "civilized" behaviour is unmistakable. Here, it is not yet in all respects so profound and all-embracing as later in bourgeois society; for it is only towards their peers that the courtier and the court lady need to subject themselves to such constraint, and far less so towards their social inferiors. Quite apart from the fact that the pattern of drive- and affect-control is different in courtly from that in bourgeois society, the awareness that this control is exercised for social reasons is more alive. Opposing inclinations do not yet wholly vanish from waking consciousness; self-constraint has not yet become so completely an apparatus of habits operating almost automatically and including all human relationships. But it is already quite clear how human beings are becoming more complex, and internally split in a quite specific way. Each man, as it were, confronts himself. He "conceals his passions", "disavows his heart", "acts against his feelings". The pleasure or inclination of the moment is restrained in anticipation of the disagreeable consequences of its indulgence; and it is, indeed, the same mechanism as that by which adults—whether parents or other persons—increasingly instil a stable "super-ego" in children. The momentary drive and affect impulses are, as it were, held back and mastered by the fore-knowledge of the later displeasure, by the fear of a future pain, until this fear finally opposes the forbidden behaviour and inclinations by force of habit, even if no other person is directly present, and the energy of such inclinations is channelled into a harmless direction not threatened by any displeasure.

In keeping with the transformation of society, of interpersonal relationships, the affective make-up of the individual is also reconstructed: as the series of actions and the number of people on whom the individual and his actions constantly depend are increased, the habit of foresight over longer chains grows stronger. And as the behaviour and personality structure of the individual change, so does his manner of considering others. His image of them becomes richer in nuances, freer of spontaneous emotions: it is "psychologized".

Where the structure of social functions allows the individual greater scope for actions under the influence of momentary impulses than is the case at court, it is neither necessary nor possible to consider very deeply the nature of another person's consciousness and affects, or what hidden motives may underlie his behaviour. If at court calculation meshes with calculation, in simpler societies affect directly engages affect. This strength of the immediate affects, however, binds the individual to a smaller number of behavioural options: someone is friend or foe, good or evil; and depending on how one perceives another in terms of these black and white affective patterns, so one behaves. Everything seems directly related to feeling. That the sun shines, or lightning flashes, that someone laughs or knits his brow, all this appeals more directly to the affects of the perceiver. And as it excites him here and now in a friendly or unfriendly way, he takes it as if it were meant this way especially for him. It does not enter his head that all this, a flash of lightning that almost strikes him, a face that offends him, are to be explained by remote connections that have nothing directly to do with himself. People only develop a more long-sighted view of nature and other people to the extent that the advancing division of functions and their daily involvement in long human chains accustom them to such a view and a greater restraint of the affects. Only then is the veil which the passions draw before the eyes slowly lifted, and a new world comes into view—a world whose course is friendly or hostile to the individual person without being intended to be so, a chain of events that need to be contemplated dispassionately over long stretches if their connections are to be disclosed.*

Like conduct generally, the perception of things and people also becomes affectively more neutral in the course of the civilizing process. The "world picture" gradually becomes less directly determined by human wishes and fears, and more strongly oriented to what we call "experience" or "the empirical", to sequences with their own immanent regularities. Just as today, in a further spurt in this direction, the course of history and society is gradually emerging from the mists of personal affects and involvement, from the haze of collective longings and fears, and beginning to appear as a relatively autonomous nexus of events, so too with nature and—within smaller confines—with human beings. It is particularly in the circles of court life that what we would today call a "psychological" view of man develops, a more precise observation of others and oneself in terms of longer series of motives and causal connections, because it is here that vigilant self-control and perpetual observation of others are among the elementary prerequisites for the preservation of one's social position. But this is only one example of how what we call the "orientation to experience", the observation of events within a lengthening and broadening nexus of inter-dependence, slowly begins to develop at exactly the point where the structure of society itself compels the individual to restrain his momentary affects and transform his libidinal energies to a higher degree.

Saint-Simon in one place observes someone with whom he is on an uncertain footing. He describes his own behaviour in this situation as follows: "I soon noticed that he was growing colder; I closely followed his conduct towards me to avoid any confusion between what might be accidental in a man burdened with prickly affairs, and what I suspected. My suspicions were confirmed, causing me to withdraw from him entirely without in the slightest appearing to do so."[144]

This courtly art of human observation—unlike what we usually call 'psychology" today—is never concerned with the individual in isolation, as if the essential features of his behaviour were independent of his relations to others, and as if he related to others, so to speak, only retrospectively. The approach here is far closer to reality, in that the individual is always seen in his social context, *as a human being in his relations to others, as an individual in a social situation.*

It was pointed out above[145] that the precepts on behaviour of the sixteenth century differ from those of the preceding centuries less in terms of their content than in their tone, their changed affective atmosphere; psychological insights, personal observations, begin to play a larger part. A comparison between the precepts of Erasmus or Della Casa and the corresponding medieval rules shows this clearly. Investigation of the social changes of this time, the transformation of

* See in this context Norbert Elias, "Problems of Involvement and Detachment", *British Journal of Sociology*, 7 (1956), pp. 226–52. [*Author's note to the translation*]

human relationships that took place, provides an explanation. This "psychologiz-ation" of rules of conduct, or, more precisely, their greater permeation by observation and experience, is an expression of the accelerated courtization of the upper class and of the closer integration of all parts of society in this period. Signs of a change in this direction are certainly not to be found only in writings recording the standard of "good behaviour" of the time; we find them equally in works devoted to the entertainment of this class. The observation of people that life in the courtly circle demands finds its literary expression in an art of human portraiture.

The increased demand for books within a society is itself a sure sign of a pronounced spurt in the civilizing process; for the transformation and regulation of drives that is demanded both to write and read books is always considerable. But in courtly society the book does not yet play quite the same part as in bourgeois society. In the former social intercourse, the market of prestige values, forms the centre of existence for each individual; books, too, are intended less for reading in the study or in solitary leisure hours wrung from one's profession, than for social conviviality; they are a part and continuation of conversation and social games, or, like the majority of court memoirs, they are substitute conversations, dialogues in which for some reason or other the partner is lacking. The high art of human portraiture in court memoirs, letters or aphorisms thus gives a good impression of the complex human observation instilled by courtly life. And here, as in many other respects, bourgeois society in France develops the courtly heritage with a singular continuity. The persistence of a Parisian "good society" as beneficiary and further developer of the instruments of prestige evolved in courtly society long beyond the Revolution and up to the present day, may have contributed to this. At any rate, we can say that from the courtly human portraits of Saint-Simon and his contemporaries to the portrayal of the "high society" of the nineteenth century by Proust—by way of Balzac, Flaubert, Maupassant and many others—and finally to the depiction of the life of broader classes by writers such as Jules Romains or André Malraux, and by a large number of French films, there is a direct line of tradition, characterized by precisely this lucidity of human observation, this capacity to see people in their entire social context and to understand them through it. The individual figure is never artificially isolated from the fabric of his social existence, his simple dependence on others. This is why the atmosphere and plasticity of real experience is never lost in the descriptions.

And much the same that can be said of this "psychologization" applies also to the "rationalization" which slowly becomes increasingly perceptible from the sixteenth century onwards in the most varied aspects of society. This, too, is not an isolated fact; it is only *one* expression of the change in the *whole* personality that emerges at this time, and of the growing foresight that is from now on required and instilled by an ever-increasing number of social functions.

Here, as in many other instances, the understanding of socio-historical developments requires a suspension of the habits of thinking with which we have grown up. This often-noted historical rationalization is not something that arose from the fact that numerous unconnected individual people simultaneously developed from "within", as if on the basis of some pre-established harmony, a new organ or substance, an "understanding" or "reason" which had not existed hitherto. What changes is the way in which people are bonded to each other. This is why their behaviour changes, and why their consciousness and their drive—economy, and, in fact, their personality structure as a whole, change. The "circumstances" which change are not something which comes upon men from "outside": they are the relationships between people themselves.

Man is an extraordinarily malleable and variable being. The changes of human attitude discussed here are examples of this malleability. It is by no means confined to what we generally distinguish as the "psychological" from the "physiological". The "physis", too, indissolubly linked to what we call the "psyche", is variously moulded in the course of history in accordance with the network of dependencies that extend throughout a human life. One might think, for example, of the moulding of the facial muscles and thus of facial expression during a person's lifetime, or of the formation of reading or writing centres in the brain. The same applies to what we refer to by the reifying terms "reason", "ratio" or "understanding". All that does not exist—though our use of words suggests otherwise—relatively untouched by socio-historical change, in the way that, for example, the heart or stomach exists. Rather, these terms express a particular moulding of the whole personality; they are aspects of a moulding which takes place very gradually, repeatedly advancing and slipping back, and which emerges more strongly the more clearly and totally the spontaneous impulses of the individual threaten to bring about, through the structure of human dependencies, loss of pleasure, decline and inferiority in relation to others, or even the ruin of one's social existence. They are aspects of that moulding by which the libidinal centre and the ego-centre are more and more sharply differentiated, until finally a comprehensive, stable and highly differentiated agency of self-constraint is formed. There is not actually a "ratio", there is at most "rationalization".

Our habits of thinking incline us to look for "beginnings"; but there is nowhere in the development of people a "point" before which one could say: hitherto there was no "ratio" and now it has "arisen"; hitherto there were no self-compulsions and no "super-ego" and now, in this or that century, they are suddenly there. There is no zero-point of all these data. But it does no more justice to the facts to say: everything was always there as it is now. The habits of self-constraint, the conscious and affective make-up of "civilized" people, clearly differ *in their totality* from those of so-called "primitives"; but both are, in their structure, different yet clearly explainable mouldings of largely the same natural functions.

Traditional habits of thinking continually confront us with static alternatives; they are schooled, in a sense, on Eleatic models: we can imagine only numerous individual points, separate abrupt changes, or no change at all. And it is clearly still very difficult to see ourselves as situated in a gradual, continuous change with a particular structure and regularity, a change which is lost to our gaze in the darkness of the more distant past, and as part of a movement which, as far as is possible, should be seen as a whole, like the flight of an arrow or the flow of a river, not as the recurrence of always the same thing at different points or as something that jumps from point to point. What changes in the course of the process which we call history are, to reiterate, the mutual relationships, the figurations, of people and the moulding the individual undergoes within them. But at the very moment when this fundamental historicity of man is clearly seen, we also perceive the regularity, the structural characteristics of human existence which remain constant. Each single aspect of human social life is comprehensible only if seen in the context of this perpetual movement; no particular detail can be isolated from it. It is formed within this moving context—which may seem slow, as in the case of many primitive peoples, or rapid, as in our own—and must be grasped within it, as a part of a particular stage or wave. Thus social drive-controls and restrictions are nowhere absent among people, nor is a certain foresight; but these qualities have a different form and degree among simple herdsmen or in a warrior class than among courtiers, state officials or members of a mechanized army. They grow more powerful and more complete the greater the division of functions and thus, the greater the number of people to whom the individual has to attune his actions. Likewise, the nature of "understanding" or "thinking" to which an individual is accustomed resembles or differs from that of other people in his society to the same extent as his own social situation and function and those of his parents or the most important influences moulding him resemble or differ from those of others. The foresight of the printer or the fitter is different from that of the book-keeper, the engineer's from that of the sales director, the finance minister's from that of the army commander, even though all these different surface mouldings are to an extent equalized by the interdependence of functions. At a deeper level, the rationality and affect-moulding of someone who has grown up in a working-class family are different from those of someone who grew up in secure, well-to-do surroundings. And finally, the rationality and affect-patterns, the self-images and drive economy of the Germans, the English, the French and Italians differ in keeping with their different histories of interdependence, and the social moulding of people in the West as a whole differs from that of Orientals. But all these differences are comprehensible precisely because the same human and social regularities underlie them. The individual differences *within* all these groups, such as those of "intelligence", are merely nuances within a framework of very specific historical forms, differentiations for which a society offers greater or lesser scope depending on its structure. Thus, for example, the venture of highly individualized independent thought, the stance by which a person proves himself to be a "creative intelligence", not only has a very special individual "natural talent" as a pre-condition. It is only possible at all within a particular structure of power balances; its precondition is a quite specific *social structure*. And it depends further on the access which the individual has, within a society so structured, to the kind of schooling, and to the not very numerous social functions, which alone permit his capacity for independent individual thought to develop.

Thus the foresight or "thought" of the knight is different from that of the courtier. A scene described by Ranke[146] gives a good impression of how the typical personality structure of knights was doomed by the growing monopolization of force. More generally, it provides an example of the way in which a change in the structure of social functions enforces a change of conduct. The Duke of Montmorency, the son of a man who had played a major part in the victory of Henry IV, had rebelled. He was a knightly, princely man, generous and brilliant, brave and ambitious. And he served the king; but that power and the right to rule should be confined to the latter or, more precisely, to Richelieu, he neither understood nor approved. So, with his followers, he began to fight against the king, as in old times knights, feudal lords, had often fought against each other. There was a confrontation. The king's general, Schomberg, was in a tactically weak position. This, however, Ranke tells us:

> was an advantage to which Montmorency paid but little attention; seeing the enemy army, he suggested to his friends that they should attack without delay. For he understood war primarily as a brave cavalry charge. An experienced companion, Count Rieux, begged him to wait until a few guns that were being drawn up had shaken the enemy's position. But Montmorency was already gripped by a belligerent frenzy. There was no more time to lose, he said, and his advisor, though foreseeing disaster, did not dare to oppose the clear will of the knightly leader. "Lord", he cried, "I shall die at your feet."
>
> Montmorency was recognizable by a stallion splendidly adorned with red blue and dun feathers. It was only a small group of followers who leapt with him over the ditch. They cut down everyone who was in their way, battling forward until they finally arrived in front of the enemy's actual position. There they were met by close and rapid musket fire: horses and men were wounded and killed. Count Rieux and most of the others fell; the Duke of Montmorency, wounded, fell from his stricken horse and was taken prisoner.

Richelieu had him tried, certain of the outcome, and soon afterwards the last Montmorency was beheaded in the courtyard of the town hall of Toulouse.

To give way directly to impulses and not to take thought of the further consequences was, in the preceding phases when warriors could compete more freely with each other, a mode of behaviour which—even if it led to the downfall of the individual—was adequate to the social structure as a whole and therefore to "reality". Martial fervour was a necessary precondition of success and prestige for a man of the nobility. With advancing monopolization and centralization all that changed.

The different structure of society now punishes affective outbursts and actions lacking the appropriate forethought with certain ruin. And anyone who does not agree with the existing state of affairs, with the omnipotence of the king, must change his ways. Let us listen to Saint-Simon. He, too, scarcely more than a generation after Montmorency, is and remains throughout his life a duke in opposition. But all he can do is form a kind of faction at court; if he is skilful he can hope to win over the king's successor, the Dauphin, to his ideas. But this is a dangerous game at the court of Louis XIV, demanding utmost caution. The prince must first be very carefully sounded out and then gradually guided in the desired direction:

> My principal intention [thus Saint-Simon describes his tactics in a conversation with the Dauphin] was to sound his opinion on everything that concerned our dignity. I thus took care gently to break off all discussion that led away from this goal, to draw the conversation back and conduct it through all the different chapters . . . the Dauphin, eagerly attentive, appreciated all my arguments became heated . . . and groaned at the ignorance and lack of reflection of the King. I did little more than mention all these different subjects in presenting them successively to the Dauphin, and then followed after him, leaving him the pleasure of talking, showing me that he was educated. I let him persuade himself, work himself up, grow angry, while I was able to see his feelings, his way of thinking, and to gain impressions from which I could profit . . . I sought less to press my arguments and parentheses than . . . gently and firmly to imbue him with my feelings and views on each of these subjects. . . .

This brief sketch of the attitude of these two men, the dukes of Montmorency and Saint-Simon, when giving expression to their opposition to the king's omnipotence, helps to complete our picture. The former, one of the last knights, seeks to reach his goal by physical combat; the latter, the courtier, by conversation. The former acts from impulse with little thought of others; the latter perpetually adjusts his behaviour to his interlocutor. Both, not only Montmorency but Saint-Simon too, are in a highly dangerous situation. The Dauphin can always break the rules of courtly conversation; he can, if he so wishes, break off the conversation and the relationship for any reason he chooses, and lose very little; if Saint-Simon is not very careful, he can divine the duke's seditious thoughts and inform the king. Montmorency hardly registers the danger; he is wholly bound by the straight-forward behaviour his passion dictates; he seeks to overcome danger precisely by the fury of his passion. Saint-Simon perceives the exact compass of the danger; he thus goes to work with utmost self-control and forethought. He seeks to attain nothing by force; he works with a longer view. He holds back, in order to "imbue" the other imperceptibly but enduringly with his feelings.

What we have in this autobiographical anecdote is a very revealing piece of that *courtly rationality* which—though this is not generally appreciated—played a no less important part, and at first an even more important one, than the urban–commercial rationality and foresight instilled by functions in the trade network, in the development of what we call the "Enlightenment". But, certainly, these two forms of foresight, rationalization and psychologization—in the courtly group of the nobility and in the leading middle-class groups—however different in their pattern, developed in close conjunction with each other. They indicate an increasing intertwining of nobility and bourgeoisie; they spring from a transformation of human relationships throughout the whole of society: they are connected in the closest possible way to the change by which the relatively loosely knit estates of medieval society gradually become subordinate formations in a more centralized society, an absolute state.

The historical process of rationalization is a prime example of a kind of process which hitherto has been hardly or only vaguely grasped by systematic thought. It pertains—if we adhere to the traditional pattern of academic disciplines—to a science that does not yet exist, historical psychology. In the present structure of scholarly research a sharp dividing line is generally drawn between the work of the historian and of the psychologist. Only Western people living at present appear in need of or accessible to psychological investigation, or at most also so-called primitive peoples living today. The path leading, in Western history itself, from the simpler, more primitive psychological structure to the more differentiated one of our day remains in the dark. Precisely because the psychologist thinks unhistorically, because he approaches the psychological structures of present-day people as if they were something without evolution or change, the results of his investigations are in general of little use to the historian. And because the historian, preoccupied by what he calls facts, avoids psychological problems, he on his side has little to say to the psychologist.

The situation is little better with sociology. As far as it is concerned at all with historical problems, it accepts entirely the dividing line drawn by the historian between the seemingly immutable psychological structure of man and its different manifestations in the form of arts, ideas or whatever. That a historical social psychology, a study at once psychogenetic and sociogenetic, is needed to draw the connections between all these different manifestations of social human beings, remains unrecognized. Those concerned with the history of society, like those concerned with the history of mind, perceive "society" on the one hand and the world of "ideas" on the other as two different formations that can be meaningfully separated. Both seem to believe that there is either a society outside ideas and thoughts, or ideas outside society. And they merely dispute which of the two realms is more "important": some say that it is society-less ideas which set society in motion, and the others that it is an idea-less society that moves "ideas".

The civilizing process and, within it, such trends as psychologization and rationalization, do not fit into this kind of scheme. Even in thought they simply cannot be severed from the historical change in the structure of interpersonal relationships. It is quite pointless to ask whether the gradual transition from less to more rational modes of thought and conduct changes society; for this process of rationalization, like the more all-embracing process of civilization, is itself both a psychological and a social event. But it is equally meaningless to explain the civilizing process as a "superstructure" or "ideology", i.e. solely from its function as a weapon in the struggle between particular social groups and interests.

The gradual rationalization and, further, the whole civilizing process, undoubtedly takes place in constant conjunction with the struggles of different social strata and other groupings. The totality of European society, the substratum of what is hitherto the last and strongest civilizing spurt, is certainly not the peaceful unity it sometimes appears in harmonistic edifices of thought. It is not an originally harmonious whole into which—as if by the ill-will or incomprehension of particular people—conflicts are accidentally introduced. Rather, tensions and struggles—as much as the mutual dependencies of people—are an integral part of its structure; they decisively affect the direction in which it changes. Undoubtedly, a civilizing movement can take on considerable importance as a weapon in these struggles. For habituation to a higher degree of foresight and greater restraint of momentary affects—to recall only these two facets—can give one group a significant advantage over another. But a higher degree of rationality and drive inhibition can also, in certain situations, have a debilitating and adverse effect. "Civilization" can be a very two-edged weapon. And whatever its effect may be in particular cases, at any rate the spurts in the civilizing process take place by and large independently of whether they are pleasant or useful to the groups involved. They arise from powerful dynamics of intertwining group activities the overall direction of which any single group on its own is hardly able to change. They are not open to conscious or half-conscious manipulation or deliberate conversion into weapons in the social struggle, far less so, indeed, than for instance, ideas. Just as the personality structure characteristic of a particular stage of social development, so specific traits of civilized conduct are at the same time a product of and a lever in the workings of the larger social process within which individual classes and interests form and transform themselves. Civilization, and therefore rationalization, for example, is not a process within a separate sphere of "ideas" or "thought". It does not involve solely changes of "knowledge", transformations of "ideologies", in short alterations of the *content* of consciousness, but changes in the whole human make-up, within which ideas and habits of thought are only a single sector. We are here concerned with changes in the whole personality throughout all its zones, from the steering of the individual by himself at the more flexible level of consciousness and reflection to that at the more automatic and rigid level of drives and affects. And to grasp changes of this kind, the pattern of thought summoned to mind by the concepts of "super-structure" or "ideology" is not enough.

The idea that the human "psyche" consists of different zones functioning independently of each other and capable of being considered independently, has become deeply rooted in human consciousness over a long period. It is common, in thinking about the more differentiated personality structure, to sever one of its functional levels from the others as if this were really the "essential" factor in the way men steer themselves in their encounter with their human fellows and with non-human nature. Thus the humanities and the sociology of knowledge stress above all the aspect of knowledge and thought. Thoughts and ideas appear in these studies as it were as that which is the most important and potent aspect of the way men steer themselves. And the unconscious impulses, the whole field of drive and affect structures, remains more or less in the dark.

But every investigation that considers only the consciousness of men, their "reason" or "ideas", while disregarding the structure of drives, the direction and form of human affects and passions, can be from the outset of only limited value. Much that is indispensable for an understanding of men escapes this approach. The rationalization of men's intellectual activity itself, and beyond that the whole structural changes of the ego and super-ego functions, all these interdependent levels of men's personality—as has been shown above and will be shown in more detail later—are only very imperfectly accessible to thought as long as enquiries are confined to changes in the intellectual aspects of men, to changes of ideas, and pay little regard to the changing balance and the changing pattern of the relationships between drives and affects on the one hand and drive- and affect-control on the other. A real understanding, even of the changes of ideas and forms of cognition, can be gained only if one takes into account too the changes of human interdependencies in conjunction with the structure of conduct and, in fact, the whole fabric of men's personality at a given stage of social development.

The inverse accentuation, with a corresponding limitation, is to be found often enough in psycho-analytical research today. It frequently tends, in considering human beings, to extract something "unconscious", conceived as an "id" without history, as the most important thing in the whole psychological structure. Although recently this image may have undergone corrections in therapeutic practice, these corrections have not yet led to theoretical elaboration of the data supplied by practive into more adequate conceptual tools. On the theoretical level it still usually appears as if the steering of the individual by unconscious libidinal impulses has a form and structure of its own, independently of the figurational destiny of the individual, the changing fortunes of his relationships with others throughout his life, and independently too of the pattern and structure of the other self-steering functions of his personality, conscious and unconscious. No distinction is made between the natural raw material of drives, which indeed perhaps changes little throughout the whole history of mankind, and the increasingly more firmly wrought structures of control, and thus the paths into which the elementary energies are channelled in each person through his or her relations with other people from birth onward. But nowhere, except perhaps in the case of madmen, do men in their encounter with each other find themselves face to face with psychological functions in their pristine state, in a state of nature that is not patterned by social learning, by a person's experience of other persons who satisfy or frustrate his or her needs in accordance with a specific social setting. The libidinal energies which one encounters in any living human being are always already socially processed; they are, in other words, sociogenetically transformed in their function and structure, and can in no way be separated from the corresponding ego and super-ego structures. The more animalic and automatic levels of men's personality are neither more nor less significant for the understanding of human conduct than their controls. What matters, what determines conduct, are the balances and conflicts between men's malleable drives and the built-in drive-controls.

Decisive for a person as he appears before us is neither the "id" alone, nor the "ego" or "super-ego" alone, but always *the relationship* between these various sets of psychological functions, partly conflicting and partly co-operating in the way an individual steers himself. It is they, these relationships *within* man between the drives and affects controlled and the built-in controlling agencies, whose structure changes in the course of a civilizing process, in accordance with the changing structure of the relationships *between* individual human beings, in society at large. In the course of this process, to put it briefly and all too simply, "consciousness" becomes less permeable by drives, and drives become less permeable by "consciousness". In simpler societies elementary impulses, however transformed, have an easier access to men's reflections. In the course of a civilizing process the compartmentalization of these self-steering functions, though in no way absolute, becomes more pronounced.

In accordance with the sociogenetic ground rule (see *The History of Manners* p. xiii) one can observe processes in the same direction directly in every child. One can see that, in the course of human history and again and again in that of each individual civilizing process, the self-steering in the form of ego and super-ego functions on the one hand and that through drives on the other become more and more firmly differentiated. Hence it is only with the formation of conscious functions less accessible to drives that the drive automatisms take on more and more that specific character which one today commonly diagnoses as "ahistoric", as a peculiarity of man throughout the ages which is purely natural, and independent of the developmental condition of human societies. However, the peculiarity of man discovered by Freud in men of our own time and conceptualized by him as a strict division between unconscious and conscious mental functions, far from being part of man's unchanged nature is a result of a long civilizing process in the course of which the wall of forgetfulness separating libidinal drives and "consciousness" or "reflection" has become harder and more impermeable.*

In the course of the same transformation, the conscious mental functions themselves develop in the direction of what one calls increasing "rationalization": only with the sharper and firmer differentiation of the personality do the outward-directed psychological functions take on the character of a more rationally functioning consciousness less directly coloured by drive impulses and affective fantasies. Thus the form and structure of the more conscious and more unconscious psychological self-steering functions can never be grasped if they are imagined as something in any sense existing or functioning in isolation from one another. Both are equally fundamental to the existence of a human being; both together form a single great functional continuum. Nor can their structure and changes be understood if observation is confined to individual human beings. They can only be comprehended in connection with the structure of relationships *between* people, and with the long-term changes in that structure.

Therefore in order to understand and explain civilizing processes one needs to investigate—as has been attempted here—the transformation of both the personality structure and the entire social structure. This task demands, within a smaller radius, psychogenetic investigations aimed at grasping the whole field of individual psychological energies, the structure and form of the more elementary no less than of the more self-steering functions. Within a larger radius, the exploration of civilizing processes demands a long-range perspective, *sociogenetic* investigations of the overall structure, not only of a single state society but of the social field formed by a specific group of inter-dependent societies, and of the sequential order of its evolution.

---

* To understand this fact is not only of theoretical but also of practical significance. Differences in the extent to which thinking is charged with affects make themselves felt again and again in the relationships between states at different stages of social development. As a rule, however, the leading statesmen of highly differentiated societies devise their strategies on the assumption that the level of restraint, the code of conduct, represented by the foreign policy of all countries is the same. Without an understanding of the different stages of a civilizing process interstate policy must necessarily be somewhat unrealistic. However, to work out foreign policy based on the knowledge of these differentials in affectivity is far from easy. It will need to a good deal of experimenting—and of wisdom—before an effective political dialogue and co-operation between societies at different levels of development can be worked out. The same applies to those cases in which, under stress, the affectivity and the fantasy character of the foreign policy of one of the more developed countries increases again to a higher level than the regarded at present as normal in the interstate relations of the leading industrial nation state. Nor are these levels in the degree of affectivity entirely dependent on the differentials of the economic or industrial development of countries. Thus, in the political strategies of China, for instance, once can discover a level of self-restraint at least on a par with that of the most highly developed industrial nations. Although in terms of its own economic development China still lags behind, its state formation process in terms of duration and continuity surpasses that of most other existing state societies of our time. [*Author's note to the translation*]

But for an adequate enquiry into such social processes a similar correction of traditional habits of thinking is needed to the one that proved necessary earlier to obtain an adequate basis for psychogenetic enquiry. To understand social structures and processes, it is never enough to study a single functional stratum within a social field. To be really understood, these structures and processes demand a study of the *relationships between the different functional strata* which are bound together within a social field, and which, with the slower or more rapid shift of power-relationships arising from the specific structure of this field, are for a time reproduced over and over again. Just as in every psychogenetic enquiry it is necessary to take account not only of the "unconscious" or the "conscious" functions alone, but of the continuous circulation of impulses from the one to the other, it is equally important in every sociogenetic study to consider from the first the whole *figuration* of a social field which is more or less differentiated and charged with tensions. It is only possible to do this because the social fabric and its historical change are not chaotic but possess, even in phases of greatest unrest and disorder, a clear pattern and structure. To investigate the totality of a social field does not mean to study each individual process within it. It means first of all to discover the basic structures which give all the individual processes within this field their direction and their specific stamp. It means asking oneself in what way the axes of tension, the chains of functions and the institutions of a society in the fifteenth century differ from those in the sixteenth or seventeenth centuries, and why the former change in the direction of the latter. To answer these questions knowledge of a wealth of particular facts is of course necessary. But beyond a certain point in the accumulation of material facts, historiography enters the phase when it ought no longer to be satisfied with the collection of further particulars and with the description of those already assembled, but should be concerned with those problems which facilitate penetration of the underlying regularities by which people in a certain society are bound over and over again to particular patterns of conduct and to very specific functional chains, for example as knights and bondsmen, kings and state officials, bourgeois and nobles, and by which these relationships and institutions change in a very specific direction. Beyond a certain point of factual knowledge, in a word, a more solid framework, a structural nexus can be perceived in the multitude of particular historical facts. And all further facts that can be discovered serve—apart from the enrichment of the historical panorama they may offer us—either to revise the insight already gained into these structures, or to extend and deepen it. The statement that every sociogenetic study should be aimed at the *totality* of a social field does not mean that it should be directed at the sum of all particulars, but at its structure within the entirety of its interdependencies. In the last resort the boundaries of such a study are determined by the boundaries of the interdependencies, or at least by the immanent articulation of the interdependencies.

It is in this light that what was said above about rationalization is to be understood. The gradual transition to more "rational" behaviour and thought, like that to a more differentiated, a more comprehensive type of self-control, is usually associated today only with bourgeois functions. We often find firmly lodged in the minds of our contemporaries the idea that the bourgeoisie was the "originator" or "inventor" of more rational thought. Here, for the sake of contrast, certain rationalization processes in the aristocratic camp have been described. But one should not deduce from this that the courtly aristocracy was the social "originator" of this spurt of rationalization. Just as the courtly aristocracy or the bourgeoisie in the age of manufacture did not have "originators" in any other social class, so this rationalization equally lacked an originator. The very transformation of the whole social structure, in the course of which these figurations of bourgeois and nobles come into being, is itself, considered from a certain aspect, a rationalization. What becomes more rational is not just the individual products of men, nor, above all, merely the systems of thought set down in books. What is rationalized is, primarily, the modes of conduct of certain groups of people. "Rationalization" is nothing other—think, for example, of the courtization of warriors—than an expression of the direction in which the moulding of people in specific social figurations is changed during this period. Changes of this kind, however, do not "originate" in one class or another, but arise in conjunction with the tensions *between* different functional groups in a social field and *between* the competing people within them. Under the pressure of tensions of this kind which permeate the whole fabric of society, the latter's whole structure changes, during a particular phase, in the direction of an increasing centralization of particular dominions increasing centralization of particular dominions and a greater specialization, a tighter integration of the individual people within them. And with this transformation of the whole social field, the structure of social and psychological functions is also changed—first in small, then in larger and larger sectors—in the direction of rationalization.

The slow defunctionalization of the first estate and the corresponding diminution of its power potential, the pacification of the second estate and the gradual rise of the third, none of these can be understood independently of the others any more than, for example, the development of trade in this period is comprehensible independently of the formation of powerful monopolies of physical force and the rise of mighty courts. All these are levers in the comprehensive process of increasing differentiation and extension of all chains of action, which has played such a decisive role in the whole course of Western history. In this process—as was shown from particular aspects—the functions of the nobility are transformed, and with them bourgeois functions and the form of the central organs. And hand in hand with this gradual change in the totality of social functions and institutions, goes a transformation of individual self-steering—first in the leading groups of both the nobility and the bourgeoisie—in the direction of greater foresight and a stricter regulation of libidinal impulses.

In perusing the traditional accounts of the intellectual development of the West, one often has the impression of a vague conception in the minds of their authors that the rationalization of consciousness, the change from magical–traditional to rational forms of thinking in the history of the West, had its cause in the emergence of a number of geniuses and outstanding individuals. These enlightened individuals, such accounts appear to suggest, taught Western man how to use his innate reason properly.

Here, a different picture emerges. What the great thinkers of the West have achieved is certainly considerable. They gave to what their contemporaries experienced in their daily actions without being able to grasp it clearly in thought, comprehensive and exemplary expression. They tried to articulate the more reality-oriented or in their own language, more rational forms of thinking which had gradually developed along with the overall changes in the structure of social interdependencies, and with their help to clarify the problems of human existence. They gave other people a clearer view of their world and themselves. And so they also acted as levers within the larger workings of society. They were to a greater or lesser degree, depending on their talent and personal situation, interpreters and spokesmen of a social chorus. But they were not on their own the originators of the type of thought prevalent in their society. They did not create what we call "rational thought".*

This expression itself evidently is somewhat too static and insufficiently differentiated for what it is intended to express. Too static, because the structure of psychological functions changes at the same rate as that of social functions. Insufficiently differentiated because the pattern of rationalization, the structure of more rational habits of thinking, was and is very different in different social classes—for instance, in the courtly nobility or the leading bourgeois strata—in accordance with their different social functions and their overall historical

---

* The waning supremacy of the Church, the changing balance of power between religious and secular rulers—between priests and warriors—in favour of the latter opened the way, to, was, in other words, the *conditio sine qua non* of the secularization of thought without which all that one means if ones speaks of "rationalization" could not have come into its own. The emergence not only of one but of a whole group of tightly organized and competing large territorial states ruled by secular princes which is one of the major distinguishing characteristics of the European development was one of its factors; the growth of large urban markets and long-distance trade and the growth of capital indispensable for it was another. A whole complex of social levers—levers of "rationalization"—worked in the direction towards a strengthening of less affective, less fantasy-oriented modes of though and experience. The great intellectual pioneers, above all the philosophical pioneers of rational thought, thus worked from within a powerful process of social change which gave them direction, but they themselves were also active levers within this movement, not merely its passive objects. In fact one has to take into consideration the whole concourse of basic processes forming the core of the overall development of society—basic processes such as the long-term process of state formation, of capital formation, of differentiation and integration, of orientation, of civilization, and others. [*Author's note to the translation*]

situation. And finally, the same is true of rationalization as was said above of changes of consciousness in general: in it only *one* side of a more comprehensive change in the whole social personality is manifested. It goes hand in hand with a corresponding transformation of drive structures. It is, in brief, *one* manifestation of civilization among others.

VI

Shame and Repugnance

No less characteristic of a civilizing process than "rationalization" is the peculiar moulding of the drive economy that we call "shame" and "repugnance" or "embarrassment". Both these, the strong spurt of rationalization and the (for a time) no less strong advance of the threshold of shame and repugnance that becomes more and more perceptible in the make-up of Western men broadly speaking from the sixteenth century onwards, are different sides of the same transformation of the social personality structure. The feeling of shame is a specific excitation, a kind of anxiety which is automatically reproduced in the individual on certain occasions by force of habit. Considered superficially, it is fear of social degradation or, more generally, of other people's gestures of superiority. But it is a form of displeasure or fear which arises characteristically on those occasions when a person who fears lapsing into inferiority can avert this danger neither by direct physical means nor by any other form of attack. This defencelessness against the superiority of others, this total exposure to them does not arise directly from a threat from the physical superiority of others actually present, although it doubtless has its origins in physical compulsion, in the bodily inferiority of the child in face of its parents or teachers. In adults, however, this defencelessness results from the fact that the people whose superiority one fears are in accord with one's own super-ego, with the agency of self-constraint implanted in the individual by others on whom he was dependent, who possessed power and superiority over him. In keeping with this, the anxiety that we call "shame" is heavily veiled to the sight of others; however strong it may be, it is never directly expressed in noisy gestures. Shame takes on its particular coloration from the fact that the person feeling it has done or is about to do something through which he comes into contradiction with people to whom he is bound in one form or another, and with himself, with the sector of his consciousness by which he controls himself. The conflict expressed in shame–fear is not merely a conflict of the individual with prevalent social opinion; the individual's behaviour has brought him into conflict with the part of himself that represents this social opinion. It is a conflict within his own personality; he himself recognizes himself as inferior. He fears the loss of the love or respect of others, to which he attaches or has attached value. Their attitude has precipitated an attitude within him that he automatically adopts towards himself. This is what makes him so defenceless against gestures of superiority by others which somehow trigger off this automatism within him.

This also explains why the fear of transgression of social prohibitions takes on more clearly the character of shame the more completely alien constraints have been turned into self-restraints by the structure of society, and the more comprehensive and differentiated the ring of self-restraints have become within which a person's conduct is enclosed. The inner tension, the excitement that is aroused whenever a person feels compelled to break out of this enclosure in any place, or when he has done so, varies in strength according to the gravity of the social prohibition and the degree of self-constraint. In ordinary life we call this excitement shame only in certain contexts and above all when it has a certain degree of strength; but in terms of its structure it is, despite its many nuances and degrees, always the same event. Like self-constraints, it is to be found in a less stable, less uniform and less all-embracing form even at simpler levels of social development. Like these constraints, tensions and fears of this kind emerge more clearly with every spurt of the civilizing process, and finally predominate over others—particularly the physical fear of others. They predominate the more, the larger the areas that are pacified, and the greater the importance in the moulding of people of the more even constraints that come to the fore in society when the representatives of the monopoly of physical violence normally only exercise their control as it were standing in the wings—the further, in a word, the civilization of conduct advances. Just as we can only speak of "reason" in conjunction with advances of rationalization and the formation of functions demanding foresight and restraint, we can only speak of shame in conjunction with its sociogenesis, with spurts in which the shame-threshold advances or at least moves, and the structure and pattern of self-constraints are changed in a particular direction, reproducing themselves thenceforth in the same form over a greater or lesser period. Both rationalization and the advance of the shame and repugnance thresholds are expressions of a reduction in the direct physical fear of other beings, and of a consolidation of the automatic inner anxieties, the compulsions which the individual now exerts on himself. In both, the greater, more differentiated foresight and long-term view which become necessary in order that larger and larger groups of people may preserve their social existence in an increasing differentiated society, are equally expressed. It is not difficult to explain how these seemingly so different psychological changes are connected. Both, the intensification of shame like the increased rationalization, are different aspects of the growing split in the individual personality that occurs with the increasing division of functions; they are different aspects of the growing differentiation between drives and drive-controls, between "id" and "ego" or "superego" functions. The further this differentiation of individual self-steering advances, the more clearly that sector of the controlling functions which in a broader sense is called the "ego" and in a narrower the "super-ego", takes on a twofold function. On the one hand this sector forms the centre from which a person regulates his relations to other living and non-living beings, and on the other it forms the centre from which a person, partly consciously and partly quite automatically and unconsciously, controls his "inner life", his own affects and impulses. The layer of psychological functions which, in the course of the social transformation that has been described, is gradually differentiated from the drives, the ego or super-ego functions, has, in other words, a twofold task within the personality: they conduct at the same time a domestic policy and a foreign policy—which, moreover, are not always in harmony and often enough in contradiction. This explains the fact that in the same socio-historical period in which rationalization makes perceptible advances, an advance in the shame and repugnance threshold is also to be observed. It also explains the fact that here, as always—in accordance with the sociogenetic ground rule—a corresponding process is to be observed even today in the life of each individual child: the rationalization of conduct is an expression of the foreign policy of the same super-ego formation whose domestic policy is expressed in an advance of the shame threshold.

From here many large trains of thought lead off in different directions. It remains to be shown how this increased differentiation within the personality is manifested in a transformation of particular drives. Above all, it remains to be shown how it leads to a transformation of sexual impulses and an advance of shame feelings in the relations of men and women.* It must be enough here to

---

* This particular problem, important as it is, must be left aside for the time being. Its elucidation demands a description and an exact analysis of the changes which the structure of the family and the whole relationship of the sexes have undergone in the course of Western history. It demands, furthermore, a general study of changes in the upbringing of children and the development of adolescents. The material which has been collected to elucidate this aspect of the civilizing process, and the analyses it made possible have proved too extensive; they threatened to dislocate the framework of this study and will find their place in a further volume.

The same applies to the middle-class line of the civilizing process, the change it produced in bourgeois–urban classes and the non-courtly landed aristocracy. While this transformation of conduct and of the structure of psychological functions is certainly connected in these classes, too, with a specific historical restructuring of the *whole* Western social fabric, nevertheless—as already pointed out on a number of occasions—the non-courtly middle-class line of civilization follows a different pattern to the courtly one. Above all, the treatment of sexuality in the former is not the same as in the latter—partly because of a different middle-class professional functions demand. Something similar emerges if the civilizing transformation of Western religion is investigated. The change in religious feeling to which sociology has paid most attention hitherto, the increased inwardness and rationalization expressed in the various Puritan and Protestant movements, is obviously closely connected to certain changes in the situation and structure of the middle classes. The corresponding change in Catholicism, as shown, for example, in the formation of the power position of the Jesuits, appears to take place in closer touch with the absolutist central organs, in a manner favoured by the hierarchical and centralist structure of the Catholic Church. These problems, too, will only be solved

indicate some of the main connections between the social processes described above and this advance of the frontier of shame and repugnance.

Even in the more recent history of the West itself, shame feelings have not always been built into the personality in the same way. To mention only one difference, the manner in which they are built in is not the same in a hierarchical society made up of estates as in the succeeding bourgeois industrial order.

The examples quoted earlier, above all those showing differences in the development of shame on the exposure of certain bodily parts,[148] give a certain impression of such changes. In courtly society shame on exposing certain parts is, in keeping with the structure of this society, still largely restricted within estate or hierarchical limits. Exposure in the presence of social inferiors, for example by the king in front of a minister, is placed under no very strict social prohibition, any more than the exposure of a man before the socially weaker and lower-ranking woman was in an earlier phase. Given his minimal functional dependence on those of lower rank, exposure as yet arouses no feeling of inferiority or shame; it can even be taken, as Della Casa states, as a sign of benevolence towards the inferior. Exposure by someone of lower rank before a superior, on the other hand, or even before people of equal rank, is banished more and more from social life as a sign of lack of respect; branded as an offence, it becomes invested with fear. And only when the walls between estates fall away, when the functional dependence of all on all increases and all members of society become several degrees more equal, does such exposure, except in certain narrower enclaves, become an offence in the presence of any other person. Only then is such behaviour so profoundly associated with fear in the individual from an early age, that the social character of the prohibition vanishes entirely from his consciousness, shame appearing as a command coming from within himself.

And the same is true of embarrassment. This is an inseparable counterpart of shame. Just as the latter arises when someone infringes the prohibitions of his own self and of society, the former occurs when something outside the individual impinges on his danger zone, on forms of behaviour, objects, inclinations which have early on been invested with fear by his surroundings until this fear—in the manner of a conditioned reflex—is reproduced automatically in him on certain occasions. Embarrassment is displeasure or anxiety which arises when another person threatens to breach, or breaches, society's prohibitions represented by one's own super-ego. And these feelings too become more diverse and comprehensive the more extensive and subtly differentiated the danger zone by which the conduct of the individual is regulated and moulded, the further the civilization of conduct advances.

when we have a more exact overall picture of the intertwining of the non-courtly, middle-class and the courtly lines of civilization, leaving aside for the time being the civilizing movement in worker and peasant strata which emerges more slowly and much later.

It was shown earlier by a series of examples how, from the sixteenth century onwards, the frontier of shame and embarrassment gradually begins to advance more rapidly. Here, too, the chains of thought begin slowly to join up. This advance coincides with the accelerated courtization of the upper class. It is the time when the chains of dependence intersecting in the individual grow denser and longer, when more and more people are being bound more and more closely together and the compulsion to self-control is increasing. Like mutual dependence, mutual observation of people increases; sensibilities, and correspondingly prohibitions, become more differentiated; and equally more subtle, equally more manifold become the reasons for shame and for embarrassment aroused by the conduct of others.

It was pointed out above that with the advancing division of functions and the greater integration of people, the major contrasts between different classes and countries diminish, while the nuances, the varieties of their moulding within the framework of civilization multiply. Here one encounters a corresponding trend in the development of individual conduct and sentiment. The more the strong contrasts of individual conduct are tempered, the more the violent fluctuations of pleasure or displeasure are contained, moderated and changed by self-control, the greater becomes the sensitivity to shades or nuances of conduct, the more finely attuned people grow to minute gestures and forms, and the more complex becomes their experience of themselves and their world at levels which were previously hidden from consciousness through the veil of strong affects.

To clarify this by an obvious example, "primitive" people experience human and natural events within the relatively narrow circle which is vitally important to them—narrow, because their chains of dependence are relatively short—in a manner which is in some respects far more differentiated than that of "civilized" people. The differentiation varies, depending on whether we are concerned with farmers or hunters or herdsmen, for example. But however this may be, it can be stated generally that, insofar as it is of vital importance to a group, the ability of primitive people to distinguish things in forest and field, whether it be a particular tree from another, or sounds, scents or movements, is more highly developed than in "civilized" people. But among more primitive people the natural sphere is still far more a danger zone; it is full of fears which more civilized men no longer know. This is decisive for what is or is not distinguished. The manner in which "nature" is experienced is fundamentally affected, slowly at the end of the Middle Ages and then more quickly from the sixteenth century onwards, by the pacification of larger and larger populated areas. Only now do forests, meadows and mountains gradually cease to be danger zones of the first order, from which anxiety and fear constantly intrude into individual life. And now, as the network of roads becomes, like social interdependence in general, more dense; as robber-knights and beasts of prey slowly disappear; as forest and field cease to be the scene of unbridled passions, of the savage pursuit of man and beast, wild joy and wild fear; as they are moulded more and more by intertwining peaceful activities, the production of goods, trade and transport; now, to pacified men a correspondingly pacified nature becomes visible, and in a new way. It becomes—in keeping with the mounting significance which the eye attains as the mediator of pleasure with the growing moderation of the affects—to a high degree an object of visual pleasure. In addition, people—more precisely the townpeople for whom forest and field are no longer their everyday background but a place of relaxation—grow more sensitive and begin to see the open country in a more differentiated way, at a level which was previously screened off by danger and the play of unmoderated passions. They take pleasure in the harmony of colour and lines, become open to what is called the beauty of nature; their feelings are aroused by the changing shades and shapes of the clouds and the play of light on the leaves of a tree.

And, in the wake of this pacification, the sensitivity of people to social conduct is also changed. Now, inner fears grow in proportion to the decrease of outer ones—the fears of one sector of the personality for another. As a result of these inner tensions, people begin to experience each other in a more differentiated way which was precluded as long as they constantly faced serious and inescapable threats from outside. Now a major part of the tensions which were earlier discharged directly in combat between man and man, must be resolved as an inner tension in the struggle of the individual with himself. Social life ceases to be a danger zone in which feasting, dancing and noisy pleasure frequently and suddenly give way to rage, blows and murder, and becomes a different kind of danger zone if the individual cannot sufficiently restrain himself, if he touches sensitive spots, his own shame-frontier or the embarrassment-threshold of others. In a sense, the danger zone now passes through the self of every individual. Thus people become, in this respect too, sensitive to distinctions which previously scarcely entered consciousness. Just as nature now becomes, far more than earlier, a source of pleasure mediated by the eye, people too become a source or visual pleasure or, conversely, of visually aroused displeasure, of different degrees of repugnance. The direct fear inspired in men by men has diminished, and the inner fear mediated through the eye and through the super-ego is rising proportionately.

When the use of weapons in combat is an everyday occurrence, the small gesture of offering someone a knife at table (to recall one of the examples mentioned earlier) has no great importance. As the use of weapons is restricted more and more, as external and internal pressures make the expression of anger by physical attack increasingly difficult, people gradually become more sensitive to anything reminiscent of an attack. The very gesture of attack touches the danger zone; it becomes distressing to see a person passing someone else a knife with the point towards him.[149] And from the most highly sensitized small circles of high courtly society, for whom this sensitivity also represents a prestige value, a means of distinction cultivated for that very reason, this prohibition gradually spreads throughout the whole of civilized society. Thus aggressive associations, infused no doubt with others from the layer of elementary urges, combine with status tensions in arousing anxiety.

How the use of a knife is then gradually restricted and surrounded, as a danger zone, by a wall of prohibitions, has been shown through a number of examples. It is an open question how far, in the courtly aristocracy, the renunciation of physical violence remains an external compulsion, and how far it has already been converted into an inner constraint. Despite all restrictions, the use of the table knife, like that of the dagger, is still quite extensive. Just as the hunting and killing of animals is still a permitted and commonplace amusement for the lords of the earth, the carving of dead animals at table remains within the zone of the permitted and is as yet not felt as repugnant. Then, with the slow rise of bourgeois classes, in whom pacification and the generation of inner constraints by the very nature of their social functions is far more complete and binding, the cutting up of dead animals is pushed back further behind the scenes of social life (even if in particular countries, particularly England, as so often, some of the older customs survive incorporated in the new) and the use of the knife, indeed the mere holding of it, is avoided wherever it is not entirely indispensable. Sensitivity in this direction grows.

This is one example among many of particular aspects of the structural transformation or society that we denote by the catchword "civilization". Nowhere in human society is there a zero-point of fear of external powers, and nowhere a zero-point of automatic inner anxieties. Although they may be experienced as very different, they are finally inseparable. What takes place in the course of a civilizing process is not the disappearance of one and the emergence of the other. What changes is merely the proportion between the external and the self-activating fears, and their whole structure. People's fears of external powers diminish without ever disappearing; the never-absent, latent or actual anxieties arising from the tension between drives and drive-control functions become relatively stronger, more comprehensive and continuous. The documentation for the advance of the shame and embarrassment frontiers found in the first volume of this study, consists in fact of nothing but particularly clear and simple examples of the direction and structure of a change in the human personality which could be demonstrated from many other aspects too. A very similar structure is exhibited, for example, by the transition from the medieval–Catholic to the Protestant super-ego formation. This, too, shows a pronounced shift towards the internalization of fears. And one thing certainly should not be overlooked in all this: the fact that today, as formerly, all forms of adult inner anxieties are bound up with the child's fears of others, of external powers.

VII

Increasing Constraints on the Upper Class: Increasing Pressure from Below

It was pointed out earlier that in certain pictures[150] attributed to the knightly-courtly upper class of the late Middle Ages, the depiction of lower-class people and their gestures was not yet felt as particularly repugnant, whereas the stricter selection corresponding to the structure of repugnance of the absolutist-courtly upper class permits the expression only of large, calm, refined gestures in art, while everything reminiscent of lower classes, everything vulgar, is kept at a distance.

This repulsion of the vulgar, this increasing sensitivity to anything corresponding to the lesser sensibility or lower-ranking classes, permeates all spheres of social conduct in the courtly upper class. It has been shown in more detail[151] how this is expressed, for example, in the courtly moulding of speech. One does not say, a court lady explains, "un mien ami" or "le pauvre deffunct"; all that "smells of the bourgeois". And if the bourgeois protests, if he replies that after all a large number of people of good society use these expressions themselves, he is told: "It is quite possible that there are a number of decent people who do not have sufficient feeling for the delicacy of our tongue. This 'delicacy' . . . is entrusted to but a few."

This is categorical, like the demands of this sensitivity themselves. The people who select in this way are neither able, nor do they attempt, to justify further why in a particular case this form of a word is pleasing and that displeasing. Their particular sensitivity is very closely bound up with the heightened regulation and transformation of libidinal impulses imposed on them by their specific social situation. The certitude with which they are able to say: 'This combination of words sounds well; those colours are ill-chosen", the sureness of their taste, in a word, derives rather from a more or less unconsciously operating psychological self-steering agency than from conscious reflection. But it is clear, here too, how it is first of all small circles of courtly society who listen with growing sensitivity to nuances of rhythm, tone and significance, to the spoken and written word, and how this sensitivity, this "good taste", also represents a prestige value for such circles. Anything that touches their embarrassment-threshold smells bourgeois, is socially inferior; and inversely: anything bourgeois touches their embarrassment-threshold. It is the necessity to distinguish themselves from anything bourgeois that sharpens this sensitivity; and the particular structure of court life, by which it is not professional competence or even the possession of money, but polished social conduct, that is the main instrument in the competition for prestige and favour, provides the occasion for the sharpening of taste.

In the course of this study it was indicated by means of a number of examples how from the sixteenth century onwards the standard of social conduct is caught up in a quicker movement, how it remains in motion during the seventeenth and eighteenth centuries in order, during the eighteenth and nineteenth centuries, to spread, transformed in some respects, throughout the whole of western society. This advance of restrictions and libidinal transformations sets in with the conversion of the knightly into a courtly nobility. It is very closely bound up with the change already discussed in the relationship of the upper class to other functional groups. The *"courtois"* warrior society is not remotely under the same pressure, does not live in anything like the same interdependence with bourgeois strata, as the courtly aristocracy. This courtly upper class is a formation within a much denser network of interdependencies. It is held in a pincer comprising the central lord of the court on whose favour it depends on the one hand, and the leading bourgeois groups with their economic advantages on the other, groups which are forcing their way upwards and contesting the aristocracy's position. Tensions between courtly aristocratic and bourgeois circles do not increase only at the end of the eighteenth or the beginning of the nineteenth century; from the first the existence of the courtly aristocracy is strongly and constantly threatened by the aspiring bourgeois classes. Indeed, the courtization of the nobility takes place only in conjunction with an increased upward thrust by bourgeois strata. The existence of a high degree of interdependence and tension between nobles and bourgeois is a basic constituent of the courtly character of the leading groups of the nobility.

We should not be deceived by the fact that it took centuries for this continuous tug of war between noble and bourgeois groups to be decided in favour of some of the latter. Nor should we be misled by the fact that the constraints on the upper class, the functional interdependence and latent tension between different strata in the absolutist society of the seventeenth and eighteenth centuries were less than in the various national societies of the nineteenth and twentieth centuries. As compared with the functional constraints on the free medieval warrior nobility, those on the courtly aristocracy are already very great. Social tensions, particularly between the nobility and bourgeoisie, take on a different character with increasing pacification.

As long as control of the instruments of physical violence—weapons and troops—is not very highly centralized, social tensions lead again and again to warlike actions. Particular social groups, artisan settlements and their feudal lords, towns and knights, confront each other as units of power which—as only states do later—must always be ready to settle their differences of interest by force of arms. The fears aroused in this structure of social tensions can still be discharged easily and frequently in military action and direct physical force. With the gradual consolidation of power monopolies and the growing functional interdependence of nobility and bourgeoisie, this changes. The tensions become more even. They can be resolved by physical violence only at infrequent climaxes or turning points. And they therefore express themselves in a continuous pressure that each individual member of the nobility must absorb within himself. With this transformation of social relationships, social fears slowly cease to resemble flames that flare rapidly, burn intensely and are quickly extinguished, only to be rekindled just as quickly, becoming instead like a permanently smouldering fire whose flame is hidden and seldom breaks out directly.

From this point of view as well, the courtly aristocracy represents a type of upper class different from the free warriors of the Middle Ages. It is the first of the more constrained upper classes, which is followed in modern times by even more heavily fettered ones. It is threatened more directly and strongly than the free warriors by bourgeois classes in the whole basis of its social existence, its privileges. As early as the sixteenth and seventeenth centuries there is in France, among certain leading bourgeois groups, particularly the high judicial and administrative courts, a strong desire to establish themselves in place of, or at least alongside, the nobility of the sword as the upper class of the country. The policy of these bourgeois strata is largely aimed at increasing their own privileges at the expense of the old nobility, even though they are at the same time—and this gives their relationship its peculiarly ambivalent character—bound to the old nobility by a number of common social fronts. For just this reason the fears that such continuous tensions bring with them express themselves, in these leading bourgeois strata, only in a concealed form controlled by strong super-ego impulses. And this applies all the more to the genuine nobility who now find themselves on the defensive, and in whom the shock of the defeat and loss they have suffered with pacification and courtization, long shows its aftereffects. The courtly aristocrats too must contain more or less within themselves the agitation aroused by the constant tug of war with bourgeois groups. With this structure of interdependencies, the social tension produces a strong *inner* tension in the members of the threatened upper class. These fears sink down in part, though never entirely, into the unconscious zones of the personality and re-emerge from them only in changed form, as specific automatisms of self-control. They show themselves, for example, in the special sensitivity of the courtly aristocracy to anything that remotely touches the hereditary privileges on which their existence is based. They manifest themselves in the affect-laden gestures of revulsion from anything that "smells bourgeois". They are partly responsible for the fact that the courtly aristocracy is so much more sensitive to lower-class gestures than were the warrior nobility of the Middle Ages, that they strictly and emphatically exclude everything "vulgar" from their sphere of life. Finally, this permanently smouldering social fear also constitutes one of the most powerful driving forces of the social control that every member of this courtly upper class exerts over himself and other people in his circle. It is expressed in the intense vigilance with which members of courtly aristocratic society observe and polish everything that distinguishes them from people of lower rank: not only the external signs of status, but also their speech, their gestures, their social amusements and manners. The constant pressure from below and the fear it induces above are, in a word, one of the strongest driving forces—though not the only one—of that specifically civilized refinement which distinguishes the people of this upper class from others and finally becomes second nature to them.

For it is precisely the chief function of the courtly aristocracy—their function for the mighty central ruler—to distinguish themselves, to maintain themselves as a distinct formation, a social counterweight to the bourgeoisie. They are completely free to spend their time elaborating the distinguishing social conduct of good manners and good taste. The rising bourgeois strata are less free to elaborate their conduct and taste; they have professions. Nevertheless, it is at first their ideal, too, to live like the aristocracy exclusively on annuities and to gain admittance to the courtly circle; this circle is still the model for a large part of the ambitious bourgeoisie. They become "Bourgeois Gentilhommes". They ape the nobility and its manners. But precisely this makes modes of conduct developed in courtly circles continually become useless as means of distinction, and the noble groups are forced to elaborate their conduct still further. Over and again customs that were once "refined" become "vulgar". Manners are polished and polished and the embarrassment-threshold constantly advances, until finally, with the downfall of absolutist-courtly society in the French Revolution, this spiral movement comes to an end or at least loses its force. The motor which, in the courtly phase, drives forward the civilizing transformation of the nobility—and with it the shame and repugnance frontier, as the examples in the first volume showed—is propelled both by the increased competition for the favour of the most powerful within the courtly stratum itself, and by the constant pressure from below. In this phase the *circulation of models* proceeds, as a result of the greater interdependence and therefore closer contact and more constant tension between different classes, far more quickly than in the Middle Ages. The "good societies" that come after the courtly one are all interwoven directly or indirectly, into the network of professional occupations, and even though "courtly" orientations are never entirely lacking in them, these no longer have remotely the same influence; from now on profession and money are the primary sources of prestige, and the art, the refinement of social conduct ceases to have the decisive importance for the reputation and success of the individual that it had in courtly society.

In every social stratum that area of conduct which is functionally of most vital importance to its members is the most carefully and intensively moulded. The exactitude with which, in courtly society, each movement of the hands while eating, each piece of etiquette and even the manner of speech is fashioned, corresponds to the importance which all these functions have for courtly people both as means of distinction from below, and as instruments in the competition for royal favour. The tasteful arrangement of house or park, the ostentatious or intimate—depending on the fashion—ornamentation of rooms, the witty conduct of a conversation or even a love affair, all these are in the courtly phase not only the private pleasures of individuals, but vital demands of their social position. They are pre-conditions for the respect of others, for the social success which here plays the same role as professional success in bourgeois society.

In the nineteenth century, with the gradual ascendancy of economic, of commercial and industrial bourgeois strata, and their increasing pressure for access to the highest power positions in the state, all these skills cease to hold the central place in the social existence of people; they cease to be of primary significance for success or failure in their status and power struggles. Other skills take their place as primary skills on which success or failure in life depends—skills such as occupational proficiency, adeptness in the competitive struggle for economic chances, in the acquisition or control of capital wealth, or the highly specialized skill needed for political advancement in the fierce though regulated party struggles characteristic of an age of increasing functional democratization. While the aristocratic courtiers' personality structure is to a large extent determined by the need to compete for status and power chances within one of the ruling court establishments of their age, the social personality structure of the rising bourgeois strata is determined by the competition for a greater share of the growing capital wealth, or else for jobs or for positions which endow their occupants with greater political or administrative chances of power. These and related competitive struggles now become the main factors of constraint which leave their imprint upon the personality of individuals. Even though certain strata of the new economic and political bourgeoisie again and again form "good Societies" of their own, and thus develop, or take over, some of the skills more highly cultivated in aristocratic societies, the pattern of social constraints acting upon the members of bourgeois "good Societies" is in one decisive respect different from that acting upon aristocratic courtiers and gentlemen. The social existence of the latter is not only *de facto* founded upon unearned income of one kind or another, but living on unearned income and thus without any occupational work, in these circles, has a very high value. It is an almost indispensable condition for those who wish to "belong". With the rise of the economic and political bourgeoisie this aristocratic ethos changes. Its members, or at least its male members, are expected to work for a living, even if they form "good Societies" of their own. Forms of sociability, the ornamentation of one's house, visiting etiquette or the ritual of eating, all are now relegated to the sphere of private life. They preserve their vital function most strongly in that national society where, despite the rise of bourgeois elements, aristocratic social formations remained longest and most vigorously alive: in England. But even in the peculiar amalgam that developed here from the interpenetration over centuries of aristocratic and bourgeois models of conduct, middle-class traits gradually move into the foreground. And generally in all Western societies, with the decline of the purer aristocracy, whenever and however this takes place, the modes of conduct and affective forms which are developed are those necessary to the performance of money-earning functions and the execution of precisely regulated work. This is why professional bourgeois society, in everything that concerns social conduct, takes over the ritual of courtly society without developing it with the same intensity. This is why the standard of affect-control in this sphere advances only slowly with the rise of the professional bourgeoisie. In courtly society, and partly in English society too, this division of human existence into professional and private spheres does not exist. As the split becomes more general a new phase begins in the civilizing process; the pattern of drive-control that professional work necessitates is distinct in many respects from that imposed by the function of courtier and the game of courtly life. The exertion required by the maintenance of bourgeois social existence, the stability of the super-ego functions, the intensity of drive-control and drive-transformation demanded by bourgeois professional and commercial functions, are in sum considerably greater, despite a certain relaxation in the sphere of social manners, than the corresponding social personality structure required by the life of a courtly aristocrat. Most obvious is the difference in the regulation of sexual relationships. However, the courtly-aristocratic moulding of the personality passes over in this or that form into the professional bourgeois one and is propagated further by it. We find this impregnation of broader strata by behavioural forms and drive-controls originating in courtly society particularly in regions where the courts were great and wealthy and their influence as style-building centres correspondingly strong. Paris and Vienna are examples of this. They are the seats of the two great rival absolutist courts of the eighteenth century. An echo of this can still be heard in the present day, not only in their reputation as centres of "good taste" or of luxury industries whose products are intended particularly for the use of "ladies", but even in the cultivation of sexual relationships, the erotic character of the population, even though reality in this respect may no longer quite match the reputation so frequently exploited by the film industry.

In one form or another, however, the models of conduct of courtly-aristocratic *bonne compagnie* have penetrated industrial society at large even where the courts were less rich, powerful and influential. That the conduct of the ruling Western groups, the degree and kind of their affect-control, show a high degree of uniformity despite all national variations, is certainly, in general terms, a result of the closely knit and long-ranging chains of interdependence linking the various national societies of the West. But within this general framework the phase of the semi-private power monopolies and of courtly–aristocratic society, with its high interdependence all over Europe, plays a special part in the moulding of Western civilized conduct. This courtly society exercised for the first time, and in a particularly pure form, a function which was afterwards transmitted in differing degrees and with various modifications to broader and broader strata of Western society, the function of a "good society", an upper class under pressure from many sides, from the organized monopolies of taxation and physical force on the one hand, and from the rising middle and lower classes on the other. Courtly society was indeed the first representative of the particular form of upper class which emerged more clearly the more closely, with the advancing division of functions, the different social classes became mutually dependent, and the larger the number of people and the geographical areas that were placed in such interdependence. It was a highly constricted upper class, whose situation demanded constant self-restraint and intense drive-control. Precisely this form of upper class from now on predominated in Western regions. And the models of this self-restraint, first developed in courtly-aristocratic society for the sphere of sociability, were passed on from class to class, adjusted and modified, like the upper-class function itself. The heritage of aristocratic society had greater or lesser importance depending on whether its character as "good society" played a greater or lesser role for a class or a nation. As we have said, this was the case to a greater or lesser degree with increasingly broad classes and finally entire nations in the West, particularly nations which, having early developed strong central institutions, early became colonial powers. In such nations there was an increase—under the pressure of social integration embodied both in the intensity of competition within the upper class itself and in the necessity of preserving its higher living standard and prestige *vis-à-vis* lower strata—in the strength of a particular kind of social control, in sensitivity to the behaviour of other members of one's own class, in individual self-control and in the strength of the individual "super-ego". In this way modes of conduct of a courtly-aristocratic upper class were amalgamated with those of various bourgeois strata as these rose to the position of upper classes; *civilité* was incorporated and perpetuated—with certain modifications depending on the situation of its new host—in what was now called "civilization" or, more precisely, "civilized conduct". So, from the nineteenth century onwards, these civilized forms of conduct spread across the rising lower classes of Western society and over the different classes in the colonies, amalgamating with indigenous patterns of conduct. Each time this happens upper-class conduct and that of the rising groups interpenetrate. The standard of conduct of the rising class, its pattern of commands and prohibitions, reflects in its structure the history of the rise of this class. So it comes about that the typical "drive- and conduct-pattern" of the different industrial nation states, their "national character", still represents the nature of the earlier power-relationships between nobility and bourgeoisie and the course of the century-long struggles between them, from which a specific type of middle-class groups in the end emerged for a time as the dominant establishment. Thus, to give one out of many examples, the national code of conduct and affect-control in the United States has to a higher extent middle-class characteristics than—in spite of many similarities—the corresponding English code. In the making of this English code features of aristocratic descent fused with those of middle-class descent—understandably, for in the development of English society one can observe a continuous assimilating process in the course of which upper-class models (especially a code of good manners) were adopted in a modified form by middle-class people, while middle-class features (as for instance elements of a code of morals) were adopted by upper-class people. Hence, when, in the course of the nineteenth century, most of the aristocratic privileges were abolished, and England with the rise of the industrial working classes became a nation state, the English national code of conduct and affect-control showed very clearly the gradualness of the resolution of conflicts between upper and middle classes in the form, to put it briefly, of a peculiar blend between a code of good manners and a code of morals. Analogous processes were shown in Part One of *The History of Manners* by the example of the differences between the German and French national characters. And it would not be difficult to add further illustrations relating to the national characters of the other European nations.

In each case, the waves of expansion of the standards of civilized conduct to a new class go hand in hand with an increase in the social power of that class, and a raising of its standard of living to that of the class above it, or at least in that direction. Classes living permanently in danger of starving to death or of being killed by enemies can hardly develop or maintain those stable restraints characteristic of the more civilized types of conduct. To instil and maintain a more stable super-ego agency, a relatively high standard of living and a fairly high degree of security are necessary.

However complex the leverage of intertwining processes within which the civilization of conduct and experience in European societies takes place may at first sight appear, the basic connections are clear enough. All the individual trends mentioned so far, e.g. the slow rise in the living standards of broad sections of population, the greater functional dependence of the upper class, or the increasing stability of the central monopolies, all these are parts and consequences of a division of functions advancing now more rapidly, now more slowly. With this division of functions the productivity of work increased; this greater productivity is the precondition for the rise of the living standards of ever-larger classes; with this division of functions the functional dependence of the upper classes increases; and only at a very advanced point in the division of functions, finally, is the formation of more stable monopolies of physical force and taxation with highly specialized administrations possible, i.e. the formation of states in the Western sense of the word, through which the life of the individual gradually gains greater "security". But this rise in the division of functions also brings more and more people, larger and larger populated areas, into dependence on one another; it requires and instils greater restraint in the individual, more exact control of his affects and conduct, it demands a stricter regulation of drives and—from a particular stage on—more even self-restraint. This is the price, if we may call it so, which we pay for our greater security and related advantages.

Moreover—and this is of decisive importance for the standard of civilization in our day—the restraint and self-control characteristic of all phases of civilization up to now, result not merely from the necessity for each individual to co-operate constantly with many others; they are no less determined by the split of society into upper and lower classes. The kind of restraint and drive patterning produced in people of the upper classes takes its special stamp primarily from the tensions running through society. The ego and super-ego formation of these people reflects both the competition within their own class and the constant pressures from below, produced in ever-changing forms by the advancing division of functions. The strength of the social constraints and the many contradictions within it, to which the behaviour of each individual member of the upper class, the establishment, is subject and which are represented by his own "super-ego", are not determined solely by the fact that it is a control exerted by competitors, some of them even in free competition, but above all by the fact that the competing members of the established groups at the same time have to make common cause in their endeavour to preserve their distinguishing prestige and their higher status from those pressing from below—still more or less as outsiders. Often enough, under these conditions, the preservation of the higher status and the distinguishing personality characteristics requires a form of foresight, self-restraint and prudence beset by anxieties.

If the outline of these processes is followed over centuries, we see a clear tendency for standards of living and conduct to be equalized and contrasts levelled out. In each of the waves of expansion which occur when the mode of conduct of a small circle spreads to larger rising classes, two phases can be clearly distinguished: a phase of colonization or assimilation in which the lower and larger outsider class is still clearly inferior and governed by the example of the established upper group which, intentionally or unintentionally, permeates it with its own pattern of conduct, and a second phase of repulsion, differentiation or emancipation, in which the rising group gains perceptibly in social power and self-confidence, and in which the upper group is forced into increased restraint and isolation, and the contrasts and tensions in society are increased.

Here, as always, both tendencies, equalization and distinction, attraction and repulsion, are certainly present in both of these phases; these relationships too are fundamentally ambivalent. But in the first phase, which is usually that in which people rise individually from the lower to the upper class, the tendency for the upper class to colonize the lower and for the lower to copy the upper is more pronounced. In the second phase, when the social power of the lower group is increasing while that of the upper group declines, the self-consciousness of both groups increases with their rivalry, with a tendency to emphasize differences and—as far as the upper class is concerned—to consolidate them. Contrasts between the classes increase, the walls grow higher.

In phases of the first kind, phases of assimilation, many individuals in the rising outsider class are, however reluctantly, very dependent on the upper class, not only in their social existence but also in their conduct, their ideas and ideals. They are frequently, though not always, still unformed in many areas in which members of the upper class are highly developed, and they are so impressed, in their social inferiority, by the affect-control and code of conduct of the upper class, that they try to control their own affects according to the same pattern. Here we come upon one of the most remarkable characteristics of this civilizing process: the people of the rising class develop within themselves a "super-ego" modelled on the superior, colonizing upper class. But on closer inspection this super-ego is in many respects very different from its model. It is less balanced and therefore often much more severe. It always reveals the immense effort which individual social advancement requires; and it shows equally the constant threat from below as from above, the crossfire from all sides to which individuals are exposed in their social rise. Total assimilation to a higher established group succeeds only very exceptionally in one generation. In most people from the aspiring outsider groups the effort to rise inevitably leads to specific deformations of consciousness and attitude. These are known in the Orient and colonies as "Levantinism"; and in the petty-bourgeois circles of Western societies they are often enough to be found in the form of "half-education", the pretension to be what one is not, insecurity of taste and conduct, "vulgarity" not only of furniture and clothing but also of the mind: all this expresses a social situation which gives rise to an urge to imitate models of a higher social group. The attempt does not succeed. It remains clearly an imitation of alien models. The education, standards of living and fears of the rising groups and the upper class are in this phase still so different that the attempt to achieve the poise of the upper class leads in most cases to a peculiar falseness and incongruity of behaviour which nevertheless conceals a genuine distress, a desire to escape the pressure from above and the sense of inferiority. And this shaping of the super-ego on upper-class models also brings about in the rising class a specific form of shame and embarrassment. These are very different from the sensibilities of lower groups with no chance of individual rise. Their behaviour may be coarser, but it is more uniform and in a way more of a piece. They live more vigorously in their own world without any claim to upper-class prestige, and therefore with greater scope for discharge of the affects; they live more fully in accordance with their own manners and customs. Their inferiority *vis-à-vis* the upper class, their gestures both of subordination and resistance, are clear and relatively unconcealed like their affects, bound by clear, definite forms. In their consciousness they and the other classes have for better or worse their clearly defined positions.

By contrast, the feelings and gestures of inferiority in people rising socially as individuals take on their particular coloration from the fact that these people identify to a certain extent with the upper class. They have the same structure as was described earlier in the case of shame feelings; people in this situation acknowledge in one part of their consciousness the upper-class norms and manners as binding on themselves, without being able to adopt them with the same ease and matter-of-factness. It is this peculiar contradiction between the upper class within themselves, represented by their own super-ego, and their incapability of fulfilling its demands, it is this constant inner tension that gives their affective life and their conduct its particular character.

At the same time their predicament shows, from a new angle, the importance which a strict code of manners has for the upper class. It is a prestige instrument, but it is also—in a certain phase—an instrument of power. It is not a little characteristic of the structure of Western society that the watchword of its colonizing movement is "civilization". For the people of a society with a high division of functions it is not enough simply to rule subject people and countries by force of arms like a warrior caste, although the old, simple goals of most of the earlier expansionist movements, the expulsion of other peoples from their land, the acquisition of new soil for cultivation and settlement, doubtless play no small part in Western expansion. But it is not only the land that is needed but the people; these must be integrated, whether as workers or consumers, into the web of the hegemonial, the upper-class country, with its highly developed differentiation of functions. This in turn requires both a certain raising of living standards and the cultivation of self-control or super-ego functions in the subject peoples on the Western models; it demands a "civilization" of the colonized. Just as it was not possible in the West itself, from a certain stage of interdependence onwards, to rule people solely by force and physical threats, so it also became necessary, in maintaining an empire that went beyond mere plantation-land and plantation-labour, to rule people in part through themselves, through the moulding of their super-egos. In established-outsiders relationships of this type one can observe figurational characteristics akin to, though of course not identical with, those to be observed in established-outsiders relationships between social classes at a comparable stage of development. One can observe, for instance, characteristics of an early form of rise, not yet of the outsider groups as a whole but of some of its individual members. They absorb the code of the established groups and thus undergo a process of assimilation. Their own affect-control, their own conduct, obeys the rules of the established groups. Partially they identify themselves with them, and even though the identification may show strong ambivalences, still their own conscience, their whole super-ego apparatus, follows more or less the pattern of the established groups. People in that situation attempt to reconcile and fuse that pattern, the pattern of occidentally civilized societies, with the habits and traditions of their own society with a higher or lesser degree of success.*

But to observe such processes we do not need to go far afield. A very similar phase is to be found in the rise of the Western bourgeoisie itself: the courtly phase. Here too it was initially the highest aspiration of many individuals from leading bourgeois groups to behave and live like nobles. They inwardly acknowledged the superiority of courtly-aristocratic conduct; they sought to mould and control themselves according to that model. The conversation on correct speech of a bourgeois in a courtly circle, quoted earlier, is one example of this. And in the history of the German language, this courtly phase of the bourgeoisie is clearly marked by the well-known tendency of speakers or writers to insert a French word after every three or four German ones, if they did not prefer simply to use French, the court language of Europe. Nobles and even bourgeois members of courtly circles often enough made fun at this time of other bourgeois unsuccessfully trying to act in a "refined" or courtly manner.

As the social power of the bourgeoisie grows, this mockery disappears. Sooner or later all the characteristics of the second phase of social elevation move into the foreground. Bourgeois groups emphasize more and more their specifically bourgeois self-image; they oppose their own codes and manners more and more confidently to the courtly-aristocratic ones. Depending on their particular situation, they contrast work to aristocratic idleness, "nature" to etiquette, the cultivation of knowledge and morals to that of good manners and conversation, not to mention the special bourgeois demands for control of the central key monopolies, for a new structure for the administration of taxation and the army. Above all they counterpose "virtue" to "courtly frivolity". The regulation of sexual relations, the fences surrounding the sexual sphere of libidinal life, are far stronger in middle and rising bourgeois classes, in keeping with their professional position, than in the courtly-aristocratic upper class; and later it is repeatedly stronger here than in high bourgeois groups which have already reached the social

---

* While going over the translation with my friend Johan Goudsblom I repeatedly had to resist the temptation to change the original text in accordance with the present state of my knowledge. The temptation was particularly strong when we came to the problems of ascending social units discussed in these pages and of the influence which social rise, or, alternatively, social hegemony, has on their social code, especially on the restraints inherent in such a code. The problems discussed above now form part of an established-outsiders theory. Not all forms of social oppression of one group by another have the form of class relations. At present one often tries to use the conceptual apparatus developed in connection with class relations for all forms of group oppression or, alternatively, group emancipation. However, the class model is too narrow; one needs a broader overall concept to deal with the varieties of group oppression and group rise. I have found it helpful to use the term established-outsiders relationships as a more comprehensive concept in that sense. With its help one can work out more clearly the common features of group domination and group subjection as well as the distinguishing characteristics of each particular type. [*Author's note to the translation*]

summit and taken on an upper-class character. But however sharp this opposition may be during the phase of social struggle, however great the emancipation of the bourgeoisie from the models and predominance of the nobility, the code of conduct which the leading bourgeois groups develop when they finally take over the function of the upper class is, because of the preceding phase of assimilation, the product of an amalgamation of the codes of the old and new upper classes.

The main line of this movement of civilization, the successive rises of larger and larger groups, is the same in all Western countries, and incipiently so in increasingly large areas elsewhere. And similar, too, is the structural regularity underlying it, the increasing division of functions under the pressure of competition, the tendency to more equal dependence of all on all, which in the long run allows no group greater social power than others and nullifies hereditary privileges. Processes of free competition also follow a similar course: they veer toward the formation of monopolies controlled by a few and may finally lead to the passing of control into the hands of broader classes. All this emerges very clearly, at this stage in the struggle of the bourgeoisie against noble privileges, in the "nationalization" of the monopolies of taxation and force previously administered in the interests of very small circles; all this takes the same course, earlier or later, by one path or another, in all the interdependent countries of the West. But within this common framework of basic similarities each country develops structural characteristics of its own; and corresponding to the different social structures are the specific patterns of affect regulation, the structure of the drive economy and the super-ego, which finally emerge in the various nations.

Thus in England, where the courtly-absolutist phase was relatively short, and where contacts and alliances between urban-bourgeois circles and the landed nobility came about early on, the amalgamation of upper and middle-class behaviour patterns took place gradually over a long period. Germany, on the other hand—which, through its lack of centralization and the Thirty Years' War resulting from this, remained a relatively poor land with a low standard of living for far longer than its Western neighbours—had an extraordinary long phase of absolutism with a large number of small, far from luxurious, courts, and, likewise through its lack of centralization, reached the phase of external, colonial expansion only relatively late and incompletely. For all these reasons, internal tensions, the isolation of the aristocracy from the bourgeoisie, were strong and enduring there, and access by bourgeois groups to the central monopolies difficult. In the Middle Ages urban-bourgeois groups had for a time been politically and economically more powerful, more independent and self-confident than in any other country in Europe. The shock of their political and economic decline was therefore particularly keenly felt. If specifically bourgeois traditions had earlier developed in a particularly pure form in many German regions because the urban formations were so rich and independent, they now persisted as specifically bourgeois traditions because their bearers were particularly poor and socially impotent. And accordingly, it was only very late that bourgeois and noble circles interpenetrated and their modes of conduct were amalgamated. For a long period the codes of both classes persisted disconnectedly side by side; and because throughout this period the key positions of the tax monopoly and the police and army administration were monopolies of the nobility, habituation to a strong external state authority became deeply ingrained in the bourgeoisie. Whereas in England, owing to its island situation,[152] for a long period neither the army nor a centralized police force played any major role in moulding the population, though the navy did to some extent, in Prussia/Germany, with its long, vulnerable land frontiers, the army led by the nobility, by privileged classes, was, like the powerful police force, of the utmost significance for the social personality structure of its people. This structure of the monopoly of physical force did not, however, compel individual people to adopt the same kind of self-control as in England. It did not force individuals to become integrated in relations of "teamwork" based on a high degree of individual self-control and self-attunement to others; instead, it habituated the individual from childhood on to a very much higher extent to a strict order of superiority and inferiority, an order of obedience and command on many levels. Understandably, this type of state control and the use made within it of the monopoly of physical force was less conducive to a transformation of controls through others, or alien controls, into self-controls. Also lacking in Germany for a long period was a particular function which in some other countries, especially England, enhanced in both noble and bourgeois classes a common foresight, and a similar pattern of firmly differentiated self-control: the central function in a very extensive network of interdependencies, as the upper class of a colonial empire. Thus the drive-control of the individual remained in Germany highly dependent on strong external state power. The emotional balance, the self-control of the individual, was endangered if this external power was lacking. From generation to generation a super-ego was reproduced in the bourgeois masses which was disposed to relinquish to a separate, higher social circle the specific kind of foresight demanded by the ruling and organization of society at large. It was shown at the beginning of this study how this situation led, at an early phase of the rise of the bourgeoisie, to a very specific kind of bourgeois self-image, a turning away[153] from everything to do with the administration of the power monopolies, and to a cultivation of inwardness, and the elevation of spiritual and cultural achievements to a special place in the table of values.

It was also shown how the corresponding movement took a different course in France. Here, more continuously than in any other country in Europe and from the early Middle Ages on, courtly circles were formed, first by *courtois* groups and then by larger and larger courts, until finally the competition between the many lords culminated in the formation of a single powerful and wealthy royal court to which flowed the taxes from the entire territory. Accordingly, a centrally controlled protectionist economic policy was adopted at an early stage. Although this primarily served the interests of the monopoly ruler and his desire to maximize his fiscal income, nevertheless it also promoted the development of trade and the emergence of wealthy bourgeois classes. Thus there were early contacts between rising bourgeois and court aristocrats with their constant need of money. Unlike the many relatively small and poorly endowed absolutist dominions in Germany, the rich, centralized, absolutist regime in France furthered both a comprehensive transformation of alien constraints into self-restraints and the amalgamation of courtly-aristocratic and bourgeois patterns of conduct. And when at the end of this stage, the rise from below was completed, and with it the levelling and equalization of social standards characteristic of this whole phase of the civilizing process; when the nobility had lost its hereditary rights and its status as a separate upper class and bourgeois groups took over the upper-class function, they continued, as a result of the long preceding interpenetration, the models, the drive patterns and the forms of conduct of the courtly phase more undeviatingly than any other bourgeois class in Europe.

VIII

Conclusion

If we survey these past movements in their entirety, it is a change in a quite definite direction that we see. The deeper we penetrate the wealth of particular facts to discover the structure and regularities of the past, the more clearly emerges a firm framework of processes within which the scattered facts are taken up. Just as in past times people observing nature, after following many blind alleys in thought, gradually saw a more coherent vision of nature take shape before them, in our time the fragments of the human past gathered in our minds and books by the work of many generations, are beginning slowly to fall into place in a cohesive picture of history and of the human universe in general. The contribution made here to this picture will be briefly summarized by presenting it from a particular point of view, that of our own day. For the profile of past changes in the social fabric becomes most sharply visible when seen against the events of one's own time. Here, too, as so often, present events illuminate the understanding of the past, and immersion in the past illuminates the present. In many respects, the dynamics of intertwining to be observed in our own day, with their numerous ups and downs, represent a continuation in the same direction of the moves and countermoves of former changes in the structure of Occidental societies.

At the point of utmost feudal disintegration in the West, as was shown above,[154] certain dynamics of social intertwining come into play which tend to integrate larger and larger units. Out of the competition of small dominions, the territories, themselves formed in the struggles of even smaller survival units, a few, and finally a single unit slowly emerges victorious. The victor forms the centre about which a new larger dominion is integrated; he forms the monopoly centre of a state organization within the framework of which many of the previously freely competing regions and groups gradually grow together into a more or less unified and well-balanced society of a higher order of magnitude.

Today these states in turn form analogous power balances of freely competing survival units. These states too, under the pressure of the tensions of competition that keep our whole society in a perpetual ferment of conflicts and crises, are now in their turn gradually being forced more and more clearly into mutual opposition. Again, many rivalling dominions are so closely intertwined that any that stands still, that does not grow stronger, runs the risk of growing weaker and becoming dependent on other states. As in every system of balances with growing competition and without a central monopoly, the powerful states forming the primary axes of tensions in the system force each other in an incessant spiral to extend and strengthen their power. The struggle for supremacy and thus, knowingly or otherwise, for the formation of monopolies over still larger areas, is already in full swing. And if at present it is supremacy over continents that is at issue, there are already clear signs, concomitant with the interdependence of larger and larger areas, of struggles for supremacy over a system embracing the entire inhabited earth.

In the present no less than in the past, the dynamics of interdependencies which have been so often mentioned in these enquiries, keep men moving and press towards changes in their institutions and indeed in the overall structure of their figurations. The experiences of our day, too, refute the notion which has now dominated men's thinking for more than a century, the idea that a balanced system of freely competing units—states, concerns, craftsmen or whatever else— can be maintained indefinitely in this state of precarious equilibrium. Now, as of old, this state of monopoly-free competition finds itself driven towards monopoly formation. Why this equilibrium is so exceedingly unstable, and the probability of its breakdown so high, has been shown in the analysis of the dynamics of competition and monopolization given earlier.[155]

And today, no more than formerly, is it "economic" goals and pressures *alone*, or *only* political motives, which are the primary driving forces of these changes. Neither the acquisition of "more" money or "more" economic power is the actual goal of state rivalry and the extension of state rule, nor the acquisition of greater political and military power merely a mask, a means to an economic end. Monopolies of physical violence and of the economic means of consumption and production, whether co-ordinated or not, are inseparably connected, without one ever being the real base and the other merely a "superstructure". Both together produce specific tensions at particular points in the development of the social structure, tensions pressing towards a transformation of this structure. *Both together form the lock joining the chain by which men are mutually bound.* And in both spheres of human bonding, the political and the economic, the same mechanisms, in permanent interdependence, are at work. Just as the tendency of the big merchant to enlarge his enterprise springs finally from tension within the *whole* human network of which he is a part, and above all from the danger of diminished control and loss of independence if rival concerns grow larger than his, likewise competing states drive each other further and further up the competitive spiral under the pressure of tensions immanent in the entire structure which they constitute. Many individual people may wish to put a stop to this spiral movement, the breakdown of equilibrium between "free" competitors, and to the struggles and changes this breakdown brings with it. In the course of history so far the constraints of human bonding have always proved stronger in the long run than such wishes. And so today international relationships, not yet regulated by an encompassing monopoly of force, are again driven towards such monopolies and thus to the formation of dominions of a new order of magnitude.

Precursors of such hegemonial units such as united states, empires or leagues of nations, certainly already exist. They are all still relatively unstable. As earlier, in the centuries of struggle between territorial dominions, it is as yet unresolved in the struggle of states today, and impossible to resolve, where the centres and frontiers of the larger hegemonial units of the future will lie. As earlier, it is impossible to predict how long it will take for this struggle, with its many spurts and counter-spurts, to be finally decided. And like the members of the smaller units whose struggles slowly produced the states, we too have scarcely more than a vague idea of the structure, organization and institutions of the larger units towards which the actions of today tend, whether the actors know or not.[156] Only one thing is certain: the direction in which the integration of the modern world is veering. The competitive tension between states, given the pressures which our social structure brings with it, can be resolved only after a long series of violent or non-violent trials of strength have established monopolies of force, and central organizations for larger dominions, within which many of the smaller ones, "states", can grow together in a more balanced unity. Here, indeed, the compelling forces of social interweaving have led the transformation of Western society in one and the same direction from the time of utmost feudal disintegration to the present.

And the case is very similar with many other movements of the "present". They are all seen in a new light when viewed as moments in that stream that we variously call "the past" or "history". Even *within* the different hegemonial units of today we see a number of monopoly-free competitive struggles. But this free competition is in many places nearing its final phase. Everywhere in these struggles fought with economic weapons, private monopoly organizations are already forming. And as earlier, in the formation of monopolies of taxation and physical force in the hands of single dynasties, compelling forces were already discernible that finally led to a broadening of control, whether by subordinating the monopoly executive to an elected public legislator or by any other form of "nationalization", in our day we already see the immanent figurational dynamics at work curtailing the possibility of private control of the recent "economic" monopolies and bringing their structure closer to the older ones, so that eventually they are likely to veer towards an integration of both.

The same can be said of the other tensions leading towards changes within the different hegemonial units, the tensions between those people directly controlling certain instruments of monopoly as a hereditary possession, and those excluded from such control and who engage in unfree competition, all being dependent on opportunities distributed by the monopoly rulers. Here too we find ourselves in the midst of a historical spurt which, like a great wave of an advancing tide, takes up the smaller ones preceding it and carries them further in the same direction. In the analysis of the monopoly mechanism, it was shown in more general terms[157] how and why, in the tension between monopoly rulers and monopoly servants at a certain degree of overall pressure, the balance tends to be more or less quickly overturned. It was shown that spurts in this direction already take place in an early period of Western society. We find them, for example, in the process of feudalization even though this involves only a shift within the upper class itself; moreover, this change in favour of the many at the expense of the few led, as a result of the low degree of division of functions, to the disintegration of control over monopolized opportunities and the decay of the monopoly centres.

As the division of functions, and with it the mutual interdependence of all functions, advances, this kind of change in the balance of power is no longer expressed by a tendency to disperse monopolized opportunities among many individuals, but by a tendency to control the monopoly centres and the opportunities they allocate in a different way. The first great transitional phase of this kind, the struggle of bourgeois classes for control of the old monopoly centres, controlled by the kings and, partly, by the aristocracy, as a hereditary possession—the first complete monopolies of modern times—shows this clearly enough. For many reasons, the pattern of rising classes in our day is more complex. One reason is that it is now necessary to struggle not only for the old monopoly centres of taxation and physical violence, or only for the recent economic monopolies still in the process of formation, but for control of both at once. But the elementary pattern of forces at work here is very simple even in this case: every monopoly opportunity restricted by heredity to particular families leads to specific tensions and disproportions in the society concerned. Tensions of this kind tend towards a change of relationships and thus of institutions in all societies, though when differentiation is low and, particularly, when the upper class consists of warriors, they often remain unresolved. Societies with a highly developed division of functions are far more sensitive to the disproportions and malfunctions caused by such tensions, the effects of which are permanently felt throughout the whole society. And though in such societies there may be more than one way in which such tensions might be resolved and removed, the *direction* in which they tend towards transcending themselves is predetermined by the mode of their becoming, by their genesis. The tensions, disproportions and malfunctions resulting from monopoly control of opportunities in the interests of a few can only be resolved by breaking this control. What cannot be decided in advance, however, is how long the ensuing struggle will take.

And something very similar, finally, is happening in our time to the conduct of people and to their whole personality structure. In the course of this study it has been attempted to show in detail both that and how the structure of psychological functions, the particular standard of behavioural controls at a given period, is connected to the structure of social functions and the change in relationships between people. To trace these connections in detail in our own time is a task yet to be undertaken. The most general points can be quickly made. The structural forces working so perceptibly today towards a more or less rapid change of institutions and of interpersonal relationships, are leading no less clearly to corresponding changes in the personality structure. Here, too, we only gain a clear picture of what is happening by comparing it, as a spurt in a particular direction, with the past movements of which it is a continuation. In the birth pains of other social upheavals the dominant standard of conduct of the upper classes was finally loosened to a greater or lesser extent. A period of uncertainty preceded the consolidation of a new standard. Behaviour patterns were transmitted not only from above to below but, in line with the shift in the social centre of gravity, from below to above. Thus, in the course of the rise of the bourgeoisie, for example, the courtly-aristocratic code of conduct lost some of its hold. Social forms became more relaxed and in some ways more coarse. The stricter taboos placed in middle-class circles on certain spheres, above all those of money and sexuality, pervaded broader circles in varying degrees until finally, as this specific balance of tensions disappeared, in alternating waves of relaxation and renewed severity, elements of the behaviour patterns of both classes were fused into a new, more stable code of conduct.

The upheavals in the midst of which we live are different in structure from all those preceding them, however much they may continue these earlier movements and be based upon them. Nevertheless, certain structural similarities with the change just described are encountered in our own time. Here too we find a relaxation of traditional patterns of behaviour, the rise of certain modes of conduct from below, and increased interpenetration of the standards of different classes; we see an increased severity in some spheres and a certain coarsening in others.

Periods like this, periods of transition, give a particular opportunity for reflection: the older standards have been called into question but solid new ones are not yet available. People become more uncertain in their conduct. The social situation itself makes "conduct" an acute problem. In such phases—and perhaps only in such phases—much is open to scrutiny in conduct that previous generations took for granted. The sons begin to think further where their fathers brought their reflection to a halt; they begin to ask for reasons where their fathers saw no reason to ask: why must "one" behave in this way here and that way there? Why is this permitted and that forbidden? What is the point of this precept on manners and that on morals? Conventions that have long gone untested from generation to generation, become problems. In addition, as a result of increased mobility and more frequent meetings with different human types, people are learning to see themselves from a greater distance: why is the code of conduct different in Germany from that in England, different in England from that in America, and why is the conduct of all these countries different from that of the Orient or of more primitive societies?

The preceding investigations attempt to bring some of these questions closer to resolution. They really raise only problems that are "in the air". They try, as far as one person's knowledge permits, to clarify the questions and to prepare a way which, in the crossfire of discussion, may lead enquiry forward in collaboration with many others. The behaviour patterns of our society, imprinted on the individual from early childhood as a kind of second nature and kept alert in him by a powerful and increasingly strictly organized social control, are to be explained, it has been shown, not in terms of general, ahistorical human purposes, but as something which has evolved from the totality of Western history, from the specific forms of behaviour that develop in its course and the forces of integration which transform and propagate them. These patterns, like the whole control of our behaviour, like the structure of our psychological functions in general, are many-layered: in their formation and reproduction emotional impulses play their part no less than rational ones, drives and affects no less than ego functions. It has long been customary to explain the control to which individual behaviour is subject in our society as something essentially rational, founded solely on logical considerations. Here it has been seen differently.

Rationalization itself, and with it the more rational shaping and explanation of social taboos has been shown[158] to be only one side of a transformation affecting the *whole* personality, the level of drives and affects no less than the level of consciousness and reflection. The motive force of this change of individual self-steering is provided, it was shown, by pressures arising out of the manifold intertwining of human activities, pressures operating in a particular direction, and bringing about shifts in the form of relationships and in the whole social fabric. This rationalization goes hand in hand with a tremendous differentiation of functional chains and a corresponding change in the organization of physical force. Its precondition is a rise in the standard of living and in security, or, in other words, increased protection from physical attack or destruction and thus from the uncontrollable fears which erupt for more powerfully and frequently into the lives of individuals in societies with less stable monopolies of force and lower division of functions. At present we are so accustomed to the existence of these more stable monopolies of force and the greater predictability of violence resulting from them, that we scarcely see their importance for the structure of our conduct and our personality. We scarcely realize how quickly what we call our "reason", this relatively farsighted and differentiated steering of our conduct, with its high degree of affect-control, would crumble or collapse if the anxiety-inducing tensions within and around us changed, if the fears affecting our lives suddenly became much stronger or much weaker or, as in many simpler societies, both at once, now stronger, now weaker.

It is only when we penetrate these connections that we gain access to the problem of conduct and its control by the social code valid at a particular time. The degree of anxiety, like the whole pleasure economy, is different in every society, in every class and historical phase. To understand the control of conduct which a society imposes on its members, it is not enough to know the rational goals that can be adduced to explain its commands and prohibitions; we must trace to their source the fears which induce the members of this society, and above all the custodians of its precepts, to control conduct in this way. We therefore only gain a better understanding of the changes of conduct and sentiment in a civilizing direction if we are aware of the changes in the structure of inbuilt fears to which they are connected. The direction of this change was sketched earlier:[159] the direct fear of one person for others diminishes; indirect or internalized fears increase proportionately; and both kinds become more even; the waves of anxiety no longer rise so frequently or steeply, only to fall away just as sharply; with some oscillation, slight by comparison with the earlier phase, they normally remain at a middle level. When this is the case, as has been seen, conduct takes on—by degrees and stages—a more "civilized" character. Here as everywhere, the structure of fears and anxieties is nothing other than the psychological counterpart of the constraints which people exert on one another through the intertwining of their activities. Fears form one of the channels—and one of the most important—through which the structure of society is transmitted to individual psychological functions. The driving force underlying the change in drive economy, in the structure of fears and anxieties, is a very specific change in the social constraints acting on the individual, a specific transformation of the whole web of relationships, above all the organization of force.

Often enough it seems to people as if the codes regulating their conduct towards one another, and thus also the fears moving them, are something from outside the human sphere. The more deeply we immerse ourselves in the historical processes in the course of which prohibitions, like fears and anxieties, are formed and transformed, the stronger grows an insight which is not without importance for our actions as well as for our understanding of ourselves: *we realize to what degree the fears and anxieties that move people are men-made.* To be sure, the possibility of feeling fear, just like that of feeling joy, is an unalterable part of human nature. But the strength, kind and structure of the fears and anxieties that smoulder or flare in the individual never depend solely on his own "nature" nor, at least in more complex societies, on the "nature" in the midst of which he lives. They are always determined, finally, by the history and the actual structure of his relations to other people, by the structure of society; and they change with it.

Here, indeed, is one of the indispensable keys to all the problems posed by the steering of human conduct and the social codes of commandments and "taboos". The child and adolescent would never learn to control his behaviour without the fears instilled by other people. Without the lever of these men-made fears the young human animal would never become an adult deserving the name of a human being, any more than someone's humanity matures fully if life denies him sufficient joy and pleasure. The fears which grown-ups consciously or unconsciously induce in the child are precipitated in him and henceforth reproduce themselves more or less automatically. The malleable personality of the child is so fashioned by fears that it learns to act in accord with the prevailing standard of behaviour, whether these fears are produced by direct physical force or by deprivation, by the restriction of food or pleasure. And men-made fears and anxieties from within or without finally hold even the adult in their power. Shame, fear of war and fear of God, guilt, fear of punishment or of loss of social prestige, man's fear of himself, of being overcome by his own affective impulses, all these are directly or indirectly induced in him by other people. Their strength, their form and the role they play in the individual's personality depend on the structure of his society and his fate within it.

No society can survive without a channelling of individual drives and affects, without a very specific control of individual behaviour. No such control is possible unless people exert constraints on one another, and all constraint is converted in the person on whom it is imposed into fear of one kind or another. We should not deceive ourselves: the constant production and reproduction of human fears by people is inevitable and indispensable wherever people live together, wherever the desires and actions of a number of people interact, whether at work, in leisure or in love-making. But one should not believe or attempt to be persuaded that the commands and fears which *today* set their stamp on human conduct have as their "purpose" simply and fundamentally these basic necessities of human co-existence, or that they are restricted in our world to those constraints and fears necessary to a stable equilibrium between the desires of many and for the maintenance of social collaboration. Our codes of conduct are as riddled with contradictions and as full of disproportions as are the forms of our social life, as is the structure of our society. The constraints to which the individual is subjected today, and the fears corresponding to them, are in their character, their strength and structure decisively determine by the particular forces engendered by the structure of our society just discussed: by its power and other differentials and the immense tensions created by them.

It is clear in what turmoils and dangers we live, and the structural forces determining their direction have been discussed. It is these forces, far more than the simple constraint of working together, it is tensions and entanglements of this kind which at present constantly expose the individual to fear and anxiety. The tensions between states arising from the compelling dynamics of their contests for supremacy over larger and larger dominions find their expression in the make-up of the individual people, in specific frustrations and restraints; they impose upon these individuals a mounting work-pressure and also a profound insecurity which never ceases. All this, the frustrations, the restlessness, the pressure of work, no less than the never-ending threat to life, inherent in these inter-state tensions, produces anxieties and fears. The same holds true of the tensions within each of the different state societies. The uncontrollable, monopoly-free competition between people of the same class on the one hand, and the tensions between different classes and groups on the other, likewise give rise, for the individual, to continuous anxiety and particular prohibitions or restrictions. They too engender their own specific fears: the fears of dismissal, of unpredictable exposure to those in power, of falling below the subsistence level, which prevail in the lower classes; and the fears of social degradation, of the reduction of possessions or independence, of loss of prestige and status, which play so great a part in the life of the middle and upper classes. And it is precisely fears and anxieties of this kind, fears of the loss of distinguishing hereditary prestige, as was pointed out earlier,[160] that have had to this day a decisive part in shaping the prevailing code of conduct. Precisely these fears, it was also seen, are particularly disposed to internalization; they, far more than the fear of poverty, hunger or direct physical danger, become rooted in the individual member of such classes, through his upbringing, as inner anxieties which bind him to a learned code almost automatically, under the pressure of a strong super-ego, even independently of any control by others. The continuous concern of parents whether their child will attain the standard of conduct of their own or even a higher class, whether it will maintain or increase the prestige of the family, whether it will hold its own in the competition within their own class, fears of this kind surround the child from its earliest years, and they do so in the middle classes, in those ambitious to rise, far more than in the upper class. Fears of this kind play a considerable part in the control to which the child is subject from the beginning, in the prohibitions placed on him. Perhaps only partly conscious in the parents, and partly already automatic, they are transmitted to the child as much by gestures as by words. They continuously add fuel to the fiery circle of inner anxieties, which holds the behaviour and feelings of the growing child permanently within definite limits, binding him to a certain standard of shame and embarrassment, to a specific accent, to particular manners, whether he wishes or not. Even the rules imposed on sexual life and the automatic anxieties now surrounding it to such a high degree, stem not only from the elementary necessity of controlling and balancing the desires of many who live together. They likewise have their origins to a considerable extent in the pressures and tensions in which the upper and particularly the middle classes of our society live. They too are very closely related to the fear of losing opportunities or possessions and prestige, of social degradation, of reduced chances in the harsh struggle of life, induced from early on in the child by the behaviour of parents and educators. And even though these parental constraints and anxieties may sometimes bring about precisely what they are supposed to prevent, even though the child might be made incapable, by such blindly instilled automatic anxieties, of succeeding in the struggle of life and attaining social prestige—whatever the outcome, it is always the tensions of their society that are projected by the parental gestures, prohibitions and fears on to the child. The hereditary character of monopolized chances and of social prestige finds direct expression in the parents' attitude to their child; and so the child is made to feel the dangers threatening these chances and this prestige, to feel the entire tensions of his society, even before he knows anything about them.

This connection between the external fears of the parents directly conditioned by their social position, and the inner, automatic anxieties of the growing child, is certainly a fact of far more general significance than can be shown here. We shall only gain a fuller understanding of the personality structure of the individual, and of the historical changes in its moulding over successive generations, when we are better able to observe and analyse long chains of generations than is possible today. But one thing has become clear enough even here: how deeply the stratification, the pressures and tensions of our own time penetrate the structure of the individual personality.

We cannot expect of people who live in the midst of such tensions, who are thus driven guiltlessly to incur guilt upon guilt against each other, that they should behave to each other in a manner representing—as seems so often to be believed today—an ultimate pinnacle of "civilized" conduct. The continuous intertwining of human activities again and again acts as a lever which over the centuries produces changes in human conduct in the direction of our standard. The same pressures quite clearly operate within our own society towards changes transcending present standards of conduct and sentiment in the same direction—although, today as in the past, these trends can go at any time into reverse gear. No more than our kind of social structure, is our kind of conduct, our level of constraints, prohibitions and anxieties, something definitive, still less a pinnacle.

To begin with, there is the constant danger of war. War, to repeat the point in different words, is not the opposite of peace. Through a necessity the reasons of which have become clear, wars between smaller units have been, in the course of history up to now, inevitable stages and instruments in the pacification of larger ones. Certainly, the vulnerability of the social structure, and so the risks and upheavals brought on all concerned by the explosive violence of wars, increase the further the division of functions advances, the greater the mutual dependence of the rivals. We therefore feel in our own time a growing disposition to resolve future interstate conflicts by less dangerous means. But the fact that, in our day, just as earlier, the dynamics of increasing interdependence are impelling the figuration of state societies towards such conflicts, to the formation of monopolies of physical force over larger areas of the earth and thus, through all the terrors and struggles, towards their pacification, is clear enough. And as mentioned above, beyond the tensions between continents and partly involved in them, the tensions of the next stage are already emerging. One can see the first outlines of a worldwide system of tensions composed by alliances and supra-state units of various kinds, the prelude of struggles embracing the whole globe, which are the precondition for a worldwide monopoly of physical force, for a single central political institution and thus for the pacification of the earth.

The case is no different with economic struggles. Free economic competition, too, as we have seen, is not just the opposite of a monopolistic order. It is constantly veering beyond itself towards this opposite. From this aspect too our epoch is anything but a final point or pinnacle, no matter how many partial downfalls, as in structurally similar transitional periods, it may contain. In this respect too it is full of unresolved tensions, of unconcluded processes of integration the duration and exact course of which are not predictable and whose direction alone is clear: the tendency of free competition or, which means the same thing, the unorganized ownership of monopolies, to be reduced and abolished; the change in human relationships by which control of opportunities gradually ceases to be the hereditary and private preserve of an established upper class and becomes a function under social and public control. And here, too, beneath the veil of the present tensions, those of the next stage are becoming visible, the tensions between the upper and middle functionaries of the monopoly administration, between the "bureaucracy" on the one hand and the rest of society on the other.

Only when these tensions between and within states have been mastered can we expect to become more truly civilized. At present many of the rules of conduct and sentiment implanted in us as an integral part of one's conscience, of the individual super-ego, are remnants of the power and status aspirations of established groups, and have no other function than that of reinforcing their power chances and their status superiority. They help members of these groups to such distinction not simply through their own achievement—which in moderation is justified—but through the monopolistic appropriation of power chances the access to which is blocked for other interdependent groups. Only when the tensions between and within states have been mastered is there a chance that the regulation of men's affects and conduct in their relations with each other can be confined to those instructions and prohibitions which are necessary in order to keep up the high level of functional differentiation and interdependence without which even the present levels of civilized conduct in men's co-existence with each other could not be maintained, let alone surpassed. Only then is there a chance, too, that the common pattern of self-control expected of men can be confined to those restraints which are necessary in order that men can live with each other and with themselves with a high chance of enjoyment and a low chance of fear—be it of others, be it of themselves. Only with the tensions and conflicts between men can those within men become milder and less damaging to their chances of enjoyment. Then it need no longer be the exception, then it may even be the rule that an individual person can attain the optimal balance between his imperative drives claiming satisfaction and fulfilment and the constraints imposed upon them (and without which man would remain a brutish animal and a danger as much to himself as to others)—that condition to which one so often refers with big words such as "happiness" and "freedom": a more durable balance, a better attunement, between the overall demands of man's social existence on the one hand, and his personal needs and inclinations on the other. If the structure of human figurations, of men's interdependencies, has these characteristics, if the co-existence of men with each other, which after all is the condition of the individual existence of each of them, functions in such a way that it is possible for all those bonded to each other in this manner to attain this balance, then and only then can humans say of themselves with some justice that they *are* civilized. Until then they are at best in the process of becoming civilized. Until then they may at best say: the civilizing process is under way, or, with the old Holbach: "la civilisation . . . n'est pas encore terminèe."

Notes

1. James Westfall Thompson, *Economic and Social History of Europe in the Later Middle Ages (1300–1530)* (New York and London, 1931), pp. 506–7.

2. This is exemplified by the consequences resulting from the Carolingian estates or fisc. These were perhaps not as extreme as they appear from the following quotation; but undoubtedly the situation of the Carolingian fisc played a part in the formation of the national frontiers:

> The widespread character of the Carolingian fisc . . . made the fisc like a vast net in which the Empire was held. The division and dissipation of the fisc was a more important factor in the dissolution of the Frankish Empire than the local political ambition of the proprietary nobles . . .
>
> The historical fact that the heart of the fisc was situated in central Europe accounts for the partitions of central Europe in the ninth century, and made these regions a battle-ground of kings long before they became a battle-ground of nations. . . .
>
> The dividing frontier between future France and future Germany was drawn in the ninth century because the greatest block of the fisc lay between them.

James Westfall Thompson, *Economic and Social History of the Middle Ages (300–1300)* (New York and London, 1928), pp. 241–2. Cf. by the same author: *The Dissolution of the Carolingian Fisc* (Berkeley, University of California Press, 1935).

3. A. Luchaire, *Les premiers Capétiens* (Paris, 1901), p. 180.

4. C. Petit-Dutaillis, *Las monarchie féodale en France et en Angleterre* (Paris, 1933), p. 8 with following map. For details on the eastern frontier of the western Frankish empire and its movements, cf. Fritz Kern, *Die Anfänge der Französischen Ausdehnungspolitik* (Tübingen, 1910), p. 16.

5. Paul Kirn, *Das Abendland vom Ausgang der Antike bis zum Zerfall des Karolingischen Reiches*, Propyláen-Weltgeschichte, vol. 3 (Berlin, 1932), p. 118.

6. Brunner, *Deutsche Rechtsgeschichte*, quoted by A. Dopsch, *Wirtschaftliche und soziale Grundlagen der europäischen Kulturentwicklung* (Vienna, 1924), pt. 2, pp. 100–1.

7. A. Dopsch, *Wirtschaftliche und soziale Grundlagen der europäischen Kulturentwicklung aus der Zeit von Cäsar bis auf Karl den Grossen* (Vienna, 1918–24), pt. 2, p. 115.

8. Kirn, op. cit., p. 118.

9. A. von Hofmann, *Politische Geschichte der Deutschen* (Stuttgart and Berlin, 1921–8), vol. 1, p. 405.

10. Ernst Dümmler, *Geschichte des ostfränkischen Reiches* (Berlin, 1862–88), vol. 3, p. 306.

11. Paul Kim, *Politische Geschichte der deutschen Grenzen* (Leipzig, 1934), p. 24.

12. F. Lot, *Les derniers Carolingiens* (Paris, 1891), p. 4; also J. Calmette, *Le monde féodale* (Paris, 1934), p. 119.

13. Beaudoin, quoted by J. Calmette, *La société féodale* (Paris, 1932), p. 27.

14. Luchaire op. cit., pp. 176–7. A sketch of the distribution of rule at the time of Hugh Capet is given by M. Mignet, "Essai sur la formation territoriale et politique de la France", *Notices et Mémoires historiques* (Paris, 1845), vol. 2, pp. 154f.

15. A. Luchaire, *Histoire des Institutions Monarchiques de la France sous les premiers Capétiens (987–1180)* (Paris, 1883), vol. 2, Notes et Appendices, p. 329.

16. Karl Hampe, *Abendländisches Hochmittelalter*, Propyläen Weltgeschichte, vol. 3 (Berlin, 1932), p. 306.

17. Kirn, *Das Abendland vom Ausgang der Antike bis zum Zerfall des Karolingischen Reiches*, p. 119.

18. A. Dopsch, *Die Wirtschaftsentwicklung der Karolingerzeit, vornehmlich in Deutschland* (Weimar, 1912), vol. 1, p. 162; cf. also the general account of manor and village in Knight, Barnes and Flügel, *Economic History of Europe* (London, 1930), "The Manor", pp. 163ff.

19. Marc Bloch, *Les caractères originaux de l'histoire rurale française* (Oslo, 1931), p. 23.

20. Dopsch, *Wirtschaftliche und soziale Grundlagen der europäischen Kulturentwicklung aus der Zeit von Cäsar bis auf Karl den Grossen*, pt. 2, p. 309: "The greater the real power, the economic and social base, of these officials became, the less the monarchy could contemplate transferring the office outside the incumbent's family on his death."

21. Calmette, *La société féodale*, p. 3.

22. Ibid., pp. 4–5. Cf. on this problem the contrast between European and Japanese feudalism in W. C. Macleod, *The Origin and History of Politics* (New York, 1931), pp. 160ff. Here, admittedly, the explanation of Western feudalization is sought rather in the preceding late-Roman institutions than in contemporary forces of integration: "Many writers appear to believe that Western European feudalism has its institutional origins in pre-Roman Teutonic institutions. Let us explain to the student that the fact is that Germanic invaders merely seized upon those contractual institutions of the late Roman Empire which . . ." (p. 162). The very fact that analogous feudal relationships and institutions are formed in the most different parts of the world can only be fully understood through a clear insight into the compelling force of the actual relationships, into the dynamics of a specific figuration; and only analysis of them can explain why the feudalization processes and feudal institutions in different societies differ from one another in certain ways.

Another comparison between different feudal societies is to be found in O. Hintze, *Wesen und Verbreitung des Feudalismus*, Sitzungsberichte der Preussischen Akademie der Wissenschaften, phil.-hist. Klasse (Berlin, 1929), pp. 321ff. The author, influenced by the ideas of Max Weber on the methodology of historical and social research, attempts "to describe the *ideal type* underlying the concept of feudalism". But while this study does begin to transform the older historiographical method into one more concerned with actual social structures and so gives rise to useful particular insights, its comparison of different feudal societies is one of the many examples of the difficulties arising when a historian takes over the methodological guiding ideas of Max Weber and tries—in the words of Otto Hintze—to construct "visual abstractions, types". The similarities confronting the observer of different people and societies are not ideal types that have in a sense to be mentally constructed by the observer, but a real, existing kinship between the social structures themselves; if this is lacking the historian's whole concept of types miscarries. If we are to oppose another concept to that of the "ideal type", it could be the "real type". The similarity between different feudal societies is not an artificial product of thought but, to reiterate, the result of the fact that similar forms of social bonding have a strong compelling tendency to develop in a way which in fact, and not only "in the idea", produces related patterns of relationships and institutions at different times and at different locations of global society.

A number of examples for which I am indebted to Ralph Bonwit have shown how remarkably similar the forces of social interweaving that led to feudal relations and institutions in Japan are to the structures and forces which have been established here in relation to Western feudalism. A comparative structural analysis of this kind would prove a more useful way of explaining the peculiarities by which the feudal institutions of Japan and their historical change differ from those of the West.

Similar results have been produced by a preliminary investigation of the Homeric warrior society. To explain the production of large epic cycles—to mention only this feature—in ancient as in Western knightly society and in other societies with a similar structure, we do not need any speculative biologistic hypothesis, the notion of a "youth" of social "organisms". It is quite enough to examine the specific forms of social life that develop at medium and large feudal courts or on military campaigns and travels. Singers and minstrels with their versified reports of the fates and heroic deeds of great warriors that are passed from mouth to mouth, have in the daily life of such feudal warrior societies a specific place and function which differ from those of singers and songs in a tribe living more closely together, for example.

We also gain access to the structural changes in ancient warrior societies from a different angle by examining stylistic changes in the vases and vase paintings of early antiquity. When, for example, in vase paintings originating in particular periods, "baroque" elements appear, affected or—positively expressed—refined gestures and garments, we should think, instead of assuming a biological "ageing" of the society concerned, of processes of differentiation, the emergence of wealthier houses from the mass of warrior society and a greater or lesser transition from warriors to courtiers; or, depending on circumstances, we should look for a colonizing influence from more powerful courts. Insight into the specific tensions and processes within a feudal society which the more abundant documentation from the early European period makes possible can, in a word, in some respects sharpen and focus our observation of material from antiquity. But, of course, suppositions of this kind should in each case be supported by a rigorous examination of material pertaining to the structural history of antiquity itself.

Comparative studies of sociogenesis or structural history of this kind have scarcely begun. Indispensable for their success is an undertaking that has been made especially difficult by the over-sharp distinction between academic disciplines and the lack of collaboration between them which have characterized research hitherto. Essential for an understanding of earlier feudal societies and their structure, for example, is an exact comparative study of living feudal societies before it is too late. A rich knowledge of details and structural connections necessary for an understanding of any society, which the material from the past is too fragmentary to provide, will only become available for interpretation if ethnology bases its research less exclusively on simpler societies, "tribes", and history concerns itself less with past societies and processes, and if both disciplines together turn their attention to those living societies which in their structure are close to the medieval society of the West. Both together should investigate the structure, in the strictest sense of the word, of such societies, the functional dependencies by which people in them are bound together in very specific ways, and the forces of interweaving which under certain circumstances bring about a change of these dependencies and relationships in a quite specific direction.

23. On this and the following discussion, cf. A. and E. Kulischer, *Kriegs- und Wanderzüge* (Berlin and Leipzig, 1932), pp. 50f.

24. J. B. Bury, *History of the Eastern Roman Empire* (1912), p. 373, quoted by Kulischer, op. cit., p. 62.

25. Henri Pirenne, *Les villes du moyen âge* (Brussels, 1927).

26. Kim, *Politische Geschichte der deutschen Grenzen*. For further details on the differences in pace and structure between German and French feudalization, cf. J. W. Thompson, "German Feudalism",

American Historical Review, vol. 28, 1923, pp. 440ff. "What the ninth century did for France in transforming her into a feudal country was not done in Germany until the civil wars of the reign of Henry IV." Ibid., p. 444.

Here, admittedly (and subsequently in, for example, W. O. Ault, *Europe in the Middle Auges*, 1932) the decline of the western Frankish area is explained primarily in terms of the greater external threat: "Germany being less exposed to attack from outside and possessed of a firmer texture within than France, German feudalism did not become as hard and set a system as was French feudalism. 'Old' France crumbled away in the ninth and tenth centuries; 'old' Germany, anchored to the ancient duchies, which remained intact, retained its integrity" (Thompson, op. cit., p. 443). But another decisive factor in the speed and degree of feudal disintegration in the western Frankish area was precisely the fact that after the Normans had settled invasions by foreign tribes, and therefore the external threat, was less than in the eastern Frankish area. The question whether larger areas, once unified, decay more slowly and whether conversely, once decayed, they re-integrate with greater difficulty than smaller ones, this problem of social dynamics remains to be investigated. But at any rate, hand in hand with the gradual weakening of the Carolingian house brought about at least in part by the unavoidable reduction in its wealth in the course of generations, by the loss of part of its land to pay for services or its division between different family members (this too remains to be examined in more detail), went a phase of disintegration embracing the whole Carolingian dominion. It may be that even in the ninth century this disintegration in the western Frankish area went somewhat further than in the later German region. But it was certainly more quickly arrested in the latter precisely because of the stronger external threat. Over a long period this threat gave individual tribal leaders the chance to become strong central rulers through military successes over common enemies and so to re-invigorate and extend the Carolingian central organization. And for a time the possibility of colonial expansion, the acquisition of new land on the eastern frontier of the German region, acted in the same direction to strengthen the central authority. In the western Frankish area, by contrast, from the ninth century on both factors were less: the threat of invasion by foreign tribes and the possibility of joint expansion across the frontier. Proportionately smaller was the chance of forming a strong monarchy; the "royal task" was lacking; and so feudal disintegration took place more quickly and completely. (Cf. pp. 275ff. and 291–2.)

27. E. Levasseur, *La population française* (Paris, 1889), vol. 1, pp. 154–5.
28. Bloch, op. cit., p. 5.
29. W. Cohn, *Das Zeitalter der Normannen in Sicilien* (Bonn and Leipzig, 1920).
30. H. See, *Französische Wirtschaftsgeschichte* (Jena, 1930), p. 7.
31. Kurt Breysig, *Kulturgeschichte der Neuzeit* (Berlin, 1901), vol. 2, pp. 937ff., partic. p. 948.

If the actions of the three monarchies are compared . . . in seeking the reasons for their varying success, the ultimate cause will not be found in isolated events. The Norman–English monarchy benefited from a circumstance that lay neither in its power nor in that of any mortal being, but was founded in the whole structure of England's external and internal history. By virtue of the fact that in 1066 a new state was established in England from the foundations upwards, it was possible to make use of the experiences gathered by the great monarchies, most of all the closest, the French. The fragmentation of the high nobility and the hereditariness of offices were in a sense only the conclusions drawn by the Norman monarchy from the fate of its nearest example.

32. Pirenne, *Les villes du moyen âge*, p. 53. The opposite view has been taken more recently by D. M. Petruševki, "Strittige Fragen der mittelalterlichen Verfassungs- und Wirtschaftsgeschichte", *Zeitschrift für die gesamte Staatswissenschaft*, vol. 85 (Tübingen, 1928), pp. 468ff. This work is not without interest in that, through its onesidedness in the opposite direction, it puts into proper perspective certain obscurities in the traditional historical view and certain inadequacies of existing concepts.

So, for example, the idea that the cities of antiquity had completely disappeared by the early

Middle Ages is countered by one no less imprecise. Cf. the more balanced account by H. Pirenne, *Economic and Social History of Medieval Europe* (London, 1936), p. 40: "When the Islamic invasion had bottled up the ports of the Tyrrhenian Sea . . . municipal activity rapidly died out. Save in southern Italy and in Venice, where it was maintained thanks to Byzantine trade, it disappeared everywhere. The towns continued in existence, but they lost their population of artisans and merchants and with it all that had survived of the municipal organisation of the Roman Empire."

To the static view whereby the "barter economy" and the "money economy" appear, not as expressions of the *direction* of a gradual historical process, but as two separate, successive and irreconcilable physical states of society (cf. pp. 284–5 and pp. 299–300 above), Petruševski opposed the different conception that no such thing as the "barter economy" ever existed: "We do not wish here to discuss in detail the fact that, as Max Weber has shown, the barter economy is one of those scholarly Utopias which not only do not exist and have never existed in actual reality, but which, unlike others . . . which are likewise Utopian generalizations on account of their logical character, can never have any application to actual reality" (p. 488). To this we may compare Pirenne's account (op. cit., p. 8):

> From the economic point of view the most striking and characteristic institution of this civilisation is the great estate. Its origin is, of course, much more ancient and it is easy to establish its affiliation with a very remote past . . . [p. 9]. What was new was the way in which it functioned from the moment of the disappearance of commerce and the towns. So long as the former had been capable of transporting its products and the latter of furnishing it with a market, the great estate had commanded and consequently profited by a regular sale outside . . . but now it ceased to do this, because there were no more merchants and townsmen now that everyone lived off his own land, no-one bothered to buy food from outside. . . . Thus, each estate devoted itself to the kind of economy which has been described rather inexactly as the "closed estate economy", and which was really simply an economy without markets.

Finally Petruševski opposes to the notion whereby "feudalism" and "barter economy" appear as two different spheres of existence or storeys of society, the latter as the infrastructure producing or causing the former as the superstructure, his own view that the two phenomena have nothing to do with each other: ". . . notions wholly at variance with historical fact, such as that of the contingency of feudalism on the barter economy or its incompatibility with a comprehensive state organisation" (p. 488).

It has been attempted to show the real state of affairs in the preceding text. The specific form of barter economy prevailing in the early Middle Ages, the relatively undifferentiated and market-less economies associated with the great courts, and the specific form of political and military organization which we call feudalism, are nothing other than two different aspects of the same forms of human relationships. They can be conceptually *distinguished* as two different aspects of the same human relationships, but even conceptually they cannot be *separated*, like two substances which can exist independently. The political and military functions of the feudal lord and his function as the owner of land and bondsmen are fully interdependent and indissolubly bound together. And likewise the changes which gradually took place in the situation of these lords and in the whole structure of this society cannot be explained *solely* in terms of an autonomous movement of economic relations and functions, or *solely* in terms of changes of political and military functions, but only in terms of the intertwining human activities comprising both these two inseparably connected areas of functions and forms of relationship.

33. Cf. the Introduction by Louis Halphen in A. Luchaire, *Les communes Françaises à l'époque des Capétiens directs* (Paris, 1911), p. viii.

34. Ibid., p. ix.

35. Ibid., p. 18.

36. Hans von Werveke, "Monnaie, lingots ou marchandises? Les instruments d'échange au XIe et XIIe siècles", *Annales d'histoire économique et sociale* (Sept. 1932), no. 17, p. 468.

37. Ibid. The corresponding process in the opposite direction, the recession of the use of money and the advance of payment in natural produce, sets in at an early stage of late antiquity: "The further the third century proceeds the faster the decline becomes. The only money remaining in circulation is the antonianus. . . ." (F. Lot, *La fin du monde antique* (Paris, 1927), p. 63.) "Wages for the army tend more and more to be paid in produce" (p. 65) . . . "As for the ineluctable consequences of a system which allows services to be rewarded only by payment in kind, the distribution of land, they are readily perceived: they lead to what is called the feudal system or to an analogous régime" (p. 67).

38. M. Rostovtsev, *The Social and Economic History of the Roman Empire* (Oxford, 1926), pp. 66–7, p. 528 and many other places. Cf. Index: Transportation.

39. Lefebvre des Noettes, *L'Attelage. Le cheval de selle à travers les âges. Contribution à l'histoire de l'esclavage* (Paris, 1931).

The investigations of Lefebvre des Noettes, on account both of their results and of their direction of enquiry, have an importance which can scarcely be overestimated. Beside the value of these results, which no doubt need confirmation on particular points, it is no great matter that the author stands the causal connection on its head, seeing the development of haulage technology as the cause of the elimination of slavery.

Indications of the necessary corrections are to be found in a critique of the book by Marc Bloch, "Problèmes d'histoire des techniques", *Annales d'histoire economique et sociale* (Sept. 1932). In particular, two aspects of Lefebvre des Noettes' work are partly accentuated and partly rectified. 1. The influence of China and Byzantium on the inventions of the Middle Ages appears to require closer examination. 2. Slavery had ceased to play an important part in the structure of the early medieval world long before the new harness appeared: "In the absence of any clear temporal succession how can one speak of a cause and effect relationship?" (p. 484). A comprehensive account of the essential results of this work by Lefebvre des Noettes in German is to be found in L. Löwenthal, "Zugtier und Sklaven", *Zeitschrift für Sozialforschung* (Frankfurt/Main, 1933), no. 2.

40. Lefebvre des Noettes, "La 'Nuit' du moyen âge et son inventaire", *Mercure de France* (1932), vol. 235, pp. 572ff.

41. Von Werveke, op. cit., p. 468.

42. A. Zimmern, *Solon and Croesus, and other Greek essays* (Oxford, 1928), pp. 113–14. Cf. also A. Zimmern, *The Greek Commonwealth* (Oxford, 1931).

For some time it has been emphasized—no doubt quite rightly—that in Rome freemen as well as slaves did manual work. Above all the research of M. Rostovtsev (cf. *The Social and Economic History of the Roman Empire*), and then specialized studies like that of R. H. Barrow, *Slavery in the Roman Empire* (London, 1928), e.g. pp. 124ff., have clarified these relationships. But the fact that freemen worked, however highly the share of their work in total production may be estimated, in no way contradicts what was illustrated earlier by the quotation from the work of A. Zimmern—the fact that the social processes and regularities within a society where manual work is done to any considerable extent by slaves differ in a very specific way from those within a society where all urban work at least is done exclusively by freemen. As a social tendency, the urge of freemen to distance themselves from work performed by slaves with the resulting formation of a class of "idle poor" in ancient society, as in modern ones with a large slave-labour sector, is always detectable. It is not difficult to understand that under the pressure of poverty a number of freemen are nevertheless forced to perform the same work as slaves. But it is no less clear that their situation, like that of manual labourers in general in such a society, is decisively influenced by the existence of slave labour. These freemen, or at least a part of them, are forced to accept conditions similar to those of slaves. Depending on the number of slaves available to such a society and on the degree of interdependence of their work with slave labour, the freemen always face a greater or lesser degree of competitive pressure from slave labour. This too is one of the structural regularities of any society of slavemasters. (Cf. also Lot, *La fin du monde antique*, pp. 69ff.)

43. According to A. Zimmern Greek society in its classical period was not a slave society in the typical sense of the word: "Greek society was not a slave-society; but it contained a sediment of slaves

to perform its most degrading tasks, while the main body of its so-called slaves consisted of apprentices haled in from outside to assist together and almost on equal terms with their masters in creating the material basis of a civilisation in which they were hereafter to share" (*Solon and Croesus*, pp. 161–2).

44. Pirenne, *Les villes du moyen âge*, pp. 1ff.

45. Ibid., pp. 10ff.

46. Ibid., p. 27. This "recourse to inland areas" and its significance for the development of Western society find confirmation in the fact that the evolution of land transport technology beyond its state in antiquity began, as far as we can see today, about a century earlier than that of nautical technology. The former begins between about 1050 and 1100, the latter clearly not before 1200. Cf. Lefebvre des Noettes, *De la marine antique à la marine moderne. La révolution du gouvernail* (Paris, 1935), pp. 105ff. Cf. also E. H. Byrne *Genoese shipping in the twelfth and thirteenth centuries* (Cambridge, Mass., 1930), pp. 5–7.

47. A. Luchaire, *Louis VII, Philippe Auguste, Louis VIII* (Paris, 1901), p. 80.

48. Calmette, *La société féodale*, p. 71. Cf. by the same author, *Le monde féodale*.

49. Law is, of course, through its fixation by an independent legal apparatus and the existence of bodies of specialists with a vested interest in the preservation of the status quo, relatively impervious to movement and change. Legal security itself, always desired by a considerable part of society, depends partly on the law's resistance to change. This immobility is indeed increased by it. The larger the areas and the number of people which are integrated and interdependent, the more necessary becomes a uniform law extending over such areas—as necessary, for example, as a uniform currency; the more strongly, therefore, the law and its apparatus, which like currency becomes itself in turn an organ of integration and a producer of interdependence, opposes any change, and the more serious are the disturbances and shifts of interest that any change brings with it. This too contributes to the fact that the mere threat of force by the "legitimate" organs of power is for long periods enough to make individuals and whole social groups comply with what has once been established as the norm of law and property on the basis of a particular stage of social power relationships. The interests identified with the preservation of existing legal and property relationships are so great, and the weight which law receives through growing integration is so clearly felt, that the constant testing of social power relations in physical struggles to which people in less interdependent societies are always inclined is replaced by a long-enduring readiness to abide by the existing law. Only when upheavals and tensions within society have become extraordinarily great, when interest in the preservation of the existing law has become uncertain in large parts of society, only then, often after intervals lasting centuries, do groups in a society begin to test in physical struggles whether the established law corresponds to the actual social power relationships.

When society had a predominantly barter economy and people were far less interdependent, and when, therefore, the most real though not yet visually representable network of society as a whole did not yet constantly confront the individual with its greater strength, the social power maintaining each legal claim by an individual had to be always fairly directly visible. If it became doubtful, the claim lapsed. Every property owner had to be ready to prove in physical combat that he still had enough military and social power to back his "legal claim". Corresponding to the closer intertwining of human activities at a later stage over large areas with relatively good communications, however, a law has developed that largely disregards local individual differences, a so-called general law, i.e. a law applicable and valid equally over the whole area for all the people within it.

The different kind of social interweaving and dependence existing in feudal society, with its largely barter economy, entrusted small groups and often single individuals with functions that are today exercised by "states". Thus "law", too, was incomparably more individualized and local. It was an obligation and bond entered into by this liege lord and that vassal, this group of tenants and that landlord, this civic corporation and that lord, this abbey and that duke. And a study of these "legal relationships" gives a very vivid idea of what it means when we say that in this phase social integration and interdependence were less and the relation of man to man correspondingly different.

We should take care [says Pirenne for example in *Les villes du moyen âge*, pp. 168–9] not to attribute exaggerated importance to urban charters. Neither in Flanders nor in any other region of Europe do they contain the totality of urban law. They confine themselves to fixing the main outlines, formulating some essential principles and resolving some particularly important conflicts. For most of the time they are products of special circumstances and have taken account only of questions being debated when they were drawn up. . . . If the burghers watched over them for centuries with extraordinary solicitude, it was because they were the paladium of their liberty, because they permitted them to justify revolt in cases of violation, but it was not because they enclosed the whole of their law. They were, as it were, no more than its skeleton. All around their stipulations proliferated a rich vegetation of customs, usages, privileges which were not less indispensable for being unwritten.

This is so true that a good number of charters themselves foresaw and recognized in advance the development of urban law. . . . In 1127 the Count of Flanders granted the burghers of Bruges 'ut de die in diem consuetudinarias leges suas corrigerent', that is, the permission to add from day to day to their municipal customs.

Here again we see how, on that different level of integration, formations of a different order of magnitude, a town and a major feudal lord, stand in the same sort of relationship to each other as today only "states" do; and their legal agreements show the same pattern as those of the latter, following fairly directly shifts of interest and social strength.

50. Calmette, *La société féodale*, pp. 70–1.

51. A. Luchaire, *La société française au temps de Philippe Auguste* (Paris, 1909), p. 265.

52. C. H. Haskins, *The Renaissance of the Twelfth Century* (Cambridge, 1927), p. 55.

53. Ibid., p. 56.

54. Ibid.

55. Eduard Wechssler, *Das Kulturproblem des Minnesangs* (Halle, 1909), p. 173.

56. Ibid., p. 174.

57. Ibid., p. 143.

58. Ibid., p. 113.

59. Hennig Brinkmann, *Entstehungsgeschichte des Minnesangs*, (Halle, 1926), p. 86.

60. Wechssler, op. cit., pp. 140–1.

61. Luchaire, *La société française au temps de Philippe Auguste*, p. 374.

62. Ibid., p. 379.

63. Ibid., p. 380.

64. Pierre de Vaissière, *Gentilshommes campagnards de l'ancienne France* (Paris, 1903), p. 145.

65. Brinkmann, op. cit., p. 35.

66. Wechssler, op. cit., p. 71.

67. Ibid., p. 74. Similarly in Marianne Weber, *Ehefrau und Mutter in der Rechtsentwicklung* (Tübingen, 1907), p. 265.

68. De Vaissière, op. cit., p. 145.

69. Wechssler, op. cit., p. 214.

70. Brinkmann, op. cit., pp. 45ff., 61, 86ff. Cf. on this and what follows C. S. Lewis, *The Allegory of Love; a Study in Medieval Tradition* (Oxford, 1936), p. 11.

The new thing itself, I do not pretend to explain. Real changes in human sentiment are very rare, but I believe that they occur and that this is one of them. I am not sure that they have 'causes', if by a cause we mean something which would wholly account for the new state of affairs, and so explain away what seemed its novelty. It is, at any rate, certain that the efforts of scholars have so far failed to find an origin for the content of Provençal love poetry.

71. In England the corresponding term is found in later periods restricted, sometimes even

explicitly, to servants. An example of this is the way in which, in an English account of what constitutes a good meal, the "curtese and honestie of servantes" is contrasted to the "kyne frendeshyp and company of them that sytte at the supper", G. G. Coulton, *Social Life in Britain* (Cambridge, 1919), p. 375.

72. F. Zarncke, *Der deutsche Cato* (Leipzig, 1852), p. 130, v.71 and v.141f. For other aspects of this first main phase in the transition from warriors to courtiers (the education and codes of knightly orders in different countries) cf. E. Prestage, *"Chivalry"*; *a series of studies to illustrate its historical significance and civilizing influence* (London, 1928); including A. T. Byles, "Medieval courtesy-books and the prose romances of chivalry" (pp. 183ff.).

73. Luchaire, *Les premiers Capétiens*, p. 285; cf. also A. Luchaire, *Louis VI le Gros* (Paris, 1890), Introduction.

74. Luchaire, *Histoire des Institutions Monarchiques de la France sous les premiers Capétiens* (987–1180), vol. 2, p. 258.

75. Cf. pp. 17ff., partic. pp. 31–2.

76. Suger, *Vie de Louis le Gros*, ed. Moliner, ch. 8, pp. 18–9.

77. A. Vuitry, *Études sur le régime financier de la France* (Paris, 1878), p. 181.

78. Luchaire, *Louis VI*.

79. "The land from Northumberland to the Channel was easier to unify than from Flanders to the Pyrenees." Petit-Dutaillis, *La monarchie féodale*, p. 37. On the question of size of territory, cf. also R. H. Lowie, *The Origin of the State* (New York, 1927), "The size of the state", pp. 17ff.

MacLeod in *The Origin and History of Politics* points out how astonishing it really was that given the simplicity of their means of transport such large dominions as the Inca or Chinese empires should have proved so stable. Only a detailed structural–historical analysis of the interplay of centrifugal and centralizing tendencies and interests in these empires could, indeed, make the agglomeration of such vast areas and the nature of their cohesion comprehensible to us.

The Chinese form of centralization, compared to that developed in Europe, is certainly very peculiar. Here the warrior class was eradicated relatively early and very radically by a strong central authority. This eradication—however it happened—is connected with two main peculiarities of the Chinese social structure: the passing of control of the land into the hands of the peasants (which we encounter in the early Western period only in a very few places, for example, Sweden) and the manning of the governmental apparatus by a bureaucracy always recruited in part from the peasants themselves and at any rate wholly pacified. Mediated by this hierarchy, courtly forms of civilization penetrate deep into the, lower classes of the people: they take root, transformed in many ways, in the code of behaviour of the village. And what has so often been called the "unwarlike" character of the Chinese people is not the expression of some "natural disposition". It results from the fact that the class from which the people drew many of their models through constant contact, was for centuries no longer a warrior class, a nobility, but a peaceful and scholarly officialdom. It is primarily their situation and function which is expressed in the fact that in the traditional Chinese scale of values—unlike the Japanese—military activity and prowess hold no very high place. Different as the Chinese way to centralization was to that in the West in detail, therefore, the foundation of the cohesion of larger dominions in both cases was the elimination of freely competing warriors or landowners.

80. On the importance of the monopoly of physical force in the building of "states", cf. above all Max Weber, *Economy and Society* (New York, 1968).

81. Cf. pp. 341–2 above. It has not been necessary here to follow the present-day custom and offer a mathematical expression for the regularity of the monopoly mechanism. No doubt it would not be impossible to find one. Once it has been found it will be possible to discuss also from this aspect a question which generally speaking is hardly raised today: the question of the *cognitive* value of mathematical formulation. What, for example, is gained in terms of possibilities of knowledge and of

clarity by a mathematical formulation of the monopoly mechanism? This question can only be answered on the basis of simple experience.

What is certain, however, is that for many people the formulation of general laws is associated with a value which—at least as far as history and sociology are concerned—has nothing to do with their cognitive value. This untested evaluation often enough leads research astray. Many people regard it as the most essential task of research to explain all changes by something unchangeable. And the regard for mathematical formulation derives not least from this evaluation of the immutable. But this scale of values has its roots not in the cognitive task of research itself but in the researcher's longing for eternity. General regularities like that of the monopoly mechanism and all other general patterns of relationships, whether mathematically formulated or not, do not constitute the final goal or culmination of historical and sociological research. Understanding of such regularities is fruitful as a *means* to a different end, a means of orientating man with regard to himself and his world. Their value lies solely in their function in elucidating historical change.

82. On this see "On the Sociogenesis of Feudalism", especially pp. 57–59. On "social power" see also the "Note on the concept of social power", pp. 62–3, note.

83. Auguste Longnon, *Atlas historique de la France* (Paris, 1885).

84. Luchaire, *Histoire des Institutions Monarchiques* (1891), vol. 1, p. 90.

85. Petit-Dutaillis, *La monarchie féodale en France et en Angleterre*, pp. 109ff.

86. A. Cartellieri, *Philipp II August und der Zusammenbruch des angevinischen Reiches* (Leipzig, 1913), p. 1.

87. Cf. A. Longnon, *La formation de l'unité française (Paris, 1922), p. 98.*

88. *Luchaire, Louis VII, Philipp Augustus, Louis VIII*, p. 204.

89. C. Petit-Dutaillis, *Études sur la vie et le règne de Louis VIII* (Paris, 1899), p. 220.

90. A. Vuitry, *Études sur le régime financier de la France*, nouvelle série, vol. 1 (Paris, 1883), p. 345.

91. Ibid., p. 370.

92. A more exact compilation of these feudal houses is to be found in Longnon, *La formation de l'unité française*, pp. 224f.

93. Vuitry, op. cit., p. 414.

94. Cf. e.g. Karl Mannheim, "Die Bedeutung der Konkurrenz im Gebiete des Geistigen", *Verhandlungen des siebenten deutschen Soziologentages* (Tübingen, 1929), pp. 35ff.

95. G. Dupont-Ferrier, *La formation de l'état français et l'unité française* (Paris, 1934), p. 150.

96. L. Mirot, *Manual de geographie historique de la France* (Paris, 1929), Map 19. This also contains maps relating to the foregoing discussion.

97. P. Imbart de la Tour, *Les origines de la réforme* (Paris, 1909), 1, p. 4.

98. Mirot, op. cit., Map 21.

99. Henri Hauser, review of G. Dupont-Ferrier, "La formation de l'état français", *Revue Historique* (1929), vol. 161, p. 381.

100. L. W. Fowles, Loomis Institute, USA, quoted in *News Review*, No. 35, p. 32.

101. Luchaire, *Les communes françaises à l'epoque des Capétiens directs*, p. 276.

102. Documentation for these and a number of other passages could not be included for reasons of space. The author hopes to append this in a separate volume.

103. P. Lehugeur, *Philipp le Long (1316–1322). Le mécanisme du gouvernement* (Paris, 1931), p. 209.

104. Dupont-Ferrier, op. cit., p. 93.

105. Brantôme, *Oeuvres complètes*, publiées par L. Lalanne, vol. 4, pp. 328ff.

106. J. H. Mariéjol, *Henri IV et Louis XIII* (Paris, 1905), p. 2.

107. Ibid., p. 390.

108. Cf. A. Stölzel, *Die Entwicklung des gelehrten Richtertums in deutschen Territorien* (Stuttgart, 1872), p. 600.

109. Richelieu, *Politisches Testament*, pt. 1, ch. 3, p. 1.

110. E. Lavisse, *Louis XIV* (Paris, 1905), p. 128.

111. Saint-Simon, *Memoiren*, tr. by Lotheisen, vol. 1, p. 167.

112. Cf. Lavisse, op. cit., p. 130.

113. Saint-Simon, op. cit., vol. 1, p. 167.

114. Saint-Simon, *Mémoires* (nouv. éd. par A. de Boislisle) (Paris, 1910), vol. 22, p. 35 (1711).

115. Thomas Aquinas, *De regimine Judaeorum*, Rome edit., vol. 19, p. 622.

116. Vuitry, op. cit., pp. 392ff.

117. Ibid., nouvelle série, vol. 1, p. 145. For another form of the monetarization of feudal seigneurial rights under the pressure of the kings' growing need for money, the liberation, for payment, of bondsmen by the king and his administration, cf. Marc Bloch, *Rois et Serfs* (Paris, 1920).

118. Paul Viollet, *Histoire des institutions politiques et administratives de la France* (Paris, 1898), vol. 2, p. 242.

119. Ibid.

120. Vuitry, op. cit., nouv. sér., vol. 2, p. 48.

121. G. Dupont-Ferrier, "La Chambre ou Cour des Aides de Paris", *Revue historique*, vol. 170 (Paris, 1932), p. 195; cf. on this and what follows the same author, *Études sur les institutions financières de la France*, vol. 2 (Paris, 1932).

122. Léon Mirot, *Les insurrections urbaines au début du règne de Charles VI* (Paris, 1905), p. 7.

123. Ibid., p. 37.

124. Dupont-Ferrier, "La Chambre ou Cour des Aides de Paris", p. 202. Cf. also Petit-Dutaillis, *Charles VII, Louis XI et les premières années de Charles VIII* (Lavisse, *Hist. de France*, IV, 2) (Paris, 1902).

125. Viollet, op. cit., vol. 3 (Paris, 1903), pp. 465–6. Cf. also Thomas Basin, *Histoire des règnes de Charles VII et de Louis XI*, ed. Quicherat (Paris, 1855), vol. 1, pp. 170ff. Details on financial organization are in G. Jacqueton, *Documents relatifs à l'administration financière en France de Charles VII à François Ier (1443–1523)* (Paris, 1897), partic. no. XIX in question-and-answer form, "Le vestige des finances". (A manual for future finance officials of the time?)

126. E. Albèri, *Relazioni degli Ambasciatori Veneti al Senato*, 1st series, vol. 4 (Florence, 1860), pp. 16–18 (Relazione di Francia di Zaccaria Contarini, 1492).

127. L. von Ranke, *Zur venezianischen Geschichte* (Leipzig, 1878), p. 59, and H. Kretschmayr, *Geschichte von Venedig* (Stuttgart, 1934), p. 159ff.

128. Albèri, op. cit., 1st series, vol. 1 (Florence, 1839), pp. 232–5.

It has been frequently pointed out, no doubt with a certain justification, that the first absolutist princes in France had learned much from the princes of the Italian city states. For example, G. Hanotaux, "Le pouvoir royale sous François Ier", in *Études historiques sur le XVIe et le XVIIe siècle en France* (Paris, 1886), pp. 7ff: "The court at Rome and the Venetian Chancellery would have sufficed on their own to spread the new doctrines of diplomacy and politics. But, in reality, in the profusion of petty states which shared the peninsula, there was not one that could not have furnished examples. . . . The monarchies of Europe went to school at the courts of the princes and tyrants of Naples, Florence and Ferrara."

No doubt structurally similar processes took place here, as so often, first in smaller regions then in larger ones, and the leaders of the large regions profited up to a point from their knowledge of the organization of the smaller ones. But in this case as well, only a precise examination in terms of structural history could determine how far the centralization processes and the organization of government in the Italian city states resemble those of early absolutist France, and how far, since differences of size always bring with them qualitative differences of structure, they also diverge from them. At any rate the account given by the Venetian ambassador and its whole tone does not indicate that he regarded the specific power position of the French king and the organization of finances connected to it as something long familiar in Italy.

129. There is today a widespread notion that the forms of social life and particular social institutions are to be explained primarily by the purpose they have for the people who are thus bound together. This idea makes it appear as if people, understanding the usefulness of these institutions,

once took a common decision to live together in this way and no other. But this notion is a fiction and if only for that reason not a very good instrument of research.

The consent given by the individual to live with others in a particular form, the justification on grounds of particular purposes for the fact that he lives for example within a state, or is bound to others as a citizen, official, worker, or farmer and not as a knight, priest or bondsman, or as a cattle-rearing nomad—this consent and this justification are something retrospective. In this matter the individual has little choice. He is born into an order with institutions of a particular kind; he is conditioned more or less successfully to conform to it. And even if he should find this order and its institutions neither good nor useful, he could not simply withdraw his assent and jump out of the existing order. He may try to escape it as an adventurer, a tramp, an artist or writer, he may finally flee to a lonely island—even as a refugee from this order he is its product. To disapprove and flee it is no less a sign of conditioning by it than to praise and justify it.

One of the tasks still remaining to be done is to explain convincingly the compulsion whereby certain forms of communal life, for example our own, come into being, are preserved and changed. But access to an understanding of their genesis is blocked if we think of them as having come about in the same way as the works and deeds of individual people: by the setting of particular goals or even by rational thought and planning. The idea that from the early Middle Ages Western men worked in a common exertion and with a clear goal and a rational plan, towards the order of social life and the institutions in which we live today, scarcely answers the facts. How this really happened can be learned only through a study of the historical evolution of these social forms by accurately documented empirical enquiries. Such a study of a particular segment, the aspect of state organization, has been attempted above. But this has also given rise to some insight of broader significance, for example a certain understanding of the nature of socio-historical processes. We can see how little is really achieved by explaining institutions such as the "state" in terms of rational goals.

The goals, plans and actions of individual people constantly intertwine with those of others. But this intertwining of the actions and plans of many people, which, moreover, goes on continuously from generation to generation, is itself not planned. It cannot be understood in terms of the plans and purposeful intentions of individuals, nor in terms which, though not directly purposive, are modelled on teleological modes of thinking. We are here concerned with processes, compulsions and regularities of a relatively autonomous kind. Thus, for example, a situation where many people set themselves the same goal, wanting the same piece of land, the same market or the same social position, gives rise to something that none of them intended or planned, a specifically social datum: a competitive relationship with its peculiar regularities as discussed earlier. Thus it is not from a common plan of many people, but as something unplanned, emerging from the convergence and collision of the plans of many people, that an increasing division of functions comes into being, and the same applies to the integration of larger and larger areas in the form of states, and to many other sociohistorical processes.

And only an awareness of the relative autonomy of the intertwining of individual plans and actions, of the way the individual is bound by his social life with others, permits a better understanding of the very fact of individuality itself. The coexistence of people, the intertwining of their intentions and plans, the bonds they place on each other, all these, far from destroying individuality, provide the medium in which it can develop. They set the individual limits, but at the same time give him greater or lesser scope. The social fabric in this sense forms the substratum from which and into which the individual constantly spins and weaves his purposes. But this fabric and the actual course of its historical change as a whole, is intended and planned by no-one.

For further detail on this cf. N. Elias, *What is Sociology?*, trans. Stephen Mennell and Grace Morrissey (London, 1978).

130. For a discussion of the problem of the social process, cf. *Social Problems and Social Processes*, Selected Papers from the Proceedings of the American Sociological Society (1932), ed. E. S. Bogardus (Chicago, 1933).

For a criticism of the earlier biologistic notion of social processes, cf. W. F. Ogburn, *Social Change* (London, 1923), pp. 56f.:

> The publication of the *Origin of Species*, setting forth a theory of evolution of species in terms of natural selection, heredity and variation, created a deep impression on the anthropologists and sociologists. The conception of evolution was so profound that the changes in society were seen as a manifestation of evolution and there was an attempt to seek the causes of these social changes in terms of variation and selection. . . . Preliminary to the search for causes, however, attempts were made to establish the development of particular social institutions in successive stages, an evolutionary series, a particular stage necessarily preceding another. The search for laws led to many hypotheses regarding factors such as geographical location, climate, migration, group conflict, racial ability, the evolution of mental ability, and such principles as variation, natural selection, and survival of the fit. A half-century or more of investigations on such theories has yielded some results, but the achievements have not been up to the high hopes entertained shortly after the publication of Darwin's theory of natural selection.
>
> The inevitable series of stages in the development of social institutions has not only not been proven but has been disproven. . . .

For more recent tendencies in the discussion of the problem of historical change cf. A. Goldenweiser, "Social Evolution", in *Encyclopedia of Social Sciences* (New York, 1935), vol. 5, pp. 656ff. (with comprehensive bibliography). The article concludes with the reflection:

> Since the World War students of the social sciences without aiming at the logical orderliness of evolutionary schemes have renewed their search for relatively stable tendencies and regularities in history and society. On the other hand, the growing discrepancy between ideals and the workings of history is guiding the sciences of society into more and more pragmatic channels. If there is a social evolution, whatever it may be, it is no longer accepted as a process to be contemplated but as a task to be achieved by deliberate and concerted human effort.

This study of the civilizing process differs from these pragmatic efforts in that, suspending all wishes and demands concerning what ought to be, it tries to establish what was and is, and to explain in which way, and why, it became as it was and is. It seemed more appropriate to make the therapy depend on the diagnosis rather than the diagnosis on the therapy.

Cf. F. J. Teggart, *Theory of History* (New Haven, 1925), p. 148: ". . . the investigation of how things have come to be as they are . . .".

131. Cf. E. C. Parsons, *Fear and Conventionality* (New York, London, 1914). The divergent view, e.g. in W. G. Summer, *Folkways* (Boston, 1907), p. 419: "It is never correct to regard any one of the taboos as an arbitrary invention or burden laid on society by tradition without necessity . . . they have been sifted for centuries by experience, and those which we have received and accepted are such as experience has proved to be expedient."

132. See the fine account by I. Huizinga, *The Waning of the Middle Ages* (London, 1924), ch. 1.

What was said above also applies, for example, to societies with a related structure in the present-day Orient and, to various degrees depending on the nature and extent of integration, to so-called "primitive" societies.

The extent to which children in our society—however imbued with characteristics of our relatively advanced civilization—still show glimpses of the other standard with its simpler and more straightforward affects and its proneness to sudden changes of mood, is shown, for example, by the following description of what children like in films (*Daily Telegraph*, 12 February, 1937): "Children, especially young children, like aggression. . . . They favour action, action and more action. They are not averse from the shedding of blood, but it must be dark blood. Virtue triumphant is cheered to the echo; villainy is booed with a fine enthusiasm. When scenes of one alternate with scenes of the other, as in sequences of pursuit, the transition from the cheer to the boo is timed to a split second."

Also closely connected to the different force of their emotional utterances, their extreme reaction in both directions, fear and joy, revulsion and affection, is the specific structure of taboos in simpler societies. It was pointed out above (cf. pp. 445ff, especially pp. 450–1; cf. *The History of Manners*, pp. 71ff.) that in the medieval West not only the manifestations of drives and affects in the form of pleasure but also the prohibitions, the tendencies to self-torment and asceticism were stronger, more intense and therefore more rigorous than at later stages of the civilizing process.

Cf. also R. H. Lowie, "Food Etiquette", in *Are we civilised?* (London, 1929), p. 48: ". . . the savage rules of etiquette are not only strict, but formidable. Nevertheless, to us their table manners are shocking."

133. Cf. C. H. Judd, *The Psychology of Social Institutions* (New York, 1926), pp. 105ff. Also pp. 32ff. and 77ff.

134. Introduction to the French translation of Gratian's "Hand Oracle" written by Amelot de la Houssaie, Paris, 1684. *Oraculo Manuale* published in 1647, went through about twenty different editions during the seventeenth and eighteenth centuries in France alone under the title *L'Homme de Cour*. It is in a sense the first handbook of courtly psychology, as Machiavelli's book on the prince was the first classical handbook of courtly-absolutist politics. Machiavelli, however, seems to speak more from the point of view of the prince than does Gratian. He justifies more or less the "reason of state" of emergent absolutism. Gratian, the Spanish Jesuit, despises reason of state from the bottom of his heart. He elucidates the rules of the great courtly game for himself and others as something with which one has to comply because there is no alternative.

It is not without significance, however, that despite this difference, the conduct recommended by both Machiavelli and Gratian appears to middle-class people as more or less "immoral", although similar modes of conduct and sentiment are certainly not lacking in the bourgeois world. In this condemnation of courtly psychology and courtly conduct by the non-courtly bourgeoisie is expressed the specific difference of the whole social moulding of the two classes. Social rules are built into the personality of non-courtly bourgeois strata in a different way than in the courtly class. In the former the super-ego is far more rigid and in many respects stricter than in the latter. The belligerent side of everyday life certainly does not disappear in practice from the bourgeois world, but it is banished far more than in the courtly class from what a writer or any person may *express*, and even from consciousness itself.

In courtly-aristocratic circles "thou shalt" is very often no more an expression of expediency, dictated by the practical necessities of social life. Even adults in these circles always remain aware that these are rules that they must obey because they live with other people. In middle-class strata the corresponding rules are often rooted far more deeply in the individual during childhood, not as practical rules for the expedient conduct of life, but as semi-automatic promptings of conscience. For this reason the "thou shalt" and the "thou shalt not" of the super-ego is far more constantly and deeply involved in the observation and understanding of reality. To give at least one example from the innumerable ones that might be quoted here, Gratian says in his precept "Know thoroughly the character of those with whom you deal" (No. 273): "Expect practically nothing good of those who have some natural bodily defect; for they are accustomed to avenge themselves on Nature. . . ." One of the middle-class English books of manners of the seventeenth century, that likewise had wide circulation and had their origin in the well-known rules of George Washington, *Youth's Behaviour* by Francis Hawkins (1646), gives pride of place to "thou shalt not" and so gives behaviour and observation in the same case a different, moral twist (No. 31): "Scorne not any for the infirmityes of nature, which by no art can be amended, nor do thou delight to put them in minde of them, since it very oft procures envye and promotes malice even to revenge."

In a word, we find in Gratian, and after him in La Rochefoucauld and La Bruyère in the form of general maxims, all the modes of behaviour which we encounter, for example in Saint-Simon, in the practice of court life itself. Again and again we find injunctions on the necessity to hold back the affects (No. 287): "Never act while passion lasts. Otherwise you will spoil everything." Or (No. 273):

"The man prejudiced by passion always speaks a langugage different from what things are; passion, not reason, speaks in him." We find the advice to adopt a "psychological attitude", a permanent observation of character (No. 273): "Know thoroughly the character of those with whom you deal." Or the result of such knowledge, the observation (No. 201): "All those who appear mad are mad, and so are half of those who do not appear mad." The necessity of self-observation (No. 225): "Know your dominant fault." The necessity for half-truths (No. 210): "Know how to play with truth." The insight that real truth lies in the truthfulness and substantiality of the whole existence of a person, not in his particular words (No. 175): "The substantial man. It is only Truth that can give a true reputation; and only the substance which can be turned to profit." The necessity for farsightedness (No. 151): "Think today of tomorrow, and of a long time beyond." Moderation in all things (No. 82): "The sage has compressed all wisdom into this precept: Nothing to Excess." The specifically courtly-aristocratic form of perfection, the temperate polishing of a moderated and transformed animalic nature all around, the levity, charm, the new beauty of the animal-made man (No. 127): "Le JE-NE-SAIS-QUOI. Without it all beauty is dead, all grace is graceless . . . the other perfections are ornaments of Nature, the 'Je-ne-sais-quoi' is that of perfection. It is noticeable even in the manner of reasoning. . . ." Or, from a different aspect, the man without affectation (No. 123): "The man without affectation. The more perfections there are the less there is affectation. The most eminent qualities lose their price if we discover affectation in them, because we attribute them rather to an artificial constraint than to a person's true character." War between man and man is inevitable; conduct it decently (No. 165): "Make good war. To conquer villainously is not to conquer but to be conquered. Anything that smells of treason infects one's good name." Over and again in these precepts recurs the argument based on regard for other people, on the necessity to preserve a good reputation, in a word, an argument based on *this-worldly*, social necessities. Religion plays a small part in them. God appears only in the margin and at the end as something outside this human circle. All good things, too, come to a man from other people (No. 111): "Make friends. To have friends is a second being . . . all the good things we have in life depend on others."

It is this justification of rules and precepts not by an eternal moral law but by "external" necessities, consideration of other people, which above all causes these maxims and the whole courtly code of conduct to appear "amoral" or at least "painfully realistic" to the bourgeois observer. Betrayal, for example, the bourgeois world feels, should be forbidden not for practical reasons, concern for one's "good reputation" with other people, but by an inner voice, conscience, in a word, by morality. The same change in the structure of commands and prohibitions that was seen earlier in the study of eating habits, washing and other elementary functions, reappears here. Rules of conduct which in courtly aristocratic circles are observed even by adults largely from consideration and fear of other people, are imprinted on the individual in the bourgeois world rather as a self-constraint. In adults they are no longer reproduced and preserved by direct fear of other people, but by an "inner" voice, a fear automatically reproduced by their own super-ego, in short by a moral commandment that needs no justification.

135. Cf. *The History of Manners*, pp. 88ff.

136. C. H. Haskins, "The Spread of Ideas in the Middle Ages", in *Studies in Mediaeval Culture* (Oxford, 1929), pp. 92ff.

137. Cf. p. 314 above. Apart from the *Minnelieder* there is a wealth of material showing this standard, in some cases even more clearly, e.g. the small prose piece by Andreas Capellanus in Marie de Champagne's cycle "De Amore", and the whole literature of the medieval controversy over women.

138. Haskins, op. cit., p. 94.

139. *The History of Manners*, pp. 167ff.

140. Cf. pp. 269ff. above.

141. La Bruyère, *Caractères*, 'De la cow' (Paris, Hachette, 1922), *Oeuvres*, vol. 2, p. 237, No. 64; cf. also p. 248, No. 99: "In a hundred years the world will still exist in its entirety. It will be the same theatre with the same decoration, but not the same actors. All those who rejoice at a favour

received or are cast into sorrow and despair by a refusal, all will have vanished from the stage. Already other men are moving on to the stage who will play the same parts in the same play. What a back ground for a comic part!" How strong the sense of immutability still is here, and of the ineluctability of the existing order; how much stronger than in the later phase when the concept of "civilization" begins to displace that of "civilité".

On this development cf. also the passage "Des Jugements": "All foreigners are not Barbarians, nor all our Compatriots civilized."

142. La Bruyère, op. cit., p. 247, No. 94.

143. Ibid., p. 211, No. 2; cf. also p. 211, No. 10: "The court is like an edifice of marble; I mean it is composed of men who are very hard, but very polished." Cf. also n. 134.

144. Saint-Simon, op. cit., p. 63.

145. *The History of Manners*, pp. 56ff, partic. 62–3.

146. Ranke, *Französische Geschichte*, bk. 10, ch. 3.

147. Saint-Simon, op. cit., vol. 22, p. 20 and pp. 22f. (1711). What is at stake in these conversations is nothing less than an attempt to win over the heir to the throne to a different form of rule, in which the balance between members of the leading bourgeois and noble groups at court is to be shifted in favour of the latter. The power of the "peers"—this is the goal of Saint-Simon and his friends—is to be restored. In particular the higher offices of state, the ministries, shall be transferred from the bourgeois to the high nobility. An attempt in this direction is actually made directly after Louis XIV's death by the regent with the active involvement of Saint-Simon. It fails. What the English nobility achieve by and large successfully, a stabilization of aristocratic rule whereby various groups and cliques of the nobility contest the occupancy of the decisive positions of political power while observing fairly strict rules, the French nobility fail to achieve. The tensions and conflicts of interest between the leading groups of the nobility and those of the bourgeoisie are incomparably greater in France than in England. Under the cover of absolutism they are constantly discernible. But as in every strong autocracy the struggle being waged around the ruler, in the highest circles, takes place behind locked doors. Saint-Simon is one of the chief exponents of this secret combat.

148. *The History of Manners*, pp. 169ff. On the general problem of shame feelings cf. *The Spectator* (1807), vol. 5, no. 373: "If I was put to define Modesty, I would call it, The reflection of an ingenuous Mind, either when a Man has committed an Action for which he censures himself, or fancies that he is exposed to the Censure of others." See also the observation there on the difference of shame feelings between men and women.

149. *The History of Manners*, pp. 99ff.

150. Ibid., pp. 167ff.

151. Ibid., pp. 88ff.

152. Attempts have often been made to explain the national character of the English or particular features of it by the geographical situation of their country, from its island character. But if this island character were simply responsible for the national character of its inhabitants as a natural datum, then all other island nations would have to show similar characteristics, and no people should be closer to the English in its character and make-up than, for example, the Japanese.

It is not the island situation as such which sets its stamp on the national character of the population, but the significance of this situation in the total structure of the island society, in the total context of its history. As a result of a particular historical development the lack of land frontiers, for example, has led in England, unlike Japan, to a low evaluation of military prowess and more concretely to the fact that soldiers do not enjoy very high social prestige.

In England the relatively pacified nobility, together with leading bourgeois groups, succeeded very early in sharply restricting the king's control of weapons and the army, and particularly the use of physical violence within the country itself. And this structure of the monopoly of physical force, made possible, to be sure, only by the country's island character, played no small part in the formation of the specifically English national character. How closely certain features of the English super-ego, or, in other words, the English conscience, are bound up with the structure of the monopoly of physical force is shown even today by the social latitude given in England to the "conscientious objector", or the widespread sentiment that general conscription represents a major and dangerous restriction of individual freedom. We would probably not be wrong in assuming that non-conformist movements and organizations have been able to remain as strong and vigorous as they have over the centuries in England only because the official Church of England was not backed by a police and military apparatus to the same extent as were, for example, the national churches in the Protestant states of Germany. At any rate, the fact that in England the pressure of foreign military power on the individual was from an early stage much less heavy than in any other major Continental country, is extremely closely connected to the other fact that the constraint which the individual had to exert on himself, particularly in all matters related to the life of the state, grew stronger and more all-round than in the great Continental nations. In this way, as an element of social history, the island character and the whole nature of the country have indeed, in a great variety of ways, exerted a formative influence on the national character.

153. *The History of Manners*, pp. 13ff., pp. 59ff. and p. 241 n. 30. On this question cf. also A. Loewe, *The Price of Liberty* (London, 1937), p. 31: "The educated German of the classical and post-classical period is a dual being. In public life he stands in the place which authority has decreed for him, and fills it in the double capacity of superior and subordinate with complete devotion to duty. In private life he may be a critical intellectual or an emotional romantic. . . . This educational system has come to grief in the attempt to achieve a fusion of the bureaucratic and the humanist ideals. It has in reality created the introverted specialist, unsurpassed in abstract speculation and in formal organization, but incapable of shaping a real world out of his theoretical ideas. The English educational ideal does not know this cleavage between the world within and the world without. . . ."

154. Cf. *State Formation and Civilization*, pp. 314ff.

155. Cf. *State Formation and Civilization*, pp. 341–3 and pp. 345ff. That the strength of tensions between different hegemonial units is indissolubly bound up with the strength of tensions and the whole social order within them has already been stressed on a number of occasions. It was shown that connections of this kind existed even in the early Western feudal society with its primarily barter economy. The population pressure which led in it to various kinds of expansionist and competitive struggles, the desire for a piece of land in the poorer warriors and the desire for more land at the expense of others in richer ones, counts, dukes and kings, this population pressure is not simply a result of the increase in population but of this in connection with the then existing property relations, the monopolization of the most important means of production by a section of the warriors. From a certain time on land was in fixed possession; access to it by families and individuals who did not already "own" became increasingly difficult; property relationships hardened more and more. In this social constellation a further increase of population in both the peasant and warrior classes and the constant sinking of many people below their previous standard of existence, exerted a pressure which intensified tensions and competition within the whole society from top to bottom, within the individual territories and *between* them, and which kept the competitive mechanism in motion (see pp. 293, 298 and 308ff.). In exactly the same way in industrial society it is not the absolute level of population and still less simply an increase in population which is responsible for pressure within particular states, but the density of population in conjunction with the existing property relations, the relationship of those who control property chances through an unorganized monopoly to those who do not have such chances.

That the social pressure in different Western states varies in degree is obvious. But we do not yet possess any very useful conceptual tools for analysing these pressure relationships, nor any precise framework within which the degree of pressure can be precisely measured, for example, by a comparison of different states. What is clear is that this "internal pressure" is most accessible to observation and analysis from the point of view of the standard of living, if by this we do not mean only the purchasing power of income but also the time and intensity of work needed to obtain this income. Moreover, we cannot gain a proper understanding of the relationships of pressure and tension within a society by comparing the living standards of its different classes statically, i.e. at a particular time, but only by a comparison over extended periods. The degree of tension and the population pressure within a society are very often not explained by the absolute level of the living standard, but rather by the abruptness with which this standard falls in certain classes from one level to another. We must have in view the curve, the historical movement of the standard of living of different classes of a society in order to understand the relationships of pressure and tension within it.

This is the reason why we should not look at one industrial nation on its own if we wish to gain a clear picture of the nature and strength of the relationships of pressure and tension within it. For the level of the living standard, different as it is in different classes of the same society, is always partly determined by the position of this whole society in the global network of different nation states and empires with its further division of functions. In most if not all the industrial nation states of Europe the living standard, which was itself attained in conjunction with industrialization, can be maintained only by constant imports of agrarian products and raw materials. These imports can only be paid for either by income from correspondingly large exports or by income from investments in other countries or from gold reserves. So it happens that it is not only internal pressure, the imminent or actual fall in the living standard of broad classes, which maintains and sometimes intensifies the competitive tension between different industrial nation states, but this inter-state tension in its turn can sometimes contribute to a very considerable extent to an increase in the social pressure within one or other of the competing nation states.

Up to a certain point this no doubt also applies to countries which primarily export agrarian products or raw materials. It applies, indeed, to all countries which have grown into a particular function within the division of labour between different nations, and whose living standard therefore can be maintained only if enough scope for the relevant exports or imports exists. But the sensitivity of different countries to fluctuations in international exchange, to defeats, to slow or rapid decline in the competition of nation states, varies very widely. It is clearly particularly high in nations with a relatively high standard of living in which the balance between their own industrial and agrarian production has tilted sharply to the disadvantage of the latter and which are dependent in both sectors on substantial imports of basic materials, particularly when they are not able to offset such deficits by earnings from foreign investments or from their gold reserves, and when, furthermore, human exports, too, for example in the form of emigration, become impossible. This, however, is a question in its own right which needs more detailed examination than is possible here. Only by such an investigation could we gain better understanding of why, for example, the tensions in the figuration of European states are so much greater than those between, for example, the South and Central American states.

However that may be, one often has the idea that it is only necessary to leave the economic competition between such highly industrialized states to the free play of forces for all the partners to prosper. But this free play of forces is in fact a hard competitive struggle which is subject to the same regularities as such struggles in all other spheres. The balance between the competing states is extremely unstable. It tends towards specific shifts the direction of which, certainly, can only be established through long-term observation. In the course of this economic competition between highly industrialized nations preponderance gradually moves in favour of some and against the others. The export and import capacity of the weakening parties becomes more restricted. To a state in this situation there remain—if, as we have said, it is unable to offset these losses by investments or gold reserves—only two possibilities. It must either force up exports, for example by lowering export prices, or restrict imports. Both actions lead directly or indirectly to a lowering of the living standards of the members of this society. This fall is passed on by those controlling the monopoly of economic opportunities to those who do not control them. The latter thus find themselves surrounded by a double circle of monopoly rulers: those within their own society and those representing foreign societies. The pressure emanating from them contributes to impelling their own representatives and their state as a whole into a competitive struggle with other societies. And thus the tensions within different states and those between them mutually reinforce each other. This spiral movement is, to be sure—it must be emphasized—only one of a large number of different sequential orders of change. But the mention of this sequential order, however fragmentary, may give an impression of the power of the compelling forces which today keep the inter-state competition and monopoly mechanisms in motion.

156. Cf. pp. 388–9 above. A summary of present-day theories on the origins of states is to be found in Macleod, *The Origin and History of Politics*, pp. 139ff.

157. Cf. pp 345ff. above.

158. Cf. pp. 475ff., esp. pp. 479ff.

159. Cf. pp. 447ff., p. 463, and pp. 465ff.

160. Cf. pp. 462ff., p. 469, pp. 472–3, pp. 492ff; on this question cf. Parsons, *Fear and Conventionality*, p. xiii: "Conventionality rests upon an apprehensive state of mind . . .", and p. 73: "Table manners are, I suppose, one of our most marked class distinctions". Also quoted there W. James, *Principles of Psychology* (New York, 1890), p. 121: "Habit is thus the enormous flywheel of society, its most precious conservative agent. It alone is what keeps us all within the bounds of ordinance, and saves the children of fortune from the envious uprisings of the poor. It alone prevents the hardest and most repulsive walks of life from being deserted by those brought up to tread therein."

The more general question, to the solution of which the present work seeks to make a contribution, has also been posed for a long time by American sociology. For example, Sumner, *Folkways*, p. 418, writes: "When, therefore, the ethnographers apply condemnatory or depreciatory adjectives to the people whom they study, they beg the most important question which we want to investigate; that is, what are standards, codes, and ideas of chastity, decency, propriety, modesty, etc. and whence do they arise? The ethnographical facts contain the answer to this question, but in order to reach it we want a colourless report of the facts." It scarcely needs to be said that this is true not only of the investigation of foreign and simpler societies, but also of our own society and its history.

The problem to which the present work is addressed has more recently been particularly clearly formulated by Judd, *The Psychology of Social Institutions*, even if he attempts a different solution to the problems than is offered here (p. 276): "This chapter will aim to prove that the types of personal emotions which are known to civilised men are products of an evolution in which emotions have taken a new direction. . . . The instruments and means of this adaptation are the institutions, some of which have been described in foregoing chapters. Each institution as it has become established has developed in all individuals to come under its influence a mode of behaviour and emotional attitude which conform to the institution. The new mode of behaviour and the new emotional attitude could not have been perfected until the institution itself was created. . . . The effort of individuals to adapt themselves to institutional demands results in what may be properly described as a wholly new group of pleasures."

Index